# SECURITY STUDIES

*Security Studies* is the most comprehensive textbook available on security studies.

Comprehensively revised for the new edition including new chapters on Polarity, Culture, Intelligence, and the Academic and Policy Worlds, it continues to give students a detailed overview of the major theoretical approaches, key themes and most significant issues within security studies.

- Part 1 explores the main theoretical approaches currently used within the field from realism to international political sociology.
- Part 2 explains the central concepts underpinning contemporary debates from the security dilemma to terrorism.
- Part 3 presents an overview of the institutional security architecture currently influencing world politics using international, regional and global levels of analysis.
- Part 4 examines some of the key contemporary challenges to global security from the arms trade to energy security.
- Part 5 discusses the future of security.

Security Studies provides a valuable teaching tool for undergraduates and MA students by collecting these related strands of the field together into a single coherent textbook.

**Paul D. Williams** is Associate Professor in the Elliott School of International Affairs at the George Washington University, USA.

# SECURITY STUDIES
# AN INTRODUCTION

2nd edition

Edited by
Paul D. Williams

 Routledge
Taylor & Francis Group

LONDON AND NEW YORK

First edition published 2008 by Routledge

Second edition published 2013 by Routledge
2 Park Square, Milton Park, Abingdon, Oxon, OX14 4RN

Simultaneously published in the USA and Canada
by Routledge
711 Third Avenue, New York, NY 10017

*Routledge is an imprint of the Taylor & Francis Group,
an informa business*

*British Library Cataloguing in Publication Data*
A catalogue record for this book is available from the British Library

*Library of Congress Cataloging in Publication Data*
Security studies: an introduction/edited by Paul D. Williams. – 2nd ed.
    p. cm.
    Includes bibliographical references and index.
    1. Security, International. I. Williams, Paul, 1975–
JZ5588.S4297 2012
    355'.033—dc23                                         2011041150

ISBN 13: 978–0-415–78280–7 (hbk)
ISBN 13: 978–0-415–78281–4 (pbk)
ISBN 13: 978–0-203–12257–0 (ebk)

Typeset in Adobe Garamond by
Florence Production Ltd, Stoodleigh, Devon

# CONTENTS

# Boxes, figures and tables

## Boxes

## Figures

## Tables

# CONTRIBUTORS

**Richard J. Aldrich** is Professor of International Security and Director of the Institute of Advanced Study at the University of Warwick, UK.

**Deborah D. Avant** is Professor in the Josef Korbel School of International Studies at the University of Denver, USA.

**Sita Bali** is Senior Lecturer in International Relations at Staffordshire University, UK.

**Michael N. Barnett** is University Professor of International Affairs and Political Science at the George Washington University, USA.

**Alex J. Bellamy** is Professor of International Security at Griffith University, Australia.

**Didier Bigo** is Professor in the Department of War Studies at King's College, London, UK.

**Pinar Bilgin** is Associate Professor of International Relations at Bilkent University, Ankara, Turkey.

**Ken Booth** is Senior Research Associate and formerly E.H. Carr Professor of International Politics at Aberystwyth University, Wales, UK.

**Barry Buzan** is the Montague Burton Professor of International Relations at the London School of Economics and Political Science, UK.

**Stuart Croft** is Professor of International Security and Pro-Vice Chancellor for Research at the University of Warwick, UK.

**Simon Dalby** is Professor of Geography and Political Economy at Carleton University in Ottawa, Canada.

**John S. Duffield** is Professor of Political Science at Georgia State University in Atlanta, USA.

**Colin Elman** is Associate Professor of Political Science in the Maxwell School of Syracuse University, USA.

**Louise Fawcett** is CUF University Lecturer in Politics and Wilfrid Knapp Fellow in Politics at St Catherine's College, Oxford University, UK.

**Lawrence Freedman** is Professor of War Studies and Vice Principal (Research) at King's College, London, UK. He was awarded the KCMG in 2003.

**James M. Goldgeier** is Dean of the School of International Service at the American University, Washington DC, USA.

**Fen Osler Hampson** is the Director of The Norman Paterson School of International Affairs, Carleton University, Ottawa, Canada.

**William D. Hartung** is Director of the Arms and Security Project at the Center for International Policy and Senior Research Fellow at the New America Foundation, Washington DC, USA.

**Michael Jensen** is a post-doctoral fellow in the Moynihan Institute at Syracuse University, USA.

**Adam Jones** is Associate Professor of Political Science at the University of British Columbia, Canada.

**Stuart J. Kaufman** is Professor of Political Science and International Relations at the University of Delaware, USA.

**Michael T. Klare** is the Five College Professor of Peace and World Security Studies (a joint appointment at Amherst College, Hampshire College, Mount Holyoke College, Smith College, and the University of Massachusetts at Amherst), and Director of the Five College Program in Peace and World Security Studies (PAWSS).

**Peter Lawler** is Senior Lecturer in International Relations at the University of Manchester, UK and a Faculty Member of the International MA programme in Peace and Development Studies at Universitat Jaume I, Castellón, Spain.

**Matt McDonald** is Senior Lecturer in International Relations at the University of Queensland, Australia.

**Colin McInnes** is Professor of International Politics and Director of the Centre for Health and International Relations (CHAIR) at Aberystwyth University, Wales, UK.

**Cornelia Navari** is Visiting Professor at the University of Buckingham, UK and a Visiting Lecturer in International Law and Organisation at King's College, London, UK.

**Paul R. Pillar** is a Visiting Professor and member of the core faculty of the Security Studies Program at Georgetown University, USA.

**Michael Pugh** is Professor of Peace and Conflict Studies at the University of Bradford, UK.

**Srinath Raghavan** is Senior Fellow at the Centre for Policy Research, New Delhi, India and a Lecturer in Defence Studies at King's College, London, UK.

**Paul Rogers** is Professor of Peace Studies at the University of Bradford, UK.

**Waheguru Pal Singh Sidhu** is Senior Fellow in the Center on International Cooperation at New York University, USA.

**Joanna Spear** is Associate Professor and Director of the Security Policy Studies programme in the Elliott School of International Affairs at the George Washington University, USA.

**Caroline Thomas** was Deputy Vice Chancellor and Professor at the University of Southampton, UK. Caroline passed away in 2008 after the first edition of this volume was completed.

**Thomas G. Weiss** is Presidential Professor of Political Science at the Graduate Center of City University of New York, USA and Director of the Ralph Bunche Institute for International Studies, where he is also co-director of the United Nations Intellectual History Project and Chair of the Academic Council on the UN System.

**Nicholas J. Wheeler** is Professor of International Relations and Director of the Centre for Global Cooperation and Security at the University of Birmingham, UK.

**Sandra Whitworth** is Professor of Political Science and Women's Studies at York University in Toronto, Canada.

**Paul D. Williams** is Associate Professor in the Elliott School of International Affairs at the George Washington University, USA.

**Phil Williams** is Professor of International Security in the Graduate School of Public and International Affairs at the University of Pittsburgh, USA.

**Danielle Zach** is a PhD student in the Department of Political Science at The CUNY Graduate Center, USA.

**Frank C. Zagare** is UB Distinguished Professor of Political Science at the University at Buffalo, SUNY, USA.

# Acknowledgments

For their permission to reproduce material within this book, thanks go to the United Nations, specifically the Department of Public Information and the Cartographic Section, and the editors of the *Journal of Peace Research*.

# LIST OF ABBREVIATIONS

| | |
|---|---|
| ABM | Anti-Ballistic Missile Treaty |
| ACC | Arab Cooperation Council |
| AECA | Arms Export Control Act (US) |
| AMU | Arab Maghreb Union |
| ANWR | Arctic National Wildlife Refuge |
| ANZUS | Australia, New Zealand, US Security Treaty |
| APEC | Asia-Pacific Economic Cooperation |
| AQI | al-Qa'ida in Iraq |
| AQIM | al-Qa'ida in the Islamic Maghreb |
| ARF | ASEAN Regional Forum |
| ARTs | Anti-retroviral therapies |
| ASEAN | Association of Southeast Asian Nations |
| ATOP | Alliance Treaty Obligations and Provisions database |
| AU | African Union |
| AWACS | Airborne Warning and Control System |
| BATF | Bureau of Alcohol, Tobacco, and Firearms (US) |
| BMD | Ballistic Missile Defence |
| BWC | Biological Toxins and Weapons Convention |
| CACO | Central Asian Cooperation Organization |
| CARICOM | Caribbean Community |
| CAT | Conventional Arms Transfer |
| CEMAC | Economic and Monetary Community of Central Africa |
| CENTO | Central Treaty Organization |
| CFSP | Common Foreign and Security Policy (EU) |
| CIA | Central Intelligence Agency (US) |
| CICS | Centre for International Cooperation and Security (Bradford, UK) |
| CIS | Commonwealth of Independent States |
| CIVPOL | Civilian Police (UN) |
| CNA | Center for Naval Analyses |
| CND | Campaign for Nuclear Disarmament |
| COIN | Counterinsurgency |
| COW | Correlates of War Project |
| CPA | Coalition Provisional Authority (Iraq) |
| CSCE | Conference on Security and Cooperation in Europe |
| CSIS | Center for Strategic and International Studies (US) |
| CSTO | Collective Security Treaty Organization |
| CTBT | Comprehensive Test Ban Treaty |
| CTBTO | Comprehensive Test Ban Treaty Organization |
| CTC | UN Counter-Terrorism Committee |
| CWC | Chemical Weapons Convention |
| CWC | Commission on Wartime Contracting |

| | |
|---|---|
| DDR | Disarmament, demobilization and reintegration |
| DOD | Department of Defence (US) |
| DoE | Department of Energy (US) |
| DPA | UN Department of Political Affairs |
| DPKO | UN Department of Peacekeeping Operations |
| DPRK | Democratic People's Republic of Korea |
| DPT | Democratic peace theory |
| DRC | Democratic Republic of the Congo |
| EC | European Community |
| ECO | Economic Cooperation Organization |
| ECOSOC | UN Economic and Social Council |
| ECOWAS | Economic Community of West African States |
| END | European Nuclear Disarmament |
| EO | Executive Outcomes |
| ESDP | European Security and Defence Policy (EU) |
| ETA | *Euskadi ta Askatasuna* (Basque Fatherland and Liberty) |
| EU | European Union |
| EUFOR | EU Force |
| FARC | Revolutionary Armed Forces of Colombia |
| FBI | Federal Bureau of Investigation (US) |
| FDI | Foreign Direct Investment |
| FMCT | Fissile Material Cutoff Treaty |
| G77 | Group of 77 |
| G8 | Group of 8 |
| GCC | Gulf Cooperation Council |
| GDP | Gross Domestic Product |
| GNI | Gross National Income |
| GWOT | Global War on Terror |
| HPAI | Highly pathogenic avian influenza / bird flu |
| HST | Hegemonic stability theory |
| IAEA | International Atomic Energy Agency |
| ICC | International Criminal Court |
| ICISS | International Commission on Intervention and State Sovereignty |
| ICJ | International Court of Justice |
| ICO | Islamic Conference Organization |
| ICTY | International Criminal Tribunal for the Former Yugoslavia |
| IDPs | Internally displaced persons |
| IED | Improvised explosive device |
| IFOR | Implementation Force (Bosnia) |
| IGAD | Intergovernmental Authority on Development |
| IGADD | Inter-Governmental Authority on Drought and Development |
| IMF | International Monetary Fund |
| INF | Intermediate Range Nuclear Forces Treaty |
| INGOs | International non-governmental organizations |

| | |
|---|---|
| IOM | International Organization for Migration |
| IPCC | Intergovernmental Panel on Climate Change |
| IPE | International Political Economy, academic subfield of |
| IPS | International Political Sociology, academic subfield of |
| IR | International Relations, academic discipline of |
| IRA/PIRA | Provisional Irish Republican Army |
| ISAF | International Security Assistance Force (in Afghanistan) |
| KLA | Kosovo Liberation Army |
| LAS | League of Arab States |
| LDCs | Least Developed Countries |
| LTTE | Liberation Tigers of Tamil Eelam (Sri Lanka) |
| MAD | Mutually Assured Destruction |
| MDGs | Millennium Development Goals |
| MERCOSUR | The Southern Common Market |
| MONUC | UN Mission in the Democratic Republic of the Congo |
| MRTA | Tupac Amaru Revolutionary Movement (Peru) |
| MTCR | Missile Technology Control Regime |
| NAFTA | North American Free Trade Agreement |
| NAM | The Non-Aligned Movement |
| NATO | North Atlantic Treaty Organization |
| NEPDG | National Energy Policy Development Group (US) |
| NFZ | No-fly-zone |
| NGOs | Non-governmental organizations |
| NNSA | National Nuclear Security Administration (US) |
| NPT | Treaty on the Non-Proliferation of Nuclear Weapons |
| NSA | National Security Agency (US) |
| NSG | Nuclear Suppliers Group |
| NWFZs | Nuclear Weapon Free Zones |
| OAS | Organization of American States |
| OAU | Organization of African Unity |
| OECD | Organization for Economic Cooperation and Development |
| OECS | Organization of Eastern Caribbean States |
| OPCW | Organization for the Prohibition of Chemical Weapons |
| OPEC | Organization of Petroleum Exporting Countries |
| OSCE | Organization of Security and Cooperation in Europe |
| P-5 | Permanent five members of the UN Security Council |
| PIF | Pacific Islands Forum |
| PMSC | Private military and security company |
| PRI | Institutional Revolutionary Party (Mexico) |
| PRIO | Peace Research Institute of Oslo (Norway) |
| PSI | Proliferation Security Initiative |
| PTBT | Partial Test Ban Treaty |
| R2P | Responsibility to protect |
| RAWA | Revolutionary Association of the Women of Afghanistan |
| RMA | Revolution in Military Affairs |
| RRW | Reliable replacement warhead |

| | |
|---|---|
| RSCT | Regional Security Complex Theory |
| RUF | Revolutionary United Front (Sierra Leone) |
| SAARC | South Asian Association for Regional Cooperation |
| SACEUR | Supreme Allied Commander Europe (NATO) |
| SADC | Southern African Development Community |
| SADCC | Southern African Development Coordination Conference |
| SALT | Strategic Arms Limitation Talks |
| SALW | Small arms and light weapons |
| SANG | Saudi Arabian National Guard |
| SARS | Severe Acute Respiratory Syndrome |
| SAS | Special Air Services (UK) |
| SCO | Shanghai Cooperation Organization |
| SEATO | Southeast Asia Treaty Organization |
| SFOR | Stabilization Force (Bosnia) |
| SIPRI | Stockholm International Peace Research Institute (Sweden) |
| SORT | Strategic Offensive Reductions Treaty |
| SPF | South Pacific Forum |
| SSR | Security sector reform |
| START | Strategic Arms Reduction Treaty |
| TB | Tuberculosis |
| UCDP | Uppsala Conflict Data Program |
| UfP | 'Uniting for Peace' resolution (UN General Assembly) |
| UN | United Nations |
| UNAIDS | The Joint UN Programme on HIV/AIDS |
| UNAMIR | UN Assistance Mission to Rwanda |
| UNAMSIL | UN Mission in Sierra Leone |
| UNASUR | Union of South American Nations |
| UNDP | UN Development Programme |
| UNGA | UN General Assembly |
| UNHCR | UN High Commission for Refugees |
| UNICEF | UN Children's Fund |
| UNIFIL | UN Interim Force in Lebanon |
| UNITA | The National Union for the Total Independence of Angola |
| UNMIK | UN Mission in Kosovo |
| UNMIS | UN Mission in Sudan |
| UNMOVIC | UN Monitoring, Verification, and Inspections Commission (Iraq) |
| UNODC | UN Office for Drugs and Crime |
| UNOMIL | UN Observer Mission in Liberia |
| UNPOL | UN Police |
| UNPROFOR | UN Protection Force (former Yugoslavia) |
| UNSCOM | UN Special Commission (Iraq) |
| WEU | Western European Union |
| WFP | World Food Programme |
| WHO | World Health Organization |
| WMD | Weapons of mass destruction |
| WTO | World Trade Organization |

# Security Studies

## An Introduction

Paul D. Williams

Security matters. It is impossible to make sense of world politics without reference to it. Every day, people somewhere in the world are killed, starved, tortured, raped, impoverished, imprisoned, displaced, or denied education and healthcare in the name of security. The concept saturates contemporary societies all around the world: it litters the speeches of politicians and pundits; newspaper columns and radio waves are full of it; and images of security and insecurity flash across our television screens and the internet almost constantly. All this makes security a fascinating, often deadly, but always important topic.

But what does this word mean, what political effects does it generate and how should it be studied? Some analysts think security is like beauty: a subjective and elastic term, meaning exactly what the subject in question says it means; neither more nor less. In the more technical language of social science, security is often referred to as an 'essentially contested concept' (see Gallie 1956), one for which, by definition, there can be no consensus as to its meaning. While in one sense this is certainly true – security undoubtedly means different things to different people – at an abstract level, most scholars within International Relations (IR) work with a definition of security that involves the alleviation of threats to cherished values.

Defined in this way, security is unavoidably political, that is, it plays a vital role in deciding who gets what, when, and how in world politics (Lasswell 1936). Security studies can thus never be solely an intellectual pursuit because it is stimulated in large part by the impulse to achieve security for 'real people in real places' (see Booth 2007). This involves interpreting the past (specifically how different groups thought about and practised security), understanding the present, and trying to influence the future. Indeed, perceptions of the future are arguably the key terrain on which competing approaches to security compete. As such, the concept of security has been likened to a trump-card in the struggle over the allocation of resources. Think, for example, of the often huge discrepancies in the size of budgets that many governments devote to ministries engaged in 'security' as opposed to say 'development' or 'health' or 'education' or 'justice'.

An extreme example of prioritizing regime security would be the case of Zaire during President Mobutu Sese Seko's rule (1965–1997). For much of this period the only thing that the Zairean state provided its people with was an ill-disciplined and predatory military. In contrast, Mobutu's government spent almost nothing on public health and education services. In similar fashion, many of the protesters who formed the core of the Arab awakening in early 2011 were incensed by their government's decisions to invest more in security forces designed to stifle dissent and retain power than in the future prosperity and education of their people.

Security can therefore be thought of as 'a powerful political tool in claiming attention for priority items in the competition for government attention' (Buzan 1991: 370). Consequently, it matters a great deal who gets to decide what security means, what issues make it onto security agendas, how those issues should be dealt with, and, crucially, what happens when different visions of security collide. This is the stuff of security studies and the subject matter of this book.

Before moving to the substantive chapters in this volume, this introductory chapter does three things. First, it provides a brief overview of how the field of security studies has developed. Second, it discusses four central questions which help delineate the contours of the field as it exists today. Finally, it explains what follows in the rest of this book.

## What is security studies? A very short overview

As you will see throughout this book, there are many different ways to think about security; and hence security studies. Rather than adopt and defend one of these positions, the aim of this textbook is to provide you with an overview of the different perspectives, concepts, institutions and challenges that exercise the contemporary field of security studies. Consequently, not everyone agrees that all of the issues discussed in this book should be classified as part of security studies. The approach adopted here, however, is not to place rigid boundaries around the field. Instead, security studies is understood as an area of inquiry loosely focused around a set of basic but fundamental questions; the answers to which have changed, and will continue to change over time. Indeed, the first major attempt to provide an intellectual history of how international security has been studied argued that the interplay of five forces is 'particularly central' to understanding how the field has evolved: great power politics, technology, key events, the internal dynamics of academic debates, and institutionalization (the process through which networks form and resources allocated) (Buzan and Hansen 2009). These five forces roughly equate to concerns about material power, knowledge, history, prevailing social constructions, and wealth and organizational dynamics respectively.

Not surprisingly, security has been studied and fought over for as long as there have been human societies. As any study of the word's etymology will show, security has meant very different things to people depending on their time and place in human history (Rothschild 1995). But as the subject of professional academic inquiry, security studies is usually thought of as a relatively recent and largely European and American invention that came to prominence after the Second World War (see Booth 1997, McSweeney 1999: Part 1, Buzan and Hansen 2009). In this version – and it is just one, albeit popular version – of the field's history, security studies is understood as one of the most important subfields of academic IR. (The other core areas of IR are usually defined as international history, international theory, international law, international political economy and area studies.) Although it was given different labels in different places (National Security Studies was preferred in the US while Strategic Studies was a common epithet in the UK), there was general agreement that IR was the subfield's rightful disciplinary home. This resulted in the immediate exclusion of some key areas of study, notably domestic policing and issues related to the welfare of populations.

According to some analysts, the field enjoyed its 'golden age' during the 1950s and 1960s – a time when some civilians began to attain credibility as experts on military strategy and enjoyed relatively close connections with Western governments and their foreign and security policies (see Garnett 1970). 'During this golden age', as Lawrence Freedman (1998: 51) noted, 'Western governments found that they could rely on academic institutions for conceptual innovation, hard research, practical proposals, and, eventually, willing recruits for the bureaucracy. Standards were set for relevance and influence that would prove difficult to sustain'. In particular, security analysts busied themselves devising theories of nuclear deterrence (and nuclear warfighting), developing systems analysis related to the structure of armed forces and resource allocation, and with refining the tools of crisis management.

Particularly as it appeared during the Cold War, the dominant approach within security studies can be crudely summarized as advocating political realism and being preoccupied with the four 'S's of states, strategy, science and the status quo. It was focused on *states* inasmuch as they were considered (somewhat tautologically) to be both the most important agents and referents of security in international politics. It was about *strategy* inasmuch as the core intellectual and practical concerns revolved around devising the best means of employing the threat and use of military force. It aspired to be *scientific* inasmuch as to count as authentic, objective knowledge, as opposed to mere opinion, analysts were expected to adopt methods that aped the natural, harder sciences such as physics and chemistry. Only by approaching the study of security in a scientific manner could analysts hope to build a reliable bank of knowledge about international politics on which to base specific policies. Finally, traditional security studies reflected an implicit and conservative concern to preserve the *status quo* inasmuch as the great powers and the majority of academics who worked within them understood security policies as preventing radical and revolutionary change to international society while maintaining the position of their own states within it.

Although dissenting voices were always present during the Cold War, they did not make a great deal of intellectual or practical headway with respect to changing the foreign policies of the major powers. Arguably the most prominent dissenters were scholars engaged in peace research and those who focused on the security predicament of peoples and states in the so-called 'third world' (for more detail see Barash 2011, Thomas 1987, Buzan and Hansen 2009: ch.5).

A key development in theorizing about security occurred in 1983 with the publication of Barry Buzan's book *People, States and Fear* (see also Ullman 1983). This book fundamentally undermined at least two of the four 'S's of traditional security studies: security was not just about states but related to all human collectivities; nor could it be confined to an 'inherently inadequate' focus on military force. Buzan's alternative approach argued that the security of human collectivities (not just states) was affected by factors in five major sectors, each of which had its own focal point and way of ordering priorities:

- *Military security*: concerned with the interplay between the armed offensive and defensive capabilities of states and states' perceptions of each other's intentions. Buzan's preference was that the study of military security should be seen as one subset of security studies and referred to as strategic studies in order to avoid unnecessary confusion (see Buzan 1987).
- *Political security*: focused on the organizational stability of states, systems of government and the ideologies that give them their legitimacy.
- *Economic security*: revolved around access to the resources, finance and markets necessary to sustain acceptable levels of welfare and state power.
- *Societal security*: centred on the sustainability and evolution of traditional patterns of language, culture, and religious and national identity and custom.
- *Environmental security*: concerned with maintenance of the local and the planetary biosphere as the essential support system on which all other human enterprises depend.

Buzan's framework paid little attention to the gendered dimensions of security and the philosophical foundations of the field, particularly its dominant epistemology. As a consequence, his book did far less to disrupt the traditional focus on scientific methods or concerns to preserve the international status quo. Nevertheless, the considerably revised and expanded second edition of *People, States and Fear*, published in 1991, provided a timely way of thinking about security after the Cold War that effectively challenged the field's preoccupation with military force and rightly attempted to place such issues within their political, social, economic and environmental context.

Despite such changes, there are several problems with continuing to think of security studies as a subfield of IR – even a vastly broadened one. First of all, it is clear that inter-state relations are just one, albeit an important, aspect of the security dynamics that characterize contemporary world politics. States are not the only important actors, nor are they the only important referent objects for security. Second, there are some good intellectual reasons why security studies can no longer afford to live in IR's disciplinary shadow. Not least is the fact that IR remains an enterprise dominated by Anglo-American men where the orthodoxy remains wedded to the tradition of political realism (see Hoffmann 1977, Smith 2000). More specifically, and not surprisingly given its origins, traditional security studies stands accused of being written largely by Westerners and for Western governments (Barkawi and Laffey 2006). What this means is that the questions, issues and ways of thinking traditionally considered most important within the field were neither neutral nor natural but were, as Robert Cox famously put it, always 'for someone and for some purpose' (Cox 1981).

In addition, studying the traditional cannons of IR may not be the best preparation for a student whose primary interest is understanding security dynamics in contemporary world politics. Many of today's security problems are so complex and interdependent that they require analysis and solutions that IR cannot provide alone. Students should therefore look for insights across a variety of disciplines, and not only those within the humanities or social sciences. For example, analysing issues related to weapons of mass destruction (WMD) requires a degree of scientific and technical knowledge; understanding the causes of terrorism will involve a psychological dimension; assessing health risks requires some access to medical expertise; understanding environmental degradation involves engaging with biology and environmental history; combating transnational crime will necessarily involve a close relationship with criminology; while providing cyber security demands knowledge of many areas from computer programming to robotics. All this raises big questions about who are the real 'security' experts in world politics and where we might find them.

In sum, while security studies has its professional roots in the discipline of IR, today's world poses challenges that require students to engage with topics and sources of knowledge traditionally considered well beyond the IR pale. It is therefore unhelpful to think of security studies as just a subfield of IR. Instead, this book begins from the assumption that security studies is better understood as an area of inquiry revolving loosely around a set of core questions.

## Defining a field of inquiry: four fundamental questions

If we think about security studies as a field of inquiry, arguably four basic yet fundamental questions stand out as forming its intellectual core:

▨ What is security?

▨ Whose security are we talking about?

▨ What counts as a security issue?

▨ How can security be achieved?

Of course, depending on one's theoretical orientation and priorities, other foundational questions could be added to the list. For some feminists, for instance, 'where are the women and what are they doing?' remain guiding concerns; for critical theorists, 'who benefits from existing security policies?' is a fundamental issue; while for political sociologists, the research agenda should revolve around investigating the question 'what practices does "security" enable?'. But all theoretical approaches must grapple – either implicitly or explicitly – with these four core questions. So let us briefly examine what is entailed by posing each of them.

## What is security?

Asking what security means raises issues about the philosophy of knowledge, especially those concerning epistemology (how do we know things?), ontology (what phenomena do we think make up the social world?) and method (how should we study the social world?). If we accept the notion that security is an essentially contested concept then, by definition, such debates cannot be definitively resolved in the abstract. Instead, some positions will become dominant and be enforced because of the application of power.

With this in mind, security is most commonly associated with *the alleviation of threats to cherished values*; especially those which, left unchecked, threaten the survival of a particular referent object in the near future. To be clear, although security and survival are often related, they are not synonymous. Whereas survival is an existential condition, security involves the ability to pursue cherished political and social ambitions. Security is therefore best understood as what Ken Booth (2007) has called, 'survival-plus', 'the "plus" being some freedom from life-determining threats, and therefore some life choices'.

Put in rather stark terms, it is possible to identify two prevalent philosophies of security, each emerging from fundamentally different starting points. The first philosophy sees security as being virtually synonymous with the accumulation of power. From this perspective, security is understood as a commodity (i.e., to be secure, actors must possess certain things such as property, money, weapons, armies, territory, etc.). In particular, power is thought to be the route to security: the more power (especially military power) actors can accumulate, the more secure they will be.

The second philosophy challenges the idea that security flows from power. Instead, it sees security as being based on emancipation, that is, a concern with justice and the provision of human rights. From this perspective, security is understood as a relationship between different actors rather than a commodity. These relationships may be understood in either negative terms (i.e. security is about the absence of something threatening) or positive terms (i.e. involving phenomena that are enabling and make things possible). This distinction is commonly reflected in the ideas of 'freedom from' and 'freedom to'.

Understood in a relational sense, security involves gaining a degree of confidence about our relationships that comes through sharing certain commitments with other actors, which, in turn, provides a degree of reassurance and predictability. This view argues that it is not particular commodities (such as nuclear weapons) that are the crucial factor in understanding the security–insecurity equation but rather the relationship between the actors concerned. Thus while US decision-makers think Iran's possession of nuclear weapons would be a source of considerable insecurity, they do not feel the same way about the nuclear arsenals held by India or Israel. Consequently, in the second philosophy, true or stable security does not come from the ability to exercise power over others. Rather, it comes from cooperating to achieve security without depriving others of it. During the Cold War, such an approach was evident in Olaf Palme's call for 'common security', particularly his suggestion that protagonists 'must achieve security not against the adversary but together with him'. 'International security', Palme argued, 'must rest on a commitment to joint survival rather than on the threat of mutual destruction' (1982: ix). In practical terms, this means promoting emancipatory politics that take seriously issues about justice and human rights.

As the chapters in this book make clear, different perspectives and particular security policies subscribe to these philosophies to varying degrees. In practice, the differences are often stark with advocates of the former philosophy prioritizing military strength while supporters of the latter emphasize the importance of promoting justice and human rights.

## Whose security?

Asking whose security we are talking about is the next important and unavoidable step in the analytical process. Without a referent object there can be no threats and no discussion of security because the concept is meaningless without something to secure. As a result, we need to be clear about the referent objects of our analysis. In the long sweep of human history, the central focus of security has been people (Rothschild 1995). As noted above, however, within academic IR, security was often fused with 'the state'. Even more specifically, it was fused with a particular conception of 'the national interest' exemplified in the US National Security Act of 1947. This helped promote the rather confusing idea that security in international politics was synonymous with studying (and promoting) 'national security'. In fact, it is more accurate to say that what was being studied (and protected) was 'state security', not least because many states were often hostile to particular nationalities contained within their borders.

There are many plausible answers to the question 'whose security should we be talking about?' Not surprisingly, therefore, debate continues over who or what should constitute the ultimate referent object for security studies. For many decades, the dominant answer was that states were the most important referents. Particularly after the end of the Cold War, this position came under increasing challenge. In contrast, some analysts argued for priority to be given to human beings since without reference to individual humans, security makes no sense (e.g. Booth 1991a, McSweeney 1999). The problem, of course, is which humans to prioritize. This view has underpinned a large (and rapidly expanding) literature devoted to 'human security' (see Chapter 19 this volume). According to one popular definition, 'Human security is not a concern with weapons. It is a concern with human dignity. In the last analysis, it is a child who did not die, a disease that did not spread, an ethnic tension that did not explode, a dissident who was not silenced, a human spirit that was not crushed' (ul Haq 1995: 116).

A third approach has focused on the concept of 'society' as the most important referent object for security studies because humans do not always view group identities and collectivities in purely instrumental terms. Rather, to be fully human is to be part of specific social groups (Shaw 1994). Another perspective approached the question as a level-of-analysis problem, that is, it offered an analytical framework for thinking about possible referent objects from the lowest level (the individual) through various sources of collective identities (including bureaucracies, states, regions, civilizations etc.), right up to the level of the international system. In this schema, the analyst's job was to focus on the unavoidable relationships and tensions between the different levels of analysis (Buzan 1991, 1995).

In recent decades, a fifth approach has gained increasing prominence, calling for greater attention to be paid to planet Earth rather than to this or that group of human beings who happen to live upon it. This perspective argues that at a basic level, security policies must make ecological sense. In particular, they must recognize that humans are part of nature and dependent on ecosystems and the environment (Hughes 2006). After all, as Buzan (1991) put it, the environment is the essential support system on which all other human enterprises depend. Without a habitable environment, discussions of all other referents are moot.

### What is a security issue?

Once an analyst has decided on the meaning of security and whose security they are focusing upon, it is important to ask what counts as a security issue for that particular referent. This involves analysing the processes through which sources of insecurity are identified and threat agendas are constructed. In other words, who decides which of a referent object's cherished values are threatened, and by what or whom?

In one sense, every thinking individual on the planet operates with a unique set of security priorities shaped, in part, by factors such as their sex, gender, age, religious beliefs, class, race, nationality as well as where they are from, where they want to go, and what they want to see happen in the future. In spite of our individual concerns and anxieties, most of life's insecurities are shared by other individuals and groups. This means that when studying security it is important to pay attention to how representatives of particular groups and organizations construct threat agendas. It is also important to recognize that not all groups, and hence not all threat agendas, are of equal political significance. Clearly, what the US National Security Council or the United Nations Security Council considers a threat will have more significant and immediate political consequences for world politics than, say, the threat agendas constructed by Ghana's National Security Council, or, for instance, the concerns of HIV/AIDS sufferers living in one of Africa's many slums. The huge inequalities of power and influence that exist across individuals and groups in contemporary world politics raise significant methodological issues for students of security. Put bluntly, should we focus on the agendas of the powerful or the powerless or both? And where should an analyst's priorities lie if these agendas conflict with one another, as they almost always do?

One illustration of the politics of constructing threat agendas was the UN Secretary-General's High-Level Panel on Threats, Challenges and Change (2004), comprising sixteen eminent international civil servants and former diplomats. After much debate, the Panel's report, *A More Secure World*, identified six clusters of threats exercising the world's governments: economic and social threats, including poverty, infectious disease and environmental degradation; inter-state conflict; internal conflict, including civil war, genocide and other large-scale atrocities; nuclear, radiological, chemical and biological weapons; terrorism; and transnational organized crime (High-Level Panel 2004: 2). It quickly became apparent, however, that there was no consensus as to which of these clusters should receive priority: some, mainly developed Western states, considered threats from terrorism and WMD to be most pressing, while many states in the developing world thought that most resources should be devoted to tackling armed conflict and economic and social threats.

Arguments about what should count as a security issue also animate the academic field of security studies. One perspective argues that security analysts should focus their efforts on matters related to armed conflict and the threat and use of military force (e.g. Walt 1991, Brown 2007, Miller 2010). From this point of view, not only is armed conflict in the nuclear age one of the most pressing challenges facing humanity but the potentially endless broadening of the field's focus will dilute the concept of security's coherence, thereby fundamentally limiting its explanatory power and analytical utility.

On the other hand, there are those who argue that if security is supposed to be about alleviating the most serious and immediate threats that prevent people from pursuing their cherished values, then for many of the planet's inhabitants, lack of effective systems of healthcare are at least as important as the threat of armed conflict (e.g. Thomas 1987, 2000). After all, the biggest three killers in the developing world are maternal death around childbirth, and paediatric respiratory and intestinal infections leading to death from pulmonary failure or uncontrolled diarrhoea. To combat these killers, the world's governments have been urged to focus on building local capacities to achieve two basic but fundamental goals: increased maternal survival and increased overall life expectancy (Garrett 2007). In a world in which a girl born in Japan in 2011 has a life expectancy of roughly 86 years compared to 34 years for a girl born during the same year but in Zimbabwe, such issues are increasingly viewed as a legitimate part of the global security equation. Security analysts have traditionally focused on the challenges posed by war and the careers and needs of soldiers, who now number over 20 million on active duty and an additional 45 million reservists globally (International Institute for Strategic Studies 2011: 477). Perhaps in the future they should pay more attention to the challenges posed by sickness and the careers and needs of healthcare workers, of whom, according to one estimate, the world needs at least four million more (Garrett 2007: 15).

### How can security be achieved?

In the final analysis, studying security is important because it may help people – as individuals and groups – to achieve security. (Although it is important to note that for some analysts, 'security' has often been a way of legitimating oppressive structures of surveillance and control, see Chapter 9 this volume.) Asking how security might be achieved implies not only that we know what security means and what it looks like in different parts of the world, but also that there are particular actors which, through their conscious efforts, can shape the future in desired ways. In this sense, how we think about security and what we think a secure environment would entail will unavoidably shape the security policies we advocate. Most analysts reject the idea of total or absolute security as a chimera: all human life involves insecurities and risks of one sort or another. The practical issue is thus what level of threat are actors willing to tolerate before taking remedial action? As the US government's response to the 9/11 attacks demonstrates, tolerance levels can vary significantly in the light of events and as circumstances change.

In contemporary world politics, the agents of security can come in many shapes and sizes. IR students are usually most familiar with the actions of states and the debates about how they formulate and implement their security policies. Similarly, the actions of international organizations have long been a staple of security studies courses. Less attention has been devoted to analysing a wide range of non-state actors and the roles they can play as agents of both security and insecurity (but see Ekins 1992, Evangelista 1999, Keck and Sikkink 1998). Important examples might include social movements, humanitarian and development groups, private security contractors, insurgents, and criminal organizations. In addition, some individuals have the capacity to help provide security for particular referents in certain contexts. Sometimes this is because of the military power they may wield. On other occasions, however, their power may stem from their ability to disseminate a persuasive message; think, for example, of how Archbishop Desmond Tutu's ideas about reconciliation helped South Africans deal with apartheid's powerful legacies.

In sum, the world is full of actors engaged in the politics of security provision, whether or not they articulate their agendas in such terms. Understanding the environments in which these actors operate and how analysts should respond when their agendas conflict, is a central theme of this book.

## How to use this book

No textbook, even one as long as this, can be completely comprehensive in its coverage, not least because the field's focus will alter as political priorities and conceptions change. But, hopefully, the chapters that follow add up to more than just a snap-shot of the field. They are intended to provide students with a clear yet sophisticated introduction to some of the enduring theories, concepts, institutions and challenges that animate security studies.

As we have seen, all security policies rest on assumptions, concepts and theories, whether or not their proponents recognize it or make these assumptions explicit. Consequently, Part 1 of this book examines eight major theoretical approaches that lie beneath contemporary security policies. Although significant cracks have appeared in political realism's central assumptions, its various strands retain their powerful influence within many of the world's governments. As a result, it is important to recall that some of the theoretical approaches examined in this book are reflected in the current security policies of powerful actors to a greater degree than others.

But theories do not just reflect political practices, they also help construct them. Like tinted lenses that illuminate certain features of our environment at the expense of others, each theoretical approach offers a different perspective on what security studies is, and should be, about. Whether these perspectives are mutually exclusive or whether some or all of them can be combined in some form of eclectic synthesis remains the subject of ongoing debate but is not discussed in great detail in this book. Instead, each chapter sets out what security studies looks like from the perspective concerned. Of course, students should decide their preferences for themselves but in making such judgments one should carefully assess what a particular theory has to say about the core questions identified above.

While this plurality of theoretical perspectives has inevitably encouraged debates about the terms in which security studies is discussed, some concepts have proved a more durable part of the lexicon than others. The chapters in Part 2 therefore analyse fifteen concepts that appear at the centre of contemporary debates about security. Some of them, including polarity, war, coercion, intelligence and the security dilemma, formed the traditional core of the field, while others, such as poverty, environmental security, crimes against humanity and health are more recent, but important, arrivals.

Parts 1 and 2 of the book thus provide students with an introduction to the theoretical menu for choice in security studies and the central conceptual vocabulary used to debate important issues. Parts 3 and 4 build on this foundation to explore the institutional framework and some of the most urgent practical challenges exercising security analysts.

Part 3 surveys the current institutional architecture of world politics as it relates to security studies. It does so through three chapters which examine relevant institutions at the national, regional and global levels, and an additional three chapters which analyse the institutions of international peacekeeping, nuclear disarmament and non-proliferation and private security firms.

While the theoretical perspectives analysed in Part 1 differ in the significance they accord to such institutions, all of them agree that they should be judged in large part on how well they help humanity cope with a variety of contemporary security challenges. The chapters in Part 4 of this book therefore reflect upon seven key challenges related to armaments, terrorism, insurgency, mass atrocities, organized crime, population movements, and energy provision. As the authors make clear, overcoming these challenges will be far from easy and will require changes of attitude as well as behaviour.

Part 5 looks to the future with James Goldgeier offering an assessment of the interactions between the academic and policy worlds of security and Stuart Croft discussing the emerging trends within academia and how security is animating research across a variety of disciplines.

As long as it is, reading this book alone is not enough. In particular, I would encourage you to supplement this book with some area studies and also to look for insights in disciplines other than IR. Hopefully, you will relate what you read in this book to the real places and real people that interest you, and reflect upon which arguments resonate most with developments in specific parts of the world. Security studies without area studies encourages ethnocentric ways of thinking and is likely to exacerbate exactly the kind of tensions that most people are trying to avoid. If we do not take the time to study areas of the world other than our own and understand why others may see us in very different ways than we see ourselves, negative political consequences and insecurity will undoubtedly follow.

Finally, security studies has not been confined to IR; and nor should it be. The next generation of security analysts should thus continue to resist one of the negative consequences of the professionalization of academia, namely, the erection of rigid boundaries between disciplines. While a degree of specialization has its uses, it can degenerate into academic hair-splitting that loses sight of the bigger historical picture and the important links between different forms of human activity. Future students of security should happily dismantle disciplinary boundaries wherever they stifle innovative and critical thinking. In the twenty-first century, security is simply too important and too complex to be left to one group of specialists. This may make for longer and more complicated reading lists but it might just help produce more sophisticated analysis of the fundamental issues that lie at the heart of this fascinating and important subject.

# PART 1
# THEORETICAL APPROACHES

REALISMS

LIBERALISMS

GAME THEORY

CONSTRUCTIVISMS

PEACE STUDIES

CRITICAL THEORY

FEMINISMS

INTERNATIONAL POLITICAL SOCIOLOGY

# Realisms

Colin Elman and Michael A. Jensen

## Abstract

In this chapter, students will learn about the various strands of the realist research tradition and their different approaches to security studies: classical realism, neorealism, rise and fall, neoclassical, offensive structural, and defensive structural realism. Although sharing a pessimistic outlook about the continuity of inter-group strife, each of these research programmes is rooted in different assumptions and provides different explanations for the causes and consequences of conflict. These differences are illustrated with a discussion of what the contemporary strands of realism anticipate will happen in international politics as China's power continues to grow.

## Introduction

Looking back over the development of the security studies field, there is little doubt that the realist tradition has exercised an enormous influence. Even its harshest critics would acknowledge that realist theories, with their focus on power, fear, and anarchy, have provided centrally important explanations for conflict and war. Even when disputed, these accounts have often set scholars' baseline expectations. Proponents of other approaches often frame their value by claiming superiority over realist alternatives, especially their traction over deviant or puzzling cases for realism.

This chapter discusses several different realist approaches to security studies. Although there are significant differences among variants of realism, they largely share the view that the character of relations among states has not altered. Where there is change, it tends to occur in repetitive patterns. State behaviour is driven by leaders' flawed human nature, or by the preemptive unpleasantness mandated by an anarchic international system. Selfish human appetites for power, or the need to accumulate the wherewithal to be secure in a self-help world, explain the seemingly endless succession of wars and conquest. Accordingly, most realists take a pessimistic and prudential view of international relations (Elman 2001, though for an unusually optimistic realist approach see Glaser 1994/95, 1997).

In describing and appraising the realist tradition, it is customary to take a metatheoretic approach which differentiates it from other approaches, and which separates realist theories into distinct sub-groups (see Elman and Elman 2002, 2003). Accordingly, accounts of twentieth century realism typically distinguish political realist, liberal and other traditions, as well as describe different iterations of realist theory. As noted in Figure 2.1, this chapter distinguishes between six different variants of realism – classical realism, neorealism, and four flavours of contemporary realism: rise and fall, neoclassical, offensive structural, and defensive structural realism. While this ordering is not intended to suggest a strict temporal or intellectual succession, classical realism is usually held to be the first of the twentieth century realist research programmes.

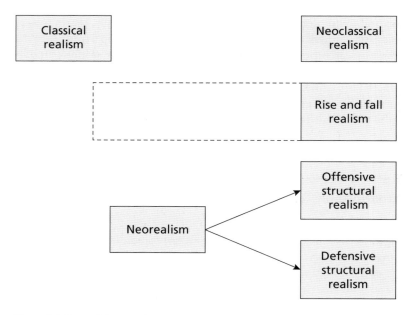

*Figure 2.1* Six realist research programmes

Realism's proponents argue that realist thinking extends well before the twentieth century, and often suggest that current theories are the incarnations of an extended intellectual tradition (e.g. Walt 2002: 198, Donnelly 2000). Hence scholars make the – often disputed – claim that realist themes can be found in important antiquarian works from Greece, Rome, India, and China (e.g. Smith, M. 1986, Haslam 2002: 14. Garst 1989 is a contrasting view). Since this chapter begins with twentieth-century classical realism we need not dwell on this controversy. It should be noted, however, that while realism's interpretation of particular episodes has been disputed, even its critics (e.g. Wendt 2000) acknowledge that humankind has, in most times and in most places, lived down to realism's very low expectations.

## Classical realism

Twentieth-century classical realism is generally dated from 1939, and the publication of Edward Hallett Carr's *The Twenty Years' Crisis*. Classical realists are usually characterized as responding to then-dominant liberal approaches to international politics (e.g. Donnelly 1995: 179) although scholars disagree on how widespread liberalism was during the interwar years (e.g. Kahler 1997: 24). In addition to Carr, work by Frederick Shuman (1933), Harold Nicolson (1939), Reinhold Niebuhr (1940), Georg Schwarzenberger (1941), Martin Wight (1946), Hans Morgenthau (1948), George F. Kennan (1951) and Herbert Butterfield (1953) formed part of the realist canon. It was, however, Hans Morgenthau's *Politics Among Nations: The Struggle for Power and Peace* which became the undisputed standard bearer for political realism, going through six editions between 1948 and 1985.

According to classical realism, because the desire for more power is rooted in the flawed nature of humanity, states are continuously engaged in a struggle to increase their capabilities. The absence of the international equivalent of a state's government is a permissive condition that gives human appetites free rein. In short, classical realism explains conflict with reference to human failings. Wars are explained, for example, by particular aggressive statesmen, or by domestic political systems that give greedy parochial groups the opportunity to pursue self-serving expansionist foreign policies. For classical realists international politics can be characterized as evil: bad things happen because the people making foreign policy are sometimes bad (Spirtas 1996: 387–400).

Although not employing the formal mathematical modelling found in contemporary rational choice theory (see Chapter 4 this volume), classical realism nevertheless posits that state behaviour can be understood as having rational microfoundations. As Morgenthau notes:

we put ourselves in the position of a statesman who must meet a certain problem of foreign policy under certain circumstances and we ask ourselves

> what the rational alternatives are from which a statesman may choose who must meet this problem under these circumstances (presuming always that he acts in a rational manner), and which of these rational alternatives this particular statesman is likely to choose. It is the testing of this rational hypothesis against the actual facts and their consequences that gives theoretical meaning to the facts of international politics.
>
> (Morgenthau 1985: 5)

State strategies are understood as having been decided rationally, after taking costs and benefits of different possible courses of action into account.

## Neorealism: Waltz's *Theory of International Politics*

Kenneth Waltz's 1979 *Theory of International Politics* replaced Morgenthau's *Politics Among Nations* as the standard bearer for realists. In *Theory of International Politics*, Waltz (1979: 77) argues that systems are composed of a structure and their interacting units. Political structures are best conceptualized as having three elements: an ordering principle (anarchic or hierarchical), the character of the units (functionally alike or differentiated), and the distribution of capabilities (Waltz 1979: 88–99). Waltz argues that two elements of the structure of the international system are constants: the lack of an overarching authority means that its ordering principle is anarchy, and the principle of self-help means that all of the units remain functionally alike. Accordingly, the only structural variable is the distribution of capabilities, with the main distinction falling between multipolar and bipolar systems (see Chapter 11 this volume).

One difference between classical realism and neorealism is their contrasting views on the source and content of states' preferences. Contra classical realism, neorealism excludes the internal make-up of different states. As Rasler and Thompson (2001: 47) note, Morgenthau's (1948) seminal statement of classical realism relied on the assumption that leaders of states are motivated by their lust for power. Waltz's (1979: 91) theory, by contrast, omits leaders' motivations and state characteristics as causal variables for international outcomes, except for the minimal assumption that states seek to survive.

In addition, whereas classical realism suggested that state strategies are selected rationally, Waltz is agnostic about which of several microfoundations explain state behaviour, several of which are mentioned in his book (1979). States' behaviour can be a product of the competition among them, either because they calculate how to act to their best advantage, or because those that do not exhibit such behaviour are selected out of the system. Alternatively, states' behaviour can be a product of socialization: states can decide to follow norms because they calculate it is to their advantage, or because the norms become internalized.

Since the theory provides such a minimal account of preferences and microfoundations, it makes only indeterminate behavioural predictions, and Waltz is correspondingly reluctant to make foreign policy predictions (Waltz 1996, see also Elman 1996a, 1996b, Fearon 1998, Wivel 2005). Waltz nevertheless suggests that systemic processes will consistently produce convergent international outcomes. Waltz notes that international politics is characterized by a disheartening consistency; the same depressingly familiar things happen over and over. This repetitiveness endures despite considerable differences in internal domestic political arrangements, both through time (contrast, for example, seventeenth- and nineteenth-century England) and space (contrast, for example, the United States and Germany in the 1930s). Waltz's purpose is to explain why similarly structured international systems all seem to be characterized by similar outcomes, even though their units (i.e. member states) have different domestic political arrangements and particular parochial histories. Waltz concludes that it must be something peculiar to, and pervasive in, international politics that accounts for these commonalities. He therefore excludes as 'reductionist' all but the thinnest of assumptions about the units that make up the system – they must, at a minimum, seek their own survival.

By focusing only minor attention on unit-level variables, Waltz aims to separate out the persistent effects of the international system. Jervis (1997: 7) observes that: 'We are dealing with a system when (a) a set of units or elements is interconnected so that changes in some elements or their relations produce changes in other parts of the system; and (b) the entire system exhibits properties and behaviors that are different from those parts.' Because systems are generative, the international political system is characterized by complex nonlinear relationships and unintended consequences. Outcomes are influenced by something more than simply the aggregation of individual states' behaviour, with a tendency toward unintended and ironic outcomes. As a result, there is a gap between what states want and what states get. Consequently, unlike classical realists, neorealists see international politics as tragic, rather than as being driven by the aggressive behaviour of revisionist states (Spirtas 1996: 387–400). The international political outcomes that Waltz predicts include that multipolar systems will be less stable than bipolar systems; that interdependence will be lower in bipolarity than multipolarity; and that regardless of unit behaviour, hegemony by any single state is unlikely or even impossible.

Waltz's *Theory of International Politics* proved to be a remarkably influential volume, spinning off new debates and giving new impetus to existing disagreements. For example, the book began a debate over whether relative gains concerns impede cooperation among states (e.g. Grieco 1988, Snidal 1991a, 1991b, Powell 1991, Baldwin 1993, Grieco, Powell and Snidal 1993, Rousseau 2002), and added momentum to the extant question of whether bipolar or multipolar international systems are more war prone (e.g. Deutsch and Singer 1964, Wayman 1984, Sabrosky 1985, Hopf 1991, Mansfield 1993).

Partly because of its popularity, and partly because of its own 'take-no-prisoners' criticism of competing theories, Waltz's *Theory of International Politics* became a prominent target. As time went by, detractors chipped away at the book's dominance (e.g. Keohane 1986). Non-realist work, in particular neoliberal institutionalism and investigations of the democratic peace, became more popular (see Keohane and Martin 2003, Ray 2003). Realism's decline in the 1990s was amplified by international events. The closing years of the twentieth century seemed to provide strong support for alternative approaches. The Soviet Union's voluntary retrenchment and subsequent demise; the continuation of Western European integration in the absence of American–Soviet competition; the wave of democratization and economic liberalization throughout the former Soviet Union, Eastern Europe and the developing world; and the improbability of war between the great powers all made realism seem out-dated (Jervis 2002). It appeared that liberal or constructivist theories could better appreciate and explain the changes taking place in the international arena. Not surprisingly, the post-9-11 arena seems much more challenging, and it comes as no revelation that political realism claims to be better suited to address threats to national security. It is, however, ironic that its renaissance is at least partly owed to transnational terrorist networks motivated by religious extremism, actors and appetites that both lie well outside realism's traditional ambit.

Excluding neorealism, there are at least four contemporary strands of political realism: rise and fall realism, neoclassical realism, defensive structural realism, and offensive structural realism. All four take the view that international relations are characterized by an endless and inescapable succession of wars and conquest. The four groupings can be differentiated by the fundamental constitutive and heuristic assumptions that their respective theories share. Briefly, the approaches differ on the sources of state preferences – the mix of human desire for power and/or the need to accumulate the wherewithal to be secure in a self-help world – while agreeing that rational calculation is the microfoundation that translates those preferences into behaviour.

## Defensive structural realism

Defensive structural realism developed, but is distinct, from neorealism (Glaser 2003, Walt 2002). Defensive structural realism shares neorealism's minimal assumptions about state motivations. Like neorealism, defensive structural realism suggests that states seek security in an anarchic international system – the main threat to their well-being comes from other states (Glaser 2003, Walt 2002).

There are three main differences between neorealism and defensive structural realism. First, whereas neorealism allows for multiple microfoundations to explain state behaviour, defensive structural realism relies solely on rational choice. Second, defensive structural realism adds the offence–defence balance as a variable (see Van Evera 1999: 10). This is a composite variable combining a variety of different factors that make conquest harder or easier (for outstanding reviews of the offence–defence literature see Lynn-Jones 1995, 2001). Defensive structural realists argue that prevailing technologies or geographical circumstances often favour defence, seized resources do not cumulate easily with those already possessed by the metropole, dominoes do not fall, and power is difficult to project at a distance (see, respectively, Christensen and Snyder 1990, Liberman 1993, Jervis and Snyder 1991, Mearsheimer 2001). Accordingly, in a world in which conquest is hard it may not take too much balancing to offset revisionist behaviour. Third, combining rationality and an offence–defence balance that favours defence, defensive structural realists predict that states should support the status quo. Expansion is rarely structurally mandated, and balancing is the appropriate response to threatening concentrations of power (e.g. Walt 1987, 1996). Rationalism and an offence–defence balance that favours defence means that states balance, and balances result.

Perhaps the best known variant of defensive structural realism is Stephen Walt's 'balance of threat' theory (e.g. Walt 1987, 2000. See also Van Evera 1999, Snyder 1991, Glaser 1994/95, 1997). According to Walt, 'in anarchy, states form alliances to protect themselves. Their conduct is determined by the threats they perceive and the power of others is merely one element in their calculations' (1987: x). Walt suggests that states estimate threats posed by other states by their relative power, proximity, intentions, and the offence–defence balance (2000: 200–201). The resulting dyadic balancing explains the absence of hegemony in the system:

> Together, these four factors explain why potential hegemons like Napoleonic France, Wilhelmine Germany, and Nazi Germany eventually faced over-whelming coalitions: each of these states was a great power lying in close proximity to others, and each combined large offensive capabilities with extremely aggressive aims.
>
> (Walt 2000: 201)

Because balancing is pervasive, Walt (1987: 27) concludes that revisionist and aggressive behaviour is self-defeating, and 'status quo states can take a relatively sanguine view of threats. . . . In a balancing world, policies that convey restraint and benevolence are best'.

One difficult problem for defensive structural realism is that the research programme is better suited to investigating structurally constrained responses to revisionism, rather than where that expansionist behaviour comes from. To explain how conflict arises in the first place, defensive structural realists must appeal to either domestic level factors (which are outside of their theory), or argue that extreme security dilemma dynamics make states behave as if they were revisionists. John Herz (1950: 157) was an early exponent of the concept of the security dilemma, arguing that defensive actions and capabilities are often misinterpreted as being aggressive (see also Butterfield 1951: 19–20; Chapter 10 this volume). Steps taken by states seeking to preserve the status quo are ambiguous, and are often indistinguishable from preparations for taking the offence. 'Threatened' states respond, leading to a spiralling of mutual aggression that all would have preferred to avoid. This is international relations as tragedy, not evil: bad things happen because states are placed in difficult situations.

Defensive structural realism has some difficulty in relying on security dilemma dynamics to explain war. It is not easy to see how, in the absence of pervasive domestic level pathologies, revisionist behaviour can be innocently initiated in a world characterized by status quo states, defence–dominance and balancing (see Schweller 1996, Kydd 2005). Because increments in capabilities can be easily countered, defensive structural realism suggests that a state's attempt to make itself more secure by increasing its power is ultimately futile. This is consistent with Arnold Wolfers' (1962: 158–9) reading of the security dilemma, that states threatened by new, potentially offensive capabilities respond with measures of their own, leaving the first state in as precarious a position, if not worse off than before. Hence, defensive realists suggest that states should seek an 'appropriate' amount of power, not all that there is. If states do seek hegemony, it is due to domestically generated preferences; seeking superior power is not a rational response to external systemic pressures.

## Offensive structural realism

Offensive structural realists disagree with the defensive structural realist prescription that states look for only an 'appropriate' amount of power. The flagship statement, John Mearsheimer's (2001) *The Tragedy of Great Power Politics*, argues that states face an uncertain international environment in which any state might use its power to harm another. Under such circumstances, relative capabilities are of overriding importance, and security requires acquiring as much power compared to other states as possible (see also Labs 1997, Elman 2004). The stopping power of water means that the most a state can hope for is to be a regional hegemon, and for there to be no other regional hegemons elsewhere in the world.

Mearsheimer's (2001: 30–31) theory makes five assumptions: the international system is anarchic; great powers inherently possess some offensive military capability, and accordingly can damage each other; states can never be certain about other states' intentions; survival is the primary goal of great powers; and great powers are rational actors. From these assumptions, Mearsheimer deduces that great powers fear each other; that they can rely only on themselves for their security; and that the best strategy for states to ensure their survival is maximization of relative power (2001: 32–36).

In contrast to defensive structural realists, who suggest that states look for only an 'appropriate' amount of power (e.g. Glaser 1994/95, 1997, Van Evera 1999), Mearsheimer argues that security requires acquiring as much power relative to other states as possible. Mearsheimer (2001: 417, n. 27) explicitly rejects Glaser's (1997, and thus Wolfer's 1962) reading of the security dilemma, and argues that increasing capabilities can improve a state's security without triggering a countervailing response. Careful timing by revisionists, buckpassing by potential targets, and information asymmetries all allow the would-be hegemon to succeed. Power maximization is not necessarily self-defeating, and hence states can rationally aim for regional hegemony.

Although states will take any increment of power that they can get away with, Mearsheimer does not predict that states are 'mindless aggressors so bent on gaining power that they charge headlong into losing wars or pursue Pyrrhic victories' (2001: 37). States are sophisticated relative power maximizers that try 'to figure out when to raise and when to fold' (2001: 40). Expanding against weakness or indecision, pulling back when faced by strength and determination, a sophisticated power maximizer reaches regional hegemony by using a combination of brains and brawn.

Mearsheimer (2001: 140–155) argues that ultimate safety comes only from being the most powerful state in the system. However, the 'stopping power of water' makes such global hegemony all but impossible, except through attaining an implausible nuclear superiority. The second best, and much more likely, objective is to achieve regional hegemony, the dominance of the area in which the great power is located. Finally, even in the absence of either type of hegemony, states try to maximize both their wealth and their military capabilities for fighting land battles. In order to gain resources, states resort to war, blackmail, baiting states into making war on each other while standing aside, and engaging competitors in long and costly conflicts. When acting to forestall other states' expansion, a great power can either try to inveigle a third party into coping with the threat (i.e. buckpass), or balance against the threat themselves (2001: 156–162). While buckpassing is often preferred as the lower cost strategy, balancing becomes more likely, *ceteris paribus*, the more proximate the menacing state, and the greater its relative capabilities.

In addition to moving Mearsheimer's focus to the regional level, the introduction of the stopping power of water also leads to his making different predictions of state behaviour depending on where it is located. While the theory applies to great powers in general (2001: 5, 403 n. 5), Mearsheimer distinguishes between different kinds: continental and island great powers, and regional hegemons. A continental great power will seek regional hegemony but, when it is unable to achieve this dominance, such a state will still maximize its relative power to the extent possible. An insular state, 'the only great power on a large body of land that is surrounded on all sides by water' (2001: 126), will balance against the rising states rather than try to be a regional hegemon itself. Accordingly, states such as the United Kingdom act as offshore balancers, intervening only when a continental power is near to achieving primacy (2001: 126–128, 261–264). The third kind of great power in

Mearsheimer's theory is a regional hegemon such as the United States. A regional hegemon is a status quo state that will seek to defend the current favourable distribution of capabilities (2001: 42).

Mearsheimer's theory provides a structural explanation of great power war, suggesting that 'the main causes . . . are located in the architecture of the international system. What matters most is the number of great powers and how much power each controls' (2001: 337). Great power wars are least likely in bipolarity, where the system only contains two great powers, because there are fewer potential conflict dyads; imbalances of power are much less likely; and miscalculations leading to failures of deterrence are less common. While multipolarity is, in general, more war prone than bipolarity, some multipolar power configurations are more dangerous than others. Great power wars are most likely when multipolar systems are unbalanced; that is, when there is a marked difference in capabilities between the first and second states in the system, such that the most powerful possesses the means to bid for hegemony. Mearsheimer hypothesizes that the three possible system architectures range from unbalanced multipolarity's war proneness to bipolarity's peacefulness, with balanced multipolarity falling somewhere in between (2001: 337–346).

## Rise and fall realism

Rise and fall realism emerged as a powerful alternative to the balance of power theories that predominated international relations scholarship during the 1950s (Kugler and Lemke 2000: 130). A.F.K. Organski's classic 1958 volume, *World Politics*, challenged the popular belief that power parity is a virtue in international relations by insisting that throughout history 'world peace has coincided with periods of unchallenged supremacy of power, whereas the periods of approximate balance have been the periods of war' (Organski 1968a: 364). Organski's claim that hegemony is the foundation for peace, while balance is often associated with war has since become a central theme of rise and fall realism.

In particular, the research programme emphasizes that war between major powers is least likely when the international system is dominated by a single state, and when there are no rising challengers vying for system leadership. Given its privileged position, a dominant state is capable of shaping the rules and practices of the international system in such a way as to satisfy its selfish interests. Stability is a product of this hegemonic order, as states which are dissatisfied with the status quo lack the capabilities to change it. However, when power becomes more evenly matched as a result of differential growth patterns, war over system leadership is likely to occur. As the power gap between the leading state and its rival(s) narrows, the declining hegemon may rationally calculate the need for preventative war in order to preserve its status as the world's top power (Gilpin 1981). In the absence of a preventative attack, a dissatisfied rising challenger could initiate a war in an attempt to capture the top spot and all of the benefits that go along with it (Organski 1968a, 1968b).

Rise and fall realism depicts the course of human history, or some significant portion of it, as the successive rise and fall of great powers. In order to explain this historical trend, the research programme pays particular attention to the mechanisms that cause states to grow at different rates and at different times. In contrast to neorealism, which sees changes in the distribution of capabilities in the international system as being primarily the product of alliances and war, rise and fall realists contend that differential growth rates are mainly caused by processes which are internal to states. These include the timing of industrialization (Organski 1958, 1968b), social formation and type of economic system (Gilpin 1981), bureaucratic politics and productivity (Doran 1983), and military, economic, and technological innovation (Modelski 1978). Since these dynamics are not at work in all states at the same time or to the same extent, states tend to rise and fall in relation to one another. Thus, internal developments and the timing of their onset produce the periods of transition from one system leader to the next which are often marked by war.

The rise and fall research programme has spawned a number of theories to explain differential growth patterns and the onset of major power war. These include power transition theory (Organski 1958, 1968a, 1968b, Organski and Kugler 1980, Kugler and Organski 1989, Kugler and Lemke 1996, 2000, Lemke 1995, 1996, DiCicco and Levy 1999, 2003), hegemonic war theory (Gilpin 1981, 1988), power cycle theory (Doran 1983, 1989, 2000, Doran and Parsons 1980), leadership long cycle theory (Modelski 1978, Modelski and Morgan 1985, Thompson 1983, 1986, 1990, Rasler and Thompson 1983, 1985, 1991, 1994, 2000) and dynamic differentials theory (Copeland 2001). These theories are differentiated from each other by the position they take on a number of key issues, including (1) whether it is the rising challenger or the declining hegemon that initiates war; (2) what specific internal process(es) drive differential growth; and (3) whether the theory is applicable across time and space, or limited to a period of history or a particular region of the world.

While continuing to emphasize the onset of major power war, in recent years rise and fall realists have extended the scope of their studies to other important aspects of international relations. For example, Douglas Lemke (1995, 1996) has applied power transition theory to dyads other than those involving states directly contesting for system leadership, while Lemke and Jacek Kugler (2000) have studied the theory's implications for nuclear deterrence. Moreover, recent theoretical emendations, such as Woosang Kim's (1991, 1992, 1996, 2002) addition of alliances to the calculation of differential growth and Dale Copeland's (2001) use of security concerns and polarity to explain great power competition, have enriched the explanatory power of the research programme and provided a solid foundation for future research on power trends and war.

## Neoclassical realism

In part responding to what were perceived as the anti-reductionist excesses of neorealism (e.g. Snyder 1991: 19), neoclassical realism suggests that what states do depends in large part on influences located at the domestic-level of analysis. Neoclassical realism employs a 'transmission belt' (Rose 1998) approach to foreign policy, which illustrates how systemic pressures are filtered through variables at the unit-level to produce specific foreign policy decisions.

While neoclassical realists agree that the distribution of capabilities is a good starting point for the analysis of foreign policy decision-making, they also insist that pressures from the international system are often unclear and indeterminate. The international arena is murky and difficult to read, threats and opportunities are not easily identifiable, and the range of possibilities open to statesmen for meeting strategic goals is practically infinite. Given these challenges, variables at the unit-level often intervene between the international system and state behaviour to determine the precise nature and direction of a state's foreign economic and military policy. In particular, neoclassical realists stress the role that the perceptions of key decision-makers (Christensen and Snyder 1990, Wohlforth 1993) and the unity and extractive capacity of the state (Christensen 1996, Zakaria 1998, Schweller 2006, Taliaferro 2006, Lobell, Ripsman, and Taliaferro, 2009) play in shaping how states respond to systemic imperatives.

Randall Schweller's (2006) theory of 'under-balancing' is a good example of the transmission belt approach favoured by neoclassical realists. Schweller starts with a central tenet of structural realism, which posits that how states behave in international politics is foremost determined by relative distributions of material power in the international system. Schweller notes, however, that exactly how states choose to react to threatening accumulations of power depends on the degree to which they embody structural realism's unitary actor assumption. When systemic pressures are transmitted through states which are unified at the elite and societal levels, decision-makers find it easy to recognize threats and carry out appropriate balancing strategies to counter them. Fragmented states, on the other hand, find it quite difficult to do the same because elite decision-makers cannot come to an agreement on the nature of a threat or how best to deal with it, and the state apparatus lacks the necessary extractive power to tap society for the resources needed to restore a balance of power. According to Schweller, both France and Britain were fragmented states prior to the Second World War, and this explains why they both under-reacted to the threat posed by a rising Germany.

Similar frameworks have been used by a host of scholars to explain a variety of foreign policy behaviours, particularly those that seem to deviate from the baseline predictions of defensive structural realism and neorealism. Neoclassical realists have developed theories to explain over-extension (Dueck 2006, Layne 2006, Snyder 1991), under-expansion (Zakaria 1998, Schweller 2009), under-balancing (Schweller 2006, Lobell 2009); risk-taking behaviour

(Taliaferro 2004), poor alliance decisions (Christensen and Snyder 1990), and unwarranted antagonism (Christensen 1996; Sterling-Folker 2009), to name just a few.

## Realisms and the rise of China

As the preceding discussion illustrates, realism is a diverse research tradition consisting of a range of perspectives on international politics and foreign policy behaviour. The tradition's theoretical diversity is nowhere more apparent than in the different, and sometimes contending, predictions that realists make about how China's growth in power is likely to shape international relations in the coming years (see Friedberg 2005, Christensen 2006, Legro 2007, and Fravel 2010). While offensive structural realists and rise and fall realists share a pessimistic view of the consequences of China's tremendous growth for global security, defensive structural realists are more optimistic that relations between China and the rest of the world can remain peaceful. Neoclassical realism, on the other hand, is open to a wide range of potential outcomes, ranging from mutual accommodation to outright war. This section will briefly review how the four contemporary varieties of realism – offensive structural, defensive structural, rise and fall, and neoclassical – see the rise of Chinese power influencing the course of international relations in the future.

### Offensive structural realism

Offensive realism paints a bleak picture of the future of international relations if China continues its ascent (see Mearsheimer 2001, 2006, Wang 2004, Fravel 2010, Kirshner forthcoming). Offensive realists argue that, given the required capabilities, states will pursue regional hegemony as the best means of staying safe in a dangerous world. The United States did so in the nineteenth century, when it pushed the European powers out of the western hemisphere and went on to dominate the region. Most offensive realists stress that there is no reason to assume that, if given the chance, China will behave any differently (although for a contrasting view see Elman 2004).

In particular, offensive realism predicts that if China's power continues to grow it is likely to assert greater control in Asia. China will invest more of its resources in military capabilities in order to become the predominant power in the region. While China may not use those capabilities to conquer its regional neighbours, it will use them to try to dictate how they behave. China will also look to force the United States from the region through a mix of military might and its own version of the Monroe Doctrine (Mearsheimer 2006: 162).

For their part, China's neighbours and the United States are not likely to sit idly by and watch as China takes over. Fearing for their security, powerful countries, like Japan, Russia, and India, and small ones, like South Korea and Vietnam, will join the United States in a balancing coalition to counter

China's rise (Mearsheimer 2006). Intense security competition between China and the American-led coalition is expected to result, with the United States pursuing aggressive policies in an attempt to remain the world's only regional hegemon. While this rivalry will not guarantee violent conflict, it will create a situation where war is significantly more likely.

## Defensive structural realism

Defensive realists are far more optimistic about China's rise and the future of international security. As they see it, the international system is relatively benign. Aggressive behaviour and power maximization usually trigger self-defeating balancing coalitions, technology and geography make offensive action difficult, and states can signal their peaceful intentions. Rational states, therefore, have little reason to worry about each other based on considerations of power alone. Thus, while China's rise in power will not be welcomed by its neighbours or the United States, it need not be feared by them either.

To be sure, defensive realists expect that as China continues to rise it will devote more of its resources to military technology and capabilities. And although these developments could spark the security dilemma dynamics that can lead to arms racing and war, defensive realists stress that measures can be taken by China to signal to other states that these investments are meant for security purposes alone (see Glaser 1994/95). For example, China could limit its military investments to technologies that work well for defence, but have little or no offensive use. When paired with the belief that conquest is difficult because of defensive advantage and the pervasiveness of balancing, defensive realists expect that any security competition that occurs as a result of China's growth in power will be countered by a healthy dose of assurance and rational restraint. This is not to say that defensive realists believe that war between China and an American-led coalition is impossible. Rather, defensive realism stresses that if war were to occur it would not be because structure mandated it. Some domestic-level pathology, such as log-rolling interest groups (Snyder 1991) or misperception (Van Evera 1999), would be to blame.

## Rise and fall realism

Rise and fall realism shares offensive realism's pessimism about a rising China and the prospects for cooperation and peace in international politics (e.g. Fravel 2010). According to this view, increased security competition and major power war are most likely when a rising challenger and declining hegemon approach power parity. Thus, as China rises relative to the United States, relations between the two countries will become increasingly antagonistic, reaching crisis levels as they near each other on measures of material power (see Kugler and Lemke 2000). If this occurs, the United States is unlikely to willingly or peacefully cede to China its position atop the international system, and the remarkable advantages that go along with it. Instead, American officials could deem that preventative actions, including war, are necessary to forestall China's rise and preserve United States hegemony. Likewise, as China's power increases, Chinese leaders are likely to demand more influence in international politics and a greater share of international spoils. If these expectations are not met, China could try to dethrone the United States by launching a hegemonic war.

For rise and fall realism, whether or not China's rise ultimately results in contained security competition or a catastrophic war depends in large part on China's ability to continue its unprecedented growth. China's rise is driven primarily by domestic processes, including industrialization, that could break down or end before it becomes powerful enough to challenge the United States for international dominance. Rise and fall realism also stresses that even if Chinese growth were to continue at current levels, much of how the two states behave toward each other in the future will come down to American and Chinese evaluations of the status quo. American officials are more likely to be open to taking preventative action to stop the rise of China if they believe that the decline of the United States is deep and inevitable (Copeland 2001). Similarly, Chinese leaders are more likely to evaluate the status quo unfavourably if they deem that the policies and actions of the United States significantly limit their ability to achieve benefits in line with the country's growing power (Kugler and Lemke 2000).

## Neoclassical realism

Neoclassical realism does not make a determinate prediction about China's rise and its implications for the future of Sino-American relations and international security. However, neoclassical realists agree that basing predictions on objective power trends alone will lead to inaccurate forecasts about the foreign policy decisions that China, its neighbours, and the United States are liable to make. A more accurate understanding of what these players are likely to do requires a consideration of the domestic-level factors that shape how states interpret and respond to systemic constraints.

In particular, neoclassical realism expects that the perceptions of key decision-makers and the ability of the state to mobilize resources for the purposes of foreign policy will play a decisive role in determining how China behaves and how others respond. Thomas Christensen's (1996) study of Sino-American relations during the early part of the Cold War showed that Chinese and American leaders frequently prolonged short-term crises between the two countries, often risking war, in order to mobilize resources from their domestic societies for the purpose of long-term grand strategy. If this were to be the case again, neoclassical realism would expect future relations between China and the United States to be more hostile than they are today as a result of leaders in both countries trying to cope with weak state institutions and the inability to extract resources from their citizens.

Neoclassical realism also expects that perceptions of China's rise in the United States and Asia will play a large part in determining whether China's growth is met with suspicion and fear, or reassurance and collaboration. If

American and Asian officials perceive China's growth to be threatening, they are considerably more likely to adopt aggressive containment strategies than they are if they view China to have benign intentions. Given that perceptions are based on a number of complex factors, including past behaviours, shared expectations, and the cognitive biases of individual leaders, it is impossible to predict how China's growth will be viewed years from now by individuals who are tasked with making foreign policy decisions.

## Conclusion

This chapter has reviewed six variants of realism: classical realism, neorealism, rise and fall realism, neoclassical realism, defensive structural realism and offensive structural realism. As the discussion has shown, realism is a multifaceted and durable tradition of inquiry in security studies, with an extraordinary facility for adaptation. The development of the realist tradition within these separate components has at least three significant ramifications.

First, while the research programmes have some common characteristics with each other, none makes wholly overlapping arguments or predictions. Although it is possible to support some general remarks about the realist tradition (for example the observations about realism's continuity and pessimism in the introduction to this essay) one should otherwise be leery of statements that begin 'Realism says . . .' or 'Realism predicts . . .'. Different realist theories say and predict different things. They will also have very different implications when considered as the basis for prescriptive policy. For example, the best offensive structural realism has to offer the world is an armed and watchful peace anchored in mutual deterrence, punctuated by wars triggered by structurally driven revisionism when a state calculates it can gain at another's disadvantage. The best defensive structural realism has to offer is a community of status quo states that have successfully managed to signal their peaceful intentions and/or refrained from obtaining ambiguously offensive capabilities.

Second, realism's capacity for change opens the tradition to some criticisms. For example, realists have been scolded for making self-serving adjustments to their theories to avoid contradiction by empirical anomalies. John Vasquez (1997) argues that balance-of-power theory, as described and defended by Kenneth Waltz (1979), Stephen Walt (1987), Thomas Christensen and Jack Snyder (1990), Randall Schweller (1994) and Colin Elman and Miriam Fendius Elman (1995) is degenerative when judged by Imre Lakatos's (1970) criteria. Vasquez suggests that balance of power theory is empirically inaccurate, but that succeeding versions of the theory have become progressively looser to allow it to accommodate disconfirming evidence. A related critique was launched by Jeffrey Legro and Andrew Moravcsik (1999), who argue that recent realists subsume arguments that are more usually associated with competing liberal or constructivist approaches. The result, they argue, is that realist theories have become less determinate, coherent and distinctive. These critiques have provoked vigorous and ongoing responses from realist scholars (e.g. Feaver *et al.* 2000, Vasquez and Elman 2003).

Finally, despite its internal divisions and external critics, the realist tradition continues to be a central contributor to security studies. Now fully recovered from the excessive optimism of the immediate post-Cold War milieu, the tradition is likely to provide a substantial share of our explanations and understandings of the causes of conflict and war.

## Further reading

Robert Gilpin, *War and Change in World Politics* (Cambridge University Press, 1981). A leading work in the 'rise and fall' realist tradition, which investigates the consequences of unequal growth rates for great power politics.

John J. Mearsheimer, *The Tragedy of Great Power Politics* (W.W. Norton, 2001). The flagship statement of offensive structural realism suggests that states pursue sophisticated power maximization to achieve security.

Hans Morgenthau, *Politics Among Nations: The Struggle for Power and Peace*, 6th edition (McGraw-Hill, 1985). The most important classical realist text, and one of the two most influential realist books written since the Second World War, this volume suggests that unchanging human nature is the root cause of conflict.

Randall L. Schweller, *Unanswered Threats: Political Constraints on the Balance of Power* (Princeton University Press, 2006). A groundbreaking neoclassical realist volume which illustrates how unit-level factors influence foreign policy decisions.

Stephen M. Walt, *The Origins of Alliances* (Cornell University Press, 1987). An important contribution to the defensive structural realist research program, which argues that threat (and not just aggregate capabilities) determines how states respond to one another.

Kenneth N. Waltz, *Theory of International Politics* (Addison Wesley, 1979). The seminal neorealist work, and the second of the two most important realist volumes, this book shifted the realist research tradition away from the individual and towards the international system.

# Liberalisms

Cornelia Navari

**Abstract**

In this chapter, students will learn about the major debates concerning security within various strands of liberal thought. The first section outlines traditional/Kantian liberalism. The second section introduces liberal economic thought regarding peace and war and the idea of *douce commerce*. The third section describes the democratic peace thesis, and reviews the major discussions on the idea that liberal states do not fight wars with other liberal states. The last section outlines the major arguments in neoliberal institutionalism. It concludes by highlighting the main differences between realist approaches to security and liberal approaches.

## Introduction

> True internationalism and world peace will come through individual freedom,
> the free market, and the peaceful and voluntary associations of civil society.
> Richard M. Ebeling (2000)

The liberal tradition in thinking about security dates as far back as the philosopher Immanuel Kant (1724–1804), who emphasized the importance of 'republican' constitutions in producing peace. His pamphlet, *Perpetual Peace* contains a peace plan, and may fairly be called the first liberal tract on the subject. But liberal thinking on security has been elaborated by different schools within a developing tradition of more general liberal thought. Andrew Moravcsik (2001) has distinguished between ideational, commercial and republican liberalism following Michael Doyle (1998) who had earlier distinguished between international, commercial and ideological liberalism, each with rather different implications for security planning; and Zacher and Mathews (1995) who identified four different tendencies in liberal security thought. Each of these thinkers is reflecting upon a family of loosely knit concepts, containing in some cases rather opposed approaches. Kant believed that trade was likely to engender conflict, while later 'commercial' liberals saw in trade a beneficial and beneficent development. Republican liberals argue that peace is rooted in the liberalism of the liberal state – the internal approach – while neoliberal institutionalists emphasize the role of international institutions, which could ameliorate conflict from without.

## Traditional or Kantian liberalism

Immanuel Kant was an enlightenment philosopher (some would say the greatest enlightenment philosopher), often noted for his approach to ethics. (Kant argued that moral behaviour resulted from moral choices and that these were guided by an inner sense of duty – when individuals behaved according to duty, they were being moral.) But he was not only an ethicist; he philosophized the 'good state' as well as its international relations. According to Kant, the only justifiable form of government was *republican government*, a condition of constitutional rule where even monarchs ruled according to the law. Moreover, the test of good laws was their 'universalizability' – the test of universal applicability. The only laws that deserved the name of 'law' were those one could wish everyone (including oneself) obeyed. Such laws became 'categorical imperatives'; they were directly binding, and monarchs as well as ordinary citizens were subject to them.

Kant argued that republican states were 'peace producers'; that is, they were more inclined to peaceful behaviour than other sorts of states. He attributed this to habits of consultation; a citizenry which had to be consulted before going to war would be unlikely to endorse war easily. He also attributed it to the legal foundations of the republican state: he believed a state built on law was less likely to endorse lawless behaviour in international relations.

But being republican was not sufficient to ensure world peace. According to Kant – and it was the critical argument of *Perpetual Peace* – the situation of international relations, its lawless condition, unstable power balances and especially the ever-present possibility of war endangered the republican state and made it difficult for liberal political orders to maintain their republican or liberal condition. Hence, he argued, it was the duty of the republican state to strive towards law-regulated international relations; they could not merely be liberal in themselves.

A critical part of Kant's argument, which initiated the debate between liberals and realists, was his critique of the concept of the 'balance of power': he refuted the argument, becoming prevalent in his day, that the balance of power was a peacekeeper. The idea of conscious balancing was fallacious, he argued, since 'It is the desire of every state, or of its ruler, to arrive at a condition of perpetual peace by conquering the whole world, if that were possible' (Kant 1991b, a view shared by some leading realists; e.g. Mearsheimer 2001). As to the automatic operations of such a balance, he held Rousseau's view that such tendencies did indeed exist. Rousseau (1917) argued that states were naturally pushed into watching one another and adjusting their power accordingly, usually through alliances. However, this practice resulted merely in 'ceaseless agitation' and not in peace.

Kant's peace programme consisted of two parts (Kant 1991a). There were the 'preliminary articles' – the initial conditions that had to be established before even republican states could make much contribution to a more peaceful international environment. These included the abolition of standing armies, non-interference in the affairs of other states, the outlawing of espionage, incitement to treason and assassination as instruments of diplomacy, and an end to imperial ventures. These had to be abolished by a majority of states, non-liberal as well as liberal, to end the condition philosopher Thomas Hobbes had described as 'the war of all against all'. There were then the three definitive articles; these went further and provided the actual foundations for peace:

1 The civil constitution of every state should be republican.

2 The law of nations shall be founded on a federation of free states.

3 The law of world citizenship shall be limited to conditions of universal hospitality.

Spreading republican constitutions meant, in effect, generalizing the striving for peace, since according to Kant, striving for peace was part of the natural orientation of the republican state. The 'federation of free states' would provide for a type of collective security system; and the provision of 'universal hospitality' would, in Michael Howard's formulation, 'gradually create a sense of cosmopolitan community' (2000: 31). Kant distinguished between the end of war and the establishment of positive peace, and his plan made peace 'more than a merely pious aspiration'. Accordingly, he can properly be regarded as 'the inventor of peace' (Howard 2000: 31).

During the nineteenth century, liberals tended to emphasize only Kant's views that liberalism inclined to peace. Through most of the nineteenth century, the liberal approach to peace consisted of critiques of the ancient regime, and promised that peace would automatically follow the overthrow of autocracy and the establishment of constitutional regimes. This led Raymond Aron (1978), to charge that nineteenth-century liberals had no peace plan. With the outbreak of the First World War, however, the emphasis changed. Then, the dangers that Kant had foreseen for liberalism in a dangerous international environment were rediscovered; and liberal thinkers turned from internal reform towards emphasizing arbitration, the development of international law and an international court, to protect liberalism from without. When the League of Nations failed, moreover, some would go so far as to recommend either the abolition of, or severe restrictions upon, state sovereignty.

## Douce commerce

According to Moravcsik, 'commercial liberalism' focuses on 'incentives created by opportunities for trans-border economic transactions' (2001: 14). This contemporary formulation attempts to make specific the causal mechanisms behind the inclination of economically liberal states to prefer peace to conflict. According to Moravcsik, 'trade is generally a less costly means of accumulating wealth than war, sanctions or other coercive means' (2001: 50). But it is not the only theory – other commercial liberals stress the structure of a liberal economy, not merely the preferences of individual economic actors.

The origins of modern commercial liberalism lay in the developing liberal critique of mercantilism, the aggressive economic policies recommended to, and to a degree practised by, the autocrats of the ancient regime. Mercantilist doctrine had advised doing all to increase the amount of bullion held by a country, in an environment where bullion was believed to be a fixed quantum. The effect of generalizing mercantilism was made explicit by Voltaire in 1764: 'It is clear that a country cannot gain unless another loses and it cannot prevail without making others miserable.' The economic *philosophes* (called physiocrats) such as François Quesnay and Victor de Mirabeau identified a structural proclivity in mercantilism towards trade wars and territorial conquests. If your own nation was to be wealthy, it could only be so by making others poorer. Tariff walls were needed to protect the prosperity of domestic producers from the 'attacks' of foreign competitors. Subsidies were required for export producers so that they could 'seize' the wealth of others in foreign markets. Resources in foreign lands had to be militarily 'captured' to keep them out of the hands of commercial rivals in opposing nation-states who would use them to defeat 'our' nation-state.

The explicit association between non-mercantilist, open trading orders and peace was, however, not French but a British development. It first appeared in Adam Smith's *The Wealth of Nations*, where he argued that 'the hidden hand' besides increasing wealth also promoted a lessening of economic hostilities. Even earlier, Smith's Scottish colleague and friend David Hume had demonstrated that an international division of labour and trade benefited all participants. Moreover, David Ricardo had formulated the theory of comparative advantage which argued wealth accrued in the degree to which states concentrated production in areas where they had 'comparative advantage' and traded for other products. Ricardo's theory underpinned the notion of a benevolent division of labour as well as the idea that trade was non-hostile competition.

But British commercial liberalism is above all associated with Richard Cobden, the early nineteenth-century Manchester manufacturer. In 1835 he published his first pamphlet, 'England, Ireland and America by a Manchester Manufacturer', where he advocated the principles of peace, non-intervention, retrenchment and free trade. The pamphlet, 'Russia' of 1836, so titled because it was intended to combat contemporary Russo-phobia, contained an indictment of the system of foreign policy founded on ideas of the balance of power and the necessity of armies for the protection of commerce. Cobden was returned as MP for Stockport in the British general election of 1841 and undertook the campaign for the repeal of the Corn Laws, the legislation preventing the import of cheap grain into England. The bill to repeal the Corn Laws passed the House of Commons on 16 May 1846 by 98 votes. He also led the negotiations for the 1860 commercial treaty with France, which laid the foundations for the general progress of free trade throughout Europe. His efforts in furtherance of free trade were always subordinated to what he deemed the highest moral purposes: the promotion of peace on earth and goodwill among men. Cobden considered the commercial treaty with France but a critical step in that direction. During much of what remained of the nineteenth century, the free trade movement was unchallenged, and free trade remained the orthodoxy until the onset of the late nineteenth-century tariff reform movement in Britain, when open trading orders once more became controversial.

As formulated by Cobden and other free trade enthusiasts, nineteenth-century liberal trade doctrine held that trade among states, like trade among individuals, was mutually beneficial. All men would gain through participation in a global division of labour – a way of life in which they offered to each other the various products in the production of which they specialized. Market competition was not conflict but rather peaceful cooperation: each producer helped to improve the quality of life for all through the production and sale of superior and less expensive products than the ones offered by his market rivals. The market was civil society and peace; economic policy in the hands of governments was conflict and war.

Commercial liberalism also took on a sociological aspect. James Mill described the British Empire as outdoor relief for the upper classes. Joseph Schumpeter argued that conquest and imperialism had economically favoured the old aristocratic elites, and that the social changes which accompanied capitalism made modern states inherently peaceful, since they led to the decline of the aristocratic class.

The only formal non-liberal nineteenth-century riposte to the commercial liberals (that is, the only argument credited with some respect) was the mid-nineteenth century idea of protecting infant industries. The German nationalist

Jahn argued that because of the time lag between developed and developing countries, there was an argument for initial protection for 'infant' industry, but even then only until it could compete in an open market. In the twentieth century, under the press of the Great Depression, liberals would also argue that there was some justification for protecting economies from storms in the world economy, but again temporary measures only. (The liberal tendency came to be to improve international regimes so that storms could be avoided or ridden out without closures.) There also developed a more refined critique of the argument that everyone benefited through trade (e.g. Johnson 1958). This made it clear that the wealth accruing through opening economic exchange did not automatically benefit everyone in society; this depended on social policies which, among other things, deliberately fostered the skills which would allow individuals to participate in market economies.

During the twentieth century, the initial successes of Nazism, government-directed labour programmes and the much vaunted 'Soviet model', led the commercial liberals to focus on government involvement in the economy and on protectionist ideologies. Indeed, twentieth-century commercial liberals spoke less of economy than of ideology, particularly attacking ideas of economic closure and planning that derived from 'scientific socialism' and especially economic nationalism. The most famous of these is Friedrich Hayek's *Road to Serfdom*, but it had many echoes, especially in central Europe. During the 1930s, the German economist Wilhelm Röpke declared that the 'genuinely liberal principle' required 'the widest possible separation of the two spheres of government and economy.' He recommended the largest possible 'depoliticization' of the economic sphere. In 1936, the Swiss economist and political scientist William Rappard (the Rappard Chateau which houses the World Trade Organization in Geneva is named after him) in a lecture entitled, "The Common Menace of Economic and Military Armaments" identified 'economic armaments' with all of the legislative and administrative devices governments use to politically influence imports and exports as well as the allocation of commodities. Rappard argued that a new world order of peace and prosperity would only come about when governments exited from control of the economy. In similar fashion, in 1952, the free-market economist Michael A. Heilperin delivered a lecture entitled 'An Economist's Views on International Organization'. He told his audience,

> It is an elementary, but often forgotten, knowledge that policies of national governments have always been the principal obstacle to economic relations between people living in various countries, and that whenever these relations were free from government restrictions, equilibrium and balanced growth would follow by virtue of the spontaneous and anonymous mechanism of the market.
>
> (cited in Ebeling 2000)

Attacks on ideology came to include refutation of some liberal ideas, particularly the idea that peace could come through abolitions of sovereignty, a favourite liberal idea of the late 1930s and 1940s. According to the Austrian economist Ludwig von Mises:

> Classical liberalism did not and does not build its hopes upon abolition of the sovereignty of the various national governments, a venture which would result in endless wars. It aims at a general recognition of the idea of economic freedom. If all peoples become liberal and conceive that economic freedom best serves their own interests, national sovereignty will no longer engender conflict and war. What is needed to make peace durable is neither international treaties and covenants nor international tribunals and organizations like the defunct League of Nations or its successor, the United Nations. If the principle of the market economy is universally accepted, such makeshifts are unnecessary; if it is not accepted, they are futile. Durable peace can only be the outgrowth of a change in ideologies.
>
> (Mises 1949: 686)

The notion that economic openness produces a more peaceful international posture has become the subject of close empirical examination. In 1997, Oneal and Russett (1997) declared the 'the classical liberals were right' in their study of the record in the post-war period. Similarly, Mansfield and Pollins (2001) have summarized a large body of empirical work that, for the most part, supports the thesis. There are various exceptions and qualifications which are seen to limit the circumstances under which economic interdependence results in conflict reduction. Stephen van Evera (1994) has argued that the more diversified and complex the existing transnational commercial ties and production structures the less cost-effective coercion is likely to be. By extension, the less diverse the production structure of a country and the more it is characterized by monopolies, the more fragile will be the inclination to peace.

Moving beyond economic interdependence to the issue of economic freedom within states, Erik Gartzke (2005) has found empirical evidence that economic freedom (as measured by the Fraser Institute Economic Freedom Index) is about 50 times more effective than democracy in reducing violent conflict. Gartzke's conclusions are critical for the direction of liberal reforms, since they imply that it is less important what sort of political regime a country has than its degree of economic freedom.

The policy prescriptions enjoined by the commercial liberals – often called 'economic disarmament' – focus on limiting the power of governments to impose trade restraints, primarily through international regulation. Foreign exchanges were to be open; tariffs were to be reduced to the minimum and quotas and other quantitative restrictions positively forbidden. Governments were to pledge themselves to open tariff borders, to abolish quotas and to allow currencies to move in line with market forces. These policy prescriptions were immensely influential in the architecture of the newly established international economic organizations, set up at the end of the Second World War.

Recently, the literature on globalization has suggested that globalization, in its aspect as unfettered free trade on a global scale, is a peace producer. Graham Allison has opined that 'global networks, particularly in economics, create demands by powerful players for predictability in interactions and thus for rules of the game that become, in effect, elements of international law' (2000: 83). Thomas Friedman's *The Lexus and the Olive Tree* declares that 'When a country reaches the level of economic development, when it has a middleclass big enough to support a McDonald's network, it becomes a McDonald's country. And people in McDonald's countries don't like to fight wars any more, they prefer to wait in line for burgers' (2000: 14).

But it is not obvious that globalization has firmly entrenched economic liberalism. Commenting on America's foreign economic policy of the 1980s, Professor Richard Ebeling, of the Future of Freedom Foundation, has observed the emergence of traditional mercantilist methods:

> If some of America's Asian trading partners 'capture' a large share of the American consumer market, the government responds with a tariff-wall 'defense.' If American agriculture cannot earn the profits it considers 'fair,' the U.S. government takes the 'offensive' by 'attacking' other lands through export price-subsidies. If other nations will not comply with the wishes of the Washington social engineers in some international dispute, the American government influences and persuades them with government-to-government financial loans, grants and subsidized credits – all at American taxpayers' expense, of course.
>
> (Ebeling 1991)

The reputed peace effects of globalization are also countered in the literature by some reputed war effects. These include increased vulnerability to threats from the failure of the complex systems globalization relies upon, as well as from non-state actors whose access to weapons and potential for disruption increases in a globalized world. Advances in technology may also have made states more vulnerable to coercive threats than would have been possible earlier (on some of the implications of globalization for security, see Navari 2006). Liberal unease with globalization is well-represented in a recent collection of essays (Held 2007), where Michael Doyle, among other noted liberals, outlines the problem of democratic accountability in a globalized political system.

## The democratic peace thesis

The 'democratic peace' thesis is the argument that liberal states do not fight wars against other liberal states. It was first enunciated in a keynote article by Michael Doyle in the journal *Philosophy and Public Affairs* (Doyle 1983). Doyle argued that there was a difference in liberal practice towards other liberal societies and liberal practice toward non-liberal societies. Among liberal societies, liberalism had produced a cooperative foundation such that 'constitutionally liberal states have yet to engage in war with one another'. Doyle based his findings on David Singer's Correlates of War Project (COW) at Michigan University and the COW's list of wars since 1816 (see Small and Singer 1982). Using the list, Doyle observed that almost no liberal states had fought wars against other liberal states, and that in the two instances in which it seemed that liberal states had fought against other arguably liberal states, liberalism had only recently been established. Doyle sourced the tendency in Kant's 'three preconditions'; namely republican constitutions, collective security arrangements and civic hospitality, in which Doyle included free trade.

The specific causes of the 'liberal peace' have become the subject of robust research and discussion. The two major contending theories focus on liberal institutions and liberal ideology respectively. Liberal institutions include the broad franchise of liberal states and the need to ensure broad popular support; the division of powers in democratic states which produces checks and balances; and the electoral cycle, which makes liberal leadership cautious and prone to avoid risk (Russett 1996). But liberal institutions would tend to inhibit all wars, whereas liberal states have fought robust wars against non-liberal states. The other contender, which can explain the difference, is liberal ideology or 'culture'. According to the liberal culture argument, liberal states tend to trust other liberal states and to expect to resolve conflict through discussion and compromise. But, equally, they distrust non-liberal states. The major argument for liberal ideology has been put forward by John M. Owen who suggests that, 'Ideologically, liberals trust those states they consider fellow liberal democracies and see no reason to fight them. They view those states they consider illiberal with suspicion, and sometimes believe that the national interest requires war with them' (1996: 153).

Since Doyle first produced his findings, the theory has developed two variants: one maintains that democracies are more peaceful than non-democracies: that is that they are more pacific *generally* (see Russett 1993). This is sometimes referred to as the *monadic* variant. The other maintains that liberal states are not necessarily more peaceful than non-liberal states, but that they eschew the use of force in relation to other democracies; that is the use of force depends on the recipient's form of government. In the later variant, sometimes called the *dyadic* variant, a few have argued that democracies may be even more robust in the use of force than non-democracies, due partially to the ideological nature of democratic wars and partially to the fact that liberal democracies are generally strong states with a large wealth base (see Barkawi and Laffey, 2001).

From the security point of view, the recommendations of democratic peace theory are clear – in the final analysis, security depends on encouraging liberal institutions; and a security policy must have as its long-term aims the spread of liberalism. In the short term, it must protect liberalism, including liberal tendencies in non-liberal states. Doyle himself argues that where liberalism has been deficient 'is in preserving its [liberalism's] basic preconditions under changing international circumstances' (1983: 229). The route to peace is to encourage democratic systems, the universal respect for human rights and the development of civil society.

But such a conclusion depends on an untroubled and robust correlation between the democratic nature of a state and a peaceful inclination, at least towards other liberal states, and it is not entirely clear that such a direct correlation exists. Chris Brown (1992) has pointed out that liberal states have, during the period that many states became liberal, faced determined enmity from non-liberal states. The fact that liberal states have faced enemies of liberalism distorts the historical record; we do not know how they may have diverged in the absence of such an enmity. It may also be that in a world of diverse states in situations of conflict; that is, in an anarchical society, liberal states make more reliable allies – that they do not fight one another because they ally with one another. (This is called the liberal alliance thesis and is compatible with Realist approaches, see Chapter 2 this volume.) There is also the not insignificant fact that the majority of liberal states are locked into economic integration, via the European Union (a fact that may support the *douce commerce* variant). Finally, the democratic transition phenomenon may be a statistical aberration. David Spiro (1996), for instance, has argued that historically there have not been many liberal states, and that most states do not fight wars against one another anyway. The fact that liberal states have not fought wars against one another may not be statistically significant.

As to whether liberal states are more intrinsically peaceful than other states, this is perhaps even more contentious. Kant, for his part, seemed to support the monadic theory; he claimed not only that republics would be at peace with each other, but that republican government is more pacific than other forms of government. But the empirical work is indeterminate since it has so far concentrated on traditional state-to-state wars and has ignored interventions – intervention could also be considered an intrinsically hostile act involving the use of force outside of one's borders. Recent 'liberal' attempts to bring other states to liberal democracy (in Iraq, for example) have raised fears that, far from being a recipe for peace, liberal foreign policy may have its own tendencies towards war. This 'dark side of liberalism' has occupied much of the recent research, which has turned to the conditions which may lead liberal states to fight wars (see Geis, Brock and Muller 2006).

Despite some hesitation from the academy, the theory that democracies do not fight wars against other democracies has been immensely influential in public policy. For example, it underpinned President Clinton's *A National Security Strategy for a New Century* (United States 1998); it was also extensively used to support the neo-conservative case for war in Iraq and has guided post-war reconstruction in insisting on a broadly inclusive post-war government in Iraq and an early move to self-government with elections. The democratic transition thesis has also come to dominate the peace-building programme of the UN. Michael Barnett (2006) has been critical of what he calls the 'civil society' model for post-war reconstruction, since it places emphasis on mobilizing social forces in often unstable and divided societies, when more attention should be placed on building state capacity and strengthening governmental powers (see also Paris 1997).

The association between war, democracy and rights, prevalent in the immediate aftermath of the Second World War has also been revived. Founded upon the principles of territorial integrity and state sovereignty, the UN has recently begun to give greater emphasis to the rights of human beings compared to the rights of states in the international realm. In a discussion on the relevance of the Security Council, UN Secretary-General Kofi Annan clearly indicated that 'the last right of states cannot and must not be the right to enslave, persecute or torture their own citizens'. In fact, rather than rally around sovereignty as its sole governing idea, the Security Council should 'unite behind the principle that massive and systematic violations of human rights conducted against an entire people cannot be allowed to stand' (Annan 1999a: 514).

## Neoliberal institutionalism

Neoliberal institutionalism concentrates on the role of international institutions in mitigating conflict. Robert Keohane (1984) and Robert Axelrod (1984), who have played a central role in defining this field, point to the ability of institutions such as the UN to redefine state roles and act as arbitrators in state disputes. Although institutions cannot transform anarchy, they can change the character of the international environment by influencing state preferences and state behaviour. International institutions do this by a variety of methods that either create strong incentives for cooperation like favourable trade status, or through powerful disincentives like trade sanctions.

'Under what conditions will cooperation emerge in a world of egoists without central authority?' This question was posed by Robert Axelrod (1984) in his central contribution to the theory, where he identified several critical factors. The first was the practice of tit-for-tat. He argued that when agents returned good for good, this initiated a potential spiral of cooperative behaviour. If this practice were repeated, egoistic agents would gradually learn to trust one another, particularly when their interests coincided. This situation was formally modelled as a reiterated prisoner's dilemma situation (see Chapter 4 this volume). It implied that if states repeatedly found themselves in a situation in which they feared that their self-restraint would be taken advantage of, they would not defect but would, instead, devise reinsurance devices that would allow cooperation to ensue. Reinsurance devices produce institutions. He also theorized the 'shadow of the future'; arguing that once cooperation was institutionalized, states would hesitate to abandon it, for fear of what lay ahead. Axelrod went further by advising participants and reformers to increase the likelihood of mutual cooperation by enlarging the shadow of the future, by making interactions more durable and/or more frequent – for example, by breaking issues under negotiation into smaller pieces – and by changing the payoffs faced by the players.

Central to neoliberal institutionalism is the notion of transaction costs. These include 'the costliness of information, the costs of measuring the valuable attributes of what is being exchanged and the costs of protecting rights and policing and enforcing agreements' (North 1990: 27). Thus, institutions are desirable, despite the constraints they impose on states, because they reduce transaction costs associated with rule-making, negotiating, implementing, enforcing, information gathering and conflict resolution. They are also durable. Existing regimes persist even after the conditions that facilitated their creation have disappeared 'because they are difficult to create or reconstruct' (Keohane 1984: 12–14, 50). This is the logic that lies at the core of neoliberal institutionalism: cooperation in situations modelled by an iterated prisoner's dilemma can be achieved in highly institutionalized settings, because institutions can serve as a means of providing information, reducing transaction costs, and altering the payoffs associated with cooperation. In consequence, many neoliberal institutionalists argue that international actors should promote institutionalization as a means of promoting the collective interest in international stability.

Constructivist institutionalism, on the other hand, conceptualizes institutions as a collection of norms, rules and routines, rather than a formal structure (see Chapter 5 this volume). In contrast to rational choice theories like Axelrod's, institutions do not simply change the preferences of actors, but can also shape their identity (Barnett and Finnemore 1999). Constructivism focuses on the central role of ideology, rules, and norms that institutions diffuse to constitute agents. Against a 'logic of instrumentality' or 'logic of consequences' of rational choice institutionalism, constructivism posits a 'logic of appropriateness', arguing that individuals' actions are guided by social expectations rather than utility maximization calculations. Institutional routines are followed even when there is no obvious self-interest involved (see March and Olsen 1989, Finnemore and Sikkink 1998).

There is, however, no single model of the most desirable sort of institution. On the contrary, the notion of transaction costs points to very different sorts of institutions for different cooperation problems. For example, the Strategic Arms Limitation Talks (SALT II) during the 1970s between the US and Soviet Union required a set of specialists to determine what might be meant by a 'technical advance', while avoiding the dangers of misreading technical information required a telephone hotline between the major nuclear antagonists. Neoliberal institutionalism has spawned a voluminous institutional design literature that points to the variation in international institutions and outlines the different institutional arrangements necessary to address different types of cooperation problems (e.g. Koremos, Lipson and Snidal 2004, Mitchell 2006).

In this approach, unlike other liberal approaches, states are central. They are the agents who design institutions to advance their joint interests. Interests are first defined outside the institutional context (in the formal language 'individual preferences are exogenous'; they are defined outside of institutional contexts), and then institutions are designed by state actors to facilitate the achievement of their joint interests (Keohane 1989, Jupille and Caporaso 1999). Thus, institutions emerge and survive because they serve to maximize the exogenously determined interests and preferences of their members, especially those founding members who designed the institution.

But state-centredness has also led to a central ambiguity in the approach: what if the state is no longer able to cope with the pressures of interdependence? This has led to a radical liberal school exemplified by David Held (1995) and Seyom Brown (1996). In this version, the state is no longer able to cope with international crises such as degradation of the environment, mass migration, starvation and disease. In such a situation, Brown (1996) recommends that we substitute world interests for the state interests envisioned by more conservative neoliberals. These world interests would include survival of the human species, reduction in world violence, provision of conditions for healthy subsistence to all people, preservation of cultural diversity and preservation of the world's ecology. But the approach is rather vague as to who should build these new 'world interest' organizations.

Neoliberal institutionalism contrasts in several critical areas with realism. Both agree that powerful states influence the formation and shape of international institutions, but for different reasons. According to liberals, states create institutions to maximize shared interests; for realists, however, it is to realize and maintain domination. According to a leading American realist John Mearsheimer, 'The most powerful states in the system create and shape institutions so that they can maintain their share of world power, or even increase it' (1994/95: 13). Realism also focuses on the extent to which powerful states dominate institutions; they argue that latecomers or less powerful members will have less control over institutional decisions and outcomes, benefit less from their creation and will have less commitment to maintaining the institution (Gruber 2000). This is quite apart from the general critique that realists make of institutional approaches. 'Realists maintain that institutions are basically a reflection of the distribution of power in the world. They are based on the self-interested calculations of the great powers, and they have no independent effect on state behavior' (Mearsheimer 1994/95: 7). Neoliberal institutionalists argue, on the contrary, that the 'shadow of the future' – the possibility to attain gains in the future – provides a strong incentive for all states to cooperate and create institutions that benefit all parties.

An equally harsh realist critique of neoliberal institutionalism is Grieco (1993) with his concept of relative gains. Grieco argues that relative gains, what a state in a competitive situation might gain from cooperation relative to what his opponent might gain, are more important than 'absolute gains' – the overall calculus of gains versus loses. This is so, he argues, because power is a relational concept; power can only be measured in relation to another's power; that is, by comparison with another power-seeker. It matters not if the other gains and I lose, but it does matter if the other gains more than I do. He maintains that the calculus of relative gains often sabotages hoped-for cooperative ventures, if the cooperative venture threatens to change the balance of power (on the relevance of the absolute vs. relative gains argument to neoliberal institutionalism, see also Snidal 1991b, Powell 1991).

The question is, how suitable is neoliberal insitutionalism with regard to security issues? Jervis has observed that the realm of security has special characteristics that at the same time make regime creation more difficult and increase its need: 'Security regimes, with their call for mutual restraint and limitations on unilateral actions, rarely seem attractive to decision-makers' under the security dilemma (Jervis 1982: 360). Basic to the neoliberal institutionalists is the idea of common interests that states could achieve together. But what if antagonists do not share common interests? According to Jervis (1999: 54), 'states will establish an institution if and only if they seek the goals that the institution will help them reach.' It does not seem, superficially, that institutions could do much to increase security.

The notion that security might lay outside the scope of neoliberal cooperation has led neoliberal institutionalists to focus on cooperation in low politics such as economy, society and environment and pay much less attention to military security cooperation. But the persistence and expansion of NATO after the end of the Cold War created a theoretical puzzle for realists and an opportunity for neoliberal institutionalism to move into high politics. Wallander and Keohane (1999), for instance, explicitly regard NATO as a security institution and try to theorize the concept of 'security institution'. First, due to transaction costs and uncertainty, it is easier to maintain than to create new institutions, which is a basic assumption argued by Keohane (1984) in *After Hegemony*. Second, the duration of an institution mainly relies on the function and extent of institutionalization and organization. Third, most importantly, the conditions and objects for a security institution's persistence are not as narrow as those of alliances. An alliance is for dealing with common threats while an institution is for coping with risks, including regional uncertainty. David A. Lake distinguishes hierarchic institutions from anarchic ones. He argues that the former are effective in taking actions but can be evanescent, while the latter, lacking dominant authorities, are less effective but more adaptable to a changing environment and can last (Lake 2001: 136). In short, Lake, Keohane and Wallender argue that NATO persisted because it was not a simple alliance; rather it was becoming a security institution.

The distinction drawn by Wallander and Keohane (1999) between an alliance and a security institution has led to a significant new typology. Dittgen and Peters (2001) have contrasted two ideal-type security systems – the alliance-type system and the community of law-type system – which provide models for the construction of the respective security systems (see Table 3.1). One is rooted in a realist perspective; the second in a liberal

*Table 3.1* Realist and liberal security systems

| Theoretical base | | Realist (Alliance) | Liberal (Community of Law) |
|---|---|---|---|
| *Structure of the international system* | | Material; Static; Anarchic; Self-help system | Social; Dynamic; Governance without government |
| *Conceptions of security:* | *Basic principles* *Strategies* | Accumulation of power Military deterrence Control of allies | Integration Democratization Conflict resolution Rule of Law |
| *Institutional features:* | *Functional scope* *Criterion for membership* *Internal power structure* | Military realm only Strategic relevance Reflects distribution of power; most likely hegemonic | Multiple issue areas Democratic system of rule Symmetrical; high degree of interdependence |
| | *Decision-making* | Will of dominant powers prevails | Democratically legitimized |
| *Relation of system to its environment* | | Dissociated; perception of threat | Serves as an attractive model; open for association. |

perspective. The key difference is the response to the threat. In a liberal community of law, potential disturbances are not dealt with by mobilizing superior power but rather diffused through integration, by reinsurance and by conflict resolution. Threats are circumvented by common membership in a security institution.

## Conclusion

In liberal International Relations theory, the state is not an actor but an institution 'constantly subject to capture and recapture, even construction and reconstruction' by coalitions of social actors (Moravcsik 2001: 5). The theory has distinct variants which supply different motivations for action and which have different implications for security theory. In ideational liberalism, the underlying motive is social identity and conflict will ensue if borders do not accord with social identity. Conflict will also ensue across social identities. In commercial liberalism, the underlying motivation is economic benefit, which does not necessarily lead to cooperation, but which identifies under what sorts of circumstances the economy can be a peace-producer. In republican liberalism, the critical factor is state form and states can be integrated into long-term peace arrangements which at the same time encourage democratization and internal state reform. The contribution of these variants of liberalism to security theory is dense, specified and progressive.

## Further reading

David Baldwin (ed.), *Neorealism and Neoliberalism: The Contemporary Debate* (Columbia University Press, 1993). Contains the major articles in the debate between realists and liberals, which still constitutes, arguably, the major axis of theory in contemporary International Relations.

Michael E. Brown, Sean Lynn-Jones and Steven Miller (eds.), *Debating the Democratic Peace* (MIT Press, 1996). Contains all the classic writings on the democratic peace and the major criticisms.

Michael Howard, *War and the Liberal Conscience* (Cambridge University Press, 1978). Presents what has become the classic account of real liberals in their encounters with war.

Robert O. Keohane, *After Hegemony: Cooperation and Discord in the World Political Economy* (Princeton University Press, 1984). Lays out the first systematic statement of neoliberal institutionalism.

Andrew Moravcsik, *Liberal International Relations Theory: A Social Scientific Assessment* (Harvard University Press, 2001). Sets out what the various liberal theories explain, their limits, and how to operationalize them.

# Game Theory

Frank C. Zagare

## Abstract

In this chapter, students will learn about the basic assumptions behind the major concepts of game theory illustrated with examples drawn from the security studies literature. For instance, an arms race game is used to illustrate the strategic form of a game, the meaning of an equilibrium outcome, and the definition of a dominant strategy. Backwards induction and the definition of subgame perfection are explained in the context of an explication of an extensive-form game that features threats. A short review of the many applications of game theory in international politics is provided. Finally, the chapter concludes with a discussion of the usefulness of game theory in generating insights about deterrence.

## Introduction

Game theory is the science of interactive decision-making. It was created in one fell swoop with the publication of John von Neumann and Oskar Morgenstern's *Games and Economic Behavior* by Princeton University Press (1944). Widely hailed when it was published, the book became an instant classic. Its impact was enormous. Almost immediately, game theory began to penetrate economics – as one might well expect. But soon afterward, applications, extensions, and modifications of the framework presented by von Neumann and Morgenstern began to appear in other fields, including sociology, psychology, anthropology and, through political science, international relations and security studies.

In retrospect, the ready home that game theory found in the field of security studies is not very surprising. Much of the gestalt of game theory can easily be discerned in the corpus of diplomatic history and in the work of the most prominent theorists of international politics (see Jervis 1988). And its key concepts have obvious real-world analogues in the international arena.

## Primitive concepts

The basic concept is that of a game itself. A *game* can be thought of as any situation in which an outcome depends on the choices of two or more decision-makers. The term is somewhat unfortunate. Games are sometimes thought of as lighthearted diversions. But in game theory the term is not so restricted. For instance, most if not all interstate conflicts qualify as very serious games.

In game theory, decision-makers are called *players*. Players can be individuals or groups of individuals who in some sense operate as a coherent unit. Presidents, prime ministers, kings and queens, dictators, foreign secretaries, and so on can therefore sometimes be considered as players in a game. But so can the states in whose name they make foreign policy decisions. It is even possible to consider a coalition of two or more states as a player. For example, in their analysis of the July crisis of 1914, Snyder and Diesing (1977) use elementary game theory to examine the interaction between 'Russia–France' and 'Austria–Germany'.

The decisions that players make eventually lead to an *outcome*. In game theory, an outcome can be just about anything. Thus, the empirical content associated with an outcome will vary with the game being analysed. Sometimes, generic terms, such as 'compromise' or 'conflict' are used to portray outcomes. At other times, the descriptors are much more specific. Snyder and Diesing use the label 'Control of Serbia' by Austria–Germany to partially describe one potential outcome of the July crisis.

Reflecting perhaps the intensity of the Cold War period in the United States in the early 1950s, almost all of the early applications of game theory in the field of security studies analysed interstate conflicts as *zero-sum games*. A zero-sum game is any game in which the interests of the players are diametrically opposed. Examples of this genre include an analysis of two World War II battles by A.G. Haywood (1950) and a study of military strategy by McDonald and Tukey (1949).

By contrast, a *nonzero-sum game* is an interactive situation in which the players have mixed motives, that is, in addition to conflicting interests, they may also have some interests in common. Two states locked in an economic conflict, for instance, obviously have an interest in securing the best possible terms of trade. At the same time, both may also want to avoid the costs associated with a trade war. It is clear that in such instances, the interests of the two states are not diametrically opposed.

The use of nonzero-sum games became the standard form of analysis in international politics toward the end of the 1950s, due in no small part to the seminal scholarship of Thomas Schelling (1960, 1966). When Schelling's book *The Strategy of Conflict* was republished in 1980 by Harvard University Press he remarked in a new preface that the idea that conflict and common interest were not mutually exclusive, so obvious to him, was among the book's most important contributions. In 2005, Schelling was awarded the Nobel Prize in economics for his work on game theory and interstate conflict. The award was well-deserved.

Most contemporary studies also make use of the tools and concepts of non-cooperative game theory. A *non-cooperative game* is any game in which the players are unable to irrevocably commit themselves to a particular course of action. By contrast, binding agreements are possible in a *cooperative game*. Since it is commonly understood that the international system lacks an overarching authority that can enforce commitments or agreements, it should come as no surprise that non-cooperative game theory holds a particular attraction for theorists of interstate conflict.

## Strategic-form games and Nash equilibria

Game theorists have developed a number of distinct ways to represent a game's structure. Initially, the *strategic-form* (sometimes called the *normal-* or the *matrix*-form) was the device of choice. In the strategic-form, players select *strategies* simultaneously, before the actual play of the game. A strategy is defined as a complete contingency plan that specifies a player's choice at every situation that might arise in a game. Figure 4.1 depicts a typical arms race game between two states, State A and State B, in strategic-form. (For obvious reasons, such a game is called a two-person game. Games with three or more players are referred to as *n-person games* but are not discussed in this short chapter.) Although the generic name for this game is Prisoners' Dilemma, it is referred to here as the *Arms Race Game* (for details see Zagare 1984).

In this representation, each state has two strategies: to *cooperate* (C) by not arming, and to *defect* from cooperation (D) by arming. If neither arms, the outcome is a compromise: a military balance is maintained, but at little cost. If both arm, both lose, as an arms race takes place, the balance is maintained, but this time at considerable cost. Finally, if one state arms and the other does not, the state that arms gains a strategic advantage, and the state that chooses not to arm is put at a military disadvantage.

Each cell of the matrix contains an ordered pair of numbers below the names of the outcomes. The numbers represent the payoff the row (State A) and the column player (State B) receives, respectively, when that outcome

**State B**

|  |  | Not arm (C) | Arm (D) |
|---|---|---|---|
| **State A** | Not arm (C) | *Tacit arms control*<br><br>(3,3) | *B gains advantage*<br><br>(1,4) |
|  | Arm (D) | *A gains advantage*<br><br>(4,1) | *Arms race*<br><br>(2,2)* |

*Key*: (x,y) = payoff to State A, payoff to State B
  \* = Nash equilibrium

*Figure 4.1* Arms race game (Prisoners' Dilemma)

obtains in a game. Payoffs are measured by a *utility* scale. Sometimes, as in this chapter, only *ordinal utilities* are, or need be, assumed. Ordinal utilities convey information about a player's relative ranking of the outcomes. In many studies of interstate conflict, however, *cardinal utilities* are assumed. A cardinal scale indicates both rank and intensity of preference.

In this example, the outcomes are ranked from best (*i.e.*, '4') to worst (*i.e.*, '1'). Thus, the ordered pair (4, 1) beneath the outcome *A Gains Advantage* signifies that this outcome is best for State A and worst for State B. Similarly, the outcome *Tacit Arms Control* is next-best for both players.

In game theory the players are assumed to be instrumentally *rational*. Rational players are those who maximize their utility. Utility, though, is a subjective concept. It indicates the worth of an outcome *to a particular player*. Since different players may evaluate the same outcome differently, the rationality assumption is simply another way of saying that the players are purposeful, that they are pursuing goals (or interests) that they themselves define.

Rationality, however, does not require that the players are necessarily intelligent in setting their goals. It may sometimes be the case that the players are woefully misinformed about the world and, as a consequence, have totally unreasonable objectives. Still, as long as they are purposeful and act to bring about their goals, they can be said to be instrumentally rational (see Zagare 1990).

Rationality also does not imply that the players will do well and obtain their stated objective, as is easily demonstrated by identifying the *solution* to the Arms Race Game. A solution to any strategic-form game consists of the identification of 1) the best, or optimal, strategy for each player, and 2) the likely outcome of the game. The Arms Race Game has a straightforward solution.

Notice first that each player (State) in the Arms Race Game has a *strictly dominant strategy*, that is, a strategy that is always best regardless of the strategy selected by the other player. For instance, if State B chooses not to arm, State A will bring about its next-best outcome (3) if it also chooses not to arm, but will receive its best outcome (4) if it chooses to arm. Thus, when State B chooses (C), State A does better by choosing (D). Similarly, if State B chooses to arm, State A will bring about its worst outcome (1) if it chooses not to arm, but will receive its next-worst outcome (2) if it chooses to arm. Again, when State B chooses (D), State A does better by choosing (D). Regardless of what strategy State B selects, therefore, State A should choose (D) and arm. By symmetry, State B should also choose to defect by arming. And, when both players choose their unconditionally best strategy, the outcome is an *Arms Race* – which is next-worst for both players.

The strategy pair (D, D) associated with the outcome labelled *Arms Race* has a very important property that qualifies it to be part of the solution to the game of Figure 4.1. It is called a *Nash equilibrium* – named after John Nash, the subject of the film *A Beautiful Mind* and a co-recipient of the Nobel Prize in economics in 1994 which, not coincidentally, was the fiftieth anniversary of the publication of von Neumann and Morgenstern's monumental opus. If a strategy pair is a Nash equilibrium, neither player has an incentive to switch to another strategy, provided that the other player does not also switch to another strategy.

To illustrate, observe that if both States A and B choose to arm (D), State A's payoff will be its second best (2). But if it then decides to not arm (C), its payoff is its worst (1). In consequence, State A has no incentive to switch strategies if both states choose to arm. The same is true of State B. The strategy pair (D, D), therefore, is said to be stable or in equilibrium.

There is no other strategy pair with this property in the Arms Race Game, as is easily demonstrated. For instance, consider the strategy pair (C, C) associated with the outcome *Tacit Arms Control*. This outcome is second-best for both players. Nonetheless, both players have an incentive to switch, unilaterally, to another strategy in order to bring about a better outcome. State B for instance, can bring about its best outcome (4) by simply switching to its (D) strategy. Thus, the payoff pair (C, C) is not a Nash equilibrium. The same is true for the remaining two strategy pairs in this game, (C, D) and (D, C).

For reasons that will be more fully explained below, strategy pairs that form a Nash equilibrium provide a *minimum* definition of rational choice in a game. By contrast, strategy pairs that are not in equilibrium are simply inconsistent with rational choice and purposeful action. This is why only Nash equilibria can be part of a game's solution.

But notice that *both* players do worse when they are rational and select (D) than when *both* make an irrational choice and select (C). In other words, two rational players do worse in this game than two irrational players! Paradoxically, however, it is also true that *each* player always does best by choosing (D). All of which raises a very important question for the two states in our game: Can they, if they are rational, avoid an arms race and, if so, under what conditions? More generally, can two or more states ruthlessly pursuing their own interests find a way to cooperate in an anarchic international system?

Space considerations preclude an answer, game-theoretic or otherwise, to this question here. Suffice it to say that it is an issue that lies at the heart of the ongoing debate between realists and liberals about the very nature of international politics. That the (Prisoners' Dilemma) game of Figure 4.1 both highlights and neatly encapsulates such a core problem must be counted among game theory's many contributions to the field of security studies (see Oye 1986, Baldwin 1993, Axelrod 1984).

Even though rational players do not fare well in this game, the game itself has a well-defined solution that helps to explain, *inter alia*, why great states sometimes engage in senseless and costly arms competitions that leave them no more secure than they would have been if they had chosen not to arm, or why trade wars sometimes break out to the detriment of all involved. The solution is well-defined because there is only one outcome in the game that is consistent with rational contingent decision-making by all of the players, the unique Nash equilibrium (D, D).

Not all games, however, have a solution that is so clear-cut. Consider, for example, the two-person game of Figure 4.2 that was originally analysed by John Harsanyi (1977), another 1994 Nobel Prize laureate in economics. As before, the two players, States A and B, have two strategies: either to cooperate (C) or to defect (D) from cooperation. State A's strategies are listed as the

**State B**

|  |  | Cooperate (C) | Defect (D) |
|---|---|---|---|
| **State A** | Cooperate (C) | *Outcome CC* <br><br> (1,3)* | *Outcome CD* <br><br> (1,3) |
|  | Defect (D) | *Outcome DC* <br><br> (0,0) | *Outcome DD* <br><br> (2,2)* |

*Key*: (x,y) = payoff to State A, payoff to State B
  * = Nash equilibrium

*Figure 4.2* Strategic-form game with two Nash equilibria (Harsanyi's game)

rows of the matrix, while B's strategies are given by the columns. Since each player has two strategies, there are 2 x 2 = 4 possible strategy combinations and four possible outcomes. The payoffs to State A and State B, respectively, are again represented by an ordered pair in each cell of the matrix.

Of these four strategy combinations, two are Nash equilibria, as indicated by the asterisks (*). Strategy pair (D, D) is in equilibrium since either player would do worse by switching, unilaterally, to its other strategy. Specifically, were State A to switch from its (D) strategy to its (C) strategy, which would induce Outcome CD, State A's payoff would go from '2' – A's best – to '1' – its next-best. And if State B were to switch to its (C) strategy, B's payoff would go from '2' – its next-best – to '0' – its worst. Thus, neither player benefits by switching unilaterally to another strategy, so (D, D) is a Nash equilibrium. For similar reasons, strategy pair (C, C) is also a Nash equilibrium; neither player benefits by switching, unilaterally, to its (D) strategy. By contrast, neither of the remaining two strategy pairs is stable in the sense of Nash because at least one player would gain by changing to another strategy.

The existence of two or more Nash equilibria in a strategic-form game can confound analysis. When only one Nash equilibrium exists in a game, it is easy to specify a game's solution. But when two or more equilibria exist, it is clearly more difficult to identify the likely outcome of a game or the best strategy of the players – unless there are criteria that allow discrimination among equilibria and the elimination of some stable strategy pairs from the solution set.

Of course, the possible existence of multiple Nash equilibria in a strategic-form game would not be problematic if all equilibria were *equivalent* – that is, if all extant equilibria have exactly the same consequences for the players – and *interchangeable* – in the sense that every possible combination of equilibrium strategies are also in equilibrium.

John Nash (1951) proved long ago that when multiple equilibria exist in a zero-sum game, all equilibrium pairs are both equivalent and interchangeable. But this is clearly not the case in the nonzero-sum game of Figure 4.2. The two equilibria are not equivalent simply because the player's payoffs are different under each equilibrium. For instance, State A's best outcome is associated with the strategy pair (D, D); its next-best outcome with the strategy pair (C, C). The two equilibria are also not interchangeable. Although the strategy pairs (C, C) and (D, D) are in equilibrium, the pairs (C, D) and (D, C) are not. This means that the players cannot use the strategies associated with the two Nash equilibria interchangeably.

Although the two Nash equilibria in the game of Figure 4.2 are neither equivalent nor interchangeable, there is one way in which they are can be distinguished. Notice that State B's defection (D) strategy *weakly dominates* its cooperation (C) strategy, that is, it provides State B with a payoff that is at least as good, and sometimes better, than its other strategy, no matter what strategy State A selects. Thus, there is a good reason to expect that State B will choose (D). By contrast, a *strictly dominant strategy* always provides a player with a higher payoff than any other strategy, no matter what strategies other players select. Both players in the Arms Race Game of Figure 4.1 possess strictly dominant strategies (for details see Zagare 1984).

Notice also that, if State B defects, State A does better by also defecting. Given that State B defects, State A will receive its highest payoff (2) by defecting, but only its second-highest payoff (1) by cooperating. Since the strategy pair (D, D) is associated with State B's unconditionally best (or *dominant*) strategy, and State A's best response to B's unconditionally best strategy, one might very well argue that it, and not strategy pair (C, C) is the equilibrium that best qualifies as the solution to Harsanyi's game.

But before this conclusion is accepted, there is one significant objection that must be considered: the fact that strategy pair (D, D) favours State A at the expense of State B. State B's payoff is clearly better under (C, C) than it is under (D, D), while it is the other way around for State A. Is there nothing that State B can do to induce the more preferred payoff associated with the equilibrium (C, C)?

One might argue that State B could do better in this game by threatening to choose (C) if State A selects (D), thereby inducing State A to choose (C) and bringing about State B's most-preferred outcome. But this line of argument is deficient. To understand why, we next explore an alternative representation of Harsanyi's game, the *extensive-form*.

## Extensive-form games, backwards induction and subgame perfect equilibria

Figure 4.2 represents Harsanyi's game in strategic-form; Figure 4.3 represents it in extensive-form. There are a number of important differences between the two forms of representation. In the strategic-form, each player selects a strategy which, it will be recalled, is a complete plan of action that specifies what a player will do at every decision point in a game. As well, the players are assumed to make their choices simultaneously or, in what amounts to the same thing, without information about what strategy the other player has selected.

By contrast, in the extensive-form, the players make *moves* sequentially, that is, they select from among the collection of *choices* available at any one time. In the extensive-form, moves are represented by *nodes* on a game tree. The *branches* of the tree at any one node summarize the choices available to a player at a particular point in a game. The payoffs to the players are given by an ordered pair at each terminal node. In an extensive-form game of *perfect information*, the players know where they are in the game tree whenever there is an opportunity to make a choice. Harsanyi's game is an example of a game of perfect information. In a game with *imperfect information*, the players may not always know what prior choices have been made.

To solve any extensive-form game, a procedure known as *backwards induction* must be used. As its name suggests, backwards induction involves working backwards up the game tree to determine, first, what a rational player

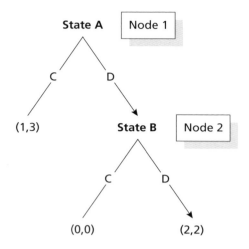

**State A** — Node 1

C          D

(1,3)          **State B** — Node 2

C          D

(0,0)          (2,2)

*Key:* (x,y) = payoff to State A, payoff to State B
——————▶ = rational choice

*Figure 4.3* Extensive-form representation of Harsanyi's game

would do at the last node of the tree, what the player with the previous move would do given that the player with the last move is rational, and so on until the first node of the tree is reached. We will now use this procedure to analyze the extensive-form representation of Harsanyi's game. More specifically, we now seek to establish why State B cannot rationally threaten to select (C) at node 2 in order to induce State A's cooperation at node 1, thereby bringing about State B's highest ranked outcome (1, 3).

To this end, we begin by considering the calculus of State A at the first node of the tree. At node 1 State A can either select (C) and induce its second-best outcome, or select (D), which might result either in State A's best or its worst outcome. Clearly, State A should (rationally) choose (C) if it expects State B to also select (C), since the choice of (D) would then result in State A's worst outcome. Conversely, State A should select (D) if it expects State B to select (D), since this induces State A's best outcome. The question is: what should State A expect State B to do? Before we can answer this question, we must first consider State B's choice at the last node of the tree.

If State A assumes that State B is rational, then State A should expect State B to select (D) if and when State B makes its choice at node 2. The reason is straightforward: State B's worst outcome is associated with its choice of (C), its next-best outcome with its choice of (D). To expect State B to carry out the threat to choose (C) if A chooses (D), then, is to assume that State B is irrational. It follows that for State B to expect State A to select (C) is to assume that State B harbours irrational expectations about State A. To put this in a slightly different way, State B's threat is not credible, that is, it is not rational to carry out. Since it is not credible, State A may safely ignore it.

Notice what the application of backwards induction to Harsanyi's game reveals: State B's rational choice at node 2 is (D). In consequence, State A should also choose (D) at node 1. Significantly, the strategy pair (D, D) associated with these choices is in equilibrium in the same sense that the two Nash equilibria are in the strategic-form game of Figure 4.2: neither player has an incentive to switch to another strategy provided the other player does not also switch. But, also significantly, the second Nash equilibrium (C, C) is nowhere to be found. Because it was based on an incredible threat, it was eliminated by the backwards induction procedure.

The unique equilibrium pair (D, D) that emerges from an analysis of the extensive-form game of Figure 4.3 is called a *subgame perfect equilibrium*. (A *subgame* is that part of an extensive-form game that can be considered a game unto itself (see Morrow 1994: Ch. 2).) The concept of subgame perfection was developed by Reinhard Selten (1975), the third and final recipient of the 1994 Nobel Prize in economics. Selten's perfectness criterion constitutes an extremely useful and important refinement of Nash's equilibrium concept. It is a refinement because it eliminates less than perfect Nash equilibria from the set of candidates eligible for consideration as a game's solution. As well, Selten's idea of subgame perfection helps us to understand more deeply the meaning of rational choice as it applies to individuals, to groups, or even to great states involved in a conflictual relationship.

It is important to know that all subgame perfect equilibria are also Nash equilibria, but not the other way around. As just demonstrated, those Nash equilibria, such as the strategy pair (C, C) in the game of Figure 4.2, which are based on threats that lack credibility, are simply not perfect. As Harsanyi (1977: 332) puts it, these less than perfect equilibria should be considered deficient because they involve both 'irrational behavior and irrational expectations by the players about each other's behavior'.

## Applications of game theory in security studies

Speaking more pragmatically, the refinement of Nash's equilibrium concept represented by the idea of a subgame perfect equilibrium and related solution concepts – such as *Bayesian Nash equilibria* and *Perfect Bayesian equilibria* – permits analysts to develop more nuanced explanations and more potent predictions of interstate conflict behaviour when applying game theory to the field of security studies. (Nash and subgame perfect equilibria are the accepted measures of rational behaviour in games of *complete* information, in which each player is fully informed about the preferences of its opponent. In games of *incomplete* information in which at least one player is uncertain about the other's preferences, rational choices are associated with *Bayesian Nash equilibria* (in strategic-form games) and with *perfect Bayesian equilibria* (in extensive-form games) (see Gibbons 1992, 1997).) It is to a brief enumeration of some of these applications, and a specific illustration of one particular application, that we turn next.

As noted earlier, applications, extensions, modifications and illustrations of game-theoretic models began to appear in the security studies literature shortly after the publication of *Games and Economic Behavior* (1944). Since then, the literature has grown exponentially and its influence on the field of security studies has been significant (see Bueno de Mesquita 2002, Brams 2002). As Walt (1999: 5) has observed:

> Rational choice models have been an accepted part of the academic study of politics since the 1950s, but their popularity has grown significantly in recent years. Elite academic departments are now expected to include game theorists and other formal modelers in order to be regarded as 'up to date,' graduate students increasingly view the use of formal rational choice models as a prerequisite for professional advancement, and research employing rational choice methods is becoming more widespread throughout the discipline.
>
> Walt (1999: 5)

Walt (1999: 7) goes on to express the fear that game-theoretic and related rational choice models are becoming so pervasive, and that their influence has been so strong, that other approaches are on the cusp of marginalization. Although Martin (1999: 74) unquestionably demonstrates, empirically, that Walt's fear is 'unfounded,' there is little doubt that game-theoretic studies are now part and parcel of the security studies literature.

Among the subject areas of security studies that have been heavily influenced by game-theoretic reasoning are the onset (Bueno de Mesquita and Lalman 1992) and escalation (Carlson 1995) of interstate conflict and war, the consequences of alliances (Smith 1995) and alignment patterns (Zagare and Kilgour 2003), the effectiveness of missile defence systems (Powell 2003, Quackenbush 2006), the impact of domestic politics on interstate conflict (Fearon 1994), the dynamics of arms races and the functioning of arms control (Brams and Kilgour 1988), the spread of terrorism (Bueno de Mesquita 2005), the dangers of nuclear proliferation (Kraig 1999), the implications of democratization for coercive diplomacy (Schultz 2001), the characteristics of crisis bargaining (Banks 1990, Powell 2002), regime change (Bueno de Mesquita 2010), and the operation of balance of power politics (Niou, Ordeshook and Rose 1989), to name just a few (for further discussion see O'Neill 1994a, 1994b, 2007, Snidal 2002, Zagare and Slantchev 2010). And, as noted above, game-theoretic models have played a central role in the debate between realists and liberals about the relative importance of absolute and relative gains and about the possibility of significant great power cooperation.

It is clear, however, that there has been no area of security studies in which game theory has been more influential than in the study of deterrence.

Accordingly, I now turn to a brief discussion of this subject and attempt to illustrate, with a simple example, how game theory can help not only to clarify core concepts, but also to shed light on the conditions that lead to successful deterrence (for recent empirical tests of game-theoretic models of deterrence see Signorino and Tarar 2006, Quackenbush 2010, Zagare 2011).

Although it may be somewhat of a stretch to say that Schelling was the inventor of classical deterrence theory, as does Zakaria (2001), his work is a good place to start (for an overview see Zagare 1996). Like all classical deterrence theorists, Schelling's work is characterized by two core assumptions: (1) that states (or their decision-makers) are rational; and (2) that, especially in the nuclear age, war or conflict is the worst possible outcome of any deterrence encounter. It is not difficult to demonstrate that these two assumptions are incompatible with the conclusion of most deterrence theorists that bilateral nuclear relationships, such as that between the United States and the Soviet Union during the Cold War, are inordinately stable.

To see this, consider now the *Rudimentary Asymmetric Deterrence Game* as given in Figure 4.4. In this, perhaps, the simplest deterrence game one can imagine, State A begins play at node 1 by deciding whether to *concede* (C) and accept the status quo, or to *demand* (D) its alteration. If State A chooses (C), the game ends and the outcome is the *Status Quo*. But if State A defects, State B must decide at node 2 whether to *concede* (C) the issue – in which case the outcome is *A Wins* – or *deny* (D) the demand and precipitate *Conflict*. Notice that the endpoints of this simple deterrence game list outcomes rather than player payoffs. I list outcomes and not payoffs in this example in order to use the same game form to analyse the strategic implications of more than one payoff configuration.

Next we determine what rational players would do in this game – given the assumption that *Conflict* is the worst outcome for both players – by

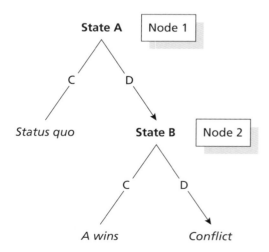

Figure 4.4 The rudimentary asymmetric deterrence game

applying backwards induction to the game tree. Since the application of this procedure requires one to work backwards up the game tree, we begin by considering State B's move at decision node 2.

At node 2, State B is faced with a choice between choosing (C), which brings about outcome *A Wins*, and choosing (D), which brings about *Conflict*. But if *Conflict* is assumed to be the *worst* possible outcome, State B, if it is rational, can *only* choose to concede since, by assumption, *A Wins* is the more preferred outcome.

Given that State B will rationally choose to concede at node 2, what should State A do at node 1? State A can concede, in which case the outcome will be the *Status Quo*, or it can defect, in which case the outcome will be *A Wins* – because a rational State B will choose to concede at node 2. If State A has an incentive to upset the *Status Quo*, that is, if it needs to be deterred because it prefers *A Wins* to the *Status Quo*, it will rationally choose (D). Thus, given the core assumptions of classical deterrence theory, the *Status Quo* is unstable and deterrence rationally fails.

To put this in a slightly different way, one can reasonably assume that states are rational, and one can also reasonably assume that war is the worst imaginable outcome for all the players, but one cannot make both these assumptions at the same time and logically conclude, as classical deterrence theorists do, that deterrence will succeed.

Logically inconsistent theories are clearly problematic. Since *any* conclusion can be derived from them, inconsistent theories can explain *any* empirical observation. Inconsistent theories, therefore, are non-falsifiable and of little practical use. When used properly, formal structures, like game-theory, can help in the identification of flawed theory.

If the core assumptions of classical deterrence theory are inconsistent with the possibility of deterrence success, what assumptions are? It is easy to demonstrate that in the Rudimentary Asymmetric Deterrence Game the *Status Quo* may remain stable, and deterrence may succeed, but only if State B's threat is credible in the sense of Selten, that is, if it is rational to carry out.

To see this, assume now that State B prefers *Conflict* to *A Wins*. (Note that this assumption implies that *Conflict* is not the worst possible outcome for State B.) With this assumption, State B's rational choice at node 2 changes. Given its preference, its rational choice at node 2 is now to choose (D) and deny State A's demand for a change in the *Status Quo*.

But State B's rational choice is not the only rational choice that changes with this new assumption. The rational choice of State A is also different. Applying backwards induction to State A's decision at node 1 now reveals a choice between *Status Quo* and *Conflict*. This means that the *Status Quo* will persist, and deterrence will succeed, *as long as State A's preference is for peace over war*. On the other hand, it will fail whenever this latter preference is reversed, even when State B's node 2 threat is credible.

At this juncture, two final observations can be made. The first is about the relationship between credible threats and deterrence success. Apparently, credibility is not, as Freedman (1989: 96) claims, the 'magic ingredient' of deterrence. As just demonstrated, a credible threat is not sufficient to ensure deterrence success. Deterrence may rationally fail even when all deterrent threats are rational to execute.

Still, in order to explain even the possibility of deterrence success in this simple example, a core assumption of classical deterrence theory had to be modified. But any analysis that proceeds from a different set of assumptions will constitute an entirely different theory. This is no small matter. As illustrated in the films *Sliding Doors* and *Run Lola Run*, and as demonstrated in Zagare (2004) and Zagare and Kilgour (2000), small differences in initial assumptions can have important theoretical consequences and significant policy differences. It is one of the strengths of game theory that its formal structure facilitates the identification of inconsistent assumptions, highlights the implications of initial assumptions, and increases the probability of logical argumentation.

## Coda

This chapter provides a gentle introduction to the key concepts and assumptions of game theory as it applies to the field of security studies. The examples used to illustrate many of these terms were meant to be suggestive, and not definitive. In the space of such a short chapter, this is the best that could be done. And although an attempt has been made to point the reader to relevant applications of the theory, this effort, too, can only be thought of as being cursory. The security studies literature that draws on, or has been influenced by, game-theoretic reasoning is vast. Nonetheless, the reader should now possess the conceptual tools that are a prerequisite for further exploration of this increasingly important body of literature.

## Further reading

Michael Brown, Owen R. Coté Jr., Sean M. Lynn-Jones, and Steven E. Miller (eds.), *Rational Choice and Security Studies* (MIT Press, 1999). Contains a spirited debate about the contributions of game-theoretic and related approaches to the security studies literature.
Sylvia Nasar, *A Beautiful Mind* (Simon & Schuster, 1998). A very readable biography of John Nash, one of the central figures of game theory.
Thomas C. Schelling, *Arms and Influence* (Yale University Press, 1966). One of the earliest and certainly one of the most influential works to draw on game theory in the analysis of interstate conflict.
Duncan Snidal, 'Rational Choice and International Relations' in Walter Carlsnaes, Thomas Risse and Beth A. Simmons (eds.), *Handbook of International Relations* (Sage, 2002). A fair and balanced assessment of the strengths and weaknesses of the rational choice approach.

Frank C. Zagare *The Games of July: Explaining the Great War* (University of Michigan Press, 2011). Uses simple and advanced game-theoretic models to explain the initiation, escalation, and expansion of major power war in 1914.

# Constructivisms

Matt McDonald

## Abstract

In this chapter, students will learn about several constructivist approaches to security studies. Constructivism has become an increasingly prominent theoretical approach to International Relations since its emergence in the 1980s. Focusing on the role of ideational factors and the social construction of world politics, it is perhaps best described as a broader social theory which then informs how one might approach the study of security. The exception in the broad constructivist tradition is the Copenhagen School, whose conceptual framework of securitization points to the construction of security through 'speech acts' that designate particular issues or actors as existential threats. This chapter begins by drawing out some of the shared assumptions of constructivist approaches to security studies. It then outlines the securitization framework in more depth, exploring the nature of its contribution to contemporary understandings of security.

## Introduction: constructivism and security

Constructivism has become an increasingly prominent theoretical approach to International Relations since its emergence in the 1980s. Drawing on insights from cognate disciplines such as sociology, constructivists argue that the world is constituted socially through inter-subjective interaction; that agents and structures are mutually constituted; and that ideational factors such as norms and identity are central to the constitution and dynamics of world politics. It is less a theory of International Relations or security, however, than a broader social theory which then informs how analysts might approach the study of security. The exception in the broad constructivist tradition is the Copenhagen School, whose conceptual framework of securitization suggests that security issues are constructed through 'speech acts' that designate particular issues or actors as existential threats. This chapter begins by drawing out some of the shared assumptions of constructivist approaches to the study of security. It then outlines the Copenhagen School framework of securitization in more depth, exploring the nature of its contribution to security studies.

## Constructivism: central tenets and shared assumptions

Constructivism, a term first elaborated by Nicholas Onuf in his ground-breaking book *World of Our Making* in 1989, is a broad theoretical approach to the study of International Relations that has been applied to a range of issues, from political economy (Blyth 2002) to international organization (Ruggie 1999: 41-130, Barnett and Finnemore 2004) and security (Katzenstein 1996b, Weldes *et al.* 1999). Despite attention to security issues, however, the extent to which constructivists have developed a *theory* of international security is limited. This distinguishes constructivists from critical theorists (with their conception of security defined as a commitment to emancipation) and realists (whose theory of world politics as a whole orients around a concern with achieving security in an inherently dangerous world) (see Chapters 7 and 2 this volume). A popular view among realists is that constructivism has generally eschewed a focus on the power politics of security and focused instead on the development of benign norms for managing interstate competition and institutionalizing broader forms of political community (see Mearsheimer 1994/95).

Such a portrayal is little more than a caricature of constructivism. Constructivists argue that their approach enables a more sophisticated and complete understanding of dynamics traditionally associated with realist approaches to security, from that of the nature of power generally (Barnett and Duvall 2007) to the security dilemma and the balance of power (Hopf 1998). As Kratochwil (1993) and Wendt (1992) have argued, constructivist approaches are also able to come to terms with periods of structural change enabled by strategic actors in world politics; most prominently the end of the Cold War. This places them in a particularly strong position relative to structuralist theories such as neorealism that assume state interests to be determined by the nature of the international system.

## Security as social construction: identity and norms

The central shared assumption of these constructivist approaches is that security is a social construction. As Karin Fierke has argued, 'to construct something is an act which brings into being a subject or object that otherwise would not exist' (2007: 56). This does not necessarily mean that there is no such thing as 'security' or that the concept is devoid of meaning. Drawing on Arnold Wolfers' (1952) classic definition, security could be understood as the preservation of a group's core values, for example. But such a broad definition of security tells us little about who constitutes the group; what its core values are; where threats to those values may come from; and how the preservation or advancement of these values might be achieved. For constructivists, answers to these questions are different in different contexts and develop through social interaction between actors. And it is the answers to these questions – articulated and negotiated in a particular social and historical context through social interaction – that ultimately define security in concrete terms, bringing it into being for particular actors in world politics.

Constructivists therefore tend to avoid advancing universal and abstract definitions of security, focusing instead on how *particular* security perspectives and practices emerge. Hopf (1998), for example, points to the impossibility of developing universal criteria for what constitutes a threat to security for states in world politics. For Hopf, state political leaders designate other states as 'friend' or 'enemy' – and approach them as such – on the basis of conceptions of identity. During the Cold War, for example, the USA interpreted the actions of the USSR as if it was an 'evil empire' eager to expand its power relative to the United States and challenge the spread of liberty and democracy that Americans viewed as central to their own national identity. This played a significant part in the American interpretation of Soviet attempts to supply Cuba with nuclear capabilities in 1962 as aggressive rather than defensive in intent (Weldes 1996). While all constructivists share a belief in the centrality of identity to the construction of security, however, different strands of constructivism see the relationship between identity and security quite differently. Different constructivist approaches to the relationship between security and identity are illustrated in Box 5.1.

Acknowledging the relevance of identity to security in constructivist approaches leads to a more general and fundamental shared assumption for constructivists: that non-material or ideational factors in general are central to security practices and dynamics in world politics. Aside from identity (perceptions of who we are) the most prominent ideational dimension of world politics addressed by constructivists is the role of norms. Norms can be defined as shared expectations about appropriate or legitimate behaviour by actors with a particular identity. Most commonly, this is applied to expectations about what constitutes appropriate behaviour for the key members of international society: states. Such a research programme builds on English School approaches to International Relations (Reus-Smit 2002). Constructivists have devoted a significant amount of time and research activity to exploring how international

## BOX 5.1  CONSTRUCTIVISMS AND IDENTITY

Debates over 'identity' are a useful site for exploring the difference between 'conventional' and 'critical' constructivist frameworks (Hopf 1998: 181–185). *Conventional constructivism* is closer to traditional theories of International Relations such as realism and liberalism in suggesting the possibility of depicting a world external to the analyst – a world 'out there' to be discovered and described objectively. *Critical constructivism*, on the other hand, points to the importance of forms of representation in constituting the 'real' world.

For *conventional constructivists*, the central concern in outlining the relationship between security and identity is to point to how national identity (and associated historical experience or cultural context) helps determine the content of a state's interests and therefore the way it will 'act' in global politics. Here, identity is something to be discovered or unearthed through analysis. This view is consistent with a commitment to a positivist epistemology: a belief that analysts can objectively examine a world 'out there'. Within this framework, identities are approached as relatively stable or sedimented, enabling the analyst to explore 'why' states act the way they do. The work of Katzenstein (1996a) and Wendt (1999) is emblematic of this approach: both have suggested the possibility of working within the epistemological and methodological frameworks of traditional International Relations theory, and both ultimately position constructivism as an ideational supplement to materialist approaches within the discipline. In the case of exploring the identity–security relationship, this might entail advancing the argument that Germany or Japan's particular experience in World War II *explains* their reluctance to use force in contemporary International Relations.

For *critical constructivists*, the central concern in exploring the relationship between security and identity is to outline how narratives of national identity become dominant and help set the limits for legitimate or feasible political action in particular settings at particular times. Here, identity is inherently unstable, contingent and a site of constant competition. Representations of security and threat can be central in this regard, serving to define who 'we' are and the 'other/s' from whom 'we' need protection. The study of identity, then, becomes the study of different representations that compete with others to provide realistic accounts of who a particular group is and how that group should act. For critical constructivists, analysts attempting to define a state's 'national identity' risk engaging in this power-political struggle by privileging some narratives of identity and marginalizing others. Such a position is consistent with a post-positivist epistemology, where it is impossible for the analyst to stand outside the world s/he is attempting to define or describe. The concern here is less with 'why' states act the way they do and more with how certain actions become possible: 'how meanings are produced and attached to various social subjects/objects, thus constituting particular interpretive dispositions which create certain possibilities and preclude others' (Doty 1993: 298). Key theorists working in this strand of constructivism include Weldes (1993), Lynn Doty (1993), Fierke (1998) and Krebs (2005). The analyses of the role of narratives of identity in the Israeli–Palestinian conflict noted later in this chapter (in Box 5.2) illustrates such an approach to the security–identity relationship.

norms evolve and come to provide limits to acceptable state behaviour in general (Finnemore 1996), and regarding issues as disparate as colonialism (Crawford 2003) and the use of nuclear weapons (Tannenwald 2007).

The example of international concerns about the nuclear ambitions of North Korea or Iran provides a useful illustration of the role of norms and identity in underpinning conceptions of threat. While it might seem self-evident that a nuclear North Korea or Iran constitutes a significant threat to international security, we might also ask why the possibility that North Korea or Iran *might* be developing nuclear weapons has been presented as far more of a threat to the so-called 'international community' than the existing nuclear arsenals of the United States, Russia, China, France, Britain, Pakistan, India or Israel, indeed enough to consider pursuing military intervention and regime change? Constructivists have pointed here to the increasing prominence and power of norms associated with the use and proliferation of nuclear weapons in general (e.g. Farrell ed. 2010), which goes some way to explaining international concerns about emergent nuclear states. Here, powerful and institutionalized expectations that legitimate states do not seek to acquire nuclear weapons conditions responses to stated nuclear ambitions and broader assessments of the regimes themselves.

This non-proliferation norm is important in determining the extent to which would-be violators are seen as a threat to international security, and in conditioning the type of response to possible violations (e.g. economic sanctions and arguments in favour of military intervention). Also important is the identity ascribed to would-be violators of this norm. In these particular cases, a constructivist analysis might also emphasize the importance of a range of social, cultural and historical factors that encourage particular forms of meaning to be given to particular actors and their intentions. Judgements about the political legitimacy of these regimes themselves and perceptions or representations of these states as 'rogue states' or part of an 'axis of evil' matter in influencing the way these states are viewed and approached, including the associated scale of the threat deemed to be posed by a possible nuclear programme. The important point to note here is not that constructivists would reject the idea of a nuclear North Korea or Iran as a threat, but that an understanding of the extent or scale of this threat and responses to it requires some attention to the role of norms, identity and representation more broadly.

## Negotiation and contestation

For constructivists, then, security is a context-specific social construction. Instead of developing abstract definitions of security, constructivists work from the premise that we would do better to focus on how security is given meaning within these contexts and analyse the implications this has for political practice. In exploring how security is given meaning, constructivists have emphasized that security is a site of negotiation (between political leaders and domestic audiences in particular) and contestation (between different actors elaborating different visions of 'our' values and how 'we' should act).

The idea of security as a site of negotiation between actors claiming to speak for a particular group and members of the group is a prominent feature of constructivist approaches. In realist approaches, security is enacted at the level of policy elites with negotiation between policy elites and the public having little or no role. In post-structural approaches, meanwhile, a state's general public is a relatively passive target of elite policy discourses that bind the individual to the nation-state (Campbell 1992). Constructivist approaches challenge these positions and point to the importance of public support for or acquiescence to elite discourses. They would further suggest that they are in a strong position to account for instances where non-state actors both within and beyond states are able to effect change in foreign or security policy discourse and practices. Such change might occur, for example, through the activism of NGOs, which have in some instances enjoyed success in promoting global political change on issues such as environmental change and human rights (Keck and Sikkink 1998).

Constructivists, particularly 'critical constructivists', have attempted to make sense of the relationship between political leaders and domestic audiences in a range of ways, emphasizing the role of representation. Fierke (1998) points to the role of 'language games' in suggesting that representations of security policy must be located in particular frameworks of communication to make sense, frameworks that change across different social contexts. Weldes (1996) meanwhile, develops Althusser's concepts of articulation and interpellation to suggest that representations of security can become acceptable if they are able to 'hail' individuals into particular subject positions. A prominent question here might be whether – in elite representations of the key beliefs and values of a nation-state – individuals recognize themselves as members of such a community.

If public support or acquiescence – however defined – is important to the construction of security and enabling for political action, it follows that security itself becomes a site of contestation. This contest takes place between actors searching to put forward their own visions of society and templates for action. In the invasion of Iraq in 2003, for example, a range of constructivist analyses pointed to dynamics of contestation within states over this issue. More directly, these analyses have pointed to the ways in which particular actors and the security policy they were advocating were able to 'win out' over competing actors and policy frameworks, in no small part due to their capacity to link military intervention with resonant narratives of national identity effectively. The success of neo-conservatives in the United States in 'selling' military intervention in Iraq, was due, in part, to their success in depriving political opponents of resources to challenge the case for invasion without subsequently being seen as weak on the threat of terrorism or simply unpatriotic (e.g. Williams and Schmitt 2008, Cramer 2007, Krebs and Lobasz 2007).

Some constructivists would agree with post-structuralists that representations of security and threat are potentially *performative*, that is, they enable or constrain certain types of action. This raises the central question of where dominant security discourses come from. For Weldes *et al.* (1999: 16), definitions of security and threat are contestable and contested, and 'considerable ideological labour' is required to ensure that particular security discourses become and remain dominant. Political elites are central figures in this process, but a range of other actors engage in the construction of security. Croft (2006), for example, has pointed to the role of the media and popular culture in both reproducing and contesting the security narratives of the US Government in the context of the 'war on terror'. For critical constructivists, competition over how to define security and threats to it are played out in a range of different contexts, all potentially with important political implications.

Dynamics of negotiation and contestation over security are therefore central to the process of the construction of security for constructivists. Different actors within states compete to define the nature of 'our values' and how they might be protected or advanced, and do so in the context of attempting to sell particular policy preferences to domestic audiences. The analysis of the Israeli–Palestinian conflict in Box 5.2 illustrates elements of these dynamics in action, in the process suggesting what a constructivist analysis of security has to offer our understanding of global security dynamics.

## Agents, structures and change

If the above account of security as a site of negotiation and contestation positions world politics generally as a social realm, nowhere is this conception more apparent in constructivist thought than in the view of the relationship between agents and structures and associated possibilities for structural change. For constructivists, agents and structures are mutually constituted. This view is most neatly captured in Wendt's seminal 1992 article, 'Anarchy is What States Make of it'. Here, Wendt engages with Waltz's neorealist theory of International Relations, which holds that state interests and actions are determined by the structure of the international system itself and its central feature: anarchy (see Chapter 2, this volume). For Waltz, the absence of a higher authority than states in the international system means that states have to provide their own security, which requires a kind of paranoid vigilance and constant preparation for conflict.

For Wendt, there is nothing inevitable about anarchy conditioning state interests and action in the way Waltz suggests. Drawing on the sociologist Anthony Giddens' conception of 'structuration', Wendt suggests that agents (in this case, states) can influence the content and effects of a particular structure (in this case, international anarchy) through the way they act. The meaning states ascribe to anarchy is not a simple reflection of the absence of a higher authority, but is developed through inter-subjective interaction with other states in the international system. To the extent that anarchy seems to encourage self-help, an overwhelming concern with survival and a view of conflict as an inevitable feature of world politics, it is one of several particular *cultures* of anarchy, rather than a timeless reality. Through their practices, states can either maintain this culture of anarchy or disrupt it, in turn either validating or questioning the normative basis of the international system itself (see Chapter 12 this volume).

## BOX 5.2  BARNETT, KAUFMAN AND THE ISRAELI–PALESTINIAN CONFLICT

How should we understand the relationship between political elites, public audiences and security policy in the context of the Israeli–Palestinian conflict? Barnett (1999) begins by suggesting that Rabin's proposed withdrawal from the occupied territories would previously have been seen as an abdication of national responsibility and security. He goes on to argue that Rabin was able to position such a withdrawal as a legitimate and even desirable policy option. He did this by locating this policy within particular narratives of Israeli identity and particular historical representations or 'frames'. In the process, not only did Rabin strategically draw on available cultural resources to ensure his policy resonated with domestic constituents, but he was also effective in marginalizing alternative stories of national identity and history. Rabin was thus able to emphasize an emergent liberal democratic narrative of national identity while marginalizing the traditionally powerful Jewish-Zionist narrative, thus enabling a more conciliatory approach to Palestinians.

Kaufman (2009) draws different conclusions about the Israeli–Palestinian conflict, albeit using similar constructivist insights. For Kaufman, the continued violence and mistrust characteristic of the Israeli–Palestinian conflict is fed by narratives of identity on both sides of the conflict that justify hostility towards the other. The intractable nature of the conflict is to be found in the continued resonance of exclusionary and violent narratives of identity on both sides that limit the extent to which political leaders in Israel and Palestine can compromise in dealings with the other without a loss of legitimacy among their respective domestic constituents. Kaufman points to a range of Israeli and Palestinian identity narratives while arguing that none are sufficiently moderate to enable a fundamental breakthrough in the peace process.

Both these analyses point to dynamics of negotiation and contestation over security policy, in which identity narratives play a central part. In their different emphases, they also illustrate the often complex relationship between sedimented social contexts that constrain actors on the one hand, and possibilities for effective strategic action that may enable change on the other. This nexus point between constraint and possibility, and between structures and agents, has been a central theme of constructivist thought in international relations.

This belief in the mutual constitution of agents and structures, and in the socially constructed nature of world politics generally, leads constructivists to conclude that change is always possible. Some care is required here. Constructivists believe that shared understandings about appropriate and legitimate behaviour can become particularly sedimented and even hegemonic. Indeed a range of constructivist analyses point to the ways in which particular expectations of appropriate behaviour can become so powerful as to effectively limit the range of possibilities for political action globally. This is particularly applicable to norms surrounding trade and the organization of political economy, in which opting out of the international economic framework or acting according to different sets of principles carries penalties for those 'deviants' (Sharman 2009).

Nevertheless, the belief that structures are socially constructed necessarily suggests the possibility of these structures becoming other than they are. An important example here is the end of the Cold War, which was enabled by actors such as Mikhail Gorbachev 'acting as if' an alternative normative structure was in place and subsequently changing the nature of the structure itself (Fierke 1998). Other constructivists have focused on the possibility for the security dilemma to be ameliorated in different contexts. This is apparent in literature exploring the possibilities for the emergence and development of 'security communities,' namely, groups of actors (usually states) for whom the use of force in resolving disputes between each other has become unthinkable over time (Adler and Barnett 1998, and Chapter 10 this volume). Here, European security cooperation since 1945 is taken as emblematic of the possibility of building alternative security futures through the development and institutionalization of shared norms. This focus is similarly based on the recognition that the security dilemma and the assumption of mutual distrust upon which it is based is not an inevitable feature of world politics produced by anarchy. Rather, it should be viewed as a social construction that is specific to particular historical moments and particular forms of identity politics.

In summary, constructivists share a belief that security is a social construction, meaning different things in different contexts. Security is also seen as a site of negotiation and contestation, in which actors compete to define the identity and values of a particular group in such a way as to provide foundation for political action. Identity and norms are seen as central to the study of security, together providing the limits for feasible and legitimate political action. Finally, agents and structures are mutually constituted and because the world is one of our own making, even structural change is always possible even if difficult.

Despite these insights into security dynamics and practices in world politics, however, constructivists have generally not attempted to develop a more specific framework for the study of security in international relations. One exception to this in the broad constructivist tradition is the Copenhagen School. This school's securitization framework is the most significant attempt to develop a theory of international security revolving around the central claim that security is a social construction.

## The Copenhagen School and securitization

The Copenhagen School was a label given to the collective research agenda of various academics at the (now defunct) Copenhagen Peace Research Institute in Denmark, centred around the work of Barry Buzan and Ole Wæver. From the early 1990s, various combinations of authors developed a series of insights about the operation of security in Europe. This collaborative work culminated in the 1998 text, *Security: A New Framework for Analysis*, co-authored by Barry Buzan, Ole Wæver and Jaap de Wilde. The 'school' itself and its central concepts developed over time, less initially as a specific project for the study of security than a series of interventions on different concepts and cases.

To the extent that a core theme animates the Copenhagen School, it is a primary concern with how security is constructed and 'works' in world politics. This approach developed in the context of post-Cold War calls to broaden security to include a range of pressing and hitherto neglected concerns such as environmental change, poverty and human rights on state security agendas. The Copenhagen School simultaneously contributed to these calls for broadening the concept and attempted to place analytical limits on the concept by suggesting that analysts should focus on the extent to which consequential political actors viewed and constructed particular issues (from nuclear warfare to climate change) as security threats. As such, the Copenhagen School has focused on how these powerful actors represent security and threat, and what political effects these representations of threat have in practice.

Wæver (2004) has suggested that the central concepts of the Copenhagen School are 'sectors,' 'regional security complexes,' and 'securitization'. Building on Buzan's earlier work (1991), sectors are defined as arenas entailing particular types of security interaction (Buzan *et al.* 1998: 7–8). Including military, political, economic, societal and environmental fields, for the Copenhagen School these sectors encourage different forms of relationships between relevant actors to develop and generally encourage different definitions of referent object (who or what is to be secured). Regional security complexes are defined as sets of units whose security processes and dynamics 'are so interlinked that their security problems cannot reasonably be analysed or resolved apart from one another' (Buzan *et al.* 1998: 201, Buzan and Wæver 2003: 44). These security complexes are defined in terms of mutually exclusive geographic regions such as Europe, the Americas, Asia, the Middle East and Africa. They also argue that the regional level of analysis is becoming increasingly important for global security dynamics but has been poorly theorized.

While these are all important ideas, the central contribution of the Copenhagen School is the concept of 'securitization'. This was first outlined in depth by Wæver in 1995 as referring to the discursive construction of threat. More specifically, securitization can be defined as a process in which an actor declares a particular issue, dynamic or actor to be an 'existential threat' to a particular referent object. If accepted as such by a relevant audience, this enables the suspension of normal politics and the use of emergency measures in responding to the perceived crisis. Security, in this sense, is a site of negotiation between speakers and audiences, albeit one conditioned significantly by the extent to which the speaker enjoys a position of authority within a particular group. Ultimately, Wæver (1995: 57) suggests that successful securitization tends to involve the articulation of threat 'only from a specific place, in an institutional voice, by elites'.

The articulations of threat themselves come in the form of 'speech acts'. Borrowing from the language theory of John Austin, speech acts are conceived as forms of representation that do not simply depict a preference or view of an external reality but also have a performative effect. A parallel illustration here would be that of a marriage, in which saying 'I do' at a particular moment and context *creates* the marriage itself, bringing it into being. Using the language of security and threat 'a state-representative moves a particular development into a specific area, and thereby claims a special right to use whatever means are necessary to block it' (Wæver 1995: 55). This is one example of conceptual development in the Copenhagen School: from originally positioning the speech act itself as securitization, by 1998 these 'speech acts' were defined as securitizing moves, with an 'issue securitized only if and when the audience accepts it as such' (Buzan *et al.* 1998: 25). This acceptance is itself conditioned by the existence of a series of 'facilitating conditions,' including the form of the speech act; the position of the securitizing actor; and the 'conditions historically associated with that threat' (Wæver 2000: 252–53, Buzan *et al.* 1998: 31–33).

There is nothing about the securitization framework that prevents it from being applied to groups other than states, but this is how it has been most frequently employed. Here, political leaders can, from a position of authority, claim to be speaking on behalf of the state or the nation, command public

---

## BOX 5.3  THE COPENHAGEN SCHOOL'S KEY TERMS

*Facilitating conditions*: particular contexts (including the form of the speech act; position of the speaker; and historical conditions associated with threat) that enable the acceptance of a particular securitizing move by the relevant audience.

*Securitizing move*: an actor's attempt to construct an issue or actor as an existential threat to a particular group through a security 'speech act'.

*Securitization*: the process whereby a securitizing actor defines a particular issue or actor as an 'existential threat' to a particular referent object and this move is accepted by a relevant audience.

*Desecuritization*: the process whereby particular issues or actors are removed from the security realm and (re-)enter the realm of 'normal politics'.

*Regional security complex*: a set of units in a particular geographical area whose security processes and dynamics are interlinked to the extent that their security problems need to be understood or addressed in conjunction with each other.

*Security sectors*: fields of activity or arenas (military, societal, political, economic and environmental) that entail particular forms of security interactions and particular definitions of referent objects.

attention and enact emergency measures (such as the deployment of troops). This is less a normative choice for the Copenhagen School – a belief in where the study of security *should* be focused – than an analytical one based on the commitment to the idea that 'at the heart of the (security) concept we still find something to do with defence and the state' (Wæver 1995: 47).

While Copenhagen School theorists defend the focus on states and elites as an analytical choice, there is a normative component to the theory in the form of an expressed preference for desecuritization: the removal of issues from the security agenda. For the Copenhagen School, security is defined in opposition to a conception of 'normal politics' characterized by the rule of law, open political deliberation and ultimately suggestive of politics in a Western liberal democratic state. Once an issue is securitized, these dynamics of 'normal politics' are suspended as an issue enters the realm of security and is dealt with in urgency (and often secrecy), with few actors able to contribute to political debate about how that issue should be addressed. This form of negative, 'panic politics' (Buzan *et al.* 1998: 34), associated with the work of political theorist Carl Schmitt, is for the Copenhagen School characteristic of securitization, and helps explain Wæver's (1995: 56–57) expressed normative preference for desecuritization.

It is when applied to the depiction and treatment of immigrants by liberal democratic states that the securitization framework is arguably at its explanatory best. In Australia after 2001, for example, political leaders suggested that asylum-seekers arriving by boat constituted a threat to the social cohesion of the Australian nation and the sovereignty of the Australian state, with some elected government representatives even suggesting that those seeking asylum in Australia might be terrorists (see Gelber and McDonald 2006). These representations in turn served to justify the denial of entry to asylum-seekers in contravention of Australia's international obligations, in part achieved through deploying military personnel and excising some islands from Australia's migration zone.

In this instance, the securitization framework is able to effectively illustrate the importance of linguistic depictions of threat. It also points to the ways in which an issue such as immigration – viewed in traditional security studies as largely irrelevant to security – may be addressed politically in very similar ways to traditional security 'threats'. Exceptional measures such as closing off borders, excising land and deploying troops followed representations of threat. And securitization in this instance did indeed have negative implications, limiting public discussion and encouraging the denial of ethical obligation to vulnerable outsiders.

In developing a relatively elegant and tight theoretical framework for security, a number of questions are left unanswered in the Copenhagen School framework. How do we know when an issue has been successfully securitized? Which audience needs to be convinced of the legitimacy of a securitizing move? Can forms of representation other than speech (images, for example) be considered as securitizing moves? How significant is the room to move of actors in positioning different actors or issues as threats? For its central theorists, the answers to these questions should depend on the case being explored. For others, there are costs associated with the relatively narrow framework the Copenhagen School has developed (McDonald 2008). Hansen (2000), for example, suggests that the Copenhagen School's ultimate focus on 'dominant voices' contributes to further silencing those already marginalized from security debates. It could also be suggested that the Copenhagen School's expressed preference for *desecuritization* – the removal of issues from the realm of security – is a product of a narrow view of the logic of security (what security *does* politically). This is a point taken up by Pinar Bilgin in Chapter 7 of this volume. These debates and controversies notwithstanding, the Copenhagen School framework has become increasingly prominent in international relations, providing students of security with tools for exploring the construction of security through depictions of threat.

The status of the Copenhagen School's normative preference for desecuritization also raises an important question of constructivist approaches to ethics and normative theorizing in general. Along with the stated desire of destabilizing dominant (state-based) security practices articulated in some critical constructivist scholarship (e.g. Weldes *et al.* 1999), the preference for desecuritization suggests that constructivists can and do advance normative concerns in their analyses of security. The manner in which these preferences are expressed, however, generally suggests that constructivists continue to draw largely from the philosophical contributions of alternative theories (such as critical theory) more comfortable with making claims about appropriate ethical action in world politics. Indeed there is little in constructivist thought to suggest that it can provide guidance in terms of telling us how security should be defined or practised in global politics. For some, employing a constructivist approach should entail eschewing normative concerns (e.g. Farrell 2002), while others suggest the possibility of employing constructivist insights to better understand possibilities for progressive change (e.g. Price 2009). This is an important issue for constructivist thought as it becomes an increasingly prominent theoretical approach in International Relations, and given ongoing debate about whether constructivists would be best advised to pursue dialogue and cooperation with critical theorists (Price and Reus-Smit 1998) or with mainstream scholars such as realists and liberals (Wendt 1999, Farrell 2002).

## Conclusion

Within International Relations, constructivism is often more readily associated with the development of norms for global governance and the role of ideational factors in world politics generally than with the militarized power politics that characterizes realist accounts of security in global politics. Yet constructivists would argue that the tools of their analysis enable a far more sophisticated understanding of 'traditional security' dynamics than traditional security approaches. Can we really understand the security dilemma or a state's perceptions of threat without some attention to the role of representation, standards of legitimacy or the politics of identity, for example? And of course, security has always been understood in a wider sense than solely as the protection of the territorial integrity or sovereignty of the state. Constructivists, with their shared emphasis on the social construction of security, are in a particularly strong position to give us a deeper insight into how security 'works' in world politics, and how politically important conceptions of security and threat actually come into being in different contexts.

## Further reading

Barry Buzan, Ole Wæver and Jaap de Wilde, *Security: A New Framework for Analysis* (Lynne Rienner, 1998). The key statement to date on the Copenhagen School's approach to security.

Karin Fierke, *Critical Approaches to International Security* (Polity, 2007). An excellent introduction to what it means to think of security as a social construction.

Ted Hopf, 'The Promise of Constructivism in International Relations Theory', *International Security*, 23(1) (1998): 171–200. An excellent overview of the constructivist contribution to the study of International Relations.

Peter Katzenstein (ed.), *The Culture of National Security: Norms and Identity in World Politics* (Columbia University Press, 1996). One of the key texts outlining a (largely conventional) constructivist approach to security and applying it to various cases.

Jutta Weldes *et al.* (eds.), *Constructing Insecurity* (University of Minnesota Press, 1999). A key text in outlining a critical constructivist approach to security and applying this to various cases.

Alexander Wendt, 'Anarchy is What States Make of It: the Social Construction of Power Politics', *International Organization*, 46(2) (1992): 391–425. A seminal article pointing to the mutual constitution of structures and agents.

# Peace Studies

Peter Lawler

## Abstract

In this chapter, students will learn about peace research with reference to the work of one of its most famous and prolific contributors, Johan Galtung. It surveys the evolution of contemporary peace studies out of early peace and conflict research, a process which involved both the redefinition of violence and peace, the constant expansion of peace studies' purview, and ultimately a decisive shift away from the foundational commitment to positivism. Given the developments in cognate fields of enquiry, arguably the defining feature of peace studies is a normative commitment to non-violence. The chapter concludes by offering two views of contemporary peace studies: a celebratory reading and a more critical view that speculates as to whether the widening of peace studies concerns has come at a price, not least the capacity to address contemporary forms of armed conflict.

## Introduction: What is peace studies?

The central concerns of peace studies – the reduction and eventual eradication of war and the control and resolution of violent conflict by peaceful means – do not self-evidently mark it out as a distinct field. Such concerns have also threaded through the discipline of International Relations (IR). Indeed, most histories of IR start by identifying its 'idealist' origins in the wake of the carnage of the First World War. Although the supposedly naive aspirations of IR's liberal founders were supplanted by a more hard-headed realism after the Second World War, even a realist-dominated IR discipline could plausibly claim war and peace at the heart of its concerns.

Peace studies' other key focus – the definition of peace itself – is arguably a better basis for distinguishing it from other cognate fields, not least because it highlights peace studies' overt, and often controversial, normative content. Certainly, in its earlier days, and in spite of considerable efforts by its key figures to present their work as an example of social *science*, it was the normative commitment to promote peace that principally marked it out from IR as well as such fields as strategic studies. These largely took war and other forms of violent conflict to be perennial, if tragic, features of an anarchical international system of sovereign states. In contrast, peace studies has always presented war as a problem in need of eradication. At the very least, someone who chose to identify themselves as working within 'peace research' or 'peace and conflict research' (the preferred labels of peace studies' key founding figures in the 1950s) was signalling a normative standpoint of sorts. In spite of the efforts of the early pioneers to mask their normative leanings beneath a commitment to otherwise orthodox social scientific methods, this was enough to ensure a sceptical or even hostile reception within cognate fields. With the more recent development of post-positivist, critical approaches in IR, however, such overt normativity alone is no longer a particularly distinguishing or, indeed, controversial feature (see Chapter 7 this volume).

Peace studies has also been marked from the outset by the interdisciplinary origins of its key figures. It has provided a site for researchers initially trained in the natural sciences, economics, psychology, anthropology, education, and sociology, more so in fact than the obvious disciplinary starting points of political science and IR, to come together in the pursuit of peace. To this day, it remains an interdisciplinary field of enquiry, although, again, this has become a decreasingly distinctive feature because of the growth of inter-disciplinary approaches and outlooks in the social sciences more generally. The multi-disciplinary origins of the founders of peace research helped arguably to stymie their original goal of establishing a methodologically distinctive and theoretically robust field of social scientific enquiry. This was not least because of widely varying conceptual assumptions and methodological commitments, disputes about the ultimate origins of violence and war (whether it stems from intrapersonal, interpersonal, inter-communal, or international politics for example), as well as disagreements about what the condition of peace actually entails.

Does peace merely refer to the absence, perhaps permanently, of war, what in peace studies is now referred to as 'negative peace'? If peace does refer to something more than this, what peace studies calls 'positive peace', what is it and would we agree on when it could be said to have arrived? Today an intellectual or practical concern with the problem of peace clearly overlaps with explorations of such things as conflict resolution (at all social levels), global exploitation, human rights, international social justice, environmental security, alternative world orders and so on. These are evidently issue areas of concern to a wide range of scholars working under a variety of disciplinary labels. Peace studies is perhaps now best understood, then, as a site or intellectual space for the bringing together of scholars who, by and large, openly declare a commitment to non-violence, or – to borrow from the title of a book by peace research's most famous figure – the realization of 'peace by peaceful means' (Galtung 1996). This commitment also highlights the historical and, again, at times controversial connections between peace studies as an academic field and the activism of peace movements.

It is important to note from the outset that peace studies does not aim to eliminate all conflict. Just as the medical sciences acknowledge the useful, indeed essential functions of some bacteria, so too do peace researchers recognize the social functions of conflict. Again, violence is key. As the editors of a leading peace studies textbook see it:

> Peace and conflict studies does, where possible, seek to develop new avenues for cooperation, as well as to reduce significantly (and eventually to eliminate) violence, especially organized and increasingly destructive state-sanctioned violence. It is this violence, by any definition the polar opposite of peace, that has so blemished history and that – with the advent of nuclear weapons, biochemical weapons and other weapons of global destruction – now threatens the future of all life on this planet. And it is the horrors of such violence, as well as the glorious and perhaps even realistic hope of peace (both negative and positive) that makes peace and conflict studies especially frustrating, fascinating, and essential.
>
> (Barash and Webel 2002: 26)

## Peace studies: a brief history

The field of peace studies is a relatively recent creation, but thinking about peace has a much longer history. The prevalence of violent conflict and war in human history has spawned innumerable reflections on war's causes as well as on the possibility (or impossibility) of 'perpetual peace' (the title of a famous and influential essay by the philosopher Immanuel Kant). All of the great religious traditions offer reflections on war and peace, although few absolutely prohibit recourse to war. As Pascal, the seventeenth-century philosopher, mathematician and devout Catholic, famously observed: 'Men never do evil so completely and cheerfully as when they do it from religious conviction'. What religious thought does offer is an enormous and often highly ambiguous body of reflection on the moral constraints surrounding war. The Christian tradition has been particularly influential here. Initially pacifist, since the fourth century it has been a key source for the contemporary laws of war which attempt to set down the moral limitations of either going to war (*jus ad bellum*) or fighting in war (*jus in bello*). As Barash (2000: 202) notes, however, 'there is a powerful and persistent tradition of explicit pacifism and antiwar activism within Christianity, as within most of the world's traditions'. Although peace studies is not characterized by a particular emphasis on religious imperatives to pursue peace, many of its modern founders were undoubtedly impelled by private religious commitments and organized religions remain a key source of funding.

The secular view that war is an inhibitor of human progress and thus irrational emerges out of Enlightenment philosophers such as Jean-Jacques Rousseau and Immanuel Kant. It was Kant who argued that universal justice and perpetual peace were categorical imperatives that humanity was compelled to pursue by virtue of its rational nature. In so doing, Kant's name became synonymous with an 'idealist' or 'utopian' tradition of thinking about global reform, founded upon a conception of universal reason and human perfectibility coupled with a more pragmatic pursuit of the domestication of international politics through the institutionalization of interaction between states and the development of international law (see Chapter 3 this volume). As noted above, it is widely held that such thinking underscored the foundation of the modern IR discipline as well as concrete, and largely unsuccessful, efforts in the early twentieth century to eradicate the scourge of war such as the failed 1928 Kellogg-Briand Pact, which sought to outlaw war, and the League of Nations. Prominent scholars such as E.H. Carr in Britain and Hans Morgenthau in the US railed against what they saw as the naiveté of early inter-war IR scholarship, focusing particularly on the failure to adequately conceptualize the role of power in international politics.

Of course, in many respects the widespread presentation of thinking about war, peace and the international system within a simplistic dualism of realism versus idealism resulted in the caricaturing of protagonists on both sides of the equation which has persisted until relatively recently (see Osiander 1998, Rosenthal 1991). This meant the early founders of peace research in the 1950s had to battle against a widespread scepticism in intellectual and policy circles premised on the view that it was symptomatic of a return to a now discredited inter-war idealism, or was little more than an intellectual protest movement tainted by its connections with an emerging public campaign in some Western states against the spread of nuclear weapons. They did this largely through adherence to the dominant trends within the social sciences more generally, notably the emergence of positivist empiricism and the trappings of objectivity.

## Peace research as science

Peace research emerged during the 1950s in both the United States and Europe, in the latter case principally in Britain and the Scandinavian states. On both sides of the Atlantic it was marked initially by an emphasis on the possibility of systematic and rigorous research into peace, underscored by a belief in the redemptive and universal power of scientific knowledge. The early focus was less on peace itself and more on the systematic analysis of war. The difficult relationship between the commitment to science and a normative concern with the problem of war was personified in the British academic Lewis Richardson who, alongside the US scholar Quincy Wright, pioneered the large-scale quantitative study of war. A Quaker and a mathematician, Richardson argued that 'science ought to be subordinate to morals' while simultaneously insisting that science itself required moral neutrality in the name of objectivity (Eckhardt 1981a). Wright was an international law specialist who in 1942 published the first edition of his monumental *A Study of War*, the product of a 15-year inter-disciplinary research project. In it Wright surveyed the history and causes of war from primitive conflict onwards and in subsequent editions the study went on to look at the advent of nuclear weapons. Wright used anthropological data and scaling techniques to hypothesize a definitive relationship between aggression and levels of civilization (Eckhardt 1981b).

The then less prominent work of the US psychologist Theo Lentz arguably most clearly foreshadowed the foundational model of a self-consciously labelled peace research. Lentz saw positivist scientific method as sound but subject to abuse. Through a process of 'democratization' and expansion he thought science could divorce itself from prejudice and transcend social and political barriers. Inspired by the adage that 'war is made in the minds of men', Lentz argued for extensive research into human character and attitudes which, in contrast to what he saw as the earnest amateurism of peace movements, would be thoroughly professional. He expressed a paradoxical 'faith' in science's capacity to assist in the release of a human potentiality to harmonize diverse purposes and achieve universal betterment (Lentz 1955). Of course the belief in the possibility of putting science and positivist social science to work in the cause of peace was a minority position in the 1950s. A lot of scientific research was servicing a weapons industry undergoing rapid techno-logical advancement spurred on by the strategic rivalries of the Cold War. Nonetheless, the invention of nuclear weaponry did stimulate the founding of the *Bulletin of Atomic Scientists* by former Manhattan Project physicists in 1945 and the establishment of the Pugwash Conferences on Science and World Affairs in 1957. This was in response to the 1955 Russell–Einstein Manifesto, named after its two key signatories, Bertrand Russell and Albert Einstein (who signed just eight days before his death), which called upon scientists to alert the public to the danger of weapons of mass destruction and for world leaders to seek the peaceful resolution of conflicts.

Much, perhaps most, of the social science at the time was more focused on systematically categorizing, explaining and indeed shoring up conventional social and political practices and policies. In this context the development of an explicitly normative branch of social science was improbable. What did ensue, notably in the US, was the establishment of 'conflict research' as an intellectual orientation that led to the establishment of the *Journal of Conflict Research* in 1957 and the Center for Research on Conflict Resolution at the

University of Michigan in 1959. Both of these developments reflected some of the normative sentiments of Huxley and Lentz and certainly were interdisciplinary in structure. The founders of the Michigan Center all shared an enthusiasm for the application of new social scientific techniques (culled from the fields of economics, social psychology and sociology) to the study of large-scale social conflict. Their research output fell into a limited range of categories: psychological studies of the origins, management and resolution of conflict; game-theoretic analysis of the dynamics of conflict; and statistical analyses of arms races and the correlates of war.

Although the field of conflict research was very much a precursor of contemporary peace studies, a noticeable absence was reference to the word 'peace' in their endeavours. There was undoubtedly a political dimension to this; conflict research quickly acquired respectability and its boundaries soon blurred with developments in other disciplines, notably IR. Nonetheless, even conflict research had an oppositional political dimension to it insofar as its output was from its inception designed to counteract that of well-established institutes of strategic studies and the pessimism and perceived moral silence of mainstream realist IR. There is an irony to be detected in the attempts of some scientifically minded philosophers to eschew the uncertainties of philosophy and political theory yet at the same time embrace, however hesitantly, a need to provide an ethically driven counterpoint to the political and philosophical assumptions that underpinned orthodox thinking about international relations and the provision of national security in particular. This ambiguity about the tensions between moral and political commitment to the cause of peace and the conduct of scientistic social and political research arguably dogged the early years of peace research, not only in the US but also in Europe where a more overtly named peace research community was also emerging.

The first appearance of peace research as a disciplinary label was in Norway. In 1959 the International Peace Research Institute of Oslo (PRIO) was established, initially as part of Oslo University, and this was followed five years later by the founding of the Stockholm International Peace Research Institute (SIPRI) in Sweden. The setting up of PRIO (and, in a related development, the first Chair in Peace and Conflict research) was not an easy task. The driving force behind it was Johan Galtung, who as a young, US-trained, Norwegian sociologist and Ghandi-inspired conscientious objector embodied the tensions between the commitments to applied research on peace and positivist methodology (Lawler 1995). He overcame considerable official political reluctance – particularly over the inclusion of the seemingly unscientific word 'peace' – to garner the financial support of the Norwegian government. Galtung was later to admit that the mantle of science proved very useful in the quest for legitimacy and, of course, funding (interview with author; Galtung 1975a: 17–18). The fact that Norway and Sweden were social-democratic welfare states beginning to develop distinctly internationalist dimensions to their foreign policies no doubt also helps explain why they were the first states in the world to support the establishment of institutionalized peace research. In 1964 the Scandinavian peace research community came of age and to greater prominence moreover with the founding of the *Journal of Peace Research* under Galtung's editorship.

## From peace research to peace studies

Galtung's influence on the subsequent development of peace research, initially in Europe but eventually pretty much everywhere it emerged, cannot be overstated. It was Galtung who set its tone and helped distinguish it from conflict studies. He introduced much of its distinctive lexicon, some of which – notably the concepts of positive and negative peace as well as structural violence and cultural violence – was to flow well beyond its boundaries. Under Galtung's aegis, the purview of peace research expanded dramatically and rapidly. Although the first decade of his work and that of peace research more generally was to retain a commitment – honoured perhaps more in the breach than in the observance – to the dictates of positivistic social science, his later work helped establish the breadth of peace studies as it is today. It is perhaps because the foundational project of establishing a field of peace research, with its own distinctive research methodology that would accord with the (then) mainstream views of what constituted social scientific research, failed to consolidate that peace studies now more openly exhibits its normative leanings and promotes itself as a broad church. Positivistic peace research has not disappeared. However, it constitutes only part of what is now a wide-ranging field of enquiry that cannot be defined by any particular methodology or disciplinary orientation alone. As Galtung himself was to write nearly 40 years after the establishment of PRIO,

> peace and violence have to be seen in their totality, at all levels of organisation of life (and not only human life). . . . Moreover, as the purpose of the whole exercise is to promote peace, not only peace studies, a non-positivistic epistemology is indispensable, with explicit values and therapies, rather than stopping once the diagnosis has been pronounced.
>
> (Galtung 1996: vii)

The problem for contemporary peace studies remains that of clearly marking itself off from other fields of scholarly enquiry, notably IR and critical security studies, which have also undergone considerable expansions of their purview as well as extensive methodological diversification. Many scholars working in such fields today would, to all intents and purposes, share the normative orientation and research interests of those who choose to overtly locate themselves in peace studies. Perhaps then the distinctiveness of peace studies today boils down to rejection of any role for violence of any kind in the pursuit of a better or preferred world, as suggested by Galtung's formulation of 'peace by peaceful means' as the departure point (see Box 6.1). If so, this would suggest that, ultimately, a commitment to pacifism constitutes the defining hallmark of peace studies today. As we shall see, however, defining violence has not been without its controversies.

## Key concepts

In reflection of his background as a physician's son, Galtung's earlier work frequently drew upon an analogy between peace research and medicine, a theme to which he would return throughout his subsequent work and which still permeates much of peace studies today. For Galtung, medicine offered an attractive benchmark. It was a relatively young science, multidisciplinary in orientation and focused on restoring bodily health. Medicine's professional ethics, encapsulated in the Hippocratic oath, also appealed to him. To be professional was 'to stand in a contractual relationship to the rest of society' and in medicine's case, professional ethics obliged the physician to always try and save life regardless of whose life was in question. Although aware that the analogy between the bodily health of individuals and the health of the international body politic was imperfect, nonetheless Galtung depicted medicine and peace research as both in the business of ensuring survival. The early depiction of the peace researcher was as an 'oriented' scientist who, drawing upon an expanding methodological and empirical toolbox, would help to put a professional peace research 'at the disposal of the development of international order' (Galtung, 1975b: 170–172, Galtung 1975c). Writing in 1967, Galtung acknowledged that this vision was perhaps utopian but speculated nonetheless that perhaps in fifteen to twenty years peace research institutions would be flourishing as 'as a matter of course, as a matter of survival' (1975b: 172).

---

**BOX 6.1 JOHAN GALTUNG'S CONCEPTION OF THE 'POINT OF DEPARTURE' FOR PEACE STUDIES: 'PEACE BY PEACEFUL MEANS'**

To start with, two compatible definitions of peace:

*Peace is the absence/reduction of violence of all kinds.*

*Peace is nonviolent and creative conflict transformation.*

For both definitions the following holds:

*Peace work is work to reduce violence by peaceful means.*

*Peace studies is the study of the conditions of peace work.*

Galtung (1996: 9)

---

Of course in drawing an analogy between health and peace, Galtung was presenting the value of peace in a commonsensical form that seemingly put it above politics. Indeed, a key theme throughout his early depictions of the young 'science' of peace was an attempt to lift it out of the overly abstracted realm of philosophy or the biases and prejudices of politics, hallmarks of what he pejoratively termed 'traditional peace thinking'. In the case of IR, for example, peace was treated in an unscientific and value-laden way, largely 'for ritualistic and expressive purposes' and not with the intent of clarifying or realizing a clearly defined end state. For Galtung, orthodox IR scholarship relied too heavily on dictums – such as 'if you want peace, prepare for war' – which had acquired the status of apodictic truth. It was also excessively and, in his view, unjustifiably state-centric and relied on insufficiently tested assumptions about such things as the centrality of the 'balance of power'. Additionally, 'traditional peace thinking' was replete with biases; it was predominantly the product of the upper social echelons of developed Western states. Galtung's ideal-type peace researcher, on the other hand, would adopt a resolutely global and more sociological focus. Thus: the peace researcher's 'field of identification' was to be 'world problems in a world perspective'; the object domain was to be the global social system; and the research focus was to be '*human* survival', a conception of the peace researcher which retains considerably currency in the field today. How then might peace research escape the partisanship and looseness of traditional scholarship? For Galtung the answer lay in a combination of multi-disciplinarity, political autonomy, a commitment to the scientific pillar of intersubjective agreement and a Hippocratic-like professional commitment to look beyond personal preferences and biases.

## Positive and negative peace

Galtung's idealized peace researcher was not to survive unscathed, not least because the scientism underpinning it was vulnerable to the swathe of anti-positivist criticism that at the same time was building within the social sciences more widely. Nonetheless, the notions that peace research was to be global in focus, take a broadly sociological view, and try to rise above a range of social and political prejudices arguably still remain key features of peace studies. The fleshing out of those early commitments also required a redefinition of peace. It was in the editorial of the first edition of the *Journal of Peace Research* that Galtung introduced his famous dual definition of peace (1964: 1–4). There peace was defined as having two aspects: *negative* peace, being the absence of war and actual physical violence; and *positive* peace, initially described as 'the integration of human society'. This dualism was premised upon the identification of two global empirical tendencies that undermined the widespread image of an anarchical world order condemned to a perpetual condition of anticipating war.

The first was that 'man identifies'; humans display a capacity for mutual empathy and solidarity. Echoing a theme that was to become a hallmark of liberal scholarship in IR under the guise of the concept of interdependence (Keohane and Nye 1977), Galtung argued that individuals 'see (themselves) as a member of groups where a norm of reciprocity is valid and cooperation a dominant mode of interaction . . . In the real world integration is a fact'. Although Galtung acknowledged that outside of spheres of 'amity and mutual aid' it could be said that 'enmity and mutual destruction may rule', the implication was clearly that there was an identifiable and demonstrable human capacity to identify with others that was universalizable. Galtung eschewed reference to states preferring the less rigid and more flexible categories of groups and spheres. The task confronting the peace researcher was, therefore, how to extend community and achieve consonance between an innate human sociability and global social structure.

The second empirical observation, also familiar to liberal IR scholars, was that no matter how bellicose relations between human communities are, 'man rarely uses all of his means of destruction against all enemies all of the time'. There were 'limitations and rules . . . elements of a game in the fight'. Again, the clear implication was that there is an evident capacity to constrain the resort to violence and this was amenable to extension. Galtung went on to propose that if we imagined the extrapolation of these two demonstrable human capacities then a vision of the elimination of violence and the dissolution of the distinction between the domestic and international social realms appears on the horizon. The extrapolation of the capacity to limit recourse to violence would only produce the condition of negative peace, whereas the extrapolation of the human capacity to cooperate would realize a condition of positive peace. In combination, however, they would produce a 'general and complete peace'.

The distinctiveness of peace research lay, then, in its commitment to simultaneously research and promote both negative and positive peace. It can now be seen how Galtung was then presenting peace research as a form of functionalist sociology. Violence arises from the relations between sub-systemic groups, but humanity displayed also a capacity to cooperate and integrate. Cast in this light, the value of peace, like that of health, was not seen to be in need of defence. 'If this is a value', Galtung claimed, 'it is amongst the most consensual ones'. If peace could acquire an objective and hardly disputable quality then, by extension, so too could the depiction of the peace researcher as a kind of technician-physician dedicated to the preservation *and* improvement of the health of the global body politic.

The term 'positive peace' remains one of Galtung's most enduring legacies, but quite what belonged under the category rapidly became a matter of dispute. As the peace research community evolved, it also diversified and within a few years Galtung's foundational dual definition of peace came under critical scrutiny. Galtung never fleshed out his original conception of positive peace very much and he soon became embroiled within a heated schism in peace research. For all of Galtung's appeals to the principles of scientific research and the role model of the physician, peace research was bound to attract critical attention not only from a sceptical orthodoxy but also from more radical intellectual quarters. The latter were in turn the product of the late 1960s when not only the social scientific research community but also Western society more widely was undergoing a wave of radical upheaval. This led ultimately to the introduction by Galtung of another concept that also remains as a hallmark of contemporary peace studies: the concept of structural violence.

## Structural violence

At a series of conferences held in 1968 and 1969 a group of young European peace researchers questioned the broad direction the field was taking. Reflecting widespread concern about the Vietnam War, they challenged the depiction of peace research as a science that aspired to be above politics and which aspired to a balanced or 'symmetric' analysis of actual conflicts. The resulting schism largely but not entirely reflected a division between peace and conflict research as it was evolving in the US and the European or 'Galtungian' wing. At the heart of the dispute was the question of whether peace research should more openly embrace a more critical standpoint and abandon the quest for symmetrical analysis in favour of an openly asymmetrical approach that would explicitly adopt an overtly political stance (key examples of the radical critique include Schmid 1968 and Dencik 1970). Although Galtung was very much the architect of the European approach to peace research which, though differing from its US counterpart in the emphasis on positive peace otherwise largely shared its positivism, and as such he was initially a target of criticism. At the same time he was revising his own conception of the field. The critics were mostly young Marxists and at its highpoint the debate became very heated with many US peace researchers choosing to disassociate themselves from what they saw as an increasingly unscientific trend in European peace research. Many older European peace researchers recognized the legitimacy of some of the questions raised but also deeply resented the aggressive manner in which they were put (Boulding 1970). As one put it, for the radical critics 'pacifism has been replaced by Marxism, conflict-resolution by class-struggle, peace by revolution and if necessary bloody revolution', an assessment the leading radical described as 'essentially correct' (Goldmann and Dencik cited in Lawler 1995: 72). Although the radical critics saw Galtung's original conception of positive peace as largely vapid, Galtung managed to stay relatively aloof from the debate. This was not least because in 1969 he published an article entitled 'Violence, Peace and Peace Research' in the *Journal of Peace Research* (Galtung 1969). Here he proposed a reconstruction of the conceptual fundamentals of peace research that clearly moved it closer to the emergent radical position, while maintaining a pacifist taboo on violence.

Galtung's revision did not directly address the question of the relationship between peace research and policymaking – the core focus of the radical critics – but it did take up the demand that peace research should focus more on the social origins of conflict and address the question of 'invisible' or 'latent' conflict that, the radicals claimed, arose out of economic, social and political inequalities. The implications of Galtung's revisions were highly significant.

Above all, they signalled a considerable expansion of peace research's purview and began in effect the transition from peace research (understood here in the sense of a commitment to a quasi-objectivist scientism) to a more openly normative peace studies. Henceforth peace research would embrace not merely the analysis of visible, large-scale violent conflicts and wars but would also now look at inequality and injustice, understood as breeding grounds for future violent conflicts. Although continuing to espouse non-violence as a *sine qua non* for anything worthy of the name peace research, Galtung also accepted that pacifism could not provide an excuse for failing to tackle the issue of social conflict. Equally, he recognized that peace research should not descend into a kind of behaviouralism in which conflict resolution was largely seen in terms of attitudinal or behavioural modification, something that was prominent in US peace and conflict studies. Although not a Marxist, Galtung shared with the radicals the view that peace research had to address the *structural* determinants of conflict.

Galtung's revised depiction of peace research commenced with a revised understanding of violence. Retaining the maxim that 'peace is the absence of violence', Galtung went on to propose that 'Violence is present when human beings are being influenced so that their actual somatic and mental realisations are below their potential realisations' (1969: 168). An important qualification is that 'potential' was to be understood as a contingent category connected to 'the given level of insights and resources'. Thus a failure to realize potential is only indicative of violence if it is knowingly avoidable. Thus the research focus of peace research needed to extend beyond the realm of direct or manifest violence into anything that inhibits individual human development. In other words, peace research had to begin to analyse 'structural violence' in which 'the violence is built into the structure and shows up as unequal power and consequently as unequal life chances' (Galtung 1969: 171).

One clear consequence of the redefining of violence was the need to revise also the definition of positive peace. Galtung now equated it with 'social justice'. Although this formulation moved Galtung much closer to peace research's Marxist critics, he argued that both liberal and Marxist political systems produced structural violence: the former through economic inequality and the latter through the unequal distribution of political power. This refusal to firmly come down on the side of Marxism (or, indeed, to firmly locate himself within any of the main schools of political and social thought), in spite of the fact that much of his subsequent work on global inequality clearly drew from it (see Galtung 1971), was to remain a hallmark not only of Galtung's work but also of peace studies more generally. Thus he subsequently preferred to equate positive peace with the less economistic notion of 'human fulfilment'.

### Cultural violence

In Galtung's subsequent work he began to explore the idea of alternative world orders, a theme that was also emerging on the reformist and more critical wing of IR. Through his involvement in the World Order Models Project, Galtung developed his interest in the multifaceted nature of violence and his criticism of dominant models of global social development. Bringing together human needs theory, a lifelong interest in Gandhi, and a growing ecological sensibility, Galtung's *The True Worlds* (1980) signalled a much more open drawing of the connections between peace research and peace activism and a depiction of peace studies as embracing a multifaceted approach to addressing the multiple crises of a global modernity. As with all of his work, the normative foundations of this rapidly expanding purview remained radically under-explored even if they were much more visible (Lawler 1995: 135–190).

A key theme in Galtung's work from that point on was the need for peace studies to escape the confines of Western modernist thinking and orthodox political and economic solutions to the various crises that underpinned the emergence of violence in its myriad forms. In 1990, Galtung introduced the term 'cultural violence' thus beginning the connection of peace studies with what remains one of the most difficult and controversial areas of research today: the politics of identity (Galtung 1990).

For Galtung, the West (or the Occident in Galtung's language) is under-stood as a civilization underpinned by a social cosmology. Indeed, social cosmology is to a civilization as 'the psychological construct of a personality' is to a human being (1981: 147; see also 1996: 211–222). Seen thus, the West is a kind of metanarrative that permeates all aspects of social life to cement together a cacophony of voices resulting in the dominance of a single narrative of intellectual and social practice. Somewhat controversially, Galtung's Occident includes Islam because, as with the other two major religions of the West, it is seen to promote the notion of people in a sub-ordinate relationship to a singular God. Galtung's Occident is exclusionary, virulently hierarchical, and proselytizing and, perhaps not surprisingly, seen as a poor source of peace thinking. Above all it is a key, but by no means the only practitioner of cultural violence.

The meaning of cultural violence is grasped through its relationship to the other two categories of violence. Thus, it refers to 'those aspects of culture, the symbolic sphere of our existence . . . that can be used to justify or legitimate direct or structural violence'. In comparison to other forms of violence, cultural violence is an 'invariant' or a 'permanence'; it flows steadily through time providing a 'substratum from which the other two can derive their nutrients' (Galtung 1990: 291, 294, see also 1996: 210). A violent culture 'preaches, teaches, admonishes, eggs on and dulls us into seeing exploitation and/or repression as normal or natural, or into not seeing them (particularly exploitation) at all' (Galtung 1990: 295). Galtung posits a causal flow from cultural violence via structural violence through to direct violence, while also suggesting that violence can emerge from any of the three corners of the violence triangle.

Of course, in the spirit of the foundational emphasis on negative and positive peace, peace studies is not confined to the analysis of violence but also to the realization of peace. The antithesis of cultural violence is, according to Galtung (1990: 291, 301–303), 'cultural peace', a condition brought about by 'aspects of a culture that serve to justify and legitimise direct peace and structural peace'. As Galtung admits, however, this sets peace research a rather gargantuan task. In addition to the issue of how one goes about identifying, analysing and changing extant cultures or social cosmologies, there is the question of how to construct a preferred, peaceful cultural form. In both cases the question of values haunts analysis as well as prescription.

As I have argued at length elsewhere, Galtung's own work has been marked throughout by a positivistic preoccupation with classification and the development of taxonomies (of peace, violence, forms of exploitation etc) (Lawler 1995). His analysis of cultures and cosmologies is no exception in this regard. However his rather idiosyncratic taxonomy (his inclusion of Islam within the 'Occident' being a case in point) runs the risk of setting definitive boundaries around features of social life that are highly resistant to definitive classification. Thus, as was the case with Huntington's controversial 'Clash of Civilisations' thesis (Huntington 1996), his depictions of specific cultures as inherently more violent or peaceable than others could be accused of simplifying, essentializing, and even caricaturing highly complex fluid aspects of collective identity. On a more positive note, the identification of deep cultural dimensions to the problematics of violence and peace has pushed peace studies much more towards notions of promoting ongoing, open-ended dialogue between cultures, epistemologies, and civilizations. As Galtung (1988: 78) himself observes, 'dialogue is not neutral, not above or below politics, it *is* politics'. The foundational enthusiasm for defining violence and peace and the possibility of a science of peace has given way then to a much looser and diverse enterprise which spans a still growing number of sub-fields of social and political enquiry and which is not confined to a singular epistemological approach or level of analysis.

## The future of peace studies?

Peace studies is clearly not reducible to Galtung's work alone, nor has everyone followed his path. Nonetheless given that he is easily peace studies' most prolific and prominent writer, Galtung's work tells us a lot about the field's evolution. Within contemporary peace studies one can now find work which still focuses on some of its earliest concerns, such as arms control, analysis of the causes of wars, critical studies of contemporary wars (including the so-called 'war on terror'), and conflict mediation and resolution; in short the pursuit of negative peace. Much of this output overlaps very strongly with a range of cognate fields such as IR and critical security studies (see Chapter 7 this volume). Since the rupture in the 1960s, the relationship between violence, exploitation, and development has become a central concern producing today a considerable overlap between peace studies and development studies. Additionally, there is a huge volume of work on the much more difficult area of building positive peace, including on human rights, environmental security and ecological wellbeing, gender and violence, peace education, and explorations of non-Western thinking such as Gandhian conceptions of non-violence and the various branches of Buddhism as the basis for constructing a culture of non-violence (see, for example, Galtung 1996, Jeong 1999, Barash and Webel 2008). It is this area of writing that can arguably be more fully described as unique to peace studies.

Two views can be taken on the state of contemporary peace studies. Positively one might celebrate its diversity and ever-expanding range, in spite of the fact that peace studies cannot be said to represent in and of itself a distinctive philosophical or theoretical viewpoint. It could be understood as a very large exercise in collation, of ideas, analyses, proposals, and prescriptions that straddle the boundaries between formal social scientific research, normative enquiry and political activism and which is loosely connected by an imprecise normative orientation that can be derived from a number of sources. Peace studies can be conceived of as a site or a space in which critical cognitive intent is brought to bear in myriad ways upon the problem of violence and the prospects for its eventual eradication. Peace studies is on the curricula of hundreds of universities, predominantly in the US but also in most corners of the globe. There are also public and private research institutes dedicated to the analysis of peace and conflict throughout the world (a directory can be found at http://ipra.terracuranda.org), along with the half a dozen or so dedicated journals, some being as old as the field itself.

A more critical view might wonder if the constant expansion of the purview of peace studies has meant that it has acquired the qualities of an intellectual black hole wherein something vital – a praxeological edge or purpose – has been lost, not least because the ostensible subject domains of violence and peace remain so essentially contested. On this view, a case might be made for restoring a focus on the continuing problem of direct violence at all levels of social life. A sobering fact remains that if peace studies is to be judged by the relative prevalence of direct violence during its half-century life span then it would be hard to declare it a success. This is not to suggest that peace studies should abandon its traditions of interdisciplinariness, epistemological diversity, or its historical relationship with peace activism. However, the changing nature of warfare and the growing salience of the issue of armed humanitarian intervention in the post-Cold War era present a raft of new challenges to peace studies. More controversially, it opens up the possibility that if peace studies is to offer viable, less violent alternatives to the currently dominant modalities of intervening in the various wars and complex political emergencies that are hallmarks of the present era, then its historical association with an absolute prohibition on the resort to violence in the name of peace may warrant critical review (Lawler 2002). In the absence of such a prohibition of course, the maintenance of a distinctive quality to peace studies would in itself become a real challenge.

## Further reading

David P. Barash and Charles P. Webel, *Peace and Conflict Studies*, 2nd edition (Sage, 2008). One of the more comprehensive textbooks available that gives a good sense of the range of issues now falling under the label of peace studies.

Johan Galtung, *Peace by Peaceful Means: Peace, Conflict, Development and Civilisation* (SAGE and PRIO, 1996). Perhaps one of the easiest entry points into Galtung's voluminous work as it distils much of his earlier and more recent work into a single volume.

Ho-Won Jeong (ed.), *The New Agenda for Peace Research* (Ashgate, 1999). Offers an insight into some of the more recent conceptual and policy-oriented developments in peace research.

Peter Lawler, *A Question of Values: Johan Galtung's Peace Research* (Lynne Rienner, 1995). This remains the only comprehensive, critical overview of Galtung's work in English. The focus is predominately theoretical and conceptual.

Ghanshyam Pardesi (ed.), *Contemporary Peace Research*, (Brighton: The Harvester Press, 1982). A collection of some of the key contributions to peace research, focusing on the debate between some of the founding figures and their Marxist critics.

Various authors, 'The Future of Peace Studies', *Peace Review* 14(1) (2002). This issue of one of the leading US peace studies journals is devoted to a series of short essays on the current state and future of peace studies.

# Critical Theory

Pinar Bilgin

## Abstract

In this chapter, students will learn about the critical approach to security studies which takes Gramscian and Frankfurt School critical theory as its guiding framework. This approach is also known as the 'Aberystwyth School' or 'emancipatory realism'. The chapter begins by tracing the origins of critical security studies. It then explores the key concepts of approaches to security that have been inspired by critical theory by using empirical illustrations from regions such as the Middle East and Southern Africa, and issues such as nuclear weapons, 'state failure' and the post-9/11 prospects for emancipation in the Muslim world.

## Introduction: the need for a critical perspective

Although the origins of critical security studies as a distinct school of thought go back to the early 1990s, the ideas and struggles it feeds upon have been around for much longer. Citizens, social groups and movements, intellectuals and activists have long called for thinking beyond the Cold War categories that restricted ways of 'thinking' about and practising security. Examples include the Non-Aligned Movement whose underlying principle reminded the world that there existed insecurities other than the United States–Soviet Union standoff; the calls for a New International Economic Order in the 1970s which underscored that the North–South tension was of no less significance for world politics than East–West rivalry; contributors to the World Order Models Project who during the 1960s and 1970s outlined visions of alternative and sustainable world orders; the 'Alternative Defence' school that helped transform security relations across 'Europe' during the 1980s through informing various social movements including the US-based 'Freeze', UK-based CND (Campaign for Nuclear Disarmament) and END (European Nuclear Disarmament); the disciples of Mahatma Gandhi who have sought non-violent ways of practising security and contributed to academic peace research; women's movements that have pointed to the 'arms vs. butter' dilemma as a cause of disproportionate suffering for women; feminist scholars who have underlined the relationship between the personal, the political and the international; and students of North/South and 'Third World' security who turned on its head the prevalent assumption that the inside/domestic realm was one of security whereas the outside/foreign realm was one of insecurity by pointing to the ways in which 'national security projects' imported from (and supported by) the West have had a mixed record in the rest of the world.

In the years of euphoria that followed the end of the Cold War, the contributions of these groups were often forgotten not only by those who claimed victory on the part of the Ronald Reagan administration in the USA (to the neglect of a variety of other factors and actors that helped to bring the Cold War to an end) but also by the more theoretically oriented students of critical security studies who approached the task of rethinking security on mostly metatheoretical grounds, thereby failing to challenge existing ways of 'thinking' about and 'doing' security. The 11 September, 2001 attacks and other al-Qa'ida-linked bombings that shook various parts of the world were tantamount to a wake-up call in more ways than one. For students of security studies who were sceptical of the contributions of critical perspectives, 9/11 served as a reminder that prevalent approaches to security are far from being able to account for let alone address the world's current insecurities. For students of critical security studies, 9/11 underscored the need to engage directly with issues related to war and peace, hard and soft power, state and non-state actors in world politics. It is in this context that the call for rethinking security (in theory and in practice) has gained new urgency.

## Rethinking security

While scarcely a day passes without some mention of 'security', what it means is often far from clear. This is not because of a lack of effort, but because security is a 'derivative concept'; one's understanding of what 'security' is (or should be) derives from one's political outlook and philosophical worldview (Booth 1997: 104–119). Failure to recognize this point and practices shaped by ostensibly universal conceptions of security have rendered the world less secure.

## BOX 7.1  SECURITY AS A DERIVATIVE CONCEPT: THE CASE OF ISRAEL

One may observe the 'derivative' character of security by analysing the views of different groups within the same political community. In the state of Israel, for example, those who have remained sceptical of the virtues of making peace with the Arabs in general and the Palestinians in particular have insisted on an agreement that would deliver 'peace with security', which often meant holding on to the territories acquired in the 1967 War in order to gain 'strategic depth'. When, during a brief period in the early 1990s the Israelis and the Palestinians seemed to be on the same 'peace' track, members of the 'Peace Now' movement celebrated by putting up banners that read 'Peace is my security' (Sharoni 1996: 116). This latter view rested on the belief that positive relations with the Palestinians 'inside' and the Arabs 'outside' Israel would provide the kind of 'security' for Israelis that the search for 'strategic depth' had thus far failed to deliver. The point being that it is possible to find within the same political community struggles informed by different conceptions of security (see Booth 1979).

Differences in understanding security and defining threats partly derive from but cannot be reduced to the psychological process of mis/perception. While applying cognitive psychology to decision-making (Jervis 1976) went some way towards explaining differences between, say, India and Pakistan's definitions of threat and conceptions of 'security', understanding their respective 'national security projects' also requires an analysis of political processes within the two states (Pasha 1996, Abraham 1998). After all, it is politics that helps shape historical memory, through the prism of which emerge the psychological processes that produce our interpretations of current events. As such, it is not mis/perception alone that produces different conceptions of security; rather, it is different conceptions of security which derive from one's political outlook that allow different perceptions of threat to emerge. The process is political through and through.

Understanding security as a derivative concept, thereby recognizing its culture-bound character, does not render the search for security any more difficult. This is because security is also an 'instrumental value . . . that frees people(s) to some degree to do other than deal with threats to their human being' (Booth 2005a: 22). While no single universal definition of security may be possible, working definitions are nevertheless needed to inform our practices. Notwithstanding their differences, all philosophical worldviews agree on the human need for security, since 'it frees possessors to a greater or lesser extent from life-determining constraints and so allows different life possibilities to be explored' (Booth 2005a: 22). Recognizing security as an 'instrumental value' also guards against the tendency to treat it as an end-point rather than as a process through which human beings find 'anchorages . . . as [they] contemplate navigating the next stage of history' (Booth 1995: 119). This, in turn, opens up the possibility for people with different political outlooks to negotiate with each other and to work towards finding ways of coexistence without depriving the others of their life chances (Alker 2005: 203–207).

Since the early 1990s, attempts to rethink security have generated lively debates and insightful writings – an important milestone was a conference held at York University in Canada in December 1994 which brought together analysts working on the fringes of security studies. Those scholars were on the fringes at the time due to the defiant character of the questions they asked and the answers they sought. The brand of critical security studies introduced in this chapter is different from the understanding that shaped the York Conference and the book that followed (see Krause and Williams 1997), in that while locating its roots in the aforementioned ideas and historical struggles originating in different parts of the world it is firmly grounded in 'critical theory' as the guiding framework.

The precursor of this approach is Ken Booth who, in his seminal article 'Security and Emancipation', called for a rethinking of security, defined it as 'emancipation' and coined the phrase 'critical security studies' (1991a). Together with Richard Wyn Jones (1999, 2005), Booth set up the first postgraduate-level course on critical security studies at Aberystwyth University in 1995, which eventually became the core course of a Master's degree in security studies. What distinguishes the 'Aberystwyth School' or 'emancipatory realism' from other strands of critical security studies is the influence of the Gramscian and Frankfurt School tradition of 'critical theory' (see Bilgin *et al.* 1998, Booth 2007).

## Critical theory

It was Robert W. Cox who familiarized students of International Relations with the ideas of the Italian political theorist and activist Antonio Gramsci (1891–1937), most notably through his distinction between 'critical theory' and 'problem-solving theory'. The distinction between the two rests on the purpose for which theory is built. Whereas critical theory 'stands apart from the prevailing order and asks how that order came about', problem-solving theory is content with fixing glitches in the prevailing system so as to make 'existing relationships and institutions work smoothly' (Cox 1981: 129). The labels used for the two strands of theorizing often confuse readers into thinking that 'critical theory' is not interested in solving problems but merely presents a critique and/or a utopia. This is a misnomer. 'Critical theory' does engage with present problems but without losing sight of the historical processes that have produced them, and proposes alternatives that are 'feasible transformations of the existing world' (Cox 1981: 130, see also Booth 1991b).

---

## BOX 7.2 PROBLEM-SOLVING AND CRITICAL THEORY: THE CASE OF SOUTH AFRICA

Between 1948 and 1994, South Africa was governed by the National Party's apartheid regime, which rested on assumptions of white supremacy. During this period, problem-solving accounts portrayed South Africa as an embattled 'bastion of Western civilization' (quoted in Booth and Vale 1995: 287) and represented South African security in terms of 'Western security' – a term that served to cloak the interests of the ruling whites. The recommended security strategy, in turn, was one of 'forward defence', designed to overpower potential threats at home and in the neighbouring region.

Critical perspectives, in turn, recognized apartheid for what it is – just another idea reified into being through intersubjective understandings and coalescing practices. Viewed through the lens of critical approaches, security in South Africa was conditional upon a non-racial and freely elected government that would seek security not at the expense of, but together with, its people and its neighbours (Booth and Vale 1995). Whereas problem-solving accounts took the status quo as given and considered its maintenance as the only possible way of producing 'security', critical theory laid bare the ways in which beliefs about white supremacy had facilitated the establishment of the apartheid regime and warranted policies that maintained the status quo. It also proposed alternative policies which eventually contributed to apartheid's demise (see Ungar and Vale 1985/86).

---

Another source of inspiration for critical scholars is the Frankfurt School theorist Max Horkheimer (1895–1973) who drew an important distinction between 'critical theory' and 'traditional theory' (Horkheimer 1982 [1937]). According to Horkheimer, traditional theory is defined by its reification of ideas into institutions, which are then represented as immutable 'facts of life' that have to be lived with – all this while denying the role played by theory and the theorist. In contrast, critical theory rejects such rigid distinctions between subject and object, observer and observed, and lays bare the role played by theories and theorists throughout the process of reification. Pointing to the role played by certain actors in bringing about the existing order of things (i.e. denaturalizing the present which some analysts take as pre-given) opens up room for human agency to come up with solutions that go beyond mere 'problem-solving' within the parameters of the existing order (Wyn Jones 1999: 100–102).

In security studies, 'traditional' and 'critical' approaches differ most notably in their treatment of the state. Traditional security studies views the world from a state-centric (if not statist) perspective (see Box 7.3). In contrast, critical security scholars have argued that states are a means and not the ends of security policy, and hence they should be de-centred in scholarly studies as well as in policy practice (Booth 1991a). Proponents of traditional approaches to security, however, have brushed aside such concerns and continued to point to the centrality of the roles states play in contemporary world politics. On

---

## BOX 7.3  STATISM AND STATE-CENTRISM

'Statism' is a normative position that treats the state as the ultimate referent object and agent of security, where all loyalty and decision-making power is assumed to be concentrated. Statism in security studies has taken many guises: while some elements of the literature are unabashedly statist, others deny their statism by identifying their stance as one of state-centrism. State-centrism, in contrast to statism, is a methodological choice that involves treating the state as the central actor in world politics and concentrating on its practices when studying international phenomena. Statism and state-centrism are thus not the same thing, although the distinction between the two may be difficult to sustain given the constitutive relationship between theory and practice. For instance, the realist argument that since it is states that act to provide security, the security of states should be given analytical primacy is a clear case of confusing agents with referents. With this rather uncritical acceptance of the centrality of the state's agency, the potential of human agency is at best marginalized and at worst rendered invisible. Broadly speaking, state-centric perspectives do not simply reflect a state-dominated field, they also help constitute it. According primacy to states in our analyses does not simply reflect a 'reality' out there; it also helps reinforce statism in security studies by making it harder to move away from the state as the dominant referent and agent (Bilgin 2002).

---

closer inspection, however, this traditional (realist) argument turns out to be rather unrealistic. As Wyn Jones (1999: 96) has pointed out,

> Although no one can doubt the elegant simplicity of this position, crucial questions remain: Is the realist's statism analytically useful? Can the internal politics of the state be ignored, thus allowing analysts to concentrate their attentions on the determining influence of the international realm of necessity?

The failure of traditional accounts to capture the end of the Cold War – in terms of how and when it happened – attests to their limited analytical value. The roles played by ideas and transnational movements in helping to bring the Cold War to an end were not visible to those who looked through the state-centric lens of traditional security studies (Wyn Jones 1999: 94–102).

Although the end of the Cold War underscored the inadequacy of theoretical frameworks that fail to take into account transnational and subnational factors, traditional approaches to security soon returned to business as usual. Even the 9/11 attacks, which reminded the world of the increasingly influential role non-state actors play in world politics, seem to have made only a minor impact on the traditional approach, which has included such actors in its analysis but failed to change the way it approaches actor–system dynamics. Part of the problem is that post-9/11 security studies treats non-state actors in a way that is reminiscent of how structural realists treat states – that is, as unitary actors the behaviour of which can be understood without becoming curious about their internal dynamics and the transnational factors which help shape those dynamics.

Viewed as such, traditional security studies fails not only by the standards set by critical theory (in terms of serving emancipatory interests; see below) but also according to its own standards. Comparing outcomes with stated objectives is what Hegel meant by his concept of 'immanent critique' (also employed by Frankfurt School scholars; see Wyn Jones 2005: 220–229). This type of critique re-evaluates a position from its own standpoint (as opposed to some externally imposed criteria) to reveal its shortcomings. The aim of critique, however, is not only to deconstruct but also to reconstruct. As Stamnes has shown in her study of UN peace operations, whereas the deconstructive task involves uncovering 'unfulfilled potential for change inherent in an organization of, or arrangement within, society', the reconstructive task 'makes possible a choice between the various alternatives – it points out potentialities for *emancipatory change*' (2004: 164). The growing critical security studies literature is replete with examples of such critique (see below).

---

## BOX 7.4  REALISM'S NOT-SO-REALISTIC APPROACH TO 'STATE FAILURE'

Viewed through the lens of traditional security studies, 'state failure' is a problem not because those states fail to provide security for their citizens, but because they fail to fulfil their responsibilities towards the 'international community' by allowing non-state actors to use their territories to stage attacks against Western interests. From this perspective, it is not state security per se that is privileged, but the security of some (Western) states. Identified as such, the problems caused by 'state failure' are addressed through intervention and regime-building often to the neglect of the interests of the citizens of those states. A more sophisticated understanding of 'state failure' would involve taking stock of the ways in which the 'standard' concepts, and practices shaped by those concepts have contributed to such 'failure' (Bilgin and Morton 2004).

A critical security studies perspective begins by asking the question 'Who has failed the "failed state"?' It then goes on to consider the possibility that the 'failure' may rest with 'standard' conceptions of the 'state' rather than with those individual states (Milliken and Krause 2002). It then identifies the socioeconomic context which allows some states to 'fail' while others 'succeed'. Such contextual factors include (but are not limited to) the academic division of labour between 'economics' and 'politics' (to the impoverishment of both); remnants of 'orientalism' in international studies that condition and limit understandings of the 'non-West'; and the legacy of imperialism which finds new guises in the global economic order (Bilgin and Morton 2002). The difficulties faced in rebuilding Afghanistan's institutions attest to the need for a comprehensive understanding of the state (and sub-state actors) in the study of 'state failure' cognizant of inside–outside dynamics in the realms of 'security' as well as 'political economy'.

## Theory/practice

Critical theorists can identify processes through which ideas are reified into institutions and then treated as 'reality' (as with 'apartheid' and 'state failure') because they reject an objectivist conception of the theory/practice relationship and instead see theory as constitutive of the very reality it seeks to explain. In Steve Smith's words, 'Theories do not simply explain or predict. They tell us what possibilities exist for human action and intervention; they define not merely our explanatory possibilities but also our ethical and political horizons' (1996: 13). Theories help organize knowledge, which, in turn, informs, enables and privileges (or legitimizes) certain practices while inhibiting or marginalizing others. That said, not all theories get to shape practices. The reason why some theories may become self-constitutive (such as traditional security studies) but others do not (as with peace research) is rooted in the power–knowledge relationship.

The competition between theories over shaping practices and therefore the future never takes place on equal terms. To conceive of theory as constitutive of reality is not to suggest that once we get our theories right a better world will simply follow. What shape the future might take will depend on whose theories get to shape practices. For example, the reason why the lands to the southwest of Asia and north of sub-Saharan Africa were lumped together and labelled the 'Middle East' as opposed to something else is rooted in the dominance of British and US security discourses. The sources of their dominance could, in turn, be found in the material (military and economic) as well as representational power enjoyed by these states (Bilgin 2004).

Here I draw an analytical distinction between the representational and material dimensions of power to stress that the workings of the power–knowledge relationship cannot be understood if one adopts a narrow or purely material conception of power. Rather, power includes a representational dimension; that is, the power to shape ideas (on the Gramscian conception of hegemony see Cox 1983). One potential problem involved in trying to account for the representational dimension of power is that it cannot be observed in the same way as the material dimension can be. In the absence of overt (or latent) conflict, no observable changes in behaviour take place. However, the absence of an observable power relationship does not necessarily mean one is absent (see Lukes 1986).

Neither material nor representational dimensions of power can be monopolized by one actor only. This is especially true in the latter case. Although a combination of ideas and material resources is what enables some discourses to prevail, history is replete with examples of the ideas of the weak coming to the fore (by being taken up by those who are in power, or directly through revolutions). One example of this phenomenon is the 1989 revolutions in Eastern Europe and the role played by Pope Jean Paul II and the Catholic Church. Previously Stalin had famously ridiculed the lack of material power possessed by the Vatican when he quipped 'how many divisions has the Pope?' It was therefore somewhat ironic that Pope Jean Paul II would play a significant role in the 1989 revolutions that eventually culminated in the dissolution of the Soviet Union (Booth 2005b: 350).

Students of critical theory consider theory as a form of practice – but not the only form! They are equally attentive to other forms of practice, as may be seen in relation to nuclear strategy. Whereas traditional security studies views technology (including nuclear technology) in neutral terms – as a realm with an autonomous logic of its own – and considers the production and use of nuclear weapons as a process which overrides cultural particularity, critical approaches recognize its 'ambivalent nature' (Wyn Jones 1999: 134–139). Technology, writes Wyn Jones, 'opens up a range of options or choices for society, and the options chosen depend in part on the configuration of power relationships within that society and almost invariably serve to reinforce the position of the hegemonic group' (1999: 139). This understanding illuminates how both superpowers throughout the Cold War made decisions regarding nuclear procurement that reflected 'bureaucratic and political power struggles rather than any rational enemy threat' (Wyn Jones 1999: 140). Similarly, India's decision to acquire nuclear weapons as partly (but not wholly) in consequence of a postcolonial search for security through modernity (nuclear weapons constituting an aspect of being/becoming 'modern'; see Abraham 1998) allows analysts to rethink the 'fetishism of nuclear weapons' and to ponder their removal from world politics as a *realistic* possibility. The idea would be to replace a MAD (mutual assured destruction) world with a SANE (security after nuclear elimination) one (Booth 1999a, 1999b).

## The 'Aberystwyth School' of critical security studies

Ken Booth (1997) laid out the rationale for critical security studies as follows:

> Security is what we make of it. It is an epiphenomenon intersubjectively created. Different worldviews and discourses about politics deliver different views and discourses about security. New thinking about security is not simply a matter of broadening the subject matter (widening the agenda of issues beyond the merely military). It is possible – as Buzan (1991) has shown above all – to expand 'international security studies' and still remain within an asserted neorealist framework and approach.
>
> (Booth 1997: 106)

The first analytical move made by the 'Aberystwyth School' of critical security studies is to deepen our understanding of security. This reveals the politics behind scholarly concepts and policy agendas, which allows analysts to de-centre states and consider other referent objects above and below the state level. The second move is to broaden our understanding of security in order to consider a range of insecurities faced by an array of referent objects. In this sense, students of critical security studies do not 'securitize' issues, but 'politicize security' (Booth 2005a). They do this to reveal the political and constitutive character of security thinking and to point to 'men's and women's experiences of threat' (Alker 2005: 195) so as to be able to de-centre the military and state-focused threats that dominate traditional security agendas. This stance is at odds with the Copenhagen School (Buzan *et al.* 1998) which calls for 'desecuritization' out of a fear that those issues that are labelled as 'security' concerns will be captured by state elites and addressed through the application of zero-sum military and/or police practices, which may not necessarily help address human insecurities (see Chapter 5, this volume). Critical scholars, while sympathetic to those concerns, prefer to hold on to 'security' as a concept for scholarly studies while scrutinizing its use in practice.

The divide between the two schools on this issue (whether to seek 'desecuritization' or to use 'security' for raising and addressing the concerns of referents other than the state/regime) is not one of 'objectivist' vs. 'constitutive' understandings of theory, since both approaches understand theorizing as 'a form of practice'. Whereas the Copenhagen School makes a

---

## BOX 7.5 'POLITICIZING SECURITY': THE CASE OF THE MIDDLE EAST

Standard textbooks informed by traditional security studies invariably define security in the Middle East in terms of the uninterrupted flow of oil at a 'reasonable' price to Western markets, the cessation of the Arab–Israeli conflict, and the prevention of the emergence of a regional hegemon. A distinguishing feature of this conception of regional security is its top–down character that views security in the Middle East from the perspective of extra-regional actors, and privileges the security of (some) states and military stability.

Critical approaches juxtapose non-regional actors' conception of regional security with that of many (but not all) regional states who voice other concerns shaped along the axis of Arab/non-Arab or Islamic/non-Islamic. Their agendas, in turn, often clash with that of non-state actors of various persuasions who call for more democratic accountability and political participation, respect for human rights and the expansion of women's rights, to name a few. Such concerns reveal the fact that although the standard textbook perspective – that military instability in the Middle East threatens global security – is valid, it captures only one dimension of regional insecurity (Bilgin 2004, 2005). What is more, conceiving security in the Middle East solely in terms of military stability helps to gloss over the structurally based (economic, political, societal) security concerns. 'Politicizing security,' therefore, refers to rethinking security to uncover the 'political' character of different definitions of security and the construction of security agendas, to open up space to include other issues identified by myriad actors, and to de-centre the statist concerns of some by highlighting human insecurities.

case for 'desecuritization' (taking issues outside of the security agenda and addressing them through 'normal' political processes), the Aberystwyth School re-theorizes security as a 'derivative concept' and calls for 'politicizing security'.

The Aberystwyth School prefers 'politicizing security' as opposed to 'desecuritization' for three main reasons. The first reason is *strategic*. Desecuritization, they argue, would amount to leaving security as a tool with a high level of mobilization capacity in the hands of state elites who have not, so far, proven to be sensitive towards the security concerns of referents other than the state and/or regime. While the Copenhagen School calls for desecuritization for exactly this reason, the Aberystwyth School turns that argument around and asks: 'Are existential threats to security simply to be abandoned to traditional, zero-sum, militarized forms of thought and action?' (Wyn Jones 1999: 109). Politicizing security thus facilitates questioning of how state elites use security and the merits of policies based on zero-sum, statist and militaristic understandings.

The second argument is *ethico-political*. The fact that security has traditionally been about the state and its concerns does not mean it has to remain that way. When defined by state elites, 'security' could include anything and everything depending on their policy agenda. Depending on the historico-political context, security agendas of states may indeed translate into zero-sum, militarist, statist and, at times, dehumanizing practices. But when 'security' is defined by other actors such as environmental or humanitarian NGOs, it may be more likely to be conceived globally and practised locally with an eye on the negative future implications of current thinking and practices. Of course, some actors are more capable of voicing their insecurities than others. Nevertheless, opportunities remain to open up room for dialogue, debate and dissent. From this perspective, the role of the scholar is to amplify the voices of those who otherwise go unheard (Said 1994; Enloe 1996).

The third argument is *analytical*. Ultimately, the question of whether it is 'desecuritization' or 'politicizing security' that would help address those concerns is one that 'must be answered empirically, historically, discursively' (Alker 2005: 198). Empirical evidence suggests that the framing of HIV/AIDS as a global security issue has been of immense help in addressing its pernicious effects in Africa (Elbe 2006). Representing migration to Western Europe in an alarmist language, on the other hand, has generally rendered 'constructive political and social engagement with the dangerous outsider(s) more difficult' (Huysmans 2006: 57).

## Emancipation

In his 1991 article, Booth summarized the relationship between security and emancipation as follows:

> Security means the absence of threats. Emancipation is the freeing of people (as individuals and groups) from those physical and human constraints which stop them carrying out what they would freely choose to do. War and the threat of war is one of those constraints, together with poverty, poor education, political oppression and so on. Security and emancipation are two sides of the same coin. Emancipation, not power or order, produces true security.
>
> (Booth 1991a: 319)

Understanding security and emancipation as 'two sides of the same coin' is not some utopian and/or imperialistic project, but rests on the ideas and struggles of individuals and social groups in different parts of the world. In Wyn Jones' words, 'security in the sense of the absence of the threat of (involuntary) pain, fear, hunger, and poverty is an essential element in the struggle for emancipation' (1999: 126). Deepening and broadening our conception of security (in our scholarly studies) is in fact necessary to catch up with and lend a helping hand to already existing struggles in the world.

While it is difficult to precisely define emancipation in abstract, theoretical terms, it is easier to define it in practical cases. Let us take the hard case of the 'Muslim world'. It is a hard case because it is considered by some to be antithetical to the very idea of emancipation (of women in particular). Al-Qa'ida has framed the 9/11 attacks in terms of its opposition to Western imperialism and interventionism. The 9/11 attacks were interpreted by some Westerners as the non-West's rejection of modernity. 'Al Qaeda does not simply oppose the United States because of its presence in the Middle East generally and its support for the West specifically', wrote Steve Smith, [al-Qa'ida] 'opposes the United States, and regimes such as Saudi Arabia in the Middle East, because it sees them as pursuing modernization, which it deems as diametrically opposed to authentic Islamic identity' (2005: 43).

Statements by prominent al-Qa'ida leaders seem to give credence to this view. Moreover, such representations, when coupled with mainstream understandings of emancipation as a uniquely 'Western' idea and process, makes it very difficult to engage with the 'non-West' on this emancipatory ground. The problem is not only that some Islamic fundamentalists do not have a conception of women's emancipation, but also that some do: some Muslim clerics, for instance, have declared women's participation in suicide bombings in Israel/Palestine as emancipatory! Students of security should indeed question whether the desire for emancipation is universally valid. This should not, however, stop them interrogating claims that women undertaking acts of 'suicide bombing' could be considered as emancipatory for those taking part and helping secure the others who stay behind. Considering such intricate and politically and culturally sensitive issues would require students of security to rethink various dimensions of power (hard and soft, material and representational) including the power to define what is 'security' and 'emancipation' within a given cultural community – be it the 'West' or the 'Muslim world'.

In the face of the currently prevailing dichotomized representations and seemingly irreconcilable positions, the Aberystwyth School's response has been critical engagement rather than despair. Alker, for example, has called for 'culturally sensitive concepts of emancipation' to 'be linked in a posthegemonic way to similarly culturally sensitive, concretely researchable conceptions of existential security' (2005: 208). Elements of such a project are already underway. The universality of some notion of human rights is common to all cultures, notwithstanding the claims of those who have the power to define what is 'true knowledge' and what is not in the 'Muslim world'. After all, there is nothing that makes authoritarian regimes such as Saudi Arabia and groups like al-Qa'ida more representative of Muslim traditions than those Muslims writing about 'non-violent' thought and action (see e.g. Satha-Anand 1990). As Booth reminds us, 'the debate about authenticity takes place at the level of texts and interpretation, but at base it is about the distribution of political/cultural power. Cultural authenticity . . . is not a fact, it is an interpretation; and what prevails at any period is not some absolute truth' (1995: 114).

One can make a case for defining security in terms of emancipation in, say, Saudi Arabia, purely on the grounds of Muslim women's calls for emancipation (see Mernissi 1989). The fact that these women have little power (in comparison to the Saudi regime or some Muslim clerics) does not make their call for emancipation less authentic. Nor does it render imperialistic the Aberystwyth School's understanding of security as a 'vital precursor to the fuller development of human potential' in the Muslim world and elsewhere (Wyn Jones 1999: 126).

## Conclusion

Writing in 1998, the Aberystwyth School proposed a 'next stage' of security studies (Bilgin et al. 1998). The growing number of contributions to this approach attests to that potential. Examples include studies on security in Africa (Williams, P. 2007), Southern Africa (Booth and Vale 1995, 1997, Vale 2003), Asia-Pacific (Burke and McDonald 2007), South Asia (Nizamani 2008), Turkey (Bilgin 2007, Özet 2010) and Burundi (Stamnes and Wyn Jones 2000), South African foreign policy (Williams 2000), regional security in the Middle East (Bilgin 2002, 2004, 2005), human rights in Kosovo (Booth 2000), Canadian security discourse (Neufeld 2004) and peace operations (Stamnes 2004, Whitworth 2004), 'state failure' (Bilgin and Morton 2002, 2004), international political economy (Tooze 2005), women's emancipation in Central Asia (Kennedy-Pipe 2004) and rape in war (Kennedy-Pipe and Stanley 2000), identity and security in Northern Ireland and Western Europe (McSweeney 1999), trust-building in the Mediterranean (Bilgiç 2010), the peace process and emancipation in Northern Ireland (Ruane and Todd 1996), human security (Linklater 2005), nuclear strategic thinking (Booth 1999a, 1999b, Wyn Jones 1999: 125–144) and nuclear proliferation in Latin America and South Asia (Davies 2004). In addition to a critical theory anchorage, what unites this body of work is taking seriously both the deconstructive and reconstructive aspects of critique in critical security studies.

## Further reading

Pinar Bilgin, Ken Booth and Richard Wyn Jones, 'Security studies: the next stage?', *Naçao e Defesa*, 84(2) (1998): 129–57. A basic introduction to critical security studies.

Ken Booth (ed.), *Critical Security Studies and World Politics* (Lynne Rienner, 2005). An introduction to critical security studies structured around three key concepts: security, community and emancipation.

Ken Booth, *Theory of World Security* (Cambridge: Cambridge University Press, 2007). The most comprehensive elaboration of 'emancipatory realism'.

Keith Krause and Michael C. Williams (eds.), *Critical Security Studies: Concepts and Cases* (UCL Press, 1997). A broad range of perspectives not necessarily grounded in 'critical theory'.

Richard Wyn Jones, *Security, Strategy and Critical Theory* (Lynne Rienner, 1999). This book lays out the foundations of a Frankfurt School critical theory approach to security studies.

Shannon Brincat, Laura Lima and Joao Nunes (eds.) *Critical Theory in International Relations and Security Studies* (Routledge, 2012). Provides interviews with four key critical IR theorists, Ken Booth, Richard Wyn Jones, Robert W. Cox, and Andrew Linklater as well as reflections by IR scholars on the achievements of Critical Theory.

**CONTENTS**

# Feminisms

Sandra Whitworth

## Abstract

In this chapter, students will learn about a number of feminist perspectives and the kinds of questions they raise about international security. It also examines some of the empirical research conducted by feminists around questions of security, including work that focuses on the impacts of armed conflict on women, the ways in which women are actors during armed conflict, and the gendered associations of war-planning and foreign policy-making. The argument here is that, whichever feminist perspective one adopts, greater attention to gender – the prevailing ideas and meanings associated with masculinity and femininity rather than the facts of biological differences between men and women – enriches our understanding and expectations associated with international security.

## Introduction

When feminist scholars and activists first began to engage with both the academic and policy practitioners of global politics, the idea that feminist thought might contribute to thinking about international security was sometimes met with hostility or ridicule. What could feminist theory – which surely concerned only the activities of women – tell us about the workings of global politics, national militaries, nuclear deterrence, or the decision-making of Great Powers? That kind of reaction was very revealing, since it illustrated well part of the point that feminism sought to make. For most feminists, whatever their particular theoretical orientation within feminism, the workings of security have long been presented as though they are gender-neutral when in fact international security is infused with gendered assumptions and representations. The effects of presenting international security as though it is gender-neutral are numerous, and not least that it makes invisible the gender-differentiated understandings and impacts of security on women and men and the ways in which security is constituted in part through *gender* – the prevailing ideas and meanings associated with masculinity and femininity rather than the facts of biological differences between men and women.

The early ridicule that greeted feminist interventions in global politics is now far more difficult to sustain. For one, more traditional theoretical orientations within International Relations (IR) have been critiqued for a variety of exclusions, as numerous chapters in this collection have highlighted. Within this context, raising issues of gender no longer seems out of step with the rest of the literature on global politics. Explicit attention to the gendered dimensions of security is now also more widespread within some of the more mainstream sites of global politics. The UN Security Council, for example, adopted Resolution 1325 in October 2000 on 'Women, Peace and Security' – a resolution which noted both that women and girls are affected by armed conflict in ways that differ from the impact on men and boys, and the importance of incorporating a 'gender perspective' into peace operations (see Chapter 26 this volume). This kind of acknowledgment underscores the feminist observation that gender permeates all aspects of international peace and security.

One question that continues to surface, however, is *how* does gender permeate international security? Even sympathetic observers of feminist thought and global politics do not always find a simple or straightforward answer to this question. The reason for this is that there is no single or straightforward answer to be given, because the answer is in part dependent on the particular feminist perspective one adopts in exploring questions of security. As with the study of IR itself, feminists are not agreed on one theoretical perspective, rather feminist thinking approaches political questions using a variety of theoretical lenses. How to understand the gendered nature of questions of peace and security is thus dependent on the theoretical perspective one adopts. This chapter will outline some of those perspectives and illustrate the kinds of questions about international security that result from them. The argument here is that, whichever perspective one adopts, greater attention to gender enriches our understanding and expectations associated with international security.

## Feminist approaches in international security

A theoretical lens, as V. Spike Peterson and Anne Sisson Runyan (1999: 1) have written, 'focuses our attention in particular ways', helping to 'order' or make sense of the world around us. These lenses draw our attention to specific features of our world, ways of looking at the world and usually offer prescriptions for ways of acting in the world. In focusing our attention to certain areas or concerns, our attention is simultaneously drawn away from other areas or concerns – in order to simplify the world that we are observing, some elements are emphasized over others. This has been true of the study of IR and international security which traditionally focused our attention towards states and away from 'people'. But it is true also within feminist thinking. Most feminists may share an interest in focusing attention on (gender-differentiated) people, but beyond this, there is no single feminist lens or perspective which directs us to the single best way in which to study international peace and security. Each feminist perspective draws our attention to different ways of thinking about gender, different ways of conceptualizing the gendered nature of international security and different ways of responding to the problems of global politics. This does not mean there will not be overlap between these perspectives; and indeed, as theoretical perspectives are adapted and modified, they may incorporate the insights of one or another perspective. Nonetheless, it is useful to map out some of the basic differences between the most important approaches to feminist theory in order to understand their different emphases and insights.

*Liberal feminists* privilege notions of equality and have tended to focus on questions of women's representation within the public sphere (see Whitworth 2008). Feminists who work from this perspective collect empirical information about women's roles – are women present as decision-makers in areas of international security? If not, why not? Are they present in national militaries? When they are present, what is the impact of their presence, and if they are not present, what are the barriers to their participation? Many liberal feminists focus on the ways in which within governments and international institutions, women remain highly under-represented. Where women are present, they are still largely relegated to clerical and support work, and do not figure prominently in the middle and upper management levels of institutions. As of 31 December 2009, for example, women in the UN comprise some 60 per cent of General Service employees, but less than 40 per cent in the Professional categories (and only 22 per cent of the highest professional category of Under Secretary General) (UN Women 2010). For liberal feminists, the barriers to women's participation need to be identified so that they can be removed, in this way permitting those women who are interested an equal opportunity to take on the challenges of political and public life.

*Radical Feminists*, by contrast, focus less on notions of equality and more on notions of difference. For radical feminists, women and men are essentially quite different from one another (and essentially quite similar *to* one another).

Whether a result of biology or socialization, radical feminists tend to agree that men as a group are less able to express emotion, are more aggressive and more competitive while women as a group are more nurturing, more holistic and less abstract. By this view, much of the way in which society is organized supports the power of men over women and their bodies – what is called patriarchy – and the privileging of masculine norms. This impacts both the ways in which the world actually operates, and also the ways in which we think about the world. Radical feminists differ from liberal feminists in that they view the political as existing everywhere – it includes, but is not limited to the public spheres of life. Indeed, many of the most pernicious ways in which patriarchy impacts women's lives is affected through control of the 'private' – through domestic violence, control over women's reproductive freedoms and control of women's sexuality. On questions of representation, radical feminists might agree with liberals that women ought to be represented in positions of public power, but not for the equality rights reasons the liberals give, rather because women bring a different point of view to politics, one that is more focused on cooperation and peace.

Whereas liberal and radical feminists tend to focus on 'women' and 'men,' some of their insights hint at an emphasis that is seen most clearly in some other approaches to feminist thought, those that examine prevailing assumptions around 'gender'. Focusing on gender attempts to distinguish between the biological and the social – between the facts of biological differences and the prevailing ideas and meanings associated with masculinity and femininity. It is these kinds of observations that have informed a variety of what are called 'post positivist' approaches to feminist theory. *Feminist critical theory*, for example, examines prevailing assumptions about both women and men: what it is to be a man or woman, what is appropriately feminine or masculine behaviour, the appropriate roles of women and men within society, within the workforce, the family and so on (Whitworth 1994: 24). Critical feminist theorists often argue that prevailing norms associated with masculinity, as much as with femininity, must be examined, and likewise that these norms can have an enormous impact on men, particularly marginalized men (Connell 1995, Hooper 2001). Critical feminists insist also that the assumptions that exist around women and men/masculinity and femininity take place not just at the level of discourse, but that gender depends also on the real, material, lived condition of women and men in particular times and places, which includes but is not limited to the lived conditions of race, class, sexuality, ethnicity, and religion.

This draws on an insight made by *feminist postmodernists* who argue that any definition or standpoint will necessarily be partial and any attempt to posit a single or universal truth needs to be deconstructed (Steans 1998: 25). Deconstruction entails exploring, unravelling and rejecting the assumed naturalness of particular understandings and relationships, and examining the impact that otherwise 'taken for granted' assumptions and understandings have on our ability to act in the world. For *feminist postmodernists*, as Zalewski (2000: 26) explains, any truth claim is an assertion of power which silences or makes invisible possibilities that do not fit easily into prevailing discursive practices.

*Postcolonial feminist theorists* also draw on these insights and argue further that of the partial truths in circulation around gender, imperialism constitutes one of the crucial moments, or processes, through which modern identities in all of their guises become established. For postcolonial theorists, although some feminists acknowledge the interrelationships between race, class and gender there is nonetheless 'a discernible First World feminist voice' in IR which does not sufficiently foreground the 'erasures surrounding race and representation' (Chowdhry and Nair 2002: 10). Postcolonial feminist theory attempts to do precisely this, further unpacking the assumed universality of experience between women that earlier (and particularly liberal and radical) feminisms relied upon.

These latter approaches remind us that gender relations are informed by, and in turn sustain, relations of power. As Cohn, Hill and Ruddick (2005: 1) write:

Gender is not only about individual identity or what a society teaches us a man or woman, boy or girl should be like. Gender is also a way of structuring relations of power – whether that is within families where the man is often considered the head of the household, or in societies writ large, where men tend to be the ones in whose hands political, economic, religious and other forms of cultural power are concentrated. These two phenomena – individual identity and structures of power – are significantly related to each other. Hence it is the meanings and characteristics culturally associated with masculinity that make it appear 'natural' and just for men to have the power to govern their families and their societies.

The manifestations of these relations of power will emerge in a variety of ways, and in the case of questions of security, can inform how we understand what security means and how it (and insecurity) is experienced by women and men. The next section explores these issues.

## Women, gender and security: The impacts of armed conflict

What have gendered analyses of security focused on and revealed? This too requires a multi-faceted response. One common set of questions within security is to focus on war and armed conflict, what Peterson and Runyan (1998: 115) describe as 'direct violence'. Some of the work examining gender and armed conflict takes a largely liberal feminist position and documents the differential impact of armed conflict on women and girls as compared to men and boys. By itself this is a very large undertaking, as the impact of armed conflict on all people is enormously complex, and highlighting the ways in which its impact differs for women requires nuanced and detailed analyses. 'Gender neutral' analyses of armed conflict regularly do not focus on people at all – conflict is conducted between states or armed groups, the specific impact on people's lives is a marginal concern and instead the focus of analysis is on territory and resources gained (or lost) and the outcome (in terms of winners and losers) of battles and wars.

Where some analysts do focus on people affected by war, the tendency has been to focus on the experiences of men – the central players in most war stories – whether it is as combatants, prisoners of war, generals, war planners, fighter pilots, infantrymen, war criminals, and so on. More rarely women are assumed to be combatants in armed conflict, and so they are assumed to be impacted only indirectly by war. Their lives may be disrupted during war, and they are sometimes injured or killed as a result of 'collateral' or indirect damage, but women's particular experiences were generally not thought to be worthy of specific or sustained study, or in any way important in determining how we might understand both 'security' and 'insecurity'.

Early feminist work in IR disrupted these assumptions. Cynthia Enloe (1983, 2000b), for example, has documented the varieties of ways that militaries require women's work, whether or not that work was ever formally acknowledged. As Enloe (1983: 3) writes:

> thousands of women were soldiers' wives, cooks, provisioners, laundresses, and nurses. Sometimes they served in all of these roles simultaneously. When they weren't being reduced verbally or physically to the status of prostitutes, camp followers were performing tasks that any large military force needs but wants to keep ideologically peripheral to its combat function and often tries to avoid paying for directly.

But women do not merely take up the invisible jobs associated with supporting fighting forces; they are regularly and directly impacted by the violence of armed conflict itself. This has always been true, but during the post-Cold War era it became increasingly apparent that in the new forms of conflict that began to emerge, women were targeted specifically, and in specifically gendered ways.

Studies by scholars, human rights organizations and international institutions began to focus on the impact of armed conflict on women. Much of this work focuses on the ways in which, most commonly, women and girls are subjected to heightened levels of sexual violence during wartime, including sexual torture, enforced prostitution, sexual slavery and mutilations and sexual trafficking (UN Secretary-General Study 2002: 17, International Alert 1999,

International Committee of the Red Cross 2001; see also Kumar 2001, Moser and Clark 2001, Turshen and Twagiramariya 1998). In some conflicts, acts of sexual violence have been so widespread, and so widely and clearly documented, that international protective measures have been developed which acknowledge the systematic use of sexual violence as a weapon of war. In both the International Criminal Tribunals for Yugoslavia and Rwanda, as well as in the Rome Statute which formed the basis for the newly established International Criminal Court, there has been an acknowledgment that sexual violence in wartime constitutes a violation of the laws of war (UN Secretary-General Study 2002: ch. 3) (see also Chapter 17 this volume).

Though in very important ways the widespread use of sexual violence during armed conflict demands our collective attention, and a focus on sexual violence against women has received the most sustained empirical analysis from feminist researchers, exclusive focus on sexual violence during war obscures a number of important issues. One is that most formal acknowledgements of women's experiences during wartime, especially in the form of legal redress, tend to reproduce very stereotypical assumptions about women: they are visible, valued and deemed worthy of protection primarily in terms of the sexual and reproductive aspects of their lives (Gardam and Jarvis 2001: 94). This means that other ways in which armed conflict impacts women may be ignored or not receive equally necessary legal recognition and protections.

These other impacts can include being targeted for acts of violence – women are not only sexually assaulted during wartime, they are also regularly killed and maimed. They can also be sexually and physically assaulted and exploited by those ostensibly sent to 'protect' them – peacekeepers, refugee and aid workers, guards and police. Women are also affected by the economic impact of armed conflict – they struggle with the loss of economic livelihoods and the inflation that normally accompanies conflict, making the cost of basic items or foodstuffs prohibitively high. In some cases local sources of food have been destroyed altogether, with the destruction of agricultural lands, market places and the poisoning of water sources. The same is true of sources of shelter – when home communities become part of the battleground or combatants force civilians to flee, women and their families become internally displaced persons (IDPs) or, when they cross borders, part of the burgeoning number of global refugees. During conflict, women also struggle for continued access to health care or other social services such as educational facilities, after these have been destroyed or are simply unavailable to internally displaced people and refugees (Gardam and Jarvis 2001: ch. 2, UN Secretary-General Study 2002: ch. 2, Giles and Hyndman 2004, Whitworth 2004).

Thus, focusing strictly on the sexual violence perpetrated against women and girls during armed conflict directs our attention away from the many other effects of armed conflict on their lives. Importantly however, it also draws our attention away from the sexual violence perpetrated against men and boys during armed conflict. Whereas women are presumed to be targets of sexual violence during wartime, the same assumption is not made of men. Yet, sexual violence – including rape, torture and sexual mutilation – is also used against men and boys during war and conflict, usually in an effort to attack their sense of manhood (UN Secretary-General Study 2002: 16). Female prisoners of war often find they are disbelieved if they report they were not sexually abused or assaulted while held prisoner – this was true of US prisoners of war Melissa Rathbun-Nealy who was taken prisoner during the 1991 Gulf War and Jessica Lynch, who was taken prisoner a little more than a decade later during the US invasion of Iraq. By contrast, male prisoners are rarely even asked whether they were sexually assaulted, their captivity is assumed to be asexual where a woman's captivity is highly sexualized, in both cases irrespective of whether sexual violence actually takes place (see Nantais and Lee 1999: 183–186, Howard and Prividera 2004: 90–91).

The United States' own sexual torture techniques against Iraqi prisoners of war illustrates well the ways in which men can be targets of sexual violence, with an explicit intention to injure and humiliate. The interrogations involved smearing fake menstrual blood on prisoners' faces, forcing them to masturbate or simulate and/or perform oral and anal sex on one another, to disrobe in one another's presence, to touch one another, to touch women, and to be photographed in these and other positions (Highman and Stephens 2004). Prisoners were also made to walk on all fours with a leash around their necks, or to stand balanced precariously on boxes, or to pile on one another to form a pyramid of naked bodies. Most often, it was female soldiers who were photographed perpetrating these and other acts. Eisenstein (2004) has written of the ways in which the male targets of this violence were depicted as 'humiliated' precisely because they were treated like women. Male Iraqi prisoners were the targets of a violence aimed in one instance directly at themselves, but as Eisenstein and other feminist commentators have noted, in another instance they were also the subjects of a violence that sent a larger message about empire and imperialist masculinity. Manipulating racialized and gendered assumptions of appropriately masculine (and feminine) behaviour, the sexual torture at Abu Ghraib also illustrates the gendered dimensions of contemporary imperialism and empire-building (Eisenstein 2004, Richter-Montpetit 2007, Philipose 2007, Sjoberg 2007, Enloe 2007b).

## Women, gender and security: Action and activism

Feminist accounts of armed conflict do not focus only on the 'impacts' of war on women (and men), they also explore the ways in which women are actors in armed conflict. We have seen above that women and men can both be 'victims' of conflict and political violence. They can also both be active 'agents' in armed conflict. It is normally men who are depicted as the primary actors in war, most often serving as combatants in armed conflicts. But women also regularly take up arms and commit acts of violence in war. In some cases it is because they are forced to do so, but in others it is because they are committed to the goals of the conflict, they choose to become combatants themselves. Women have also been documented as serving as messengers for combatants, as spies, as suicide bombers and as providing assistance through smuggling weapons and providing intelligence (Sjoberg and Gentry 2007, UN Secretary-General Study 2002: 3, 13, Mansaray 2000, Moser and Clark 2001, Turshen and Twagiramariya 1998, Jacobs *et al.* 2000).

The positioning of women and men as either combatants (men) or victims (women) has implications for both women and men (Whitworth 2004: 27). Because women are seldom viewed as having served as combatants they may experience greater freedom in organizing informal peace campaigns. Much feminist analysis focuses on the varieties of peace campaigns that women are involved in, from peace marches to silent vigils, to working across combatant groups to establish communications. Some authors note the ways in which some women peace activists have used prevailing assumptions about their roles as 'mothers' to protect themselves against state and non-state authorities who would otherwise prohibit public criticisms of local and foreign policies concerning a conflict (Samuels 2001, see also Giles *et al.* 2003). However, at the same time that women have been documented as being actively involved in informal campaigns, they are usually ignored when formal peace processes begin, they are rarely invited to formal 'peace tables' and are normally excluded from disarmament, demobilization and reintegration (DDR) programmes which give former combatants access to educational, training and employment opportunities (UN Secretary-General Study 2002: ch. 4).

Men, on the other hand, are presumed to have held power and decision-making authority prior to the emergence of conflict and to have been combatants and instigators throughout the conflict itself. This assumption can make all men (and boys) targets of violence within a conflict, whether or not they are actually combatants or directly involved in the conflict. Some critics point out that the assumption of men as combatants – or at the very least 'able to take care of themselves' – has resulted in their exposure to greater dangers and levels of violence during armed conflict. In the former Yugoslavia, the protection of women and children was prioritized as the goal of UN peacekeeping forces, resulting in a massacre of unarmed Bosnian Muslim men and boys who were left largely unprotected (Carpenter 2005).

The assumption of men as combatants also sometimes makes their motivations suspect when they become involved in efforts to bring conflict to an end – they are often assumed to have alternative agendas. At the same time, however, it is men who are normally invited to the formal 'peace table' once it has been established, and they are the ones who primarily receive the benefits of DDR and other post-war activities (UN Secretary-General Study 2002: ch. 4). The assumption of men's 'activity' in conflict is what may impact their insecurity when conflict is ongoing, but is also what ensures a 'place at the table' when the formal efforts to bring a conflict to an end are underway.

Women and men can thus both be 'active' in wars and armed conflicts in a variety of ways, either as perpetrators of violence or as participants in peace processes. However, the prevailing understandings and assumptions about women and men in conflict – whatever their actual experience – can significantly shape and limit those experiences in both profoundly positive and negative ways.

## Women, gender and security: Talking and making weapons and war

Although many feminist analyses of security focus on the impact on and involvement of women and men in war and armed conflict, as discussed in previous sections, these are not the only forms of scholarly intervention taken by feminists who explore questions of international security. Instead, many feminists focus on the ways in which gender is constructed through security (and insecurity) and on the ways in which security is constructed through gender. The previous sections already pointed to some of these types of arguments – it is prevailing assumptions about women and men/masculinity and femininity that position men and women differently in conflict: as targets of violence, as targets of sexual violence, as actors and as victims. Other feminist scholars have examined the practices of national security think tanks, of nuclear strategy, of foreign policy decisions and even of weapons of mass destruction, to uncover the way in which assumptions around gender impact, and are impacted by, these processes.

One of the most important early interventions in this area was the work of Carol Cohn (1987), who argued that the apparently gender-neutral and objective (or by contrast highly sexualized) language of defence strategists and planners was used as an 'ideological curtain' to obfuscate and naturalize the deployment and possible use of nuclear weapons (see also Cohn 1993, Taylor and Hardman 2004: 3). She showed how the language used by defence planners either drew attention away from the real implications of their plans and analyses (for example by describing hundreds of thousands of civilian casualties in a nuclear confrontation with highly sanitized terms such as 'collateral damage'), or how sexualizing weapons and weapons systems made them appear more controllable by symbolically equating them with women's bodies (for example through such terms as 'pat the bomb').

Cohn has also examined the ways in which the 'symbolic dimensions' of weapons or foreign policy decisions can impact decision-makers in ways clearly tied to their own sense of masculinity. As Cohn, Hill and Ruddick (2005: 3) write:

When India exploded five nuclear devices in May 1998, Hindu nationalist leader Balasaheb Thackeray explained 'we had to prove that we are not eunuchs.' An Indian newspaper cartoon depicted Prime Minister Atal Behari Vajpayee propping up his coalition government with a nuclear bomb. 'Made with Viagra' the caption read. Images such as these rely on the widespread metaphoric equation of political and military power with sexual potency and masculinity.

When linked to notions of manliness in this way, the decision to choose nuclear weapons, as Cohn *et al.* point out, is characterized as 'natural'. A symbolic association with strength and potency, in other words, becomes a substitute for careful and rational analysis that would explore all costs and benefits associated with of acquiring nuclear weapons.

These kinds of concerns are in keeping with questions asked by Enloe (2000a: 1) of foreign policy more generally: 'Are any of the key actors motivated by a desire to appear "manly" in the eyes of their own principal allies or adversaries? What are the consequences?' These questions have been raised in assessing the US reaction to the events of 11 September 2001, where calls for an appropriately 'manly' response were made almost immediately after the attacks on New York and Washington D.C. (see Whitworth 2002). Former Defense Intelligence Agency officer Thomas Woodrow (2001) wrote within days of the attacks that 'To do less [than use tactical nuclear capabilities against the bin Laden camps in the desert of Afghanistan] would be rightly seen . . . as cowardice on the part of the United States'. Journalist Steve Dunleavy (2001) commented that 'This should be as simple as it is swift – kill the bastards. A gunshot between the eyes, blow them to smithereens, poison them if you have to. As for cities or countries that host these worms, bomb them into basketball courts'. Not to be outdone, George W. Bush sought to establish his credentials when he said of Osama bin Laden: 'Wanted Dead or Alive'.

For feminists, this kind of masculinist frame can lead decision-makers down paths that could be avoided, and predisposes decision-makers to naturalize highly militarized and violent responses. In turn, it likely forecloses other policy options precisely because they are not deemed to be 'manly' enough. Some observers suggested that the US government could make an enormously profound statement after 11 September by 'bombarding Afghanistan with massive supplies of food instead of warheads. Such an approach would surely earn America's commander-in-chief the media label of wimp – and much worse. Obviously, it's the sort of risk that the president wouldn't dare to take' (Solomon 2001).

The expectation that the terrorist attack on the US demanded a swift and manly response was simultaneously linked to a sudden concern for the 'plight' of Afghan women. Part of the justification for the intervention focused on the Taliban's treatment of women in Afghanistan. As Hunt (2002: 117) argues, representation of Afghan women as passive is part and parcel of the way in which 'we' will dehumanize 'them,' depicting the women of Afghanistan as uncivilized and in need of saving. As Hunt points out, the United States', and the West's sudden interest in the plight of Afghan women was, at best, suspicious. There had long been information available about the systematic abuse of women in Afghanistan – much of it raised by the Revolutionary Association of the Women of Afghanistan (RAWA) – which until 11 September went largely ignored by Western governments and the international media. For Hunt, this means not only that women's bodies are being 'written' in a way which justifies particular forms of military response, but moreover, that the enormous impact on women which will result from that military response will be rendered if not invisible, at least 'justified'.

This is not to suggest, however, that the situation of women in Afghanistan was *not* horrifying, and another set of questions which feminists raise about 11 September concerns the relationship between the deep misogyny inherent in fundamentalisms (*all* fundamentalisms) and the kinds of violence which erupt from them. The group Women Against Fundamentalisms (2007) writes that: 'Fundamentalism appears in different and changing forms in religions throughout the world, sometimes as a state project, sometimes in opposition to the state. But at the heart of all fundamentalist agendas is the control of women's minds and bodies'. How much does the violence which we saw on 11 September emerge from a complex of factors, one part of which is the offer to 'desperate, futureless men the psychological and practical satisfaction of instant superiority to half the human race' (Pollitt 2001)?

Finally, these kinds of questions also point feminists to explore the context and conditions out of which violence emerges. As Cockburn has noted, 'war-fighting between two armies is only the tip of the iceberg' (2010: 147). By this view, militarism is a continuum that involves not only the moments in which acts of violence or conflict erupt, but also the large machineries of war that function in a constant state of readiness through periods ostensibly described as 'peaceful'. These machineries include but are not limited to the maintenance of militaries and large defence establishments. But the preparedness for war usually goes much deeper in any given society and involves also the ways in which militarized activities or practices become 'normalized' in everyday life. When militaries are called in to quell a labour dispute, a society is being militarized, as it is when war toys and war clothing are considered natural or ordinary. As feminists such as Enloe (2007a) have pointed out, preparing a society for war by militarizing its citizens is both highly gendered and is as central a part of war making and conflict as is the production of weapons and amassing of armies.

## Conclusions

This chapter has outlined some of the kinds of interventions feminists make into questions of international security: those that focus on the differential impact of armed conflict on women and men, the impact on women and men of naturalized assumptions about their behaviour and actions, and the ways in which assumptions around masculinity and femininity figure into conflict and decision-making and the continuum of militarization. The argument here has been that the ways in which gender is implicated in questions of international security are multi-faceted, but in all of its variations, feminist analyses of security direct our attention to a much broader set of practices and concerns than more traditional perspectives which insist international security is a gender neutral set of practices.

## Further reading

Sanam Anderlini, *Women Building Peace; What They do, Why it Matters* (Lynne Rienner, 2007). Examines through a series of case studies the ways in which women contribute to peace and security processes and the ways in which women's experiences need to figure into peacebuilding efforts.

Wenona Giles and Jennifer Hyndman (eds.), *Sites of Violence: Gender and Conflict Zones* (University of California Press, 2004). Focuses on the gendered and racialized dimensions of contemporary armed conflict by exploring over half a dozen specific examples (including the former Yugoslavia, Sudan, Ghana, Guatemala, Sri Lanka, Iraqi Kurdistan and Afghanistan).

Cynthia Enloe, *Nimo's War, Emma's War: Making Feminist Sense of the Iraq War*, (University of California Press, 2010). By examining the lives of eight different women – four in Iraq and four in the United States – this book explores the complex set of issues women confront in conflict in a highly concrete way.

V. Spike Peterson and Anne Sisson Runyan, *Global Gender Issues*, 2nd edition (Westview Press, 1999). Provides a general introduction to both theoretical approaches and empirical examples of issues in gender and international relations, explicitly focusing on questions of security, economics, power and ecology.

Laura J. Shepherd (ed.), *Gender Matters in Global Politics* (Routledge, 2010). Provides an introduction to feminist contributions in International Relations, including overviews of feminist theories and specific chapters that examine feminist perspectives on war, peace and security.

Laura Sjoberg and Caron E. Gentry, *Mothers, Monsters, Whores: Women's Violence in Global Politics* (Zed, 2007). A detailed exploration of the ways in which women are understood when they commit acts of violence in situations of conflict.

Sandra Whitworth, *Men, Militarism and UN Peacekeeping: A Gendered Analysis*. (Lynne Rienner, 2004). Explores from a feminist perspective some of the issues that arise in UN peacekeeping missions, including charges of sexual harassment and assault, and examines also UN responses to these concerns through the strategy of gender mainstreaming.

## CONTENTS

# International Political Sociology

Didier Bigo

▌ **Abstract**

In this chapter, students will learn how security is analysed from an international political sociology (IPS) approach by looking at its epistemology, methods and major findings. Instead of focusing on premises and hypotheses derived from political science and international relations (IR), IPS is based on an interdisciplinary perspective. It reformulates the question of the relationship between the international and the political by drawing on ideas from reflexive political sociology and political theory. When dealing with security, IPS bridges different approaches to knowledge coming from IR, the sociology of surveillance studies and critical criminology and questions their respective assumptions. Security is thus conceived as a process of (in)securitization, which is centrally driven by competition among multiple actors to police the line between security and insecurity. This is done to create obedience among populations and legitimize their practices of coercion, surveillance, information gathering and the drawing up of personal profiles. This process of (in)securitization is a mixture of discursive and non-discursive practices, which operates at different scales.

## Introduction

What is International Political Sociology (IPS)? In a nutshell, it is a different way to conduct research about international relations which is simultaneously 'constructivist' and 'empiricist'. It is constructivist in the sense that it is reflexive and deconstructs essentialist claims to knowledge – what has been also called post-structuralism. It is empiricist inasmuch as it is sensitive to the practices of human beings and their relationships to objects and starts its theories from these sociological and historical relationships rather than by applying abstract categories to so-called 'case studies'. These two characteristics are bound together by contemporary IPS to give a different perspective on how to analyse security by focusing on specific 'practices' and by being reflexive towards those practices.

Security studies as a discipline has often been based on knowledge coming from political science and government studies, especially in the US. These displayed a preference for rational choice theory and general abstraction, as well as a 'case study' approach, i.e., transforming historical and sociological trajectories into (dependent and independent) 'variables'. Consequently, the key concepts in these disciplines have been naturalized and essentialized – that is, they have lost their specific historicity. Theory has been associated with pure abstraction and minimalist statements in an attempt to mimic 'scientific laws'. Historical practices of human beings in their specific trajectories have been considered as testable and reversible 'empirical elements' that theory, through comparison, can illuminate and order, to produce knowledge for policy-makers. In addition the 'international' has been seen as different from the national; thereby justifying the need for a different discipline – IR – with its own specific objects and methods. This 'separatist' move had the effect that international politics has been cut from its domestic roots and considered as either an equivalent of interstate relations or, more recently, as a turbulent world, not yet unified, but leading towards a new world order (Walker 2010). These simplified abstractions have inhibited our understanding of international politics in general and security in particular.

## Interdisciplinarity, relations and practices

There are two key starting points for IPS research. First, it reconciles IR with a humanistic tradition permitting constructive dialogue between IR and the fields of sociology, history, political theory, criminology and law. Second, IPS analyses concepts like security in a reflexive and transversal way by analysing the limits and disconnections among the terminologies of security seen through the eyes of IR specialists, historians, sociologists or criminologists, and the possibilities opened by confronting these with different bodies of knowledge (Madsen 2011).

The very notions of states, boundaries, sovereignty, security, risk, freedom, justice, privacy, and democracy need to be discussed in order to understand their genesis and transformations (see, for example, Balibar 2003, Bartelson 1995, 2010, Bourdieu and Accardo 1993, Ranciere 2006, Walker 2007). No single discipline can claim to have a monopoly on knowledge about one of them. These notions make sense only by the way they relate to other notions, as they are mutually interdependent inside a specific episteme (or discursive frame) (Foucault 1971). This discursive frame itself makes sense only in *relation* to the practices the notions encompass, and ignore.

If some authors prefer to speak of a social genesis of these concepts linked with their institutional emergence, and others speak of a genealogy uncovering the change of their meanings and relations with other concepts over time, they all have a critical stance questioning common sense and disciplinary knowledge, instead of relying on them. This critical stance begins with the discussion of the relevance of specialized sub-disciplines such as IR or security studies. These bodies of knowledge should engage in a dialogue (even a difficult one) with the other disciplines which use the same terminology for describing other practices, or choosing to qualify the same practices by exact opposite terms or connotations. For example, in IR's version of security studies, most scholars see security in positive terms as the opposite of insecurity. Conversely, in surveillance studies and critical criminology, security often has negative connotations related to securitarian ideology and conservative politics. Atemporal concepts fixed by a discipline are valueless; for example, security cannot be seen as an innate reaction of protection against the world. Equally security cannot be seen as the necessity to survive in a dog-eat-dog world generating fear from others and the need to secure oneself. Security, as a social concept, has no 'essence'.

If IPS research has a central common characteristic it is this reflexive attitude that distances itself from the liberal and illiberal philosophical narratives of modern Western thought. IPS refuses to accept that these narratives deliver 'truth' about man, state, and war as well as the many other practices which constitute world politics. Rather, they are myth and dogma and should be analysed as such. Consequently, research should be informed by an anthropological attitude – analysing the belief of a specific culture about its own universality and the benefits of appearing universal. This has already informed many postcolonial studies and feminist approaches (see Chapters 8 and 12 this volume).

From an IPS perspective, concepts are significant only in relation to certain localized contexts (spatially and temporally) and if they are understood as emerging in relation to specific practices, which themselves are moulded by power and politics (Veyne 1984). The constructivism of IPS thus derives from its reflexive stance towards actors' practices and to their variations, distinctions, differences and heterogeneities. To do so is certainly not to revert to positivism, to abandon theory, or to abandon all attempts at generalization. But this approach does have to stem from the study of specific practices. As Bourdieu put it, 'theory without empirical research is *empty*, empirical research without theory is *blind* (1988: 775). Being reflexive towards empirical data is not the same as accepting the choices of particular authors about philosophy and episteme. Reflexivity is against any dogma, and its object is to analyse what the actors in diverse social universes are actually 'doing'.

The starting point for research is therefore to study practices: what is it that actors do and what do they think they are doing (Thévenot cited in Schatzki *et al.* 2001)? Such sociological reasoning leads to a very different research agenda from traditional political 'science'. As one analysis put it, it is necessary to 'go onto the veranda'; to meet the actors, to question them and to respect their reasoning (Eckl 2008). Reflexivity should involve an effort to explain the reasoning of actors and the material and discursive aspects of specific practices (Bigo and Walker 2007b). As Schatzki *et al.* suggest, 'to speak of practices is to depict language as a discursive activity in opposition to structuralist, semiotic, and poststructuralist conceptions of it, as structure, system, or abstract discourse' (2001: 10).

International Political Sociology is then deconstructionist, post-positivist and embedded in a sociological constructivism (see Berger and Luckmann 1966, Bourdieu 1996, Bigo and Walker 2007a). This is different from both the simplifications of rational choice theory and the primacy of norms that idealist forms of constructivism develop (see Chapters 2, 4 and 5 this volume). IPS thus uses a relational approach to explore the logic and practices of actors which rejects the false oppositions between general theory and empirical research or structure and agency which dominate much traditional IR theorizing.

Instead of opposing society and individuals, IPS proposes a relational version of a 'society of individuals'. This is meant to capture the collective character of individual agents (they belong to a series of specific social universes or fields) and the individual dimension of change and uncertainty incorporated into the agents' *habitus* and the practical reasons given for their actions (Elias and Etoré-Lortholary 1991). This leads to a focus on immanent (i.e. habitual, unthinking) practices instead of rational choice as a starting point for analysis (see Bigo and Madsen 2011). This is also how we should analyse the institutions and practices of *security*.

The traditional division between IR and other disciplines has been destabilised as more analysts have focused on the concrete practices of actors and the networks and dynamics their activities generate. For example, in January 2011, the self-immolation of one Tunisian man – Mohammed Bouazizi – in protest against his regime may have a worldwide impact. To divide it into levels-of-analysis is irrelevant; what is central is to follow and trace the cascade of actions of human and institutional actors which have followed this action, their relevance and coincidence, the immanent reasons and the strategic calculus of some powerful actors. (This does not mean simply focusing on the stories of 'great men and elites'.) For IPS social practices emerge, persist, and constrain actors beyond their individual imaginations and beliefs through the specific social universes they live in. This is different from a soft idealist constructivist perspective founded in ideas and beliefs of actors as the central element of the social. For IPS, the actors are less individuals than 'dividuals' as their relations are more important than they are themselves. Nevertheless, IPS argues against a structuralist or functionalist perspective, that the central element of the analysis is the relations between actors and not a predetermined structure. The actors (human beings) or actants (human beings in relation to objects) are what matter (Latour and Lepinay 2008). To analyse the social is to follow their relations, whatever the scale of these relations is. Institutions matter but they live only through the relations engaged by the practices of the actors. If the actors do not act, institutions die. Society is a society of individuals, not a different level of analysis. It is the same for the state. The state is not an actor; it is a field of actions.

Most IPS scholars share these core ontological, epistemological and methodological views. Their attention to practices is what enables them to reconcile political sociology, political theory, criminology and international relations. Reflexivity permits them to focus on the interconnection between different forms of knowledge. Consequently, in contrast to traditional political science, the task of the IPS researcher is not to substitute his/her reasoning for those of the actors in order to anticipate what they will do, but to understand their practical reasons, and their historicity. This should help eliminate the false distinctions between levels (man, state and war) as well as privileging the state and the interstate over human action (compare Walker 2010 to Waltz 1954).

## An international political sociology of security

As discussed above, for IPS 'security' is not divided into different disciplinary 'objects'. It makes no sense to analyse security as 'something', as an object belonging to a specific discipline (for example military or strategic studies, or even international relations). Security is the name given to certain practices that might otherwise be called violence, coercion, fear, insecurity, freedom, mobility, or opportunity. The boundaries of these practices, which are subsumed into the catchall term 'security', vary according to the trajectory of disciplinary bodies of knowledge, as well as historical and political reasons. Therefore, like Lewis Caroll's hunting of the snark, the quintessential meaning of security has no end(s). The right question is not what security means, but what security *does* (Balzacq *et al.* 2009, CASE Collective 2006).

Security should therefore be analysed as a process of (in)securitization by which some practices are subsumed by actors under a claim that they provide security in order to generate acceptance for their activities; even if it implies use of (physical and symbolic) violence. The process is driven by the permanent struggles among the actors concerning these claims, the refusal to accept them, and the competitions they engage to determine in their own social universes what is security, what is insecurity and what is fate. In brief, if security is meant to be about reassurance, protection and giving certainty about the future, the process at work shows that this is never the case. Rather, security generates unease, uncertainty, and new struggles, at whatever scale the security claim is launched (Bigo 1995).

To understand how to analyse this process of (in)securitization empirically, it is necessary to look at its episteme, the methods to use, and the major findings of the IPS approach to date.

## Episteme

Security as a term of art is historically determined with very different meanings over time (Burgess 2011, Foucault 2007, Gros 2006, Wæver 2010). The term is also used to describe very different practices in different disciplines (e.g. survival, deterrence, human needs for IR, personal safety, fear of crime, urban policing and computer hacking for criminology, self identity for psychology, social security in a welfare state, risk management for sociology, personal guarantee and human rights for law). And these practices may be seen as in opposition. For example, privacy as personal safety may be described as a danger in IR security discourses. More importantly, security, as a notion, and whatever the social universe, is always the object of competition between actors seeking to control its content (Bigo 1994, Huysmans 1995). This is why security claims belong to the realm of politics and politicization.

Security claims imply a struggle about the legitimacy of some ambiguous practices involving violence or control of an actor's behaviour. Certainly, many practices, which we call security or protection in everyday life are not, as such, an object of direct contestation. Often these practices are seen as forms of freedom. For instance, in my home country I can choose what to eat, drink, wear, as well as where I want to go, or what I publish on the internet about myself. But these practices can become a security issue when they reach the boundaries of somebody else's freedom, for example because of scarcity, lack of equality and redistribution, forms of property, etc. Why? Because the temptation is to refuse to change the previous practices when they are contested, and to continue by claiming that they are vital to assure security, that they are a legitimate reaction versus a danger, a risk, a threat, and are *de facto* justified. The claim may also be used to mobilize support in favour of previous actions, which themselves were considered illegitimate. This logic operates at the personal level, but also with regard to collectivities and their identities. Politicization comes from the dispute about the boundaries of security.

Security is therefore a label which sets the limit to other labels like freedom, mobility, and privacy. It has no autonomy and does not describe a class of specific objects or facts. The label of security often reveals its political origin, or more exactly the process of politicization, through its justificatory claim, and it may be a site of contestation about the legitimacy of an action. Security is then never absolute, integral, total, or global; it always reaches a limit, and appears as a reversal, a tipping point, against other qualifications. Security presupposes political judgements about freedom, property, mobility, privacy and democracy and to recognize the practices associated with these other concepts.

Contrary to many contemporary discourses affirming that 'more security is always the solution' and that 'security is for all and needs to be global', IPS examines security studies in relation to 'liberty' studies, 'human rights' studies, 'criminology and risk' studies etc. An IPS approach to 'security' is about these relations between different forms and bodies of knowledge, it is a nexus where disciplines may converge or reveal fundamental contradictions (Baldaccini and Guild 2007, Bigo *et al.* 2008, Guild 2009, Guild and Geyer 2008).

One of the main sites of disagreement with traditional approaches is about this 'isolation' of security and its closure as an objective category, an eternal value, a central concept organizing life, a right more fundamental than freedom, or even a justification to save a collectivity. Any academic definition, which tries to stabilize the meaning of security, is either naïve or politically oriented. What is central in the game of the actors concerned with security claims, are the struggles for legitimacy of the actors themselves around their own ambiguous practices of coercion, surveillance, protection, reassurance of the public, gathering of information, elaboration of profiles, establishment of patterns about dangerous actions or risky outcomes, in order to label them security to produce obedience.

The episteme of security is about the uncertainty and ambiguity of human action. What is called security is the result of legitimacy struggles between actors, who tend to mask this element of uncertainty and to claim their monopoly over the certainty of the boundaries of security (for them and for the others), to affirm their capacity to know the future and to have preventive actions, and to eliminate the ambiguity of the practices included in this process.

## Methods

Contemporary terminologies of security have been framed more often as a 'struggle against insecurity' or as 'freedom from threats' than they have been framed positively as protection and reassurance. This vision supposes the simplicity to categorize insecurity as the exact opposite of security and to think that more security automatically diminishes insecurity. But is this true? Security discourses may generate feelings of insecurity as in the case of warnings concerning everyday products (contaminated food, for example). Troubling people may develop insecurity, fear and sense of unease. Insecurity and security may grow simultaneously. The 'constellation' of (in)security can expand, fuelled by new security discourses.

Ambiguity arises from the fact that the qualification of practices put under the label of security, or the label of insecurity (killing, coercing, detaining, torturing etc.), depends on the identity of the actors practising them (Bigo *et al.* 2006, Guittet 2004). Deconstructing security while believing in the objectivity of threats and insecurity is therefore insufficient. The deconstruction of the label 'security' has to reach the boundaries between security and insecurity, security and freedom, security and mobility, security and danger, and to discuss all these terminologies.

Violence in the name of peace, freedom, human rights may also exist by displacing the boundaries with security, and by mobilizing supports of ambiguous practices. They are labelled simultaneously peace and security operations or freedom and security practices; many Western interventions have played with these double registers.

Far from being natural, the categorization of facts, individuals or groups, as a danger, risk, threat, or simply unwanted, is produced by institutional interests and strategies of justification. By naming what is insecurity, and what is freedom, institutions engaged in security practices draw a veil over what may be challenged as arbitrary choices. It is why, methodologically, a social genesis of the practices and a genealogy of each concept are central to re-situate them in relation to one another, and to understand what practices they capture.

This is why IPS starts its analysis of security by deconstructing the meaning of (in)security in order to trace its origins. Each historical case where the label is used needs to be analysed in order to understand the interests of the actors using it, and the authority that these actors claim they have to draw the limits between security and insecurity. This method applies across the various disciplinary definitions.

The practices subsumed into the term security are rarely determined by rational choices, even in IR. To try to secure oneself or something is not a grand strategy, or even a strategy, it is in most cases an immanent practice, a reaction, an intuition of the sense of the game coming from previous situations. It is a 'regression to the *habitus*' more than a carefully prepared strategy. It comes immediately to mind, and is seen as a reaction to someone else's aggressive move. It is a pragmatic justification, which is enacted in order to protect oneself, to keep freedom of action, to have some room for manoeuvre, to control the situation, to avoid risk etc. If security claims are sometimes about international security, they are also about personal safety, fear of crime, computer security, 'firewalls', food safety, climate change and its potential outcomes. The process at work is not radically different when it comes to tracing the origins of the dynamic of actions and the competition over meaning given by the actors. And it is rarely a rational choice, even if it may happen on some occasions where the players have lost their bearings, their sense of the game, because they were engaged in multisectorial social spaces.

The second step in an IPS approach is then to analyse what immanent practices are captured under the label of security (or insecurity), by whom, and for what reasons. Whose security is at stake (Heisler and Layton-Henry 1993)? Who is claiming to act in favour of security and against a danger, a threat or just a risky situation where the dangers overcome the opportunities (Aradau *et al.* 2008, Dupuy 2004)? Who is targeted as a potential source of insecurity and by what forms of reasoning?

In addition, as a third step, it is important to reflect on the conditions of reflexivity. Is it possible or not for the academic studying specific ambiguous practices to have an informed judgement and to decide about their contradictory meanings? Is the result of what is included in security or rejected as insecurity or fate, not dependent on who is judging the legitimacy of the actions? To what extent does describing a process of life as a security practice constitute participation in the game of folding into the term 'security', practices which are otherwise about mobility, freedom, or opportunity? (For example, migration, mobility, tourism of poor people in rich countries) (Guild 2009, Huysmans 2005, Squire 2010). The same acts can be judged as acts of violence or acts of protection depending on the identity of the actor. (Think about the difference of appreciations concerning a bombing, a riot, a revolution, a humanitarian intervention, an interdiction to travel by sea in small boats, a warning about potential dangers, a statistic permitting profiling of undesirable persons in a community.)

Definitive and simplistic definitions of security have also mostly disappeared from the language of the actors themselves. Usually the researcher encounters a list of actions described as security measures, or a list of 'threats'. A common practice among security institutions consists of enumerating a long list of actions without context by associating them to a label (terrorism, serious crime, fraud), and justifying action as a struggle against these threats. But such definitions of what is dangerous are always subject to different appreciations, and cannot be accepted as a truth. A positivist approach to terrorism (or security) enumerating acts, without an analysis of the configuration of the relations between actors does little more than validate the value system of the actor enunciating the list (Bigo *et al.* 2006, Bigo and Hermant 1998, Bigo and Tsoukala 2008, Jackson 2007). Transforming such political and moral judgements into a positive legal system may give them legality/the 'force of law' but it does not necessarily legitimate them (Borradori *et al.* 2003). One day a person can be a terrorist, the next, a Nobel Peace Prize winner, as happened to Nelson Mandela. Meanings of acts of violence, coercion, protection, or surveillance, depend on the practical regime of justification they have at the time they are enacted. However their outcome and the historically negotiated settlements about these outcomes can reverse the meaning of these practices, hence the problem of revisionism.

To say that security is an essentially contested concept has to be taken seriously (Gallie 1956, Booth ed. 2005, Collier *et al.* 2006). It is not just a formula to reach a new consensus. It is not a contestation coming from some radical researchers. It comes from the everyday practices of the actors themselves when they engage in a process of securitization. The contestation here does not mean that an epistemic community will not finally agree, but that any agreement will be against some actors and in favour of others. Fundamentally it means that political and ethical judgements are embedded in practices (Frost 1986).

Sociologically, it implies that the analyst pay attention to the spokespersons of groups claiming the necessity of a practice because it enhances security or reduces insecurity. As many sociologists of politics stress, one has always to remember the fact that speaking in the name of a group, is also speaking instead of the group (Cohen *et al.* 2009, Lacroix 1994). A study of any claim to define security has to be related to the representativity of the person claiming authority to draw a line between security and insecurity, because once this line is fixed, security operates as a sacrifice, a banning mechanism.

The line divides groups to normalize, to protect, to care about, and groups of people to coerce, to exclude, to filter, to reform, to re-socialize in order to integrate them into the former group, it divides the normal and the abnormal inside a society (Bonditti 2004, Foucault 2003). If researchers recognize the exclusion created by some security claims, sometimes they fail to grasp the most important factor, that of normalization, where the security claim is capable of rallying people to a cause and creating obedience. It is nevertheless of the utmost importance as it explains the power of a security claim.

## Major findings

IPS researchers have different opinions concerning the nature of the security claim itself, its conditions of possibilities, of enunciation, of success as well as its frequency, the necessity of its repetition, and its relation to everyday practices, to normality, to strategic choices. Ole Wæver (1995) has proposed the terminology of 'speech act' to describe the process of securitization. It supposes that because 'saying is doing', a security claim transforms by the simple fact of its enunciation a practice into a practice of *security*. The security claim tends to secure a referent object by insisting on the existential threat menacing it, and has as a consequence to justify exceptional measures, harder than would be the case in normal politics in democratic debate (see Chapter 5 this volume). Balzacq (2010) agrees only partially by insisting on the importance of how the speech act is received in the communication process. For him the audience is central, more central than the enunciation. Hansen (2006), for her part, insists that the securitization process is not a purely linguistic effect; rather it is a discursive practice, an activity embedded into a certain frame concerning collective identity, and that securitization works with repetitions, with controversies. It is more a long process than a specific moment with a clear origin. I have insisted, with my colleagues, that the securitization process has a semantic element but that it includes centrally bureaucratic and technological practices, implying categorizations, classifications, and boundary formations among the labels of security, insecurity, freedom etc. (Bigo *et al.* 2010a, 2010b).

The security claim is not only a discursive practice – it is a mix of discursive and non-discursive practices. To analyse the process of (in)securitization one has to examine how actors construct an (in)security continuum. This operates transversally by transferring the legitimacy of the fights against certain threats to other less legitimate priorities of the authorities, for example, the transfer of measures, special laws, technologies reserved to major violence and bombing, to drug trafficking, and migration management in the name of their 'illegality' or 'unwantedness'. Because the different categories of threats, risk, illegality, information concerning victims, are increasingly managed in a coordinated way by diverse bureaucracies in the public realm (intelligence services, police, border guards, immigration officers, consulates, asylum offices), and because they are often managed in the same network of interconnected databases, it creates a virtualization of the world generating a fear of the future and worst case scenarios. This, in turn, creates spirals of preventive discourses and (in)security claims. All these elements have favoured the emergence of transnational guilds of professionals, of experts, sharing the same way of justifying their ambiguous practices.

As Huysmans observed, security claims are not always about exceptional measures and existential threats, there may be more mundane examples other than big international crises. Security claims are an everyday practice of many actors. Their exceptionality is often embedded in law-making processes but does not suspend them (Basaran 2010, Neal 2009). Security routines by the work of (public and private) bureaucracies are a large part of their activities. Technologies play a central role in developing interconnections between previously separated domains of activities and they develop categories of thoughts concerning proactivity, intelligence-led policing, prevention, precaution which transforms security practices logics and have the tendency to orient them towards a monitoring of the future, a virtualization.

From this interdisciplinary perspective developed by IPS and through the support of different multiannual and multidisciplinary research projects (e.g. Elise, Challenge, Inex, Cast, Surveillance and Society), some findings may open new avenues of research which are truly original and interdisciplinary.

The first central finding is that the line of demarcation between security/ insecurity is the result of competition between different authorities with different priorities regarding their personal and institutional hierarchy of dangers. Any definition of security, which does not address this competition, is irrelevant.

Second, the lines of demarcation between security/insecurity, security/ freedom, security/democracy have to be investigated on both sides to see the transformation of the practices subsumed by both labels and the nature of the relationship between them. Sometimes the line of demarcation between security/insecurity is hard and the others are constructed as enemies or traitors within. Sometimes the line is fuzzier; the others are not seen as enemies but as potential adversaries or neighbours who cannot be trusted and hence require surveillance. It blurs the line with risk management when categories of unknown individuals whose personal data fits specific patterns are put under surveillance or cast out.

Third, these groups of 'professionals of (in)security' may temporarily agree about central priorities, common struggles and technologies, and negotiate the lower limits of what needs to be secured. Or, they can – because they want to or because they are be obliged to – reverse their opinions, and merge what were separated lists of priorities before, or disaggregate elements, which have previously been homogenized into one list under the label of security. But in all these cases, it has to be remembered that the lines change through time and a *longue durée* explanation is necessary to have some reflexivity concerning the contemporary fights and the endless argument of the novelty of threats and dangers which fuel the rise of security claims.

Think, for example, about the long struggles between the church and the state about the priority to save the soul over the body, the legitimization of torture during the Inquisition in the name of this priority and the capacity of the state to prioritize later the survival of the (collective) body (Delumeau 1989). Remember the way medicine was practised before Louis Pasteur in the event of epidemics and its fusion with policing practices; practising medicine meant at that time controlling populations, disciplining them (Vigarello 1993). Now policing and medicine look like different sets of practices, but fear of pandemics could reconnect them.

Bear in mind the canonical distinction drawn by IR specialists during the Cold War between 'real' security dealing in the international realm about the survival of the nation-state on the one hand, and on the other hand, inside the state, the terminology of law and order was used to express internal security and policing (see, for example, Walt 1991). It is also worth recalling the reaction of sociologists and criminologists when the discourse of enlargement of security in IR turned into an expansionist project to colonize the 'inside' instead of learning what the other disciplines had concluded after analysing these practices for decades. What is at stake here is the recognition of the different boundaries of the security label and the process of policing them (Ericson 2006, Haggerty and Ericson 1999, McSweeney 1996, Tsoukala 2009).

Fourth, if the line of demarcation between security/insecurity is a discursive competition over categorizations by the actors, and especially the politicians, it is not exclusively that. The transformation of the relations between war and policing has also been at the heart of contemporary fights among public and private bureaucracies and experts. The dynamics of expanding security claims is nourished by the simultaneous transformation of threat priorities and the reallocation of the people in charge of responding to the main threats. For example, the terminology of global terrorism has tended to fuse petty criminality, the radicalization of ideas, and strategic thinking about state enemies coming both from inside and outside, and by doing so, has created relationships between police, intelligence and military missions, thereby opening up opportunities for each institution to enlarge its own scope of action. But once these inter-relationships exist, institutions with different resources in terms of technologies, and especially information management, have an incentive to further expand the list of practices put under the label of global terrorism.

Fifth, the networked activities and actions of violence, of coercion, of risk management, of data-gathering, retention and exchange have expanded the range of practices that are connected with a security claim. Local practices have been seen as the result of so-called global trends, even when they were specifically local. This expansion of the process of (in)securitization to diverse spheres of activities of social life is due to the redefinition of the boundaries between internal and external security issues, but also to the redefinition of public and private boundaries.

The extension and privatization of the technologies of information management have enlarged hugely the recourse to the (in)securitization process to other domains of life: economic life, insurance and bank activities, the welfare system, information management, risk management strategies and the elaboration of profiles. It has changed what is at stake when speaking about security. Security is no longer reserved for the military experts and their deterrence games. Criminologists and specialists of IR interested in private military or security companies have shown the strength of this trend of entanglements of external and internal logics, of military and police logics, of public and private logics of practice, which are now captured by the label of security (Abrahamsen and Williams 2009, Leander 2005, Olsson 2009, Zedner 2009). This has occurred in a contemporary context where the securitization of crime, migration, urban life, community activities etc. have become the 'daily bread' of the political spectacle (Bonelli 2008).

## Conclusion

Theorizing about security is not about finding new consensual definitions. It should be to explain the reasons why accepted definitions change and with them political practices. That is why the process of labelling some specific practices as *security* practices constitutes a technique to govern others; the goal of which is to create acceptance, obedience, possibly even enthusiastic consensus around a practice which would otherwise be considered violent and producing insecurity (Bigo 2008, Foucault 2007, Huysmans 2005).

Hopefully, this chapter has demonstrated that students using an IPS approach will overcome the schizophrenia coming from the contradictory visions of security they get in various specialized disciplines of social science. They will not be obliged to forget what they learnt in their history, criminology or penal law courses to understand the definition of security in International Relations and vice versa. In IPS, they have an approach which encourages them to examine the multiple and always changing practices named (in)security through an analysis of a common process of (in)securitization which is deployed by actors at very different scales.

## Further reading

Didier Bigo *et al.*, *Europe's 21st Century Challenge: Delivering Liberty and Security* (Ashgate, 2010). An interdisciplinary analysis of the transformation of the relationships between security and liberty discussing how it changes our practices concerning sovereignty, authority, border, mobility and democracy.

Thierry Balzacq *et al.*, 'Security practices' in Robert A. Denemark (ed.), *International Studies Online Encyclopedia* (Blackwell, 2009). A short, synthetic article giving an explanation of the concept of (in)security.

Jeff Huysmans, *The Politics of Insecurity: Fear, Migration and Asylum in the EU* (Routledge, 2005). A key book to understand the relationship between security and insecurity and why (in)security is a politics.

Mikael R. Madsen, 'Reflexivity and the International Object of Study'. *International Political Sociology*, 5:3 (2011), pp. 259–75. An analysis of the key concepts of reflexivity, practices, practical sense, habitus and field.

R.B.J. Walker, *After the Globe, Before the World* (Routledge, 2010). A crucial book analysing sovereignty, security and freedom in the contemporary 'international'.

The quarterly journal *International Political Sociology*, which belongs to the International Studies Association, published by Wiley-Blackwell.

# PART 2
# KEY CONCEPTS

- UNCERTAINTY

- POLARITY

- CULTURE

- WAR

- COERCION

- TERRORISM

- INTELLIGENCE

- GENOCIDE AND CRIMES AGAINST HUMANITY

- ETHNIC CONFLICT

- HUMAN SECURITY

- POVERTY

- CLIMATE CHANGE AND ENVIRONMENTAL SECURITY

- HEALTH

# CHAPTER 10

# Uncertainty

Ken Booth and Nicholas J. Wheeler

## Contents

## Abstract

In this chapter, students will learn about the concept of the security dilemma. This concept engages with the existential uncertainty that lies in all human relations, and especially in the arena of international politics. After defining the meaning of the security dilemma, the chapter explores its dynamics, giving illustrations from current and future dangers. It argues that if security studies is to live up to its name in the twenty-first century, uncertainty and security dilemma dynamics must be given a central place on the syllabus.

## Introduction

The term 'security dilemma' describes a familiar predicament experienced by decision-makers in a world already overflowing with dilemmas. Despite its ubiquity, our claim is that the concept has been invariably misconceived by academic theorists, yet – properly understood – it should be regarded as one of the most fundamental concepts in security studies, and as such should be at the centre of a reformed agenda of this field (see Booth and Wheeler 2008). The security dilemma is a foundational concept because, above all, it engages with the *existential condition of uncertainty* that characterizes all human relations, not least those interactions in the biggest and most violent arena of all – international politics. That its significance has not been properly recognized has been the result of orthodox thinking failing to give due credit to the work and insights of its major early theorists (John H. Herz and Herbert Butterfield, and later Robert Jervis) and at the same time missing the opportunity (as a result of paradigm blinkers) to appreciate the extent of the theoretical and practical horizons it opens up. Our claim is that an understanding of the dynamics and potentialities involved in thinking about the security dilemma gets to the heart of the central questions of security studies.

## The house of uncertainty

By describing uncertainty as the 'existential' condition of human relations we mean that it is not an occasional and passing phenomenon, but rather an everyday part of the existence of individuals and groups. It is uneven in its significance and how it is felt, but it is ultimately inescapable. Insecurity, however, cannot be simply correlated with uncertainty, since uncertainty is a house in which there are many rooms, and in some life is much less insecure than in others. It is preferable to live with the uncertainties of what Kenneth Boulding (1979) called 'stable peace' than with the insecurities described in Stanley Hoffmann's (1965) 'state of war'. When states practise cooperation, or societies even embed trust in security communities, significant degrees of security are attained, even within the house of uncertainty.

In the context of International Relations, the existential condition of uncertainty means that governments (their decision-makers, military planners, foreign policy analysts) can never be 100 per cent certain about the current and future motives and intentions of those able to harm them in a military sense. We call this situation one of *unresolvable uncertainty*, and see it as the core of the predicaments that make up the security dilemma.

The drivers of unresolvable uncertainty are multiple, but they can be reduced to material and psychological phenomena, and primarily the *ambiguous symbolism* of weapons and the psychological dynamic philosophers call the 'Other Minds Problem'. Together, these create the conditions for the concept first theorized by Herz (1951) and Butterfield (1951). Students of disarmament are familiar with the idea of the *ambiguous symbolism* of weapons, if not this actual label. The term refers to the difficulty (many would say the impossibility) of safely distinguishing between 'offensive' and 'defensive' weapons. As the old adage has it, whether you regard a gun as defensive or offensive depends on whether or not you have your finger on the trigger. This subjective interpretation, in principle, is the same in international politics, though in practice it is more complex. If, for example, it is argued that it is possible to distinguish between what is clearly offensive (a sword) from what is clearly defensive (a shield) with respect to individual weapons, strategists are likely to reply, unanimously, that such distinctions are operationally

---

## BOX 10.1  THE SECURITY DILEMMA DEFINED

The security dilemma is a *two-level strategic predicament* in relations between states and other actors, with each level consisting of two related lemmas (or propositions that can be assumed to be valid) which force decision-makers to choose between them. The first and basic level consists of *a dilemma of interpretation* about the motives, intentions and capabilities of others; the second and derivative level consists of *a dilemma of response* about the most rational way of responding.

*First level*: a dilemma of interpretation is the predicament facing decision-makers when they are confronted, on matters affecting security, with a choice between two significant and usually (but not always) undesirable alternatives about the military policies and political postures of other entities. This dilemma of interpretation is the result of the perceived need to make a decision in the existential condition of *unresolvable uncertainty*, about the motives, intentions and capabilities of others. Those responsible have to decide whether perceived military developments are for defensive or self-protection purposes only (to enhance security in an uncertain world) or whether they are for offensive purposes (to seek to change the status quo to their advantage).

*Second level*: a dilemma of response logically begins when the dilemma of interpretation has been settled. Decision-makers then need to determine how to react. Should they signal, by words and deeds, that they will react in kind, for deterrent purposes? Or should they seek to signal reassurance? If the dilemma of response is based on misplaced suspicion regarding the motives and intentions of other actors, and decision-makers react in a militarily confrontational manner, then they risk creating a significant level of mutual hostility when none was originally intended by either party; if the response is based on misplaced trust, there is a risk they will be exposed to coercion by those with hostile intentions. When leaders resolve their dilemma of response in a manner that creates a spiral of mutual hostility, when neither wanted it, a situation has developed which we call the *security paradox*.

(Booth and Wheeler 2008: 4–5)

---

meaningless when the two weapons are employed together, because a shield can be a vital part of an offensive move when used in combination with a sword.

Such an understanding has informed Russian, Chinese, and other strategic planners in their interpretation of various plans for US ballistic missile 'shields' up to the present day. In the early twenty-first century, the Administration of George W. Bush attempted to justify deploying missile defence systems with the argument that they would help protect the US homeland against limited missile attack from 'rogue states' in general, and crucially Iran and North Korea in particular. Washington's critics (in potential target countries and elsewhere) claimed to the contrary that the shield of missile defence can potentially be used in combination with the sword of US offensive nuclear missiles in a disarming strike against their enemies at some point in the future. The domestic critics of such a deployment in the USA for this reason see the move as destabilizing. 'What is not a weapon in the wrong hands?' is the question delegates at the World Disarmament Conference asked themselves in the early 1930s.

The closely related second dimension of unresolvable uncertainty is the 'Other Minds Problem'. This refers to the inability of the decision-makers of one state ever to get fully into the minds of their counterparts in other states, and so understand their motives and intentions, hopes and fears, and emotions and feelings. Even when decision-makers are able to exhibit some degree of understanding, sympathy, and empathy, when it comes to matters of national security, the degree of confidence required by national security planners has to be very high, for the cost of getting it wrong is never trivial. A serious misjudgement could result in a waste of money and the loss of prestige through the pursuit of imprudent policies; ultimately, defeat in war and foreign occupation might be the outcome.

The challenges posed by the 'Other Minds Problem' are evident from the numerous illustrations of misperception in international history. On many occasions, decision-makers and analysts have made more or less serious mistakes when trying to get into the minds of those with whom they have been dealing (Jervis (1976) is still the key work). These mistakes have ranged from misreading a signal in a diplomatic conference to misinterpreting intelligence information, and so failing to predict hostile military moves. We all know how difficult it can be sometimes to understand what is going on in the minds of those we know best; it is not surprising, therefore, that the decision-makers of one country invariably fail to get inside the minds of people from a different cultural lifeworld, and so misinterpret their motives and intentions. What is more, the problems of interpretation in international politics are compounded by the fact that governments will normally go out of their way to keep secret a great deal of what they say and do, while on important strategic issues they may engage in deliberate deception.

The interaction of the ambiguous symbolism of weaponry and the 'Other Minds Problem' helps ensure that politics among states takes place under the shadow of *the certainty of uncertainty*. This is why the security dilemma is such a fundamental concept in security studies; it alone describes the existential condition of the future environment in which political groups frame their thinking.

## The quintessential dilemma

The dilemmas deriving from ambiguous symbolism and the 'Other Minds Problem' are as old as international history and as new as today's newspaper headlines (The Washington Post declared in a headline on 12 July 2011: '[Russian foreign minister] Lavrov: Missile defense remains the biggest irritant in US–Russian relations'). On the former, it is fascinating to recall that in the first significant account of war in the West the security dilemma was thought to be the underlying cause. Writing in the fifth century BCE, the historian (and General) Thucydides argued that what led to war in ancient Greece between Athens and Sparta was the growth of Athenian power and the fear that this had caused in Sparta (Thucydides 1972: 49). The leaders of both these major powers of the time faced a dilemma of interpretation and a dilemma of response regarding the other's military plans and political motives and intentions. This two-level predicament constituting the security dilemma links twenty-six centuries of politics among states and nations down to the present day, from the era of city-states and spears to today's era of globalization and intercontinental missile systems.

Those responsible for the security of a political community (be it a superpower in the Cold War or ethnic groups in the Balkan wars in the early 1990s) face the complexities of the dilemma of interpretation: they have to decide whether perceived military developments on the part of others are for defensive or self-protection purposes only (to protect the status quo but without provoking the fears of others) or whether they are for offensive purposes (to seek to change the status quo to their advantage). Logically, the dilemma of response kicks in when the dilemma of interpretation has been settled (to the extent it ever can be, because in practice, interpretation must be continuous if it is rational). Decision-makers must decide how they will react to what they perceive to be happening: should they signal by words and deeds that they wish to show reassurance, or should they seek to send deterrent signals because of anxiety about what they fear is developing (Jervis 1976: 58–111)? When those responsible for policy remain divided or unsure in the face of a dilemma of interpretation, then arriving at a decision on their dilemma of response – and turning it into diplomatic and military moves – becomes all the more difficult. In the mid-1930s, unsure about the motives and intentions of the new Nazi regime in Germany, the British government had to decide whether its response should be to try and confront rising German military power (and perhaps provoke German nationalism, already stoked by the 'humiliation' of the Treaty of Versailles) or to reassure Germany about its place in Europe by accepting its changing military status (and so risk allowing German rearmament to steal a march if an arms race developed).

When a dilemma of interpretation is settled in favour of the view that another state is a definite threat to one's own national security, there is no longer a security dilemma; the relationship is best understood as a *strategic challenge*. It may be, of course, that the interpretation is faulty, and the other state's defensive moves are misread as being aggressive. In such a situation, decision-makers who react in a militarily confrontational way risk creating a significant level of mutual hostility when none was initially intended by either party. The result is a spiral of security competition which makes everybody more insecure; this is best understood as a *security paradox* (see Box 10.2). The paradox derives from a condition of *security dilemma dynamics*, but is not synonymous with the security dilemma itself, though many authors erroneously confuse the issue by thinking of the paradox and the dilemma as the same phenomenon (see Booth and Wheeler 2008: 6–10, Tang 2010).

> ## BOX 10.2  THE SECURITY PARADOX
>
> A security paradox is a situation in which two or more actors, seeking only to improve their own security, provoke through their words or actions an increase in mutual tension, resulting in less security all round.
>
> (Booth and Wheeler 2008: 9)
>
> This idea was inspired by Jervis's concept of the 'spiral model', which is predicated on policy-makers failing to 'recognize that one's own actions could be seen as menacing and the concomitant belief that the other's hostility can only be explained by its aggressiveness.'
>
> (Jervis 1976: 75 – see also Wheeler 2008)

It should be clear by now that what underlies the dynamics of the security dilemma is fear. Indeed, as traditionally understood, the international system can be conceived as a fear system. It is a competitive self-help system in which states fear being attacked, fear leaving themselves open to attack, fear dropping in the prosperity league, fear losing prestige, fear being oppressed by outsiders – and on and on. For many, fear makes the world go around.

Fear was central to the thinking of Herz, who first coined the term 'security dilemma,' for he argued that the issue at the base of social life was 'kill or perish' (1951: 3). For Butterfield, the other pioneer, the inability of one set of decision-makers to enter into the counter-fear of others was the 'irreducible dilemma' (1951: 20). In other words, for Herz fear created a structure of conflict between groups, while for Butterfield this fear derived from an inescapable inability of people(s) to understand how their own peaceful motives and defensive/reactive intentions could be interpreted as threatening by others. The operating principle for those responsible for national security planning tends to be: 'You have nothing to fear from us, but we must be concerned that your motives, even if peaceful now, might change in the future.' Clearly, the problems of mistrust are maximized when present predicaments are set against a historical record of a conflictual relationship.

The idea of *future uncertainty* therefore appears to construct international politics as an inescapable insecurity trap. Even if, today, the government of State A considers the leadership group in State B to be peacefully inclined, can it afford to rely indefinitely on 'best-case' thinking in a situation where bad judgements of interpretation and response can have such negative consequences for one's own state (Mearsheimer 2001, Copeland 2000, 2003)? The conclusion drawn so often through history has been that those charged with responsibility for a state's or people's security must never rely on best-case forecasting when assessing potential threats to their well-being. Instead, the guiding principle must be very conservative. Barry Posen put it very baldly, when he advised that states 'must assume the worst because the worst is possible' (1993: 28). The corollary of all this, in the language of US security dilemma theorists, is that defensively motivated states cannot 'signal type' (Glaser 1992, 1997, 2010, Kydd 1997a, 1997b, 2000, 2001, 2005, Mitzen 2006). That is, however peaceful State A believes itself to be, it can never transmit such intent with 100 per cent effectiveness to State B (and C, D etc) because others know that 'the worst is possible' in a world of future uncertainty.

If uncertainty and fear logically exist at the best of times in relations between states – when all the parties hold weapons only for self-protection, but cannot effectively signal this to others – then can there ever be any hope that humans can live together in a more peaceful world? In this understanding, the security dilemma depicts politics among nations as being a potential or actual war system *even* when all the units believe themselves as having peaceful motives and defensive/reactive intentions. This is why it is the quintessential dilemma in international politics.

Butterfield, as a historian, claimed that it was only much later, when the guns had fallen silent, that it became possible to reconstruct the past, and so understand the motives and intentions of the key actors. But we now know that such a view belongs to an older and more confident era of historiography. Today we are more familiar with the idea of an endless interpretative debate among historians. If the latter cannot make up their minds about the interpretations and responses made by policy-makers in the past, with the critical distance and abundant information that hindsight allows, students of security studies should show sympathy to the predicaments that had to be faced by those decision-makers on whose shoulders rest great responsibilities, when operating with always limited information and often very compressed time in the face of terrible risks.

## Three logics

The previous section finished by recognizing the limited time and knowledge often faced by decision-makers in international politics. When this is the case, what tends to fill the gaps in their knowledge are their philosophical and theoretical understandings of how the world works. With this in mind, we identify below three a priori logics that have framed the way theorists and practitioners of international politics have thought about the security dilemma:

- *Fatalist logic* is the idea that security competition can never be escaped in international politics. Human nature and the condition of international anarchy determine that humans will live in an essentially conflictual world.

- *Mitigator logic* is the idea that security competition can be ameliorated or dampened down for a time, but never eliminated. Here, notions of regimes and societies are key, blunting the worst features of anarchy.

- *Transcender logic* is the idea that human society is self-constitutive, not determined. Humans have agency, as individuals and groups, and so human society can seek to become what it chooses to be, though inherited structural constraints will always be powerful. A global community of peace and trust is in principle possible if in practice it currently looks improbable.

From these three logical positions derive characteristic forms of international behaviour.

Fatalist voices say that the search for security is primordial, and because groups cannot trust each other in conditions of anarchy, relations between states are essentially competitive, sometimes violent, and always characterized by a degree of insecurity. The logic of interstate anarchy (there is no supreme authority above states) is to maximize power and especially military power. In such a worldview, rational behaviour consists of mistrusting all around, and taking what advantage one can whenever it is prudent to do so. Cooperation can take place, but only when it is in one's immediate interests to do so. States are conceived as 'rational egoists' – where actors place 'primary value on [their] own security . . . and [do] not care much about others' well-being as an end in itself' (Jervis 1982: 364. See also Glaser 1997: 197). The ideal type of this worldview in contemporary International Relations theorizing is 'offensive realism' (see Chapter 2, this volume).

Mitigator logic accepts that the international system is technically anarchic, but does not believe that this must necessarily mean that anarchy is synonymous with chaos and violent conflict. A major strand of thought within mitigator logic has focused on the concept of 'security regimes' which seek through mutual learning and institutionalization to bring a degree of predictable order into security relationships (see Jervis 1982: 357). An alternative strand of mitigator logic is that of the English school, though its exponents have strangely neglected comprehensive and constructive engagement with the theory and practice of security. English school thinking about

---

### BOX 10.3  JOHN MEARSHEIMER'S CONCEPTION OF OFFENSIVE REALISM

The sad fact is that international politics has always been a ruthless and dangerous business, and it is likely to remain that way. Although the intensity of their competition waxes and wanes, great powers fear each other and always compete with each other for power . . . But great powers do not merely strive to be the strongest of all the great powers . . . Their ultimate aim is to be the hegemon – that is, the only great power in the system . . . Why do great powers behave this way? My answer is that the structure of the international system forces states which seek only to be secure nonetheless to act aggressively toward each other . . . This situation, which no one consciously designed or intended, is genuinely tragic.

(Mearsheimer 2001: 2–3)

'society' has focused on the building of the institutions of international law, developing processes of moderate diplomacy, and experimenting with norms such as mutual military transparency. As a result, a society of states can exist with predictable order, and hence the amelioration of the security dilemma.

The view identified earlier with Butterfield that it is impossible to enter into another's counter-fear has been challenged by certain ideas within mitigator logic. In the 1980s 'common security' thinking in particular attempted to reduce the most dangerous features of the superpower confrontation. The key here was the idea of security not *against* others (the fatalist logic) but security *with* others (which requires that the parties are able to understand to a reasonable degree the counter-fear of the other parties). In practice, this was most notably demonstrated by Mikhail Gorbachev, leader of the USSR after 1985, who was able to begin to wind down the Cold War because he began to understand how the West felt threatened by Soviet forces and postures. As a result he sought to address the causes of such fears by offering to eliminate the most threatening parts of Soviet military deployments and foreign policy positions (Wiseman 2002: ch.5). Here, Gorbachev showed his appreciation of how mutual mistrust and suspicion could result from security dilemma dynamics, and in seeking to dampen these dynamics down through his trust-building initiatives, he exercised what we call *security dilemma sensibility* (see Box 10.4).

What has characterized transcender logic has been the variety of viewpoints and theories it has sponsored, from the centralization of power globally necessitated in world government to the decentralization of traditional anarchist theory. Some strands have been reformist, others very revolutionary. What they all share is the belief that history rather than necessity has got us where we are, and that it is possible (if extremely difficult) to construct a radically different world order – including one in which dilemmas of interpretation and response are replaced by a successful politics of trust-building. One of the difficulties facing transcender logic as a whole is that the separate strands tend to reduce the problem of insecurity in world politics to one cause (such as 'capitalism', 'patriarchy', or 'anarchy') and one related solution (abolish capitalism, overcome patriarchy, transcend anarchy). One

---

## BOX 10.4 SECURITY DILEMMA SENSIBILITY DEFINED

*Security dilemma sensibility* is an actor's intention and capacity to perceive the motives behind, and to show responsiveness towards, the potential complexity of the military intentions of others. In particular, it refers to the ability to understand the role that fear might play in their attitudes and behaviour, including, crucially, the role that one's own actions may play in provoking that fear.

(Booth and Wheeler 2008: 7)

of the problems of the transcender logic is that its various strands have little agreement about the causes of international insecurity, or the prescriptions for a safer world.

Despite the generally limited success of much transcender thinking, all is not lost for those who hope for a more peaceful world. The most significant theory and practice within transcender logic – the one with most purchase in the real world – is the idea of 'security community'. Its political manifestation has been the project that developed in Western Europe from the late 1940s onwards, to bring peace, prosperity, and security to the traditional cockpit of realist thinking and war. In this laboratory – now extending far across the continent – militarized security competition appears to have been *transcended* indefinitely, though some uncertainty can never be escaped – as in all human relations. In the security community of Europe there are interactions between states and societies at multiple levels; states have stopped targeting each other in a military sense; and war has become unthinkable (Deutsch 1957).

It is for each student of security studies to decide which of the three logics, and which strand within each, gives the best account of international politics. Each logic – or combination of logics – generates alternative guides for future policymaking (see Booth and Wheeler 2008: ch.10). In our view, offensive realism may offer some short-term security (especially for the most powerful) but ultimately its effect is to replicate the 'war system' (Falk and Kim 1980), and to do so with ever-more dangerous weaponry. Security regimes may offer mitigator possibilities, but as Jervis showed in relation to the Concert of Europe, they may contain 'the seeds of their own destruction' (1982: 368). A more sophisticated approach within mitigator thinking has been that of the English School, which for all its conceptual and practical lacunae, has crucially focused on the potentialities for diplomats to construct lasting order in international society through developing shared interests and values that promote practices of common security. Within transcender logic we identify the idea of security communities as the most hopeful project for those who do not think human society must live fatalistically in a condition of war and the preparation for war.

---

## BOX 10.5  KARL DEUTSCH'S DEFINITION OF A SECURITY COMMUNITY

[A] group of people which has become 'integrated'. By *integration* we mean the attainment, within a territory, of a 'sense of community' and of institutions and practices strong enough and widespread enough to assure . . . dependable expectations of 'peaceful change' among its population. By *sense of community* we mean a belief . . . that common social problems must and can be resolved by processes of 'peaceful change'.

(Deutsch 1957: 5)

The concept of the security dilemma has been much contested, and its empirical manifestations have been interpreted in a variety of not always positive ways; nonetheless, the practices of security communities have challenged in a fundamental manner some of the basic patterns of thought ('the logic of anarchy') associated with the Westphalian era. In drawing special attention to the promise of security communities, we are not saying that their members have 'escaped' the security dilemma finally, for uncertainty is the existential condition, as was argued above. What we do claim, however, is that the workings of such a security community have so shifted the conditions for politics that the security dilemma has effectively been *transcended* because war has become practically unthinkable. In the case of the EU, the ambiguous symbolism of weapons has become irrelevant, because the members do not target each other, and the 'Other Minds Problem' has shifted from the life-and-death agenda of military competition to the normal politics of life under capitalism and liberal democracy. In the house of uncertainty, the rooms marked 'security community' are promising places to live.

## The security dilemma in the twenty-first century

The security dilemma should be at the heart of security studies not only because its significance pervades the 'very geometry' of human conflict as Butterfield put it, but also because it speaks directly and urgently to some of the main challenges of our time. There are strong grounds for thinking that world politics has entered a period of unprecedented insecurity – a 'Great Reckoning', when human society locally and globally will increasingly come face-to-face with its most fundamental self-created difficulties (Booth 2007: ch. 9). The coming decades will see a potentially disastrous convergence of dangers unless sensible collective action is quickly taken to head them off. In a new era of uncertainty human society will be challenged by a novel combination of old and new security predicaments in relation to such issue areas as nuclear proliferation, terrorism, 'climate chaos', competition for non-renewable (especially traditional energy) resources, mass migration, great power rivalry, cultural and religious clashes, ethnic conflict, food and water security, and the growing gap between haves and have-nots. All these risks threaten to be exacerbated by the huge but uneven growth in the global population – a topic with which security studies and indeed International Relations in general has not yet begun to seriously engage. In most of these key risk areas, as we discuss in the four major illustrations below, security dilemma dynamics threaten to heighten fear, provoke mistrust, and close down possibilities for building cooperation and trust:

*First: the danger of a new cold war with China*. Students of International Relations have long been concerned with the instabilities supposedly posed by power transitions between rising and falling powers. In today's world, this concern focuses on the Sino–US relationship. Despite some common interests, the crisis area of the Taiwan Straits continues to represent the functional equivalent of the Central Front in US–Soviet Cold War rivalry, that is, the symbolic and actual face-to-face line of confrontation. The Straits are an active theatre of security dilemma dynamics, being highly weaponized and the site of potentially uncontrollable military escalation. Two issues that continue to fuel mistrust between Beijing and Washington are missile defences and the weaponization of space. What worries strategic planners in Beijing is that Washington might view its own Ballistic Missile Defence (BMD) as part of an offensive strategy of nuclear pre-emption designed to give the United States dominance over the process of escalation in any future crisis (Lieber and Press 2006: 52). Even if Chinese leaders are persuaded that a particular US administration does not currently harbour aggressive intent, what guarantees can they have that future US leaders will not seek to employ missile defences as part of an offensive strategy? At the same time, the White House has not been persuaded that China's motives and intentions are peaceful when it comes to outer space, a perception which Beijing did nothing to allay by its successful launch of an anti-satellite weapon in early 2007 (though the Chinese could easily justify this as a countervailing move in the light of US plans). Beijing has claimed that it wants to limit not accelerate the competition in space weapons, but the problem with such professions of peaceful intent is that the boundary between 'peaceful' and 'military' uses of technology is invariably blurred when it comes to outer space. Fatalist logic would argue that because the United States and China cannot 'signal type', there is no alternative but for planners to assume the worst and treat all deployments in space as potentially offensive. While cautioning against the trap of applying offensive realist prescriptions to outer space, Blair and Yali recognized that 'there is nothing China can do to convince American worst-case analysts that China could not possibly adapt its dual-use space capabilities for "possibly" posing military threats to the United States' (2006: 5). Consequently, under fatalist logic, there is no prospect of Sino–US cooperation in preventing space from becoming weaponized. Each set of decision-makers will feel compelled to seek security in space at the expense of the other, replicating key aspects of the dynamics that have historically driven security competition on Earth.

*Second: the danger of new arms races.* In several interstate relationships, security dilemma dynamics appear to have been working in well understood ways, with future uncertainty about motives and intentions feeding existing mistrust, and provoking the dangers of new arms competition. These might be global (Russia versus United States) or regional (India and China), and they might be conventional (South versus North Korea), nuclear (the Middle East), or both conventional and nuclear (India and Pakistan). The latter two are the regional hotspots where fears of new arms races are most acute.

The nuclear armaments competition between the two South Asian powers is driven by Pakistani fears of India's conventional superiority, and is complicated by New Delhi facing a Chinese nuclear adversary which has played a key role in the development of Pakistan's nuclear programme. At the same time, the Pakistani military and intelligence services have supported the growth of Islamic militant groups fighting for Kashmiri independence (though how far elements within the Pakistani state can now control these groups is a matter of considerable controversy). Moreover, as the attacks against the Indian Parliament in 2001 and against Mumbai in 2008 showed, these groups are prepared to attack targets in India itself. India's response to sub-conventional warfare of this kind centres on the development of rapid reaction conventional forces to deter such attacks (the Indian planning assumption is that the Pakistani Government could ultimately shut down this terrorist activity), and in the event that this does not deter future terrorist attacks like Mumbai, the Indian military has plans to strike deep into Pakistan territory. These multiplying fears and uncertainties threaten the continuance of competition between the two states in both the conventional and nuclear spheres.

The growing risk of a nuclear armaments competition in the Middle East centres on the fear, both within and outside the region, that Iran is building nuclear weapons under the cover of a civil nuclear power programme. The government in Tehran is seeking mastery of the nuclear fuel-cycle by developing an indigenous capability to enrich uranium. It claims that this is to produce fuel for its planned programme of power reactors: the worry for outsiders is that uranium enriched to higher levels (90 per cent plus) provides the fissile material necessary for the construction of a nuclear weapon. If Iran does become a nuclear-armed state, or moves to the point where it could rapidly become one, then the fear is that such a momentous step by the Iranian leadership would lead inexorably to similar decisions on the part of Saudi Arabia, Turkey, and other neighbours. Even before arms competition spirals in this way (with the consequent diffusion of great fear and tension), the prospect of preventive military action against Iran by states which already possess nuclear weapons cannot be discounted.

*Three: the danger of a world of many nuclear powers*. The threat here is of the breakdown of the Treaty on the Non-Proliferation of Nuclear Weapons (NPT), and with it the spread of nuclear weapons technology to an increasing number of states (see Chapter 27 this volume). Few believe that a world of many nuclear powers will be a safer world (Waltz (1981) is an important counter thesis – see also the Sagan and Waltz (2003) debate), yet there continues to be a diffusion of proliferation-sensitive civilian nuclear technologies (e.g. uranium enrichment and plutonium separation facilities), to an increasing number of states. This fuels uncertainties about states developing nuclear weapons under the guise of a civilian nuclear programme. If, as a consequence of the resulting dilemmas of interpretation, states begin to hedge against the collapse of the NPT, the outcome will be a self-fulfilling prophecy of regime breakdown. This will multiply the range of nuclear risks including accidental war, 'loose nukes', nuclear entrepreneurship, acquisition by terrorists, inadvertent nuclear war, crises resulting from non-nuclear weapon states rapidly moving towards nuclear status (especially in tense regional situations), and the problems of stability between nascent nuclear powers without sophisticated command-and-control arrangements.

*Four: the danger of terrorism*. The 9/11 attacks on the United States by the al-Qa'ida jihadists, and then the Bush Administration's declaration of a global 'war on terror' marked the apogee of the globalization of 'international terrorism', which had been perceived to be on the rise for some time. In many parts of the world, the use of terror tactics are ever more feared, though their actual occurrence (as yet) falls short of public perceptions of the actual risks. International terrorism feeds off local problems but increasingly has been synergistic with regional- and global-level confrontations between identity groups associated with cultural or religious markers. The danger of terrorism has become globalized and multilevel, with potential dangers ranging from individual attacks in cafes or public transport to 'dirty' bombs, biological attacks, and 'spectaculars' of various sorts – notably, so far, the bringing down of the Twin Towers of the World Trade Center in New York (see Chapter 15 this volume). The 'signature' of al-Qa'ida has been attacks aiming to bring about mass casualties disrupting life on a huge scale and producing commensurate political effects (Bergen 2011, Booth and Dunne 2011). The classic example of the globalization of the security dilemma in this new age of uncertainty are those situations in which fellow citizens may no longer be trusted to share the same values – the phenomenon of the 'home-grown terrorist'. Here, where one may fear that a fellow citizen may be ready to use violence – including suicidal tactics – to further extremist causes, the security dilemma becomes individualized as well as globalized: one is made to look with suspicion at fellow commuters on the subway, and wonder what might be in the backpack of the young man opposite from a different identity group. Moreover, in a world where nuclear materials are predicted to be more plentiful than previously, with significant proportions of it being unaccountable, the prospect of terrorists who represent strategic challenges becoming armed with nuclear devices has to be taken very seriously (compare Jenkins 2008 and Mueller 2010). Security dilemma dynamics come into play here most importantly in relation to contemplating the possible state sponsorship of such groups and, if the latter is thought probable, calculating the utility of preventive or demonstrative strikes against the state concerned.

It should be evident from these illustrations that the security dilemma – its vocabulary, dynamics, and insights – speaks directly to some of the major issues of our time. Back in the 1950s, Herz had claimed that the security dilemma had reached its 'utmost poignancy' (1959: 241). There could be no doubt at that time about the relevance of the concept to the potential catastrophe of the Cold War spiralling out of control through failures to appreciate security dilemma dynamics. Nonetheless, we would claim that the global predicament has moved even beyond Herz's judgement in the late 1950s that bipolarity and the threat of nuclear annihilation had created conditions for the security dilemma's 'utmost' relevance. We believe world politics has entered a new age of uncertainty. Its terrain is being shaped by manifold risks and dangers, by mistrust and long-term fear, by the fragility of cooperation and unwillingness to trust, and by the expectation of a prolonged season of uncertainty. When Tony Blair introduced the British government's White Paper on the renewal of its Trident nuclear weapons system in December 2006 – in the view of many people well ahead of when he needed do it – he argued that the United Kingdom should continue as a nuclear weapons state for at least the next fifty years. He spoke for many governments around the world when he said 'the one certain thing about our world today is uncertainty' (Blair 2006). This view, given authoritatively on the part of one of the most territorially secure states in the world, is a token of the power of the unresolvable uncertainty that characterizes the security dilemma.

Our general claim is that uncertainty in the twenty-first century is set to be intense and globalized, multi-level, and multi-directional, and that many of the key issue areas are likely to be subject to security dilemma dynamics, and hence amenable to analysis in terms of relevant frameworks (including the injunction to explore mitigator and transcender themes, such as security dilemma sensibility and security communities). Without doubt, the dynamics described by the concept continue to have impact in real sites of power and violence across the globe, and so the prospects for building world security would suffer if policy-makers and scholars conspire to marginalize the insights and prescriptions offered by security dilemma theorizing – as they did in the Cold War (Buzan 1991: 4). In the fast changing terrain of contemporary security and insecurity, the security dilemma deserves a special place for those wanting to understand our times and engage with them if human society in whole and in part is to have hope of developing in decent shape.

## Towards a new agenda for security studies

Space allows only the briefest discussion of what a reformed agenda might look like, so we will confine ourselves to indicating some ways in which the concept of the security dilemma is central to answering some of the most basic questions of philosophy and social science: What is real? What can we know? How might we act? (Booth 2007).

*What is real?* In today's world, students of security studies must analyse a wider set of referents and issue areas than was the case with the traditional agenda – namely states and military power/force. This certainly does not mean in our view that states and military force are irrelevant: far from it. We would oppose any approach to security studies that eschewed the military dimension of world politics, or the referent of sovereign states. However, the traditional agenda should be approached through the perspective of what Robert Cox (1981) called 'critical' rather than orthodox or 'problem-solving' theorizing. This means shifting the weight of the agenda from focusing on the problems *in* the status quo to the problems *of* the status quo (Booth 2005a). This means that insecurity should be understood first as the consequence of a wider range of threats (poverty, the environment, the global economy, etc.) than that of military violence and second, contemplating a wider range of referents (individuals, regions, and common humanity for example) than sovereign states. It took a decade or so before academic theorizing began to grasp the changes brought about by the advent of the atomic bombs and then hydrogen weapons and intercontinental delivery systems, and so began what has been called the 'golden age' of strategic studies. If security studies for the era of globalization is to produce its own golden age, then it is necessary to reorient its research into a deeper understanding of the role of uncertainty in world politics, and its potentialities. The security dilemma is fundamental to this, recognizing the existential reality of uncertainty in human affairs, but at the same time looking towards a realization that uncertainty is a house with many rooms.

*What can we know?* In the light of the changing dynamics of world politics, security studies needs a much wider group of experts than those who dominated the mainstream during the Cold War and who still now set the agenda in a broadly business-as-usual direction. Security studies in the twenty-first century needs not only deterrence theorists but also those who understand economic development; not just conflict managers but confidence builders; and not just tinkerers with the status quo but global trust builders. This is an argument for disciplinary pluralism, to keep everybody honest, and for challenging the ethnocentrism in the Anglo-American orthodoxy. By focusing research on uncertainty, and its acute manifestation in the security dilemmas between political entities, there is an opportunity for issues to be addressed by a fruitful collaboration across a spectrum of theoretical perspectives – allowing each to bring their special insights, as opposed to the dialogues of the deaf that presently take place. In other words, as the agenda of security studies is broadening and deepening under the pressure of real events, it is necessary to broaden the bases of knowledge accordingly, which in turn means inviting a wider range of areas of expertise to the academic conversation on security.

*What might be done?* It is evident that human societies will continue to want problem solvers *in* the status quo, though two warnings must be given. First, on matters of immediate policy relevance, academics can have only limited impact, because bureaucracies have relative advantages in terms of information and access. And second, the status quo in the security field is overwhelmingly dominated by the agendas and perspectives of nations and states, and the tribal analyses and perspectives that tend to emerge are rarely best calculated to advance the interests of world security in an age threatened by global dangers. As the twenty-first century unfolds, the special role for academics lies in the opportunities they have for understanding the manifold dimensions of uncertainty in human relations and opening up pathways of thought and action regarding the global challenges that are moving from the horizon onto centre-stage. These, overwhelmingly, derive from the problems *of* the status quo. If we are right, and the most important and interesting work relating to international and world security lies in the borderlands between, on the one hand certain strands of mitigator thinking (largely common security advocates and English school solidarists concerned with military confidence building and post-national identity formation) and on the other, the reformist strand of transcender thinking (concerned with security community building and maintenance) then the implications for security studies are enormous. Unless one espouses the fatalist outlook of offensive realism, a reformed agenda must seek to open up the potential for human agency to build cooperation and trust at all levels of political community. At the heart of this is the notion of security dilemma sensibility, which seeks to do what Butterfield thought impossible, namely, overcome the challenge of successfully signaling peaceful intent. This would reduce the likelihood of relations spiralling into armed competition, and the trap of the security paradox.

Security dilemma sensibility offers human society globally some hope of coming through the dangerous decades ahead in more positive shape than presently seems conceivable if governments and societies remain wedded to the global politics of business-as-usual. If security studies is to be other than an activity in which its exponents focus entirely on their own nation, then its students must accept that future uncertainty cannot be escaped by a mix of technology and rational egoism. Fatalism about global insecurity will be self-fulfilling. In contrast, a comprehensive understanding of the dynamics of the security dilemma and the requirements of the political conditions of trust (notably security communities) offers at least a glimpse into the theory and practice of a radically different but still realistic world. This would be a world characterized by the political, economic, social, and philosophical uncertainties of human existence, yet one in which people might hope to progressively emancipate themselves from direct and structural violence.

## Further reading

Ken Booth and Nicholas J. Wheeler, *The Security Dilemma: Fear, Cooperation and Trust in World Politics* (Palgrave-Macmillan, 2008). The most up-to-date and comprehensive exegesis of the concept, together with an extensive discussion of historical illustrations and its contemporary relevance.

Charles L. Glaser, *Rational Theory of International Politics: The Logic of Competition and Cooperation* (Princeton University Press, 2010). A sophisticated rationalist analysis of the conditions which promote either security competition or cooperation between states.

John Herz, 'Idealist Internationalism and the Security Dilemma', *World Politics*, 2: 2 (1950), pp. 157–80. The first article on the security dilemma.

John Herz, *Political Realism and Political Idealism: A Study in Theories and Realities* (Chicago University Press, 1951). This book locates the concept of the security dilemma in the context of realist and idealist theories of International Relations. In the second half of the book Herz opens up the possibilities for 'mitigating' the security dilemma.

John Herz, *International Politics in the Atomic Age* (Columbia University Press, 1959). The book develops Herz's position on the security dilemma, particularly his disagreements with Butterfield on the ubiquity of the security dilemma. It also sets out his view that world conditions (the threat of nuclear annihilation) were creating the basis for a new universal politics of global survival.

Herbert Butterfield, *History and Human Relations* (Collins, 1951). Chapter One provides the first elucidation of the psychological dynamics driving the security dilemma, particularly the inability of decision-makers to realize that others do not necessarily see them as they see themselves.

Robert Jervis, *Perception and Misperception in International Politics* (Princeton University Press, 1976). This remains the most sophisticated and influential analysis of the psychological factors influencing security dilemma dynamics.

Robert Jervis, 'Cooperation under the Security Dilemma', *World Politics*, 40: 1 (1978), pp.167–214. This article remains the seminal discussion of the role that offence–defence dynamics play in exacerbating or ameliorating security dilemma dynamics in international politics. It focuses on the interrelationship between the material and psychological dimensions of the security dilemma.

# Polarity

**Barry Buzan**

## Abstract

In this chapter, students will learn about the concept of polarity as it relates to security studies. It reviews the origins of the concept in neorealism, and its dependence on a distinction between great powers and all other states. It then looks at how polarity was used during the Cold War and post-Cold War debates in International Relations (IR). Looking forward, the unipolarity debates basically set up two scenarios: either other rising powers will challenge the US as sole superpower, with a possible return to bi- or multi-polarity; or the US will hang on as sole superpower, either dominating the system, or increasingly having to act as *primus inter pares* within a group of leading powers. The chapter questions these framings, arguing that in a truly global system, the simple distinction between superpowers and the rest does not work, and that the key distinction is among superpowers (globally operating), great powers (influential in more than one region) and regional powers (influential mainly within one region). This taxonomy opens the possibility of another scenario, a world with no superpowers, only great and regional ones.

# Introduction

Polarity is a materialist concept. It assumes that the distribution of capabilities largely determines what the behaviour of the actors in the system will be: power politics is always the game. The basic propositions underlying polarity are:

- Power is *the* (in the harder versions) or one of the (in the more moderate versions) key driving force(s) behind international relations.
- The most powerful actors in the system are states.
- As a matter of historical record, international relations has been dominated by a relatively small number of great power states varying between one and nine.
- Taken collectively, these great powers control most of the material resources (military capability, production capacity, wealth, technology) in their system. Because of this, their activities, and often their ideas and identities, dominate international systems, and their interests are sufficiently wide ranging to give them a strong stake in international order.
- Numbers matter, especially when they are small. Thus systems with four or five or more great powers, can be lumped together as multipolar and treated as a single category, but as the numbers drop towards one, sharply distinct system dynamics emerge, with tripolar, bipolar and unipolar systems each having their own unique qualities.

As Hansen (2000: 18) notes: 'neorealism makes only one stratification of states: into great powers and other states'. I will return below to the problems raised for polarity theory by this single differentiation. Polarity refers to the number of great powers in the international system, not to the coalition structure among the powers. Polarity is therefore a big simplifying idea. It offers to reduce international politics to relations among the great powers, and to establish a basic set of benchmarks (shifts in polarity) against which to conduct systematic cause–effect analysis in which a simple variable can be tested against a variety of questions. Polarity offers two possibilities for insight: first, what are the effects on the behaviour of states of being inside any particular polarity structure?; and second, what are the likely consequences of changes from one degree of polarity to another?

Polarity is probably still the most widespread way of capturing in shorthand form the essentials of the global power structure. The terms bipolarity and unipolarity, and to a lesser extent multipolarity, act as a common currency across academic journals, government statements, diplomatic discourse and media reporting and commentary. Polarity is most closely associated with realism and especially neorealism (see Chapter 1, this volume), but it is also prominent in realist-influenced approaches to international political economy (IPE) where polarity fits nicely with analyses of markets in analogous terms: monopoly, oligopoly, pure. Indeed, this economistic mode of analysis was influential in Waltz's (1979) formulation of polarity thinking within IR.

The implications of polarity for security studies can be understood through Wendt's (1999) idea that international social structures are built around relationships of enemy, rival and friend. Realists assume that the international system is composed of enemies and rivals, and that polarity therefore matters primarily in relation to military and political security. Leaving out the possibility of friends is one thing that differentiates neorealism from the other IR theories, and makes its use of polarity heavily orientated towards traditional security issues. In the IPE perspective, something like friendship is allowed, or at least ideological compatibility along liberal lines, and this opens another angle on security, where the hegemon is benign and stabilizing, but hegemonic transitions can cause breakdowns of international order and war (Gilpin 1981).

The next section reviews the debates about polarity both during the Cold War and after. Following that is a discussion of the problems created by the single distinction between great powers and other states. The penultimate section looks ahead to the future of polarity, and the conclusions address the utility of the concept.

## The debates about polarity

Modern history can be simplified in terms of neorealist polarity as follows: before the Second World War the international system was multipolar with generally quite a few great powers; during the Cold War it was bipolar with just two superpowers (the US and the USSR); and after the Cold War it became unipolar with just one hyperpower (the US). Within an IPE view, unipolarity plays more strongly with Britain playing the hegemonic role in the international political economy during the eighteenth and nineteenth centuries, and the US, after a chaotic transition period, picking up this role after the Second World War. Either way, a polarity perspective offers clear structural transitions as benchmarks for analysing international systems.

### Polarity during the Cold War

Although polarity can be applied across time, the concept itself only became explicit during the Cold War, when the number of great powers dropped down to two, and the small number effect of bipolarity kicked in. Only once polarity became an established way of thinking, was it applied retrospectively to the analysis of historical international systems. During the Cold War, academic IR was not far behind the policy community in its enthusiasm for the concept of bipolarity. The leading figure in this development was Kenneth N. Waltz, who laid down the theory that became known as neorealism (Waltz 1959, 1979, 2000; see also Keohane 1986, Buzan, Jones and Little 1993). Neorealism provided explanations in terms of polarity for both balance of power behaviour in general and Cold War behaviour in particular. Here was a relatively clear and simple way of characterizing the structure of international security which, in principle, could be extended into a general theory for all times and places. One could count the number of great powers in any international system to determine its polarity, and then test those numbers for correlations with phenomena such as war, peace, crisis, arms racing, trade and suchlike. Changes in the number of great powers could then be used as benchmarks for identifying points of significant change in international systems. The interest in polarity theory that followed generated a very substantial literature not only during the Cold War, but continuing vigorously until the present day (see Bueno de Mesquita 1975, Cederman 1994, Deutsch and Singer 1964, Gaddis 1992-93, Huntington 1999, Kapstein and Mastanduno 1999, Kegley and Raymond 1994, Midlarsky and Hopf 1993, Singer *et al.* 1972).

The understanding that the international power structure was durably bipolar became dominant during the 1970s, though it remained a focus of contestation and argument (Wagner 1993). For those engaged in public policy debates, bipolarity was a handy simplifier. In one word it seemed to capture all of the main features that made the Cold War period different from what had come before. Rather than being several great powers there were only two relatively huge superpowers whose global economic and political dominance was reinforced by possession of vast arsenals of nuclear weapons. Rather than being a multitude of national and ideological divisions among states and peoples there was an overriding worldwide ideological division between the communist and capitalist worlds. And rather than international security being managed through shifting patterns of alliance, there were two relatively fixed and durable camps. The superpowers consciously pursued their rivalry in a bipolar (and bipolarized) framework (first world versus, second world), and everyone else, whether allies, or the 'third world', or even peace activists, took their positions in relation to that idea. The ending of the Cold War ended bipolarity in two senses: the breakdown of a material power structure based on two superpowers; and the ending of an ideational confrontation in which totalitarian communism and democratic capitalism staked rival claims to the future of industrial society worldwide. The comprehensive collapse of both the Soviet Union and communist ideology raised the question: after bipolarity, what?

While bipolarity was in some ways an accurate structural description of the Cold War international system, it also unquestionably served the political interests of the two superpowers. It lifted them and their ideological rivalry to the centre of world politics, and helped to justify their assertions of hegemony and/or suzerainty over their respective camps. As Freedman (1999: 23–5) notes, it enabled them to form a kind of diplomatic club from which all others could be excluded. Since polarity is an American theory, this self-serving aspect is important. It perhaps goes some way to explaining both why insufficient attention was paid to the difficulties of defining a 'pole', and why the designation of bipolarity effectively resisted the mounting evidence against it that accumulated from the 1960s onwards.

Even during the Cold War there were three obvious problems with bipolarity as a blanket designation of military–political system structure. First was the growing realization from the 1970s onwards that the Soviet Union was an 'incomplete' superpower (Dibb 1988, Kennedy 1989: 554ff.). It possessed first rank military forces, and could compete in space and nuclear technology. But it increasingly failed to register as a significant element in the world economy, eventually being surpassed by Japan.

Second, and in some ways related, was the marked disaggregation of power that emerged during the Cold War (Buzan, Jones and Little 1993: 51–65). This was principally to do with the re-surfacing of Japan and West Germany as economic great powers, but prevented by the deep hangover of their behaviour during the Second World War from taking on 'normal' great power roles and functions. More broadly it was also expressed in the rise of the European Community/Union (EC/U) as an economic giant with some actor quality, but not enough by way of political–military institutions to count as a state. Could such an entity be counted as a great power? Did great powers have to have nuclear weapons or could 'civilian powers' count? The problem of disaggregated power was registered even more broadly in the globalization perspective, which saw international power generally as shifting away from the state to other institutions (firms, markets, international and transnational non-governmental organizations), and from the military–political sector to the economic one. What kind of bipolarity was it when one of the two poles of power had an economy smaller than some states outside that inner circle, and where military power seemed increasingly less relevant to understanding the driving forces of international relations?

The third problem was the re-emergence of other regional powers, in particular China. The pace of China's real development, as well as its endlessly mooted potential, seemed to cast it in a role in Asia similar in some ways to Germany's role in nineteenth-century Europe: big, centrally located, rapidly industrializing, authoritarian, and perceived as a threat by most of its neighbours. Since China, unlike Germany and Japan, was evidently aiming to be a full-spectrum power, it was a clear potential challenger to bipolarity. Its significance was underlined by the importance attached to the US opening to China during the early 1970s, and the subsequent way in which 'the China card' was played in US–Soviet relations. This empirical challenge to bipolarity was never properly addressed by polarity theory. One fudge was to talk of a 'great power triangle' *in Asia*, thereby avoiding the question of China's global standing (Segal 1982, Thomas 1983). Another fudge was to talk of China as a 'half' pole (Hinton 1975), while avoiding the crucial definitional question of what this might mean for polarity theory.

Despite these problems, the bipolar designation of the global power structure largely clung on among both academics and practitioners down to the end of the Cold War.

## Polarity after the Cold War

The ending of the Cold War and the demise of the Soviet Union brought a decisive end to the era of bipolarity. What remained unclear was how to designate the polarity of the post-Cold War system. Without a clear answer to this, neorealist theory was in deep trouble. Confusion about this question reigned for much of the 1990s in both academic and public policy circles. Since polarity theory rested on the idea of a single distinction between great powers and other states, there were only three possibilities. The system could be unipolar, in which case the US was the only candidate for sole remaining superpower (Wohlforth 1999). It could be multipolar, in which case Russia, China, Japan and the EU had to be elevated to parity with the US as great powers (Kupchan 1998). Or it could be that polarity had somehow become obsolete, as some enthusiasts for globalization maintained (Held *et al.* 1999: 7–9, Woods 2000: 6, Scholte 2000: 2–3). Dismissing polarity as obsolete required not only abandoning a longstanding tradition of thought, but also buying into a globalist conception of international reality that many found suggestive, but less than fully convincing as a replacement. The globalist critique raised the question of whether the Cold War had been a perhaps unique era in which analysis in terms of great power polarity seemed to produce a passing moment of clarity. Perhaps *bipolarity* was interesting, but polarity theory generally not.

For much of the 1990s, opting for unipolarity seemed to give more weight to the US than it deserved. The case for unipolarity rested on the unique position of the US. It alone had world class capabilities across a broad spectrum, and its military capabilities in particular were far ahead of any other state. Yet the US seemed to be in long-term relative decline (Kennedy 1989) as measured by the steady shrinkage of its share of the global GNP from nearly 50 per cent in 1945, towards a more natural level of around 20–25 per cent. Nevertheless, given the disparity of capability, role, global reach, and status between the US and the next group of great powers the system could not simply be described as multipolar without giving Russia, China, Japan and the EU more weight than they deserved. The EU was not a state, Russia was an economic basket case for a decade after the fall of the Soviet Union, Japan's power was almost all in its economy which went sour from the mid-1990s, and China, while presenting a balanced profile of power, was still pretty weak and had a lot of internal restructuring still to do.

One problem with the multipolar image was where and how to draw the line under what counted as a 'pole'. How did one deal with big, but partial powers such as Russia, Japan and the EU? And after them what? The list of potential candidates faded steadily from rising transregional powers (China, India) down to powers influential only in their region (Brazil, Nigeria, South Africa and suchlike). Because of these other powers, the US was nowhere near dominant enough to transform the international system from anarchy to hierarchy. If the political and security structure of the post-Cold War world was to be understood as unipolar, it was not unipolarity in the sense of being the potential suzerain core of a world empire or federation. It was not even global hegemony in the sense of having its leadership universally acknowledged and accepted.

The main initial position among those who still accepted the utility of polarity was to see a unipolar 'moment' (of unspecified duration) to be followed inevitably by multipolarity (Layne 1993, Waltz 1993a, Mastanduno 1997, Haass 1999, Kupchan 2002). Another position was to attempt descriptive mixtures, such as Huntington's (1991) idea of 'uni-multipolarity', but without thinking through the consequences of this move for the theory overall. But by the late 1990s unipolarity emerged as the dominant interpretation of the international power structure, the unipolar moment looked more like an era in its own right (Kapstein 1999), and multipolarity looked increasingly to be a long way down the line. The claim of the US to be a unipole was strengthened both by the gloss being taken off Asia by the economic crisis of the later 1990s, and by successive demonstrations of huge US military superiority in the first Gulf War, former Yugoslavia, Afghanistan, and the invasion of Iraq. Those inclined towards a unipolar thesis also drew strength from the increasing unilateralism that began to mark US foreign and defence policy. September 11, 2001, which many pundits pronounced as changing the basic character of the international security environment, in fact reinforced the idea that we live in a unipolar world. The attacks on the US underlined its unique position, and the war against international terrorism both strengthened US inclinations towards unilateralism, and amplified the widening gap in military capability between it and the rest of the world. September 11 and the responses to it can be interpreted as unipolar politics in action.

Yet the neorealist unipolar interpretation meant that the US was the only 'great power', differentiated from all other states. But if the 'other' category contained states ranging from China and Japan to the Maldives and Lesotho it seemed to cry out for some further internal differentiation. There was certainly room for argument that there was a big structural difference between a system with one superpower and a host of minor powers, and a system with one superpower and three or four large, possibly 'great' powers, in a rank just beneath the superpower.

And despite the emergent consensus on it, unipolarity was also a problem because neorealist theory had never developed a coherent image of it (Hansen 2000: 1), and the very idea seemed to go against the grain of Waltz's theory. In his original formulation, to which he has remained true, Waltz never explicitly discussed unipolarity. The closest he got was a discussion of world government, which suggests that unipolarity collapses the deep structure of anarchy and replaces it with a hierarchical system structure, in other words some form of world government. Waltz's theory suggests that stable unipolarity should be impossible because unipolarity means the end of balance of power, and therefore effectively a drastic political transformation of the international system into some form of hierarchical structure. Within Waltz's theory, the only room for a unipolar structure under anarchy should be a brief, and probably turbulent period of transition, in which the unipole either succeeds in creating a world empire or federation, or else triggers vigorous balancing efforts by others which restores a system of two or more poles. Until the reality on the ground of the post-Cold War system demanded it, Waltz (1979, 1993a, 1993b) didn't consider unipolarity, because if the system was still anarchic, and no frenzy of balancing was taking place, it could not be unipolar. More recently Waltz (2000: 5, 24, 27–8) acknowledges the post-Cold War system as unipolar, and finesses the problem of the absence of balancing by saying that the balancing mechanism will restore itself, but that his theory cannot say when. Waltz (2000: 13, 27, see also 1993b: 189) has managed to tweak his theory to deal with the apparent fact of unipolarity within anarchy, but still argues, contra Hansen (2000: 80), that 'unipolarity appears as the least durable of international configurations' on the grounds that 'unbalanced power is a danger no matter who wields it', and because unipoles will be tempted (as he thinks the US has been) into foolish policies of over-extension. The US-led invasion of Iraq in 2003, and the seeming dominance of the crusading 'neocons' in Washington did much to widen the perception that the US was heading down this route.

The puzzle of stable unipolarity can be solved if one adopts the more IPE-centred view of polarity mentioned above. Hegemonic stability theory (HST) was *de facto* about a kind of unipolarity (Gilpin 1981, 1987). Because its main concerns were about the stability of liberal international economic orders, it did not really consider balance of power issues, emphasizing instead the role of hegemonic leader in the world economy, which combined power and elements of consent. Unipolarity in this version had many positive qualities in underpinning the global economy. Ironically, its main worry was that the burdens of hegemonic leadership tended to undermine the power providing it, therefore periodically destablising the system. While HST and neorealism might agree that unipolarity was unsustainable, HST had no difficulty imagining that it might last for decades or even a century or more. With the notable exceptions of Kapstein (1999) and Guzzini (1993, 1998), no attempt was ever made to reconcile the contradiction between HST's assumption of relatively durable unipolarity, and mainstream neorealism's rejection of that possibility.

The post-Cold War crisis of polarity posed less of a problem for practitioners than for academics. The public policy debates could quite easily take a pragmatic view that the system was indeed a mixture of one superpower and some great powers without worrying about the theoretical consequences. As the end of the Cold War has receded into history, most practitioners have remained comfortable talking about a mixed system in these terms. For the more theory-minded in the academic community, however, a mixture of one superpower and several great powers posed problems.

## The problem with polarity

Waltz's theory was strict about *great power* representing a single category, differentiated from all other states, and useable to designate the polarity of an international system. Yet as is clear from the previous section, there have been persistent empirical difficulties with this single differentiation. While the two superpowers were at least militarily clearly in a class by themselves, there were other players with a meaningful claim to great power status. Yet to accept a mixture of *great powers* and *superpowers* would be to undo the whole logic of identifying system polarity. Leading polarity theorists had to treat the two terms as synonyms, with *superpower* simply corresponding to low-number polarities (two or three). This reasoning might be extended to cover the label *hyperpower* sometimes applied (Ash 2002) to the US as the 'sole superpower'. In terms of polarity theory, there was no problem if great power, superpower and hyperpower were just labels reflecting different degrees of polarity (multi-, bi-, and uni-). The difficulty arose if these labels represented different types of major power that could co-exist within the same international system at the same time. The Cold War talk about China as a 'half-pole', and the post-Cold War talk of one superpower and several great powers raised exactly this problem. If there were two or more different levels of 'great power', how did one count poles?

Practitioners continued to talk about one superpower and several great powers. The logic of HST also seemed open to this formulation inasmuch as the role of hegemonic leader was about a particular role rather than about one power outweighing the other great powers. But neorealist theory required a stricter formulation if its understanding of polarity was to remain coherent.

This problem of how to designate a 'pole' is not new. The conventional list of great powers given for 1914 is nine: Austria-Hungary, Britain, France, Germany, Italy, Japan, the Ottoman Empire, Russia, and the US. A standard of entry that allows the likes of Italy and the Ottoman Empire in 1914 to be called great powers seems to debase the simple distinction between great powers and others. The range of difference between those two at one end of the scale, and the US at the other, is enormous. Kennedy (1989: 314, 429) notes that in 1914 the national income of the US was already more than three times as great as that of Britain and Germany, nine times that of Italy, twelve times that of Austria-Hungary and eighteen times that of Japan. Schweller (1993: 75) in a study of the run-up to the Second World War, agrees with the need to differentiate classes of great power, and does so on the material basis that to count as a 'pole' of power, a state must possess 'more than half the resources of the most powerful state'. On his measures, he sees the international system of the 1930s as tripolar, with the Soviet Union, the US and Germany counting as poles, and Britain, Japan, France and Italy counting as 'middle powers'. Wight (1979: 56, 63) notices what in my view is the more important idea of distinguishing between 'world powers' 'with interests in the world at large', and 'regional great powers'. This gets close to a distinction between superpowers and great powers as different classes of power that exist at the same time. Once one is thinking on a global scale, rather than just a European one, the range of power projection becomes at least as important as mere material capabilities. Britain operated globally in a way that Germany did not.

A distinction between superpowers and great powers based on the operational range of power, holds regardless of changes in the factors that generate power. It works as well before the industrial revolution as after it. Pushing the global perspective harder back into the pre-1945 period than is usually done makes what happened after 1945 much easier to understand. An oversimplified version of the story would be that in the course of two world wars, the three globally operating superpowers (Britain, US, Russia/ USSR) either eliminated (Austria-Hungary, Ottoman Empire) or demoted (Japan, France, Germany, Italy) all of the more regionally based great powers. This rendition of course greatly understates the role of Germany, which played the major part in demoting France, and twice came close to eliminating Russia and Britain, and establishing itself as a globally operating superpower.

This history shows why polarity theory's single differentiation between great powers/others is so problematic as a basis for determining structure. As the international system becomes less Eurocentric and more global it becomes increasingly necessary to make differentiations within the 'great power' category, particularly between system-spanning superpowers and great powers with influence mainly in one or more regions. These labels do not simply correlate with multipolarity and bipolarity: they represent important distinctions about types of power coexisting within an international system. In this perspective, as I have argued elsewhere (Buzan 2004), the polarity structure of international systems would need to be understood using both superpowers and great powers. This logic can be extended down to the regional level, where regional powers also play a role in determining the polarity structure within their regions (Buzan and Wæver 2003, see also Haas 1970, Walt 1987, Lake and Morgan 1997).

Thinking along these lines inevitably makes polarity more complicated, but against that one has to weigh the cost of the distortion created by staying with a single differentiation between great powers and all others. This greater complexity has its costs, but it also brings opportunities. One can, for example, think about scenarios that are impossible within neorealism's understanding of polarity but which seem plausible possibilities for the future. In terms of superpower numbers we have, after all, witnessed a decline from three to two to one. What if there were *no* superpowers in the system, but only great powers operating mainly in their own and in immediately neighbouring regions?

## The future of polarity

Despite these deep problems with polarity theory it remains a very influential way of contemplating the future, particularly in the US. For neorealists, two alternatives dominate: either the US hangs onto its position as sole superpower, maintaining the unipolar structure, or another power, generally China, rises to share superpowerdom in a re-creation of bipolarity. In the unipolarity scenario, the debate is about ways to preserve US hegemony/leadership either by maintaining and exploiting a power advantage or by re-legitimizing its leading role using institutions to accommodate rising powers (Brooks and Wohlforth 2008, Ikenberry 2009, Lake 2009). In the bipolar scenario the question is whether there will be a power transition crisis or the US and China can find a way of living together. Given the still formidable assets of the US, there is little if any consideration of a unipolar structure in which China is the superpower and the US falls down into 'other' status.

On the basis of the differentiation between superpowers and great powers established above, there is a third option: one in which there are no superpowers, only great powers. This scenario of a world without superpowers has not yet been much explored. Its logic is that with 'the rise of the rest' no state will any longer be able to command sufficient relative power to operate globally in a dominant way. In the short term, the unnatural dominance of the US in the years following the Second World War has been steadily eroded both by the recovery of Europe and Japan and by the rise of new economic powers. In the longer term, the huge predominance that enabled the West to overwhelm the rest of the world during the nineteenth century, of which superpowers were one expression, is steadily giving way as modernization spreads more widely through the international system. Diffusing the foundations of power makes it increasingly difficult for any state to achieve the relative capability necessary for superpower status. The world is returning to something like the more natural and even distribution of power that existed before power became extremely concentrated in the West. The rise of the rest will therefore create a system with many great and regional powers, of which China, Russia and the EU might be taken as current models. A good case can be made that such a world would take a more regionalized form, and so mark a sharp move away from polarity theory, with its assumption that all of the 'great power poles' are operating strongly at the system level (Buzan 2011). A world with no superpowers, only great powers plus regional powers, might still be thought 'multipolar', but this would not carry the systemic implications associated with polarity theory.

Speculations about the nature of a benign regionalized international order have been around for a long time in the IR literature (Helleiner 1994, Kupchan 1998), and the practice of regionalization is already well established in a host of institutions ranging from the EU, through Mercosur to ASEAN. There are reasons to think that a regionalized international order would work quite well. The generic worry about such an order stems from the experience of most of the twentieth century, when imperial powers competed with each other either over their spheres of influence or over whether one of them could dominate the whole world.

For several reasons the danger of a struggle for global hegemony seems no longer very salient. First, the West is in relative decline, and other regions are mainly defensive in outlook, trying to maintain their political and cultural characteristics, and find their own route to modernization, against Western pressure. Nobody else obviously wants the job of global leader. Second, any potential global hegemon will be constrained by the difficulty of acquiring the necessary material preponderance. Third, there are no deep ideological or racist differences to fuel conflict like those that dominated the twentieth century. Fourth, all the great powers fear both war and economic breakdown, and have a commitment to maintaining world trade. Nobody wants to go back to the autarchic, empire-building days of the 1930s. In addition, sufficient shared values exist to underpin a reasonable degree of global level coexistence and cooperation even in a more regionalized international order (Buzan 2010). A regionalized world under contemporary conditions would not look like that of the 1930s or the Cold War. In Wendt's terms it would be a world of friends and rivals, not one of rivals and enemies.

## Conclusion: The utility of polarity

Like most other attempts to turn IR into a hard science, polarity theory largely failed. The indeterminacies of defining a 'pole', discussed above, mean that the specification of polarity, and the ability to know when or if polarity is undergoing change, are also indeterminate. But even where acceptable common sense definitions of polarity were applied, no clear correlations or causal patterns emerged on the big questions. By itself polarity proved too simple to act as any kind of general predictor. The polarity of the system was much the same in 1920 as it was in 1914, but the intervening years of global war had greatly changed the whole prospect for peace or war. Polarity can also be accused of resting on an inaccurate realist understanding of what the international system is and how it works. It defines the system primarily in terms of states, and the dynamics of international relations primarily in terms of conflict. It assumes that the driving logic behind state behaviour is the need to accrue power in order to ensure survival in a Darwinian system whose basic rule is survival of the fittest. Many argue that this is no longer, if it ever was, a good way of understanding the international system. Boxing everything into states pushes hosts of powerful and important non-state actors such as firms, religions, and the many organizations of global civil (and uncivil) society into the background. State-centrism also emphasizes a military–political interpretation of what makes the system tick, too often at the expense of, for example, interpretations rooted in the world economy and/or international society. Polarity is essentially a material view of the system. It assumes that the drive for power to preserve security always trumps other, more potentially collaborative, motives, such as the desire to increase wealth, welfare and knowledge. And it discounts the effects of homogenization among states, such as the convergence in domestic values and structures that underlies the 'democratic peace'. On ethical grounds these assumptions have long been criticized for the danger they pose of creating self-fulfilling prophecies. Analysing international relations in terms of power politics risks increasing the possibility that actors will behave in that way.

Yet despite the challenges that can be put to it, polarity has still been extremely useful in academic thinking about world politics and international security. Not least, it stimulated a much higher awareness throughout the discipline of IR of the advantages of differentiating between structural explanations (where observed behaviour is accounted for by the principles governing the arrangement of the units in the system), and unit level explanations (where observed behaviour is accounted for by the internal processes of the actors composing the system, and the interactions between them). As with many social science concepts, its strengths are the mirror image of its shortcomings. While oversimplification is a fault from a descriptive point of view, it is a necessity for theorizing. Whatever its weaknesses, polarity points us towards a basic feature of the international power structure. So long as humankind remains divided up into political entities claiming the ultimate right of self-government (states), and so long as relations among those states are sufficiently competitive in character to carry a risk of war, the distribution of power among them is going to matter. Even if the ruthless Darwinian side of international politics is substantially overlaid by concerns carrying at least partly cooperative imperatives, such as sustaining a global economy, or managing the planetary environment, the distribution of power still matters to what kind of international orders are possible and how they will function.

Polarity is attractive as a theoretical starting point because of the immediate way it bears on the relational logic amongst the players in the game of international politics. As noted, polarity does not always determine outcomes. But it is a useful guide to understanding the logic of pressures and imperatives that are inherent in many situations, not just in military security, but also in diplomacy, international institutions, and economic management. For example, knowing the polarity of a system suggests hypotheses about how power balancing is likely to work. In a bipolar system, most balancing will have to be internal (i.e. by the rivals expanding or mobilizing their domestic resources), whereas in a multipolar system states can balance more economically by seeking other powers as allies (Waltz 1979: 168). Hansen (2000: 53–68) suggests that in a unipolar system there will be no balancing against the single great power, but a lot by other states against each other. She also suggests (2000: 14–15, 68–73) that changes in polarity create distinctive transition periods in which the analyst has to look more for effects of the transition than for effects of structure.

By extension, polarity also suggests quite a lot about the likely patterns of alliance formation: probably durable and fairly rigid under bipolarity, probably opportunistic and flexible in multipolar structures, perhaps irrelevant in unipolar ones. Polarity says a lot about the logic of nuclear deterrence, which is relatively simple between two powers (because there can be only one source of strike and one target for retaliation), but gets extremely complicated when three or more powers are in play (Buzan 1987: 173–77). A similar pattern of polarity logic works in relations to the design and implementation of arms control agreements. In the study of the international political economy, some think it crucial to how, or possibly whether, the international economy is managed, with a unipolar hegemon as the favoured option for a liberal economy (Kindleberger 1973, 1981, Keohane 1984, Gilpin 1987). Underlying much of this insight is a fairly simple general logic of coalitions. Arranging bargains of whatever kind is affected by the number of parties to the negotiation, and the effects are particularly strong when the number of parties is small (Riker 1962). Overall, polarity fitted nicely with the rational choice approach to international relations that was particularly strong in US social science.

Whatever problems academics might have with it, polarity has been hugely influential in public debates about international relations. This success is not just confined to the Cold War, when bipolarity framed the bulk of the discourse, but extends right down to the present day. The unipolar interpretation of world politics has steadily gained strength in the public discourse. Unipolarity is now a ubiquitous point of reference in public discussions about international relations, and that fact, along with the way in which it hugely flatters the US, helps to keep it in play in the academic debates. Those academics engaged in the policy debates can hardly be expected to ignore either the opportunity or the responsibility to make something out of the existence of a shared concept. Within the US, unipolarity serves as a kind of touchstone around which options for American foreign policy and grand strategy are debated. As with other elements of the analytical apparatus of IR, widespread and sustained use of a term such as unipolarity becomes part of what it purports to describe. Acceptance of unipolarity helps both to make it true and to hold that 'truth' in place, and this works for both those in favour of (or resigned to), and those opposed to, the position of the US as the unipole.

Outside the US, unipolarity serves in a general way to define the policy problem for two quite different groups. First, are those who oppose the US 'hyperpower', and would prefer a multipolar power structure (and whose voices are loud in China, Russia, France, Iran, India and elsewhere). Second, are those friendly to the US, but who worry that unipolarity is somehow fueling an increasingly unilateralist policy in Washington which is undermining a whole framework of international institutions and multilateral agreements that the US was previously instrumental in supporting. So whatever its flaws, polarity is well-established as both a theoretical approach to understanding the international power structure, and as a social fact in the public debates about world politics. Since it is so firmly embedded in this way, academics have some social responsibility for improving public understanding about what it does and does not signify and explain.

## Further reading

Barry Buzan, *The United States and the Great Powers: World Politics in the Twenty-First Century* (Polity, 2004). Uses the distinction between great powers and superpowers to explore the possible polarity configurations, and their consequences, in the coming decades.

Birthe Hansen, *Unipolarity and the Middle East* (Curzon Press, 2000). A rigorous investigation of how Waltzian polarity logic plays into the regional security of the Middle East.

Samuel P. Huntington, 'The Lonely Superpower', *Foreign Affairs,* 78(2) (1999): 35–49. Sets out the position of the US in a 'uni-multipolar' world.

Ethan B. Kapstein and Michael Mastanduno (eds.), *Unipolar Politics: Realism and State Strategies after the Cold War* (Columbia University Press, 1999). A collection of essays by many of the leading writers on polarity after the Cold War looking at the emergent politics of unipolarity during the 1990s for the US and other leading powers.

Charles A. Kupchan, 'After Pax Americana: Benign Power, Regional Integration, and the Sources of Stable Multipolarity', *International Security,* 23(2) (1998): 40–79. Sets out a vision of polarity based on core regions centred on the US, the European Union and Northeast Asia.

Harrison R. Wagner, 'What was Bipolarity?', *International Organization,* 47(1) (1993): 77–106. A thoughtful review and critique of how bipolarity was used to understand the Cold War.

Kenneth N. Waltz, *Theory of International Politics* (Addison-Wesley, 1979). The classic neorealist statement of polarity theory setting out in considerable theoretical depth why the distribution of capability is the key variable in world politics.

## CONTENTS

# Culture

Michael N. Barnett

## Abstract

In this chapter, students will learn about the complex relationships between culture and security. It begins by summarizing why security scholars began to think that culture might shape processes of global and national security. One driving reason was the observation that some states were not behaving 'rationally' – hence culture must be getting in the way. This view of culture – as the cause of irrational or dysfunctional behavior – limits our understanding for thinking about the relationship between culture and security processes. Instead, other definitions of culture see it as shaping who we are and what we want, as well as producing constraints on what we can do and what we think is appropriate. Culture is present in organizations, in societies, and in global affairs. But the challenge is to clarify what we mean by culture and how we think it matters. Contrasting rational and cultural approaches to security, the rest of the chapter examines several important issue areas: (1) the role of bureaucratic and organizational culture for understanding security issues such as military doctrine and evolution; (2) strategic culture; and, (3) how organizational and global cultural factors influence peacekeeping operations.

## Introduction

Does a volume on security studies need a separate chapter on culture? Not necessarily. The first edition of this title covered the topic without giving it special attention or even an entry in the index. Does this mean that the first edition was delinquent? Not necessarily. Depending on one's definition, attributes typically associated with culture appear in nearly all the chapters, suggesting that it is virtually impossible to discuss fundamental processes and patterns of security without incorporating it. Taking culture's simultaneous absence and omnipresence in the first edition as a point of departure, this chapter explores culture's imprint and impact on various areas of security.

It begins by showing how security studies tended to treat culture either as irrelevant at best or a scoundrel at worst, often because security scholars focused on culture to explain why behavior didn't conform to their pre-existing rationalist assumptions. Yet security scholars have increasingly recognized that culture is not only a menace but also is a constant presence. The next section then explores the world of culture, surveying the implications of two leading definitions for thinking about security and repeating some lessons learned from cultural theorists regarding how to – and not to – think about culture as a category of analysis and practice. The third section explores the relationship between security and culture with reference to strategic culture and cultures of peacekeeping and peacebuilding. Whereas strategic culture is largely interested in national styles of war-making, and thus includes attitudes toward the utility of force, grand strategy, and military doctrine, peacekeeping and peacebuilding cultures are interested in international styles of peace-making, and thus operate with assumptions regarding the conditions under which it is possible to make peace and resolve conflict. The chapter concludes by asking what is gained and what is lost by operating with a narrow or overly ambitious concept of culture.

## States behaving badly

If security scholars were to produce a film on the relationship between culture and security they would probably title it 'States Behaving Badly'. Security studies leans heavily on rational action models of state behavior. As recounted in Chapter 4, these models assume that states are unitary actors that pursue their pre-existing interests under an identifiable set of constraints, and choose the strategy that maximizes benefits and minimizes costs. They also assume that actors have full and complete information, can rank order their prefer-ences over time, and can weigh the opportunity costs of different options. Importantly, rational actor models do not pass judgment on the goals of states (or other actors), but instead are more interested in how states act in the world given their existing goals. In this sense, our assessment of Saddam Hussein's rationality depends not on whether we agree with his goals, but whether we believe that he has conformed to a rational decision process. Scholars know that most actors, especially states, hardly meet these demanding standards in the real world, but rational actor assumptions certainly make it easier to analyze the behavior of states and even recommend do's and don'ts for improving the decision process. In this rational world, culture does not (and should not) exist. Individuals, organizations, and states are information processors stripped of feelings, sentiments, passions, and history.

The problem is that our textbook models of how states and other actors should behave do not correspond with how they actually behave. Rationalist-driven security studies tends to assume that states will fluidly alter their strategies in response to changes in the security environment. Yet we often find that changes in the environment do not necessarily lead states to change their military doctrines, their strategic postures, or their tactics. The failure of states to adapt accordingly has led some security analysts to explain why states might be 'irrational', a kinder way of noting that they do stupid things. Security scholars have tended to explain such deviations with one of two responses. One is toward psychological models of decision-making, which assumes that the problems lie inside someone's head (see Goldgeier 1997). Leaders are affected by stress, exhibit motivational bias, and tend to minimize possible losses rather than maximize gains. The other response is to blame the environment. Sometimes scholars examine the institutional context in which decisions are made, as Graham Allison (1999) famously did in the case of the Cuban missile crisis and the impact of bureaucratic politics and organizational processes.

Others resort to culture. Americans and Europeans are supposed to have different attitudes toward the use of force because the former are from 'Mars' and the latter are from 'Venus'. On the eve of the first Persian Gulf War, US Secretary of State James Baker flew to Geneva to meet with his Iraqi counterpart, Tariq Ali, to try and convince him to withdraw, even partially, from Kuwait, and thus avoid a war. Saddam Hussein refused the offer, which, in retrospect, was one decision in a very long string of self-destructive actions. Why not respond in a way that, from everyone else's perspective, seemed more rational? Some suggested that Hussein did not have perfect information or believed that the US was bluffing, nothing more than a paper tiger, while others blamed an Arab culture that forces leaders to do anything to avoid public humiliation.

It is because much of security studies operates within a rational actor framework that it becomes attracted to cultural explanations when, and only when, states act in ways that deviate from rationalist premises and commit big-time blunders. But culture is more than an 'error' term. Instead, students of culture have observed that it can have both *constitutive* and *constraining* effects. Constitutive effects examine how culture shapes our identity, preferences, and what we consider to be appropriate behavior. Culture defines how we see ourselves, how we see the world, and how we make meaningful sense of our actions and the world around us. If equally powerful states facing the same strategic environment adopt alternative strategic preferences, then perhaps it owes to culture. In fact, many security scholars became interested in strategic culture precisely when they observed that the United States and the Soviet Union seemed to have different strategic preferences because of their different national styles of military strategy (Snyder 1977, Gray 1986). If there are differences in strategic preferences owing to different national styles, then we are suggesting the culture constitutes identity, preferences, and strategies. Importantly, constitutive arguments do not necessarily pass judgment on whether a goal is rational or irrational. These goals come from cultural values, and therefore are attributed to what the German sociologist Max Weber called 'value rationality'. For instance, we might think that the Taliban or al-Qa'ida have an 'irrational' ideology, but they might still be perfectly rational in terms of how they pursue their objectives. Constraining effects focus on the limits of choice. We have various objectives, but how we accomplish them, and what behavior we regard as appropriate or inappropriate, might be shaped by culture. In other words, not all is fair in love and war. American military officials might be convinced that torture is an effective way to get actionable intelligence, but might decide that the existing humanitarian norms against torture, which translate into sanctions such as being called to account before Congress or even being named at The Hague as a war criminal, makes the costs too high.

To the extent that security scholars rely on rational actor models, they have a difficult time recognizing the importance of culture and its full range of effects. Culture is about values and states, according to realists, are interested in power. Yet, culture matters not only for adding color to our drab and technical arguments, but also because it is does serious work. Over the last several decades scholars of International Relations and security have recognized that we live not only in a material world but also a social world, a world consisting of culture that shapes our identity, interests, and behavior. They have done so because rationalist explanations are inadequate for explaining everything from military doctrine, to alliances, to grand strategy, to the war on terror (see Katzenstein 1996). In short, the distribution of power and rational choice assumptions leave a lot to be explained (Desch 1998, Duffield *et al.* 1999).

It is not only scholars that are recognizing the centrality of culture. So, too, are practitioners and professionals. Consider the following confession by American Army Colonel Peter Mansoor (2011: 164), who served in Iraq during the first year of combat operations:

When U.S. forces invaded Iraq in 2003, the U.S. military was not particularly concerned about the impact of culture on its operations. U.S. leaders believed that the assault would play out as a high-tech conventional conflict and would be followed by a stabilization effort only slightly more difficult than the one U.S. troops had encountered in Kosovo a few years before ... quickly discovered that ... sectarian and ethnic identities, the role of tribes in Iraqi society, and the U.S. Army's own internal culture would weigh heavily on the course of the conflict, influence our approach to waging the war, and impact our interactions with our coalition allies.

Mansoor proceeds to describe how the military corrected its cultural blindness, and how doing so helped to turn around US operations. Culture, as he describes it, operates up and down the causal chain. Culture explains the American military's obsession with technology and belief that somehow hyper-rationality is not a cultural attribute (culture seems to be something that everyone else has, especially when you believe yourself to be rational and modern); the reaction of the Iraqi people to daily American security operations; the outcome of the counterinsurgency doctrine.

One of Mansoor's important observations is that culture is not something that 'other people have' but is something that everyone has. This is true for many Westerners who consider themselves modern and rational and somehow beyond culture. Yet modern attributes can combine to constitute a culture of rationality. We might become so obsessed with the possibility that there is a technological fix for every problem that we fail to recognize that our values might also play a role. We might become hopelessly infatuated with optimizing and decision choice models because we believe that they will improve our welfare, without sufficiently understanding the limits of these models and the presence of emotions.

The juxtaposition of 'us' as rational and 'them' as cultural has several unfortunate effects. For one, culture gets invoked when 'we' cannot understand what other people do, think, and feel. When coupled with judgments about what actions might have been more 'rational', the effect is to reduce culture to the irrational. It is only a short step from here to using culture in the most racist, ethnocentric, and unthinking ways. Take for instance, the argument that Saddam Hussein refused to take a negotiated exit from Kuwait because of an Arab culture that emphasizes honor and false pride. When American presidents also refuse to budge, and they do, rarely do we explain it with reference to an American culture but rather to personality attributes of stubbornness, a White House that is cut off from alternative sources of information and prone to groupthink, or even to domestic political considerations. In other words, while rational actor models typically overlook the presence of culture, sometimes this bias can have the positive effect of reducing prejudice, stereotyping, and racism.

## Culture

World culture. Global culture. High culture. Low culture. Organizational culture. Bureaucratic culture. World Bank culture. UN culture. European culture. Islamic culture. Asian culture. Macho culture. Military culture. Academic culture.

Not only is the world awash in cultures, it is awash in different definitions. There is no single-accepted definition of culture, not among anthropologists, who make their living studying it, and not among security scholars, who rely on anthropologists as they explore the relationship between security and culture (see Kuper 1999). Why are we awash in choices? The easy answer is that, like power, it is an essentially contested concept. The more complex answer is that different definitions are intended to serve different purposes. In other words, most definitions of culture are purpose-built – they are intended to help us analyze the world. Definitions of culture, like definitions of power, the State, and security, are not right or wrong; they are more or less useful for some identified purpose. Definitions can be better or worse, and concepts can be more or less insightful, but they are not necessarily right or wrong. Consequently, it can be an exercise in frustration to try and convince others that one definition is right and the other is wrong, but at least we can be clear and precise about our definition, how it differs from others, and what are its advantages and disadvantages.

The rich menu of choice when conceptualizing culture has, at times, caused scholars of security to lose patience and interest. Ideally, scholars of culture would offer more consensus, clarity, and precision. But the central concept of realism – power – shares these elusive qualities. There is no single definition of power. Instead, scholars recognize that it is an essentially contested concept. Power comes in many different forms. If security scholars have chosen to define power in material terms, such as geography, wealth, and military capabilities, it is not because these variables extinguish other forms of power, but rather because they are the most easily measured. In fact, many security scholars confess that this 'easy road' neglects not so easily measurable aspects of power, including those associated with beliefs, opinion, perception, determination, and so on. No wonder, then, that security scholars have been constantly puzzled by the disconnect between the distribution of power and outcomes. The most persuasive mechanisms of influence can also shift from generation to generation, from economic power to military power to cultural power. Security studies scholars might be frustrated by the concept of culture, but their central concept of power has similar characteristics.

Because there are so many definitions of culture, I want to highlight two that have been more popular among International Relations and security scholars. The first is by Clifford Geertz, one of the twentieth century's greatest and most influential anthropologists. According to Geertz, culture is 'an historically transmitted pattern of meanings embodied in symbols, a system of inherited conceptions expressed in symbolic forms by means of which men communicate, perpetuate, and develop their knowledge about and attitudes toward life' (1973: 89). The other approach is offered by two sociologists, Peter Berger and Thomas Luckmann (1967), that our view of the world is shaped not by mental states but rather by how society shapes how we see the world. Although society can have various influences on our interpretation of the world, perhaps most important is knowledge, that is, the symbols, rules, concepts, categories that individuals use to construct and interpret their world. Reality does not exist out there waiting to be discovered; instead, historically produced and culturally bound knowledge enables individuals to construct and give meaning to reality. Members of the same culture are likely to share interpretations of the world, which certainly facilitates common meanings and understandings.

There are important differences between Geertz's symbolically heavy approach and Berger and Luckmann's cognitive heavy approach, but they share various aspects that are now accepted by many students of culture and have been used by scholars interested in exploring the relationship between culture and security. First, they are interested in how actors give meaning to their world. Following Max Weber's (1949: 81) insight that 'we are cultural beings with the capacity and the will to take a deliberate attitude toward the world and to lend it *significance*', scholars of culture are interested in the meanings that actors give to their practices and the objects that they construct. These meanings are important not because they are colorful descriptions but rather because they shape our reactions and actions. For instance, the reason why advanced military technology might be valued has less to do with its technical qualities and more to do with its symbols of modernity. In this regard, conventional and nuclear weapons might spread not only because of their utility for war-fighting or deterrence but also because of their status (Eyre and Suchman 1996; Sagan 1996/97).

Second, cultures are resilient. They do not come and go with the change in the weather but rather have an enduring aspect and help to explain continuity. If cultures are durable it is because they socialize new members and sanction existing members from flying from the flock. How are cultures transmitted and maintained? Scholars offer a variety of mechanisms, including genetics (some of us are more prone to certain kinds of cultures than others), emulation (we learn by mimicking others and keep mimicking until it becomes second nature), learning, language, and incentives that reward those who follow the group and punish those who do not.

Third, cultures do change, not always dramatically but often through small adaptations. The recognition of the possibility of change alerts us to the fact that all cultures have subcultures. There are regional differences; Yankee culture is different from Southern culture. There can be class differences; Wall Street culture is different from working-class culture. There are professional cultures. There are cultures among lawyers, doctors, and academics. There is a military culture that derives from shared professional training. But there might be different military traditions that derive from different historical traditions. American military culture is different from Israeli military culture is different from Chinese military culture. Each of these national military cultures also can have subcultures identified with the different branches of the armed forces.

Fourth, culture shapes but does not determine. We should be wary of assuming that people are cultural dupes. Sometimes culture can generate fairly rigid worldviews, but because culture often includes a process of interpretation, and different people can interpret culture in different ways, we should avoid sentiments of cultural determinism. Culture, in this respect, can operate as a constraint, representing one factor among many that shapes how actors react to situations.

Fifth, we should be careful about assuming that cultural and material forces are separate and distinct. Today, most scholars agree that culture and material are interrelated. Although some scholars speak of a 'material culture', where technology and artifacts drive how we think and act, others recognize that such material forces might have symbolic meaning and thus make separating the two difficult. How confident are we, for example, that Iran's rumored quest for nuclear weapons can be reduced to either material or cultural factors?

These cautionary flags are evident in the debate between anthropologists and military officials regarding how the US Department of Defense's counterinsurgency field manual (COIN) tends to treat culture. In response to the wars in Iraq and Afghanistan, the Department of Defense decided that it had to get smarter about counterinsurgency, and that a smart counterinsurgency campaign should 'grab and hold' and 'win hearts and minds'. Both goals, though, required intimate knowledge of the local terrain, including different political networks, tribal ties, linguistic differences, ethnic allegiances, religious beliefs, how to treat women when entering a house, and on and on. In other words, from the military's perspective it required an intimate knowledge of the local culture. The military translated this into a need for a glossary of sorts that allowed analysts, soldiers, and tacticians to take into account the basic worldviews of local participants. The problem, according to some anthropologists, was that this concept was too 'static, coherent, bounded, and one-dimensional' (Albro 2010: 1089). Rather than speak of an Arab culture, an Iraqi culture, an Afghan culture, or a Pashtu culture, it is critical to bear in mind that culture: is not fixed but rather fluid and shaped by the past and the present; is not unified but rather has various faultlines and subcultures; is not something that only others have but we also have and that practices that we often believe are attributable to their culture (i.e. Arabs do not like to be humiliated) might also be part of 'our' culture (i.e. Americans do not like to be humiliated); and is only one factor among many that might be driving behavior (i.e., do we need a cultural theory to explain why someone would rather be alive than dead?).

These concerns suggest, sixthly, that cultural and material explanations are neither necessarily competing nor complementary. As scholars we typically ask: how important is X? In other words, we want to know if X is more or less causally significant than Y or Z. After all, culture might be important, but how important and in what ways? For security scholars, the default presumption is that power is the most important, and, therefore, our need to recognize culture depends on our assessment of whether it is as or more important than power. This 'how important is it?' has been a centerpiece of the debate between rationalists and constructivists, with realists insisting that constructivists demonstrate the causal importance of culture before they bother themselves with studying it. This is a highly reasonable and understandable position, but only up to a point. It makes most sense if we adopt a definition of culture as constraint, but if culture is constitutive then it will shape conceptions of threat, strategy, and appropriate tools. And, partisans of the power variable have a tendency to smuggle in variables that might be more properly claimed under the mantle of culture.

The value and limitations of thinking in terms of competing explanations is offered by Michael Gross's (2009) book on whether the laws of war are being undermined by this current age of asymmetrical warfare. He argues that international law governing war initiation and conduct during war are the relatively recent result of two primary factors: new versions of humanity, that is, what is considered to be civilized and what is not; and balances of power, which have encouraged states to recognize how their enlightened self-interest is consistent with rules of war. The juxtaposition of humanity and balance of power allows him to make predictions regarding whether combatants will comply with or violate existing laws of war – in short, even 'good states' will violate the laws of war if they believe they can get away with it, and even 'evil states' will comply with them if they believe that the costs will be too high if they violate these rules. Yet this 'materialist' hypothesis only gets him so far, because there are lots of states and combatants who comply with the laws of war not because they worry about the consequences of violating them but also because of a sense of self. In fact, they might comply with the laws of war not because they respect international humanitarian law or even know about it, but rather because of existing religious doctrine that generates a sense of justice and fairness in war. For instance, some leaders will not condone torture not only because they do not believe it is effective but also because it violates their sense of what it means to be civilized. The willingness of other states to go to extraordinary lengths to distinguish between civilian and combatant, even at the risk of their own soldiers, is related to their sense of what makes a military moral. In short, sometimes material forces make us behave, but at other times we behave even if we could misbehave without worrying about being caught and punished.

## Cultures in security

Security studies has clearly become more open to the importance of culture. Rather than sampling a long list of examples, I want to use two concepts to illustrate the insights provided by culture. The first is strategic culture, which has become a focus of debate among security scholars for the last several decades. Although different scholars have different approaches to the topic, in part because they are interested in illuminating different processes and identifying the importance of culture relative to other, more traditional, variables such as material power, I want to focus on the reasons for considering the importance of strategic culture.

The other concept is peacekeeping or peacebuilding culture, which refers to a set of practices largely associated with the UN and other agencies that are interested in maintaining and building peace. Whereas strategic culture directs our attention to national attitudes toward the use and projection of force, peacekeeping and peacebuilding cultures draw it to international attitudes toward the diminution of violence and production of peace.

## Strategic culture

Scholars began serious study of strategic culture in the 1980s in recognition that the Soviet Union and the United States varied in their strategic postures, thus defying standard realist predictions that states sitting in the same place in the international distribution of power would adopt similar strategic choices. Although students of military history had long recognized the existence of national styles of strategy, it now became acceptable for students of International Relations to try and identify its origins, content, and effects. With the emergence of constructivist International Relations theory in the 1990s, more scholars began developing, refining, and testing the concept of strategic culture, and it has now been applied to an impressive range of topics, from Iran's nuclear strategy, to the African Union's changing orientation toward intervention, to the 'ASEAN way' of non-interference, to the preference for offensive or defensive strategic postures, to European security policy.

Different scholars adopt different definitions (see Johnston 1995b, 1999, Klein 1988, Kier 1995, Poore 2003, Lock 2010). Many scholars adopt a definition of strategic culture as shared beliefs and behaviors among militaries – derived from common experiences and historical narratives – that shape identities, influence relationships, and affect the manner in which armed forces define and achieve their security objectives (Adamsky 2010). Along these lines, Iain Johnston (1995a: 36) defines strategic culture as 'an integrated system of symbols (i.e., argumentation structures, languages, analogies, metaphors, etc.) that acts to establish pervasive and long-lasting grand strategic preferences by formulating concepts of the role and efficacy of military force in interstate political affairs, and by clothing these conceptions with such an aura of facticity that the strategic preferences seem uniquely realistic and efficacious'. In contrast, Colin Gray prefers to think of culture as 'context' and as including 'the total warp and woof of matters strategic that are thoroughly woven together' (1999: 51).

Despite their definitional differences, these scholars are in heated agreement that culture is too important to ignore for several reasons. To begin, they are convinced that standard realist, power-politics models do not explain variation in the strategic choices of countries. Second, state security policies do not adapt quickly or efficiently to changes in the strategic environment. Instead, they appear to be sticky not only because of standard bureaucratic reasons (branches of the military do not want their budgets to decline or their status to diminish) but also because of 'tradition', 'history', and other references to 'just the way things are done'. In other words, we observe a fair bit of consistency in strategic preferences over time, even when the strategic environment changes radically and would seemingly force states to change their strategic profile. Third, strategic culture both constrains and constitutes. States' strategic choices are limited by what fits with an existing culture. Also, the strategic culture shapes broad worldviews, including whether states are naturally offensive or defensive minded, whether there is a culture of action or 'wait and see', whether states prefer to rely on technology or manpower for their military doctrine. In other words, culture is about identity and identity is central to forming preferences, strategies, and sense of what is appropriate and legitimate in the use of force. Because of culture's constituting properties, we can expect strategic culture to generate a limited set of grand strategic preferences because members learn from repeated interactions with their environment.

Although there is broad agreement on culture's analytical power, there is one difference that should be flagged: whether and how it is possible to turn culture into a standard causal argument that can be tested against 'material' forces. Iain Johnston argued forcefully that if scholars are going to take culture seriously, then it has to be defined clearly, operationalized systematically, and distinguished from rival hypotheses. Arguments that proclaim that 'culture is everything and everywhere' border on triviality and must be tightened so that they can be distinguished from alternative, more standard rationalist and power-politics arguments. His work has been immensely influential for precisely this reason – he offered a method for discriminating between material and cultural explanations.

Critics offered three familiar objections. First, we should be careful about confidently distinguishing between material and culture forces. Second, the focus on behavior and outcomes should not come at the expense of how actors make meaningful their world. Although Johnston builds on Geertz's definition, Geertz was primarily interested in the process of interpretation and how actors make sense of the world that they give significance and meaning. Johnston seems more interested in behavior than the process of interpretation. Third, his argument dangerously assumes that there is a single authentic culture and thereby fails to recognize the divisions, contestations, and subcultures.

One last question regarding strategic culture is the extent to which it has a gendered dimension. One of the most famous articles ever written about American strategic culture posits that a gendered discourse shapes the meaning and significance the military gives weapons systems (lots of phallic representations), what counts as strength and victory, and what is viewed as acceptable and unacceptable (Cohn 1987). One of the most famous movies ever made about war, Stanley Kubrick's *Dr. Strangelove*, is organized around the intimate relationship between sex and war. The reason why Captain Jack Ripper launches a unilateral strike is because his 'precious bodily fluids' have been corrupted by the communist infiltration of fluoride in the water system. The B-52 pilot is reading *Playboy*, surreptitiously tucked inside a copy of *Foreign Affairs*. American leaders in the war room agree that the way to save the world after a nuclear holocaust is for the remaining male survivors to retreat to an underground compound where very attractive women outnumber the men by 10 to 1. Although Kubrik's dark comedy takes tremendous liberty with reality, what makes it classic and timeless is because its themes of gender and war continue to resonate.

### Peacekeeping cultures

Security cultures exist not only at the national level – they also exist at the international level. One of the United Nations' primary functions is to address threats to international peace and security. Throughout the Cold War such debates largely centered in and around the Security Council, and its tools were limited to peacekeeping operations whose function was largely to monitor a cease-fire between two combatant states. After the Cold War, though, the definition of a threat to international peace and security expanded dramatically, and, so, too, did the UN's tools. It became more heavily involved in prevention and preventive diplomacy; expanded its operations from simply keeping the peace to enforcing the peace; and moved into post-conflict peacebuilding. As it addressed all phases of conflict, from beginning to middle to end, it also created a set of rules on all aspects of how to use force, resolve conflict, and build peace (see Chapter 26 this volume).

Barnett and Finnemore (2004) offered one of the first statements regarding the relevance of bureaucratic culture to the study of international organizations in general and peacekeeping in particular. Rules stand at the core of their definition of bureaucratic culture. They write: 'Bureaucratic rules thus shape the activities, understandings, identity, and practices, of the bureaucracy and consequently help to define the bureaucratic culture. Quoting from Diana Vaughan (1996: 64), they define bureaucratic culture as 'the solutions that are produced by groups of people to meet specific problems they face in common. These solutions become institutionalized, remembered and passed on as the rules, rituals, and values of the group'.

In other words, bureaucracies are built for a purpose – they are designed to help identify, solve, and resolve problems. Because bureaucracies are divided into different specialized units and develop standard operating procedures so that they can efficiently generate answers to challenges put in their in-boxes, these rules will reflect their overall purpose. Consequently, while it is possible to identify different aspects of a bureaucratic culture (is it gendered? does it allow for some degree of democratic decision-making or is it completely hierarchical?), Barnett and Finnemore limit their definition of culture to bureaucratic rules that are created to solve problems. Yet they also recognize that rules, much like culture, are constantly debated and being revised, in part because staff are constantly contesting how to interpret the relationship between existing rules and the fit for solving current problems. In other words, they want to capture how bureaucracies limit how staff see the world but also recognize that there usually is a vibrant debate among staff regarding whether one set of rules is more or less appropriate for current circumstances.

Barnett and Finnemore argue that this peacekeeping culture, that is, the rules governing the deployment and use of peacekeeping troops, helps explain the UN Secretariat's shocking reluctance to recommend an intervention to stop the genocide in Rwanda in 1994. One explanation is that its failure was due to pressure from member states in general and the United States in particular. Yet there is little or no compelling evidence that either immediate pressure or an anticipatory response stopped them in their tracks. Instead, Barnett and Finnemore argue that the source of their passivity was the peacekeeping culture. To understand the role of the peacekeeping culture requires a systematic consideration of the evolution of the rules and practice of peacekeeping.

Briefly, peacekeeping was a creative response by the UN Secretariat and several member states to the 1956 Suez crisis. It originally entailed the interpositioning of lightly-armed forces to monitor an existing cease-fire or political agreement between two contending states. Peacekeepers also were expected to follow the rules of impartiality, consent, and neutrality. These rules certainly reflected geopolitical constraints of that time and the functions that UN forces were to serve, but they also reflected the sources of the Secretariat's authority. One important source of authority was its delegated mandate from states to promote peace, but one condition of this delegation was that the UN operate with the consent of parties to the conflict. The UN also had moral authority but, again, this was conditioned on acting impartially in the conflicts. The Secretariat's power and influence rested on its authority, which, in turn, depended on being perceived as impartial and operating with consent.

New global pressures and opportunities gave cause for the Security Council and the Secretariat to expand the purposes of peacekeeping. Whereas during the period of classical peacekeeping peacekeepers monitored a cease-fire between two states, in these second generation operations peacekeepers became involved in domestic conflict and a host of new activities, including saving failed states and providing humanitarian assistance. This new social purpose of peacekeeping shaped the UN's bureaucratization in two principal ways. First, it led to the establishment of new units within the Secretariat that reflected its understanding of how to assist states make the transition from civil war to civil peace. More important for our purposes, it led to a reconsideration of the rules of peacekeeping and, specifically, whether the rules of consent, impartiality, and neutrality were appropriate and functional for these new conflict environments where the UN increasingly confronted parties willing to use violence to oppose the UN and the premise of its mandate. In order to discharge its responsibilities in this new environment, the UN began to adapt these rules to include non-consensual enforcement tactics.

At the very peak of its popularity the UN met several high-profile failures in places like Somalia and Bosnia. For the Secretariat, these failures represented a threat to the organization because they generated vocal opposition in important capitals and compromised its moral authority. In order to ensure that peacekeeping would be effective, and to shore up the organization's authority and political support, the Secretariat and the Security Council narrowed the conditions under which peacekeepers were deployed (emphasizing the need for stability on the ground before deployment) and restrained their actions in the field (reemphasizing consent and impartiality). Peacekeepers were no longer to be used in civil wars where there was no peace to keep.

The adaptation of the rules of peacekeeping proved to be both functional and dysfunctional. Those in New York at the time believed that adapting the rules in these ways would improve the UN's chance for success in peacekeeping and restore the organization's authority and popularity. Yet this adaptation also planted the seeds for pathological behavior. One reason why the more expansive, second-generation rules evolved after the Cold War was that the UN was responding to humanitarian emergencies, a form of action that Cold War politics had largely prevented it from attempting. Its humanitarian objectives, though, often conflicted with impartiality and consent. Humanitarian emergencies are frequently engineered by the combatants whose war aims are served by the catastrophe. The UN confronted a decision in these cases: either depart from the rules of impartiality and consent in order to confront the humanitarian emergency or allow the rules of impartiality and consent to determine the limits of its humanitarianism. In the late 1980s and early 1990s, it moved toward the former option. Somalia and Bosnia, though, caused it to retreat to the latter option. By mid-1993 the organization was so badly scarred by these failures that respecting rules about impartiality and consent became ends in themselves, eclipsing other organizational concerns. In an 'irrationality of rationalization', the organization's rules of consent, neutrality and impartiality helped to determine its goals – and made it undesirable to try to stop crimes against humanity.

Although Barnett and Finnemore argue that culture is neither inherently good nor bad, they show how a rule-obsessed bureaucratic culture can generate pathologies, situations when the organization acts in ways that violate its fundamental mandate. They identify two sources. One is that the same rules and routines that are designed to create an efficient response can also have limiting effects – enticing staff to see existing rules as infallible and even as ends in themselves rather than a means to an end. Second, bureaucracies are organized around divisions of labor, and each division is supposed to be the expert of its domain. Although it is good to have experts involved, they necessarily exclude other values that are not necessary to their work and thus create a distinctive (and limited) worldview. They proceed to identify how these two sources of pathology generate five different kinds of pathology in (international) organizations.

The peacekeeping culture – the rules governing when peacekeepers are deployed and how they operate in the field – shaped how UN staff understood and reacted to the violence in Rwanda. The Security Council established UNAMIR in October 1993 to oversee the Arusha Accords, ending the civil war between the Rwandan Patriotic Front (RPF) and the Rwandan government. Instead of supervising a peace process, however, UNAMIR confronted an increasingly dangerous security situation. Even prior to April 1994, UNAMIR confronted civilian killings and threats to peacekeepers, politicians, and the Arusha process itself. After April 6, violence escalated dramatically with the eruption of civil war and mass killings. Despite changes in the scale and kind of violence, the Secretariat's response to the changing violence was the same: operate with the consent of the parties and do not use force. Why?

There is no evidence that the Secretariat wanted to intervene to protect civilians but was prevented by the states on the Security Council. Instead, evidence indicates that the Secretariat preferred non-intervention, and that this preference was a product of peacekeeping culture. During the pre-April period the Department of Peacekeeping Operations (DPKO) leaned on the peacekeeping rules and ordered the Force Commander Romeo Dallaire to respond to the growing violence and threats to the Arusha process with consent-based means. When the violence escalated on April 6 the peacekeeping culture shaped the Secretariat's response in two important respects. It colored its categorization of what was happening in Rwanda. There were several possible ways to define the violence – including civil war, reciprocated clashes between the two ethnic groups, and ethnic cleansing and crimes against humanity. Even though General Dallaire was providing evidence that Rwanda was both a civil war and a site of crimes against humanity being organized by Hutu extremists against the Tutsi population, during April the Secretariat categorized these killings as reciprocal violence related to the civil war and as the most recent chapter in the long story of ethnic conflict between the two groups. The peacekeeping culture informed this conclusion. UNAMIR was designed to help end a civil war. Its peacekeeping activities were created for this purpose, and pre-April predictions of what would happen if the peace process collapsed always involved the return of the civil war. Accordingly, when the post-April 6 violence erupted the UN quickly categorized it as originating from the civil war and treated the killings as a consequence of the civil war. In short, the Secretariat expected killing in Rwanda to be part of a civil war and saw what it expected to see. An 'institutional ideology of impartiality' led the Secretariat to believe that it was appropriate and desirable to not try and stop crimes against humanity, or even recognize them as such, as the UN, itself, later acknowledged (UN Secretary-General 1999: 111).

Building on Barnett and Finnemore's argument regarding a peacekeeping culture, Severine Autesserre (2010) argues that there is a peacebuilding culture that shapes how UN officials understand and attempt to resolve conflict, and she illustrates the power and pathology of this culture in the case of the Congo. A legacy of colonialism, authoritarian rule, and the Rwandan genocide, the war in the Congo ranks as one of the world's great humanitarian nightmares and arguably the biggest peacebuilding challenge faced by the United Nations. Although this is not a war that lends itself to concrete beginnings or endings (at least so far), hostilities commenced in August 1998 in what was then known as Zaire, and officially ended in July 2003 with a new transitional government in the Democratic Republic of Congo. Sometimes known as Africa's world war because of the participation of dozens of armed groups, often backed by foreign governments, and the invasion by neighboring countries, several million people have died from violence, disease, and starvation, with millions more displaced, living in squalid camps, and facing daily threats of death, rape, and deprivation. To try and create, maintain, support, and extend the peace plan, the UN became deeply involved in all aspects of peacekeeping and peacebuilding, and eventually established the UN Stabilization Mission in the Democratic Republic of the Congo, with a wide-ranging mandate to build the conditions for peace and protect civilians.

The UN operation in the Congo had its own idiosyncracies, but it also had an identifiable culture because it was a culture that was present in other operations. Importantly, this culture has a particular way of understanding the causes of and solutions to civil war. From the UN's perspective, ending a civil war requires getting the central parties, that is, the main armed combatants, including the government, to negotiate a cease-fire followed by a peace treaty. Wars are caused by the central elites and they have the power to end them. Yet to what extent are the causes of civil war, and the reasons for its continuation, located among the central elites, often living in the capital city? According to Autesserre, this might be the case in other civil wars, but not in the Congo. The causes of the violence are local and due to a mixture of economic, demographic, and ethnic forces. Consequently, in order for the UN to address the causes of the civil war it would have to attend to these issues located in the periphery and outside the control of the centralized elite. However, it keeps looking in the wrong direction. Why? Because UN officials have a culture that obscures these local processes and exaggerates the role of centralized elites. The troubles in the Congo are partly due to the Congo and partly to a UN culture of conflict resolution. There is certainly no guarantee that UN mediators that incorporated local elites would have solved the conflict, but it is fairly certain that they had little chance if they did not.

## Conclusion

Students of security can deny the existence of culture, but at considerable risk. They risk failing to recognize explicitly the importance of culture in security processes, which can have immediate and long-term consequences for their theories and practices. Ignoring culture means that we are less equipped to understand the world. It also means, as Pentagon officials have acknowledged over the last decade, that militaries will be less effective at accomplishing their objectives. Scholars might want to treat culture as an 'error' term that is used as a last resort explanation, but practitioners do not have that luxury.

The conversation should move beyond asking 'does culture matter?' to the more important question: 'how does it matter?'. The substantive answer to that question is: it appears to shape strategic preferences, attitudes toward violence, willingness to take risks, readiness to suffer casualties and obey the rules of war, and on and on. The analytical answer is: it appears to shape identity, preferences, and strategies, constrain the incentives and disincentives for certain kinds of action, and shape the meanings that we give to the world and thus how we interpret it and act on it. The challenge for those who want to work with the concept of culture is thus to be very clear about how they are using it and how it helps them better explain and understand the world.

## Further reading

Scott Atran, *Talking to the Enemy: Faith, Brotherhood, and the (Un)making of Terrorists* (Ecco Books, 2010). An anthropologist's nuanced and first-hand account of the evolving and complex relationship between religion and suicide bombers.

Michael Barnett, *Eyewitness to a Genocide: The United Nations and Rwanda* (Cornell University Press, 2002). A look into whether and how UN officials developed a 'banality of indifference' to crimes against humanity.

Martha Finnemore, *The Purpose of Force* (Cornell University Press, 2003). A compelling exploration of how different global cultures shape the motives and reason for war.

Peter Katzenstein (ed.), *The Culture of National Security* (Columbia University Press, 1996). A path-breaking volume that examines the difference that culture makes in a range of security issues.

Laura Sjoberg (ed.), *Gender and International Security: Feminist Perspectives* (Routledge, 2009). A wide-ranging look at the role of gender in shaping fundamental security dynamics.

## CONTENTS

# War

Paul D. Williams

## Abstract

In this chapter students will learn about the concept of war and some of the major trends in armed conflict since 1945. With the end of the Cold War the threat of major war between the great powers has receded, but many parts of the developing world still suffer from ongoing armed conflicts or the legacies of old ones. The chapter begins by outlining some of the different philosophies of war and ways of defining them. It then summarizes some of the functions of war beyond military victory. The next section reviews five major trends in armed conflicts since 1945 before asking who is doing the fighting and the dying in the world's contemporary war zones. The chapter ends by discussing the extent to which the nature of warfare is changing.

## Introduction

Students of security ignore warfare at their peril. Commonly understood as the clash of armed actors, war is much more than that: it is an intense form of political relations that impacts upon virtually every dimension of human life. It has caused huge amounts of suffering and destruction but it has also been a major engine for social, political, economic and technological change.

It has influenced many of our most enduring cultural reference points, shaped the deep meanings of masculinity and femininity, and set the contours of many of our laws, institutions and customs. Of course, wars involve a range of strategic activities: thinking about what military means can achieve, and against whom; how to define and prioritize vital interests and values, and who might threaten them; as well as a host of practical considerations in gearing up for military campaigns and living with their aftermaths. But war is much more than the strategies and tactics of war-fighting: it is a 'full-spectrum' social phenomenon that is 'present beyond the war front and beyond wartime, in and among apparently pacific social, cultural and economic relations' (Barkawi 2011: 713, 707–708).

As such an important idea and practice, there are many reasons to study war: some do it in order to help their side win; others want to study war in order to eradicate it; still others want to know why wars begin and how they end; while some are interested in studying the sociology of war and its functions rather than its causes. Whatever one's motivation, a concern with war and the use/threat of military force has formed the traditional core of security studies. In the face of the rapid 'broadening' of security studies, some analysts think it should stay that way (e.g. Miller 2010).

Although recent decades have seen a significant decline in the number of armed conflicts around the world, huge sums of money are still spent on waging wars and preparing for future ones. During 2010, the Stockholm International Peace Research Institute estimated that worldwide military expenditure had reached $1,630,000,000,000. The end of the Cold War certainly reduced the threat of major war between the great powers but armed conflict (and its legacies) blights many parts of the developing world in particular.

This chapter examines some of the different ways of understanding war's place in world politics, some of its central social functions, some of the major trends that have been identified in armed conflicts since 1945, and the extent to which the nature of warfare has changed over time.

## Three philosophies of war

In his introduction to the Penguin edition of Carl von Clausewitz's unfinished classic, *On War*, Anatol Rapoport (1968: 11) noted that although Clausewitz was often dubbed 'The Philosopher of War', there are in fact several philosophies of war and Clausewitz was simply the most important proponent of one of them. These different philosophies are important not only because they give different answers to the question 'what is war?' but also because humans are sentient beings and consequently what they think about an issue like warfare can have an important bearing on its nature. Rapoport labelled the three philosophies the *political*, the *eschatological*, and the *cataclysmic*.

Clausewitz was arguably the most important proponent of the *political* philosophy of war. This defined warfare as 'an act of violence intended to compel our opponent to fulfil our will' (Clausewitz 1976: 75). It was essentially a rational, national and instrumental activity: the decision to employ the military instrument ought to be made on the basis of a rational calculation taken by the political authority concerned in order to achieve some specified goal. In Clausewitz's framework, the political challenge of warfare was how to achieve such rationality given the fluctuating relationships between his central trinity of actors – the people, the government and the military – given their principal characteristics – passion, reason and technique, respectively. During Clausewitz's lifetime (1780–1831), war was widely viewed as a legitimate instrument of state policy albeit one that should be used only with a clear purpose in mind. Victory in battle was the goal and it usually went to the side most accomplished in the arts of attrition and manoeuvre.

The *eschatological* philosophy, in contrast, had a teleological view of history which would culminate 'in a "final" war leading to the unfolding of some grand design – divine, natural, or human' (Rapoport 1968: 15). Rapoport offered two variants: messianic and global eschatology. In the messianic variant the agency destined to carry out the 'grand design' is presumed to exist already. Its 'mission' was to 'impose a just peace on the world' thus 'eliminating war from future history'. Expressions of such a philosophy include the Crusaders' attempts to unite the known world under a single faith in the Middle Ages, the Nazi doctrine of the Master Race, or al-Qa'ida's vision of a global caliphate. In the global variant, the 'grand design' is presumed to arise from the chaos of the 'final war'. In Christian eschatology, for example, this would involve forces which will rally around Christ at the Second Coming. Alternatively, in Communist eschatology the struggle for power was waged between classes rather than states or religions. From this perspective the emergence of the 'world proletariat' was required to convert imperialist war into class war and, after defeating the bourgeoisie, establish a world order in which wars will no longer occur.

Finally, the *cataclysmic* philosophy conceived of war 'as a catastrophe that befalls some portion of humanity or the entire human race' (Rapoport 1968: 16). Here, war could be seen as a scourge of God or as an unfortunate by-product of 'human nature' or the anarchic 'international system'. This philosophy also comes in two variants: ethnocentric and global. The ethnocentric version sees war as something that is likely to befall *us*; specifically war is something that *others* threaten to do to us. The coming war is not seen as beneficial to us; all that can be done is to forestall the impending disaster or alleviate its worst effects. The global variant views war as a cataclysm that affects humanity as a whole not just this or that group of humans. No one is held responsible and no one will benefit from it. Consequently, this philosophy focuses attention on the prevention of war; 'on uncovering the causes of war and on inventing institutionalized methods of conflict resolution' (Rapoport 1968: 40, see also Roberts 2005 and Chapter 6 this volume).

Based on these descriptions, Rapoport suggested that 'in political philosophy war is compared to a game of strategy (like chess); in eschatological philosophy, to a mission or the dénouement of a drama; in cataclysmic philosophy, to a fire or epidemic' (1968: 16).

Historically, during the period from the Napoleonic era until the First World War, European politics provided the conditions in which Clausewitz's political philosophy flourished and became dominant. By the time Europe's major armies had become bogged down in the trench warfare of the First World War, however, it was clear that developments in military technology had rendered Clausewitzean methods of attrition incredibly costly to implement and the art of manoeuvre almost impossible. The industrialized slaughter of 'the Great War' thus ceased to serve the political aims of either side.

A glance at the landscape of contemporary world politics reveals that in some important respects the political philosophy espoused by Clausewitz is under significant challenge. It is clearly alive and well in the military colleges of Western states but outside these corridors other philosophies and practices are in the ascendancy. As Box 13.1 illustrates, debate continues over whether Clausewitzean thinking is still relevant for analysing today's wars.

First, the concept of the battlefield, so central to the way in which Clausewitz understood warfare, has dissolved. The 9/11 attacks, for instance, demonstrated that today's battlegrounds might be Western (or other) cities while the US-led 'war on terror' – subsequently re-branded as the 'long war' – conceives of the battlefield as literally spanning the entire globe. Even when Western states have been able to localize the theatre of war in places such as Serbia, Sierra Leone and Somalia, the need to use military force – often in the name of maintaining 'international peace and security' – usually highlighted the failure of those governments to achieve their stated objectives by other means. In the future, however, battles are unlikely to be confined to planet earth as the US in particular will be forced to militarize space in an effort to protect the satellites upon which its communication and information systems depend (Hirst 2002). Back on planet earth, rising levels of urbanization and the desire of anti-Western forces for concealment, have contributed to more engagements being fought in urban areas including industrialized cities, shanty towns and even refugee/displacement camps (Hills 2004). Conducting military operations in urban areas poses many difficult challenges because they are far more interactive environments than jungles or deserts.

Second, as the speeches of both Osama bin Laden and former US President George W. Bush made clear, leaders on both sides of the 'war on terror' have often rejected political narratives of warfare. Instead, they have adopted eschatological philosophies in their respective rallying cries for a global jihad and a just war against evildoers.

A third problem for advocates of the political philosophy – and one which Clausewitz obviously never encountered – is war involving the 'exchange' of nuclear weapons. Far from furthering the political objectives of the participants this is more likely to resemble a mutual suicide pact between the states involved. As the technology to make nuclear weapons continues to diffuse and attempts to bolster the Nuclear Non-Proliferation Treaty continue to falter, the world may well be entering the most dangerous phase of nuclear confrontation since the second Cold War of the 1980s. In addition, the potential for nuclear weapons to fall into the hands of groups committed to carrying out 'terrorist

## BOX 13.1   IS CLAUSEWITZ'S THINKING STILL RELEVANT?

*Martin Van Creveld*: 'contemporary "strategic" thought . . . is fundamentally flawed; and, in addition, is rooted in a "Clausewitzian" world-picture that is either obsolete or wrong. We are entering an era . . . of warfare between ethnic and religious groups. . . . In the future, war will not be waged by armies but by groups whom we today call terrorists, guerrillas, bandits, and robbers, but who will undoubtedly hit on more formal titles to describe themselves. Their organizations are likely to be constructed on charismatic lines rather than institutional ones, and to be motivated less by "professionalism" than by fanatical, ideologically based loyalties. . . . If low intensity conflict is indeed the wave of the future, then strategy in its classical sense will disappear'.

(Van Creveld 1991: ix, 197, 207)

*Mary Kaldor*: 'the core of Clausewitzean theory [the inner tendency of war to lead to extremes], is no longer applicable. For Clausewitz, war was fundamentally about the "urge to decision", which was achieved through . . . combat between two warring parties, and this implied the need for speed and concentration; the suspension of belligerent action and the dispersal of forces did, of course, take place but were explained in terms of departures from the inner nature of war. Today's wars . . . are inconclusive, long lasting and have a tendency to spread. My argument is that this is because these wars have a different inner nature. In this sense, a Clausewitzean understanding of these wars can be deeply counterproductive in developing appropriate international strategies both for trying to end these wars and for the role of military forces. On the other hand, there is much in Clausewitz's method of argument that can help us think through alternative approaches'.

(Kaldor 2010: 271)

*General Sir Rupert Smith:* In today's wars, fighting occurs among the civilian populace; it is 'war amongst the people'. The aim of using military force is 'to influence the intentions of the people.' Consequently, 'I do not agree with some who dismiss Clausewitz and his trinity as irrelevant: it is my experience in both national and international operations that without all three elements of the trinity – state, military and the people – it is not possible to conduct a successful military operation, especially not over time.' 'Clausewitz's trinity of state, army and people is a useful tool with which to analyse the actors' purpose and activities, despite their [often] not being states'. Even apparently formless non-state actors 'will also have some dependency and relationship with the people, there will be an armed force of some description and there will be some political direction to the use of force'. In this type of environment, however, there must be a shift in emphasis from destruction to communication. When communication to capture the will of the people is the objective, military operations must be conducted with an appreciation of how the mass media constructs its narratives and in such a way as to influence its interpretation of events. Furthermore, military force must be used within the appropriate legal frameworks: 'to operate tactically outside the law is to attack one's own strategic objective'.

(Smith, R. 2005: 277, 58, 303, 379)

spectaculars' without making specific demands is a worrying break from Clausewitzean tradition (see Chapters 27 and 30 this volume).

Finally, when confronted by 'revolutionary' wars, which cry out for counter-revolutionary responses, Clausewitz's injunction to destroy the military forces of the adversary is problematic not just because such 'military forces' are often indistinguishable from the local populace but also because one can never be sure they have been eliminated 'unless one is ready to destroy a large portion of the population' (Rapoport 1968: 53, see also Chapter 31 this volume). The problem, as Rapoport noted, is that 'this usually conflicts with the political aim of the war' – to insure the irrelevance of the revolutionary ideology in question – 'and hence also violates a fundamental Clausewitzean principle'.

As we have seen, different philosophies understand war in different ways. But in the traditionally Anglo-American-dominated field of security studies the political philosophy has held sway (on the ethnocentric tendencies of security studies see Booth 1979, Barkawi and Laffey 2006). All that can be said in general terms is that whatever approach to understanding warfare one adopts will have consequences, opening up some avenues and closing down others. In International Relations and security studies warfare has commonly been defined in ways that highlight its cultural, legal and political dimensions but more attention should probably be given to the sociology of war (see Box 13.2).

## The functions of war

Scholars in IR and security studies have usually focused on investigating the causes of war and tracing their incidence over time/place or analysing how the threat and use of military force might be used to coerce or deter opponents. But warfare is not just an instrument of policy or an entirely negative phenomenon with 'causes' and 'effects'; it also has functions. As David Keen (2008) has pointed out, significant sectors of society may benefit from war. Thus to understand why wars are started and why they persist, analysts need to understand what these benefits are and to examine wars as positive phenomena that have functions as well as causes and effects.

For Keen, the conventional wisdom is that the point of engaging in warfare is to win a violent contest against one's opponent, sooner rather than later. But based on his analysis of a variety of recent wars including those in Sudan, Sierra Leone, Chechnya, Colombia, and Afghanistan, Keen observed a variety of practices that showed the participants in warfare were not always primarily interested in victory. Rather, war served a variety of other functions.

A first central aim of war beyond victory was to *limit violence*, especially one's own exposure or that of a key political constituency. This could be achieved in a variety of ways. Geographically, efforts could be made to fight away from one's own homeland. Politically, one could 'farm out' violence and its adverse consequences to militias or proxies. This would be particularly important if the recruitment of a large, conscript army would be unpopular

## BOX 13.2  DEFINING WAR: CULTURAL, LEGAL, POLITICAL AND SOCIOLOGICAL APPROACHES

*Cultural*: Warfare looks different and conjures up different meanings depending where and when in human history the analyst looks. As John Keegan has suggested, war 'is always an expression of culture, often a determinant of cultural forms, in some societies the culture itself' (1994: 12). In this sense, war is best understood as a socially constructed category, but one with powerful material implications like marriage, the market, or society. This means that what 'we' choose to define as an act of war may not always coincide with how 'others' see things.

*Legal*: Another approach is to define war in juridical terms, for example, as 'the legal condition which equally permits two or more hostile groups to carry on a conflict by armed force' (Wright 1983: 7). From this perspective war is distinguished from peace because it is a state of legal contestation through military means. However, this does not mean that war is synonymous with the conduct of military engagements: parties can be legally in a state of war without overt violence occurring between them. The relationship between North and South Korea following the cessation of hostilities in 1953 would be one such instance. However, because the international legal framework is primarily defined by states, analysing war through solely legal lenses has limited applicability in cases of armed conflict where either the belligerents are not states or where the government of a particular state is loath to recognize the actions of its domestic opponents as constituting warfare rather than criminal activity.

*Political*: Arguably the most popular approach within security studies has been to define war, following Clausewitz, as a particular type of political activity involving violence. Hedley Bull, for instance, defines war as:

> organised violence carried on by political units against each other. Violence is not war unless it is carried out in the name of a political unit; what distinguishes killing in war from murder is its vicarious and official character, the symbolic responsibility of the unit whose agent is the killer. Equally, violence carried out in the name of a political unit is not war unless it is directed against another political unit; the violence employed by the state in the execution of criminals or the suppression of pirates does not qualify because it is directed against individuals.
>
> (Bull 1977: 178)

*Sociological*: War is understood as a socially generative form of relations, that is, warfare 'consumes and reworks social and political orders'. It is a 'full spectrum' social phenomenon inasmuch as it involves 'the complete range of social, cultural, economic and political relations, shaping everything from matters of state to gender relations, from high politics to popular culture' (Barkawi 2011: 713). Combat and strategy are often among the most visible aspects of warfare as a social force but they represent only a small part of its sociology.

or if it was necessary to deny responsibility for atrocity crimes. Militarily, violence could be limited by avoiding direct confrontation/battles with a competent armed enemy: it was usually much better to employ one's forces to prey upon civilians or conduct commercial activities than to rapidly degrade them in destructive battles.

A second function of warfare is to fulfil the desire for *immediate gain*. This might be economic gain through the accumulation of commodities or the desire for improved safety for one's friends and supporters. But war may also deliver psychological benefits. It might, for example, be important for individuals to feel that they are fulfilling an important role as a 'freedom fighter' in the liberation struggle or a 'protector of the homeland'. Similarly, taking up arms may offer individuals a chance to invert established social hierarchies, gain respect by protecting their communities, or simply to take revenge for past humiliations.

Finally, Keen noted how war can play a crucial role in *weakening political opposition* – not solely the enemy, but also by suppressing, dividing or delegitimizing actual or potential critics within one's own camp. Once war is declared, the gloves often come off and the war leaders ask 'are you with us or against us?' In these circumstances, a range of charges can be levelled against political opponents from appeasement and weakness to consorting with the enemy and treachery.

Importantly, as Keen points out, all three of these aims 'may not only compete with the priority of winning but may also be actively counter-productive from a military point of view' (2008: 17).

## Trends in armed conflicts since 1945

According to the data compiled by the Uppsala Conflict Data Program (UCDP), five main trends can be identified in armed conflicts since 1945 (see Box 13.3). First, particularly from the mid-1970s there has been a significant decline in interstate armed conflict with intrastate conflicts accounting for the vast majority of organized violence (see Figure 13.1).

A second major trend is that since reaching a peak of 51 state-based armed conflicts in 1991–1992, the number of these conflicts has dramatically declined. According to Andrew Mack (2007), the decline in armed conflicts can be explained with reference to four main factors. First, the end of colonialism removed a major source of political violence from world politics. (Although some armed groups are still waging state-formation conflicts against what they see as colonial rule.) The second key factor was the end of the Cold War, which encouraged the superpowers to stop fuelling 'proxy wars' in the developing world. The third, and for Mack the most important factor, was the increased level of international activism spearheaded by the UN that followed the end of the Cold War. This activism involved more serious efforts at preventive diplomacy, peacemaking, peace operations, and the increased number of 'Friends of the Secretary-General' and other mechanisms designed

## BOX 13.3 THE UPPSALA CONFLICT DATA PROGRAM ON CLASSIFYING ARMED CONFLICT

1. *State-based armed conflicts* are those in which a government is one of the warring parties. There are four variants:

   *Interstate armed conflict* occurs between two or more states.

   *Intrastate armed conflict* occurs between the government of a state and internal opposition groups. These conflicts are further sub-divided into:

   civil wars, which are fought for control of an existing government;

   state-formation/secessionist conflicts, which are fought between a government and a territorially-focused opposition group that is seeking to redraw the borders of the existing state.

   *Internationalized intrastate armed conflict* occurs between the government of a state and internal opposition groups but with additional intervention from other states in the form of troops.

   *Extrastate armed conflict* occurs between a state and a non-state group outside that state's territory.

2. *Non-state armed conflicts* are those where organized, collective armed violence occurs but where a recognized government is not one of the parties. Examples might include violent intercommunal conflicts or fighting between warlords and clans.

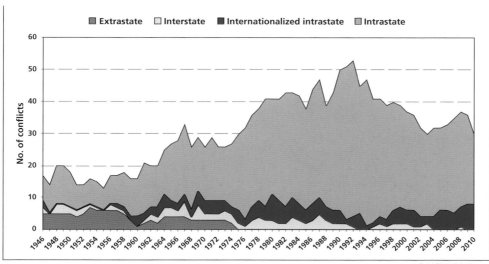

© UCDP 2010

*Figure 13.1* State-based armed conflicts by type, 1946–2010

to support local efforts to foster peace (see Chapters 25 and 26 this volume). With greater engagement, international society has become better at ending wars. A fourth factor was the increasing popularity of global norms that proscribe the use of military force in human relationships.

A third significant trend in armed conflicts since 1945 is the decline in battle-deaths. Whereas the average number of battle-deaths per conflict, per year was 38,000 in 1950, by 2005 it had fallen to just 700 – a 98 per cent decrease (Mack 2007: 7, see also Human Security Report 2009). Battle-death counts do not include either the intentional killing of civilians, or so-called 'indirect deaths' from war-exacerbated disease or malnutrition (see below).

A fourth trend was only spotted in the early 2000s when the UCDP started collecting data about non-state armed conflicts. The early results revealed more than 400 non-state armed conflicts took place around the world since the end of the Cold War (Eck, Kreutz and Sundberg 2010). Until recently, this category of armed conflicts had been almost completely hidden from view and is still not included in some databases of armed conflict. During the early 2000s there were often more than 30 non-state armed conflicts taking place in a single year, most of them in Africa. Indeed, in Africa alone, between 1990 and 2009 the UCDP registered 287 non-state armed conflict dyads which generated just under 60,000 battle-related deaths (Williams 2011: ch. 1).

The final trend worth identifying here is the shifting regional spread of armed conflicts. In global historic terms, constraints imposed by geography and climate have meant that major wars have been confined to a relatively small portion of the earth's surface (Keegan 1994: 68-73). Since 1945, it is clear that at different times, different regions have experienced far more wars than others (see Figure 13.2). Until the mid-1970s East and Southeast Asia

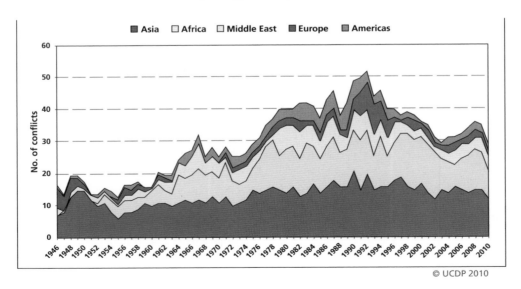

© UCDP 2010

*Figure 13.2* State-based armed conflicts by region, 1946–2010

suffered the most battle-deaths whereas during the latter stages of the Cold War most such casualties were spread between the Middle East, Asia and Africa. During much of the 1990s, however, sub-Saharan Africa proved to be, by far, the world's most conflict prone region (see Williams 2011).

## Who fights? Who dies?

As already noted, states are not the only belligerents in contemporary armed conflicts; armed actors come in many shapes and sizes, including international organizations and a variety of non-state actors. International organizations such as the UN, NATO, EU and AU have fielded troops primarily as peacekeepers or as part of counterinsurgency operations but many have engaged in combat (see Chapters 24–26 and 31 this volume). Historically, the most prevalent armed non-state actors have been mercenaries, private military companies, insurgents and a wide variety of paramilitaries, militias and self-defence forces, tribal and clan-based groups as well as the infamous suicide bombers. Another recent trend has been the rise to prominence of child soldiers in contemporary armed conflicts (see Denov 2010). Estimates suggest there are about 300,000 child soldiers currently fighting or recently demobilized, and another 500,000 in armies currently at peace (Singer 2005).

With the reduction in the number of major engagements and the subsequent drop in the number of battle-deaths, it is not surprising that civilians account for a major proportion of those killed in contemporary armed conflicts. In 2005, the Human Security Centre (2005: 75) suggested that between 30–60 per cent of violent deaths in contemporary armed conflicts were civilians. Part of the explanation for civilian deaths is the campaigns of one-sided violence/massacres conducted by governments and rebels (according to UCDP data there have been about 25–45 each year since 1989). Humanitarian aid workers have also found themselves more likely to become the targets of intentional violence. After decades of relative immunity, one study found that between 1997 and 2005 the number of humanitarian workers killed each year increased from 39 to 61, although the rate of violent assaults against aid workers had only increased marginally during the same period – from an average of 4.8 assaults per 10,000 workers between 1997 and 2001, to 5.8 between 2002 and 2005 (Stoddard *et al.* 2006).

Ultimately, however, the difficulty of extracting reliable and systematic information from the world's war zones makes it impossible to know for sure how many civilians have been killed. Moreover, as Adam Roberts has argued, 'The entire exercise of seeking universal civilian–military casualty ratios is flawed. To build up a more accurate picture, there is a need to focus on actual wars' as opposed to general categories (2010: 128).

The vast majority of fatalities in contemporary armed conflicts are so-called 'indirect deaths': people (mainly children, the elderly and women) who die from war-exacerbated disease and malnutrition, usually brought on and/or intensified by the process of displacement. Despite being the biggest single

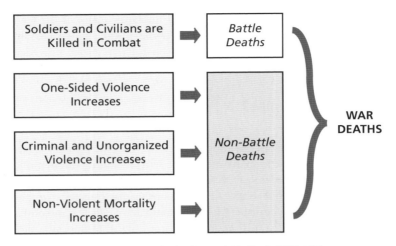

*Figure 13.3* Sources of war deaths (Lacina and Gleditsch 2005: 149)

category of war deaths, this type is arguably the least well documented and understood (see Figure 13.3). This is because measuring 'indirect deaths' is fraught with problems, not least those concerning methodology (especially how to measure and compare 'normal' as opposed to 'abnormal' mortality rates), data-collection, and because publicized estimates are commonly inflated or deflated for reasons of propaganda. Nevertheless, there is a large degree of consensus that the changing demography of victims is linked to changes in the mode of contemporary warfare.

## Is the nature of warfare changing?

Debates about whether and how the nature of warfare is changing are as old as the concept itself. In recent years, however, debates about three questions have been particularly important in addressing this issue: whether the concept of 'total war' is useful for thinking about developments in warfare; whether the processes of globalization have given rise to a 'new' type of warfare; and whether advanced industrialized democracies in the West are waging a new type of war compared to earlier historical periods.

### The idea of total war

Although the term 'total war' was coined by the German First Quartermaster General, Erich Ludendorff, in 1918, fear of such a prospect had dominated Western views of warfare since at least 1800. The fears were exemplified by the horrors of the First and Second World Wars which killed approximately 8.5 million and 55 million people respectively (see Bourne 2005, Overy 2005). Although few contemporary wars come close to matching the scale and intensity of these conflicts, the longevity of the idea of total war is evident in the continued use of the terminology of 'limited war' to refer, for instance, to the wars in Korea (1950–1953), the Falklands/Malvinas (1982), and the Gulf (1991).

At its heart, the idea of total war revolved around the notions of escalation and participation (McInnes 2002). Fears of escalation derived from the concern that once started, warfare was difficult if not impossible to control. This meant that wars were likely to increase in scale (both in terms of geographic spread and casualties) as well as intensity, thus eroding the various constraints on the conduct of war. Participation referred to the growing involvement of citizens in warfare, both as combatants willing to fight and die for their nation, and as workers willing to make important sacrifices to fuel the war effort at home. The image of national participation in the war effort was epitomized by the *levée en masse* decreed by France's revolutionary government in August 1793.

Although these trends are evident in modern history, total war is usually understood as an ideal type, that is, a set of circumstances which reality can approach but never reach. In practice, limits have always been placed or imposed on warfare. For example, some available weapons have not been deployed when they might have been, such as the US decision not to use nuclear weapons in the Korean War. Why some available weapons are not used is also a source of debate. For some analysts, the limited use of poison gas during the Second World War reflected the power that normative restraints have over the belligerents. Others argue that the non-use of poison gas is better explained by a pragmatic concern about its inconsistent and unpredictable effects. Another sense in which war is always less than total is that no belligerent has been able to commit the entirety of their resources to a war effort. Even during the Second World War, 'the major combatants mobilized between a half and two-thirds of their industrial work-force, and devoted up to three-quarters of their national product to waging war' (Overy 2005: 154). Nevertheless, some societies have come even closer to experiencing total war. For the North Vietnamese, for instance, war has often felt 'total'.

Given these practical limitations, why has the idea of total war occupied such an important place in the collective psyche of analysts and practitioners alike? One recent study has suggested that several tendencies encouraged the growing 'totality' of warfare between 1861 and 1945 (Chickering *et al.* 2005). These tendencies were arguably at their most intense from 1914 to 1945. First, technological and industrial advances during this period permitted the methods of warfare to become more destructive, thus facilitating the slaughter of people quickly and on a consistent basis. Second, governments were increasingly able to mobilize national resources (both through state institutions and the energies of private or semi-private actors) and harness them to the war effort. A third tendency was the expanding scope of war aims. In particular, as Imlay (2007: 554) has summarized, 'Limited goals such as territorial gains or economic advantage, were replaced by the determination to achieve outright victory, defined not simply as the defeat of an enemy's armed forces, but also more ambitiously as the replacement of its political regime, which often entailed a period of post-war occupation.' Fourth, the study noted war's increasingly global scope, as more and more states across the world's continents were drawn into conflicts originating in European politics.

Finally, these tendencies combined to blur the distinction between the civilian and military spheres; a key characteristic of 'total wars'. This had several effects, not least the fact that as ordinary citizens back home became more deeply involved in fuelling the war effort, it was not long before they became the targets of deliberate and large-scale violence. During the Second World War, for example, large-scale atrocities were committed by the Japanese military against Chinese civilians, on the Eastern Front in fighting between the Germans and Soviets, and with the atomic bombs and carpet bombing meted out upon Japanese cities. The temptation to target civilians was facilitated by advances in military technology which ultimately made possible the strategic bombing of cities such as Dresden, Coventry and Osaka during that war. As a result, the Second World War became the first conflict since Europe's Thirty Years' War where civilian deaths outnumbered military deaths (Imlay 2007: 556). In recent years Western states have attempted to re-solidify the distinction between civilian and military spheres (discussed below).

While the idea of total war has been a pervasive feature of the literature analysing warfare it is arguably a confusing and often unhelpful concept. Since real wars can never be 'total,' debating how closely they approximate this ideal – which wars were more total than others? – makes little grammatical sense; something is total or it is not. Hence this mode of thinking can obscure more than it clarifies. Instead, a more useful approach to studying real wars is to analyse the varying degrees of 'intensity' of warfare across various indicators such as the efforts/resources expended and the costs/losses incurred during war (Imlay 2007: 566–7).

### The 'new wars' debate

A second way of thinking about how warfare might be changing involves the argument that, especially since 1945, globalization has given rise to a distinctive form of violent conflict commonly labelled 'new wars' (Kaldor 1997, 1999, 2007b, Munkler 2004, Box 13.4). According to Kaldor (1999), in new wars the traditional distinctions between war (violence between states or organized political groups for political motives), organized crime (violence by private associations, usually for financial gain), and large-scale violations of human rights (violence by states or private groups against individuals, mainly civilians) has become increasingly blurred.

These new wars are distinct from 'old wars' in terms of their goals, methods and systems of finance, all of which reflect the ongoing erosion of the state's monopoly of legitimate organized violence (Kaldor 1999). The goals of combatants can be understood in the context of a struggle between cosmopolitan and exclusivist identity groups. The latter are understood to be seeking control of a particular territory by ethnically cleansing everybody of a different identity group or those people who espouse cosmopolitan political opinions. In terms of methods, Kaldor suggests new wars are fought through a novel 'mode of warfare' that draws on both guerrilla techniques and counterinsurgency. Yet this mode of warfare is distinctive inasmuch as decisive engagements are avoided and territory is controlled through political manipulation of a population by sowing 'fear and hatred' rather than winning 'hearts and minds'. It is thus not surprising that paramilitaries and groups of hired thugs are a common feature of these war zones as they can spread fear and hatred among the civilian population more effectively than professional armed forces (see Mueller 2000). This perspective might help explain the rise in one-sided massacres of civilians identified above. Bands of paramilitary forces are also useful because it can be difficult to trace back responsibility for their actions to political leaders. The final characteristic of Kaldor's new wars is that they are financed through a globalized war economy that is decentralized, increasingly transnational and in which the fighting units are often self-funding through plunder, the black-market or external assistance (see also Duffield 2001: ch. 6).

Wars that reflect these characteristics are often very difficult to bring to a decisive end. As a result, Kaldor suggests that the resolution of these new wars lies with the reconstruction of legitimate (that is cosmopolitan) political communities that instil trust in public authorities, restore their control of organized violence, and re-establish the rule of law. In this context, the role of concerned outsiders should be to provide what she calls 'cosmopolitan law enforcement' in the form of robust peace operations involving a combination of military, police and civilian personnel.

## BOX 13.4 COMMON HYPOTHESES IN THE 'NEW WARS' LITERATURE

*Hypothesis 1*: An essential characteristic of 'new wars' is the progressive erosion of the state's monopoly on the use of force. Consequently, traditional distinctions between combatants and civilians become increasingly blurred.

*Hypothesis 2*: 'New wars' are driven by economic aspirations with political or ideological motivations playing only a minor role. This political economy of 'new wars' reinforces and perpetuates the violence.

*Hypothesis 3*: 'New wars' are characterized by asymmetry involving the constellation of (a) actors, (b) military capabilities, (c) the methods of warfare and (d) the politics of war.

*Hypothesis 4*: 'New wars' are driven by exclusive conceptions of identity, which are instrumentalized for the purpose of seizing political power. These forms of 'identity politics' are unfolding in the context of the erosion of state structures and the insecurities of globalization.

*Hypothesis 5*: The new forms of international terrorism represent a modern variant of guerrilla warfare but unlike traditional guerrilla warfare, this new kind of terrorism poses a strategic challenge to Western societies.

(Source: Mello 2010)

Elements of Kaldor's arguments have been contested. First, many of the trends she identifies are not 'new' (see Kalyvas 2001, Shaw 2001, Berdal 2003, Newman 2004). Atrocities against civilians, for example, have been a feature of all wars and there is little evidence that suggests a temporal, qualitative shift in the use of atrocity across the twentieth century. A second set of criticisms has challenged Kaldor's view of globalization as a novel set of processes that has altered the nature of warfare after 1945. In contrast, Tarak Barkawi (2006) has argued that globalization is not the recent phenomenon that Kaldor suggests. Rather, globalization is a much older process that is essentially about circulation, that is, the processes through which people and places become interconnected. War, Barkawi observes, has been a historically pervasive and significant form of interconnection between societies and in this sense warfare has been a globalizing force for a long, long time (see Box 13.5). Understood in this manner, globalization is not a process separate from war which acts to change the nature of warfare in the way suggested by Kaldor. Instead, war has been intimately implicated in the globalization of world politics for thousands of years.

### The contemporary Western way of war

A third way of thinking about the changing patterns of warfare has focused on the ways in which Western states prefer to use military force through an analysis of the campaigns in Kosovo (1999), Afghanistan (2001), Iraq (2003), Libya (2011) and elsewhere. For some analysts, these campaigns show that in the contemporary Western world warfare has become akin to a spectator

---

## BOX 13.5  TARAK BARKAWI ON GLOBALIZATION AND WAR

'In and through war, people on both sides come to intensified awareness of one another, reconstruct images of self and other, initiate and react to each other's moves. To be at war is to be interconnected with the enemy. Such connections involve social processes and transformations that should be understood under the rubric of globalization. . . . From a war and society perspective, war can be seen as an occasion for interconnection, as a form of circulation between combatant parties. In and through war, societies are transformed, while at the same time societies shape the nature of war.'

'Militaries and war are also sites of cultural mixing and hybridity. Military travelling cultures expose soldiers to the foreign and lead them to reassess their ideas about home. Soldiers returning from abroad transmit new ideas and practice to their native lands. . . .[N]o matter how globalization is understood – as economic globalization, as transregional interconnectedness, or as consciousness of the global – war and the military play far more important roles than extant studies of globalization indicate. . . .[W]hat is needed is an assessment of the ways in which war is centrally implicated in the processes of globalization.'

(Source: Barkawi 2006: xiii, 169–172)

sport. First employed by Michael Mann, this metaphor was used to argue that:

> 'limited conventional wars involving client states aided by 'our' professional advisers and small expeditionary forces in 'our backyards,' do not mobilize nations as players but as *spectators* . . . wars like the Falklands and the Grenadan invasion are not qualitatively different from the Olympic Games. Because life-and-death are involved, the emotions stirred up are deeper and stronger. But they are not emotions backed up by committing personal resources. They do not involve real or potential sacrifice, except by professional troops'.
>
> Michael Mann (1988: 184–185)

Colin McInnes (2002) developed the idea further to argue that in contrast to the dynamic of escalation that provided the backdrop for fears of total warfare, contemporary wars waged by Western states have been localized in both their conduct and impact. This was because (1) there was no global conflict into which they can be subsumed (unlike the Cold War with its ideas of containment and expansionism); (2) Western definitions of the enemy have changed from the opposing state and its citizens to a narrower concern to change a particular regime or leader; and (3) with civilians no longer seen as legitimate targets there has been an effort to minimize 'collateral damage'. Since McInnes wrote his book, a debate has developed over the extent to which the US-led 'global war on terror' has indeed replaced the Cold War as a global conflict into which local conflicts are increasingly connected (see Freedman 2001/02, Barkawi 2004).

The other key contrast is that the West's contemporary wars don't involve high levels of societal participation but are instead fought by a small number of its professional representatives i.e. the armed forces and private contractors. As a consequence, a relatively small number of casualties can have dramatic political repercussions, even for a military superpower like the United States. In Somalia, for example, the 18 US soldiers killed in a fire-fight in Mogadishu in October 1993 were enough to induce a strategic retreat from the country by Washington and its allies. Less than two weeks later, in Haiti, just the sight of paramilitary thugs on the Port-au-Prince dockside was enough to trigger the USS Harlan County's retreat. This low tolerance of casualties is related to the fact that the wars waged by Western states in places like Bosnia, Somalia, Kosovo, Sierra Leone and Libya have been wars of choice to help achieve liberal policy objectives rather than wars of survival. When core national security interests are perceived to be on the line, as in Afghanistan or Iraq, tolerance of casualties has been much higher.

In this context, McInnes identified several key characteristics of spectator-sport wars. First, they are expeditionary – based on the localization of the conflicts concerned and a desire to fight away from the Western homeland. Second, the 'enemy' is narrowly defined as the leadership/regime of the target state rather than the whole of the enemy state's society. In a radical departure from past practice, even the enemy's military forces are no longer always a target for destruction per se and engagement with the main body of the enemy's military is no longer necessary or desirable. A third characteristic of spectator-sport wars is the desire to minimize collateral damage because only small elements of the enemy society are identified as legitimate targets. Finally, force protection, that is, the need to minimize risks to Western forces, is a significant priority. The intention is to avoid both the 'body bag' syndrome, which might damage domestic support for the war, and to protect the West's investment in its military professionals.

In pursuing these wars, Western states have emphasized the importance of airpower. Airpower is easy to deploy compared to land and sea forces; it allows quick and direct access to enemy leadership; it can be very accurate; the West enjoys a massive comparative advantage in this branch of warfare; and airpower can attack the enemy's centre of gravity directly without engaging the mass of enemy forces. In practice, however, there are significant limitations to thinking of airpower as an ideal instrument to conduct 'humane' and 'risk-free' war (see Pape 1996, McInnes 2001). First, while the separation of combatants and civilians might sound easy in theory it is often difficult in practice. Second, targeting errors, operational mistakes and technical malfunctions produce civilian deaths. Third, many 'strategically' significant installations are part of the civilian economy. Fourth, even 'surgical' strikes on cities terrorize civilians because of the constant fear of errors. Finally, the protection afforded to pilots by flying at high altitude is offset in terms of efficiency by the presence of such awkward phenomena as clouds!

Of course, the spectator-sport approach is only applicable to a small number of states and hence is not very useful for understanding the dynamics of warfare in the rest of the world. Nevertheless, it highlights some important trends in official Western thinking and therefore provides some important clues for understanding how the West wants to fight, and how its enemies will try and fight against it.

## Conclusion

Although the Clausewitzean, or political, philosophy of war has traditionally held sway in much of the security studies literature, warfare can be conceived in different ways. And in several respects, other ways of thinking about (and practising) war are gaining in prominence. On the positive side, the number of state-based armed conflicts has declined from a peak in the early post-Cold War period. The likelihood of interstate wars and wars between the great powers has also receded. On the other hand, recent data collection has revealed a large number of non-state armed conflicts which were previously missing from the discipline's databases and which remind us that warfare is not always connected to the interstate system. War certainly brings many dangers – from the deliberate targeting of civilians to the potential for nuclear Armageddon – but as a socially generative process it also serves a variety of functions which have a huge but often under-acknowledged impact on contemporary politics and society. Understanding the strategies and tactics of war, but also its broader sociology, should therefore remain near the centre of the agenda for contemporary security studies.

## Further reading

Carl von Clausewitz, *On War*. Edited and translated by Michael Howard and Peter Paret. (Princeton University Press, 1976). The seminal discussion of the political philosophy of war.

Charles Townshend (ed.), *The Oxford History of Modern War* (Oxford University Press, new edition, 2005). This book provides a useful historical discussion of the evolution and contemporary elements of modern warfare.

Mary Kaldor, *New and Old Wars: Organized Violence in a Global Era* (Polity, 2nd edition, 2006). An important statement of the argument that the processes of globalization have fundamentally changed the nature of some armed conflicts.

Tarak Barkawi, *Globalization and War* (Rowman and Littlefield, 2006). An excellent discussion of the relationship between these two crucial concepts in security studies.

Rupert Smith, *The Utility of Force: The Art of War in the Modern World* (Allen Lane, 2005). A sophisticated attempt to answer when, why and how to use military force in contemporary world politics by one of Britain's most experienced military commanders.

Hew Strachan and Sybille Schiepers (eds.), *The Changing Character of War* (Oxford University Press, 2011). An overview of the field produced as part of Oxford University's Changing Character of War research programme.

# Coercion

Lawrence Freedman and Srinath Raghavan

## Abstract

In this chapter, students will learn about coercion as a distinctive type of strategy, in which the intention is to use threats to put pressure on another actor to do something against their wishes (compellence) or not to do something they had planned to do (deterrence). The chapter considers the different forms coercion can take in terms of the ambition of the objective, the methods used (denial versus punishment) and the capacity of the target for counter-coercion. It also analyses how perceptions of an actor's strategic environment are formed and the extent to which these perceptions are susceptible to targeted threats as part of another's coercive strategy.

## Introduction

Coercion or the use of threats to influence another's conduct is a ubiquitous phenomenon in social and political intercourse. Activities as diverse as child-rearing, controlling crime and nuclear strategy involve an element of coercion. This chapter considers coercion as a distinctive type of strategy, in which the intention is to use threat to pressurize another actor to do something against their wishes, or not to do something that they intended to. The chapter will consider the different forms coercion can take in terms of the objective being pursued, the methods used, and the capacity of the target for counter-coercion. It will also consider how strategies of coercion could influence the relationship between the protagonists from a long-term perspective.

## Strategy

The concept of strategy as used in this chapter is closely related to the concept of power, understood as the ability to produce intended effects. Power is often considered merely as capacity, usually based on military or economic strength. But, confronted with certain challenges or in the pursuit of some objectives, much of this capacity may be useless. It takes strategy to unleash the power inherent in this capacity and to direct it towards specific purposes. Strategy is thus the creative element in any exercise of power.

Strategy is about choice. It depends on the ability to understand situations and to appreciate the dangers and opportunities they contain. This in turn calls for an understanding of the choices available to others and of how this might frustrate or enable one's own choices. The essence of strategy therefore is the interdependence of choice.

Strategies can be understood as falling under three broad categories along a spectrum. A *consensual* strategy involves the adjustment of strategic choices with others without the threat or use of force. By contrast, a *controlling* strategy involves the use of force to restrict another's strategic choice, for example by defending disputed territory against any attempted seizure. A *coercive* strategy (or strategic coercion) involves deliberate and purposive use of overt threats of force to influence another's strategic choices.

Consider an example of the longstanding boundary dispute between India and China. In the late 1950s, the two countries began negotiating using different propositions to find a mutually acceptable solution. In other words, they adopted a consensual strategy. By the end of 1960, it was clear that the negotiations had failed. China began sending armed patrols into disputed areas to back its claims with force, and to convince India to accept its earlier proposal. Here, the Chinese were adopting a coercive strategy. When India refused to comply and responded by sending its own armed patrols into the disputed areas, China launched a war in October 1962 which resulted in it seizing control of the disputed areas. In so doing, China had adopted a controlling strategy.

Some important aspects of strategic coercion might be noted. Central to the concept is the notion of the target as a voluntary agent. It is presumed that the opponent will retain a capacity to make critical choices throughout the course of a conflict. Whether a threat succeeds in influencing the target's strategic choices will depend on the target's perception of the threat and on the other factors that go into its decision calculus. Furthermore, the threat must be both deliberate and purposive: it must be issued intentionally, and with some aim. *B* may feel threatened by *A*, although *A* may not be interested in threatening *B*. This cannot be considered a case of strategic coercion. Lastly, although coercion is defined in terms of threats of force, it does not preclude the actual use of force, if only to reinforce the threats.

## Deterrence and compellence

Thus defined, strategic coercion can be divided into two sub-categories in terms of the objective. Deterrence is the use of threats to dissuade an adversary from initiating an undesirable act. Strategies geared to coercing an adversary to do something or to stop doing something have been described as compellence or coercive diplomacy (Schelling 1966, George and Simons 1994).

Deterrence and compellence differ on several counts: initiative, timescale, and the nature of demands. Deterrence involves making clear what the coercer considers undesirable and then waiting, leaving the overt act to the adversary. The coercer would need to act only if the adversary makes the forbidden move. Compellence, on the other hand, involves initiating an action that stops or becomes harmless, only if the target responds. Compellence, then, might require the coercer to punish until the target acts, unlike deterrence, which requires administering punishment only if the adversary carries out the undesirable act.

Deterrence has no necessary time limit. The threat might be carried out whenever the adversary acts undesirably. Indeed, the coercer would prefer to wait forever. Compellence, however, requires a clear deadline. In fact, if the adversary is not given a specific time limit by when to change his behaviour, the threat could become irrelevant.

Deterrent threats are usually clear because they aim at preserving the existing situation, which can be observed with a reasonable degree of confidence. Compellent threats, by contrast, 'tend to communicate only the general direction of compliance, and are less likely to be self-limiting, less likely to communicate in the very design of the threat just what, or how much, is demanded' (Schelling 1966: 73). A corollary to this is the role of assurances. Every coercive threat carries with it an implicit assurance that if the adversary behaves as desired, the threat will not be implemented. Since the demands of a compellent threat are not as evident as those of a deterrent threat, the former might need to be accompanied by overt assurances. In addition, with deterrence compliance is literally a non-event; it does not require any special rationalization by the target. With compellence, however, compliance will be blatant, and will carry with it the added reputational significance of humiliation. Compellence might, therefore, be more difficult than deterrence.

Notwithstanding these differences, the distinction between deterrence and compellence is not water-tight. The two might merge when *B* starts doing something that *A* has urged it not to do in the first place and the situation has to be retrieved. Another example might be a conflict in which both sides can hurt each other, but neither can forcibly accomplish its purpose. In such a situation what is compellent and deterrent can shift for both sides over time. Once engagement has begun, the difference between the two, like the difference between defence and offence, may disappear. Consider the Cuban Missile Crisis of 1962. The United States was at once warning the Soviet Union to stop constructing missile sites in Cuba (compellence) and not to pass ships carrying any more missiles through the American blockade (deterrence). When it was deciding what steps to take, Moscow in turn warned Washington that if its threats were implemented then terrible consequences would ensue. This was therefore a case of each side trying to coerce the other, with deterrence and compellence underway at the same time.

## Designing coercive strategies

The central challenge with both deterrent and compellent strategies is to find ways of ensuring that the opponent receives the threat, relates it to his proposed course of action, and decides as a result to change his behaviour. But what the coercer intends to convey might not be what the target receives. This problem would be minimized if it could be assumed that the adversary would act according to the dictates of rationally determined self-interest. This usually turns out to be difficult, if only because different actors have different views about what constitutes rational behaviour. For deterrence to work, *A* must persuade *B* to act to serve the interest of them both, but according to *B*'s conception of rationality. Even if both sides share the same framework of rationality, deterrence might still fail because *B* may misinterpret the signals sent by *A* or, even if he understands them correctly, he might be inclined to believe that *A* will not implement his threat. There are examples of misunderstanding and confusion leading either to a failure to deter someone who needs deterring, or else provoke someone who was inclined to be cautious, thereby aggravating a crisis.

The construction of effective military threats depends on two factors. First, because military signals are notoriously ambiguous, they need to be supplemented by some more direct forms of communication to ensure that the opponent receives the message being sent without distortion. The problems of interpretation grow in the psychological intensity of the crisis to the point where even interpreting straightforward communications can become problematic. In the later stages of the Cuban Missile Crisis, for instance, there was a moment when the United States received two communications from Moscow in quick succession, the second more hawkish. President Kennedy had to judge what this confusing development revealed about the real objectives of his Soviet counterpart, Nikita Khrushchev, and the pressures that were working on him. At the same time, he had also to decide whether the attack on an American U2 aircraft that same day was a separate incident or part of a new stage in the Soviet Union's strategy.

Second, the coercer's threats must be credible. This, at one level, will depend on the costs associated with implementing them, which might simply reflect the amount of resource and effort entailed. But, more seriously, it may also reflect the ability of the target to respond and impose costs on the coercer. The problem of credibility was central to nuclear deterrence during the Cold War. Since both sides possessed nuclear capabilities, the possibility of retaliation could never be eliminated. In effect, the basis of deterrence was not so much a credible threat to use decisive force if the opponent overstepped some mark, but the possibility that some force might be used, to which a response was all but inevitable, so setting in motion an inexorable process of escalation to nuclear war.

Thus when threats are no more than hints and are couched in vague terms, a coercive strategy might become feeble and unconvincing. Then again, even if threats are well constructed and are perfectly understood, they might be only one part of the target's decision calculus. His response will have to factor in all the pressure to which he is susceptible. The threat itself will be one variable among many and not necessarily the most important.

In consequence, proving that strategic coercion works is challenging, especially with deterrent strategies. The failure of deterrence is evident. B has been told not to engage in a particular action if he wishes to avoid dire consequences, but he goes ahead with it. But when deterrence succeeds, all that is known is that B did not take the proscribed step. This could well be because B never intended to do it in first instance, or was only suggesting he might for bargaining purposes. If he had the intention and then refrained, this could be because of a whole range of factors, both external and internal. Apart from threats of punishment, these might include the probability of being able to accomplish the act, the resources required, the opportunity costs, domestic opposition, problems of securing support from allies and other important but uncommitted actors, and uncertainties over the benefits.

Terrorism used by non-state actors is almost by default a coercive strategy (see Chapter 15 this volume). Consensual strategies are ruled out by groups which resort to terrorism. Similarly, their adoption of terrorism is driven by an understanding that controlling strategies are out of their reach. Radical and insurgent groups pitted against the state can seldom hope to take on the latter – at least in the short-run – by a decisive contest of force, in which the enemy is unequivocally defeated. Put differently, the gap between the ends that they pursue (overthrow of the state, for instance) and the means at their disposal is rather wide. This is why terrorism is usually described as the strategy of the weak.

Alfred Hitchcock, the master of thriller movies, observed that: 'There is no terror in a bang, only in the anticipation of it'. As coercion, strategic terror does not seek to control the target but rather to stimulate changes in the target's attitudes and behaviour. It involves the creation of a psychological effect – terror – with a view to creating a political effect that will be manifest in changes in the target's strategy. There is an interesting question as to whether retributive action, intended to do no more than punish those deemed responsible for some tragedy or humiliation, can be considered successful as soon as death and destruction have been caused. If there is no intention of affecting the target's behaviour then this is not strategic. If there is such an intention it will be coercive.

As a coercive strategy, terrorism can be deterrent as well as compellent. For instance, insurgent groups operating in Kashmir have resorted to terrorism in order to compel the Indian state to accept their demand for independence. But radical Islamist outfits such as the Indian Mujahideen have carried out terrorist attacks both to avenge the pogrom against Muslims in Gujarat in 2002 and to deter right-wing Hindu groups from perpetrating such violence against Muslims in the future.

Terrorism as a coercive strategy is difficult not only because of the gulf between means and ends. The problems associated with communicating threats, which were discussed above, tend to get magnified in the case of terrorism. Understanding the motives behind acts of terrorism requires making links between small individual actions and large political demands, with the offered explanations, often in the form of anonymous communiqués of uncertain provenance that are both bombastic and cryptic at the same time. Sometimes actions are not claimed at all, which creates further confusion in the minds of the target audience. The explosion of forms of media and social networking, often beyond the control of governments let alone individuals, has increased this problem of communicating the intended threat. It is now likely that any dramatic, violent deed, no matter how anonymous the perpetrators, will stimulate immense speculation and controversy around the identity of the perpetrators and their motives. The effect of the attack therefore depends on the perpetrator's ability to influence this commentary, which can be multimedia and global, cutting across geography and cultures, taking in politicians, the mainstream media and the internet.

## Punishment and denial

Coercive strategies could differ from one another not only in the objective (deterrence or compellence) but also in the methods used. Coercion is usually associated with the threat of punishment. The early use of the term deterrence in twentieth century strategic vocabulary, for instance in connection with air power, was close to the Latin root – *deterre* or to frighten from or away. The word has seemed most apposite when being used to convey the idea of scaring off a potential aggressor by using threats of consequential pain.

This definition, however, is restrictive in that it only touches upon one aspect of the cost/benefit calculation that the adversary must make (Snyder 1958). If he can pocket the gains without much difficulty, then he might be more willing to risk costs in retaliation. But if moving forward is going to be extremely difficult because of the obstacles erected directly in his path, then the costs of surmounting these – in the form of more troops, better equipment, greater logistical effort – will intermingle in his mind with costs resulting from the opponent's reprisal. These types of strategies have been called *denial*. In general we will consider these strategies in the following paragraphs in terms of denial. It should, however, be noted that in the case of a compellence strategy, which is more offensive, they could also be considered strategies of acquisition.

For purposes of deterrence a strategy of denial is potentially more reliable than a strategy of punishment because its quality can be measured in more physical terms and thus more confidently. Calculating the amount of military effort required to hold onto a piece of territory may not be an exact science, but is still more straightforward than an attempt to discern the effect of prospective punitive measures on an opponent's decision-making. Furthermore, it offers a greater hope of retrieving the situation if the opponent presses on regardless.

The focus on this issue in these terms has a lot to do with the association of deterrence with nuclear weapons, and the fact that the most important theorizing took place during the Cold War. At this time there did not seem to be much possibility of defending against nuclear weapons. Both passive and active defences were discussed. In practice, faced with a nuclear attack, passive or civil defences involved running for shelter or evacuation, and so were hardly passive. Active defences referred to the anti-aircraft or anti-ballistic missile systems designed to halt the enemy offensive before any targets were reached. Against numerous nuclear-tipped missiles these defences never really appeared credible; if only a few nuclear weapons out of the thousands in existence got through they would still cause catastrophic devastation. Which is why counter-threats appeared the best deterrent to a nuclear threat.

In the Cold War debate, coercion by denial developed many proponents as a means of reducing reliance on nuclear threats. John Mearsheimer (1983) argued that conventional deterrence essentially depended on the coercer's ability to convince the adversary that a blitzkrieg–type offensive (the one most likely to be adopted by Warsaw Pact forces and the one most likely to avoid a draining stalemate) would be foiled. After the Cold War, Robert Pape (1996) picked up this debate on denial versus punishment arguing that the most effective coercive strategies would be directed against the benefit side of the opponent's cost/benefit calculus. In this connection Pape described the purpose of coercion as obtaining concessions without having to pay the costs of a military victory. He further saw denial in terms of influencing the opponent's capacity to engage in battle while punishment was largely linked to the use of air power to impose civilian suffering. But, as he acknowledged, 'the distinction between coercion by denial and the pursuit of military victory is more ambiguous, for both present the target state with military failure'.

The difference between denial and war fighting can be understood in terms of control and coercion. War fighting aims at imposing control come what may, whereas denial poses a threat which makes the outcome of war fighting uncertain to impose control. Yet if denial has to be pursued to the bitter end then the conclusion is control. So long as denial falls short of asserting control over a situation, target has a choice about persisting, withdrawing or seeking some negotiated outcome; if a choice is posed to the target, then denial is a coercive strategy. With punishment, the target continues to retain choice even after the coercer inflicts some pain. In this sense, denial is closer to control than is punishment. Denial is evidently a better strategy than punishment: even if the target fails to be coerced, the coercer can proceed to impose control.

Viewing denial and punishment in this fashion clarifies yet another issue. There is no reason why we should consider punishment in terms of civilian damage alone: losses imposed on the target's armed forces can also constitute punishment as long as the target is not deprived of choice. The loss of the major part of one's army might have all sorts of dire consequences – related to internal as much as external threats. For instance, during the 1991 war in Kuwait, Saddam Hussein was anxious to protect his Republican Guard from being annihilated by the allies because of the role he saw it might have to play in the preservation of his regime against Kurdish and Shiite rebels.

In practice, denial and punishment may not necessarily lead to an altogether different use of force. This point is obscured by the excessive focus on nuclear deterrence in the strategic studies literature. The problems with preventing a successful nuclear strike made it possible to think of punishment that did not involve a prior battle. The enemy would not have to be overcome: the pain would follow soon after the decision to inflict it. But in a non-nuclear context, in order to damage an opponent's society or state, its armed forces must first be defeated in battle. The target will take steps to avoid hurt, and this can lead to a trial of strength not very distinct from a trial over the seizure of territory.

## Types of costs

To understand the relative efficacy of coercive strategies, let us consider the two types of costs with which the coercer might threaten his target: *resistance* costs and *compliance* costs. Resistance costs are those involved in defying the coercer's demands, i.e., the costs that the target will incur should the coercer implement its threat. Resistance costs have two components. First, the costs involved in trying to prevent the coercer from executing the threat; second, the pain imposed by the coercer's action. Much of the literature tends to equate resistance costs with the latter alone. This is a valid assumption when studying nuclear coercion, for the target cannot hope to resist a nuclear strike. But when examining non-nuclear coercion, we cannot overlook the costs attached to resisting the coercer's attempts to punish non-compliance. Even if the target succeeds in thwarting the coercer's efforts, it would have incurred some costs. The target, then, suffers even before the coercer fully implements its threat. If target fails to foil the coercer's efforts, it will have to incur the compliance costs. These are costs associated with forgoing benefits or accepting losses by acquiescing in the coercer's demands.

In military terms, the forms of the resistance are obvious: the destruction of civilian centres from the air first requires the penetration of enemy air defences; the imposition of a blockade at sea may require the confirmation of 'command of the sea' in a naval battle; territory may not be acquired until the defending army has been overwhelmed. These battles may not be once-and-for-all affairs, matters being settled after a single encounter. During the course of a campaign there may be many battles, which will allow the two sides to refine their assessments of their future prospects. The use of the term 'battle' does not refer only to classic encounters between armies to establish local supremacy, but any trial of strength. In fact, the same issues occur with non-military forms of pressure, such as trade boycotts. There are resistance costs in trying to circumvent economic sanctions, in setting up routes for smuggling or paying above market price for essential goods.

The resistance and compliance costs reflect the central calculation which is at the heart of coercion. Coercion can thus be understood as an attempt by *A* to present *B* with a choice between two types of costs: that of resisting *A*'s efforts to punish and incurring the subsequent pain that *A* threatens to cause, and that of complying with *A*'s demands. In the simplest version, coercion is likely to succeed if *B* is convinced that the resistance costs exceed the compliance costs. There are some compliance costs, such as loss of territory or economic privileges, that are tangible; others, such as honour are less so. Part of a target's calculation in resisting will be whether a weak performance in one encounter will result in future challenges because of a reputation for a lack of resistance.

The difference between denial and punishment can be understood in terms of these costs. Both threaten the target with resistance and compliance costs; the difference lies in linkage between the two sets of costs in each strategy. In denial, the target is presented with resistance and compliance costs *together*. The coercer threatens the target that if its resistance fails, compliance costs will automatically follow; for control will be imposed on the target leaving it with no choice. In punishment, the two sets of costs are uncoupled: even if resistance fails, the target still has the option of choosing whether or not to comply. As long as the coercer has not got what it wants, the target may have a way out. Viewed in this framework, it is the all the more clear why denial is preferable to punishment.

Two questions arise from the preceding discussion: If denial is so obviously better than punishment, why resort to the latter at all? And if denial is a feasible strategy, why not take control? In answering these, we must consider a third variable in the framework of costs – enforcement costs. As opposed to resistance and compliance costs that the coercer presents to the target, enforcement costs are those that the coercer has to bear. These are costs associated with overcoming the target's resistance and with incurring the pain or damage that the target is likely to inflict on the coercer. Enforcement costs are an integral part of the calculations involved in coercion. Coercion is a dynamic process: the target, too, will attempt to influence the coercer's cost calculus. We may call this counter-coercion. In framing a coercive strategy, the coercer will have to consider the enforcement costs, which will indicate the effort required to render the threat credible and to implement it if necessary. The target will invariably try to increase the coercer's enforcement costs. This could be done in many ways. The target may issue a deterrent threat to the coercer; it may strengthen its own defences; it may escalate militarily or invoke the support of a powerful patron to convince the coercer to back down. In most conflicts, mutual coercion, even somewhat one-sided, is much more likely than a wholly asymmetric relationship. Indeed, such an asymmetric relationship would imply scant freedom of manoeuvre for the target and hence control.

Enforcement costs play an important role in deciding which variant of coercion to employ. If enforcement costs were comparable, denial would be preferable to punishment. Yet because of the effort and costs involved in denial, punishment, at times, may seem a less costly and risky option. This, of course, was the basis of the original theory of strategic bombardment. It was assumed that mounting air raids would be much more straightforward in the threat, and much harder to resist, than launching ground invasion. This was also the calculation that led NATO to adopt a strategy of deterrence by punishment against the Warsaw Pact during the Cold War. Despite the obvious merits of denial, in that the threat would be more credible and carry far fewer risks of an escalation to a nuclear exchange, it was always undermined by the cost that was expected to be involved in building NATO's forces up to Warsaw Pact levels.

Even in situations where imposing control is a possibility, a strategy of denial may be preferred. For the coercer might reckon that the difference in enforcement costs between control and denial exceeds the difference in compliance benefits arising out of control and denial. For example, the coalition in 1991 assumed that while Iraqi forces might not put up a serious fight to hold on to Kuwait, they might be more committed to the defence of their own homeland. In such situations, it might be worth offering the opponent a deal on the basis that his alternative is still defeat and some form of conditional surrender will at least provide relief from the costs of resistance. This can be offered right up to the edge of victory – the opponent's choice is purely whether to continue to resist or to yield. This feature may be more present when the objective is more offensive, or acquisitive, than the more defensive objective associated with denial.

With denial the opponent only retains choice over whether or not to engage in battle; with punishment the choice remains even after the battle is finished, for the coercer still has not got direct access to what he is after. Put in this fashion, denial appears to be the least interesting form of coercion, because the choice is so circumscribed; and it becomes even less interesting the more irresistible the coercer appears. The interesting cases are those where either denial is not an option, or at least difficult, but there are other possibilities for imposing costs.

How do these costs affect each other and the outcome of coercion? In the simplest setting, coercion is likely to succeed when resistance costs exceed compliance costs. The latter are also related to enforcement costs. If compliance costs are low, i.e., if the target does not consider the magnitude of the coercer's demands to be high, then it might not be inclined to much resistance. In consequence, enforcement costs are likely to be proportionately low. This explains why deterrence may relatively be easier than compellence.

Conversely, if enforcement costs for the coercer are high then the value of the target's compliance should also be correspondingly high. This may seem obvious, but in practice cumulative enforcement costs over time might exceed the potential benefits arising from the target's compliance. This is evident in any counter-insurgency, where the actual costs, in resources if not always in lives, are likely to far exceed those of the insurgents, as has been evident in both Iraq and Afghanistan over the past decade. These are coercive to the extent that the aim is to persuade the insurgents to give up – there is unlikely to be the equivalent of a battlefield victory. In any situation where there might be a political settlement at some point which will depend on the perceived balance of forces, there will be an element of coercion to reach the optimum position. But coercion is unlikely to suffice. Inducements might also be need to be offered to the target. These might help reduce the target's determination to resist, which in turn could lead to a reduction in enforcement costs. Inducements could thus play an important role as supplements to coercive strategies. Alternatively, if enforcement costs seem unacceptably high, the coercer might have to settle for a less satisfactory outcome. Political objectives might need to be modified to take into account what military means can achieve.

Enforcement costs are also related to resistance costs. A threat will be credible only if resistance costs for the target exceed enforcement costs for the coercer. The calculation is complicated by the fact, evident in counter-insurgency, that the coercer and the target will not be evaluating their costs on the same scale. Their respective stakes in the contest will make a difference: for one side the interests involved may be limited and marginal, for the other the very conditions of existence might be at stake. What one side values the other might consider trivial. One side might be able to afford high expenditure which far exceeds the resources available to the other. These are the sorts of asymmetries that exist, and how well they are understood is what makes coercive strategies so complex in their design and implementation.

## Multiple audiences

Coercion does *not* refer to a type of strategic relationship between two sides, but only to one aspect. Most strategic relationships are rather complex and are unlikely to be governed by a single type of communication, however severe its implications. The fact that the Cold War involved a bipolar relationship gave an impression that the situation to be examined was stark and simple. There was, however, an inherent unreality in the presumption of a dyadic relationship involving only two actors. The circumstances in which threats were issued and received, even during the Cold War, were far more complex. To understand how coercion works in practice, we need to have a sense of how this political context impacts on the formulation and efficacy of strategic threats.

Contrary to the impression conveyed by formal theories of deterrence and compellence, threats are often issued to impress domestic audiences as much as the notional target. India's decision to resume nuclear testing in 1998 was widely understood as being aimed at keeping Pakistan in place. But it transpired that one of the motives was also to shore up the government's domestic position. Decision-makers will invariably be subject to such pressures, and in consequence coercive strategies might be fashioned to meet political as well as functional criteria, though these often tend to pull in different directions.

Similarly, international factors could be an important aspect of a coercive process. They could affect the coercer's assessment of the enforcement costs attached to a threat. On the one hand, these costs might be increased if there were a possibility of external powers supporting the target. The coercer might then be impelled to take steps to reassure these powers of its aims and intentions. On the other hand, the coercer's estimate of enforcement costs might be reduced by its expectation that external powers would keep the target in check. For instance, during the India–Pakistan crisis of 2001–2002, the expectation that the United States would help rein in Pakistan was an important factor in India's calculus. Furthermore, both the coercer and the target could try to use the external actors to convey a sense of urgency to the other or to enhance the credibility of their threats. They could also try to persuade the external actors to intercede with the target in order to achieve the desired outcome. This in turn might force the external actors to clarify their own interests at stake in the crisis.

In the case of non-state terrorism, the issue of audiences takes on a different dimension. Modern terrorism fits well with the anarchist tradition of 'propaganda of the deed'. The nineteenth-century Russian anarchists, such as Mikhail Bakunin, argued that in a repressive state, where words were censored, actions had to be eloquent. The well-placed bomb or assassin's bullet would demonstrate the vulnerability of the governing elite and give hope to the masses, awakening within them a sense of the contingency of the status quo and the revolutionary hope that it could all be quite different. Although the context has considerably changed, this idea continues to inspire contemporary radical and insurgent groups that resort to strategic terror. Acts of terrorism are not only aimed at coercing the target, but also at galvanizing their own bases of support, both existing and potential ones.

Amongst the organizations using terrorist tactics today, al-Qa'ida has most clearly understood the importance of shaping the people's understanding of the nature of the struggle, the stakes involved, the progress of operations and the eventual outcome. Osama Bin Laden's periodic press statements and video messages constantly updated and retold al-Qa'ida's version of the progress of the global jihad. In these messages, Bin Laden wove together the latest developments with the long-term trends, the tactical outcomes with the strategic objectives. It was his ability to speak to a globally dispersed audience that allowed the diffuse and loosely networked organization to continue its recruitment and operations after 2001, although eventually his inability to direct operations reduced his relevance as a strategic player.

## Reputations

Another complicating factor is the impact of one act of coercion for those that might follow. Compliance may be a form of humiliation and an acknowledgement of submission. This can have long-term consequences. From the coercer's standpoint, this might mean that a desire for a reputation for resolve may override the interests involved in a dispute. In other words, even if enforcement costs exceed compliance costs, it might be worth persisting in order to reduce the potential enforcement costs in any future attempt at coercion. Similarly, owing to concerns about reputation the target may remain defiant despite the costs threatened by the coercer. How one coerces now will have an impact on how much one might have to coerce in the future.

The most notorious statement of this view came from Thomas Schelling, who wrote that 'face' is 'one of the few things worth fighting over'. Although 'few parts of the world are intrinsically worth the risk of serious war by themselves, especially when taken slice by slice', he argued that 'defending them or running risks to protect them may preserve one's commitments to actions in other parts of the world at later times' (Schelling 1966: 124). The world, in this view, is closely interconnected. A state's behaviour during an encounter could influence the outcome of another encounter, as other states will scrutinize one's behaviour for signs of resolve or lack thereof. Thus, if a state retreated in one area of contention, it would acquire a reputation for weakness or for lacking resolve. This in turn would lead its adversaries to doubt the credibility of its threats in other areas of contention, so rendering the state incapable of preserving its commitments by using coercive strategies.

The risk involved in this line of argument lay in creating a vital interest where none truly existed or in persisting with a flawed course despite mounting costs. Not only was this idea undermined by what appeared to be its consequences in Vietnam, but empirical analysis seemed to lend it little support. Paul Huth (1988), for instance, found no evidence to suggest that losing a war against one country led another to assume a lack of resolve against them. Reputation, however, is intangible, and difficult to measure and identify. It provides an intuitive test of the quality of a policy rather than a specific goal itself. The evidence, moreover, suggests that the issue of reputation might have a greater salience in protracted regional rivalries involving the same pair of adversaries (Shimshoni 1988, Lieberman 1995).

## Long-term impact

In principle, every act of foreign policy has some significance for the creation of expectations of future performance. Coercion might influence the development of the power relationship between the protagonists. The party that emerges worse off from a crisis might want to ensure that it would fare better in any future confrontation. It could do so either by augmenting its own military capabilities or by allying itself with a powerful third-party. At least in theory, then, successful coercion could drive the target to fortify itself, and so set the stage for a failure in the future.

Furthermore, acts of coercion might have a wider impact on the management of conflict between the adversaries. Even if they do not generate a 'reputation' for the coercer, they might convince the target that certain actions are best avoided owing to the likely reaction of the coercer. Over time, this perception might become ingrained: the target might desist from certain courses despite the absence of an ever-present threat from the adversary. Land may be coveted but it is not grabbed; the unacceptable practices of foreign governments are denounced but they are left untouched; inconveniences, disruptions, outrages are tolerated; punches are pulled. All of these might result from the sensible application of what should always be the first principle of strategy: anticipate the probable responses of the opponent. This sort of deterrence is far more regular than the sort that academics and policy-makers tend to focus on, when a determined effort is made to dissuade another party from taking action one judges harmful to one's interests. Only on occasion is it necessary to resort to the explicit threats related to specific prospective acts that we commonly associate with a deterrent strategy. This perspective is critical to any understanding of how deterrence might work as a political strategy. We can call this *internalized* deterrence.

An actor may be deterred even if there is no direct interaction with the one doing the deterring. But in terms of strategy this is less important than those cases where there is such an interaction. From a longer-term perspective, the real challenge for strategic coercion is to create internalized deterrence in its targets.

## Conclusion

The study of coercion is concerned with the role of threats in international politics. The distinguishing feature of coercion is that the target always retains choice, but must weigh the choices between the cost of compliance and non-compliance. Nonetheless, because this is a bargaining situation the target might in turn be able to threaten the coercer. The negotiation in each instance will essentially be over what can be deemed acceptable compliance and over the costs of enforcement of, or resistance to, the coercer's will. In practice, however, strategic threats may be issued by *A* for a variety of reasons, not all connected with the expected behaviour of *B*; multiple audiences are being addressed at all times. The political context, both domestic and international, will impact the construction of coercive strategies, and their outcome. Furthermore, every act of coercion feeds into the set of assumptions and expectations about the behaviour of others, which conditions all power relationships in international politics. The study of coercion, therefore, is not simply about the design of effective threats. It must also consider how perceptions of a state's strategic environment are formed, and how susceptible these are to manipulation by another's coercive strategy.

## Further reading

Lawrence Freedman, *Deterrence* (Polity, 2004) provides a succinct overview of the field.

Lawrence Freedman (ed.), *Strategic Coercion: Concepts and Cases* (Oxford University Press, 1998) contains a number of studies seeking to apply the concept to a number of regional cases.

The two classic books on strategic coercion are the collection of case studies edited by Alexander George and William Simons (eds.), *The Limits of Coercive Diplomacy*, 2nd edition (Westview Press, 1994), which is largely concerned with the problems of US crisis management, and the more theoretical work by Thomas C. Schelling, *Arms and Influence* (Yale University Press, 1966).

Daniel Byman and Matthew Waxman, *The Dynamics of Coercion and the Limits of Military Might* (Cambridge University Press, 2002) provides a more contemporary analysis of the issues, although again largely from a US perspective.

An excellent discussion of the range of issues concerned with deterrence is found in Patrick M. Morgan, *Deterrence Now* (Cambridge University Press, 2003).

# Terrorism

Paul Rogers

## Abstract

In this chapter, students will learn about the definitional debates surrounding the concept of terrorism and different types of terrorism, notably the difference between state terrorism and sub-state terrorism or terrorism from below. The chapter then analyses trends in state terrorism and sub-state terrorism in the context of other more substantive threats to security. It then examines the main responses to sub-state terrorism and assesses the response to the 9/11 attacks, the state of the 'global war on terror' after ten years and the likelihood of a reconsideration of the nature of the response.

## Introduction

The 9/11 attacks in New York and Washington in 2001 brought the issue of terrorism to the forefront of Western security thinking and resulted in the declaration of a 'global war on terror' by the George W. Bush administration. Because of the suddenness of the attacks, the large numbers of people killed (*c*.3,000) and the targeting of two hugely important symbols of American life, the World Trade Center and the Pentagon, the reaction was both vigorous and extended, leading to the termination of regimes in Afghanistan and Iraq.

To some extent this concentration on the incidents and on retaliating against the al-Qa'ida movement has resulted in a concern with terrorism that may not be justified, given the many other problems of human and state security affecting the world. It therefore makes sense to seek a broader assessment of the phenomenon of terrorism, bearing in mind that it can be undertaken by states against their own populations as much as by sub-state actors, even if the latter forms of terrorism currently dominate the security agenda.

## Terrorism in perspective

Excluding the very high levels of non-combatant casualties in Iraq since 2003, terrorist activities conducted by sub-state actors across the world result in the deaths of, at most, a few thousand people each year. While this is appalling for the victims and for their families and friends, it does mean that terrorism is one of the minor causes of human suffering in the world. Far more significant are the problems arising from poverty and underdevelopment, from natural disasters, from wars, from crime and even from automobile accidents. Even so, the 9/11 attacks have resulted in an extraordinary concentration on a particular form of transnational political violence, focusing mainly on the al-Qa'ida movement and associated Islamic jihadist groups.

The 9/11 attacks killed nearly 3,000 people in just one day, but at least that number of children die every day across the global South from avoidable intestinal diseases including diarrhoea and dysentery, brought on mainly by impure water supplies. In Iraq in the closing months of 2006, the monthly death toll of civilians in the insurgency and in sectarian violence was very nearly the same as the losses in the 9/11 attacks. In Rwanda in the mid-1990s, close to a million people died in genocidal attacks, and continuing conflicts in the Great Lakes region of Africa have since killed even more people. In the mid-1970s, it was estimated that over 400 million people suffered from malnutrition, but today this has risen to at least 700 million. Across the world, more than two billion people survive on the equivalent of two US dollars a day or less. The diseases of poverty are mostly avoidable yet kill millions of people each year (see Chapter 20 this volume).

In spite of this, the global war on terror was elevated in the early 2000s into the principal challenge to security. Two regimes were terminated, partly on claims of sponsoring terrorism, the US military budget rose to the level of the peak years of the Cold War and the term 'war on terror' was for some years transformed into the 'long war against Islamofascism'. In its most extreme representation in some influential US political circles, this war was understood as the 'Fourth World War,' and was just as much a matter of the survival of civilization as were the previous world wars, including the 'Third World War' against the Soviet Union.

Any dispassionate analysis would question the centrality of the war on terror, at least in terms of overall human well-being, but it is necessary to acknowledge this representation given its potency and centrality in international security thinking after 2001. There are three elements that together offer some degree of explanation for this concentration. One is that the 9/11 attacks were deeply shocking to the United States in that a small group armed only with parcel knives could use civil aircraft as flying bombs to destroy a world-class financial centre and attack the headquarters of the US military. Moreover, the attacks came as a complete surprise to most people and their effects were witnessed live on television.

The second element that helps explain the response is that the Bush administration in mid-2001 was beginning to pursue its vision of a New American Century with some success. Unilateral stances on some key issues were being developed and there seemed every prospect that the rest of the world would come to accept American leadership as being essential for international security – a 'benign imperium' was said to be no bad thing (Krauthammer 2001). Finally, the almost inevitable focus of state-centred security, given the status of the United States as the world's sole military superpower, was that it was essential to regain control by destroying a dangerous sub-state movement and any state sponsors, not least because the al-Qa'ida movement and its presumed sponsors were based in the Middle East and South West Asia. This was a region of long-term security interest to the United States because of the critical importance of its energy resources and the close American ties to the state of Israel.

The end result of these factors is a situation that, in the absence of fundamental changes in policy, is likely to remain a major feature of international security for some years to come. Yet terrorism is still a minor issue in terms of global human security, and an aim of this short contribution is to provide a wider perspective. This will involve a brief examination of definitions of terrorism, an analysis of state and sub-state terrorism, an overview of the main forms of terrorism in recent years and a discussion of the main responses to terrorism leading to a review of the counter-terrorism methods used specifically in response to 9/11.

## Definitions

A succinct definition of terrorism is 'the threat of violence and the use of fear to coerce, persuade, and gain public attention' (NACCJSG 1976). A more complete definition, which brings in a political dimension and thereby excludes the use of terror in ordinary criminal activities such as protection rackets, is that:

> Political terrorism is the use, or threat of use, of violence by an individual or a group, whether acting for or in opposition to established authority, when such action is designed to create extreme anxiety and/or fear-inducing effects in a target group larger than the immediate victims with the purpose of coercing that group into acceding to the political demands of the perpetrators.
>
> (Wardlaw 1982: 16)

A definition used by the US government is 'premeditated, politically motivated violence perpetrated against non-combatant targets by subnational groups or clandestine agents, usually intended to influence an audience' (US Department of State 2001: 13).

Both of the latter definitions are concerned with the intention to have an effect on an audience that is larger than the group actually targeted. It follows that terrorism works through fear, but it is also the case that acts of terror may have distinct political aims rather than being, for example, acts of revenge. Moreover, the specific inducement of fear in a larger audience may be intended to ensure that a particular political response ensues, when it might not be stimulated by an act that does not elicit a wider response. The element of inducing fear in a larger population than that targeted is a key aspect of terrorism and is one explanation why it attracts so much attention compared with the many other forms of violence as well as suffering due to natural disasters or poverty and underdevelopment.

## State and sub-state terror

There is one fundamental difference between the definition given by Wardlaw and that used by the United States government in that the latter is concerned with sub-state actors, even if they may be supported or sponsored by a state, whereas Wardlaw's definition embraces the actions of states against their own populations. In broad terms, state terrorism is actually far more widespread in its effects, both in terms of direct casualties and in the inducing of fear.

Some of the most grievous examples of state terrorism have been the purges of Stalin's Soviet Union in the 1930s and Mao's China in the 1950s, but most colonial powers have used terror tactics to maintain control of colonies, especially during the early phases of colonization but also in response to the demands for independence in the early post-war years. More recently, states have readily used a wide range of terror tactics against their own populations. These have ranged from detention without trial through to torture and summary execution, but have also involved disappearances and the use of death squads. In Latin America in the 1960s and 1970s frequent use was made of such tactics, with persistent claims that the United States was involved at least indirectly (George 1991).

Even within the restricted 'sub-state' definition, which is the main concern of this chapter, there will be many controversies over who is a terrorist. Two examples illustrate this. During the long period of violence in Northern Ireland, the British government and most British people regarded the Provisional Irish Republican Army (Provisional IRA or PIRA) as a terrorist organization seeking to achieve a united Ireland by a sustained campaign of violence. Against this, though, many political supporters of Irish unity, in Northern Ireland and the Republic of Ireland, saw the PIRA volunteers as freedom fighters trying to liberate Northern Ireland from British rule. Such support extended to many members of the Irish-American community in the

United States. Furthermore, when the peace process in Northern Ireland finally made progress in the period 1997–2007, some of those with close links with PIRA became senior members of a power-sharing system, transitioning from perceived terrorists to legitimate political figures in a matter of years.

A second example is the use of terror and violence against Black Americans across the Southern states by white supremacist organizations for more than a century, right up to the 1960s and even more recently. Such groups were not, at the time, considered to be terrorists by most Americans but they would fit in with any of the three definitions given above. By a combination of beatings, torture and lynching, a substantial sector of the American population was terrorized into accepting its inferior place in society.

Sub-state terrorism can originate in very different societies and with highly variable motivations and underlying drivers. Although firm categorization is not easy, terrorism can be loosely divided into two orientations. One is terrorism that seeks fundamental change in a state or in society. Such revolutionary terrorism might be based on a political ideology of a radical persuasion that may be either left or right wing in nature, or it might be based on religious commitment. It may even combine the two. Either way, it aims for fundamental change, usually within a particular state but with this quite commonly being seen as a prelude to an international transformation. Baader Meinhof, Action Direct, Brigate Rossi and other European groups would be examples in the 1970s. More recently, the al-Qa'ida movement combines revolutionary change with religious belief.

The other form of terrorism seeks particular change for an identifiable community. This rarely has international ambitions but may link up with similar groups elsewhere. It is frequently separatist in nature but may have elements of revolutionary politics embedded in its thought. ETA in Spain and the LTTE Tamil Tigers in Sri Lanka are examples. Radical groups of this nature often arise in response to substantial political change that has damaged the prospects of the community from which they arise. Many radical Palestinian factions, for example, developed in direct response to the occupation of Palestinian territory by Israel in the Six Day War of June 1967, even if the Palestinian communities had previously been under the control of Egypt or Jordan.

## Responding to terrorism

There are three broad approaches to responding to sub-state terrorism (see also Chapter 30 this volume). The approach most commonly used might best be described as traditional counter-terrorism rooted principally in policing, intelligence and security. Paramilitary groups are identified and taken into custody before they can carry out attacks, or if this fails then those responsible for attacks are detected, detained and subsequently brought to justice. In addition, improved security is directed at providing increasing levels of protection for perceived targets. The second approach is more overtly military and involves direct military action against paramilitary organizations, especially when they have distinct physical locations. If they are clearly seen to be sponsored by a state, then that state may itself be targeted for punitive action or even regime termination.

The third approach concentrates on the underlying motivations of terrorist groups and the environment from which they draw support. While there may be a belief that the leaders and the most dedicated cadres of a paramilitary organization may have a degree of motivation and determination that is difficult to undermine, this approach is rooted in the idea that most paramilitary groups have evolved and are operating within a much wider context. They do not exist in isolation but depend for support on a sector of a particular society that shares their aims and approves, to an extent, of their methods. This approach also recognizes that there are conditions in which negotiations with paramilitary leaders may become possible, often with the utilization of mediators acceptable to both parties.

Most responses to terrorist campaigns utilize a combination of these methods, but the balance may vary widely. Many of the middle-class left-wing revolutionaries in 1970s Europe that included the Baader Meinhof Gang in West Germany and Brigate Rossi in Italy believed that their violent actions would provoke an uprising of the masses leading to a working class revolution. Even so, their campaigns did nothing to persuade the authorities to make any major changes in wage agreements or working conditions. The authorities did not see such movements as presaging a wider revolution and in this assessment they were correct. Instead, the response was very much one of intensive policing and intelligence gathering, coupled with some degree of increased security for potential targets, especially senior politicians and industry leaders.

Between 1968 and 1972 there were widespread activities by a number of radical Palestinian groups, some of them working in association with paramilitary movements in Western Europe and Japan. While Israeli security forces sought to kill some of those responsible, the greatest concern for most Western states was the development of aircraft hijacking as a means of gaining attention and, on some occasions, attempting to negotiate prisoner release. Although there were intensive efforts to identify and detain those responsible, the most substantial response was to invest in a massive increase in security measures for air travel.

In the long-running Northern Ireland conflict, all three approaches to counter-terrorism were adopted by the British authorities. Intensive policing and intelligence-gathering, in Northern Ireland and also in Britain, were accompanied by new legal regulations, including courts that sat without juries and, for one period, internment without trial. These methods were paralleled by an intensive counter-insurgency posture by the British Army and local Northern Ireland forces, mainly in Northern Ireland itself but sometimes in cooperation with the Republic of Ireland. Even as these methods were being used, not always with success, there was a recognition that much of the support for the republican movement came from within the Catholic nationalist minority community in Northern Ireland, largely because it had been in an inferior socio-economic position and had had little political power for generations. Indeed, the origins of the violence in the 1960s came largely from a robust response from the Protestant unionist government to a civil rights movement from within the nationalist community that was partly modelled on the US civil rights movement.

Because of this underlying support for the republican paramilitaries, the British authorities worked towards the greater emancipation of the nationalist community, not least through a number of economic and social measures. This was a difficult process considering the suspicions of the unionist majority, itself vulnerable through seeing itself as a minority in the island of Ireland as a whole, even if it was the controlling majority in Northern Ireland. Neverthe-less, the position of the nationalist community did improve over more than

## BOX 15.1 ECONOMIC TARGETING

Paramilitary organizations tend to be relatively conservative in their tactics, staying with particular methods that have been tried and tested. These may involve bombings, assassination, kidnappings, punishment beatings or combinations of these. This conservatism is often a reflection of the difficult environment in which they are operating and which makes it necessary to rely on those methods in which they are most practised. On occasions, changes in strategy and tactics can be significant in the effectiveness of an organization, and one of the developments of the two decades after 1990 was a tendency for a number of paramilitary groups to engage in the targeting of the economy of a target state in addition to more traditional targets such as the police and military forces and the political leadership.

Economic targeting has been practised to some extent by many paramilitary groups, with recent examples being the LTTE (Tamil Tigers) in Sri Lanka, the persistent attacks on Iraqi oil pipelines since 2003 and parallel attacks on Saudi facilities, most notably the attempt to disrupt the Abqaiq oil processing plant in Saudi Arabia, the world's largest, in February 2006.

Economic targeting was developed, in particular, by the Provisional IRA in Britain between 1992 and 1997 at a time when there was a stalemate in the long-lasting violence in Northern Ireland. The campaign was not designed to cause mass casualties but rather to attack the financial centre of the UK, the City of London, which was then competing with Frankfurt to be the financial hub of Europe. Two large truck bombs were used to cause substantial damage in the heart of the city in 1992 and 1993 with another targeting a major road interchange. At least three other bombs were intercepted but the impact of the bombing was such that rigorous counter-measures were put in place in the City while the British government looked more favourably on the possibility of negotiations.

Apart from a temporary ceasefire, the period 1992–1997 saw many more attacks, some of them large as in Canary Wharf and Manchester in 1996, with other small attacks causing substantial disruption to roads, railways and airports. PIRA tended to target facilities away from the centre of London because of improved security there, but still had a substantial impact on UK government attitudes. While other factors were involved, this change of tactics was influential in encouraging the Labour government from 1997 to devote considerable effort to resolving the conflict.

two decades and was one of the main reasons why a peace process became possible in the mid-1990s, even if particular tactics from the Provisional IRA directed at economic targeting in Britain almost certainly increased the British government's commitment to such a process (see Box 15.1).

## The 9/11 response and the War on Terror

The response to the 9/11 atrocities was unusual in that it placed far greater emphasis on military action compared with other forms of counter-terrorism. Other approaches such as improved homeland defence were utilized, but the primary focus was on the military with the main response being developed over the first decade into a global War on Terror. It was a particularly robust response for reasons already discussed above – major military campaigns were mounted against presumed state-sponsors of the al-Qa'ida movement in Afghanistan and Iraq leading to regime termination in both cases, and military operations were undertaken in a number of other countries, including Pakistan, Yemen and Somalia. Since the post-9/11 response has become a dominant feature of international security in general, and terrorism in particular, and is likely to remain so for some years to come, it is appropriate to examine this in some depth.

The group responsible for the 9/11 attacks, the al-Qa'ida movement, is a dispersed and very broadly based movement that is not narrowly hierarchical but does have clear aims and intentions. It is not a nihilistic collection of insane extremists, even if that impression is frequently given, but a rational movement involving an unusual combination of revolutionary political fervour rooted in a fundamentalist orientation of a major religion – Islam – rather than in a political ideology or nationalist or ethnic base. The movement has its theoretical origins in the writings of a number of radical Islamic thinkers, notably the Egyptian Sayidd Qutb, who was tortured and executed by his own government in 1966. In more practical terms, al-Qa'ida can be traced back to the success of the *Mujahiddin* fighters in Afghanistan and their opposition to Soviet occupation in the 1980s. Aided by the US Central Intelligence Agency and the Pakistani Inter-Services Intelligence organization, the paramilitary and guerrilla fighters were eventually able to force the Soviet Union to withdraw from the country, and many within the movement see this as leading to the collapse of the Soviet system.

Following the eviction of Iraqi forces from Kuwait in 1991, substantial US military forces remained in the region, including Saudi Arabia – the Kingdom of the Two Holy Places (Mecca and Medina). This resulted in a revitalization of elements of the anti-Soviet movement of the 1980s, with the main focus being on evicting such 'crusader' forces, especially from Saudi Arabia. Central to this were two individuals. One was Osama bin Laden, a wealthy Saudi of Yemeni extraction, who had been active in Afghanistan. The other was the Egyptian-born strategist Ayman al-Zawahiri. During the 1990s, the movement developed a more comprehensive strategy, rooted largely in

Qutb's ideas of a revival of 'true' Islam following its corruption by Western culture. By the end of the twentieth century, al-Qa'ida had developed a number of short-term aims together with an over-arching long-term vision.

There were six short-term aims. One was the eviction of US military forces from Saudi Arabia, an aim that the movement claimed to have achieved by 2005 when the last of the major US bases in the Kingdom was evacuated because of concern of the Saudi authorities over the US presence, and a second was the eviction of foreign forces from the Islamic world. A third was the replacement of the House of Saud by a 'genuine' Islamist regime, the Saudi royal family being seen as corrupt, elitist and excessively linked to the United States. The fourth aim was the replacement of other corrupt, elitist and pro-Western regimes across the region, with an initial focus on Egypt and Pakistan but extending later to Iraq and Afghanistan. Fifth, there was deep antagonism to the Zionist state of Israel and support for the Palestinian cause and, finally, there was support for other Islamist movements such as the Chechen rebels and the Southern Thailand separatists. Beyond this lay the long-term aim of establishing a pan-Islamic Caliphate, developing in the Middle East but extending eventually to other parts of the world.

In the context of these aims there is a broad distinction between the 'near enemy' which comprises the unacceptable regimes and their supporters across the Middle East and the 'far enemy,' this being the United States and its coalition partners such as the United Kingdom. A further core aspect of the strategy of the movement is the question of timescales. The short-term aims are seen as being achieved progressively over a period of several decades and the long-term aim of establishing Islamist governance through a Caliphate may take fifty to a hundred years. This is a fundamental issue as it differs so markedly from the typical timescales of Western political and economic institutions.

The 9/11 attacks were designed to demonstrate an ability to attack the far enemy of the United States, not least to increase support for the movement. It would also serve to attract US forces into Afghanistan in large numbers, enabling a guerrilla war to develop over a number of years with a similar effect on US resilience to that on the Soviet Union two decades earlier. Al-Qa'ida failed initially in this second aim in that the United States initially used a combination of air power, Special Forces and a re-arming of the Northern Alliance to terminate the Taliban regime. Even so, by mid-2011 a Taliban revival was continuing and was tying down 140,000 US and coalition forces in an entrenched insurgency.

After the apparent success in Afghanistan the Bush administration developed the war on terror to encompass pre-emptive military action against what it called an 'axis of evil' of states believed to be developing weapons of mass destruction and sponsoring terrorist organizations. The principal members of the axis were declared to be Iraq, Iran and North Korea, with Iraq being the first candidate state for regime termination in 2003. While the Saddam Hussein regime was ended within three weeks, a complex insurgency then developed which eventually combined with a degree of sectarian conflict to produce a highly unstable and violent country. Eight years after regime termination, at least 120,000 Iraqi civilians had been killed and close to four million were refugees. The United States lost over 4,000 troops killed and 25,000 wounded; many of the latter maimed for life. In spite of using a wide range of tactics, the US-led forces were unable to contain the violence and there was abundant evidence that the insurgents were able to develop techniques at a rate at least as fast as they could be countered. A marked tendency of US forces to use their overwhelming fire power against urban insurgents might be understandable from their own perspective but could be seen by opponents as little short of terror (see Box 15.2).

Perhaps most important of all was the status of Iraq as providing a jihadist combat training zone, an aspect of huge advantage to the al-Qa'ida movement and its associates. Moreover, Iraq represented a combat training zone that was far superior to Afghanistan in the 1980s in that young paramilitaries could gain experience against well-armed and well-trained US soldiers and Marines in an urban environment – far superior in paramilitary terms than poorly trained Soviet conscripts in rural Afghanistan two decades earlier. Given al-Qa'ida's decades-long timescale and its concern with terminating unacceptable

## BOX 15.2  WHOSE TERRORISM?

The difficult issue of who is the terrorist is well illustrated by the US military action in the Iraqi city of Fallujah in November 2004. Seven months earlier there had been a US attempt to gain control of the city following a particularly brutal paramilitary action when four American security guards were killed, mutilated and their bodies burnt before being hung from a bridge. The first assault failed but Fallujah was then seen as a centre of terrorism. The November assault was covered in detail by TV channels operating with US forces, and there was stark footage of the very heavy use of ordnance against the city. This was seen as an utterly just cause in the United States, and there was great satisfaction when the city was brought fully under control by the US Army and Marine Corps.

Across the Middle East, on the other hand, regional TV news stations (see Box 15.3) were reporting the effects within the city, where several thousand people were killed in the assault, many of them civilians, and most of the public buildings and more than half of all the private houses in the city were destroyed or severely damaged. Fallujah was known as the City of Mosques and the damage done to many of the mosques was a particular affront. For the US forces, though, mosques were often used by the insurgents and represented legitimate targets.

For the United States, the taking of Fallujah was an essential and fully justified military operation against a dangerously evolving insurgency that was already killing and injuring hundreds of American troops. Across the Middle East and the wider Islamic world, Fallujah was nothing less than an act of state terrorism conducted by an occupying power that was on a par with the 9/11 attacks. American opinion would be almost entirely unable to comprehend such a view, just as Arab opinion would find it extraordinary that the assault could in any sense be justified.

regimes in the Middle East, eight years or more of combat experience against US forces in Iraq seemed likely to provide a new generation of jihadists. In that sense, the US decision to occupy Iraq can be seen as an historic error of quite extraordinary magnitude. Furthermore, the extensive coverage of the carnage in Iraq, both by regional satellite TV news channels and through propagandistic outlets did much to increase support for radical Islamist movements (see Box 15.3).

In the global war on terror as a whole, ten years into the war well over 100,000 people had been detained without trial, for various periods, with at least 25,000 detained at any one time. Prisoner abuse, torture and rendition had been used and the detention centre at the US military base at Guantanamo in Cuba was still open and widely criticized. There were some significant changes in policy with the election of Barack Obama in 2008, and these included a speeding up of the withdrawal of troops from Iraq and a willingness

## BOX 15.3  TERROR AND THE NEW MEDIA

One of the most striking developments in paramilitary movements has been the use of new media to publicize their actions, promote their cause and air their grievances. New versions of old media such as television in combination with new media and communications systems such as the internet, broadband, smart-phones and DVDs have all made these aspects more effective. While the major changes have come since the mid-1990s, they are not entirely new – television coverage of aircraft hijackings in the late 1960s and early 1970s was influential in bringing the activities of Palestinian paramilitary movements to world attention.

For television, the main change has been the development of new 24-hour regional satellite TV news stations. While these may be financed or owned by local elite rulers, as in the case of Al-Jazeera and Al-Arabiya, they portray a news agenda from a strongly regional perspective rather than an Atlanticist outlook as is the case with CNN and other US and European-owned outlets. Stations such as Al-Jazeera maintain high professional standards and are exceptionally popular across the Middle East for their independence from narrowly focused and often propagandistic state broadcasting networks. Prime time news bulletins attract viewing audiences in the tens of millions, a level that is far higher than the main channels in countries such as Britain, France or Germany. They are increasingly available world-wide to diaspora audiences and are notable for their coverage of the effects of conflicts in Iraq, Afghanistan and Pakistan. As such, they illustrate the effects of Western interventions with persistence and with little self-censoring of the impacts.

Beyond this extensive conventional TV coverage, many jihadist groups have become adept at videoing their activities and using them as part of highly propagandistic packages distributed by CD, DVD and, in particular, the internet. The widespread availability of broadband makes it possible to distribute detailed coverage of paramilitary actions within hours of the events. Furthermore, statements by leaders are distributed by all the major means. Some of the outputs are in the form of extensive lectures that demonstrate a thorough familiarity with Western policies and attitudes and are attuned to have a maximum effect among target audiences.

to engage with Taliban elements as a prelude to an eventual negotiated withdrawal from Afghanistan. The killing of Osama bin Laden in May 2011 aided this change in policy but the onset of the Arab Spring seemed likely to damage the movement more, since it stemmed from popular protests and mass demonstrations rather than actions by Islamist revolutionaries. Even so, if the Arab Spring failed, then the al-Qa'ida movement could regain some impetus. Furthermore, the importance of the Persian Gulf oil resources would ensure a long-term US military presence in the region (Kubursi 2006) sustaining the al-Qa'ida propaganda message of the 'far enemy' as a persistent threat.

## Trends in terrorism

In the years after 1990 there were a number of developments in terrorism and political violence that are likely to be significant in the longer term.

### Terrorism and insurgency

The practice of employing regime termination as a major response to terrorism produced a complex reaction that effectively mixes terrorism and insurgency. This evolved in Afghanistan and Iraq into a form of warfare that may be concentrated in the two countries concerned but has a much wider impact, not least in Pakistan and in terms of support for the al-Qa'ida movement and its associates.

### Internationalism

Although there has long been an element of transnational capabilities in paramilitary movements, this has evolved rapidly in recent years. In the first six years of the war on terror, for example, the al-Qa'ida movement and its loose affiliates were able to carry out attacks in Egypt, Indonesia, Jordan, Kenya, Morocco, Pakistan, Saudi Arabia, Spain, Tunisia, Turkey, the United Kingdom and Yemen, quite apart from Iraq and Afghanistan, with attacks prevented in a number of other countries including France, Italy, Singapore and the United States.

### Suicide terrorism

As with internationalism, suicide attacks as a facet of terrorism are not new, but the intensity of the attacks in many countries, and the willingness of so many people to engage in martyrdom is novel. Suicide attacks are intrinsically more difficult to counter as an aspect of any form of political violence. Moreover, while most of the relatively rare incidents of suicide attacks until 2001 were by people with deep political or ethnic motives, such as the LTTE in Sri Lanka, the more recent trend is for suicide attacks to draw on religious motivation, especially within Islam, and for there to be a substantial increase in the numbers of motivated individuals who embrace an eschatological dimension to their aspirations.

### Speed of learning

Most paramilitary groups in the past have been relatively conservative in their operations, tending to stay with methods that they have developed and have become experienced in using. The intense environments of the insurgencies in Afghanistan and especially Iraq forced paramilitary groups to learn fast in order to survive and thrive. There is abundant evidence that these learning environments have combined with the internationalization of terrorism to allow the far more rapid spread of tactics than in the past – advanced fusing for improvised explosive devices and the production of explosively formed anti-armour projectiles being just two examples.

### Media developments

Regional satellite TV news channels, the use of the internet, CDs, DVDs and mobile phones have all increased the ability of paramilitary groups to promote their causes (see Box 15.3).

### Economic targeting

The development of sophisticated economic targeting strategies by groups such as the Provisional IRA (see Box 15.1) and insurgents in Iraq has provided a new avenue of influence and effect. Given the numerous nodes of power and economic activity in urban/industrialized societies, it is probable that this development is still in its early stages.

### Mass casualty attacks and weapons of mass destruction

Although there has been no single instance of the large-scale use of nuclear, chemical, biological or radiological weapons, the increased use of mass casualty attacks has raised fears that weapons of mass destruction will ultimately be used by some terrorist organizations. While there is clearly a risk, it remains the case that conventional forms of destruction can readily lead to casualties on a very substantial scale, as in the 9/11 attacks.

## Conclusion

The war on terror as a response to the 2001 attacks in New York and Washington came to dominate international security, not least by embracing robust military operations as the principal responses to the attacks. Given the failure of such responses to have the intended effects, it is possible that there will be a re-balancing of counter-terrorism strategies, although the long timescale of radical Islamist strategies and the long-term importance of the Persian Gulf region to the United States might militate against this. Given the developments in terrorist tactics and the factors aiding movements such as al-Qa'ida discussed above, it would appear that it would be wise to embrace a fairly fundamental re-thinking of Western policies in general, and US policies in particular.

## Further reading

Charles Allen, *God's Terrorists, The Wahhabi Cult and the Hidden Roots of Modern Jihad* (Abacus, 2006). Focuses on the long-term development of jihadism.

Sean K. Anderson and Stephen Sloan, *Historical Dictionary of Terrorism* (The Scarecrow Press, 2002). The most comprehensive coverage of sub-state terrorist movements available.

Jason Burke, *Al-Qaeda, the True Story of Radical Islam* (Penguin Books, 2007). The best single account of the development of the al-Qa'ida movement.

John Horgan, *The Psychology of Terrorism* (Routledge, 2005). One of the few examples of an analysis of motivation.

Bruce Lawrence (ed.), *Messages to the World: The Statements of Osama bin Laden* (Verso, 2005). Essential reading in understanding the al-Qa'ida movement.

Richard Jackson, Eamon Murphy and Scott Poynting (eds.), *Contemporary State Terrorism: Theory and Cases* (Routledge, 2010). A wide-ranging analysis of state involvement.

Richard Jackson, Marie Breen Smyth, Jeroen Gunning and Lee Jarvis, *Terrorism: A Critical Introduction* (Palgrave-Macmillan, 2011). An up-to-date introduction.

Ahmed Rashid, *Taliban* (I.B. Tauris, 2010). An updated edition of a standard text.

# Intelligence

Richard J. Aldrich

## Abstract

In this chapter, students will learn about intelligence; a concept which since 9/11 has rarely been off the front pages of our newspapers and websites. Little of this coverage has been flattering and a word association game would quickly link intelligence with terms like 'failure' and 'torture'. This chapter introduces students to the competing concepts of intelligence and the arguments over whether its performance can be substantially improved and whether intelligence services stabilize or disrupt the international system. It concludes that the field is dominated by an out-dated concept of intelligence as a strategic process designed to produce refined information for policy-makers. This idea is actually untypical of intelligence activity elsewhere in the wider world, which is for the most part about regime security and surveillance. It is also fundamentally unsuited for the challenges of the twenty-first century which are increasingly about the global politics of domestic security.

## Introduction

Recent debates over intelligence have taken two forms. The first is what we might call an old fashioned 'value for money' argument about intelligence failures. The American intelligence behemoth now spends close to $80 billion a year. Reportedly, some 854,000 people hold top-secret clearances allowing them to see its high-grade intelligence reports. Many of them are employed by some 2,000 private companies rather than the US government. In reality, no-one is really sure how much this sprawling enterprise costs or how many people it employs. Politicians, practitioners and the public have all been vexed about poor performance, either in the context of the failure to warn of the 9/11 attacks or the Iraqi weapons of mass destruction (WMD) fiasco. Intelligence has also under-performed in the recent wars in Iraq and Afghanistan. Countless reports have been written on how the intelligence machine can be reformed but few of these prescriptions command universal consensus. Most observers agree that the current benefits from intelligence do not appear to be commensurate with the scale of spending.

The reformist debate over 'value for money' has been overtaken by a second debate characterized by moral outrage. When public intellectuals such as Noam Chomsky, Michael Ignatieff or Philippe Sands discuss security policies, the nefarious activities of intelligence agencies are often central to their discourse. This debate is about action and kinetic effects rather than briefings. Over the last decade the US Central Intelligence Agency (CIA) has become associated with renditions, secret detention sites and torture. When the Obama administration assumed office, the emphasis shifted towards secret drone strikes over Pakistan and the Yemen. The CIA still gathers intelligence and does reporting, but the trend is moving away from 'watch and wait' towards 'capture or kill'. Unquestionably, the new roles allocated to the intelligence services are hard to reconcile with core Western values. Paradoxically, secret intelligence has now become very public and its activities are increasingly taken to be symbolic of national security policy as a whole.

This second debate about intelligence ethics is symptomatic of the troubled transformation of intelligence across much of the Western world. Intelligence services that had spent most of their time passively observing the Communist bloc in the 1980s were re-directed towards dealing with organized crime in the 1990s and then to the task of counter-terrorism after 2001. However, the changes that have occurred in the realm of intelligence are not merely about new targets. They are increasingly about action, disruption and event-shaping. Moreover, the traditional Westphalian boundaries which outline clear divisions between foreign intelligence operations and domestic surveillance are collapsing – with multiple consequences. Intelligence is becoming globalized and it is already apparent that intelligence in the context of globalization is dirty work.

## What is intelligence?

Many countries do not have a special word for 'intelligence'. The Chinese simply refer to 'information' while the French prefer the word 'research'. What is the difference between intelligence and information? Michael Warner (2002) has argued that intelligence is a particular form of information that allows policy-makers, or operational commanders, to make more effective decisions. This instrumental idea of intelligence as a special kind of information that constitutes the prelude to policy and renders strategic decision-making more effective is a classic Western conceptualization that has changed little over time. General Sir Gerald Templer, who helped to pave the way for the creation of the UK Defence Intelligence Staff, offered a similar definition as early as May 1960: 'Intelligence is not an end in itself. It is an essential aid to policy-making and military planning and should ideally provide timely warning of events which we would wish to anticipate and the intelligence background for policy decisions' (Templer 1960).

Mark Lowenthal, author of the most widely used textbook on intelligence and policy, argues that the word 'intelligence' is widely used in three different ways. First, as a *process*, through which intelligence is requested by policy-makers or operational commanders, then collected, analysed, and fed to the consumers. This is often referred to as the 'intelligence cycle', albeit the nature of this cycle is now much debated. Second, we can define intelligence as a *product*, once upon a time circulated as paper, but now distributed through multilevel secure electronic databases. Finally, we can talk of intelligence services and intelligence communities as *institutions*. As their name implies, they often deliver diverse 'services' to government and increasingly this involves active efforts to shape the world as well as merely reporting about it (Lowenthal 2008, Omand 2009).

Michael Herman (1996), author of the most influential theoretical text on the nature of intelligence, defines intelligence as a form of power, not unlike military power or economic power. Certainly for developed states, intelligence is a crucial part of 'hyper-powerness', allowing them to project military force on a global basis and allowing them to dominate. The Revolution in Military Affairs is strongly connected to a growing ability to utilize unimaginable amounts of data and so intelligence constitutes a significant component of the changing nature of war (Ferris 2004). We might also think of this in terms of Nye's observation about the relationship of soft power to hard power (Nye 2004).

Although intelligence has often bolstered the power of states, large parts of the overall national infrastructure are now in private hands. The most obvious examples are telecom and internet service providers, which are increasingly required by law to work with government as intelligence collectors. Moreover, the growing emphasis on state–private partnerships to protect national infrastructure ensures that businesses such as airlines and banks are not only collectors of intelligence, but also important consumers. Even state intelligence and security agencies have turned to contracting out a surprising range of their activities. Approximately a third of CIA employees are private contractors and so we can no longer claim that intelligence is a predominantly state-based activity (Pincus and Barr 2007, Shorrock 2008).

Regional and international organizations have also embraced intelligence. The European Union has its own satellite and sees intelligence as an essential component of a Common Foreign and Security Policy. The rise of the United

Nations as a significant military actor has resulted in the need for intelligence to support UN peacekeeping operations and hence interfacing with a small group of Western states with the required experience and global capabilities (Chesterman 2006). In the long term, UN intelligence might well take on a life of its own. This has occurred to some degree in the International Criminal Tribunal for the Former Yugoslavia (ICTY) which boasts an investigatory arm with a significant intelligence capability. Since 1997, ICTY investigators have been searching the Balkans for individuals who themselves once belonged to curious organizations that were part intelligence service, part criminal gang and part political faction. The UN has thus been involved in what might be called an 'intelligence war' (Smith 1994, Wiebes 2003).

## Warning, surprise and 'failure'

The advent of strategic airpower in the first half of the twentieth century offered new opportunities for surprise attack. Hitler's invasion of Russia in June 1941 and Pearl Harbor later that year were dramatic examples. Thereafter, the outbreak of Korean War in 1950, the Soviet invasion of Czechoslovakia in 1968, the Yom Kippur War in 1973, the invasion of the Falklands in 1982 and the Iraqi invasion of Kuwait in 1990 were all examples of successful surprise and intelligence failure. Perhaps because policy-makers have seen warning against surprise attack as one of the highest priority intelligence requirements, this area has been intensively studied and heavily theorized.

In 1973, Barton Whaley published a path-breaking study of Hitler's remarkable surprise attack on Russia, launched on 22 June 1941. Although this was primarily a historical account, it sought to draw out many of the important psychological aspects of both surprise for the victim and also the strategies used by the aggressor to achieve effective deception. This, in turn, triggered increasingly rigorous political science research into the problems of perception and deception within the intelligence cycle. Whaley himself, over the next three decades, sought to distil the concept of 'stratagem' that placed considerable emphasis on the art of surprise and deception as a component of statecraft (Whaley 1973, 2007).

In 1977, Robert Jervis published one of the first major works in the wider realm of International Relations to take intelligence seriously. Entitled *Perception and Misperception in International Politics,* it suggested that perceptions matter and that, quite often, states that develop a hostile image of their opponents will interpret information to fit that fixed image, leading to unnecessary conflict over minor issues. Jervis also began to ask where these 'images' of other states come from and how this related to intelligence. This study was peppered with references to a new wave of empirical literature that was emerging on subjects such as World War II deception planning and intelligence during the Cuban Missile Crisis. It suggested that intelligence analysts could be trained to avoid some of the perception problems (Jervis 1977: 25, 74, 172).

A little later, Richard Betts published a sophisticated comparative analysis of surprise attack. He asked why surprise attacks succeed so often, despite the existence of elaborate intelligence communities. Betts argued that weak collection of raw data – in other words inadequate field espionage – was rarely the cause of failure. Instead, the main culprits fell into three categories: first, bureaucratic dysfunction; second, psychological perception issues or 'cognitive dissonance'; and third, excessive political interference by policy-makers. Betts conceptualized the intelligence process as a long chain, arguing that mechanistic efforts to improve one part of the intelligence process only resulted in the chain pulling apart at another weak point. Partly for this reason, he famously concluded that 'intelligence failures are inevitable' (Betts 1978). The work of Betts was paralleled by that of Michael Handel, who argued that these problems could be viewed as a series of paradoxes. While these could not be resolved, they could serve to alert policy-makers to the intrinsic problems of intelligence (Betts and Mahnken 2003).

The debate on the sources of strategic intelligence failure has been greatly intensified by two recent events. The first is the failure to offer warning of the 9/11 attacks and the second is the fiasco over reporting of a supposed Iraqi WMD programme in 2002, prior to the invasion of Iraq in 2003. Governments around the world wanted to know why they had spent many billions of dollars a year on intelligence and yet seemed to receive poor value for money. Countries as disparate as the United States, UK, Israel, Australia and Denmark launched inquiries into their own local versions of the vexed WMD intelligence fiasco, hoping that they might obtain a better return on their investment in the future. Yet even as these inquiries proceeded, intelligence budgets continued to climb at a dizzying rate, suggesting an inverse – even perverse – relationship between performance and reward. Reflecting on this, Rhodri Jeffreys-Jones (2003) has likened the intelligence chief to 'the confidence man' or the 'snake oil merchant', long-established but shady figures in American folk culture. Certainly, in the world of intelligence, nothing succeeds like failure since budgets for intelligence tend to increase in the wake of a major disaster in the hope of avoiding another nasty surprise further down the line.

The over-arching narrative of the Iraqi WMD intelligence fiasco has been relayed to us largely in terms of a politicization of the intelligence process. The prevailing view in the literature is that the invasion of Iraq was 'sold' to the public by manufacturing an intelligence case that fitted prevailing political whims and facilitated a pre-existing decision to invade Iraq taken at some point in early 2002. Some have seen this intelligence 'manipulation' as an alarming failure of the marketplace of ideas in a mature democracy (Kaufmann 2004). The extent to which this involved an elaborate propaganda effort by officials who enjoyed exotic job titles such as 'Story Development' is now well documented (Danchev 2004, O'Halpin 2005). Yet subsequent inquiries have also shown significant intelligence failures as a result of poor source validation and 'groupthink'. Western intelligence agencies had badly under-estimated Iraqi chemical weapons stocks back in 1991 prior to the first Gulf War and so in 2002 they over-corrected for their past mistakes. Most national intelligence agencies, including the Germans and the French, indeed even the UN's atomic weapons expert, Hans Blix, all believed that Iraq had some capability. Only the Canadians and the Dutch got it right (Davies 2004, Jervis 2006).

We also need to make a clear distinction between intelligence failure and its effect. As former US Secretary of Defense Donald Rumsfeld has asserted, most Western intelligence agencies performed badly on the Iraqi WMD question. But it is disingenuous for Rumsfeld to claim that this was a significant contributory factor to the decision to invade Iraq. Intelligence was used to support policy promotion in public arenas such as the UN – not to illuminate the policy-making process (Rumsfeld 2011). Moreover, as Lawrence Freedman (2004) has wisely observed, Iraq was a double intelligence failure given the benign expectations of the consequences of regime change in Iraq and the reality of the traumatic insurgency that followed.

The literature on successful surprise attack and its obverse – intelligence failure – is now impressive. This, in turn, has led to a sophisticated understanding of the interaction of intelligence and security within the framework of foreign policy analysis. Box 16.1 charts the observations and prescriptions of some of the key commentators regarding intelligence reform.

---

## BOX 16.1  POSITIONS ON THE RELATIONSHIP BETWEEN INTELLIGENCE AND SECURITY POLICIES

*Pessimistic*: Richard Betts (2007) counsels that policy-makers should simply revise their expectations downwards, attributing current disappointment to unrealistic demands. Betts sees intelligence as 'tragic'.

*Methodological*: Robert Jervis (2010) also thinks too much has been expected of intelligence and partly for this reason he argues that pre-emption is a weak doctrine. Nevertheless, he thinks that good political science methods would help analysts avoid some of their more lamentable errors.

*Optimistic*: Amy Zegart (2007) argues that meaningful reform is possible and has attributed recent difficulties to a kind of institutional arteriosclerosis that obstructs substantial change.

*Domestic*: Gregory Treverton (2011) is also optimistic about structural change, but points out that some of the greatest challenges lie in the controversial area of domestic intelligence.

*Iconoclastic*: Dana Priest and Bill Arkin (2011) argue that the expansion of intelligence and security agencies has resulted in a sprawling and ineffective system that is both unaccountable and unsustainable.

---

## Intelligence, uncertainty and stability

Famously, the granite wall of the foyer in the CIA headquarters is engraved with the biblical exhortation 'And ye shall know the truth, and the truth shall make you free' (John 8: 31–32). Intelligence agencies have frequently advanced the claim that their ability to lend a general transparency to the international system helps to remove uncertainty and improves stability. Michael Herman has suggested that, while the intelligence activities of each individual country are conducted in a competitive environment, the collective result that accrues can operate as a public good or an 'international good' (1996: 375–376, 2001: 231). The overall effect of many secret agents shining their torches into dark corners is more like a street light, illuminating the broader landscape for the benefit of all. Therefore, the international system is potentially a more reassuring place – at least for the policy-makers who have access to this material.

It is clear that intelligence has made a major contribution to stability by providing verification for arms control. The most frequently cited example is Dwight D. Eisenhower and the infamous bomber and missile gaps of the Cold War. During the 1950s, Eisenhower was able to resist pressure, particularly from the US Air Force, for major expansion of strategic weapons programmes. Historical studies undertaken by the intelligence agencies themselves have probably exaggerated these claims, arguing that intelligence was a 'magic bullet' that allowed Eisenhower to defeat arms racing. Independent studies have confirmed the broad thesis, but have also shown that Eisenhower's inability to place this secret material in the public domain somewhat reduced its usefulness (Andrew 1995, Roman 1995). Surveillance satellites were an essential component of the major Cold War arms control initiatives, including the Non-Proliferation Treaty, the Strategic Arms Limitation Talks, and several atomic test bans. Indeed, one could argue that it is no coincidence that complex arms control and sophisticated satellite-based collections systems emerged at around the same time. The phrase 'National Technical Means' – a polite phrase for spying with science – first gained wide currency during the Strategic Arms Limitation Talks of the late 1960s. It could be argued that several esoteric intelligence sub-disciplines have evolved primarily in support of arms control negotiations including seismology and air sampling (Richelson 2006, Goodman 2007).

Verified information for policy-makers might be broadly viewed as exercising a stabilizing effect on the international system. However, the same does not hold true for the processes by which such information is collected. Intelligence operations are potentially provocative (Jervis 1986: 141). The historical example of a collection system which has attained iconic status in the International Relations literature is the CIA's high-flying U-2 reconnaissance aircraft programme. The U-2 usefully embodies the duality of intelligence as both a stabilizer and a source of risk. The intelligence collected by the U-2 was often benign, typically enforcer of ceasefires on behalf of the United Nations following the Middle East wars of 1968 and 1973. Yet the

---

## BOX 16.2   THE SHOOTING DOWN OF THE U-2 SPY-PLANE, MAY 1960

On 1 May 1960, the CIA launched a U-2 spy-flight over the Soviet Union to photograph missile and bomber bases. The U-2 aircraft, piloted by Francis Gary Powers was shot down near Svedlovsk using a ground-to-air missile and was recovered almost intact by the Soviets. President Eisenhower had clearly attempted to make a balanced calculation concerning the trade-off of benefits and risks of the mission. However he was surprised by the scale of negative fallout for East–West relations from this single disaster. Thirteen days later, the Paris Summit between Eisenhower, Khrushchev, and Harold Macmillan was cancelled. Khrushchev insisted on an apology but Eisenhower refused. The incident led to public accusation and counter-accusation as the paper-thin cover story deployed by Eisenhower about the scientific exploration of the upper stratosphere was exposed as patently dishonest. The incident dragged on as Gary Powers was put on trial, convicted, and then sentenced to seven years' hard labour. Powers was incarcerated for a little less than two years, being the subject of a dramatic spy-swap on the Glienicke Bridge in Berlin for the KGB spy Rudolph Abel.

(Sources: Aldrich 2002, Powers 1971, Pocock 1989)

---

missions themselves involved a degree of jeopardy. The infamous shoot-down of a U-2 in 1960 illustrates this (see Box 16.2).

## Covert action, disruption and event-shaping

The importance of intelligence for international security becomes greater once we review the full range of activities undertaken by intelligence services. Intelligence agencies not only gather intelligence on world affairs – often a rather passive activity – but also seek to intervene covertly to shape events. This mode of activity is often referred to as 'covert action' or 'special political action' and is intended to achieve plausible deniability. Because the event itself is often visible, for example an assassination, the intelligence service in question merely tries to make it difficult for the event to be traced back definitively to the perpetrator. Covert action can also take many forms from noisy paramilitary activity to the discrete covert funding of political parties. As a result, the basic facts of even widely cited covert actions, such as the CIA's intervention in Chile in 1973, remain disputed (Shiraz 2011).

Normative theorists view covert action as problematic and it is often linked to neo-imperialism. Chalmers Johnson, a respected political economist, has deployed the CIA term 'blowback' to denote the unintended consequences of covert actions that were deliberately kept from the American public. He also uses the CIA as a primary exhibit in his argument about the scale of covert political interference and economic imperialism in the world. For Johnson, many of America's current difficulties in the global south stem from vexatious retaliation against CIA activities that ironically the American public knows little about. The removal of a democratic regime in Iran and the installation of the Shah in 1953 is an obvious example. Noam Chomsky argues that the majority of covert action has focused on subverting democracies in the Third World, typically by secretly funneling money to preferred candidates. Chomsky's arguments capture the anxieties of both the anti-imperialists and those worried about the subversion of democratic norms in the international system (Johnson 2000, Chomsky and Otero 2003). These views are widely held and are by no means monopolized by the New Left. William Roger Louis, the world's foremost historian of Empire, has commented in a similar vein on the classic covert actions of the early Cold War in Iran and Guatemala:

> The greater the frustrating restraint of nuclear weapons, the more tempting the use of covert methods. Eisenhower used the CIA to help topple Mosaddeq in Iran (as well as Arbenz in Guatemala) . . . Eisenhower's policy of external interference, pursued by his successors, almost certainly contributed to the later Iranian revolution and led to the replacement of Britain by the United States as the 'great Satan'.
>
> Eisenhower was in fact as wary of the excesses of the CIA as he was of those of the American military. His wariness remains a warning for the present and the future. Nevertheless the amoral and clandestine operations of the CIA and other American agencies in Iran and Guatemala were endorsed by the Eisenhower administration. The President himself was perhaps under the impression that a Pax Americana of sorts could be created and sustained by such methods. If so there must have been a delicate balance between hoping that the United States could preserve freedom by subversive means (or 'ruling indirectly', American-style) and believing that small nations have the right to conduct their own affairs.
>
> (Louis 1985: 419)

Even hard-nosed realists have concluded that many covert actions did not go well. Episodes that seem to have been regarded as a success in the short term, for example the support given to the Mujahidin in resisting the Soviet occupation of Afghanistan in the 1980s, now appear to have resulted in long-term 'blowback'. Theorists working from a wide range of perspectives seem to regard covert actions as broadly destabilizing or at least a high-risk activity that should only be attempted as a last resort. The agencies themselves respond that the more elaborate examples of covert action – such as Iran-Contra – have tended to be the result of demands for action by politicians rather than schemes developed by the agencies (Treverton 1988, Reisman and Baker 1992).

Covert action allows presidents and prime ministers to undertake foreign policies that are unaccountable, undemocratic, and often questionable. Unsurprisingly, this issue connects with Democratic Peace Theory (DPT). Those interested in promoting DPT have argued that democracies rarely wage war against each other, and are less inclined towards aggression generally (see Chapter 3 this volume). When democracies do engage in war, they insist that it is more likely to be against non-democracies. Most DPT theorists suggest that democracy has a dual effect. They suggest democratic institutions exercise a restraining effect and in addition the elites in democratic states are imbued with nonviolent norms (Russett 1993, Russett and Starr 2000). Yet adherents of DPT have ignored the way secret intervention can evade the impact of democratic institutions upon the foreign policy process. Others have argued that covert action shows that elites in democracies actually have weak adherence to nonviolent norms and are happy to coerce other democracies as long as the process is not too visible (Kim 2005, Forsythe 1992). Enthusiasts for covert action often respond that this 'quiet option' does less damage than conventional military force. They rightly assert that more recently covert action has often involved democracy promotion, typified by CIA support to the Polish trade union movement 'Solidarity' in 1981 (MacEachin 2001).

Certainly one of the most neglected aspects of covert action is clandestine diplomacy and mediation. Intelligence services have been valuable in facilitating discussion between states that do not have diplomatic relations. They have also proved helpful in developing dialogue with violent non-state actors such as militias and terrorist groups (Newton 2011). The employment of intelligence services in this role has several possible advantages. First, the negotiations are deniable on all sides, and in the case of 'talking to terrorists', this may be essential if the discussions are to proceed at all. Second, terrorist groups often feel they enjoy a cultural commonality with clandestine operators and may prefer to interact with intelligence officers than with diplomats. The path to peace in Northern Ireland was assisted by British Secret Intelligence Service (SIS) contact with the IRA that continued for many years. Although the British premier, Margaret Thatcher, frequently asserted that she would not talk to terrorists, in reality an intense dialogue continued unbroken, even at the height of the troubles (Scott 2004). Intelligence services have often served as important mediators and arbitrators in the context of Middle East conflict (Shpiro 2003, Stempel 2007).

In the past, covert action was sometimes dismissed as not really being part of intelligence. This was always nonsense and covert action is now a major part of the 'War on Terror'. Intelligence services increasingly regard themselves as action-orientated, or as one former practitioner has put it, they are now 'hunters not gatherers' (Cogan 2004). The landscape has changed radically, underlined by the fact that we now have elaborate academic writing discussing the pros and cons of both torture and assassination. Whether activities like special rendition are strictly speaking 'covert action' is debated amongst intelligence aficionados, nevertheless rendition, torture, secret prisons and targeted killing have provoked enormous controversy during recent years. Intelligence officers from the CIA's Special Activities Division are now the subject of arrest warrants from Italian courts for a kidnapping carried out on the streets of Milan in 2002. The CIA officers had used their frequent flier cards in their own names to collect their air miles and so were easy for the Italian police to trace. These action operations have set the intelligence services on a collision course with the professed liberal and humane values of Western democratic societies. As a result, the intelligence services are often less concerned to avoid the eyes of their enemies than the steely gaze of journalists, human-rights activists and nongovernmental organizations all determinedly 'watching the watchers'.

## Intelligence cooperation

One of the most radical changes in the world of intelligence has been the recent increase in cooperation between intelligence services. This reflects the nature of the threats faced by Western governments which are increasingly transnational. Alliances have long existed between the foreign intelligence services of familiar partners such as United States, the United Kingdom, Canada, Australia, and New Zealand – or between the Nordic countries. But the pattern of sharing is now much wider and – precisely because the threats are 'transnational' rather than international – the key partners are often the domestic security agencies of the global south rather than other foreign intelligence services (Lander 2004, Jones 2006).

Globalization rather than terrorism has been the key driver of this change in intelligence culture. Elusive transnational threats, including terrorism and organized crime, have encouraged a migration from a culture of 'need to know' to 'need to share'. This trend accelerated markedly after 9/11 and resulted in closer cooperation with unfamiliar partners, including Syria, Jordan, Egypt and several African countries. The Federal Bureau of Investigation (FBI) now has as many overseas liaison officers serving abroad as the CIA. The New York Police Department – which operates its own intelligence agency – has officers in a dozen capital cities around the world. In foreign capitals, some of the heads of SIS stations have MI5 officers as their deputies. The expansion in international diplomacy between domestic security services – busily connecting what is inside with what is outside – is a sure sign of the growing impact of globalization upon intelligence services (Svendsen 2008).

Since 9/11, acrimonious transatlantic arguments have erupted over subjects such as Iraqi WMD assessments, secret prisons, and the interrogation of detainees. Yet countries that appear to be barely on speaking terms are often the closest intelligence partners (Rees and Aldrich 2005). In recent years, the Americans have worked with the security agencies of both Libya and Sudan, two countries which they had simultaneously listed as state-sponsors of terrorism. This is because intelligence cooperation is a rather specialist kind of 'low politics' that is often about specific cases or causes, allowing countries to work together in one area even while they disagree about something else. Meanwhile, the challenge of elusive transnational opponents compels intelligence agencies to work more closely together, despite their instinctive dislike of multilateral sharing. Nevertheless, the more powerful European states have so far resisted the rise of a federal EU intelligence service, preferring bilateral arrangements for the swapping of sensitive material (Aldrich 2009a).

There has also been considerable debate over intelligence to support the activities of the United Nations. Historically, the UN has been 'allergic' to intelligence, but with the expansion of its security role it has discovered that intelligence is necessary in at least three different contexts. First, effective intelligence support can greatly assist peacekeeping and all operational aspects of conflict resolution (see Chapter 26 this volume). The UN's Department of Peacekeeping Operations has over 90,000 uniformed personnel deployed and in 2006 it approved the creation of Joint Mission Analysis Centres in locations such as the Democratic Republic of the Congo and Haiti. Such support for peacekeeping forces can often be provided by the troop-contributing countries, however, the problems of sharing sensitive material such as signals intelligence amongst a kaleidoscopic coalition of peacekeepers remains difficult (Aid 2009). Second, in the wake of conflicts, the UN may well depend on intelligence support from states to monitor ceasefires and agreements on decommissioning weapons, or to serve commissions designed to investigate war crimes (Wiebes 2003). Third, and most controversially, the UN Secretary-General, together with his senior officers, requires strategic intelligence support. In the 1990s, the UN found it necessary to develop an analytical capability at its New York headquarters (Chesterman 2006).

Intelligence cooperation is often about security sector reform. The UK's Secret Intelligence Service currently gives a high priority to 'investing in newer intelligence partners to develop their capacity and skills' (SIS 2011). Over the last decade developed states have poured enormous resources into increasing the capacity of security agencies in the global south and leading security professionals have argued that well-regulated intelligence has a positive role to play in promoting good governance. In counties as far apart as Romania and South Africa, root and branch transformation of the intelligence and security services has been a core component of an impressive shift towards democratic control and improved governance (Martin 2007, Martin and Wilson 2008). Intelligence and counter-terrorism, including templates for national legislation, have been important Western exports in the security field since 2001. However, there has also been a clear tension between improving governance frameworks and improving capacity. America's key allies in the war on terror have not been the poster-boys of intelligence reformism such as South Africa. Instead they have been the much feared 'Mukhabarat' – the domestic security agencies of countries such as Jordan and Egypt. Britain's intelligence services maintained a close relationship with the shadowy agencies of Colonel Qaddafi's Libya in recent times. However, the 'Arab Spring' of 2011 swept away many of the West's favourite secret policemen in this region and a new approach to intelligence partnership will be required.

## Security and global surveillance

Global surveillance is on the rise. In 2003, America's shadowy technical intercept organization, the National Security Agency (NSA), constructed a new facility. Its purpose was to house all the internet data that it would collect over the next three years. In fact, they filled their newly constructed data warehouse in eleven months. In July 2009, President Obama gave the NSA approval for a remarkable $2 billion facility at San Antonio near Utah that will store unimaginable quantities of data. Much of this material is mundane – the 'electronic exhaust fumes of our lives'.

There is a distinct cleavage in the literature between those who attribute the rise of surveillance to short-term political factors and who therefore tend to emphasize agency, and those who favour longer-term structural explanations. There can be little doubt that recent times have seen nation-states taking extraordinary powers in areas such as data retention, communications interception, the monitoring of internet use, and the tracking of financial activities. Some have pointed directly to the pre-emptive doctrines developed by the Bush presidency, typically the National Security Strategy of 2002 (de Goede 2008). Others, especially sociologists, have tended to emphasize longer-term factors that identify modernity and globalization as the underlying drivers. David Lyon places considerable emphasis upon changing social habits which have resulted in societies that consider surveillance much more acceptable and even playful. Facebook and supermarket loyalty cards have ushered in an era of self-surveillance (Lyon 2007). Anthony Giddens has long argued that surveillance is simply an inescapable outgrowth of modernity and that the delivery of even basic services such as public health provision would be impossible without it (Giddens 1985).

James Der Derian has pointed to globalization as the driving force behind what he calls 'Speed, Simulation and Surveillance'. Der Derian's work is important because while Foucault and Bentham have been the mainstays, almost *ad nauseam*, of theoretical writing on *domestic* surveillance, his own work represents the first substantive effort to apply these ideas to security and the international system. Der Derian argues that geopolitics has been supplanted by chronopolitics, in which the real space of national geography is supplanted by the real time of international telecommunications. Notions of 'otherness' are central to the way in which he develops the themes about technological advances of international politics. Der Derian asserts that information technology, and especially its temporo-spatial impact, has resulted in a new importance being placed on 'us' and 'them'. Military simulations with computers create an alternative 'reality' and new kinds of space where much of the 'reality' of international politics now occurs and these simulations are ever-hungry for more data. Accordingly, the rise of surveillance and simulation reflects the fact that 'space is no longer in geography – it's in electronics' (Der Derian 1990: 307).

Global surveillance also transcends the local, national, regional, and international realms (Gill 2008). Arguably this constitutes a development of the first importance, since intelligence and security services have hitherto thrived on the divide between what is inside and outside the state. For more than a century, states often regulated their domestic security services quite closely, realizing that surveillance of their own citizens was deemed repellent.

By contrast, their foreign intelligence services were given more or less unlimited licence to watch, and indeed to subvert, those beyond the borders of the state. This Westphalian divide is still a normative boundary in the realm of intelligence. America's NSA has been involved in a 'domestic' wiretapping controversy which reflects a growing attention to transnational threats that sits awkwardly with its clear and long-standing legal directive not to listen in on American citizens (Aid 2009).

Global surveillance is often associated with hegemony and 'hyper-powerness', but in a curious way it also reflects anxiety and weakness – perhaps even brittleness. The obsession that Western governments have with 'risk' and its elimination also underlines the difficulty that even the most powerful secret agencies have in achieving traction against transnational groups. The intelligence agencies of nation-states continue to take the strain – especially in moments of crisis – but they are not well suited to their new tasks. Many aspects of globalization, including global civil society and global communications, have accelerated impressively, but global governance has not manifested itself strongly. The tracking and disrupting of all sorts of transnational miscreants therefore remains a task for national rather than global agencies that swim awkwardly in their novel environment. More advanced concepts are urgently required in the realm of intelligence. In the meantime, how the agencies might adapt to their new security challenges while simultaneously measuring up to the norms and values to which we aspire remains a puzzle.

## Conclusion

The practice of intelligence has changed radically over the last decade. Superficially this reflects the surge towards counter-terrorism, but more fundamentally it is symptomatic of the pressures of globalization over a rather longer period. Intelligence against transnational threats, whether it is terrorism, people-trafficking or weapons proliferation, is harder than collecting intelligence against old-fashioned static nation-state targets like the Chinese naval forces. Yet paradoxically, governments now expect rather more of intelligence, since they spend breathtaking amounts of money in this area. Moreover, intelligence underpins the tactics of pre-emption which have increasingly found favour as a form of risk-shifting in an age of global uncertainty. Pre-emption is morally hard to justify and so states often prefer secret pre-emption. Accordingly, when intelligence services uncover problems they are themselves increasingly tasked with secret pre-emptive action. The 'action' element has always existed, but it was often regarded as a fringe activity for intelligence services. Now covert action, disruption and event-shaping are centre stage.

Meanwhile, the global revolution in information and communications technologies has ushered in an era of self-surveillance in which Tesco, Amazon or Google may hold more data on us than our governments. This has increased the importance of the private actor in the security world, with airlines, banks and telecoms proving to be both large intelligence collectors and customers. The internet has also helped to galvanize an unlikely alliance of human rights campaigners, international lawyers and investigative journalists determined to keep a watchful eye on the intelligence services, set against the background of an intensified ethical debate over civil rights. Privately, most intelligence officers admit that it is hard to tackle the new security challenges of globalization and to work with exotic foreign partners while simultaneously meeting the expectations of global civil society for ethical practice. All these developments are altering what we understand intelligence to be, but as yet we lack the theoretical apparatus to interrogate these new forms of secret activity.

## Further reading

Matthew M. Aid, *Intel Wars: The Secret History of the Fight Against Terror* (Bloomsbury Press, 2012). An analysis of intelligence and special forces in the recent wars in Iraq and Afghanistan.

Richard K. Betts (1978), 'Analysis, war, and decision: Why intelligence failures are inevitable', *World Politics*, 31(2): 61–89. The classic essay on intelligence failure.

Melissa Mahle Boyle, *Denial and Deception: An Insider's View of the CIA* (Nation Books, 2005). One of the most perceptive intelligence memoirs written by a practitioner in recent years.

S.D. Gibson (2009), 'Future roles of the UK intelligence system', *Review of International Studies*, 35(4): 917–928. A prescient analysis of how intelligence is changing.

Peter Gill and Mark Phythian, *Intelligence in an Insecure World* (Polity, 2006). A critical overview of the debates on intelligence with a focus on civil rights.

Michael Herman, *Intelligence Power in Peace and War* (Cambridge University Press, 1996). The classic statement of intelligence and policy.

Robert Jervis (2006), 'Reports, politics, and intelligence failures: The case of Iraq', *Journal of Strategic Studies*, 29(1): 3–52. The Iraq WMD fiasco explained.

David Omand, *Securing the State* (Hurst/Columbia University Press, 2010). A thoughtful restatement of the virtues of intelligence as an aid to stability and good governance.

# Genocide and Crimes against Humanity

Adam Jones

## Abstract

In this chapter, students will learn about the concepts of 'genocide' – the destruction of human groups – and the range of atrocities classified as 'crimes against humanity'. Key modern instances of genocide are described, along with some central debates in the field of genocide studies, and proposals for intervention and prevention. The evolution of the related but much broader concept of crimes against humanity is also considered.

## Introduction

Is there a more potent word in the English language than 'genocide', the neologism invented by the Polish jurist Raphael Lemkin in the 1940s? Lemkin sought to encapsulate and criminalize an atrocious practice – the destruction of human groups – that had afflicted humanity since the dawn of recorded history, and probably long before. The power of the term that was first deployed in *Axis Rule in Occupied Europe* (Lemkin 1944) was evident in the United Nations' decision, just four years later, to establish a convention to prevent and punish the crime of genocide. And its power is evident today in the cartwheels that leaders and other policy-makers will turn, in order to avoid having the word 'genocide' applied to their actions. Nonetheless, the 'prohibition regime' against genocide remains weakly developed and only sporadically effective. Efforts to suppress genocide, and bring perpetrators to justice, have until recently run up against the most powerful institution in international relations: state sovereignty, which long permitted despots to annihilate members of their own populations without outside interference.

Similar observations pertain to the broader concept of 'crimes against humanity'. This term predates genocide in discourse (it featured in a joint Allied declaration of 1915), and in international law (it was used to prosecute Nazis at Nuremberg). But despite its radical novelty as a legal and philosophical concept, 'crimes against humanity' has only recently come into its own. Long regarded as a rather abstract catch-all, it has taken centre-stage for prosecutors in international tribunals, perhaps eclipsing 'genocide' in central respects. This chapter introduces readers to both of these core concepts and to the struggle to develop effective mechanisms to counter the strategies of mass atrocity that they denote.

## Genocide

'The word is new; the concept is ancient', wrote Leo Kuper in his field-defining treatise, *Genocide: Its Political Use in the Twentieth Century* (1981: 9). Only in the late nineteenth and early twentieth centuries did the vulnerability of ethnic and religious minorities in the modern state system evoke mounting humanitarian concern. It was decisive in the formation of Raphael Lemkin, a Polish-Jewish jurist who was powerfully moved by anti-Jewish pogroms in Eastern Europe, and by the slaughter of the Christian minorities of the Ottoman Empire during the First World War. But Lemkin's investigation of such persecutions extended back to antiquity. While attentive to the distinctive features of modern genocides, most genocide scholarship has likewise adopted Lemkin's broad view, conceptualizing genocide as something deeply embedded in human society, indeed in the human psyche. The subtitle of Ben Kiernan's opus, *Blood and Soil: Genocide and Extermination from Carthage to Darfur*, captures this sense of historical sweep (Kiernan 2007).

What is 'genocide'? It is simultaneously an empirical phenomenon, an analytical-legal concept, and a plea for intervention. In developing his 'catalysing idea', Raphael Lemkin was motivated above all by a need to protect threatened minorities, and to develop a legal instrument capable of mobilizing international support for their defence. This activist and interventionist dimension has characterized all subsequent applications of the term.

Lemkin was one of the great 'norm entrepreneurs' of the twentieth century. In casting about for a word to convey some of the horror of group destruction, and the damage done to the fabric of human civilization, he experimented first with 'barbarity' and 'vandalism'. In the end, he settled on a neologism combining the Greek *genos* (race, tribe) with the Latin-derived suffix *cide* (killing). As defined in *Axis Rule in Occupied Europe*, 'genocide' consisted of:

> a coordinated plan of different actions aiming at the destruction of essential foundations of the life of national groups, with the aim of annihilating the groups themselves. The objectives of such a plan would be disintegration of the political and social institutions, of culture, language, national feelings, religion, and the economic existence of national groups, and the destruction of the personal security, liberty, health, dignity, and even the lives of the individuals belonging to such groups. Genocide is directed against the national group as an entity, and the actions involved are directed against individuals, not in their individual capacity, but as members of the national group.
>
> (Lemkin 1944: 79)

As is immediately evident, the popular notion of genocide as the total *physical* extermination of a group – connected above all with the Nazi slaughter of up to six million European Jews during the Second World War – is not primary in Lemkin's formulation. He was preoccupied above all with the loss to humanity that the destruction of group cohesion and culture represented. Physical killing was one element of that destruction, but only one. The language of the UN Convention on the Prevention and Punishment of the Crime of Genocide (1948) accorded primacy to killing, but only as the first of five genocidal strategies that were outlawed 'whether committed in time of peace or in time of war':

> Article II. In the present Convention, genocide means any of the following acts committed with intent to destroy, in whole or in part, a national, ethnical, racial or religious group, as such:
>
> (a)  Killing members of the group;
>
> (b)  Causing serious bodily or mental harm to members of the group;
>
> (c)  Deliberately inflicting on the group conditions of life calculated to bring about its physical destruction in whole or in part;
>
> (d)  Imposing measures intended to prevent births within the group;
>
> (e)  Forcibly transferring children of the group to another group.

As with all such treaties, the Genocide Convention was the product of protracted negotiations and intensive haggling over language. The result was an instrument that was both revolutionary – in establishing a new standard for 'civilized' behaviour in international society – and profoundly vexing. What was meant by 'destroy'? Why was genocide limited to 'national, ethnical, racial [and] religious' groups – ignoring the vulnerabilities of political groups, social classes, and gender groups, to cite just three? What 'part' of a designated group had to be destroyed in order for the destruction to qualify as genocide? How severe did 'bodily or mental harm' have to be before it could be considered genocidal? For better or worse, though, the Convention wording still stands unaltered as the international, legal definition of genocide.

Difficulties of definition and application contributed to the Convention's sidelining as a legal instrument for several decades after it came into force. (Lemkin himself died in obscurity in 1959.) More significant than its wording, however, was the challenge the Convention posed to the essential norm of the international system: state sovereignty and the right to non-interference in the domestic affairs of a state. This was precisely the norm that Lemkin had hoped to displace, by challenging the unlimited right of governments to persecute national minorities. But any such effort ran up against the UN Charter, which anchored itself in traditional conceptions of state sovereignty. Interventions in genocide did occur between the 1950s and the dawn of the 1990s, and were sometimes successful: for example, in East Pakistan/ Bangladesh in 1971, Cambodia in 1978–1979, and Uganda in 1979 (see Wheeler 2000). But in no case did those who mounted the interventions cite the Genocide Convention – or other humanitarian grounds – to justify their actions. In general, as Leo Kuper wrote in his 1981 volume, a 'right to genocide' was observed in the domestic practice of states. The guiding understanding of 'security' was the security of states and their leaders – not that of the security of the civilian populations whose putative guardians were often their worst persecutors.

## Challenges of intervention

A number of factors contributed to a resurgence of interest in genocide from the 1970s to the 1990s, and its growing use as a buttress for legal, rhetorical and military intervention. These included the continuing evolution of the human rights regime, demonstrated by the Helsinki Accords of 1975 and the UN conventions against apartheid (1976) and torture (1985); the growing influence of non-governmental organizations such as Amnesty International and Helsinki Watch (later Human Rights Watch); and the mass movement against nuclear weapons and the 'omnicide' (destruction of all life) that they threatened to inflict. Equally significant was the end of the Cold War – which separated issues of humanitarian intervention from the previous East–West competition – and the complex nature of national and international violence in the post-Cold War period. On one hand, the end of the bipolar conflict between the superpowers allowed for a negotiated end to bloody conflicts in Southern Africa, Central America and South Asia. On the other hand, the break-up of the Soviet empire produced a wave of wars of succession, predominantly in Central Asia, some with genocidal overtones (as between Armenia and Azerbaijan, or in Chechnya in the 1990s and into the 2000s).

The collapse of communism in Central and Eastern Europe spilled over to Yugoslavia. Following the death of Marshal Tito in 1980, the Yugoslav Federation experienced economic decline and a growing crisis of political legitimacy. With the renewed impetus for national self-determination in the wake of the Soviet collapse, a generation of nationalist politicians worked to undermine the federation and to establish ethnically dominated nation states. In 1991, Yugoslavia erupted into open war – first with a brief conflict over the secession of Slovenia, and then into a vicious trilateral struggle among Croatians, Serbs, and Bosniaks (Bosnian Muslims). By 1992, it was clear that a genocidal dynamic had developed. This was especially (but not exclusively) true of the Serbian 'ethnic cleansing', conducted by local militias supported from Belgrade, of areas of Bosnia-Herzegovina in which Muslims constituted a substantial minority or outright majority.

The apparent return of genocide to the European heartland, half a century after the vanquishing of Nazism, prompted urgent debate among European and North American governments about how a successful 'humanitarian intervention' could be mounted. Western European countries experimented with a variety of measures, including diplomatic pressure and UN resolutions; the imposition of an arms embargo; the creation of an International Criminal Tribunal for the Former Yugoslavia (ICTY) to try accused war criminals and *génocidaires* on all sides of the conflict; and the dispatching of UN peacekeepers (the 'blue helmets'). These strategies, however, produced little in the way of protection for the victims. The siege of the Bosnian capital, Sarajevo, became institutionalized, despite a small UN presence and a trickle of outside aid. The uniform arms embargo favoured the Serbs, who had inherited most of the stockpiles of the Yugoslav National Army, over the landlocked and militarily strapped Bosniaks. And the policy of establishing 'safe areas' for threatened Muslim populations proved a grim chimera. When Serb forces chose to eliminate these areas in 1995, the desultory peacekeeper presence proved wholly inadequate to impede Serb designs. The 'safe area' at the town of Srebrenica was overrun in July, and the result was the worst massacre in Europe since the Second World War. Some 8,000 Bosnian men and adolescent boys were rounded up or hunted down, and slaughtered in scenes often reminiscent of the Nazi mass killings of Jewish and other civilians on the Eastern Front in 1941.

Srebrenica, however, did prove a catalyst for a resolution of the Balkans conflicts – in part because the elimination of the safe areas ratified 'ethnic cleansing' by creating a patchwork of geographically contiguous and ethnically homogeneous territories. In the aftermath of the massacre, NATO launched its most vigorous airstrikes on Serb strongholds. Croatian forces – which had rearmed with covert US assistance – launched a lightning assault on the majority-Serb Krajina region abutting Bosnian Serb territory. Some 200,000 Serbs fled (today they constitute the largest refugee population in Europe); and with Belgrade unwilling to intervene, the Bosnian Serbs were forced to the negotiating table. The signing of the Dayton Peace Accords in late 1995 led to the influx of 60,000 NATO troops to oversee the fragile peace, and to help build new and, where possible, non-sectarian institutions to stave off future genocidal outbreaks (see Innes 2006).

Intervention in the Balkans was thus generally slow, halfhearted, and ineffectual. But this was as nothing compared to the world's stunning abdication when not just genocide, but a full-blown holocaust, descended upon Rwanda in the spring of 1994. When systematic killing of ethnic Tutsis and moderate Hutus began in April of that year, and ten Belgian peacekeepers were murdered by the 'Hutu Power' regime, Western countries did intervene – but only to rescue their own nationals, leaving black Africans to the depredations of Rwandan armed forces and 'Hutu Power' militias. Government officials in the USA and elsewhere bent over backwards to avoid applying the word 'genocide' to what was in fact the most rapid and intensive genocide in recorded history. To have done so would have increased the pressure to intervene and suppress the mass killing, and that was hardly conceivable. In the scathing assessment of human rights researcher Alison Des Forges, 'Rwanda was simply too remote . . . too poor, too little, and probably too black to be worthwhile' (quoted in National Film Board of Canada 1997). Even the force of 2,500 peacekeepers deployed to Rwanda after an interim peace accord in 1993 was rapidly scaled down, leaving a skeleton force under Canadian Lt.-Gen. Roméo Dallaire to do what little it could to protect threatened Tutsis and moderate Hutus. Dallaire's troops heroically managed to save thousands of lives, but the outside world abandoned hundreds of thousands of other Rwandans to the savagery of the 'Hutu Power' *génocidaires*.

Rwanda was an abysmal low point, but it was not the final word in humanitarian intervention. It was followed several years later, in fact, by one of the most successful, and in many ways remarkable, of contemporary interventions – in September 1999, in the tiny Southeast Asian territory of East Timor. In 1975, East Timor – previously a Portuguese colony – was invaded and occupied by the military regime in Indonesia. There ensued a scorched-earth campaign of suppression that killed fully one-third of the East Timorese population (some 200,000 people): by ground-level massacres; in bombing raids; and by starvation and destitution as crops were burned and civilian populations fled into inaccessible and infertile mountain regions. While the simultaneous atrocities of the Khmer Rouge aroused international condemnation and Hollywood film treatments, however, the suffering of the East Timorese was ignored by all but a tiny international network of scholars and activists. The powerful position of Indonesia in the strategic *realpolitik* of the West trumped, for a quarter-century, the Timorese right to self-determination.

In 1999, the military regime under Indonesian President Suharto collapsed. Suharto was replaced by an elderly civilian leader, B.J. Habibie, who surprised many by approving a referendum on independence for East Timor. When

Timorese went peacefully to the polls in August 1999, they voted over-whelmingly for independence. The Indonesian military and its locally raised militias responded with a murderous crackdown. Thousands of Timorese civilians were killed, and much of the territory's infrastructure was burnt to the ground. As the small corps of international observers huddled terrified in the UN compound in Dili, machete-wielding thugs and pyromaniacs roamed beyond the walls. It seemed that, just as in Rwanda, the UN would abandon the field; the world would turn its back; and genocide would reign unconstrained.

The violence, though, erupted scant months after the Kosovo crisis of 1999. The conflict in Kosovo was a holdover from the larger Balkans wars of the 1990s: formally part of Serbia, it had an overwhelming ethnic-Albanian majority which had long agitated for freedom from Serb subjugation – first peacefully, and then via an armed rebel movement, the Kosovo Liberation Army (KLA). In April 1999, Serb forces conducted a systematic campaign, murdering thousands of ethnic Albanians, and expelling some 800,000 to neighbouring countries. With memories of the Srebrenica debacle still relatively fresh, media airwaves and government press conferences resounded to Western leaders' lofty declarations that the rights and lives of Kosovar Albanians had to be protected. The result was a sustained air campaign against Serb forces, and eventually the withdrawal of the Serb military from the province. (In February 2008, Kosovo unilaterally declared itself independent, a status recognized by over 70 UN member states including the United States and major Western European countries.) If the plight of Kosovar Albanians in Europe was sufficient to spark a major Western intervention, why should the plight of Timorese in Southeast Asia be insufficient? The well-established Timor solidarity network organized popular demonstrations that drew hundreds of thousands to the streets in major Australian cities alone.

The *realpolitik* equation had not changed. It behoved the world's most powerful countries to avoid antagonizing Indonesia, especially its still-dominant military, and to leave the Timorese to their fate. But the combina-tion of popular pressure and moral suasion, with the Kosovo precedent still fresh in public consciousness, trumped narrower conceptions of the 'national interest'. The United States placed strong pressure on its erstwhile clients in the Indonesian Army and threatened to stop loans to Indonesia coming from the World Bank and IMF. After receiving official consent for an operation from Jakarta, the Australian government led a military expedition to occupy the territory. Three weeks after the outbreak of mass violence, the first Australian soldiers stepped ashore at Dili, and a UN-sponsored protectorate took shape that oversaw the withdrawal of Indonesian forces and ushered East Timor towards its status (in 2002) as a newly independent state (see Robinson 2010).

The Timor case suggests that the world's tolerance of genocide and mass atrocity may be declining, and the notion of a 'responsibility to protect' – in the catch-phrase propounded by a Canadian-sponsored commission – may be gaining ground (see ICISS 2001, and Chapter 32 this volume). Mitigating such optimism, however, was the pallid international response to the crisis in Darfur, a territory in western Sudan. When rebel movements in Darfur demanded autonomy, the authorities in Khartoum responded as despotic regimes often have: by mobilizing military and paramilitary forces to wage a brutal counter-insurgency, featuring widespread and indiscriminate violence against Darfurese civilians. In September 2004, US Secretary of State Colin Powell announced his government's conviction that the atrocities constituted 'genocide'. The declaration, however, was accompanied by little meaningful action. A small and ill-equipped African Union peacekeeping force watched ineffectually as populations were uprooted, civilian men and adolescent boys were murdered, and women and girls were raped.

The Darfur crisis – which still simmers at the time of writing – nevertheless generated some positive developments. The outburst of protest on university and high school campuses in the USA and elsewhere was notable and encouraging. By urging their academic institutions to divest from companies linked to Sudan, staging sit-ins and street demonstrations, and using the lever of the 2008 Beijing Olympics to pressure the Chinese government to withdraw vital political and economic support from the Sudanese regime, the movement energetically countered the stereotype of the current generation of students as apathetic, narcissistic, and ill-informed.

Moreover, Darfur fell under the jurisdiction of a newly created institution, the International Criminal Court (ICC). The founding of the ICC in 2002 was the culmination of legal mechanisms developed over the decades to confront genocide (including the formative one – the Nuremberg tribunal – which functioned before the Genocide Convention came into effect). The signatories to the 'Rome Statute' which underpinned the ICC's operations sought to create a permanent body to *supplement* national legal institutions and to *supplant* the 'ad-hoc tribunals' devised for the former Yugoslavia (the ICTY, 1993) and Rwanda (the ICTR, 1994). At the time of writing in mid-2011, the ICC had handled only African cases – reflecting the less-developed national-legal mechanisms on that continent, but perhaps also signifying the court's recognition that such cases were politically 'safe', compared with (for example) launching investigations into genocidal atrocities in Western-occupied Iraq after 2003, or crimes associated with the US-led 'war on terror' (the US itself, though it signed the Rome Statute, avoided ratifying it – a policy established under George Bush, Jr. which has continued under President Obama).

As the legal machinery to confront mass atrocities has evolved, another trend has become notable, evidenced most recently in the indictments of Sudanese president Omar al-Bashir and several of his henchmen for crimes committed in Darfur. When the ICC Pre-Trial Chamber first handed down those indictments, 'genocide' was absent. Chief prosecutor Luis Moreno-Ocampo appealed, and 'genocide' was subsequently added. But the overriding preference of the ICC was to substitute instead the charge of 'crimes against humanity'. It is time now to turn to consider this parallel concept in some detail. What are the crimes that are deemed so extreme as to constitute assaults not just on the direct victims, but on all of humanity, and the sense of 'humanness' that allegedly binds it?

## Understanding crimes against humanity

'Genocide', as we have seen, is a relatively recent concept. 'Crimes against humanity' is somewhat older – indeed, use of the phrase can be traced as far back as 1860, when the US Republican Party denounced the African slave trade in precisely this language. The Martens Clause in the 1899 Hague Conventions cited 'the laws of humanity' and similar language (references to acts that 'shock' and 'offend' the 'universal conscience,' or are 'intolerable from the point of view of the entire international community'). It was not until April 1915, however, that 'crimes against humanity' became the focus of a diplomatic declaration. When widespread reports of mass atrocities against Christian minorities of the Ottoman Empire reached the West, Russia – which had long positioned itself as a defender of threatened Christians, and had occupied parts of northeastern Anatolia under this self-declared mandate – called for the Triple Alliance to denounce Ottoman 'crimes . . . against Christianity and civilization'. The other Allies, however, felt the phrasing might provoke further attacks against Christians, and instead the reference was changed to crimes 'against humanity and civilization'.

Following the Second World War, 'crimes against humanity' were codified in the Nuremberg Charter of August 1945, which set them alongside 'crimes against peace' and 'war crimes', and defined them as: 'murder, extermination, enslavement, deportation, and other inhumane acts committed against any civilian population, before or during the war . . . whether or not in violation of the domestic law of the country where perpetrated'. Though Nuremberg focused on 'crimes against peace', the Charter established two core elements of 'crimes against humanity' which have lasted to the present. These were that the crimes targeted civilians, and could occur both in war and 'peace'. The work of the Nuremberg Tribunal and the ad-hoc tribunals of the 1990s led to the benchmark definition of 'crimes against humanity' in the Rome Statute of the International Criminal Court (1998) (see Box 17.1).

Note that in this phrasing, two crucial additional elements are added to the understanding of 'crimes against humanity', beyond the targeting of civilians and the application to conditions of both war and peace. Such crimes must be 'committed as part of a widespread *or* systematic attack' (NB: not 'widespread *and* systematic'), and perpetrators must have the *mens rea* (mental element or knowledge) that their crimes are committed as part of that wider attack, not in isolation. It is also important to stress that only individuals may be charged with crimes against humanity, as is also the case with genocide. States or regimes as a collectivity cannot be held to account.

Beyond these general points, it is apparent that the crimes against humanity prohibited in the Rome Statute are a great deal broader than those banned by the Genocide Convention. (They are, moreover, open-ended, via the

## BOX 17.1 CRIMES AGAINST HUMANITY AS DEFINED BY THE ROME STATUTE OF THE INTERNATIONAL CRIMINAL COURT

For the purpose of this Statute, 'crime against humanity' means any of the following acts when committed as part of a widespread or systematic attack directed against any civilian population, with knowledge of the attack: (a) Murder; (b) Extermination; (c) Enslavement; (d) Deportation or forcible transfer of population; (e) Imprisonment or other severe deprivation of physical liberty in violation of fundamental rules of international law; (f) Torture; (g) Rape, sexual slavery, enforced prostitution, forced pregnancy, enforced sterilization, or any other form of sexual violence of comparable gravity; (h) Persecution against any identifiable group or collectivity on political, racial, national, ethnic, cultural, religious, gender . . . or other grounds that are universally recognized as impermissible under international law . . . (i) Forced disappearance of persons; (j) The crime of apartheid; (k) Other inhumane acts of a similar character intentionally causing great suffering, or serious injury to body or to mental or physical health.

addendum of 'other inhumane acts of a similar character'.) Though the language draws directly from the Nuremberg Tribunal definition, it also incorporates additional crimes which reflect the evolution of human-rights discourse in the post-World War Two period. The crime of apartheid, for example, reflects the international mobilizations to confront this institution in the South African context, culminating in the International Convention on the Suppression and Punishment of the Crime of Apartheid in November 1973. (The convention bans acts 'committed for the purpose of establishing and maintaining domination by one racial group of persons over any other racial group of persons and systematically oppressing them'.) The provision against the 'forced disappearance of persons' likewise reflected the pervasiveness of this atrocious practice in Latin America, especially, under the military regimes of the 1970s and 1980s. A campaign by Amnesty International and sympathetic regimes (notably, the democratizing ones that supplanted military rule in South America) led to the Declaration on the Protection of All Persons from Enforced Disappearance (1992). Finally, the prominence of rape and related sexual crimes in the Rome Statute's provisions was spurred by feminist mobilizations of the past several decades.

Space constraints prevent detailed attention to all the offences enumerated in crimes-against-humanity legislation. In *Crimes Against Humanity: A Beginner's Guide* (Jones 2008), I sought to provide an accessible primer on the subject. For present purposes, though, a couple of interesting points of crossover with the UN Genocide Convention are worth noting. First of all, the definition of 'extermination' is strikingly similar (indeed, almost identical) to Article 2(c) of the Genocide Convention, which bans acts 'deliberately inflicting on the group conditions of life calculated to bring about its physical destruction in whole or in part'. The Rome Statute's definition of 'extermination', drawing on the Nuremberg Tribunal's, cites 'the intentional infliction of conditions of life, inter alia [among other things] the deprivation of access to food and medicine, calculated to bring about the destruction of part of a population'. In 1996, the UN's International Law Commission acknowledged that extermination and genocide were 'closely related', but clarified that 'extermination covers situations in which a group of individuals who do not share any common characteristics are killed'. That is – and this applies to all crimes against humanity, with the exception of apartheid – victims need not belong to a particular 'national, ethnical, racial or religious group', and be targeted *as such*.

The crime against humanity of 'persecution' has served, in practice, as a context and adjunct for other offenses, rather than as a standalone offense. It is notable, nonetheless, that the Rome Statute refers to persecution on 'political, racial, national, ethnic, cultural, religious, gender . . . or other grounds'. It thus incorporates the four group protections extended by the Genocide Convention, but supplements them with other variables (political, cultural, gender) that many genocide scholars and activists have longed to see added to anti-genocide provisions (and have often incorporated in their own preferred definitions of genocide). It is, moreover, again open-ended ('. . . or other grounds'), so that persecution on the basis of, for example, social class could theoretically also be included.

On the basis of the foregoing discussion, the growing preference of international prosecutors for charges of 'crimes against humanity', rather than genocide, is perhaps understandable. A much wider range of acts is encompassed; the limited group definitions and vexing 'intent' provisions of the Genocide Convention are transcended or downplayed. Moreover, the consequences for perpetrators convicted of crimes against humanity are usually roughly the same as for genocide: twenty years to life in prison. Thus, to date, *only* in the case of Sudan's Omar al-Bashir and his confederates has the ICC issued an indictment for genocide – and then only after its original exclusion from the charge sheet was appealed by ICC prosecutors.

One can expect this trend to continue, and as it does, 'crimes against humanity' may finally emerge from the shadows of the Genocide Convention, where they have long languished. While the phrase at first glance lacks the punch of Raphael Lemkin's brilliant neologism, it is revelatory and revolutionary in its own way. The notion of a universal humanness and *humaneness* that is fundamentally undermined by this set of atrocities – all of them, like genocide, *jus cogens* offences that fall under 'universal jurisidiction', and thus may be prosecuted by any legal authority anywhere – attests to the mounting influence of a cosmopolitan vision of humankind, and a sense of collective responsibility to prevent and punish mass atrocities worldwide. Such crimes are now held to undermine the security of all.

## Conclusion

How far does the influence of this cosmopolitan, human-security vision extend beyond the realm of rhetoric? Has it truly succeeded in changing the norm of state sovereignty which for so long enabled leaders to inflict atrocities upon their populations?

Sceptics will find no shortage of evidence to challenge rosy universalist assumptions. Genocide and crimes against humanity remain pervasive features of our age. The willingness of states and leaders – and those global institutions, like the UN and International Criminal Court, that are composed and influenced by them – to intervene to 'prevent and punish' such mass atrocities is still decisively influenced by considerations of *realpolitik*. All the indictments so far handed down by the ICC, for instance, are drawn from Africa – the least politically influential and economically powerful of the world's regions. As for humanitarian and military intervention in crisis zones where atrocities rage, the record is uneven, and efforts have often been half-hearted. The willingness of the UN Security Council, as well as key regional players like the Arab League and African Union, to intervene in early 2011 to protect Libyan civilians threatened by Moammar Qaddafi's regime was a striking development. But within weeks, key Security Council members, notably Russia, were getting cold feet; the Arab League also hesitated; and when arguably even more severe atrocities against civilians broke out in Syria, the waning appetite for intervention and Syria's key strategic position combined to limit the response of the outside world to (sometimes harsh) denunciations and symbolic gestures like the withdrawal of ambassadors. Inconsistency and an *ad hoc* approach have therefore prevailed. Proposals to establish military forces under the control of regional authorities or the UN have languished.

Another difficulty has arisen with the use of a discourse of humanitarian intervention to justify actions which may be founded on neo-imperial motivations, and which evoke the opposition of a large majority of the global community. The deleterious effect of the US and UK administrations' justification for their 2003 invasion of Iraq will long linger. The invasion, carried out without UN sanction, produced the near-collapse of the Iraqi state and economy. It was followed by reciprocal bouts of genocidal killing among Shia and Sunni communities, in which tens if not hundreds of thousands of civilians were slaughtered, and in which *millions* of innocent people were displaced, whether internally or as refugees in surrounding countries. Any intervention that proceeds with the involvement of the world's leading states will almost automatically generate strong opposition from those who feel the humanitarian rhetoric masks a more sinister, neo-colonial agenda – as was evident in the controversy over NATO's Libyan action in 2011. Moreover, the great powers – notably the 'Big 5' permanent members of the Security Council – continue to enjoy something approaching a free hand with regard to the atrocities they themselves inflict and sponsor. Russia, for example, suffered no significant sanction for its successive assaults on the breakaway region of Chechnya. China's treatment of its minority Tibetan and Uighur populations continues to be both atrocious and tolerated. And the US establishment of a torture regime at Guantánamo Bay, and in numerous 'black sites' for the forcibly disappeared, proceeded without negative international consequences, beyond an erosion of US legitimacy and standing in world politics.

Nonetheless, for those willing (or desperate) to isolate more positive developments, some evidence is also at hand. A close examination of several of the great-power-led interventions in the past decade or two (Bosnia, Kosovo, East Timor, Sierra Leone, Libya) suggests that moral–ethical principles *were* influential, and may even have been decisive. Successful intervention occurred in Bosnia only after years of mounting outrage at the depredations of Serb forces, culminating in the slaughter at Srebrenica in 1995. Kosovo reflected a desire, based on the Bosnian precedent, to stop mass atrocities before they became a full-scale genocide. Forces of global civil society promoting intervention in East Timor were able to 'norm-graft' the justifications offered for the Kosovo intervention. British forces were dispatched to Sierra Leone in significant part to lend substance to the humanitarian rhetoric favoured by the Labour government (Williams 2001). The fact that French president Nicolas Sarkozy's push for intervention in Libya reflected a desire to bolster his domestic political standing does not cancel out the important fact that such acts *can* bolster a politician's standing. US support for NATO's actions in Libya, meanwhile, seem to have been strongly shaped by a small group of advisers centered around Samantha Power, the National Security Council member whose seminal book on genocide, '*A Problem from Hell': America and the Age of Genocide*, reflected the nascent norms of a state's 'responsibility to protect' (not murder) its citizens, and an international 'will to intervene' when it failed to do so (see Nicholas 2011). A reflexive neo-colonial explanation for these interventions, moreover, runs up against the fact that the territories concerned (Libya excepted) hardly offered the kind of opportunities for material plunder or geostrategic expansion that are usually held to underpin imperial campaigns. Even in the Libyan case, what could military intervention achieve, in terms of material access and exploitation, that the previous coddling of Qaddafi could not?

One way of muting neo-colonial tendencies (and anti-imperialist critiques) in these instances is for regional actors to play a greater role. There are signs that regional organizations, such as the European Union (EU), the Organization of American States (OAS), the African Union (AU), and the Economic Community of West African States (ECOWAS), increasingly recognize that part of what binds their members is a commitment to certain values and legal strictures (see Chapter 24 this volume). As well, it is regional actors who are more likely to be directly and negatively affected by the 'spillover effect' of mass atrocities – for example, by the flow of refugees fleeing them. The conflict-resolution activities of the OAS in Central and South America; the 'carrot' the EU has extended to Balkan states in return for expanding democratic freedoms and arresting war criminals and *génocidaires*; the faltering but not irrelevant role of the AU in Darfur; the Nigerian-led ECOWAS forces dispatched to Liberia – all suggest that attention to cases of mass atrocity, and a willingness to intervene to suppress them, is mounting at the regional level.

Finally, the substantial civil-society mobilizations which have developed around campaigns to prevent and suppress genocide and crimes against humanity constitute another significant and positive development. In the

Balkans, East Timor, Darfur, and Libya, such initiatives seem to have exerted considerable influence; in the Timorese and Darfuri cases, they were perhaps decisive. This points to the evolution of a vision of cosmopolitan 'human security' extending far beyond the realm of high politics, to the ordinary woman and man in the global 'street' (see Chapter 19 this volume). This vision is distinctively *modern*, but it is not *new*. In fact, the record of the past couple of centuries supplies numerous instances of civil society led mobilizations that have succeeded (in tandem with powerful state sponsors) in mitigating or vanquishing destructive and atrocious institutions. A little over two hundred years ago, chattel slavery was a legal and globalized practice. By the end of the nineteenth century it had been all but eliminated – a status which holds true today, despite the prevalence of certain 'slavery-like practices'. Barely a century ago, the vast majority of the world's territories and populations were controlled by a handful of exploitative Western powers. This arrangement was obliterated by the anti-colonial struggles of the twentieth century, and it is literally *unimaginable* that it could return – any more than South Africa could return to a white-ruled apartheid system, or that the world's women could be forced back into the politically invisible and economically powerless position they occupied at most times and in most places in the past. Genocide and crimes against humanity remain potent threats to the security of individuals and communities. But this should not blind us to the limited successes achieved in the struggles against them, and the potential that may exist to sideline or suppress them decisively in the future.

## Further reading

M. Cherif Bassiouni, *Crimes Against Humanity: Historical Evolution and Contemporary Application* (Cambridge University Press, 2011). The latest edition of the most in-depth legal study of crimes against humanity.

Frank Chalk and Kurt Jonassohn, *The History and Sociology of Genocide* (Yale University Press, 1990). An early and eclectic study, still widely used in the genocide studies field.

Adam Jones, *Genocide: A Comprehensive Introduction*, 2nd edition (Routledge, 2010). Attempts to capture the interdisciplinary breadth of genocide studies in a student-friendly volume.

Leo Kuper, *Genocide: Its Political Use in the Twentieth Century* (Yale University Press, 1981). A foundational text of comparative genocide studies.

Samantha Power, *'A Problem from Hell': America and the Age of Genocide* (Basic Books, 2002). Influential critique of US policy in contemporary genocides, and a tribute to the individuals who sought to steer it in an anti-genocide direction.

William Schabas, *Genocide in International Law: The Crime of Crimes*, 2nd edition (Cambridge University Press, 2009). Exhaustive legal survey by a past president of the International Association of Genocide Scholars (IAGS).

# Ethnic Conflict

Stuart J. Kaufman

## Abstract

In this chapter, students will learn about the relationships between ethnicity and warfare. Ethnic groups are usually distinguished by some combination of language, race and religious affiliation. These differences are not natural or primordial but socially constructed. Most countries are multiethnic, and most ethnic relationships are peaceful. However, some ethnic conflicts do become violent, and they represent a sizeable fraction of all wars that occurred in the twentieth century. Violence is most likely when government is weak; the groups have myth-symbol complexes that lead them to see each other as hostile; they fear for the survival of their group; and the sides demand political dominance over some disputed territory. While power-sharing and compromise are the internationally preferred formula for resolving ethnic conflicts, in practice most of them end only when one side wins militarily.

## Introduction

Ethnic identities have existed throughout recorded history. Even in ancient times, ethnic groups such as the Hebrews, Babylonians and Egyptians were important political actors (Smith 1986). When different linguistic and religious groups mix, political issues inevitably arise, leading to 'ethnic conflict'. These conflicts are almost always managed peacefully, however. To take one example, the Soviet Union is said to have included 120 ethnic groups, yet with all of these points of friction, there was only a handful of cases of ethnic groups clashing violently when the Soviet Union collapsed (Fearon and Laitin 1996).

Still, especially when the issue at stake is the political dominance of one group over another, violent ethnic clashes do sometimes occur. These ethnic wars are sometimes of critical international importance: Pakistan's effort to repress the Bengalis of East Pakistan in 1971, for example, provoked an Indian invasion that led to East Pakistan's becoming the independent country of Bangladesh, changing permanently the balance of power in South Asia.

In the twentieth century, ethnic civil wars – indeed, civil wars of all kinds – were more important than ever before. Though they were overshadowed by the two World Wars and then the Cold War, civil wars were more common than international wars throughout the twentieth century (Correlates of War). Many of those civil wars were ethnic – in fact, 45 per cent of all wars from 1919 to 2001 were fought for national liberation or ethnic autonomy. After the Cold War, the proportion rose: from 1989 to 2006, a full 75 per cent of all wars were ethnonationalist wars (Wimmer *et al.* 2009).

Some of these conflicts were also large and very violent. On one list of the ten bloodiest civil wars of the twentieth century (Correlates of War), for example, half of the cases were ethnic conflicts: Sudan (1963–1972 and 1983–2005), Pakistan/Bangladesh (1971), Rwanda (1994), and Bosnia (1992-1995). Nigeria's civil war of 1967–1970 was comparably bloody. Each of these conflicts is estimated to have cost upwards of a quarter of a million lives, and each was not only a catastrophe for the country that became a battlefield, but also a major source of disruption, conflict, and refugees for neighbouring countries as well. As a result, each became a major international issue, together sparking every sort of foreign intervention from mediation efforts to direct military involvement. Ethnic conflict is therefore a central issue for security studies.

Even ethnic riots can be deadly on a large enough scale to constitute a problem for international security. Hindu–Muslim riots in India in 1947 killed between 100,000 and 200,000 people and generated about 10 million refugees. A series of riots in 1966 by Muslim northern Nigerians (mostly Hausa) against Christian Ibos from the south displaced over a million people by 1967. Rioting by Sri Lankan Sinhalese aimed against the Tamil minority in 1977 killed only about one hundred people but displaced over 50,000. All three episodes catalyzed civil war causing even more death and destruction. Other cases, such as later rounds of Hindu attacks on Muslims in northern India, do not themselves lead to war, but reflect and contribute to international tensions – in this case, between India and Pakistan (Horowitz 2000).

## What is ethnic conflict?

Discussions of ethnicity and ethnic conflict are notoriously imprecise because people disagree about what counts as an ethnic conflict. Are race relations between blacks and whites in the United States an example of low-violence ethnic conflict, or is racial conflict a different category altogether? If race is different, does the distinction extend to Rwanda, where Hutus and Tutsis – both black – referred to their difference as one of race? Are relations between Muslims and Hindus in India, or between Sunni and Shi'a Arabs in Iraq, cases of ethnic conflict, or do they belong in different categories as 'religious', 'communal', or 'sectarian' conflicts?

For an anthropologist, what these cases all have in common is that the groups involved are primarily ascriptive – that is, membership in the groups is typically assigned at birth and is difficult to change. In theory, Indian Muslims can convert and become Hindu, and Iraqi Sunnis can become Shi'a, but in practice few do, and the conversion of those few is not always accepted by their new co-ethnics. Such identities are 'sticky', hard to change even if they are not marked by the kind of obvious physical differences that distinguish African Americans from white Americans. Based on this commonality, I will use the broader definition of ethnicity that encompasses all of these kinds of ascriptive groups. According to Anthony Smith (1986), a group is an ethnic group if its members share the following traits: a common name, a believed common descent, elements of a shared culture (most often language or religion), common historical memories, and attachment to a particular territory.

In the past, experts disagreed widely about where ethnicity comes from. Some, focusing on the evidence that many ethnic identities seem to go back hundreds or thousands of years, asserted that ethnicity was a 'primordial' identity, and implied that it was essentially unchangeable. They emphasized that groups often worked hard to make their identity unchangeable, sometimes carving that identity onto their bodies through tattoos or circumcision (Isaacs 1975). Even when they do not go that far, however, people tend to stick to the identities – especially the language and religion – they learn first from their parents. This view of ethnicity implies that ethnic conflict is based on 'ancient hatreds' that are impossible to eradicate and nearly impossible to manage.

There is another, more complicated side to ethnic identity, however. Most people have multiple identities that are either 'nested' (as subgroups within larger groups) or overlapping. The average Cuban-American is at the same time also an American Hispanic or Latino, an American Catholic, an American, and a member of the worldwide Catholic Church. Which identity is more important to her is likely to depend on the situation: when listening to the Pope, she is likely to respond as a Catholic; when watching the US president, as an American; and when thinking about US policy toward Cuba, as a Cuban-American.

Furthermore, identities do sometimes change, with new ones emerging and old ones disappearing, especially in times of crisis. For example, when the Soviet Union was breaking apart in the early 1990s, Ukrainians and Russians in the Transnistria region of Moldova came together as 'Russophones' – people who preferred to speak Russian rather than Moldovan – to resist the assertiveness of the ethnic Moldovans (Kaufman 2001). On the other hand, the 'Yugoslav' identity disappeared when the country of Yugoslavia did in 1991, so people who formerly called themselves Yugoslavs had to shift to another identity as Serbs, Croats, or members of some other group.

Noticing that people shift their identity – or at least the identity they use politically – based on the situation, a second group of scholars emerged to argue that ethnic identity is not 'primordial' at all, but merely 'instrumental' (Hardin 1995). From this perspective, people follow 'ethnic' leaders when it is in their interests to do so, and leaders try to create ethnic solidarity when it works for them. This view of ethnic identity implies that ethnic conflict can be blamed primarily on selfish leaders who mislead their followers in pursuit of their own power.

A third point of view about ethnic identity mixes the other two views by emphasizing the degree to which people create their identities. Expressed in book titles such as *The Invention of Tradition* (Ranger 1992), this view points out that ethnic identities are 'socially constructed'. They are not 'natural' in the sense that a simple primordialist view would assume; even racial distinctions are just a matter of custom. For example, most African Americans accept the label 'black', but in South Africa, most of them would be classified as 'coloured' – of mixed race – rather than as the darker, purely African 'blacks'. Most white Americans would not notice the difference, but in apartheid-era South Africa, the difference would have shaped every aspect of people's lives.

Furthermore, constructivists pointed out, the source of these customs was 'invented traditions': writers or scholars who created what Anthony Smith calls a 'myth-symbol complex'. This myth-symbol complex establishes the 'accepted' history of the group and the criteria for distinguishing who is a member; identifies heroes and enemies; and glorifies symbols of the group's identity. In most cases, these mythologies 'mythicize' real history, taking real events but redefining them as the morally defining experiences of their people. In many cases, these events are what Vamik Volkan (1997) has called 'chosen traumas', such as the Holocaust for Jews or the 1389 Battle of Kosovo Field for Serbs. In some cases, however, histories and myths are invented from whole cloth to create new identities.

These constructivist insights may be viewed as a way to settle the argument between primordialists and instrumentalists, because constructivist ideas explain both the insights and the problems of the other two views. For example, most Serbs honestly believe that their identity is primordial, forged in the fires of battle against the Turks at Kosovo in 1389, so their perception is that their conflicts with Muslims are the result of primordial 'ancient hatreds'. In fact, though, that view of history was the result of late nineteenth-century Serbian politics and educational policy (Snyder 2000); before then, most Serbs did not think of themselves as Serbs at all. Similarly, Serbian politicians like Slobodan Milosevic did indeed use Serbian ethnic identity instrumentally to pursue their own power in the 1990s, but that identity only worked politically because it had been socially constructed before. Any old identity will not do.

Another question is how to tell whether a particular conflict is an ethnic conflict. Most African countries are multiethnic, for example, but African civil wars often involve warlords competing for control over resources such as diamond mines, so ethnicity has little to do with who is on which side. A conflict is ethnic only if the sides involved are distinguished primarily on the basis of ethnicity. Often one or both sides in an ethnic conflict will be a coalition of ethnic groups, rather than a single one, but the conflict is still ethnic because the people involved choose sides on the basis of their ethnic group membership, rather than other considerations such as economic interests.

While most ethnic conflicts are peaceful, I will focus in this chapter on the violent ones, because in most cases it is only violent ethnic conflicts that become problems relevant for security studies. I will begin, however, with a brief overview of ethnic conflicts more generally.

## An overview of ethnic conflicts

Ethnic groups and ethnic conflicts are everywhere. One comprehensive survey found a total of 275 ethnic or communal groups in 116 countries around the world that were socially disadvantaged in some way – 'minorities at risk'. Put together, the groups included more than one billion people, or about 17.4 per cent of the world's population (Gurr 2000: 9–10). Of the fifty biggest countries in the world by population, only four – Poland, Tanzania, Nepal, and North Korea – did not have at least one 'minority at risk' (and Tanzania has many ethnic groups: they were merely judged not to be 'at risk'). Some of these groups are very small, in mostly homogeneous countries: Australia's lone 'minority at risk', the Aborigines, are only about 1 per cent of the country's population; while Japan's only minority, the Koreans, are only one-half of one per cent. Some of the groups are very large and important, however: Malaysia's Chinese minority is 27 per cent of the population, and India's oft-mistreated Muslims are11 per cent of India's population. Overall, it is accurate to say that most countries in the world are ethnically diverse.

Most of the time, the existence of minority groups does not lead to violence or even to serious conflict. In 1995, most of the 'minorities at risk' (58 per cent) were either politically inactive or mobilized only for routine politics. Another 15 per cent were a bit more volatile, engaging in demonstrations, rioting, or both. Still, violent ethnic conflicts were unfortunately plentiful: 49 (18 per cent) ethnic groups were engaged in 'small-scale rebellion' in 1995, and another 22 (8 per cent) were fighting a 'large-scale rebellion' (Gurr 2000: 28). These numbers, however, were just about the worst ever: the long-term trend is that the number of violent ethnic conflicts increased fairly steadily from the end of World War II until the mid-1990s, but then it started to drop.

What are these violent conflicts about? The simplest answer is political power in a disputed territory. Most of the conflicts involve a regional minority who want to separate and form their own state, or at least their own autonomous region. Examples include Myanmar (Karens), India (Kashmir), Palestine (vs. Israel), Philippines (Muslims), Sri Lanka (Tamils), and Iran and Turkey (Kurds). In other cases, the insurgent ethnic group wants to take over government of the whole country: thus Burundi's majority Hutus wish to take power from the minority Tutsi government.

Often the goals and stakes are unclear, as rebels may disagree with each other. For example, some Palestinians want to establish their own state alongside Israel, but others are fighting to replace Israel with a Palestinian state. The Afghanistan case is only partially ethnic: the rebel Taliban define themselves by their ideological aims – creation of an Islamic state – but in practice, virtually all of their support comes from the Pashtun ethnic group, while the Tajik, Uzbek and Hazara minorities oppose them.

Only rarely are these conflicts 'religious' in the sense of one group trying to impose its religion on another – even when the groups in conflict differ in religion. Thus even though Sri Lanka's Tamils are Hindu while the majority Sinhalese are Buddhist, neither group wants the other to convert. Rather, the rebel Liberation Tigers of Tamil Eelam want to establish their own state (Tamil Eelam) in northern and eastern Sri Lanka, while the Sinhalese-dominated government wants to prevent that outcome. The biggest exception in recent years was Sudan, where the main grievance of the Christian and animist southerners was the attempt by the Sudanese government to impose Islamic law on the whole country, including them. This conflict, however, seemed on its way to resolution after the Sudanese government accepted the results of a referendum in 2011 in which southerners voted overwhelmingly to secede and form their own state.

Another misconception is that ethnic conflicts are merely economic. Some scholars argue that the statistical link between ethnic diversity and civil war is weak, and that the main causes of civil war are poverty, weak governments, and other factors that make it easy to start a guerrilla campaign (e.g. Fearon and Laitin 2003). The truth, however, is that while economic grievances are almost always present, in ethnic conflicts they are expressed in ethnic terms. In Mindanao in the southern Philippines, for example, the poor – Christians as well as Muslims – are all disadvantaged by inadequate government spending on education and infrastructure. But the Communist New People's Army, which tries to exploit such rich/poor distinctions to gain support, has had little luck in Muslim areas. Rather, Muslims there respond to specifically Muslim rebel groups who emphasize the differences between Muslims and Christians, not between rich and poor (McKenna 1998). In other cases, it is not the poor ethnic group but the rich one that rebels: in Yugoslavia, for example, it was the relatively prosperous Slovenes and Croats who first tried to secede, because they felt they were being held back by the more 'backward' ethnic groups in the rest of the country.

## Causes of violent ethnic conflict

In the statistics about ethnic conflicts quoted above, the violent conflicts fell into two broad categories: riots, and armed conflicts or civil wars.

Deadly ethnic riots have occurred all over the world, but how and why they occur seems puzzling. Such riots typically begin suddenly, soon after a seemingly minor triggering incident. Once they begin, they mushroom in size, yielding widespread violence across a city or an entire country. Furthermore, even though many such riots involve little or no planning, they almost always involve careful selection of victims: rioters seem to be in unspoken agreement about whom they want to kill or torture. Also, there is frequently no discrimination between ages and sexes: children, women, and men of all ages may be targeted. After the killing is done, there is usually no remorse on the part of the killers or their co-ethnics: 'they had it coming' is the attitude typically expressed by rioting communities all over the globe (Horowitz 2000).

One comprehensive survey, which takes a social psychological approach, finds three main factors that lead to deadly ethnic riots (Horowitz 2000). First, there needs to be a hostile ongoing relationship between the groups – tensions of long standing to motivate the killing. Second, there needs to be authoritative social support: potential rioters need to be assured by public statements from community leaders in their group that the leaders agree killing members of the other group is justified. At the same time, this support usually extends to the security forces: riots usually become large only if the police are sympathetic, or at least do not make determined efforts to stop the killing.

Finally, there needs to be a stimulus, some event – usually implying some sort of threat – that provokes fear, rage, or hatred in the rioting group. For example, a report (true or not) of a violent attack by one of 'them' against one of 'us' might spark a widespread cry to 'teach them a lesson'. Alternatively, a political change or potential change might provoke a similar outburst. In 1958, for example, Sri Lankan Prime Minister S.W.R.D. Bandaranaike, a Sinhalese, signed a power-sharing deal with the leader of his country's Tamil minority, but quickly backed away under political pressure. *After* the deal was abrogated, ordinary Sinhalese vented their wrath at the very idea of such power-sharing by attacking innocent Tamils in a large-scale riot.

Another approach to explaining ethnic riots focuses not on psychology but on social organization. In India, for example, hostile relations between the Hindu and Muslim communities are common, but most of the riot violence is concentrated in just a few cities. Why is that? The riot-prone cities, it turns out, have 'institutionalized riot systems': community activists and extremist organizations that benefit from keeping tensions high, politicians who benefit from occasional violence, and criminals and thugs who can profit from it (Brass 1997). On the other hand, Indian cities with little or no riot violence have community organizations (business groups, labor unions, etc.) that cross communal lines, bringing Hindus and Muslims together instead of driving them apart (Varshney 2002).

Explanations of ethnic civil wars divide along similar lines: social psychology approaches, social mobilization approaches, and instrumentalist approaches. Instrumentalists start with what creates the opportunity for rebels to act: weak governments, large populations and inaccessible terrain create the opening that extremists need to act (Fearon and Laitin 2003). Also important are extremist leaders seeking to grab or hold onto power, who stir up ethnic disagreements and provoke violence to create a 'rally around the flag', in effect uniting their group around their own leadership (Gagnon 1995). From this perspective, extremist media, which seek popularity by appealing to group loyalties, play crucial roles in presenting the news in terms of 'us' against 'them' (Snyder 2000). These two factors work together: extremist leaders provide heroes for the extremist media to promote, while one-sided media portrayals seem to validate the extremist leaders' claims that their group must unite against the 'enemy'. A prominent example of an extremist leader of this kind is Slobodan Milosevic, who led the upsurge of Serbian national identity that led to the breakup of Yugoslavia in 1991.

Social mobilization approaches consider these leadership roles, but are also interested in how ethnic groups mobilize – that is, how do members of the group get together the people and resources needed for collective action? The answer, these theorists point out, is that people use social organizations and networks that already exist, like political parties and labour unions, and press them into action on ethnic issues. Successful mobilization efforts also find 'brokers', people who can link different groups and networks together to help them cooperate in a single movement (McAdam, Tarrow and Tilly 2001). This provides one answer to the question: why do people mobilize as *ethnic* groups instead, for example, of organizing as economic interest groups? It is because people's social networks tend to be mostly within their ethnic group; barriers of language, religion or custom typically separate them from members of other groups.

Social psychological approaches focus on a different puzzle: why do followers follow these extremist leaders? Even if people mobilize as ethnic groups to look out for their interests, why do they follow extremist leaders who want violence, instead of following moderate leaders who will work for peace? One answer is proposed by symbolic politics theory, which emphasizes the roles of group myths and fears. Remembering that a group is defined by its myth-symbol complex – the stories it tells about the group's history and identity – symbolic politics theory suggests that when the group's myth-symbol complex points to the other group as an enemy, its members will be predisposed to be hostile to the other group. Politicians will then be able to appeal to symbols of past hostility – such as Slobodan Milosevic referring to the Battle of Kosovo Field – to rouse people's emotions against the enemy that symbol brings to mind (Muslims, in the case of Kosovo). If the group is at the same time convinced that they are in danger of extinction – of being wiped out as a group – they can be persuaded to back extreme measures that are justified as 'self-defence' (Kaufman 2001).

To see how these complex processes play out in practice, let us consider two examples of the bloodiest ethnic conflicts in recent decades: Sudan's north–south civil wars, and the three-sided fight in Bosnia.

## Sudan

In Northern Sudan the population is overwhelmingly Muslim in religion and is led by a long-dominant Arab elite whereas the south is a mixture of Christian and animist groups, of which the largest are the Dinka and the Nuer. During and before the Mahdiyya (1885–1898), a period of Muslim fundamentalist rule, southerners' main contact with northerners came when northerners raided their lands to collect slaves. In colonial times (1899–1955) the British, nominally in partnership with Egypt, ruled the two regions separately, with the north under a form of Islamic law (Kaufman 2006).

Sudan had the preconditions for ethnic war from every perspective. Instrumentalists would note that its large population, huge land area (the biggest in Africa), hostile neighbours and weak government provide ample opportunity for rebel groups to form. Symbolists point out that northerners' myth-symbol complex glorifies the Mahdiyya as a basis for an Islamic identity for Sudan; while southerners see Islamist rule as a disaster for themselves, and they fear northerners' efforts to spread Islam as a threat to their own identities. North and south were thus primed for mutual hostility.

When Sudan gained its independence in 1955, northern elites – including descendants of the Madhiyya's leader, the al-Mahdi clan – gained almost all government jobs and government benefits, and they formulated a Muslim and Arab national identity to try to unite northerners behind their rule. They attempted to impose this identity on the south, swiftly sparking violent resistance that escalated to full-scale civil war in the early 1960s. A military coup in 1969 brought to power the secularist colonel Jaafar al-Nimeiri, who signed a peace agreement in 1972 granting autonomy to the south.

By the late 1970s, however, Nimeiri's secular coalition began crumbling under pressure from traditional northern elites like the al-Mahdi clan, while Sudan's economy sagged. To maintain his power, Nimeiri began appealing to Islamist symbols, dressing like an Arab sheikh, publicizing his mosque attendance, and forming a coalition with the Muslim Brotherhood and al-Mahdi clan leader Sadiq al-Mahdi. As part of this campaign, he revoked in 1983 the southern autonomy he had granted a decade before, and imposed Islamic law throughout the country. Since southerners' identity was threatened by this programme of forced Islamization, they immediately rebelled again.

Nimeiri's programme of appeals to symbols of Islam was popular. But it did not save him and he was overthrown in 1985. Thereafter, the group with the most enthusiastic following was the Muslim Brotherhood, which convened huge rallies promoting slogans like, "No alternative to God's law!" to block any suggestion of compromise with the south. When a new military dictatorship took power in 1989 under General Omar al-Bashir, it maintained

Islamic law and the coalition with the Islamists – and continued the war in the south for another sixteen years. A 2005 Comprehensive Peace Agreement was meant to resolve the conflict, and it resulted in the declaration, with Sudan's acceptance of a newly independent Republic of South Sudan on 9 July 2011. Tragically however, just as the war in the south was winding down, a new civil war began in Sudan's western region of Darfur. Meanwhile, disputes remain between Sudan and South Sudan especially a violent clash over ownership of the oil-rich border region of Abyei.

## Yugoslavia

Yugoslavia, formed in the aftermath of World War I, was a multi-ethnic state with no majority group. The three largest groups all spoke the same language, Serbo-Croatian, but differed in their religious tradition among Serbs (Orthodox Christians), Croats (Catholics) and Bosnian Muslims. The fourth-largest group, the Slovenes, are Catholics but speak a different (though related) language; the next-largest, the Albanians, are Muslims who speak a wholly unrelated language. Before World War II, Yugoslavia was ruled by a Serbian king and dominated by Serbian politicians. During World War II, the Germans conquered the country and placed Croatian fascists, the Ustashe, in power in the regions of Croatia and Bosnia, where they engaged in genocidal violence against the Serbs. As the war ended, Communist partisan leader Josip Broz Tito took power in Yugoslavia, massacring the Ustashe and re-creating Yugoslavia as a nominal federation of six Republics: Serbia, Croatia, Bosnia-Hercegovina, Slovenia, Macedonia and Montenegro (Kaufman 2001).

When Tito died in 1980, the loss of his charismatic authority severely weakened Yugoslavia's government. The increasingly powerful Republic governments facilitated the kind of mutually hostile mythmaking Tito had tried to stamp out. For example, nationalist Serbs began talking about the menace of the Albanian minority in the symbolically important Kosovo region, while labelling any Croatian disagreement as evidence of resurgent Ustashe fascism. As symbolists would note, ethnic myths and fears were growing. The leader of Serbia's League of Communists, Slobodan Milosevic, noticed the power of this nationalist sentiment and in the late 1980s became its spokesman, repressing the Albanians and attempting to impose Serbian control on the whole of Yugoslavia (Gagnon 1995). In response to this Serbian threat, voters in Slovenia, Croatia and Bosnia turned to supporting their own nationalist leaders – with the Croatian nationalists reviving the national symbols last used by the Ustashe fascists, raising alarm among Serbs and making Milosevic's appeals ever more plausible.

Yugoslavia was dying. Slovenia moved first, declaring independence on June 25, 1991. The Croats quickly followed, sparking a months-long war in which the Yugoslav army conquered areas in Croatia inhabited by Croatia's Serbian minority.

The agony of Bosnia-Hercegovina lasted longer. Home to a mixture of Bosnian Muslims, Serbs and Croats, Bosnia was torn three ways. Serbs wanted to remain in Yugoslavia; but fearing Serbian domination, the Muslims wanted to secede and form an independent Bosnian state, while Croats wanted their areas (especially western Hercegovina) to join Croatia. In 1992 a coalition of Muslims and Croats therefore declared Bosnian independence, sparking a three-sided civil war in which Serbia and Croatia – trying to take over chunks of Bosnian territory – provided military assistance to their co-ethnics in Bosnia, while the Muslims were the principal victims. Under the slogan, 'Only Unity Saves the Serbs', Serbs exaggerated the disadvantages of separation from Serbia into a threat to their national existence, and used this invented threat to justify (and invent the term) 'ethnic cleansing', the Serbs' programme of massacring enough of their ethnic enemies to force the rest to flee any territory they claimed. Finally, in 1995, a Croatian military counteroffensive backed by NATO air power prompted the Serb side to agree to stop the fighting. A later uprising by ethnic Albanians against Serbian rule in Kosovo led to a 1999 NATO bombing campaign against Serbia to try to stop Serbian violence aginst civilians. Serbia eventually accepted NATO's terms to stop the fighting, but when Kosovo unilaterally declared independence in February 2008, Serbia and Russia, among others, refused to recognize the fledgling nation.

## International security dimensions of ethnic conflicts

As these two examples illustrate, ethnic conflicts often have important international effects. In Bosnia, the politics of ethnic conflict transcends national boundaries, with ethnic diasporas often playing an important role. For example, the Croatian émigré community in the US provided lavish funding for the nationalists in Croatia, giving them a significant edge over moderate rivals in Croatia's first free elections in 1990. Later, a politically influential international Croatian minority in Germany tilted German foreign policy in 1991 towards supporting the Croatian cause. This support undermined international efforts to head off war. Croatian émigrés in the west thus played an important role in causing Yugoslavia's break-up and the wars that followed.

A second international effect of ethnic civil wars is the creation of refugees as people sensibly flee for their lives from combat areas. Ethnic civil wars, however, produce especially large numbers of refugees because such wars are often about which group will control disputed lands, so massacres and evictions (i.e., ethnic cleansing) are frequently used weapons. When the victims stay within their own country, as did most of Bosnia's 1.8 million homeless, they are technically 'internally displaced persons' rather than refugees, and their international effect is limited. Presenting a humanitarian problem, they often receive humanitarian aid, but provoke little more reaction.

If, however, they do cross international borders, refugees may be seen as a threat to international security in several different ways. For example, when Serbia conducted an ethnic cleansing campaign in Kosovo in 1998–1999, the hundreds of thousands of ethnic Albanian refugees who flooded across the border into Macedonia threatened to destabilize the tenuous ethnic balance between ethnic Macedonians and the Albanians already there. Alternatively, refugees might turn their refugee camps into bases from which to attack their former homeland. For example, in 1994, hundreds of thousands of ethnic Hutus (many involved in committing genocide) fled from Rwanda to Zaire when their Tutsi rivals took power. They quickly began launching attacks against Rwanda's Tutsi-led government, using international humanitarian aid to help their war effort. These attacks finally provoked Rwanda and its allies into invading Zaire, not only stopping the attacks but also toppling the country's president, Mobutu Sese Seko and sparking what eventually turned into 'Africa's first world war'.

Ethnic civil wars can also become focal points of international diplomacy. As the crises in Croatia and Bosnia grew in 1991 and 1992, respectively, diplomats wrangled over how best to avoid war. Western governments came under increasing pressure to act to stem the humanitarian emergency generated by ethnic cleansing. But Europeans were initially split over the Yugoslav crisis, with the French and British at first tilting toward the Serbs, spurring the European Union to upgrade its efforts to form a common foreign and security policy.

The result is sometimes effective diplomatic intervention, and sometimes tragically unsuccessful diplomacy. On the one hand, the short war between Slovenia and Yugoslavia was ended through mediation of European Community (EC) leaders in talks on the island of Brioni in 1991. Similarly, the war between Croatia and Serbia (Yugoslavia having by now dissolved) was ended in early 1992 through a cease-fire brokered by UN special envoy Cyrus Vance (a former US Secretary of State), building on the efforts of EC mediators. On the other hand, in January 1992 German pressure pushed the EC into formal diplomatic recognition of Croatia and Slovenia and into consideration of recognition for other Yugoslav republics declaring independence. This position faced Bosnians with the perception that it was now or never for their own prospects for independence. They went ahead, declaring independence and sparking their agonizing three-year civil war. Thus the same diplomatic moves that helped end the war in Croatia helped to start the much more violent one in Bosnia (Cohen 1995: 238).

When diplomacy alone is not enough, international actors sometimes resort to sending peacekeepers to try to manage ethnic violence. If there is a cease-fire in place, peacekeepers can be effective in helping to maintain it, especially if the peacekeepers can physically separate the warring factions. On the other hand, the peacekeepers can sometimes do their job too well: by preventing bloodshed, they can make the current situation of neither peace nor war an easier option than the tough compromises that a final peace agreement would require.

Bosnia, however, is a prominent example of the ineffectiveness of peacekeepers if they are introduced in the wrong circumstances. The United Nations Protection Force (UNPROFOR) was originally sent in to Yugoslavia in early 1992 to monitor the cease-fire between the Croats and Serbs in Croatia, which it did. But as the fighting in Bosnia escalated, the UN voted to increase UNPROFOR's size and expand its mission to guarantee the provision of humanitarian aid to beleaguered Bosnian towns. The whole idea was self-contradictory: while pretending to be neutral and refusing to engage in combat, UNPROFOR was acting to undermine the Bosnian Serbs' strategy of blockading Bosnian Muslim towns to starve them out. Not surprisingly, the Serbs obstructed UNPROFOR's efforts whenever they could.

The futility of UNPROFOR is illustrated by the fate of the town of Srebrenica: declared a UN 'safe area' in April 1993, it was intermittently supplied by UN convoys and protected by a small UNPROFOR garrison. But when an all-out Serb offensive came in July 1995, the UNPROFOR troops stood aside, the town was captured, as many as eight thousand Bosnian Muslims were slaughtered by the victorious Serb troops, and the rest of Srebrenica's civilians were forced to flee. Srebrenica was 'ethnically cleansed' (Rieff 1996).

Because international interest in ethnic conflicts is often intense, and because peacekeepers are not always effective, international actors often resort to violent intervention, either directly or indirectly. Indirect intervention in ethnic civil wars is common: foreign countries frequently provide supplies, weapons, and military training to the sides they favour. In many cases, this international aid is also ethnically motivated, with countries backing the side more closely related to them (Saideman 2001). Thus in the Yugoslav conflicts, Russia armed their fellow Eastern Orthodox Slavs, while the Bosnian Muslims received arms and volunteer fighters from the Muslim Middle East. The Western, Christian United States, similarly, not only provided arms for Catholic Croatia, but also paid a US-based private firm to train the Croatian army, readying it for the 1995 offensive that threw the Serbs out of Croatia. Similar patterns occur all over the world: Christian Kenya and Ethiopia helped the partially Christian southern Sudanese against their Muslim adversaries, for example, while Muslim Libya and other Muslim states aided the Muslims of the southern Philippines in their war against the Christian-dominated Philippine government.

Sometimes these interventions are purely opportunistic rather than ethnically based. For example, in the war in the mountainous Karabagh region of the former Soviet Republic of Azerbaijan in the early 1990s, Russia switched back and forth between aiding the (Muslim) Azerbaijanis and the (Christian) Armenians, depending on which side was more pro-Russian at the time.

When indirect military intervention is not enough and interests are strong, foreign actors sometimes resort to the direct use of force to influence ethnic civil wars. In the Bosnian case, the US and its NATO allies had only to launch a limited air campaign in 1995 to end the war, as the main effort on the ground was carried out by the US-trained Croatians. Four years later, a 78-day NATO bombing campaign against Serbia was required to persuade the Serbs to stop their campaign of ethnic cleansing in Kosovo. In 2008, Russia sent troops to throw back Georgian forces trying to reassert Georgian control over the separatist region of South Ossetia. Ethnic civil wars are dangerous in part because there is often the danger they will turn into international wars.

## Resolution of ethnic civil wars

Because of the danger that ethnic civil wars may spread, international intervention is often aimed at stopping the fighting, or even at resolving the underlying conflicts. Some theorists argue that the best way to stop an ethnic conflict is to arrange a compromise settlement, usually involving a mixture of power-sharing in the central government and regional autonomy for disgruntled minority groups (Lijphart 1985). Others maintain that ethnic civil wars end only when a rebel minority is either repressed by military force or granted its own separate state by partitioning – dividing up – the existing country (Kaufmann 1996). Either way, in this view, ethnic civil wars end only when one side wins: usually the government, but occasionally the rebel ethnic group.

In most cases, the outcome does result from a military victory; the most effective foreign intervention is therefore to help one side win. One analysis of 27 ethnic civil wars resolved between 1944 and 1994 found that 16 of the cases, or 59 per cent, ended either in a military victory or in a partition that stemmed from a military victory (Kaufmann 1996). In Bosnia, for example, the result was for all practical purposes a partition: the Serbian bid to dominate most of the country was defeated by Croatian and NATO military force, but each of the three groups received its own autonomous area under a very weak Bosnian federal government.

Some ethnic conflicts are settled in a compromise deal among the parties involved, but all too often these agreements collapse later. As mentioned above, Sudan's first civil war was settled in 1972 in a deal that gave autonomy to the non-Muslim southerners, but that deal collapsed into renewed fighting in 1983. Some experts point to peace agreements in Lebanon in 1958 and 1976, but each of them also collapsed later into even worse fighting than before. Similarly, the highly touted Oslo Accords of 1993 that seemed to put the Israeli–Palestinian conflict on the road to resolution collapsed into renewed fighting in 2000.

One way of bringing these two perspectives together is to think about conflicts in terms of whether they are 'ripe for resolution' (Zartman 1985). In this view, the best chance for negotiations to succeed comes when the conflict reaches a hurting stalemate, a situation in which neither side seems likely to win, but both sides are suffering. This was the case before each of Sudan's peace agreements, and before each of Lebanon's. The Bosnian war, too, ended more in a stalemate than a victory for one side: each side succeeded in gaining control of a share of the territory, but NATO forced all sides to recognize that they would not be able to win decisively. The Dayton Accords, the compromise peace deal of 1995, were the result.

Power-sharing advocates can point to a few cases in which violent conflicts did end in a successful power-sharing deal, arguably the most important case being the end of apartheid in South Africa. In an initiative that soon inspired many imitators, the new government worked to address the legacy of past oppression and discrimination by establishing a Truth and Reconciliation Commission to collect and publicize information about all of the apartheid government's misdeeds, many of which were kept secret or denied.

A second prominent case of power-sharing is in Northern Ireland, where the Good Friday Accords of 1998 called for power-sharing between the local Protestant majority and the Catholic minority. The Accord resulted in the

Provisional Irish Republican Army finally laying down its arms, and in 2007 after years of delay a power-sharing government uniting the region's bitterest rivals finally took shape. Though Northern Ireland remained politically united with Great Britain, the Republic of Ireland also was given a role in the new order.

Sometimes, international efforts to promote power-sharing can go terribly wrong. The 1994 Rwanda genocide, for example, was carried out by Hutu extremists trying to prevent the implementation of a UN-sponsored power-sharing deal with a minority Tutsi-led rebel group. Similarly, East Timorese voted for independence from Indonesia in another UN-sponsored deal in 1999, but shortly thereafter militia groups sponsored by the Indonesian military massacred thousands of them. In both cases, as in the case of UNPROFOR, UN peacekeepers had neither the mandate to stop the killing, nor enough military power to do so.

It is fitting that this chapter end with these negative examples of international involvement. Even though the number of violent ethnic conflicts in the world is starting to decline, the ongoing ones remain extremely difficult to settle, and many of those that have been settled are at risk of recurring. While international involvement can help, the good intentions of international actors do not guarantee that their efforts will improve the situation: misfired peace plans and ineffective peacekeepers may not just fail, but prolong the agony or even cause it to get worse.

## Further reading

Michael E. Brown (ed.), *Nationalism and Ethnic Conflict*, revised edition (MIT Press, 2001). An excellent collection of articles on the causes and management of ethnic conflict which includes prominent statements of the instrumentalist approach and a famous argument in favour of partition as the best way to resolve ethnic wars.

Ted Robert Gurr, *Peoples Versus States* (US Institute of Peace Press, 2000). The leader of the Minorities at Risk research team outlines the detailed results of their statistical data collection and analysis effort, presenting evidence for all three approaches to explaining ethnic violence.

Donald Horowitz, *Ethnic Groups in Conflict* (University of California Press, 1985). The classic statement of the social psychological approach to explaining ethnic conflict and conflict management, with myriad examples from across Asia, Africa and the Caribbean.

Stuart J. Kaufman, *Modern Hatreds: The Symbolic Politics of Ethnic War* (Cornell University Press, 2001). This book sets out the symbolic politics theory about the causes and avoidance of ethnic war, with a set of case studies from the former USSR and former Yugoslavia.

David A. Lake and Donald Rothchild (eds.), *The International Spread of Ethnic Conflict: Fear, Diffusion and Escalation* (Princeton University Press, 1998). In this collection of articles the leading instrumentalist and rational-choice scholars offer their insights for understanding ethnic conflict and its international dimensions.

# Human Security

Fen Osler Hampson

## Abstract

In this chapter, students will learn about recent academic and policy research on human security. It first summarizes the various definitions and conceptions of human security informing current academic research and thinking. It then offers a brief overview of some recent contributions to the human security literature. The final section identifies some of the key debates and issues now at the centre of human security research.

## Introduction

There is little doubt that human security studies have attracted growing attention in the wider International Relations and social science literatures. The expanding UN agenda of human security concerns (among them: war-affected children, racial discrimination, women's rights, human trafficking, transnational crime, and refugees), coupled with former UN Secretary-General Kofi Annan's personal commitment to human security activism, catapulted these questions to the forefront of the scholarly and policy research agenda in the 1990s (see MacFarlane and Khong 2006). This agenda accompanied the longstanding human security concerns of students and practitioners of international development – an agenda that has generally tended to focus on the ways that globalization dynamics have damaged the prospects for human development and the provision of basic human needs.

In second decade of the twentieth century there has been renewed focus on human security in the context of the so-called Arab Spring. On 17 March 2011, UN Security Council resolution 1973 demanded an immediate ceasefire in Libya, including an end to attacks against civilians, which it said might constitute 'crimes against humanity', imposed a ban on all flights in the country's airspace – a no-fly zone – and tightened sanctions on the Qaddafi regime and its supporters. Additionally, the Council authorized member states, 'acting nationally or through regional organizations or arrangements, to take all necessary measures to protect civilians under threat of attack in the country, including Benghazi, while excluding a foreign occupation force of any form on any part of Libyan territory'.

The rationale for the imposition of a no-fly-zone (NFZ) over Libya was ostensibly to avert a blood bath by Qaddafi's forces, specifically in the cities of Benghazi and Tobruk. Champions of the responsibility to protect (R2P) doctrine applauded the NFZ as an invocation of key R2P principles (see Chapter 32, this volume). In this case, they had a relatively easy target – a ruthless, bloody dictator who had shown repeatedly that he was prepared to murder his own citizens to stay in power. In the eyes of some, however, the West was hypocritical for not intervening in Bahrain, Syria, or Yemen where there were similar outbreaks of protest and bloody repression by autocratic leaders in 2011. Nor was this apparent double standard lost on the streets of Syria and Yemen where many lives have been lost in continuing struggles to throw off autocratic rule.

This chapter reviews some of the ideas which facilitated these events, specifically recent academic and policy research on human security. It first summarizes the various definitions and conceptions of human security informing current academic research and thinking. It then offers a brief overview of some recent contributions to the human security literature. The final section identifies some of the key debates and issues now at the centre of human security research.

## Understanding the scope of human security

Despite the major investment of research and interest in human security in the past two decades there is no real consensus on what can or should constitute the focus of what are still loosely termed human security studies (Kaldor 2007a, Reveron and Mahoney-Norris 2009, Matthew *et al.* 2009, Kent 2005, Hampson *et al.* 2002). There continues to be considerable methodological, definitional and conceptual disquiet about the real meaning of human security, and about its implications for the study or the practice of international relations. This should come as no surprise, given the nature of the academic enterprise and the different disciplinary and methodological backgrounds informing the work of scholars engaged in human security research. (Even so, the evident inability of scholars to advance beyond theoretical debates over definitions toward practical policy recommendations understandably frustrates practitioners in the policy community.)

There is also a great unevenness in the depth (and breadth) of research on particular themes. Some issues, such as anti-personnel landmines or small arms, are well ploughed; the literature on these subjects is rich not only in analysis of particular problems and causes, but also in implications for public policy. Other problems, such as gender-directed violence, have received the sort of attention they deserve as evils in their own right and as sources and symptoms of human insecurity.

There are arguably three distinct conceptions of human security that shape current debates. The first is what might be termed the natural rights/rule of law conception of human security, anchored in the fundamental liberal assumption of basic individual rights to 'life, liberty, and the pursuit of happiness', and of the international obligation of states to protect and promote these rights (Claude and Weston 2006, Morsink 1998, Lauren 1998, Alston 1992). A second view of human security is humanitarian. This is this view of human security that, for example, informs international efforts to deepen and strengthen international law, particularly regarding genocide and war crimes, and to abolish weapons that are especially harmful to civilians and non-combatants (Kaldor 2007a, Beebe and Kaldor 2010, Power 2003, Boutros-Ghali 1992, Moore 1996). This view lies at the heart of humanitarian interventions directed at improving the basic living conditions of refugees, and anyone uprooted by conflict from their homes and communities. On those rare occasions when military force has been used ostensibly to avert genocide or ethnic cleansing, it has also been justified usually on rather specific humanitarian grounds such as the need to restore basic human rights and dignity.

These two views of human security, which focus on basic human rights and their deprivation, stand in sharp contrast to a broader view, which suggests that human security should be widely constructed to include economic, environmental, social, and other forms of harm to the overall livelihood and wellbeing of individuals. There is a strong social justice component in this broader conception of human security, as well as a wider consideration of threats (real and potential) to the survival and health of individuals. According to this third and probably most controversial perspective, the state of the global economy, the forces of globalization, and the health of the environment, including the world's atmosphere and oceans, are all legitimate subjects of concern in terms of how they affect the 'security' of the individual (Battersby and Siracusa 2009, Friman and Reich 2007, Kent 2005, Matthew *et al.* 2009, UN 1995, 1999, UNDP 1994, 1997, Nef 2002).

These 'broadeners' have attracted sharp criticism. Yuen Foong Khong (2001) warns that making everything a priority renders nothing a priority – raising false hopes in the policy realm and obscuring real trade-offs between rival human security objectives. Similarly, Andrew Mack (2001, 2005) makes the sound methodological point that overly broad definitions of human security can block investigation of the very phenomena that need to be understood. Examining the relationship between poverty and violence, for example, requires us to treat them as separate variables. A definition that conflates dependent and independent variables will confound analysis of causal connections between them.

As a practical matter, many human security initiatives, such as the international campaign to ban trafficking in small and light weapons, generally, fall between the narrower and the broader definitions of human security. But, there is a lively debate among scholars and practitioners as to what legitimately should be the scope of efforts to promote and advance human security at the international level, and as to whether we should define human security in more restrictive or broader terms (Hampson *et al.* 2002, Paris 2001, Khong 2001, MacFarlane and Khong 2006).

How should human security be defined? One way is to define it negatively, i.e. as the absence of threats to various core human values, including the most basic human value, the physical safety of the individual. Alkire (2002: 2) offers a more positive definition of human security: 'The objective of human security is to safeguard the vital core of all human lives from critical pervasive threats, and to do so without impeding long-term human flourishing'.

The definition offered by the Report of the Commission on Human Security (2003: 2) is even more expansive: 'to protect the vital core of all human freedoms and human fulfilment'. What is this vital core? Does it represent all human freedoms? And should personal fulfilment be placed alongside freedom as a basic right and public responsibility? The same paragraph goes on to embrace almost every desirable condition of a happy life in its description of human security:

> 'Human security means protecting fundamental freedoms ... It means protecting people from critical (severe) and pervasive (widespread) threats and situations. It means using processes that build on people's strengths and aspirations. It means creating political, social, environmental, economic, military, and cultural systems that together give people the building blocks of survival'.

Underlying much of the human security literature is a common belief that it is critical to international security, and that international order cannot rest solely on the sovereignty and viability of states – that order depends as well on individuals and their own sense of security. This is clearly a departure from traditional liberal internationalism, which sees international order as resting on institutional arrangements which, in varying degrees, help secure the integrity of the liberal, democratic state by reducing threats in the state's external environment (see Chapter 3 this volume). Placing the individual as the key point of reference, the human security paradigm assumes that the safety of the individual is the key to global security; by implication, when the safety of individuals is threatened so too in a fundamental sense is international security. In this view, global challenges have to be assessed in terms of how they affect the safety of people, and not just of states. Proponents of the enlarged or maximalist conception of human security also argue that these threats arise not only from military sources; non-military causes, such as worsening environmental conditions and economic inequalities can, in some instances, exacerbate conflict processes (Mathew *et al.* 2009, UNDP 1994, Nef 2002, Paris 2001).

## Setting the boundaries of human security

Not surprisingly, problems of definition and boundary-setting have dominated much of the literature in human security research. To some degree, these uncertainties simply reflect the state of the art; these are, after all, relatively new approaches. But it is also fair to say that these definitional and conceptual arguments echo turmoil experienced since the Cold War in schools of both development and national security – two important sources of human security scholars and scholarship (King and Murray 2001/2).

King and Murray define human security as 'the number of years of future life spent outside the state of "generalized poverty"' (2001/2). Generalized poverty, in this definition, occurs when the individual falls below a specified threshold 'in any key domain of human well-being'. Operating the definition therefore requires choosing domains of wellbeing, constructing practical indicators, and specifying threshold values for each. King and Murray find their domains mainly in the UNDP's Human Development Index (per-capita income, health, education), and add 'political freedom' and 'democracy' (for example, by applying Freedom House measures of voting and legislative conduct).

Human security in this scheme is thus expressed as a probability – the expected number of years of life spent outside 'generalized poverty', whether for an individual or aggregated across an entire population. Leaving aside other questions of domain choice and threshold selection, the King–Murray equation (they frame it mathematically) raises provocative issues for methodology and policy. Mack (2005), on the other hand, measures human security in terms of the costs of war on human suffering. The Liu Institute's Report on Human Security documents in vivid detail the impact that war – measured in terms of civilian casualties – has had on different countries and regions of the world.

Some of the literature has attempted to define human security by integrating its disparate dimensions. Hazem Ghobarah (with Huth and Russett 2001) explored long-term health effects of civil wars with a cross-national analysis of World Health Organization (WHO) statistics on death and disability. The immediate harms done to health by specific wars are familiar; in contrast, Russett and his colleagues tracked the delayed after-effects and their mechanisms: rising crime rates; property destruction, economic disruption, diversion of health-care resources, and the like.

In *Madness in the Multitude* (2002) Fen Hampson and others situated human security approaches in the long history of liberal democratic theory, but concentrated on the distinguishing features of human security as a global public good. Among other advantages, the lens of public goods analysis focuses attention on some recurring issues in the human security discourse – namely, problems of under-provision, collective governance, and operational delivery.

The 1994 UN Human Development Report identified *inter alia* drug and human trafficking, transnational crime, migration, and terrorism as major threats to human security – issues that were highlighted more recently in the World Bank's 2011 *Development Report*. Interestingly, these threats were largely omitted from the mandate of the Independent Commission on Human Security (2003), which chose to focus on a narrower set of issues, i.e., the ways internal conflicts threaten the physical security of non-combatants; human insecurities stemming from preventable diseases, injury, or chronic ill health; insecurities flowing from a lack of basic literacy, access to education, and innumeracy; and the insecurities of poverty and economic, social and gender inequalities.

The Human Security Gateway, a useful online source, provides a wealth of information on the current state of human security studies (Human Security Report Project, 2011). Topics now covered range from the impact of conflict on human rights, children and armed conflict, the role of paramilitary and non-state armed groups, the relationship between climate change and armed conflict, conflict resolution and prevention, natural resources and armed conflict, to name but a few. As the Zurich-based Center for Security Policy notes:

Two decades after it was introduced in political debate, the concept of human security still remains a controversial matter. On the one hand, it has met with great resonance in many countries and in international organisations such as the UN. New issues were introduced to the security policy agenda, such as the ban on anti-personnel mines, efforts to curb the misuse of small arms and light weapons, or security sector reform (SSR). On the other hand, numerous questions remain unanswered. The definitory arguments between the proponents of a broad approach ('freedom from want') and the advocates of a narrow interpretation ('freedom from fear') remain unresolved. There is no general agreement on the role of the state, which can both ensure and threaten the safety of its citizens. It is in this context that one must view the occasional charge that the concept of human security is founded on an interventionist logic and attempts to undermine state sovereignty based on a 'responsibility to protect'.

(CSS 2011)

## Ongoing debates and unresolved issues

A number of key debates and/or unresolved issues are reflected in the scholarly and the policy-oriented human security literature. One of the burgeoning areas of research, especially among students of international development, involves the relationship between globalization (in its various meanings) and human security – or insecurity (Battersby and Siracusa 2009, Reveron and Mahoney-Norris 2011). There is widespread agreement that the forces of globalization are intensifying economic connections and the pace of social change and thus transforming international politics and recasting relationships between states and peoples with important implications for human security. Further, it is not just goods and capital that are exchanged across borders, but ideas, information, and people.

On one side of this argument, globalization enthusiasts argue that the breakdown of national barriers to trade and the spread of global markets are processes that help to raise world incomes and contribute to the spread of wealth. Although there are clear winners and losers in the globalizing economy, the old divisions between the advanced Northern economies and 'peripheral' South are breaking down and making way for an increasingly complex architecture of economic power (Held *et al.* 1999: 4). On the other side, globalization's critics argue that although some countries in the South have gained from globalization, many have not and income inequalities between the world's richest and poorest countries are widening.

Globalization also presents new dangers to human security, particularly in the area of public health where the spread of diseases like AIDS, which ravage many developing countries, are partially rooted in the workings of the global economy, and in externally imposed structural adjustment policies that have directly contributed to deterioration in public health delivery and in overall living standards (Leon and Walt 2001).

Much work remains to be done on the positive and negative consequences of globalization for human security, and on how globalization affects the capacity of various international, national and sub-national actors and institutions to provide for human security.

## Human security and 'failed' states

The relationship between conflict and development processes in affecting human security in the struggling states and societies of the South is also the focus of recent studies and discussion in key policy circles. The World Bank's 2011 *Development Report* argues that insecurity is the 'primary development challenge of our time'. This is because '[o]ne-and-a-half billion people live in areas affected by fragility, conflict, or large-scale, organized criminal violence, and no low-income fragile or conflict-affected country has yet to achieve a single United Nations Millennium Development Goal (UN MDG)'. These so-called 'new threats' include 'organized crime and trafficking, civil unrest due to global economic shocks', and 'terrorism' (World Bank 2011: 5). The populations most affected by such 'insecurities' are to be found in sub-Saharan Africa, Central Asia, and parts of Southeast Asia (Burma, Cambodia) and North Korea (Fund for Peace 2011).

Of special interest to scholars and practitioners is the relationship between so-called 'failed' or 'fragile' states and human security. Typically, the poorest, most conflict-wracked 'states' like Somalia, where there is an absence of effective governance and government institutions, have been classified as failed states where large swathes of the local population live in abject poverty compounded by violence and other threats to their existence such as drought and famine. However, state failure should not be construed too narrowly or simply in terms of countries that are in total collapse like Somalia (Gertz and Chandy 2011). There are many other countries in sub-Saharan Africa and South Asia, like Pakistan, Cameroon, or Djibouti, which are classified as 'middle income' by the World Bank but which nonetheless contain a large and growing sector of people who are desperately poor. In many of these countries, state institutions also have a tenuous hold on their territory and maintaining local law and order. The number of these so-called middle-income failed or fragile states (MIFFs) is growing. They may require development assistance and other kinds of support to maintain stability and alleviate local poverty, but they may not be eligible for the kinds of assistance that poorer and more stable countries, such as Tanzania, currently receive.

## The dilemmas of humanitarian intervention

Normative concerns typically surface when the imperative of human security is invoked in cases of humanitarian intervention (Kaldor 2007a, Beebe and Kaldor 2010, Holzgrefe and Keohane 2003, ICISS 2001, Power 2003, Chapter 32 this volume). There is obviously a continuing debate on whether force should be used in support of particular human security objectives, one that has only intensified with the NATO bombing of Libya in a barely disguised attempt to unseat Qaddafi. At one level, the dispute is about the proper hierarchy of humanitarian goals and international norms of state sovereignty and non-intervention. But it is also a debate about whether or when it is right to do violence against individuals – especially non-combatants who find themselves in harm's way – when force is exercised for human security purposes. Where human security concepts challenge traditional notions of what constitutes a 'just war' or a just cause, and test our sense of what are tolerable degrees of 'collateral damage' – is fertile terrain for ethicists and others concerned with the deeper ramifications of evolving human security norms.

Cultural differences figure prominently in different regional perceptions on human rights and evolving humanitarian intervention norms (Claude and Weston 2006, Mayer 2006). In the Arab world, attitudes towards intervention have been shaped by the US-led invasions of Iraq and Afghanistan. As Kodmani (2012) argues, 'Arab states (just like many other countries of the South) consider that only the UN Security Council is entitled to decide on intervention and must do so under strict conditions and that if the members of the council fail to come to an agreement, humanitarian intervention should simply not take place, whatever the human cost of not intervening'. Furthermore, she states, 'humanitarian intervention is seen as being applied selectively: Arab states and publics claim that the West only invokes human rights violations in the cases of small states or unfriendly regimes, just as the West chooses to punish "rogue states" in order to bring them in line with its strategy. Whether it is out of nationalism, a desire to keep society under control, or a fear of disintegration of the state, the Arab world remains averse to recognizing the diversity of most societies of the region and granting specific rights to their minorities' (Kodmani 2012: 243).

These debates underscore the tensions between diverse conceptions and priorities in the human security agenda. Exploring these tensions within explicit ethical and normative frames of reference can itself yield new knowledge and understanding – if not always agreement. Not only will such analysis render explicit the kinds of value trade-offs involved, but it might also help societies make more ethically informed choices as they respond to the human security threats they face.

The concept of human security also poses an interesting challenge to traditional notions of democratization, civil society development, and peacebuilding. Some scholars, citing familiar post-colonial history, hold that liberal democracy and economic liberalization by themselves will not suffice to ensure human security – especially not the security of vulnerable communities. The argument is that historical patterns of human settlement and lingering colonial legacies have too often marginalized large numbers of peoples from social, economic, and political development processes. As Swatuk and Vale report, the people of the South African homelands and townships still suffer the insecurity of poverty and pains of incorporation into the political economy of South Africa. The power of 'vested interests and established social relations in support of neocolonial political economies', along with 'fissures of identity' reflected in 'race, class, state, nation, and tribe' pose a major if not insurmountable barrier to the advancement of human security – not just in South Africa but the whole region (Swatuk and Vale 1999: 384).

There are clearly different understandings of human security particular to different social, political, and economic contexts – details that raise important questions about the limitations of traditional liberal assumptions about democratization and political development. Increasingly, scholars and the practitioners are beginning to ask difficult but essential questions about the proper sequence and priorities to be adopted in peacebuilding and democratic development, and how to ensure that these processes are informed by indigenous perspectives of what human security requires in their own lives.

Negotiated political transitions (from communist dictatorship, or from apartheid, from oppressive military or one-man rule, or in the aftermath of Western-led interventions in Kosovo, Iraq and Afghanistan) impose a sharp focus on the significance of these issues. Given the predominant role of Western governments and publics and Western-oriented intergovernmental and nongovernmental organizations in the peacemaking and peacebuilding field – and the reality that colonial legacies are seldom erased easily in developing countries – there is considerable potential for a collision between opposed human security values and priorities.

The literature also reveals telling differences in national and regional perspectives – different assessments of the subject, and different judgments on policy and political performance. Khong (2001) (with others) has speculated that the human security agenda grew out of the particulars of Canada's own history and circumstances – if not as a 'fireproof house', at least as relatively safe from the world's troubles and decently governed.

> In a world consisting primarily of Canadas, human security might command a consensus; and the kind of intrusiveness associated with implementing such an agenda might be acceptable. . . . However, too many individuals in the twenty-first century reside in makeshift shelters and thatched homes. What difference will it make to their lives for us to insist that they have become the referents of security? Not very much.

Asian perspectives get considerable attention in the literature on human security (e.g. Tow *et al.* 2000). More than one observer has remarked on the policy divergence between Canada and Japan on human security. Acharya (2001) has outlined a more expansive (but less intrusive) view of human security that goes beyond conventional issues of violence to matters of politics, culture, dignity and freedom – a definition expressed most comprehensively, of course, by the late Mahbub ul Haq at UNDP. Furtado (2000) looked to specific Asian states and reports on their particular responses to the 1997 financial shocks. Applying yet another perspective, Cocklin and Keen (2000) have described threats to human security (or wellbeing) characteristic of urbanization on South Pacific islands. These examples suggest how human security takes on different attributes in micro-level examinations.

Geisler and de Sousa (2001) have raised an awkward case of human security endeavours working disastrously at cross-purposes in Africa. They examine so-called 'ecological expropriation', the creation of millions of refugees by the closure of lands for purposes of environmental protection and repair. 'Human security and environmental security, often reinforcing, can be at odds', they note. Human security can no doubt be enhanced by environmental protection – or imperilled by it.

## Human security risk assessment

Much of the human security literature uses the language of 'threats' to characterize a wide – and, it would seem, always growing – list of challenges. To group all of these problems – from pandemic diseases to human-induced environmental catastrophes, from population displacements to terrorism, to the proliferation of nuclear or small arms – on the same long list, as if the costs (immediate as well as long-term) and probabilities (present and future) of each were the same, is unhelpful. They should be disaggregated and the costs and probabilities associated with each of these distinct problem areas specified. Changing rates of infection and mortality rates only tell us the direct, human costs of diseases such as AIDS, for instance; as some scholars now argue, there are profound, longer-term social, economic, and potential political consequences of these diseases as well. Once these costs are identified, it will be important to consider their longer-term implications for public policy and for preventive and mitigation strategies, especially if long-term social and economic costs are significant and widespread.

Mortality rates or poverty 'thresholds' are only one benchmark of human security. Although some 'threats' have major human security costs attached to them (the terrorist detonation of a nuclear bomb in a city, for example), the actual probability associated with these events may be quite low (Mueller 2006a, 2006b), especially when compared to the array of human security risks that most people confront in their daily lives. Nor do probabilities remain constant; on the contrary, some can rise suddenly, and others will fall. Resources and policy attention need to be re-allocated to those human security risks that are increasing, but only after undertaking a serious comparative assessment of relative risks (importantly including an identification of which population groups face the most risk).

The report on *Global Risks* (2007: 4) argues that 'there has been a major improvement in the understanding of the interdependencies between global risks, the importance of taking an integrated risk management approach to major global challenges and the necessity of attempting to deal with root causes of global risks rather than reacting to the consequences'. The report documents 23 core global risks which include energy supply disruptions, climate change, natural catastrophes, international terrorism, interstate and civil wars, pandemics and infectious diseases, and the breakdown of critical information infrastructures. The report measures the probabilities and costs associated with these risks on the basis of qualitative and quantitative data. In assessing severity, two indices – 'destruction of assets/economic damage and, where applicable, human lives lost' – were considered. It also offers a number of institutional recommendations on how businesses and governments can best mobilize resources and attention in order to 'engage in the forward action needed to begin managing global risks rather than coping with them'.

The relationships between political and economic variables, and their impact on conflict processes and so-called 'state failure', have also been examined in risk-assessment frameworks. The 'failed state index' developed by the Fund For Peace and *Foreign Policy* (2011) magazine, finds that nearly 60 countries in the world are dysfunctional because the government does not effectively control its territory, provide basic services to its citizens, or the country is experiencing some kind of internal unrest.

There is also now a great deal of work on organized violence and its causes (Collier 2007, Sambanis, *et al.* 2002, Stewart and Brown 2007, Duffield 2001). Three explanations dominate this literature:

1 those that stress the importance of group-based inequalities as a source of conflict, i.e. conflicts are based on 'creed';

2 those that focus on private gains – i.e. conflicts are driven by 'greed';

3 explanations which stress the failed social contract thesis, i.e. conflicts are really about 'needs'.

Those who have looked at these explanations closely find that it is not *absolute* poverty, but *relative* poverty that matters most. In other words, poor countries where some groups are, relatively speaking, much better off than others because of caste or creed are much more predisposed to experience violent conflict.

The policy implication of this research is that development strategies must be tied not simply to alleviating poverty in the poorest countries, but also to addressing the horizontal inequalities that divide those societies through, for example, redistribution of land, privatization schemes, credit allocation preferences, educational quotas, employment policies that stress balanced employment, and public sector infrastructure investment that advantages the disadvantaged (Stewart and Brown 2007). Research also shows that economic development is critical to sustaining the peace in states that have just ended a civil war (Paris 2004). Economic development is necessary to restore a state's human capital and infrastructure, raise the opportunity costs of conflict, and get buy-in from the local populace by raising their standard of living.

The subjective aspects of risk are another potentially promising research venue. We now know that most people tend to discount risks that they consider controllable, while exaggerating risks they think are uncontrollable. (This might explain why some people have a fear of flying.) People also tend to discount – and usually quite heavily – future risks (even though the probabilities associated with them are high), as against imminent risks that are relatively low. This is all to say there is a substantial literature in psychology on the cognitive biases that come into play as individuals confront the ordinary risks of daily life (Tversky and Kahneman 2000, Tversky, Slovic and Kahneman 1982). But there has been little direct application of this research to human security concerns. Do individuals in different societies perceive common human security threats through similar or different cognitive frames of reference? Are there significant cross-cultural barriers that stand in the way of coordinated policy responses to shared human security risks? To what extent are perceptions about different kinds of risks to human security at variance with more 'objective' assessments of those risks? Are there cultural taboos that stand in the way of efforts to reduce certain kinds of human security risks (family violence, violence against women, infanticide, etc.), and what kinds of strategies are appropriate to changing social attitudes? Are some social institutions better able to manage certain kinds of risks? And are there lessons to be learned about ways to reduce risk exposure for the most vulnerable groups in society? These are some questions that warrant further study.

## Governance and human security

Tension remains between still-new human security concerns and still-standing institutions and categories that continue to shape academic and political assumptions. There is an extensive consensus that prevailing institutions – state, interstate, nonstate – are performing inadequately (Thomas 2001, Reveron and Mahoney-Norris 2011, Friman and Reich 2007). But there is noisy disagreement over explanations and remedies.

Hampson *et al.* (2002) explored adaptations by international financial institutions (IFIs) to the human security agenda, and found them partial and unreliable: constrained by bureaucratic divisions or inertia, and by conflicts among their own (state) donors, IFIs 'have tended to adopt those elements among the different conceptions of human security that are most compatible with *existing* organizational mandates'.

Again, in the development discourse, there has been an early and fundamental dispute about the place of the state in the human security universe. Griffin (1995) had concluded by the mid-1990s that it was essential 'to construct new, post-cold war structures for global governance and cooperation among peoples', and to 'shift the emphasis from national sovereignty and state security to individual rights and human security'. In response, Bienefeld (1995) held that states themselves are a precondition to successful global governance – and to the achievement by any society of democracy, human security and sustainable development: 'Therefore we cannot abandon the sovereign state and strive for global governance. Instead, we must seek to protect the sovereign state in order to use it to fashion a system of global governance'.

Former Canadian foreign minister Lloyd Axworthy (2001) found it possible to resolve this polarity in the imagery of interdependence-driven coalition-building among states, NGOs, intergovernmental organizations, businesses and others. The Landmines Convention and the Rome Statute demonstrated the possibilities of diplomacy to advance human security (McRae and Hubert 2001). But even Axworthy acknowledged the present operational inadequacies of governance in some critical human security activities – which is perhaps most dramatic in the realm of coercive intervention, where norms remain inchoate or contradictory and institutions weak.

Several authors have applied human security analysis to the governance of refugee problems. Adelman (2001) detected a shift in emphasis at UNHCR, away from legal asylum issues and toward the protection of refugees and refugee operations (including protection of internally displaced people). But he does not diagnose this as a radical departure: 'It was built into the possibilities of the UNHCR from the beginning'. Again on refugees, Schmeidl (2002) found confirming evidence that refugee flows themselves can constitute a menace to human security – but especially when states encourage the transformation of refugee populations into 'refugee warrior communities'. Her assessment of the Afghan refugee experience in South Asia leads to the conclusion that 'the way local, regional and international actors responded to the refugee crisis seems to have contributed equally, or more to the security dilemma, than the migration itself'.

The Internal Displacement Monitoring Center (2011) finds that since 1998 'the number of internally displaced persons (IDP) has steadily risen from around 17 million to 27.5 million in 2010'. Although displacement 'continues to rise in the Americas, Asia, Europe and the Middle East', there has been 'a steady decline in IDP numbers in Africa, dating back from 2004'. Arguably, this positive development is because 'the African continent remains at the forefront of policy development in support of IDP rights. In 2009, the African Union adopted the Kampala Convention – the first ever instrument for the protection and assistance of IDPs to bind countries across a whole continent'. When the Convention is ratified by 15 African Union members it will go into effect. Globally the causes of much of this displacement are continuing patterns of armed violence and criminality which have forced peoples and communities from their homes. This trend is also accompanied by an increasing pattern of urban displacement, which poses its own unique challenge for international humanitarian and development responders.

## Towards a theory of human security

Running through the human security literature is a recognition – not always explicit – of the difficulty in grounding these subjects in cohesive theory or methodology. Indeed, conventional realist frameworks of International Relations theory prove quite inhospitable to human security approaches – one reason, no doubt, why the treatment of human security in the prominent journals of security studies has so far seemed brief and dismissive (Mack 2001). Systematic attempts to develop theory and methodology helpful to understanding humans' security ultimately appear to involve the abandonment, if not outright repudiation, of the various realist schools of International Relations theorizing (see Chapter 2, this volume). Some scholars have turned instead to feminist critiques to address human security questions, and more generally to constructivism (see Chapters 5 and 8, this volume).

Constructivism shares fundamental assumptions with human security approaches – the assumption, for example, that threats are constructed, not inevitable, and that they can be altered or mitigated. Furthermore, the acknowledgement by states that certain forms of economic and political organization facilitate domestic peace and stability, and that domestic conditions affect the international system, are characteristically constructivist insights (see Neuman 2001).

Similarly, some feminist approaches explicitly call for political action and focus on familiar human security issues: shifting scales, from household to substate to global; breaking down dichotomies, as between public and personal, national and international; and acknowledging mobility, whether of refugees or fugitives from human rights law (e.g. Hyndman 2001). Throughout, there is in feminist analysis a sharp and careful attention to unequal and violent relationships in families, communities, or transnational systems – the kinds of relationships that often define human insecurity.

Taken together, constructivist and feminist analyses offer promising methodologies for examining exactly the phenomena that concern human security scholars. By reorienting the research focus to life as it is lived by the most insecure in any society (women, the poor, minorities, aboriginal communities), these methodologies can advance research and make for more productive human security policy.

## Conclusion

For all their inconsistencies and uncertainties, human security studies are growing demonstrably stronger and more abundant. In fact, the diversity of disciplinary foundations accounts for some of the strength in human security scholarship: there is a kind of evolutionary advantage in drawing from a wide variety of intellectual methods and traditions. That same variety goes some way to explain a profusion of research activities that can sometimes look like incoherence.

Some scholars are still busy trying to define the boundaries of human security, organizing a discipline, arranging typologies. Meanwhile, others are exploring human security issues on the ground – and beginning a serious scholarly contribution to the design and execution of human security policy.

In all of this, policy-makers and scholars are bound to find each other at odds from time to time. Practitioners, hard-pressed to prevent the crises not already exploding on CNN and the internet, and to cope with crises underway, show understandable impatience with scholarship that renders any problem more complicated – or worse, that does not evidently address any recognizable problem at all. Policy-makers (some of them scholars *manqués* themselves) would do well to remind themselves that scholars honour their own obligations and professional standards; they are neither desk officers at the call of foreign ministries nor cheering spectators at the policy sidelines. Equally, scholars ambitious to affect policy are wise to understand the constraints of politics and resources that act on policy in every phase. They should also respect the dictatorship of deadlines that practitioners face – and the low tolerance among practitioners for elegant definitional argument. When a theory collides with reality, busy practitioners might want to know why; they will show no detectable excitement when a theory collides with another theory. In the best sort of dialogue – frank, timely, and open-minded – academic and policy communities can collaborate to their lasting and shared advantage. More to the point, together they might advance the progress of human security.

## Further reading

Mary Kaldor, *Human Security* (Polity, 2007). A broad-ranging discussion of human security by one of its principal European intellectual champions that is written in an accessible and provocative style.

Fen Osler Hampson *et al.*, *Madness in the Multitude* (Oxford University Press, 2002). Provides an overview of the history and evolution of different conceptions of human security and key policy initiatives.

International Commission on Intervention and State Sovereignty (ICISS), *The Responsibility to Protect* (Ottawa: International Development Research Centre, 2001). A key policy document that discusses the challenges of humanitarian intervention and offers major recommendations to strengthen the capacity and will of international institutions to intervene when there are major violations of human rights.

Neil S. MacFarlane and Yuen Foon Khong, *Human Security and the UN: A Critical History* (Indiana University Press, 2006). Discusses the history and evolution of the contribution of the United Nations to human security.

Jorge Nef, *Human Security and Mutual Vulnerability* (Ottawa: International Development Research Centre, 2002). One of the earliest and most definitive discussions of the meaning of human security and its importance in international development.

Samantha Power, *'A Problem from Hell': America and the Age of Genocide* (Harper Perennial, 2003). A Putlizer prize-winning discussion of the moral dilemmas associated with humanitarian intervention by one of President Obama's key policy advisers.

Derek S. Reveron and Kathleen A. Mahoney-Norris, *Human Security in a Borderless World* (Westview Press, 2011). A useful, up-to-date text on the broader conception and approaches to the study of human security that is a good introduction to the subject for students.

Report of the Commission on Human Security, *Human Security Now: Protecting and Empowering People* (UN, 2003). A key report of an international commission that discusses the different aspects of human security and the ways to address different human security challenges.

# Poverty

Caroline Thomas with Paul D. Williams

## Abstract

In this chapter, students will learn about the intimate relationship between poverty and security. The chapter's starting point is that fundamentally, the pursuit of security is about individual human beings – i.e. human security – and the protection and fulfilment of their human rights. The pursuit of other levels of security has legitimacy and relevance to the degree to which it supports human security, and the latter cannot be defined or contained within the territorial boundaries of an exclusive political unit. From this perspective, poverty is of direct relevance for security studies; indeed poverty and human insecurity are in many respects synonymous. Both refer to a human condition characterized by the lack of fulfilment of a range of human entitlements such as adequate food, healthcare, education, shelter, employment, and voice; a life lived in fear of violence, injury, crime or discrimination; and an expectation that life will continue in this way. Although the connections between poverty and security have been recognized by mainstream development and security analysts since the early 1990s, it has not yet resulted in a sustained critique of neoliberal development policy, but rather a reassertion of it.

## Introduction

Despite sixty years of official development policies, as well as the commitment made in 2000 by 189 states at the UN to the Millennium Development Goals (MDGs), one billion people continue to live in extreme poverty. Almost half of the world's seven billion people live on $2 a day or less. Poverty is the cause of far more deaths than armed conflict. This human insecurity occurs against the backdrop of a growth in global military spending (reaching an estimated $1,630,000,000,000 in 2010) (SIPRI 2011), a growth in the arms trade, and the significant proliferation in small arms and light weapons which account for the majority of violent deaths and maiming (see Chapter 29 this volume).

In addition, this routine insecurity occurs in the context of global and national political and economic systems which many believe perpetuate not only poverty but also deepening inequality. If nobody had to endure a life of poverty, then the fact that one per cent of the global population earns annually as much as the poorest 57 per cent of humanity might not be an issue. However, given the current scale of global poverty, and the spectre of increased numbers living in poverty, the continuation and, arguably, the intensification of inequalities should be of concern. These trends are evident in increased differentiation and polarization within and between states, world regions, and globally, and raise fundamental questions about the appropriateness of global and national economic, social, political and security structures, policies and values.

Globally, the political and economic challenge is defined in limited terms of 'poverty reduction' via quantitative targets set out in the MDGs. Yet with the global population on course to reach 8 billion by 2025, even the limited goal of poverty reduction appears to be a hugely ambitious target in many parts of the world. Moreover, if the current development trajectory continues – which equates neoliberal economic policy with development policy – it is reasonable to expect that even the limited MDG targets, if met, will be unsustainable over time. In other words, what is being sold as the solution to global poverty – neoliberal economic policy – is actually part of the problem.

## Is poverty an appropriate concern for security studies?

Over the last two decades, interest has grown in the relationship between security and poverty. Prior to that, 'experts' such as practising diplomats, government leaders and mainstream academics in security studies generally thought of these areas as separate. Of course, it is unlikely that their view was shared by ordinary citizens throughout the world, for their direct experience would have suggested otherwise. Security for the 'experts' was understood narrowly as protecting the national interest, usually defined as upholding the physical, territorial integrity of the state against external military attack, but in reality often involving protection against internal fragmentation or challenge

## BOX 20.1  THE MILLENNIUM DEVELOPMENT GOALS, 2000

### Goal 1  Eradicate extreme poverty and hunger

*Targets*: Halve, between 1990 and 2015, the proportion of people whose income is less than one dollar a day; and halve, between 1990 and 2015, the proportion of people who suffer from hunger.

### Goals 2  Achieve universal primary education

*Target*: Ensure that by 2015, children everywhere – boys and girls – will be able to complete primary schooling.

### Goal 3  Promote gender equality and empower women

*Target*: Eliminate gender disparity in primary and secondary schools by 2005, and all levels of education by 2015.

### Goal 4  Reduce child mortality

*Target*: Reduce by two thirds, 1990–2015, the under-five mortality rate.

### Goal 5  Improve maternal health

*Target*: Reduce by three-quarters, 1990–2015, the maternal morbidity ratio.

### Goal 6  Combat HIV/AIDS, malaria and other diseases

*Targets*: Halt and begin to reverse the spread of HIV/AIDS by 2015, and the incidence of malaria and other diseases.

### Goal 7  Ensure environmental sustainability

*Targets*: Integrate sustainable development principles; halve the proportion of people without sustainable access to safe drinking water; achieve a significant improvement in lives of 100 million slum dwellers by 2020.

### Goal 8  Develop a global partnership for development

*Targets*: Further develop a rule-based, non-discriminatory financial and trading system; address needs of least developed countries, small island and landlocked states; make debt sustainable; employment for youths; access to medicines; share benefits of new information and communications technologies.

to the ruling elite. Economic issues, insofar as they were considered at all by this group, were very much low-order issues. Poverty was relegated to the domain of development practitioners and development academics, who shared the state-based approach of their security colleagues. They understood and measured development in terms of national achievements.

During the 1990s, the mainstream security agenda merged with the mainstream development agenda under the mantle of global governance. Global political changes post-Cold War, the shift in conflicts mainly to poorer regions of the world (particularly Africa), the scale of humanitarian emergencies, the perceived threat of global terrorism, and deepening global economic integration with its attendant inequalities and political protests, created space for the exploration of the relationship between poverty and security within mainstream analysis. Nowadays, mainstream academics, diplomats and politicians speak openly of the need to integrate approaches to poverty and security. Leaders of the G8, the International Monetary Fund (IMF) and World Bank, for example, have spoken forcefully about a possible link between poverty and armed conflict.

The acknowledgement of connections between poverty and security is welcomed by those who have long advocated a holistic approach, but a word of caution is in order as such analysts remain sceptical about the direction of travel. The new global political focus on poverty reduction is seen by some as a means to ensure that opposition to global economic integration is neutralized, and the economic liberalization project continued unimpeded.

## Whose poverty? Whose security?

One of the first problems a student of poverty and security encounters is the contested nature of the key terms of the debate. In other words, what precisely are we talking about? Security means different things to different people, as has been demonstrated in this book. Likewise, poverty has different meanings, and these are often understood within the larger concept of development – itself a heavily debated term. Both have been analysed and measured in terms of individual human beings, sub-state regions, the state level, continental regions and even at the global level; both have also been thought about in terms of specific groups or categories of people who may be contained within or spread beyond a single state. Box 20.2 summarizes some of the widely utilized approaches to define 'poverty' and how to think about the category of 'the poor'.

The term 'conflict' often crops up in discussions of poverty and security, and this too takes on many different meanings according to the perspective of the respective author. It often refers to wars, for example: interstate wars, proxy wars, internal wars fought to gain regional independence or to gain political supremacy, wars initiated by outside powers (Stewart 2003: 329–330). Yet conflict is also experienced at the individual level, particularly amongst poor communities where, for example, a gun culture can flourish aided by

## BOX 20.2 APPROACHES TO POVERTY

There are different approaches to defining what is meant by 'poverty' and how researchers should understand the category of 'the poor'. Among the most widely used are the monetary, capability, social exclusion, and participatory approaches (Laderchi *et al.* 2003):

- The monetary approach defines poverty as a shortfall in consumption (or income) from some previously identified poverty line.

- The capabilities approach views poverty as deprivation in, or failure to achieve certain 'basic capabilities' defined by 'the ability to satisfy certain crucially important functionings up to certain minimally adequate levels' – or what Amartya Sen referred to as 'freedom' (in Laderchi *et al.* 2003: 253).

- A third approach defines poverty as a form of social exclusion whereby people are rendered poor through the suffocating consequences of social structures. As defined by the European Union, social exclusion is the 'process through which individuals or groups are wholly or partially excluded from full participation in the society in which they live' (in Laderchi *et al.* 2003: 257).

- The participatory approach looks at the issue from the standpoint of those who are thought to be suffering from poverty and gets these people to participate in decisions about what it means to be poor and the magnitude of poverty. The problem is that it assumes we know which people to ask and there is no satisfactory means of adjudicating between competing accounts.

the easy availability of small arms and light weapons, and also in the domestic setting where gendered power relations underpin domestic violence. In addition to all of these complexities, there is the challenge of understanding the term 'violence': for many authors, it is physical; for some, such as Galtung, it is structural, exemplifying the condition of living perpetuated by the development of the global economy over the past 500 years, whereby swathes of humanity are disenfranchised, living in routine poverty and exploitation (see Chapter 6 this volume).

These conceptual and theoretical debates are rehearsed extensively in the academic literature, and they are not repeated here; but it is important to be aware of the many claims to 'truth', and the role that perspective and position play.

For us, security at its very core is about the condition of individual human beings and humankind, rather than geographical, administrative, economic or political units, or faceless others. Fundamentally, the pursuit of security is about individual human beings – i.e. human security – and the protection and fulfilment of their human rights. (Of course, the meaning of the term 'human security' is also contested, see Chapter 19 this volume.) The pursuit of other levels of security – for example, global, regional or national – has legitimacy and relevance to the degree to which it supports human security, and the latter cannot be defined or contained within the territorial boundaries of an exclusive political unit. Thus, a government's pursuit of 'national security' should not threaten the human security either of its citizens, or indeed of people living beyond its borders.

Working with this understanding of security as being a priori about human beings, it becomes clear that poverty is of direct relevance for security studies; indeed poverty and human insecurity are in many respects synonymous. Both refer to a human condition characterized by the lack of fulfilment of a range of human entitlements such as adequate food, healthcare, education, shelter, employment, and voice; a life lived in fear of violence, injury, crime or discrimination; and an expectation that life will continue in this way. All of these elements are to varying degrees dependent facets, and the loss of one often leads to the loss of/decline in enjoyment of others, e.g. under-nutrition and poor housing contribute to ill-heath, which itself prevents productive work, and this affects the ability to grow or purchase food, which contributes to further malnutrition; living without title to land or housing opens the way to physical insecurity and the feeling of hopelessness, for example as slums are cleared; living in fear of arbitrary violence from gangs, or even from those acting in the name of or in the payroll of the government, undermines voice and obstructs economic and political development.

Improvements in human security necessarily involve poverty reduction, and likewise, poverty reduction will decrease human insecurity. Such improvements can also be seen as synonymous with improvements in the experience of human rights – economic, social, civil, political and cultural – by individual human beings.

Thus poverty is not simply a relevant area of concern for security studies; rather, it is a central concern for those who believe that security is a priori about human beings, and that it is about states, world regions and the global political system only to the extent that they help or hinder the primary goal of human security.

Therefore, in a world where half of humanity lives in a condition of poverty (read: human insecurity or lack of enjoyment of basic human rights), understanding the national and global structures and policies which sustain this situation is crucial for the articulation of policies supportive of the enhancement of human security. As a consequence, a critique of current development policy, and the articulation of alternative pathways to development, should be a key focus for security studies. Indeed, the continuation of entrenched academic silos which differentiate between and create 'experts' in the study of security, or poverty/development or human rights, obstructs the growth of knowledge and understanding about the human condition, and the enormous challenges to be faced. The need for an inclusive, integrated approach is clear (on which, see Spear and Williams 2012).

## What do we know about the poverty–security nexus?

When security is considered in human terms, the current model of development is failing to deliver to the majority of people across the world, and in

## BOX 20.3 THE BLUEPRINT FOR DEVELOPMENT: NEOLIBERAL ECONOMICS, OR 'THE WASHINGTON CONSENSUS'

By the early 1980s, with changes in the domestic politics of leading industrialized countries, the post-war liberal principle of state-guided markets gave way to the rise of neoliberal economic policy. This signalled a fundamental shift in development policy from state-led to market-led.

The 'Washington Consensus' as it came to be known was promoted as a universal blueprint for development by an increasingly coordinated set of actors – public and private international financial institutions (e.g. IMF and World Bank, private banks), think-tanks and political leaders in Washington DC, other OECD governments, all keen to ensure the repayment of Third World debt.

The causes of poverty and underdevelopment were identified as internal to the state, rather than external/structural or a combination of both. Export-led growth would generate foreign exchange necessary for debt repayment, and benefits would occur throughout society by the 'trickle down' effect. The role of the state was redefined as the enabler of the private sector, facilitating privatization, liberalization and deregulation. Good governance was crucial for competitive elections, enforcing property rights, tackling corruption etc. Global economic integration through trade and investment liberalization was the best way to promote economic growth, which in turn would deliver improvements for all worldwide.

While the theory may have looked convincing to some, when applied in the real world it has encountered many problems. The reform of domestic economies across the developing and transition countries, with an emphasis on rolling back the state in favour of market-led development, trade and investment liberalization, has not resulted in benefits for all. Indeed, many in the former Soviet bloc and East Asia have been thrown into poverty following particular crises of liberalization, whilst in parts of Africa poverty has deepened routinely as anticipated growth has failed to materialize through the combination of structural adjustment policies, plus increasing debt, falling commodity prices and disappointing levels of aid. State infrastructures have declined.

Voices of opposition from development NGOs have grown louder, criticizing the imposition and questioning the appropriateness of a universal blueprint recommended and applied irrespective of local condition or wishes. Increasingly, criticisms have been heard within the IMF and World Bank, and have resulted in significant resignations (e.g. Joseph Stiglitz left the World Bank in 2000).

By the late 1990s, the key advocates of neoliberalism were supporting a change of emphasis: growth alone is not enough, it must be 'pro-poor', and locally owned by national governments and civil society. Yet in reality, post-2000, the emphasis on domestic reform in support of the private sector plus trade liberalization remains.

some cases, such as across parts of sub-Saharan Africa, it seems to be making a significant contribution to the deterioration of the human condition.

For the one billion people living below the internationally identified poverty line of $1 a day, and the next two and a half billion living on $2 a day, poverty is a chronic condition; for others, it may be transient, for example following a specific, one-off crop failure. Specific disadvantaged groups exist within these figures e.g. the elderly, disabled, youths, refugees, internally displaced persons, HIV/AIDS sufferers. Also hidden within these figures are the poor who are made even poorer and more vulnerable by some specific event, e.g. the Asian tsunami (December 2004); or the Pakistan Kashmiri earthquake (October 2005), or the Haitian earthquake (March 2011).

Those in chronic poverty lead wholly insecure lives, routinely lack voice, basic needs, work and opportunity, often living in fear, subject to physical abuse, forced eviction and so forth. In addition to arbitrary violence often perpetrated by the authorities, those living in poverty face violent crime. In major cities they endure the normalization of the gun culture, e.g. in Lagos, Rio de Janeiro and Nairobi. The perpetrators and the victims are generally young, unemployed male youths without hope. This hopelessness amongst youths is particularly worrying, given the evolving age profile of the global population, and the fact that young people are the next generation of social

## BOX 20.4 PROBLEMS OF APPLYING THE 'WASHINGTON CONSENSUS' MODEL OF DEVELOPMENT

- Economic growth lower than expected, and of poor quality, e.g. neither job-creating nor poverty-reducing. In sub-Saharan Africa many countries experienced a drop in GDP during the 1980s and 1990s (UNCTAD 2010: vii).

- Trickle-down does not occur – inequalities increase within and between states, including those of the developing world. In countries with low per capita income, benefit from trade openness accrues to the rich not the poor.

- Debt remains a serious problem, especially for the most heavily indebted countries for whom debt as a percentage of external exports rose from 38 per cent in 1980–1984, to 103 per cent 1995–2000.

- Trade liberalization – developing countries which rely on the export of primary commodities (i.e., the poorest) suffer a continuous, significant decline in market share – they are more open to trade, but earn less (UNCTAD 2006: 20).

- Unemployment rates have increased with many countries facing their highest rates of unemployment for 40 years. This should prompt a rethink of the paradigm of export-led development based on keeping labour costs low (UNCTAD 2010: i, vi).

- Social problems increase as market-based entitlement deprives poor people of access to essential services, e.g. health care to meet the HIV/AIDS emergency in Africa.

- Official Development Assistance has been disappointing, with the expected new money failing to flow in; indeed after the deduction of debt relief, there was decline in aid to the poorest countries 1996–2000; thereafter, increases were largely absorbed by Iraq and Afghanistan.

- Foreign Direct Investment (FDI) – poorest countries lose out, with 49 of them attracting just 2 per cent of FDI to the South, or 0.5 per cent of global FDI, in 2001.

and economic actors (World Bank 2006). Opportunities missed, and behaviours/cultures developed early on in life can be very difficult to reverse.

The direct experience of poverty is often linked to significant vertical inequalities based on income, and/or horizontal social, economic and political inequalities (i.e., differences across geographical regions or social groups) which may occur within the national or global context, are often played out over many generations (HDR 2005: 163). These inequalities do not happen naturally. Rather, they are the result of actions or inactions by human beings in government or in international institutions. They are created, sustained, made worse or better, or ignored by human beings in positions of authority and/or power and influence, who chose to promote certain rules of the economic and political game over others. These inequalities erode the political legitimacy of government in both the developed and the developing world, and of global governance through institutions such as the World Trade Organization (WTO) and IMF.

These horizontal inequalities may play out within a state's borders, e.g. in Sudan, Nepal, China, Russia, India, or Mexico, where particular regions and/or groups of people feel disadvantaged by the state and a conflict situation exists. Governments can play a role in alleviating or exacerbating vertical and horizontal inequalities, and therefore human insecurity, within their states.

---

## BOX 20.5 CURRENT SETBACKS ON THE MILLENNIUM DEVELOPMENT GOALS

Progress in achieving the Millennium Development Goals has been far from uniform across the world. The greatest improvements have been in East Asia and South Asia but other developing regions continue to struggle. Sub-Saharan Africa remains at the epicentre of the crisis, making overall progress on only two of the twenty-one quantifiable development targets (UN 2011a). The World Bank's 2007 assessment continues to hold true: the largest 'MDG deficit' is in states with weak institutions and governance, and often in conflict – the 'fragile states' (World Bank 2007: 3). According to the UN, among the most significant ongoing setbacks are:

- Huge disparities between urban and rural areas.
- The poorest children have made the slowest progress in terms of improved nutrition.
- Opportunities for full and productive employment remain particularly slim for women.
- Being poor, female or living in a conflict zone increases the probability that a child will be out of school.
- Advances in sanitation often bypass the poor and those living in rural areas.
- Improving the lives of a growing number of urban poor remains a monumental challenge.
- Progress has been uneven in improving access to safe drinking water.

(UN 2011b: 4–5)

It is noteworthy that in terms of deaths through violent physical acts, more people are killed by their own governments than by foreign armies. For example, it has been estimated that in the twentieth century, while approximately 40 million people were killed in wars between states, more than four times that number – some 120 million people – were killed by their own governments (Rummel 1994: 21). Deprivation resulting from acts or omissions of government via their policies adds to the citizens' death toll. Often, economic and social policies pursued by governments are heavily influenced from outside, e.g. IMF, WTO, or a major power which ties aid to specific domestic policy reform (see below).

Many of the half of humanity living in poverty are refugees or have been forcibly displaced. Globally, in early 2011, the UN High Commissioner for Refugees estimated that there are approximately 43.7 million forcibly displaced people (some 10 million of whom are refugees), with particularly high numbers in Afghanistan and Sudan. Statelessness and mass denial of effective citizenship by governments threatens the security of individuals, and groups, and this can have a detrimental effect beyond borders.

Horizontal inequalities can also be detected from a global perspective, with entire world regions and their inhabitants disadvantaged or advantaged by the particular global rules within which all must operate, yet few set. For example, the vast majority of HIV/AIDS sufferers live in sub-Saharan Africa, yet they and their governments have no voice in developing the global rules which determine access to drugs. A further example involves the rules which determine the benefits of the globalization process in which sub-Saharan Africa and its people have been marginalized; these are legitimated by international financial institutions and the G8 governments. Another example is a system of trade that fails to take into account the needs of the poorest, especially rural agricultural workers. These inequalities are created, they are intentionally or unintentionally made worse, or simply ignored by major governments or external agents such as the IMF, the WTO, or aid donors. Through their policies, these actors can create, promote and sustain or simply even permit human insecurity, to devastating effect. The tragic history of debt accumulation and repayment by African governments (read: poor inhabitants of African states) is testimony to this.

Consider the example of food insecurity, which is one of the defining features of existence for people living in poverty. Three-quarters of poor people live in rural areas, yet rural livelihoods in agriculture are being destroyed by the unfolding of global economic integration, and inadequate alternative opportunities are being created in urban areas. The progress of trade liberalization means that food produced using huge subsidies in rich countries such as the US and within the EU, finds it way to markets in poor countries where local farmers lose their livelihoods and are left without the means to buy the imported foodstuffs. In Haiti, for example, poor rice farmers have lost their means of subsistence as US rice has flooded the national market and they have no alternative means of subsistence. Similarly, poor farmers in tropical countries who depend on the sale of their agricultural products in northern markets – such as coffee, tea or cotton farmers – find their livelihoods are completely insecure. Eleven million cotton farmers in West Africa, and 20 million coffee farmers, faced devastation in recent years.

While the contemporary effects of economic liberalization on food security are clear, it is also noteworthy that governments that have chosen over the last sixty years to prioritize food security have been able to lift their populations out of food insecurity. Diverse examples exist: Sri Lanka, countries of South East Asia, and Cuba. In sum, governments have choices, but it remains to be seen to what degree they will have leeway with the progression of rules on trade liberalization.

## What do we know about the poverty–violent conflict nexus?

Poverty causes more deaths than violent conflict but it may also contribute to violent conflict and therefore to further human insecurity. Likewise, violent conflict may contribute to poverty. What do we know about this relationship? In the post-Cold War period, and particularly since the mid-1990s, there has been a significant scaling-up of research on the poverty–violent conflict nexus by universities, institutes, NGOs and even governments (see Williams 2012). These investigations range from large projects offering detailed data gathering and analysis (e.g. Uppsala Conflict Data Programme working in partnership with the Human Security Centre, University of British Columbia; Stockholm International Peace Research Institute), political economic analysis and econometric modelling (e.g. Queen Elizabeth House, Oxford and WIDER), or case studies of regions or issues (e.g. Centre for International Coopera-tion and Security (CICS) Bradford University, Amnesty International, the International Action Network on Small Arms, and Oxfam International), to more theoretical critiques of the broad area (Duffield 2001, Stewart and Fitzgerald 2001, Wilkin 2002). Of course, many citizens on the ground would doubtless suggest that these findings simply confirm what they already knew from direct experience.

### Effect of poverty on conflict

While it is often not possible to completely disentangle a whole range of factors which may contribute to a violent conflict (e.g. environmental, social, economic, political, historical), the growing body of knowledge has provided evidence in a previously data-light area that 'poverty and falling incomes are critical drivers for violent conflict in less developed countries' (Miguel 2006: 1). Nafziger and Auvinen (2002: 153) have shown that 'stagnation and decline in real GDP, high income inequality, a high ratio of military expenditures to national income, and a tradition of violent conflict are sources of emergencies'. Collier *et al.* (2003), have shown that there can be a variety of economic motivations for conflict, born out of poverty, including economic grievance, greed and even opportunity. Econometric studies have shown that poverty feeds insecurity, and insecurity feeds poverty, both at the level of the state and the individual. The UNDP has summed this up as 'the conflict trap is part of the poverty trap' (UNDP 2005: 157).

The UN categorizes states according to their per capita income, and has identified poor countries – and therefore their inhabitants – as being far more likely to experience violent conflict than rich countries. In 2006, 50 Least Developed Countries (LDCs) were identified, each exhibiting a per capita income under $750, human resource weakness (poor health, nutrition, education, adult literacy); and economic vulnerability. Of these, 16 were landlocked and 12 were small islands. Such low-income countries accounted for over half of countries experiencing violent conflict 1990–2003. Moreover, countries with per capita income of $600 are half as likely to experience civil war as countries with per capita income of $250. In Africa, for example, it is notable that Algeria was the only state with a GNI per capita over $1,000 which suffered a state-based armed conflict between 1990 and 2009 (Williams 2011: 212). In other words, the poorer the country, the more likely its people are to experience civil war.

The majority of countries listed by the UN as least developed countries are in sub-Saharan Africa, and the problems of poverty and conflict affect Africa disproportionately. The region is caught in a trap of poverty–conflict–poverty. At the turn of the twenty-first century the situation was so bad that,

> Almost every country across the middle belt of the continent – from Somalia in the east to Sierra Leone in the west, from Sudan in the north to Angola in the south – remains trapped in a volatile mix of poverty, crime, unstable and inequitable political institutions, ethnic discrimination, low state capacity and the "bad neighbourhoods" of other crisis-ridden states – all factors associated with increased risk of armed conflict.
>
> (Human Security Centre 2005: 4)

More recently, the popular protests in North Africa and the Middle East known collectively as the 'Arab Spring' have demonstrated once again the clear connections between poverty, underdevelopment and violent conflict.

The issue of how to lift these countries and their peoples – most of whom depend on the production of basic commodities – out of the poverty trap is pressing. Those commodities have experienced a long-term decline in value compared with manufactured goods. G8, IMF and World Bank structural adjustment policies call for increased exports of such commodities to generate foreign exchange which can be used towards debt repayment. Yet more and more of these very products have to be produced and sold in order simply to stand still. And then there is the additional problem of governments of many low-income states spending more on weapons than on healthcare, e.g. Burundi, Ethiopia, Nepal, Bangladesh (UNDP 2005: 160).

### Effect of conflict on poverty

Mounting evidence shows the negative effect of conflict on development and poverty alleviation (e.g. World Bank 2011: 4). The thirteen case studies published by CICS in 2005 illustrate the vast range of possibilities, which may be short- or long-term, local, regional, national or even international. Examples include:

- depletion of the productive workforce through direct involvement in conflict and indirectly through displacement, hunger, injury and disease;
- destruction of physical and social infrastructure, including transport, power, education and health;
- destruction of the agricultural base and therefore of subsistence and livelihoods, plus a loss of local expert farming knowledge with subsequent movement of displaced into urban areas;
- disruption and destruction of markets;
- diversion of young children into military roles;
- expansion of youths in urban areas turning to crime and acceptance of violence as a legitimate way to settle differences;
- decline in economic growth and export revenues;
- rise in military expenditure by governments; and
- negative effect on growth nationally and in neighbouring states.

At a human level, conflict exacerbates the human insecurity of those directly involved or caught in the crossfire, many of whom already do not routinely enjoy basic entitlements and rights. It is a cruel irony that for some, conflict is seen as the route to secure rights and entitlements which they see their government as denying them.

## The diplomatic agenda on poverty and security

At the academic level, data-gathering and analysis regarding poverty, security and their interlinkages, as well as theoretical critique, is proceeding rapidly. What of the diplomatic level? The poverty–security connection was under the spotlight in the 2005 World Summit at the UN General Assembly, which considered the report of the High Level Panel on Threats and Challenges, *A More Secure World: Our Shared Responsibility*. This defined a threat to international security as 'any event or process that leads to large-scale death or lessening of life chances and undermines States as the basic unit of the international system' (UNGA 2004: 25). It details a number of threats, including poverty, infectious disease and environmental degradation; conflict between and within states; nuclear, radiological, chemical and biological weapons, terrorism and transnational organized crime. In his foreword, Kofi Annan commented:

> I support the report's emphasis on development as the indispensable foundation stone of a new collective security. Extreme poverty and infectious diseases are threats in themselves, but they also create environments which make more likely the emergence of other threats, including civil conflict. If we are to succeed in better protecting the security of our citizens, *it is essential that due attention and necessary resources be devoted to achieving the Millennium Development Goals.*
>
> (UNGA 2004: 2 para.7)

But is the focus on the MDGs appropriate? Of course they should be met, and their fulfilment will enhance the human security of some of the world's poorest people. And yes, violent conflict will make their achievement more difficult. Yet the mere existence of those goals is testimony to the failure of development policy to date. The fundamental issue is whether the current approach to development (still principally variants of economic neoliberalism) is appropriate for meeting the challenge of human security or poverty eradication or human rights – today and tomorrow. The evidence suggests that it is not. Consider that in 2003 the UN Development Programme report contended that if sub-Saharan Africa continues on its current course, it will take another 150 years to reach the MDG target of halving poverty, and the hunger situation will continue to worsen (UNDP 2003). Consequently, a radical critique of those policies and the development of an alternative should be at the heart of diplomatic endeavour.

At the broadest level, the failure of development post-1945 must be acknowledged, and the values underpinning the approach must be brought into question (see Stewart 2004). There are no signs that this development model is about to be overturned. The modifications of the existing approach evident in the Post-Washington Consensus are not likely to deliver poverty eradication or human security for all, or result in a sustainable future for the eight billion people who will inhabit our planet by 2025. The pursuit of growth without equal attention to equity and sustainability will perpetuate the current poverty–conflict–poverty trap.

For the countries of sub-Saharan Africa, their specific circumstances mean that the continuation of trade openness will contribute to further poverty, inequality and insecurity. These are the very countries which are currently the most conflict-ridden. In particular, progress must be made on commodities – especially basic agricultural commodities – if the world's governments are serious about the eradication of hunger and malnutrition, and improving human insecurity. Progress on the trade rules governing arms flows is also vital: human security rather than liberal free trade principles must inform the development of the rules. Much will hinge on improving the slow progress being made on the global Arms Trade Treaty at the UN (on which see Chapter 29, this volume).

Likewise, with aid: the very countries which are currently the most conflict-ridden – those in sub-Saharan Africa especially – are missing out under the current aid regime. Despite the promises made by the G8 at Gleneagles in July 2005, a tiny number of recipients outside the continent are the greatest beneficiaries of aid. The African Progress Panel was launched in April 2007 to ensure accountability of the donors – a sure sign that delivery was not matching promises.

Human security concerns must drive trade, aid and foreign investment, as well as domestic reform, and we must measure their legitimacy by their contribution to it. The contribution of internal factors to current insecurity must be matched by due acknowledgement of the role of external/structural factors. A development strategy for human security must embrace both.

## Conclusion

This chapter has explored the relationship between poverty and security. Defining security at its core in human terms, it suggests that poverty is not only an appropriate concern for students of security – it is an essential part of their studies. A significant proportion of humanity is caught in a poverty–insecurity–poverty trap. Poverty and insecurity are two sides of the same coin. A person who experiences one, will likely be familiar with the other. If governments and international institutions tackle one, they will impact on the other. Serious students of one necessarily need to study the other. All need to think about development, for without that there cannot be poverty eradication or sustainable human security.

## Further reading

Centre for International Cooperation and Security (CICS), *The Impact of Armed Violence on Poverty and Development* (Bradford University: CICS, 2005), at www.bradford.ac.uk/cics. An accessible collection of case studies examining the effect of armed violence on poverty and development across the world.

Human Security Centre, *Human Security Report 2005* (Oxford University Press, 2005). A rich compilation of data which suggests a dramatic, and unnoticed, decline in the number of wars, genocides and human rights abuse over the past decade, due it suggests in large part to the unprecedented upsurge of international activism, spearheaded by the UN.

Paul Rogers, *Losing Control: Global Security in the Twenty-first Century* (Pluto Press, 3rd edition, 2010). An engaging and accessible book which calls for a radical rethinking of Western perceptions of security, and highlights the need to address the core issues of global insecurity, including poverty and inequality.

Joanna Spear and Paul D. Williams (eds.), *Security and Development in Global Politics: A Critical Comparison* (Georgetown University Press, 2012). Analyses how experts from the security and development fields have addressed several crucial contemporary issues including poverty, aid, humanitarian assistance and trade.

Frances Stewart, 'Conflict and the Millennium Development Goals', *Journal of Human Development*, 4(3) (2003): 325–351. Shows the relationship between conflict and the fulfilment (or not) of the Millennium Development Goals.

Peter Wilkin, 'Global Poverty and Orthodox Security', *Third World Quarterly*, 23(4) (2002): 633–645. A critique of orthodox security analysis and its failure to address global social crises afflicting the twenty-first century world.

**CONTENTS**

# Climate Change and Environmental Security

Simon Dalby

## Abstract

In this chapter, students will learn about how climate change has emerged as a major issue in international politics in the last decade. If environmental changes cause people to either flee floods, droughts or starvation, or to fight over scarce resources then these are matters of security. But research has suggested that scarcities rarely actually cause wars. Neither is the military an institution that is an obvious choice to solve climate change problems. Nonetheless security agencies may have a significant role in alerting societies to coming disruptions, and in facilitating cooperative adaptations to the many political problems that may emerge in coming decades.

## Introduction: Security and environment

In the aftermath of the Cold War two decades ago numerous policy statements and academic analyses suggested that various forms of environmental change were threats to global security. This might happen, it was argued, because of major disruptions to essential human systems, wars due to struggles for scarce resources, or because of climate-induced migration in various places. Other authors suggested that security as understood during the Cold War was now no longer an appropriate conceptualization or a useful policy framework for the new circumstances where threats were from global changes rather than superpower rivalries. Empirical research in the 1990s made it clear that environmental scarcities usually didn't lead to armed conflict, contrary to earlier fears. Indeed it became clear that in many cases armed conflict was more likely in places where resources were abundant and economic options limited, than in places of scarcity. The combination of fears of disruptions, possible environmental changes causing conflict and the apparent necessity to rethink security after the Cold War gave rise to a wide-ranging debate about what has come to simply be called 'environmental security' (Dalby 2002).

Now, twenty years after the initial expressions of concern over environmental security, the discussion has been revived as numerous agencies, both military and political, raise the spectre of dangers and even possible wars as a consequence of climate change. Alarmist accounts about millions of climate refugees, food shortages and potential conflict caused by climate disruptions are now common in the media and in political discussion. In contrast, the much quoted Intergovernmental Panel on Climate Change (IPCC), the clearing-house for climate change science, has not dealt with the security dimensions of the issue in its first four assessment reports, the most recent one in 2007. Nonetheless the UN Secretary-General (2009) commissioned a report outlining the dangers of climate change in terms of possible security threats, and began a process of looking forward to possible policy innovations to head off coming disruptions. Numerous academic studies have weighed in with discussions of conflict possibilities, and think tanks and advisory committees have written a series of high profile reports.

While climate change is clearly a problem, the broader matter of global environmental change is the context within which societal adaptation will occur (Adger, Lorenzoni and O'Brien 2009). Globalization, with all the technological changes of late, and its huge use of resources, is changing both human and physical geography dramatically. As reports from the UN Environment Programme now increasingly emphasize, humanity has transformed most aspects of the biosphere in its rapid economic expansion, and our construction of an urban context for ourselves in the last few generations (UNEP 2007). The implications of this are profound; life is not a passive superficial part of the geological picture, but an active component in how our planet operates. Thus the new form of life on the planet, what might simply be called industrial humanity, has taken the future of the planet into its hands, even if it is only now beginning to realize that this is what is happening.

Discussions of environmental security require a clear analysis of how human actions are changing all aspects of the biosphere, and in the process making the world we inhabit an increasingly artificial place. According to the scientific literature on earth system science, the changes we have already made to the living part of the planet are of such a scale as to require the nomenclature of a new geological era, the 'Anthropocene' (Steffen *et al.* 2007). Not only are we changing the atmosphere, and as a result setting climate change in motion, but humanity is also changing other parts of the planet, building roads, ports and cities, clearing forests to grow crops and fishing numerous parts of the oceans to the stage where many species are endangered. These new, increasingly artificial circumstances are the world in which climate changes will render both people and states insecure in the near future (Dalby 2009).

Environmental security discussions are now changing into climate security discussions as the focus shifts to global warming and the effects it may have in coming decades. As the discussion unfolds it is important to remember the lessons learned from scholarly research in the decades since the end of the Cold War; there are reasons for cautious optimism in at least some regards, not least because the endless journalistic fears of such things as 'water wars' are usually greatly exaggerated. But if the lessons of the last couple of decades are forgotten, and the traditional military focus on national security is uncritically imposed on discussions of climate, things are likely to be made worse rather than better.

To demonstrate this argument the rest of the chapter looks first at those important discussions from the 1990s and then the more recent discussion of climate and how security agencies might be involved. Later sections examine both how security agencies have begun to think about climate change, and more recently apply risk analysis to thinking about future priorities. The crucial point in all this is that there is nothing inevitable about environmental change causing armed conflict, but, the chapter concludes, if modern societies don't prepare for what we know is coming then we might indeed get conflict and insecurity if political elites try to violently re-impose control on a rapidly changing world.

## Armed conflict and environmental change

Fears of wars over scarce resources were a theme in the much discussed World Commission on Environment and Development Commission report of 1987 on 'Our Common Future' – the document that finally focused many decision-makers' attention on the need for sustainable development. But empirical research in the 1990s that tried to tease out the causal connections between environmental scarcity and political violence had great difficulty validating the initial assumption that scarcities cause conflicts (Homer-Dixon 1999). The focus on local conflicts and matters of farmland water supplies often ignored matters of the larger-scale connections. Subsequent research suggested that violence was more often related to control over valuable sources of resources in impoverished and badly governed areas than over environmental scarcities (Le Billon 2005). The perpetual scares of water wars have turned out to be journalistic fantasy rather than a matter of historical record.

Nonetheless, while small-scale violence and political strife are related to land and food issues, starving people rarely are capable of organizing major military actions. The truly destitute don't organize rebellions; usually they starve instead. Fears of wars between the global North and South over climate change or other environmental factors turned out to have no foundation in geopolitical reality, although they do undoubtedly make good headlines. That does not mean that military agencies might not be turned loose on hapless migrants seeking shelter from floods, droughts and hurricanes if they are portrayed in such a way that desperate refugees are presented as a threat to social order or national security. On the largest scale, considering the Anthropocene and climate change it is clear that the cause of the problem is not peripheral peoples threatening peaceful metropoles, but rather the consequences of metropolitan consumption that have many effects in those peripheries.

Looking at particular cases, recent scholarship has emphasized that even in cases of ecological 'collapse', which were much discussed in the debate about Jared Diamond's (2005) book of that name, societies that get into difficulties do not disappear as a result of simple indigenous scarcity phenomena, but as a result of complex social processes, frequently ones tied into larger economic disruptions (McAnany and Yoffee 2010). None of this is obviously a matter of 'national security' to Western states. On the other hand, threatened with inundation, for Bangladesh greenhouse gas emissions are obviously a grave threat to its national security, one that its military is powerless to do much about. The Indian government has built a fence around most of Bangladesh ostensibly to stop terrorists crossing the border, but many people worry that the gates might be closed if a major storm were to set millions of Bangladeshis in motion in search of shelter and sustenance.

The larger danger is that such tropes produce a policy environment where the rich and powerful use force to keep the poor and marginal away from their prosperous states (Smith 2007). Such scenarios are the stuff of contemporary science fiction novels and movies. The British rendition of all this in the movie *Children of Men* is noteworthy because its dystopian geographical representation of an island fortress using violence to exclude the poor is encapsulated in the designation of abject others in a generic category of the 'fugee'. The apocalyptic tone of this movie, as with larger cultural themes of our age is not helpful (see Zizek 2010). Coupled with the territorial strategies of national security thinking and political logics of disconnection it is a rendition of precisely what has to be resisted if ecological thinking is to inform discussions of either global security or forms of security that take the survival and wellbeing of the majority of humanity seriously (see Box 21.1).

Geopolitics has traditionally been mostly about how great power rivalries play out. Now in the new circumstances of the Anthropocene it is about writing the rules that bring us the future parameters of the planetary system.

## BOX 21.1 FORMS OF SECURITY THINKING

*National Security* focuses on the state, sovereignty and the military control of national territory, in many cases not the appropriate scale for thinking about climate changes that have global effects. Focusing on 'threats' from migration and using huge amounts of fuel to run military institutions suggests that such policies are part of the problem rather than the solution to climate issues.

*Human Security* focuses on vulnerable people and the provision of the essential needs for people to thrive in their particular places. As humanity increasingly lives in cities and requires commodities from all over the planet to supply the global economy that keeps us alive, infrastructure and trade become more important in providing this form of security.

*Ecological Security* is concerned with maintaining the integrity of natural systems on which humanity is dependent, an especially complicated and difficult matter now that humanity is effectively changing the planet's ecology in the Anthropocene. *Climate security*, insofar as it aims to keep the planet's temperature close to what civilization has so far known, is now obviously a key to ecological security.

*Global Security* has traditionally focused on avoiding major international and particularly nuclear wars which, given their immense destructive consequences, would render people and states everywhere insecure. Now the question is whether climate change is potentially an equally important 'global' consideration.

*Cooperative Security* focuses attention on how states, militaries and other institutions can work together for common benefit, on such things as shared rivers or waterways, but also on how such efforts and the habits of working together can prevent conflict occurring in crisis situations.

Adding this key point into traditional geopolitics is what considerations of world order for the next couple of decades require us to do. There is of course no guarantee that political elites will 'get it', nor that governance structures will evolve to deal with these issues, but it seems as though many trends are moving that way as activists and political entrepreneurs find new modes of changing things, modes frequently not subject to the central control of the putative great powers. But insofar as attempts to deal with climate change are being undertaken, it is now clear that, to a very substantial extent, efforts to create effective governance structures are escaping the traditional territorial control mechanisms of states (Newell and Paterson 2010). Traditional military modes of war fighting too are useless in the face of many complex humanitarian disasters; human security is not about military predominance, it is about practical infrastructure provision, and adaptation to unpredictable patterns (Beebe and Kaldor 2010). Security in these terms is about connection, presence on the ground, and anticipation, not violent action after the fact.

## Climate change and security

Despite the refusal of the Bush administration in the United States to take climate change seriously, or facilitate strategic thinking on such matters in the early years of its 'war on terror', clearly climate change has now caught the attention of American military thinkers and it is now a matter of geopolitics, both in formal academic analysis and in popular literature (Dyer 2008). Militaries elsewhere have been thinking about the profound implications of climate change for some time, but it is only in the last few years, as the themes of Hurricane Katrina and the destruction of New Orleans in 2005 were echoed by scenarios of the future drawn from the science of climate change that the strategic implications garnered widespread attention.

Now with the practical matters of retreating glaciers in many mountain systems, especially in Greenland, getting attention people are starting to ponder the effects of such changes on how societies will work in the future. The disappearing Arctic sea ice in summer, with the much-discussed possibilities of new trade routes and resource conflicts, means that militaries are starting to pay attention. Foreign policy and strategic think tanks have focused on these themes in a series of high profile discussions, although ongoing negotiations about boundaries and large-scale undersea mapping suggest that deals will be worked out there in everyone's interest eventually (Fairhall 2010).

Some militaries play a major role in infrastructure building and maintenance; the US Army Corps of Engineers is noteworthy as the builder of dams, flood defences and other infrastructure. Militaries are also owners of huge land holdings, bases, airfields and other facilities that may be vulnerable to storms and, in particular, as sea levels rise, flooding in coastal areas. If hurricanes destroy airplane hangars or naval dockyards, military institutions may be directly affected too. So thinking about how to be ready to face such issues is increasingly part of the mandate of armed forces (Briggs 2010).

Disasters in many parts of the world have also killed many thousands of people in recent years, and set others in motion in search of sanctuary. In most cases of disaster the military is called upon to help with rescues and transportation of aid, food and supplies. The huge flood in 2010 in Pakistan, forest fires in Russia, the Haiti earthquake in 2010, the 2004 tsunami in Asia, and the 2011 one in Japan all involved military organizations in providing emergency help. Climate change science models are suggesting that as the climate changes, more severe events and unpredictable weather patterns may make such operations more frequent. If the climate system crosses some thresholds of temperature and suddenly changes into a new global pattern then numerous societies could be dramatically disrupted (Webersik 2010).

In these circumstances security in many guises will be called into question and the military may find themselves doing many things for which they are neither trained nor equipped.

Unless of course that is, they pay attention to the changing world and how new forms of insecurity may emerge in the decades ahead. However, military institutions also have a role in looking ahead and identifying dangers that their societies may face in the future. It is precisely by identifying dangers and raising the alarm that militaries may have an impact on changing the priorities of politicians and corporate decision-makers as to how to reduce the emissions of greenhouse gases and in turn reduce the likelihood of severe disruptions in the future. As Mabey (2007) argues, no other institution in contemporary society has the function of long-term thinking about threats to modern states. But clearly the military cannot solve the problem of climate change even if its forces may be used to try to deal with some of the symptoms.

The geography of threats has now changed, and the geopolitical analyses of climate change are beginning to recognize this. Climate change is only one of the potential catastrophes humanity faces (Smil 2008). But, given that burning carbon fuels to power the global economy is the cause of the changing composition of the atmosphere, it is one that is substantially of our own making; hence the recently heightened focus on these matters in the political arguments about climate change where much of the discussion is about who is endangered how and where, and who ought to respond to the increasingly obvious dangers we have unleashed upon ourselves. Unlike fears of big meteorites, or serious disease outbreaks, or even earthquakes that unleash tsunamis, the climate change situation is both of our own making and something about the consequences of which we have had plenty of warning.

But what should not be forgotten in all this is that it is the rich and powerful parts of the world that have generated the carbon dioxide and methane gases that are causing the planet to warm. This is not a traditional external military threat, even if its effects may set armed conflict in motion. As the discussion in the scholarly literature also makes clear, such conflicts do not have to happen if careful planning and cooperation among political elites make preparations for societies to adapt to the coming changes (Brauch *et al.* 2011). Here security institutions may have a role to play that is rather different from traditional war planning. In the new circumstances of the Anthropocene, new modes of security thinking and planning are clearly needed.

## Scenarios of doom

Popular concern about climate change is frequently tied into forecasts of doom and disaster if nothing is done, reprising themes that were articulated in the early 1990s in the aftermath of the end of the Cold War and the lead up to the 1992 Earth Summit in Rio de Janeiro, also, in slightly different vein, the 1980s discussions of the consequences of a nuclear winter and rapid climate change. Burning rainforests of the 1980s and the iconic pictures of blazing oil wells in Kuwait in 1991 dominated the earlier discussions; more recently images of Hurricane Katrina and New Orleans in 2005 and later the floods in Pakistan and fires in Russia that happened in the summer of 2010, came to represent fears of climate change. These images link up with other concerns about influenza and diseases of various sorts that are also part of the wider discourse of geopolitical danger (see Chapter 22, this volume). In particular, fears of migration, whether linked to climate change or not, repeatedly reprise fears of other populations; climate change will supposedly set the poor in motion with all sorts of political instabilities as the result (see also Chapter 34, this volume).

In 2007 the National War College Strategic Studies Institute in the United States held a key conference on the subject of climate change, but it was framed in terms of US national security and the logic of the arguments was framed in terms of US military roles and possible future disruptions (Pumphrey 2008). A similar CNA analysis in 2007 discussed matters in terms of 'National Security and the Threat of Climate Change' while the Center for Strategic and International Security (CSIS) study of the same year focused on 'The Age of Consequences'. It also focused, as its subtitle suggests, on 'The Foreign and National Security Implications of Climate Change' (Campbell *et al.* 2007). The book based on this analysis, published the following year by the Brookings Institution, looks to the same formulations (Campbell 2008). All of these re-impose the national focus, looking at the impacts on the United States. While these may indeed raise alarm and undoubtedly fed into the discussion of the Climate Security Act in Congress in 2009, the initial focus of all these documents is national rather than a broader-scale examination of the global security implications (Moran 2011).

Once one looks at those scenarios which are the source of alarm, the interconnections between national and international security become obvious. So too do the difficulties of trying to deal with the multiple interconnected factors which will shape the human future (Dalby 2009). The complexity of the interconnections is crucial to understanding possible outcomes, although obviously these are impossible to predict clearly. It is also imperative to try to identify where likely disruptions may occur and their modalities in particular regions. The German Advisory Council's (2008) report attempts a much more comprehensive evaluation. The focus is on multiple conflict 'constellations' involving the degradation of freshwater resources, declining food production, flood and other storm disasters, and the much discussed matter of environmentally induced migration. These 'constellations' are likely to have security implications in various locations that span the globe. But, and this is the key point, disruptions occur in many modes in different environmental circumstances.

The German Advisory Council (2008) focuses on a list which includes polar ice cap melting leading to a rise in the global sea level; accelerated North African migration to Europe; and droughts in the Sahel and in Southern Africa which may increase food shortages. Disappearing glaciers in Central Asia make this region vulnerable to water shortages. Pakistan and India depend on glacial melt-water flowing into their major rivers to feed hundreds of millions; they too may face serious difficulties with food production. China also depends on glacial melt-water and is vulnerable to sea level rise on its long coast. The Caribbean nations are especially endangered if hurricane frequency increases. The list goes on: glaciers are melting in the Andes too; deforestation in the Amazon may accelerate climate change in that region with droughts replacing tropical rainfall and hence further accelerating the destruction of rainforests. There was a serious drought in the Amazon region in 2010 which may have killed large numbers of trees there, ironically just before a major flooding event changed matters from too little rain to too much. Extreme events and global change are the world in which we live. Security planners need to take these matters seriously. To do so requires them to look to the sciences of climate change as well as to the social sciences that deal with risks and adaptations.

## Security planning and risk analysis

The British government in particular has been concerned about climate change as a security risk, and in early 2011 the environmental organization E3G published a major report that asked the basic question: what does climate change look like if viewed through the lens of military risk-planning? How is the risk to be understood, and if it is serious, how might the dangers be mitigated? It follows on from Nick Mabey's (2007) earlier argument about the role of military organizations in thinking about future threats. The overview of the issue in the early pages of the report is blunt:

> Regional and global security is inextricably linked to climate change. Climate change will bring about a significantly different strategic security environment, a fact that few countries have yet absorbed and none are fully prepared for. However, there is growing momentum within the security community to tackle the threat of climate change. The reality of climate change will require fundamental readjustments in how international relations are conducted, and will alter much of the focus of international security policy. It will change strategic interests, alliances, borders, threats, economic relationships, comparative advantages and the nature of international cooperation, and will help determine the continued legitimacy of the United Nations in the eyes of much of the world.
>
> (Mabey *et al.* 2011: 18)

All this matters greatly precisely because states have not yet taken the long-term risks seriously. Focusing on adaptation measures over the next couple of decades has been the primary preoccupation of policy-makers, but the long-term effects have not been a priority. Short-term adaptation will mostly not deal with the growing instabilities in the climate system that are likely to occur if temperature continues to rise. Unless there is a dramatic reduction of greenhouse emissions soon, rising temperatures and all the climatic disruptions that will ensue will become inevitable. How we collectively build infrastructure and societies that are resilient, and hence able to adapt to rapid change, has become an important matter, although one that security studies is only just beginning to consider (Brauch *et al.* 2011).

The 'Degrees of Risk' authors suggest that risk analysis is the appropriate framework for thinking about climate in security terms, and note bluntly that focusing on the short term or the average of scenario predictions for coming decades is missing the more important matter of extreme perturbations to the climate system. In the long run, looking out to the end of the century, rather than just to the next couple of decades:

> Estimates for projected average global temperature rise in 2100 range from 1.7°C to 7.2°C relative to preindustrial temperatures. Over half this range comes from scientific uncertainty over climate system behavior. But risks are not symmetrical. ... Recent observations show that climate models have been underestimating the rate of important climatic changes – for example the rate of Arctic sea ice melt – suggesting that climate models may be systematically underestimating the rate at which large-scale changes in the climate system will proceed in the future.
>
> (Mabey *et al.* 2011: 25)

Pointing out that the danger of crossing 'tipping points' increases greatly once a 3°C increase is reached, the document suggests that 'the "worst case scenarios" are not necessarily low probability events, even though analysts tend to assume that they are. Some major tipping points may be inevitable if current momentum economic behavior persists' (Mabey *et al.* 2011: 26). Added to this is the concern that the models used to predict climate response to greenhouse gas levels have, it seems, been systematically underestimating the speed of change. The surprise melting of the Arctic sea ice in 2007 has made it clear that some responses are coming decades faster than the models suggest, at least in part because the positive feedback mechanisms in the climate system are outweighing the negative ones.

In contrast to the German Advisory Committee (2008) report that listed five major systems in danger of rapid climate change, the 'Degrees of Risk' report suggests thirteen potential tipping systems in the climate system. This includes disruption of the Asian monsoon that is especially important as it directly relates to the food supply of a substantial part of humanity in south and southeast Asia. They add in disruption to the Boreal forests of the northern hemisphere that may turn from being places that absorb carbon to being sources of carbon from increasingly severe forest fires. Changes are not just a matter of disruptions to the poor states of the global South.

Risk management is about probabilities of outcomes and the severity of the consequences. Multiplied together they offer a template for management. 'In this formulation, two factors determine whether a risk is high or low: likelihood and severity. A high probability of an outcome with minor consequences causes only moderate concern. On the other hand, a low probability of an outcome with grave consequences may cause significant concern' (Mabey *et al.* 2011: 51). Grave concerns in security thinking about such possibilities as nuclear weapons getting into the hands of terrorists (something that the United States in particular has gone to very great lengths to try to prevent), suggest that this may be a low probability event, but the high consequences of it happening mean that preventive action has to be taken.

With the matter of climate change things are rather different. Climate change is, projecting present trends into the future, both a high probability outcome and one with grave consequences. Hence the logic in the 'Degrees of Risk' document is that it needs priority attention at least on the order of magnitude currently given to nuclear weapon threats and the policies for containment of fissile material. If we do not act we know we will indeed get dramatic disturbances to the ecological system that made human civilization possible in the first place. This is not a matter of probability and calculating the likelihood of things happening in the future if security agencies do not act. Rather, these developments are certain to happen and in a very big way too if these specialized agencies do not act along with society in general to start doing things very differently.

## Climate wars?

But will all this lead to war, the traditional focus of security studies? There are all sorts of ways that environmental change might lead to conflict, but as the research literature from the 1990s started to point out clearly, and as subsequent reworking of this material confirms, the most important point in predicting what circumstances might lead to armed conflict depends much more on political institutions and elite actions than it does on solely environmental factors (Kahl 2006). When this argument is taken seriously and applied to forecasts of climate change and related matters it becomes clear that analysis of the risks, such as those listed in the 'Degrees of Risk' report, points clearly to the need for international cooperation and planning that spells out appropriate responses to extreme events and fluctuations in such things as water supplies in key regions. Such action needs to be complemented by action to reduce the use of carbon fuels and hence slow climate change giving societies more time to adapt.

While neither the scenarios outlined in the CSIS analysis of 'The Age of Consequences', the German warnings about conflict constellations nor the 'Degrees of Risk' document focus on the extreme violence of a nuclear war, Gwynne Dyer's (2008) popular book on the possibility of climate wars does think through the possibilities of a nuclear war between India and Pakistan.

This might result from escalating tensions over water shortages when the Himalayan glaciers have finished melting a couple of decades in the future. While fluctuations in winter snowfall will probably contribute more to the uncertainty about river flows than disappearing glaciers, the point is that these events are predictable. Given that it is entirely predictable that water supplies will be especially short when there is no summer melt-water flowing into regional rivers, careful planning and cooperation can forestall the political tensions. Wars do not have to happen if cooperative security institutions are in place to deal with predictable environmental changes (Dabelko 2009). While concerns over climate change have become an increasingly important matter of international politics, agreements such as the one signed in Copenhagen late in 2009 are but very preliminary steps towards building a new security architecture to tackle the truly global issue of climate change.

While formulations of national security have frequently been the starting point for considerations of climate change, as the logic of the analyses unfold it becomes clear that a global perspective on the interconnected fate of humanity is necessary to grapple with the issue. Clearly, mapping threats in terms of borders and national territories somehow endangered by 'external' threats is simply inappropriate for dealing with the causes of disruptions set in motion by environmental change. This is about global security and inter-connections across borders, not a matter of national security, borders and territorial protection. Attempts to grapple with the coming changes by using national means alone are most likely to make adaptation more difficult by preventing cooperative efforts. At the beginning of the environmental security discussion Deudney (1990) warned that the military is not an institution designed to deal with environmental matters; indeed its mandate is very different, which makes it an unsuitable agency to implement most solutions to environmental change. Put very crudely, the military is designed to kill people and break things rather than clean up pollution or install solar panels. The American military in particular uses huge amounts of fuel, especially in its recent campaigns in Asia that involved long supply lines, making it a substantial contributor to climate change. While the Army Corps of Engineers undoubt-edly has a future role in such projects as constructing coastal flood defences, and it might be reorganized to make windmills, it is hardly the appropriate institution to do what utilities and businesses are already well equipped to do.

Bearing in mind this misfit between the institution and environmental matters, and the simple but crucial fact that environmental matters in general and climate change in particular are international concerns, it is not at all clear that military agencies, focused primarily on national security and the protection of particular states from external threats, might have much to say about climate change. But if military organizations are engaged in cooperative efforts to anticipate the future, alerting decision-makers to the risks of climate change and coordinating practical responses to change while simultaneously working to build infrastructure not dependent on carbon fuels, they might yet prove to be of very considerable use in making climate security a reality in coming decades.

## Further reading

Simon Dalby, *Security and Environmental Change* (Polity, 2009). An introduction to environmental security thinking for the Anthropocene epoch.

Gwynne Dyer, *Climate Wars* (Random House, 2008). A lucid, popular introduction to military and climate science scenarios for the future.

German Advisory Council on Global Change, *Climate Change as a Security Risk* (Earthscan, 2008). A comprehensive overview report of the global climate change issue within a broad perspective on security.

Nick Mabey, Jay Gulledge, Bernard Finel and Katherine Silverthorne, *Degrees of Risk: Defining a Risk Management Framework for Climate Security* (E3G, 2011). The key study on how to apply risk analysis to climate and security.

Daniel Moran (ed.), *Climate Change and National Security: A Country-Level Analysis* (Georgetown University Press, 2011). A series of regional studies on how climate change might play out in various places.

Cleo Pascal, *Global Warring: How Environmental, Economic and Political Crises will Redraw the World Map* (Key Porter, 2010). A popular account of the climate security issue with particularly useful emphasis on the key matter of infrastructure planning.

## CONTENTS

# Health

Colin McInnes

### Abstract

In this chapter, students will learn why health has not traditionally been seen as a security issue and why this began to change. It will look at the main health issues on the security agenda: the spread of infectious disease, especially to the West; the impact of HIV/AIDS, especially on state stability; and the risk of bioterrorism. Questions which arise include whether some of these risks have been over-stated, over whose interests are being served by securitizing health, and whether health should be a concern for security policy or development policy?

## Introduction

For more than two decades hundreds of thousands, sometimes millions, have died each year from AIDS-related illnesses. Even with the increased access to anti-retroviral therapies (ARTs) seen over the past decade, this pattern is likely to continue for the foreseeable future. The scale of suffering caused by this single illness is immense and the number of deaths dwarves that of more traditional security crises such as those in Iraq and Afghanistan, or the war on terror. Moreover HIV/AIDS is only one of a number of communicable diseases, many of which are preventable, which each year kill millions of people. These include long-established diseases such as polio and malaria as well as new diseases such as SARS and HPAI (highly pathogenic avian influenza, or bird flu), which threaten to become global pandemics with the potential to kill millions in a relatively short space of time. Further, non-communicable diseases such as tobacco-related illnesses and cardio-vascular disease again kill millions each year. In sum, the lives and livelihoods of the overwhelming majority of people on this planet are at greater risk from disease than from war, terrorism or other forms of violent conflict. But does this make global health a security issue? Indeed, given the links between poor health and poverty, is global health more properly a subject for Development Studies than International Relations? And should it be the focus of development agencies rather than ministries of defence or foreign affairs?

The focus of this chapter is on the emergence of health as a *national* security issue. It should however be noted that this is just one – albeit significant – construction of the link between health and security; others are detailed in Box 22.1. For many of the past 50 years the relationship between health and national security has been limited and unidirectional: conflict has caused health problems. (Historically, of course, the reverse has also been significant, with disease often accounting for more deaths than battle in military campaigns.) These problems have been both a direct result of warfare (largely in the form of combat casualties) and indirect (for example, the destruction of infrastructure affecting the ability of hospitals to keep working, increased prevalence of water-borne diseases as a result of disruption to the water supply, refugee flows leading to the spread of infectious disease or the overburdening of public health systems).

This was not always the case. In the nineteenth century, as trade between Europe and the rest of the world increased, so did the risk of infectious disease being brought into Europe from elsewhere. Disease was viewed as an exogenous threat which had to be dealt with by means of international cooperation and the introduction of internationally agreed health regulations. Thus the origins of international cooperation on public health lie in the security concerns of Europe in the nineteenth century. After the Second World War, however, this relationship disappeared for two main reasons. First, health was presented not as a security issue but as a human right. This move was seen in the constitution establishing the World Health Organization (WHO) in 1948 and reached a high point in the 1970s with the WHO's 'Health for All' initiative. Second, during this period the perception grew that infectious diseases were being conquered, not least through the use of antibiotics. The number of deaths in the West from these diseases fell dramatically in the early decades after the Second World War, while in the late 1970s for the first time in history a major infectious disease, smallpox, was effectively eradicated. These successes prompted the US Surgeon General in the late 1960s to declare (perhaps apocryphally) that communicable disease had been conquered, at least for the West. What was patently clear was that this was not the case elsewhere, where living conditions and levels of poverty were much worse. Therefore global health became for the West less of a security concern than one of development.

## BOX 22.1  THE DIFFERENT MEANINGS OF HEALTH SECURITY

'Health security' is not only poorly defined but used in a variety of different ways. For heuristic purposes it is possible to identify four different meanings, though often these overlap in usage.

1  *Biosecurity* is sometimes used in a vague and all-encompassing manner relating to any health issue considered a threat to a community. More narrowly it refers to the risks posed by the development of new and lethal pathogens in scientific laboratories as a result of advances in molecular biology (Enemark 2010).

2  *Global (public) health security* is largely identified with the health community and especially the WHO. It refers to the manner in which certain health threats have become global in nature requiring a global response. Global health security is therefore a form of health promotion in the face of global risks (WHO 2007).

3  *Human security* originated in the development community and especially the UN Development Programme in the 1990s. It is concerned with the insecurities of daily life on an individual scale, and is especially concerned with two freedoms: from want and from fear. Health has been a core component of human security linking to both of these fears, but also because of the manner in which poor health affects the way individuals live their lives (Chen 2003).

4  Health is a *national security* risk when it threatens the functioning of a state or the ability of a state to protect itself. It is not simply about the self-preservation of a state however, but its ability to fulfil its responsibilities to its citizens (Elbe 2009: 86–107).

By the late 1990s, however, this had begun to change. Two examples of this are the 1999 US National Intelligence Estimate on the global threat of infectious disease to the United States, and the January 2000 meeting of the UN Security Council. On the first, in 1999 the Central Intelligence Agency identified a number of risks to US security arising from infectious disease, risks exacerbated by rapid globalization and the increased movement of goods and people. These included not only risks to US citizens travelling abroad, but to citizens in the US itself given the potential ease with which diseases could spread internationally. Indeed in just over a decade the US had seen incidences of West Nile fever, ebola and monkeypox, all originating from outside its own borders and presumably unwittingly brought into the US by travellers or international trade. Crucially, however, the CIA went further than this, arguing that infectious disease also posed a risk to international stability and to economic growth, placing it firmly in the territory of national security (CIA 2000). On the second, at its first meeting of the new millennium, the UN Security Council discussed the threat of HIV/AIDS to Africa and in Resolution 1308 warned 'that the HIV/AIDS pandemic, if unchecked, may pose a risk to stability and security'. In particular the Security Council drew attention to the effects of HIV/AIDS on social stability and on peacekeeping missions. This debate raised the global political stakes on HIV/AIDS, and in subsequent years HIV/AIDS was framed not only as a humanitarian catastrophe but as a risk to national security and international stability. By the middle years of the twentieth century, health issues had begun to appear in statements from foreign and security ministers, while global health was discussed at a number of G8 summits, including Genoa, Gleneagles and St Petersburg, in the context both of humanitarianism and security.

## The emergence of health as a national security issue

Three issues contributed to the emergence of heath as a security issue: the spread of new and existing infectious diseases; the continued growth of the HIV/AIDS pandemic; and bioterrorism (discussed further below). But two other factors facilitated this emergence. The first of these was the growing acceptance during the 1990s of a broadened security agenda. The end of the Cold War saw security analysts shift their focus away from threats, especially military threats, to more diffuse risks. This opened the door for a more eclectic range of issues to be considered as security concerns. Further, the shift from threat to risk allowed security's focus to shift from the idea of a 'clear and present danger' to more probabilistic assessments of potential hazards. Both of these moves opened up a space whereby public health issues could be raised as security concerns. Moreover, questions were raised not only over the security agenda – those issues which might be considered as legitimate security concerns – but also over the referent object: whose security was to be protected? Whereas the Cold War had prioritized national security, in the post-Cold War world security at both the global and individual levels began to be considered. The idea that risks to the individual from macro-level developments could be part of the security agenda again allowed a space for the inclusion of health as a security issue. After all, individuals generally were more likely to be at risk from new infectious diseases spread as a consequence of globalization than they were from ethnic conflict, environmental disasters or terrorism.

The second facilitating factor was human agency. A number of prominent individuals used their positions of power and influence to place health on the foreign and security policy agenda. Two examples of this are the former head of the WHO, Gro Harlem Brundtland and President Clinton's ambassador to the UN, Richard Holbrooke. As WHO's Director General, Brundtland emphasized the changing nature of public health in a globalized world, and argued that global public health could not be divorced from broader social and political trends (e.g. Brundtland 1999). Significantly it was during Brundtland's tenure that the WHO coined the term 'global health security'. The second example of individual agency is that of Richard Holbrooke, who is widely acknowledged as a key player in the securitization of HIV/AIDS. According to Prins (2005), when visiting Africa in 1999 Holbrooke realized not only the scale of the HIV/AIDS pandemic but that existing aid-based approaches were failing to deal with the crisis. Moreover the potential social consequences of the pandemic were beginning to become apparent, including state instability. On his return to New York, Holbrooke was instrumental in placing HIV/AIDS on the Security Council's agenda. What is unclear is whether Holbrooke saw his actions as motivated solely by security concerns, or whether he saw the securitization of HIV/AIDS as a way of achieving greater political prominence and global action to help deal with the crisis. This potential for the securitization of health to act as a Trojan horse for greater attention and assistance to the most needy is an important theme in the debate over health and security.

## The spread of infectious disease

New infectious diseases and new forms of existing diseases have been emerging at an accelerated rate over recent years, averaging one a year for more than two decades. These new diseases include HIV/AIDS, SARS, HPAI and swine flu, all of whose impact has been, or has the potential to be global in nature (see Box 22.2). Although this phenomenon may be a by-product of increased urbanization and the speed of movement of goods and people, it may also be that changes are occurring in the microbial world that are independent of these social forces. In particular modern biology is leading, directly and inadvertently, to the creation of new pathogens in laboratories (see Box 22.3). But why have these developments triggered concerns in the security community? There are broadly three reasons for this.

---

### BOX 22.2 INFECTIOUS DISEASE AND GLOBALIZATION: THE 2009 SWINE FLU PANDEMIC

On 28 March 2009 a 4-year-old Mexican boy became the first known case of a new strain of the Influenza A virus H1N1 ('swine flu'). Two weeks later a woman in Mexico became the first person to die of this strain of the virus. On 25 April, less than a month after the first case, the rapid spread of the disease led WHO to declare an 'international public health emergency'. This was the first time it had used this power granted by the 2005 revision of the International Health Regulations. On 11 June the disease had spread to 74 countries with over 30,000 infections, leading WHO to declare a pandemic – the first flu pandemic for 41 years. On 24 October, with the disease present in all mainland states, US President Obama declared a national state of emergency. Although morbidity remained comparatively low – leading some analysts to declare it the mildest pandemic in history – the speed with which the disease spread, the global media coverage and the international competition for vaccines was remarkable.

## BOX 22.3  INADVERTENTLY INCREASING THE VIRULENCE OF MOUSEPOX

In a 2008 report on the dual use dilemmas involved in some modern biological research, WHO offered the example of the inadvertent increase in the virulence of mousepox:

'In an attempt to control mice as pests, Australian scientists unexpectedly increased the virulence of mousepox. Their research, which was published by the *Journal of Virology* in 2001, was originally aimed at producing an infectious contraceptive for mice. By inserting a gene responsible for the production of interleukin-4 into the mousepox genome, the scientists created a pathogen that overcame the immune defence of mice and even killed mice that had been vaccinated. This unforeseen result and its publication raised the questions of whether the same technique could be applied to other orthopox viruses, such as smallpox, and what the consequences in terms of vaccination circumvention might be.'

(WHO 2008: 9)

First, the spread of these diseases could pose a direct threat to the health and well-being of the very people that states are there to protect. And for the first time in perhaps half a century, this includes the populations of Western states. Although the numbers of deaths from SARS and swine flu were (thankfully) small, they nevertheless triggered high levels of concern across the globe, including in Western states. In contrast to the low morbidity levels of these diseases, HPAI ('bird flu') has a mortality rate currently well in excess of 50 per cent and if human-to-human transmission occurs, may spread as quickly as swine flu did in 2009. Infectious disease therefore poses an exogenous threat to the lives of people in a state.

Second, a pandemic may cause social disruption and threaten the effective functioning of a state. Confidence in the state may be reduced if it cannot provide a basic level of protection against disease; social inequalities may be highlighted as the rich or privileged obtain access to better drugs or health care, potentially leading to public disorder; if large numbers of people die or are unwilling/unable to go to work, public services may be placed at risk; violence and disorder may appear if the authorities become unable to cope and if groups feel they have nothing to lose. Thus the stability of states may be at risk and weak states may begin to fail. Indeed Andrew Price-Smith (2009) has argued that infectious disease can prove as great a stress on a state as invasion.

Third, a large scale epidemic may also contribute to economic decline by: forcing increased government spending on health as a percentage of GDP; reducing productivity due to worker absenteeism and the loss of skilled personnel; reducing investment (internal and external) because of a lack of business confidence; and by raising insurance costs for health provision. For the state involved, the costs may be highly significant, but in a globalized world the effects may be felt around the world. The relatively short-lived SARS outbreak of 2002–2003 led to fewer than a thousand deaths – individually tragic but, compared to annual deaths from HIV/AIDS, TB or malaria, statistically relatively insignificant. However the loss in trade and investment was calculated in tens of billions of dollars, while rumours persist that the UK and US attempted to pressurize WHO into not declaring swine flu a pandemic because of fears of the impact on the global economy. The macro-economic effects of a major epidemic may therefore be very significant, threatening to make the relatively affluent poor and the already poor poorer, with a consequent impact on the ability of states and individuals to provide for their security and well-being.

## HIV/AIDS

The HIV/AIDS pandemic has not only led to widespread humanitarian concerns, but has been identified as a security issue by the UN Security Council. The claims made by the Security Council in its initial discussion and subsequently in Resolution 1308 (both in 2000) set the agenda for the subsequent debate on HIV/AIDS as a national security issue (McInnes and Rushton 2010). The effects of the disease on economies and on governance have been consistently highlighted as a risk to state stability. HIV/AIDS appeared to pose particularly severe economic problems because of the cumulative effects of the disease over a number of years; because its full effects are postponed as those infected only become ill gradually but then pose an increasing economic burden on society; and because of its disproportionate impact upon workers in what should be the most productive period of their lives (ICG 2001: 9–13, UN Secretariat 2003: xiii–xiv). Such economic decline may increase income inequalities and poverty, exacerbating or creating social and political unrest. Fears were also expressed that, since HIV infection rates are unusually high amongst skilled professionals (including civil servants, teachers, police and health workers) and young adults, this might threaten 'the very fibre of what constitutes a nation' (ICG 2001: 1). Concerns also highlighted the potential risks to democratic development if societies became polarized as a consequence of HIV/AIDS, if disaffection with the political process set in, or as a consequence of aid-dependency. The stigma of AIDS may also lead to exclusion from work and/or society, creating alienation, fatalism and anger amongst people, especially young people, living with HIV/AIDS. These people may become prone to criminal violence or to following violent leaders (CIA 2000, Justice Africa 2004).

A second concern focused on the high rates of HIV infection amongst security forces, including the military – typically cited in the years immediately following Resolution 1308 as being up to five times higher than that of the civilian population and sometimes dramatically higher (elements of the South African military were believed to be perhaps 90 per cent HIV+). This risked combat readiness, military performance and morale. If military effectiveness is reduced as a result of HIV/AIDS, or even if it is perceived to have been affected, then states may be at greater risk from internal conflict or external aggression. Of particular concern was the potential loss of experienced military and technical specialists with 8 to 15 years' service, the 'middle management' and technical glue which holds an organization together, while the issue of whether HIV+ individuals could serve in the military posed a difficult human rights issue for states such as South Africa (ASCI 2009, Elbe 2002, 2003, ICG 2001, Heinecken 2003, UNAIDS 2003).

A third concern was the impact of HIV/AIDS on peacekeeping. Peacekeepers may be at increased risk from HIV since many of the world's conflicts are in regions with a high prevalence of HIV. They may also act as vectors for the spread of the disease, especially since the top 10 contributory nations to peacekeeping operations included states with high HIV prevalence rates (such as South Africa, Kenya, Nigeria and Ghana), as well as a number perceived to be at high risk (such as Ukraine, Bangladesh, Pakistan and India) (UNAIDS 2003: 6). HIV may also make it difficult for some armies to deploy peacekeeping forces, especially at short notice. The attempt to devolve peace-keeping to regional powers may also be hamstrung by high HIV prevalence, particularly amongst key African armies such as South Africa and Nigeria (Elbe 2002, Heinecken 2003).

Finally, concern was expressed that conflict acted as a vector for the spread of HIV/AIDS. Soldiers, already a high risk group, are willing to engage in even more risky behaviour in conflict regions; incidents of sexual violence increase in conflict; combat injuries may be treated in the field with infected blood; health education and surveillance may be poor in zones of conflict; soldiers returning from conflicts may bring HIV with them; conflicts create migration which may facilitate the spread of HIV; and refugee camps may have poor health education and access to condoms, but are also areas where sexual violence is rife. In addition HIV/AIDS may act as a disincentive to end conflicts because of fears that troops originating from low prevalence areas may act as a Trojan horse for the spread of the disease on their return home (UNAIDS 2003).

In recent years, however, the evidence supporting these four concerns has begun to appear less clear-cut, more complex and case sensitive. For example, evidence began to appear that conflict might also constrain the spread of HIV/AIDS by limiting the ability of people to move; with the exception of Sierra Leone, there appeared to be little empirical evidence linking UN peacekeeping missions and high HIV prevalence; and AIDS awareness pro-grammes in the military have significantly reduced the disparity in infection rates (ASCI 2009, de Waal 2005, McInnes 2006, 2011). Moreover the causal links between HIV/AIDS and insecurity appear less robust. It is unclear how high HIV prevalence will transform societies; what intervening variables will determine the nature of such transformations; and how significant such transformations will be. Nor is it apparent that the weakness of a state's armed forces is a causal agent in either internal or external aggression. It appears far more likely to be a contributory factor, and even then secrecy over combat readiness and HIV prevalence may limit the impression of weakness.

It is tempting to argue that some of the dangers identified have been averted through preventative action, not least AIDS awareness programmes; but in retrospect the case made in 2000 was somewhat speculative, while worst case thinking and snowballing subsequently led these concerns to a position of orthodoxy which now appears less assured. This is not to say that HIV/AIDS does not create security problems. Indeed as Garrett has commented, the lack of demonstrable proof of a security threat currently in place against any given state, regional, or transnational system does not mean the danger is nonexistent, or that it will not emerge (2005: 15). Rather it is to suggest that the case is at the very least more complex than originally articulated, and that the threat may be less direct.

## Bioterrorism

The idea of using biological agents (or pathogens) to cause disease as a weapon of war goes back several hundred years, and was a major source of concern not least during the Cold War. For much of that period concern focused upon state use, but in the 1980s and 1990s a number of political and religious extremist groups used or attempted to use biological weapons. These included a 1984 attempt by followers of Rajneesh Bhagwan to use salmonella to incapacitate voters in Oregon, thereby influencing election results; the 1995 use of sarin in the Tokyo subway by the Aum Shinrikyo cult, which followed their failed attempt at an airborne release of anthrax over Tokyo; letters purporting to contain anthrax spores being sent to abortion clinics and government offices in the US in the late 1990s; and claims that al-Qa'ida was attempting to develop an anthrax weapon for mass terror use. At the same time concerns were rising over possible proliferation of biological weapons to states. Intelligence reports suggested that the break-up of the Soviet Union might lead to biological weapons material being sold to states on the black market, including Cuba, Iran, Libya and Syria, while in 1995 a UN Special Commission reported that Iraq had been developing an anthrax weapon during the 1990–1991 Gulf War (Graham 2008: 6–10, WHO 2007: 35–7).

The terrorist attacks of 11 September, 2001 however dramatically increased the sense of risk, demonstrating the willingness and ability of terrorist organizations to inflict mass civilian casualties (e.g. Strongin and Redhead 2001). A week after these attacks a series of letters were sent to US government officials and media outlets containing anthrax spores, infecting 22 and killing 5. As WHO commented in a later report, 'coming so soon after the 11 September terrorist attacks, the anthrax offensive prompted a profound rethinking of threats to national and international security. It showed the potential of bioterrorism to cause not just death and disability, but social and economic disruption on an enormous scale both in the United States and internationally' (WHO 2007: 37). What was perhaps most surprising was that the anthrax letters were not sent by a terrorist organization but almost certainly Bruce Ivins, a US scientist working in a government laboratory with a high level of security clearance, indicating the dangers inherent in the proliferation of laboratories dealing with highly dangerous pathogens and toxins (Enemark 2010).

Although concern initially focused on anthrax, fears of other pathogens and toxins quickly emerged. Pre-eminent amongst these was smallpox, which had been eradicated outside secure laboratory storage in 1979. Unlike non-contagious agents such as anthrax which require sophisticated methods to infect large numbers of people, smallpox would spread by human-to-human contact; the lag time between infection and symptoms emerging would be several days, meaning rapid exposure of very large numbers of people as those infected wittingly or not continued to move amongst the population; and its eradication as an endemic disease meant that immunization programmes had been stopped, leaving people highly vulnerable to the disease. In a high profile, if somewhat alarmist article, Laurie Garrett wrote, 'If the smallpox virus were released today, the majority of the world's population would be defenseless (*sic*), and given the virus' 30 per cent kill rate, nearly two billion people could die . . . The world is thus completely vulnerable to a smallpox attack' (2001: 77–8). In a similar vein, controversy erupted when the journals *Science* and *Nature* published details of the successful reconstruction of the influenza AH1N1 virus responsible for the 1918 flu pandemic – the 'Spanish flu' – which killed more people worldwide than the First World War. One of the collaborators was the US Centers for Disease Control and Prevention, which acknowledged that the information could be used for bioterrorism but defended its actions by reference to the potential for developing effective health interventions strengthening defences against the disease (WHO 2008: 9).

Three problems, however, have emerged in responding to the risk of bio-terror. First, there have been clear tensions between an internationally versus domestically focused strategy. Following the anthrax attacks, the US stepped up its stockpiling of the smallpox vaccine, soon joined by other countries including the UK. Given the large-scale purchasing by a few states of the vaccine, supplies worldwide were soon in short supply. Similarly, worldwide supplies of the antibiotic Cipro used to treat anthrax rapidly became in short supply. This national strategy of stockpiling vaccines raised international concerns over hoarding by a few states to the detriment of others. Tensions also arose over the US government's decision to pull out of negotiations on the Biological Weapons Convention. The priority of the US appeared to be to focus on domestically based security measures, while others argued that a more international approach would yield better results.

This tension is also revealed in the second problem – whether it is better to try and prevent such attacks from happening or whether the priority should be on defence. The former suggests that attention should be given to international co-operation on intelligence and to the use of diplomatic efforts (including arms control) to make the supply and production of such weapons more difficult. In this, public health would be important in monitoring and surveillance of activities, but not the key element in an international strategy. The alternative approach, however, accepts that attacks are likely to be attempted and that a much more nationally focused strategy would be more appropriate. This would use domestic counter-terrorist agencies and 'at the border controls' to prevent biological weapons from entering the country, but would also make much greater use of public health systems in defending against such attacks.

The third problem is whether the risk has been overstated. Despite the comparatively recent use of such weapons in Iraq, Japan and the United States, there remain doubts both over how easy it is for sub-state groups to gain access to, or produce effective weapons and over how easy it is to use them in a manner which might cause significant loss of life. As Dando has pointed out, using non-contagious biological agents as weapons of mass destruction would require their use as an aerosol over large areas. The means to do this – especially against Western states – is almost wholly the preserve of states with relatively advanced militaries, not small terrorist groups (Dando 2005; see also Box 22.4).

## A not so perfect partnership?

Health affects every one of us – our state of well-being affects individual life, lifestyle and livelihood. Moreover our health is often intertwined with that of the communities in which we are located, either geographically or as part of a socio-economic group. Poor communities for example are more likely to be at risk from TB; malaria is common in certain parts of the world but not others. Thus health officials have long understood that well-being is as much socially determined as it is a bio-medical condition. These social determinants have an international dimension – infectious diseases for example can cross

---

### BOX 22.4 THE GRAHAM COMMISSION ON THE RISKS FROM BIOTERRORISM

Although generally expressing concern over the bioterrorist threat, the high-level Graham Commission in the US did express reservations based on the difficulties involved:

'Because of the difficulty of weaponizing (sic) and disseminating significant quantities of a biological agent in aerosol form, government officials and outside experts believe that no terrorist group currently has an operational capability to carry out a mass-casualty attack. But they could develop that capability quickly . . . [But] given the high level of know-how needed to use disease as a weapon to cause mass casualties, the United States should be less concerned that terrorists will become biologists and far more concerned that biologists will become terrorists'.

(Graham 2008: 11)

state boundaries. But the process of globalization has led to an awareness that this international dimension is becoming more important and that the ability of national health services to protect their populations is partial in the face of such change. Health therefore is increasingly globalized (Lee 2003). With this recognition has come an increased interest on the part of the public health community in foreign and security policy – an awareness both of shared interests between these different communities and the possibilities of health issues gaining increased attention and resources through 'piggy-backing' on foreign and security policy. Simultaneous to this, security communities have become increasingly aware of health issues as security risks, most notably the three issues identified above. Thus the prospect has developed of a mutually beneficial partnership between health and security. For those on the security side of this partnership, health (and in particular public health) bring valuable tools and expertise to a range of novel problems; for those on the public health side, securitizing health raises its political profile leading to the prospect of greater resources being devoted to urgent health needs.

This securitizing move, however is not unproblematic. Three issues in particular have proved worrying, especially for the health side of the partnership (see also Elbe 2006, 2010). The first of these is: who controls the agenda? At present it is clearly security policy, with global well being lagging as a policy driver. The debate at present is dominated by those health risks which are seen as threatening the national interest, regional stability or international security; it is not about promoting a healthier world. Thus diseases which kill millions each year – including TB, malaria and diarrhoeal diseases – are not considered national security risks, while bioterror (which does not rank on the list of major causes of non-natural death) dominates. Moreover it is an agenda dominated by the West – how international health issues threaten the national security interests of the West – even though the majority of those who die of preventable illnesses do so outside the West. This is not to say that Western policy more generally does not have a humanitarian dimension, though the impact of policies tends to be limited. Rather it is to say that in securitizing health, the national security interests of the West have been prioritized over the individual security of the poor elsewhere.

The next two problems both follow from this control of the agenda. The second is the relatively narrow range of health issues which are considered part of the national security agenda. Infectious diseases such as TB and malaria, as well as non-communicable diseases such as tobacco-related illnesses and cardio-vascular disease, are not considered to be part of the agenda despite the fact that they kill millions each year and may be mitigated by concerted international action. Tobacco sales for example have increased dramatically as a consequence of Western-prompted policies on the liberalization of international trade. The UK MP Frank Dobson has referred to tobacco as a 'weapon of mass destruction', but the Framework Convention on Tobacco Control provides only limited controls on the promotion and sale of tobacco.

The third problem is that of the referent object – whose health is at risk and whose security? Despite health being a risk to individuals, national security perspectives place the referent object at the state level. Tobacco is not considered a global health security issue because, despite the number of individuals who die from tobacco-related illnesses each year, there are no implications for the stability or security of the state. On the other hand, although deaths from bioterrorism are speculative rather than real, the risk to the state in terms of disruption is such that it is clearly entrenched on the agenda.

## Conclusion

Over the past decade health issues have begun to appear on the security agenda. This has led to multiple different meanings of 'health security' and different referent objects. This chapter has focused on health as a national security problem. The incorporation of health issues into the national security agenda has been aided by the post-Cold War shift away from military threats which pose a 'clear and present danger', to more diffuse and conceivably long-term risks. To date, this attention has focused on three health-related risks: the spread of infectious disease, HIV/AIDS, and bioterrorism. Although some may have seen this increased attention to heath issues as a means of gaining greater political support (and resources) for pressing global health issues, the risks have also been substantial in terms of subordinating both the health and development agendas to national security needs.

## Further reading

Lincoln Chen, Jennifer Leaning and Vasant Narashimhan (eds), *Global Health Challenges for Human Security* (Harvard University Press, 2003). A collection of essays from some leading authors using the human security perspective.

Stefan Elbe, *Virus Alert: Security, Governmentality and the AIDS Pandemic* (Columbia University Press, 2009). An excellent discussion of the relationship between HIV/AIDS and security.

Stefan Elbe, *Security and Global Health: Toward the Medicalization of Insecurity* (Polity, 2010). A more general work on security arguing that medical thinking has impacted upon security as much as security has on health.

Kelley Lee, *Health and Globalisation: An Introduction* (Palgrave, 2003). An excellent introduction. Although focused on how different aspects of globalization have impacted upon health, it has a much broader utility.

Andrew Price-Smith, *Contagion and Chaos: Disease, Ecology and National Security in the Era of Globalization* (MIT Press, 2009). An occasionally controversial book drawing on history as well as contemporary examples of securitization.

# PART 3
# INSTITUTIONS

# Alliances

John S. Duffield

## Abstract

In this chapter, students will learn about the concept and theories of alliances, paying particular attention to the question of alliance persistence and disintegration. After discussing what alliances are, the chapter surveys the scholarly literature on why alliances form and fall apart. It then reviews the somewhat puzzling case of NATO, which many observers expected would not long outlive the Cold War. The chapter asks how well existing theories explain NATO's persistence and concludes with theoretically informed observations about the alliance's future prospects.

## Introduction: Why study alliances?

Alliances are one of the most significant phenomena in security studies and world politics more generally. Indeed, the eminent American political scientist, George Modelski, once described alliance as 'one of a dozen or so key terms of International Relations' (1963: 773). For hundreds of years, great powers, and many smaller ones as well, have regularly formed, acted through, and, sometimes, broken alliances. Alliance diplomacy has typically constituted a major component of states' external policies.

Why is this so? Because alliances are one of the most valuable instruments for advancing a state's interests. In particular, alliances are a primary tool for enhancing a state's security in the face of external and, sometimes, internal threats. Focusing on the international realm, Kenneth Waltz (1979: 118) has noted that the means available to states for achieving their ends fall into just two categories: internal efforts and external efforts, including moves to strengthen and enlarge one's own alliance or to weaken an opposing one. And for smaller states with limited resources, reliance on alliances may be the only option. Thus the formation and use of alliances is a frequent response to the dangers of aggression and the opportunities for aggrandizement present in the international system.

Not surprisingly, alliances have been quite common in modern history. The most comprehensive database on alliances, based on the Alliance Treaty Obligations and Provisions (ATOP) project, lists a total of some 648 alliances between 1815 and 2003 (Leeds *et al.* 2002, http://atop.rice.edu). Most alliances have been quite small, with the average number of members being just over three. But the major powers and European states have turned to alliances quite frequently. Just six European powers – the United Kingdom, France, Germany, Austria-Hungary, Italy, and Russia/Soviet Union – account for one-quarter of all alliance memberships during that period.

Arguably, alliances have also had a major impact on international relations. After all, states would presumably not form or maintain alliances if they were not thought to serve the states' interests in ways that were otherwise impossible or less cost-effective. In addition, a number of studies have established that alliances have been an important determinant of the outbreak, spread, and results of militarized conflicts. As Walt has written, 'The formation and cohesion of international alliances can have profound effects on the security of individual states and help determine both the probability and likely outcome of war' (1997: 156).

This chapter explores the concept and theories of alliances, paying particular attention to the question of alliance persistence and disintegration. After surveying what the scholarly literature has to say about the issue, it examines the case of the North Atlantic Treaty Organization (NATO) after the Cold War.

## Definitions: What is an alliance?

The conclusions that one draws about the causes and effects of alliances depend very much on what one counts as an alliance. And, unfortunately, the process of developing theories of alliances has been complicated by the use of widely varying definitions.

A number of influential definitions of alliances have been overly broad. For example, Walt, in his seminal study on the origins of alliances, defined alliance as 'a formal or informal relationship of security cooperation between two or more sovereign states' (1987: 1). An almost identical definition was used by Barnett and Levy in their path-breaking work on the domestic sources of alliances (1991: 370). More recently, Weitsman has described alliances as 'bilateral or multilateral agreements to provide some element of security to the signatories' (2004: 27).

Such broad definitions are reflected in quantitative coding schemes. In their efforts to be comprehensive, the most complete alliance databases have grouped together defensive alliances, offensive alliances, non-aggression pacts, neutrality pacts, and consultation agreements. Further complicating matters is the fact that a high percentage of these so-called 'alliances' – more than half (364 of 648) in the case of the ATOP data set – consist of two or more types.

There are at least two potential problems with such broad definitions of alliances. First, they may be so expansive as to encompass just about any imaginable security arrangement between states. Of particular concern is the fact that they blur the important distinction between alliances, on the one hand, and collective security arrangements, on the other, which involve fundamentally different orientations. Alliances are primarily, if not exclusively, outwardly oriented, intended to enhance the security of their members *vis-à-vis* external parties. In sharp contrast, collective security arrangements and related phenomena such as arms control agreements are designed to enhance the security of their participants *vis-à-vis* each other.

The other problem is the failure to distinguish between various forms of security cooperation. The above definitions would seem to embrace all manner of security cooperation, no matter how innocuous. Thus, they include alliances that might be limited to supportive diplomacy or economic aid with security objectives. What has traditionally distinguished alliances from many other security arrangements between states, however, is the emphasis that they place on military forms of assistance, especially the use of force.

Such considerations suggest the need for a subset of alliance definitions that take these important distinctions into account. Four decades ago, Osgood defined alliance as 'a formal agreement that pledges states to co-operate in using their military resources against a specific state or states and usually obligates one or more of the signatories to use force, or to consider (unilaterally or in consultation with allies) the use of force in specified circumstances' (1968: 17). Similarly, Snyder, in his magnum opus *Alliance Politics*, wrote that 'Alliances are formal associations of states for the use (or nonuse) of military force, in specified circumstances, against states outside their own membership'. He went on to emphasize that '[t]heir primary function is to pool military strength against a common enemy, not to protect alliance members from each other' (1997: 4). And even Walt later amended his conception of alliances, noting that 'the defining feature of any alliance is a commitment for mutual military support against some external actor(s) in some specified set of circumstances' (1997: 157).

These definitions clearly exclude a number of agreements that have sometimes been treated as alliances. In particular, they would seem to militate against the inclusion of pledges by states to refrain from engaging in aggression against one another, promises to remain neutral in the event of a military conflict with a third party, and commitments to consult in the event of a crisis that threatens to lead to war. Nevertheless, hundreds of security arrangements meet the more stringent criteria contained in them.

Before proceeding, it may be useful to consider one further distinction. Even these more restrictive definitions encompass both defensive and offensive alliances. Primarily offensive alliances, however, are relatively rare and almost always short-lived. Of the 277 offensive and/or defensive alliances listed in the ATOP database, only 14 were purely offensive. Of those 14, moreover, only four lasted more than two years, and all began and ended during the nineteenth century. (The mean duration of the 14 purely offensive alliances was 4.4 years, with a standard deviation of 6.5 years.) In view of these considerations, the remainder of this chapter will focus on alliances with a defensive purpose, including those that might also have had an offensive element (about 25 per cent).

Even when the focus is limited to defensive international military alliances, there are a number of possible important issues to explore. Among the topics that have received the most attention from scholars are the following:

- *Alliance formation*: Under what conditions do states form alliances? Who aligns with whom?
- *Alliance dynamics*: How are alliance policies and strategies determined? How are burdens shared among alliance members? What determines the relative degree of alliance cohesion?
- *Alliances and state behaviour*: Do alliances influence the behavior of their members? Do states honour their alliance commitments when called upon to do so?
- *Alliances and war*: Do alliances make war more or less likely? In particular, do alliances deter aggression against their members? Do alliances embolden their members to act with less restraint? When war occurs, do alliances improve their members' prospects of victory?

Clearly, these are far too many questions to explore thoroughly in a single book, let alone in a short chapter such as this. Motivated by what some would describe as NATO's puzzling persistence after the Cold War, the remainder of this chapter will focus on the question of why some alliances endure while others disintegrate.

## Explanations of alliance persistence and collapse

Most international military alliances have ended at one point or another. But some have lived to a ripe old age while others have quickly fallen apart. How long have alliances tended to last? Of the approximately 263 defensive alliances (both purely defensive and with a combination of both defensive and offensive elements) in existence between 1815 and 2003, the mean duration was 13.4

years with a standard deviation of 13.1 years. Interestingly, defensive alliances with no offensive component have tended to last nearly twice as long on average as those with an offensive component, with average life spans of 15.1 and 8.2 years, respectively. This striking difference exists even though some 42 of the 197 purely defensive alliances in the ATOP database had not yet terminated as of 2003.

Have more recent alliances tended to last longer than earlier ones? Although such longitudinal comparisons may be problematic, there is some evidence to suggest that they do. Consider the periods 1815–65 and 1945–95. Both are long intervals of relative peace immediately following a major power war. During the first period, the mean alliance duration was 8.7 years, with a standard deviation of 10.3 years. During the latter period, the average life span was 17.7 years, with a standard deviation of 13.7 years. Similar differences in durability are found even if one considers only purely defensive alliances, even though more than one-third (42 of 124) of those that existed between 1945 and 1995 were ongoing as of 2003.

What factors cause alliances to persist or to collapse? And can they account for this seeming temporal shift in alliance longevity? One obvious factor is major war and the shifts in the map of international politics that such wars can occasion. Of the approximately 40 alliances formed before 1870, only two outlived the wars of German unification. Likewise, only two of the alliances in existence before World War I remained after that conflict was over. And only five of the alliances formed before World War II, including such peripheral pairings as Turkey-Afghanistan and Russia-Mongolia, remained standing when the conflagration came to an end. In other words, major wars tend to sweep the landscape clean of alliances.

Of greater interest, then, are the factors other than war that help alliances to endure or cause them to fall apart. The following sub-sections examine a number of such factors. The analysis is limited, however, to those theories that seem most relevant to the question of NATO's persistence after the Cold War. It does not aspire to provide a truly comprehensive survey of the causes of alliance persistence and collapse that have been hypothesized, although it encompasses most of the prominent ones.

## Theories of alliance formation

The first place to look is at explanations of alliance formation. Such an approach may at first seem counterintuitive. But, arguably, as long as the factors that caused the alliance to form in the first place remain in place, then the alliance will endure. Should those conditions change, however, then the alliance may lose the glue that held it together and fall apart.

In principle, states can freely join alliances. In practice, however, they do not enter into such arrangements lightly, for alliance membership has costs as well as potential benefits. Among those costs may be the loss of autonomy and the creation of dependence. Thus, we need to ask, under what circumstances are states willing to assume and bear these costs? For the purposes of this chapter, the most relevant theories of alliance formation fall into two broad categories: those that emphasize international determinants and those that focus on domestic factors.

## INTERNATIONAL DETERMINANTS: CAPABILITIES AGGREGATION MODELS

The most prominent international explanations of alliance formation are associated with the realist school of International Relations (see Chapter 2, this volume). Also known as capabilities aggregation models, they emphasize how states form alliances in order to combine their military capabilities and thereby improve their security positions. But when precisely will states do so?

The most parsimonious explanation is balance-of-power theory (Waltz 1979: 117–123). It posits that states form alliances to balance the power of other states, especially when they are unable to balance power through their individual efforts or when the costs of such internal balancing exceed those of alliance membership. From this perspective, unbalanced power alone represents a threat to the survival of less powerful states. Therefore, two or more relatively weak states, when confronted with a much more powerful state, will ally. An important exception to this general rule may occur when one state becomes so powerful that no combination of other states can balance its power. In that case, other states may choose to 'bandwagon' with the predominant state (Waltz 1979: 126).

Clearly, balance-of-power theory can also serve as a theory of alliance persistence and disintegration. In this case, shifts in the international distribution of power may threaten the existence of established alliances. For example, the previously predominant state may decline, to the point where an alliance of other states is no longer required to balance its power. Indeed, with the passage of time, an alliance member may become the most powerful state, prompting its erstwhile allies to cut their ties and perhaps even to form counterbalancing alliances against it.

An important refinement of balance-of-power theory is balance-of-threat theory. Sometimes, alliances appear to be unbalanced in terms of power. For example, during much of the Cold War, the alliances centred on the United States were more powerful, as measured on a number of indices of capability, than those revolving around the Soviet Union. Walt addressed such apparent anomalies by arguing that states form alliances in response to common threats, not just power. Although aggregate power is an important component of threat, it is not the only one. How threatening a particular state appears is also a function of its geographical proximity, its offensive capabilities, and the aggressiveness of its intentions. Thus the Soviet Union, by virtue of its relative proximity, its massive ground forces, and its hostile ideology, seemed to pose much more of a threat to its strong but less powerful neighbours, such as France, West Germany, Japan, and Britain, who chose to ally instead with the United States (Walt 1985, 1987).

By the same token, balance-of-threat theory should also illuminate the question of alliance durability and collapse. A decline in the magnitude of the threat posed by an adversary will cause an alliance to weaken or dissolve. This may happen, moreover, even in the absence of any shift in overall power, if, for example, an adversary significantly mutes its offensive military capabilities or seems to moderate its intentions.

Some scholars have noted that states may also use alliances to manage, constrain, and control their partners (Osgood 1968, Schroeder 1976, Weitsman 2004). Obviously, this function is contingent upon the existence of some external balancing purpose; otherwise, we could not speak of the arrangement as an alliance. But assuming that the condition of a more powerful or threatening third party is met, this function can nevertheless be an important, albeit secondary, one. Although this perspective may not be especially helpful for explaining alliance formation, it may shed additional light on the dynamics of alliance disintegration. In this case, if the ally that the alliance is intended, at least in part, to contain becomes too threatening or too powerful to manage successfully, then the alliance will not long survive.

## Domestic Determinants

Balance-of-power theory may be excessively crude as an explanation of alliance formation, persistence, and collapse. In contrast, balance-of-threat theory represents a more nuanced approach, but this refinement comes at the cost of other analytical problems. After all, is it always so obvious which state will be viewed as a threat by others? In particular, when will a state be regarded as harbouring aggressive intentions? Threat perception may depend as much, if not more, on the internal characteristics of states, a subject to which we now turn.

Fortunately, scholars have been equally productive at identifying possible domestic determinants of alliance formation. One set of explanations focuses on similarities and differences in the culture, ideologies, and political institutions of states. The general argument is that, other things being equal, states will tend to ally with states whose political orientations are similar to their own (e.g. Walt 1987). Thus conservative monarchies will prefer alliances with other monarchies, dictatorships with dictatorships, liberal democracies with liberal democracies, and so on.

Scholars have advanced several interrelated reasons for this tendency. Similar value systems may generate common interests and common interpretations of what constitutes a threat. In the case of states sharing a formal ideology, such as Marxism-Leninism, they may even be operating under an explicit injunction to join forces in the face of a hostile international environment. Not least important, forming an alliance with like-minded states may enhance the domestic legitimacy of a weak regime by suggesting that it is part of a broader, popular movement (Walt 1987: 34–35).

Such arguments also suggest possible causes of alliance disintegration. Most obviously, a sudden regime change in one partner or another as the result of a revolution, coup, or other internal upheaval will immediately loosen the bonds of affinity that held the alliance together. Even more gradual changes in political outlook can have the same effect over a longer period. And in some cases, tensions may arise even among states with a common ideology, since it may dictate that national interests must be subordinated to a single authoritative leadership (Walt 1987: 35-36).

In view of such considerations, scholars have suggested that alliances among liberal democratic states are likely to be especially strong and resilient (Gaubatz 1996). One reason is the relative stability of public preferences and the greater continuity of national leadership. Although different administrations may come and go, the democratic process ensures that leadership transitions occur smoothly and abrupt shifts are unlikely. In addition, the international commitments associated with alliances become more deeply embedded in domestic law and institutions. That tendency, combined with a more general respect for legal commitments, enhances the ability of leaders in liberal democracies to tie the hands of their successors.

## Alliance institutionalization and socialization

Thus far, the discussion has been limited to explanations of alliance formation that may also shed light on the question of alliance duration. Despite their differences, these theories have in common the idea that when the conditions that promoted the creation of an alliance are no longer present, we should expect the alliance to dissolve. There is, however, another set of factors and processes that can promote alliance persistence even in the face of significant changes in those formative conditions.

### INSTITUTIONALIZATION

One of these is alliance institutionalization. Some alliances are endowed with important institutional characteristics from the outset, and some may become increasingly institutionalized over time, with important implications for their staying power. Two particular dimensions of alliance institutionalization stand out.

First, alliances may include or develop intergovernmental organizations to facilitate cooperation among their members. These organizations often include a formal bureaucracy with a staff, budget, and physical location. Although presumably of use to the alliance members, such bureaucracies are also actors in their own right with some degree of autonomy and an inherent interest in perpetuating themselves (Walt 1997, Bennett 1997). As McCalla (1996) has noted, such actors can engage in various types of behaviour to ensure the organization's survival. For example, they can actively resist change. They can affirm the necessity of the organization. And they can try to manage change by promoting modifications in the alliance's roles and missions that will maintain member state support while not threatening the organization's core functions.

Second, alliances may contain or acquire institutional capabilities that can be used for tasks beyond those for which they were originally designed (Walt 1997, Wallander 2000). Thus even when an alliance's original *raison d'être* fades, member states may find that they can readily employ such institutional assets to address new threats and security concerns. This tendency will be especially pronounced when states are risk averse or the costs of maintaining pre-existing capabilities are clearly less than those of creating new ones from scratch.

The overall implication of such reasoning is that alliances characterized by high levels of institutionalization will last longer on average. Of course, some scholars may reply that the level of institutionalization of an alliance is itself a function of other determinants of alliance formation and persistence. For example, states facing particularly acute threats may choose to create especially capable alliance organizations, or liberal democracies may find it easier to establish and abide by the additional constraints associated with alliance institutions. Once established, however, such alliance institutions may assume a life of their own and exert an independent impact on subsequent member behaviour. Their consequences cannot simply be reduced to the influence of other factors.

In fact, there has been considerable variation in the initial level of institutionalization of alliances. Of the agreements establishing the 263 defensive alliances in the ATOP data set, 70 have contained a named organization with regularly scheduled meetings or a stand-alone organization with a permanent bureaucracy. 28 agreements provided for an integrated military command among the allies, and 63 have called for official contact among national militaries during peacetime or committed the members to conducting a common defence policy.

Moreover, the initial degree of alliance institutionalization has tended to increase over time, suggesting a possible explanation of the greater longevity of more recently formed alliances. Although some 150 (57 per cent) of the 263 defensive alliances were established after World War II, 36 (88 per cent) of the 41 with a permanent bureaucracy date from the postwar era, as do 21 (75 per cent) of those providing for an integrated military command and 49 (78 per cent) of those calling for close military contacts. Nevertheless, such indices of institutionalization leave much to be desired, as they do not directly measure organizational autonomy or the fungibility of institutional assets. Moreover, the existing data do not yet capture changes in the level of institutionalization that may occur after the alliance is established.

## SOCIALIZATION

Another process that can promote alliance longevity is the socialization of member states, or more precisely, of their political elites and possibly their general publics. Alliance-related social interactions can lead to the development of more similar world views and even a common identity. Thus, as Walt has noted, an alliance may persist because its members come to see themselves as integral parts of a larger political community (1997: 168).

Scholars have lamented that the processes of socialization in international relations are under-theorized and poorly understood (Johnston 2001, Checkel 2005). Nevertheless, it is possible to identify a number of mechanisms through which alliances might promote the socialization of their members, both directly and indirectly. For example, institutionalized alliances may facilitate substantial contact among elites through regular meetings. Within formal organizational structures, both civilian and military personnel seconded from member governments will often work side-by-side with their counterparts from other countries. And, similar to the organizational arguments presented above, international civil servants may actively seek to cultivate a sense of community among elites and attentive publics through their pronouncements and lobbying activities.

Socialization need not be limited to highly institutionalized alliances, however. The existence of even a weakly institutionalized alliance between two states may reinforce or lead to other connections between the members that facilitate socialization. Because allied states have less to fear from one another than from third parties, other things being equal, they may be more likely to engage in trade and to be receptive to the exchange of capital, technology, information, ideas, and people. And as the eminent political scientist Karl Deutsch (1957) argued more than five decades ago, it is through such mundane material and ideational flows that political communities may be forged.

## The case of NATO after the Cold War

What light does alliance theory shed on the important case of NATO? And what can an examination of NATO after the Cold War contribute to alliance theory?

### Background: NATO's origins and evolution during the Cold War

NATO, along with a handful of other alliances formed in the years immediately following World War II, is one of the longest-lived alliances. It dates back to April 1949, when the North Atlantic Treaty was signed in Washington, DC, and ratified by the twelve original members. Although the treaty does not refer to any particular adversary, it was clearly a response to the growing threat that appeared to be posed by the hostile ideology and military power of the Soviet Union. At the same time, at least some members also viewed the alliance as an insurance policy, provided primarily by the United States, against the then admittedly distant prospect of a resurgent Germany. As NATO's first Secretary-General, Lord Hastings Ismay, reportedly remarked, the purpose of the alliance was three-fold: to keep the Russians out, the Americans in, and the Germans down.

The alliance's initial organizational expression was extremely modest. The treaty called for only a Council and a defence committee. In contrast, the

Brussels Treaty Organization, founded a year early, had a much more elaborate organization, including a military command structure and regional planning groups. And so things remained until mid-1950, when the Korean War abruptly altered Western attitudes about the imminence of the military threat.

In response, the members quickly put the 'O' in NATO. They established a council of representatives in permanent session in Paris and, over time, an increasingly complex intergovernmental apparatus for consultation and joint decision-making. They created an international staff, headed by a secretary-general, to serve the council. And, not least important, they set up a Military Committee and an elaborate integrated military planning and command structure, the most prominent officer of which would be the Supreme Allied Commander Europe (SACEUR).

This is not the place to go into detail about the first four decades of NATO's history. Suffice it to say that the alliance suffered its share of internal stresses and strains. Indeed, disagreement on one important matter or another was a nearly constant theme (e.g. Osgood 1962, Daalder 1991, Duffield 1995). There were intense debates on such questions as how much emphasis to place on nuclear versus conventional weapons in NATO's military strategy, how many conventional forces each member should provide, and whether and how to modernize the alliance's nuclear arsenal. And in the 1960s, France withdrew from the alliance's military structures, precipitating the sudden transfer of NATO's civilian and military headquarters to new quarters in Belgium.

What appears most important in retrospect, however, is that the alliance survived the many challenges to its internal cohesion that arose during those decades and even outlasted the Soviet Union itself. Indeed, NATO's persistence during the Cold War is rarely, if ever, discussed, perhaps because it has subsequently seemed inevitable. After all, the Soviet Union continued to pose a serious political-military threat to the alliance's members, and, secondarily, NATO proved to be an effective vehicle for harnessing West Germany's tremendous military potential without recreating destabilizing security dilemmas in western Europe.

## The puzzle of NATO's post-Cold War and persistence

Instead, what has seemed most puzzling and, as a result, has been the object of considerable inquiry has been NATO's survival after the Cold War. Even before the disintegration of the Soviet Union and especially thereafter, some International Relations scholars argued that the alliance's days, or at least its years, were numbered and that it would sooner or later fall apart (e.g. Mearsheimer 1990, Waltz 1993a). The principal argument offered was the absence of a compelling external threat. With the end of the Cold War and the Soviet Union, the NATO members would no longer see any imperative to maintain the alliance, and it would soon lapse into ineffectuality, even if it continued to exist on paper. Later in the 1990s, Walt offered the more general argument that alliances will tend to be less robust in a multipolar world because major powers will possess more options as their numbers increase (1997: 163). Thus, he concluded, 'prudence suggests that existing alliance commitments can no longer be taken for granted' (1997: 164).

These predictions proved, at a minimum, to be premature. Rather than go out of business, NATO has, at least in some ways, thrived since 1990. It has added twelve new members, nearly doubling in size. Forces under NATO command have engaged in extensive combat operations in places such as Bosnia, Kosovo, Afghanistan, and Libya. Indeed, the core operational element of the treaty, Article V, which obligates members to provide assistance should one or more of them be the object of an armed attack, was invoked for the first time, following the terrorist attacks on the United States of 11 September, 2001. All in all, NATO has exhibited what might be regarded as a surprising degree of durability and robustness.

## Explaining NATO's persistence

Can NATO's post-Cold War persistence be accounted for in terms of the existing explanations of alliance persistence identified above? Are there any aspects of the alliance's recent history that do not fit these theories? What other explanations can be adduced to account for these anomalies?

Before proceeding, there is one methodological issue that should be aired. Some of the explanations of alliance persistence have in fact been developed with the case of NATO after the Cold War in mind. Since the goal of this chapter is not to test theories but rather to use them to illuminate a particular instance, this circularity poses no troubling methodological problems. But it does, at a minimum, raise the question of whether such explanations are in fact likely to find applications elsewhere, even though their underlying logic may be sound.

Some might argue that there is no puzzle to be explained because NATO is no longer an alliance. Rather, it has been transformed into something else, perhaps a regional collective security arrangement or what Wallander and Keohane (1999) have called a security management institution. Such an argument, however, would still beg the question of how and why NATO was able to perform this feat of re-inventing itself.

The first place to turn for answers is the explanations that emphasize the international determinants of alliance persistence. Here we might note three principal reasons for NATO's longevity. One is the residual threat posed by the remnants of the Soviet Union, notably Russia. Although greatly diminished in power and geographically separated from NATO Europe by an additional layer of buffer states, Russia nevertheless continued to possess a military capability second to none on the continent and by far the most lethal nuclear arsenal. Compounding this enduring disparity in raw capabilities has been much uncertainty about Russia's future intentions. Russia's experiment with democracy was troubled from the outset, and recent years have been marked by renewed efforts by Russia to assert itself, sometimes by coercive means, on the world stage.

A second external factor was the emergence of new threats that were largely shared by NATO members. The first to emerge, even before the Cold War was officially interred, was instability and bloody civil conflicts on or near NATO's borders, especially in the Balkans. Apart from the humanitarian imperatives that such conflicts generated, some had the potential to spill over into or draw in neighbouring states, raising the possibility of a wider conflagration. Concern about regional conflicts was followed by the growing threat of international terrorism. To be sure, NATO as an organization has thus far played a relatively minor role in the overall efforts of its members, chiefly the United States, to combat terrorists (de Nevers 2007). Nevertheless, it has made important contributions, most notably its assumption of the command of the International Security Assistance Force (ISAF) in Afghanistan in 2003.

Not to be overlooked is the continuing intra-alliance function that NATO has played in ensuring friendly relations among its members. Certainly, this function is less important than it was during the early years of the Cold War, when memories of World War II were still fresh, and it has been increasingly assumed by the European Union. Still, NATO's post-Cold War role in this regard has not been insignificant, especially its role in allaying potential concerns about a unified Germany. By increasing transparency, further denationalizing security policies, and subtly balancing power, the alliance has helped to assure its members that they have nothing to fear from one another (Duffield 1994/95). German leaders in particular have recognized the value of maintaining NATO as a vital organization for the purpose of reassuring Germany's neighbours (Duffield 1998).

What about NATO's institutionalization and the socialization of its members over time? Clearly, NATO has acquired a substantial organizational structure. Overall, more than 5,000 civilians work for NATO, with 1,200 of them concentrated in an International Staff at the alliance's headquarters in Brussels. There is little evidence to suggest, however, that this bureaucracy has exercised much influence over the relevant actions of the member countries (McCalla 1996). Although the secretary-general and his staff have sometimes played a critical role in facilitating cooperation among the members (Hendrickson 2006), the key decisions concerning the perpetuation of the alliance since the end of the Cold War have been consistent with pre-existing national interests and priorities.

Arguably more important in explaining NATO's persistence has been the fungibility of its institutional assets (Wallander 2000). In addition to the civilian bureaucracy, NATO had developed an elaborate integrated military planning and command structure and associated joint military assets, which made it unique among peacetime alliances. Although these assets were developed with Cold War challenges and contingencies in mind, they have proved to be remarkably adaptable to the new threat environment. In particular, they have enabled NATO and its members to take a number of actions, such as the operations in Bosnia, Kosovo, Afghanistan, and Libya, that other alliances or ad hoc groupings would have found difficult, if not impossible, to mount. Here, however, we must acknowledge a close, if not symbiotic, relationship between the emergence of new threats and NATO's institutional ability to deal with them. Neither factor by itself would have provided a sufficient rationale for maintaining the alliance.

Finally, we turn to the question of socialization within NATO. This is perhaps the most difficult explanation to evaluate. There is some evidence that the views of government officials and military commanders have been altered by their close association with alliance counterparts (Tuschhoff 1999). It is not clear, however, how extensive or consequential such changes may have been. Certainly, it would be difficult to conclude that interpersonal intra-alliance interactions have altered national identities or worldviews in ways that can be said to have had a measurable impact on national policies toward NATO since the end of the Cold War. Perhaps more important have been the broader contacts, especially those of a transatlantic nature, that have been facilitated and nurtured by the existence of NATO over the years. The substantial movement of goods, investments, ideas, and people has created close societal ties between the two sides of the Atlantic. But here, too, it would be nigh impossible to draw a direct link between them and NATO's persistence.

Of course, numerous though they be, the above explanations do not exhaust the possibilities. Thus before concluding, it is worth considering some additional reasons that may be unique to the case of NATO and thus impossible to generalize to other alliances. One is NATO's utility as a tool for political reform. Since the breakup of the Soviet empire, NATO countries have employed the prospect of membership to promote liberal democratic practices and institutions, such as civilian control of the military and transparency in defence budgets, in the countries of central, eastern, and southeastern Europe (Gheciu 2005). Although these efforts can be viewed as part of the alliance's overall strategy for enhancing the security of its members, they constitute an unconventional approach by historical standards, to say the least.

Another reason for NATO's longevity may be its usefulness as an enforcement arm of the UN Security Council. During the Cold War, the two security organizations had little or nothing to do with one another, and it took the trauma of the conflict in Bosnia to prompt the first halting steps toward coordination. Now, however, NATO has a long track record of enforcing Security Council resolutions. To be sure, the member countries have used the alliance in this way only where doing so served their interests, but these interests may be increasingly broadly defined, as suggested by the assistance that the alliance has provided in situations as geographically remote or as unrelated to traditional security concerns as Darfur, Libya, and the Gulf of Aden.

## Conclusion: Alliance theory and the future of NATO

The above analysis, despite its necessary brevity, suggests the usefulness of alliance theory for illuminating the reasons for NATO's persistence after the Cold War and, more generally, for understanding international relations.

Indeed, alliance theory may be too useful, insofar as the case of NATO tends to affirm the utility of multiple approaches. Typically, social scientists search for cases that will differentiate more decisively among alternative theories on the basis of their explanatory power. But that was not the goal of this chapter. Rather, the NATO case was chosen because of its practical importance in a world where significant threats to the security of states still exist. Whether or not one can draw broader conclusions about the conditions influencing the longevity of alliances is beside the point. Indeed, given the many unusual, if not unique, features of NATO, any attempts to generalize are likely to be misleading.

Instead, we might content ourselves by concluding with some discussion of what alliance theory can say about the future of NATO. Here, the theory is less useful, although no less useful than other theories when it comes to prognostication. Perhaps the best that it can do is to draw attention to the types of factors that are likely to be determinative, even if no particular weights or probabilities can be attached to them. Among the most important will be the presence or absence of threats that are sufficiently shared and intense so as to cause the NATO countries to continue to see value in addressing those threats in a collective manner. Closely related will be the ability to adapt NATO's institutions, especially in ways that are less costly than institutional alternatives, so that they can continue to address the evolving spectrum of threats.

From this perspective, NATO faces at least two significant challenges. One is a growing divergence in the principal security concerns facing NATO members. This divergence is partly a result of the alliance's successful expansion after the Cold War, which necessarily widened the range of concerns. While older members may especially value NATO for its role in promoting stability beyond the alliance's borders, some of the newer members may view it primarily as a means of providing security in the face of a potentially revanchist Russia. Although these varying motives for maintaining NATO may complement one another, they can nevertheless generate strains when it comes to establishing alliance priorities and deciding on concrete courses of action. Further complicating matters is the emergence of new threats that may not always, or even often, be best addressed through NATO. Most obvious here is the challenge posed by international terrorism, which has prompted rather divergent responses among the members of the alliance.

The other challenge is the existence of promising institutional alternatives, especially for the European members of NATO. Since the early 1990s, the European Union (EU) has made great strides toward the development of common policies and policymaking structures in the areas of foreign, security, and even defence policy. Thus far, the leaders of NATO and EU countries (many of whom are one and the same) have succeeded in ensuring that the two sets of institutions and their activities remain compatible with one another. But in view of the many tensions that have roiled transatlantic relations in recent years, it is not difficult to imagine circumstances in which European leaders would decide to assign clear priority to the use of EU structures, calling into question the preservation of NATO in anything like its present form.

## Further reading

The best recent overview of the subject of alliances is Glenn Snyder, *Alliance Politics* (Cornell University Press, 1997).

The two most thorough examinations of alliance formation and persistence are Stephen M. Walt, *The Origins of Alliances* (Cornell University Press, 1987), and Patricia A. Weitsman, *Dangerous Alliances: Proponents of Peace, Weapons of War* (Stanford University Press, 2004).

The most comprehensive study of NATO's persistence is Wallace J. Thies, *Why NATO Endures* (Cambridge University Press, 2009).

Perhaps the most authoritative and up-to-date history of NATO is Lawrence S. Kaplan, *NATO Divided, NATO United: The Evolution of an Alliance* (Praeger, 2004).

# Regional Institutions

Louise Fawcett

## Abstract

In this chapter, students will learn about the role of regional institutions in the provision of international security; the history and development of regionalism in the security sphere; and the evolving relationship between the United Nations and regional institutions. It considers the conditions behind the growth of regional security projects, and explanations for their success and failure. As the world becomes more multipolar and more states seek an active stake in the multilateral system, there is both increasing demand for and supply of regional security provision and this is reflected in the growth and development of institutions. Though the record of such institutions is mixed and shows considerable variation from region to region, there is increasing evidence of regional institutions forming part of a new multilateral security architecture. Older debates about the comparative advantage of regional versus global institutions have given way to a consensus about the need for a complementary framework.

## Introduction

The growth of regional security institutions over the past half century or so looks impressive. Before the Second World War, there were few formal international institutions of any type and even fewer dealing explicitly with security matters: the main exception was the League of Nations. Since 1945 their numbers have grown steadily if unevenly, reflecting periods of growth and change in the international system. By 2010, of a growing array of intergovernmental regional organizations, nearly 40 included a commitment to security provision (Diehl 2005, Tavares 2010). Their distribution, though uneven, is global, encompassing Europe, Africa, the Americas, Asia, and the Middle East (see Table 24.1). When one considers that much earlier institutional growth was identified primarily with economic integration this is particularly notable. Also impressive is the wide scope of their activities reflecting how the term security itself has expanded to take in a variety of new tasks: from confidence-building measures and conflict prevention to peacekeeping and arms control.

Further, while regional institutions have become more active in their own right, they have also become involved in collaborative security ventures, typically with the UN, but also with other regional/cross-regional institutions, and an array of NGOs (Pugh and Sidhu 2003). Collaboration between the UN and regional actors is particularly evident today in the area of peace operations (see Chapter 26 this volume, CIC 2006–2010). Regional organizations also collaborate among themselves, part of a wider phenomenon dubbed 'interregionalism' (Hanggi, Roloff and Ruland 2006). Though more prominent in the economic arena, it has also entered the security sphere, for example in EU efforts to promote security cooperation in a region like the Middle East, through the Euro-Mediterranean partnership and related processes (European Commission 2002).

Finally, these new security roles of regional organizations, though still understudied, have been increasingly recognized by states, the UN and other actors. Earlier and widely expressed scepticism about the value of such institutions has given way to acknowledgment of their potential as multilateral actors. They are part of an 'explosion of international activism' (Human Security Reports 2005, 2010), seen as responsible for the post-Cold War decline in

*Table 24.1* Major regional institutions with security provision 1945–2010

| | |
|---|---|
| Africa | OAU/AU, IGADD/IGAD, ECOWAS, SADCC/SADC, CEMAC |
| Europe | EC/EU, WEU, NATO, (Warsaw Pact) CSCE/OSCE, CIS, CSTO |
| Asia | (SEATO), ASEAN, SAARC, ARF, SCO, CACO, ICO |
| Middle East | LAS, (CENTO), GCC, AMU, (ACC), RCD/ECO |
| Americas | OAS, CARICOM, OECS, MERCOSUR, UNASUR |
| Australasia/other | Commonwealth, ANZUS, SPF/PIF |

Note: ( ) = defunct institutions / name change

armed conflicts. In the words of former UN Secretary-General Kofi Annan, 'multilateral institutions and regional security organizations have never been more important' (UN Press Release SG/SM/8543: 9/12/2002). Since then their area of activity has continued to expand as has their perceived legitimacy as international actors. In 2011, for example, during the popular reform movements dubbed the 'Arab Spring' the important potential roles of regional security institutions were highlighted by their involvement in attempts to promote peaceful political transition as in the case of the GCC in Yemen; and in endorsing humanitarian intervention as in the case of both the GCC and the LAS in Libya (Lynch 2011).

This chapter analyses this 'new wave of regionalism in security affairs' (Lake and Morgan 1997). It traces the start-up, the growth and progressive expansion of regional institutions and the trend towards more regionalisation in security affairs since 1945. Historical institutionalism is helpful here to understand how institutions create path dependencies, bridge gaps and lock in the practices of cooperation (Pierson 1996: 126). Few regional institutions have become defunct as Table 24.1 shows, many have survived difficult times, and their overall sphere of activity and competence has also expanded considerably. Some once exclusively economic organizations have registered advances in the security domain. They have also directly contributed to conflict resolution and peacebuilding activity in Africa, Southeast Asia, Latin America and Europe. Some have successfully promoted non-proliferation through the establishment of nuclear-free zones. In other regions, weapons proliferation problems continue but the idea that regional organizations can and should help to regulate this issue has become firmly established.

Consequently, as regionalism becomes more multifaceted and complex it is helpful to separate off its different activities and also to take a closer look at the different properties of institutions themselves (Acharya and Johnston 2007). Doing so also reveals their diversity: there is evidently no immediately regular or generalizable pattern in the development of security regionalism. States have behaved quite differently in the face of regional security challenges. A second task of the chapter, therefore, is to consider explanations for these trends by looking at some of the theories and concepts that have been deployed in explaining regionalism.

Current explanations for institutional cooperation, regional or otherwise, vary widely. At one end of the spectrum there are those (neorealists) who are sceptical that international institutions can deliver public goods or positively or permanently transform the international security environment. For them, institutions are transient and reflective of power balances in the international system. At the other are the idealists who view institutions in a positive and progressive light, with important roles to play in overcoming conflict and fostering global prosperity and peace (Higgott 2006). Most explanations of regional cooperation now rest between these two positions, clustering around inter-governmentalist and neo-functionalist approaches. Originally designed to explain the European case they have been applied elsewhere, though with varying degrees of success, since early non-European experiments in cooperation were often limited in scope. Nevertheless state bargains, functional cooperation and spill-over together constitute powerful explanations for the global spread of regionalism.

Recent additions to the debate have come from Regional Security Complex Theory (RSCT) (Buzan and Waever 2003) and constructivism (Acharya 2000). In an increasingly multipolar international order in which emerging and new powers seek to establish distinctive normative frameworks and shift the parameters of international society, the constructivist challenge is particularly important (Checkel 1998). The domain of multilateralism has become an increasingly pluralist and contested normative space (Ruggie 1992).

These two approaches help in explaining why regional groups form in the first place and why their agendas differ. They do not, however, necessarily contribute to a progressive or positive reading of security regionalism. On the one hand, a security complex can be defined by amity or enmity, producing quite different institutional outcomes. It is also subject, positively and negatively, to the influences of powerful states. On the other, there is the danger that the local norms fostered in regional institutions may conflict, either with competing regional norms or with global ones. If such normative fragmentation occurs there could be a danger of increased conflict. One example of this is the different positions adopted regarding issues like humanitarian intervention, human rights or arms control where regional institutions take stances that are at variance with each other or with the 'global' norms of the UN (see Huntington 1993, Narlikar 2010).

This divergence helps explain why some commentators remain sceptical of regionalism. Against the positive view that regional security might be a gateway to global security, a step towards a unified world, or, alternatively, that peace might be obtained 'in parts' (Nye 1971), regionalism might be considered at best complementary, secondary and at worst detrimental to global efforts to promote peace and security. For those who think the UN, or some universal body, should be the main security provider, the promotion of regional security contradicts the search for global security for both normative and material reasons – regional organizations cannot be impartial and will be susceptible to the ambitions of strong regional powers (Goulding 2002). With their competing narratives of security, they also dilute global security provision. As discussed below, the view that international security institutions should be based on the principle of universality, while resting on some very sound historical and normative foundations, has arguably given way to a more nuanced appraisal of regionalism and its possibilities.

## Definitions

What is a regional institution and what defines the security component of a regional institution? All three terms: 'regional,' 'security' and 'institutions' are subject to differing interpretations, so a brief note of clarification on their use is needed. In International Relations, institutions refer to formal organizations with 'prescribed hierarchies and capacity for purposive action' and international regimes with 'complexes of rules and organizations, the core elements of which have been negotiations and explicitly agreed upon by states' (Keohane 1988, Ruggie 1998). Regional institutions are formal organizations and regimes comprising a membership which is geographically delimited in some way, for example contiguous states or perhaps to two or more proximate regions (NATO or the ASEAN Regional Forum for example). That said, other definitions exist based around shared histories, issue areas and policies, allowing organizations like the ICO, or Commonwealth to be included (Nye 1968, Katzenstein 1996, Russett 1967).

The tendency in International Relations has been to focus on formal rather than informal institutions and state rather than non-state actors, though both are today increasingly recognised as important elements in regionalism (Hettne 2004, Van Langenhove 2011). For example ad hoc or 'informal' groups and coalitions of states are often important security providers (as in the Australia-led coalition in East Timor; or the EU-3 negotiating group with Iran); so are non-state actors like sub- or trans-state groups that engage in cross-border cooperation; and NGOs, particularly in peacebuilding. If the state remains the gatekeeper of much regional security we also need to include in our discussion a much wider range of actors.

The *security* dimension of regional institutions may be understood in different ways. First, drawing on the definition employed in the Introduction to this volume, which incorporates a wide range of threats, it could be argued that every regional organization has some security component. Assuming the association is voluntary, any attempt to promote cooperative and more predictable relations among its member states, may be seen as a step towards building a more secure community (Deutsch 1957, Adler and Barnett 1998), or promoting human security. Second and more narrowly, a regional security institution can be understood as an organization whose charter contains some explicit reference to security *provision* by member states i.e. some formal mechanism for dealing with conflict and its consequences. Such a mechanism would typically include the coordination of defence, security and foreign policy at some level. This distinction may be understood by contrasting the early European Community (EC) project with that of the later European Union (EU) which incorporated common foreign and security policy instruments and conducts its own peace operations. The distinction between these two concepts of security remains fuzzy however. Security provision does not always imply a military or peacekeeping component. Regional institutions engage in civilian as well as military missions. They provide assistance following humanitarian or natural disasters; they support democratic consolidation and institution-building, whether or not the state or states involved have been involved in conflict, and one thinks here of the role of Mercosur in the Americas in preventing democratic backsliding. The hard/soft security line can be hard to draw. While acknowledging the broader realm (and referents) of security and the role of regional institutions in promoting it, the focus here will be principally on the more measurable forms of security provision: security as conflict prevention, reduction and resolution, or post-conflict reconstruction.

## The origins and development of regional security institutions

No understanding of the contemporary role of regional security institutions is complete without historical context which provides valuable information about their start up and formative conditions. The growth of formal regional institutions dates from the Second World War and is part of a general pattern of growth in international institutions. Three main types of regional institution can be identified:

1 multipurpose institutions, like the League of Arab States (LAS), Organization of American States (OAS) or Organization of African Unity (OAU);
2 institutions with principally an economic focus, like the EC;
3 security alliances like NATO, SEATO and CENTO.

The emphasis here is on institutions with an explicit security component, or types (1) and (3). Not all regional economic institutions have developed security provision, nor do all regional security institutions have provision for economic cooperation and integration (NATO is one example). There is thus no necessary link or 'spillover' effect as some early integration theorists predicted (Haas 1958). The type of cooperation undertaken depends on local and international conditions.

In the area of regional security, three broad waves of institutional growth can be identified from 1945 to the present: the first coinciding with the immediate post-Second World War and early Cold War period, the second, less defined perhaps but distinctive nonetheless, occurring in the mid- to late Cold War period, and the third, most recent wave, in the first post-Cold War decade. There has been little *new* institution-building since the turn of the century – one exception is the Union of South American Nations, UNASUR, founded in 2008 – though a number of existing institutions have expanded and developed their capacity in different areas. The ASEAN+3 framework is one example, so far mainly concerned with economic cooperation. For each wave, institutional growth and change correlates both with change and development in the international system – with state formation and breakdown – and with parallel domestic politics. The last major systemic change, which saw both the (re)birth and death of a number of institutions (most notably the death of the Warsaw Pact), was the end of the Cold War and the break-up of the former Soviet bloc.

Prior to the Second World War formal security institutions were few and regional security institutions non-existent. The Inter-American system, with its roots in the late nineteenth century, was not a formal security institution, though it embodied ideas of an informal security regime for the Americas (Fawcett 2005). Other security regimes were evident in nineteenth-century Europe, where the idea of a 'concert' or balance of powers clearly informed understanding of regional order. It was only when this loose regime was broken by the onset of the First World War, that international statesmen, led by US President Woodrow Wilson, made the first sustained attempt at constructing a formal security institution: the League of Nations.

The League experiment, though intended to be universal, betrayed a number of regional features, not least that its dominant members were all European. A reference in the Covenant, in Article 21, to 'regional understandings', was included to attract the United States, which did not become a member, and the Monroe Doctrine was the only understanding actually mentioned (Zimmern 1945). More broadly, the League experiment set the tone for a wider and ongoing debate about how to deal with the problem of integrating regional arrangements into the framework of a general security organization. This debate was overtaken by the events of the 1930s when Europe, and much of the rest of the world, became embroiled in a new war. By this time it was evident that the League had failed in its central purpose as a collective security institution, and 'regionalism' had become negatively associated with Japan's pan-Asian project, or the Nazi's pan-European one.

## Regional security institutions in the Cold War

It was against this background that the UN was constructed and the first wave of regional institution-building also took place. The League's example informed these developments, with the aim to create a more robust set of international institutions precisely to prevent the social, political and economic upheavals that had taken the world to war after 1939. Few states questioned the need for a more ambitious universal security organization, but many also sought to protect their interests through regional or cross regional groupings. The new Third World's effort at institution-building through the development of 'pan' regionalisms, notably in Africa and the Middle East, though also in the Americas, was a case in point.

In the 1940s, the first such regional institutions, like the OAS following an overhaul of the Inter-American System, but also the Commonwealth, and League of Arab States had come into being, in a pattern that would soon be replicated in Africa with the creation of the OAU in 1963. The final design of the UN Charter, like the League Covenant before it, was strongly influenced by states with investments in such institutions. Despite the reservations of the UN founding fathers, like US President Roosevelt, about diluting its universal aspirations and competence, regional interests were simply too strong to be ignored. (Winston Churchill for example, had supported a four regional pillars approach to international security.) The UN Charter endorsed the principle of regional partnership and action, within the framework of the global security organization. This important principle continues to guide the relations between global and regional institutions to this day.

The provisions regarding the role of regional agencies, and their relationship with the UN, are principally clustered in Chapter VIII, Articles 51–54 of the UN Charter: Article 51 endorses the right of states to collective self defence; in Article 52, regional agencies are called upon to 'make every effort to achieve peaceful settlement of local disputes . . . before referring them to the Security Council'; Article 53 emphasizes that regional arrangements shall not use military force without prior approval from the Security Council; while Article 54 stipulates that regional arrangements keep the Security Council informed of their activities. The Charter is ambiguous as to which types of regional actors and institutions are appropriate for Chapter VIII partnerships, leaving this open to a variety of interpretations (Schreuer 1995, Sarooshi 1998).

The construction of the first formal regional organizations was a response to changes in the international system, brought about both by the war itself and the end of European empires. These institutions had to readapt to a new international environment characterized by the Cold War, one in which it was clear that the power of regional actors, particularly where new Third World states were concerned, would be severely constrained. As well as Cold War overlay, domestic factors, such as regime type and level of economic development, were important. Their very newness and lack of diplomatic expertise were part of the problem as were scarce resources and limited state-building capacity. Where strong states were present or able to influence regional institutions, as was the case for the US in the Americas and Western Europe, their room for manoeuvre and agenda setting was considerable.

The early general purpose organizations are often described as failures, at least in the short-term (Haas 1993). They were unable to foster security by protecting their regions against both external and internal threats. Their regions suffered from civil wars and external intervention. These new institutions, however, given the difficulties they faced, were not wholly unsuccessful in promoting regional unity and in forging common positions on issues of importance to their members such as decolonization and apartheid (in the African case) or support for Palestine (in the Arab one). Peacekeeping roles, reflecting a pattern established in the UN, were also played by the OAU, OAS and the LAS in conflicts over Chad, the Dominican Republic and Kuwait and Lebanon respectively. Regional institutions had an early role to play in conflict resolution and in framing security debates that has hitherto been under-recognized. They were therefore a tool for the 'weak in the world of the strong' (Rothstein 1977).

The rise of the Cold War alliance system complicated this picture. On one reading it can be argued that by far the most successful regional security institutions were those on either side of the East–West divide: the Warsaw Pact and NATO respectively. If the Cold War has been characterized as a 'long peace' (Gaddis 1987) it was the role of these two institutions and their superpower patrons that was critical in keeping that peace through the maintenance of a stable balance of power. On another, these security alliances and the bilateral and multilateral arrangements they promoted, both bypassed the UN system and shaped the global and regional security picture, offering little scope for regional organizations either to develop their own arrangements, or the type of security relationships detailed in Chapter VIII.

Neither NATO nor the Warsaw Pact was designed as a Chapter VIII institution; they retained full autonomy of action, bypassing the careful wording of Article 103 on the primacy of UN obligations over 'any other international agreement'. If the very presence of NATO was a major factor in removing security from the agenda of the West European states, helping to explain the EC's early successes in economic integration, the same situation did not arise in other regions. Efforts by the United States to create regional security organizations to serve similar Cold War purposes, whether in Southeast Asia (SEATO), the Middle East (Baghdad Pact/CENTO) or Australasia (ANZUS) were far less successful, except for the latter case, and deeply divisive in the case of the CENTO. Ultimately Cold War security on the periphery was achieved through bilateral alliances rather than formal institutional arrangements. Japan, for example, through its bilateral security treaty with the US was more secure than most of the states that formed part of either SEATO or CENTO.

It was in reaction to this superpower dominance of the regional security arena, the disappointing early results of multipurpose institutions and the changing regional security environment itself that a second mini wave of institution-building occurred, mainly among developing countries. This new wave of security regionalism, between 1966 and 1986, should be distinguished from the earlier wave of pan-regionalism and economic regionalism, inspired by the creation and successful early years of the EC (Nye 1968). Like the latter, this wave was mostly sub-regional in scope, encompassing a smaller geographical space and with fewer members than the pan-regional or conti-nental groups, though it also included a pan-European security institution, the CSCE, and a pan-Islamic, though not strictly regional, institution, the ICO.

Overall, this second wave was characterized by small, but important steps to improve regional self-sufficiency and cooperation in a changing global environment which afforded more flexibility to regional actors. Bipolarity had loosened in the détente era of the late-1960s to mid-1970s, while many developing countries had consolidated their statehood and autonomy. Not all these new institutions immediately assumed security roles; a number had more ostensibly economic functions: the GCC is an institution designed to meet a security threat whose charter is couched in mainly economic and cultural terms (see Article 4). Still there was a clear security dimension to this second wave of institution-building. In fact many of these second wave security institutions were constructed with a particular local threat in mind: for ASEAN it was Vietnam, for the GCC, revolutionary Iran; for SADCC apartheid South Africa. The short-lived ACC was conceived as a vehicle for containing Iraq. Nevertheless the overlay features of the Cold War remained in this phase of institution-building, and continued to restrict options. This was also true for the CSCE, a quite different European security enterprise, which by encouraging East–West convergence in several areas played a facilitating role in the end of the Cold War.

The results of this second wave, like the first, were mixed, but a couple of points should be noted. As in the first wave, institutional survival rates were high: few institutions died (except the now redundant security pacts, CENTO and SEATO, and the short lived ACC). Even where their functions were limited, they were evidently valued by their members. They were also flexible, a function in part of the uncertain environment in which they operated. However, as their raison d'être shifted with the new balance of power at the end of the Cold War, many went on to consolidate their security roles. Again, the security trajectories established in this period provided important continuities into the next.

## Regional security institutions since the Cold War

Once again, it was system change that helps explain the post-Cold War changes and developments in regional institutions. Indeed, if path dependencies had been created in the Cold War in respect of the development of regional institutions, its ending was critical in reshaping these, triggering new growth and expansion of regional security projects. The post-Cold War environment radically changed the parameters of the international security domain and made security more vulnerable, yet also more accessible to local actors. This was because of the absence of superpower overlay and an increase in regional autonomy. It was, above all, the exposure of new regional security complexes which gave rise to a new wave of regionalism. Like earlier waves, the post-Cold War regionalism has been the subject of much debate and a growing literature, but the evidence on the security side merits separate examination (Tavares 2010).

At first, there was a universalist flavour to the post-Cold War security order which did not immediately suggest an important role for regional institutions. Just as the two world wars had seen the birth and rebirth of universal paradigms of global order, reflected in the ethos of the League and the UN, the end of the Cold War era was similarly informed by idealized notions about the possibilities of global institutions and the promotion of global peace. This was picked up in the rhetoric of the 'New World Order' articulated by US President George Bush Sr., after the 1991 Gulf War, and in popular works on the end of history, ideology, geography and so on. These big ideas were captured by different understandings of the term 'globalization'. As in the past, regionalism was viewed by some as a mere stepping stone to a more unified global order by others as potentially obstructive and damaging to such a process (Baghwati 1991).

Three things illustrated regionalism's potential and possible trajectory. First, was the experience of Western Europe where the EC experiment represented an important model of how regional cooperation could be achieved. And with domestic and international conditions more favourable to regionalism after the post-Cold War wave of democratization and trade liberalization, non-European institutions did start to grow. Meanwhile, the EU itself, in furthering its process of European Political Cooperation and developing a Common Defence and Security Policy, was poised to move from a predominantly economic focus to one which also emphasized security cooperation.

Second, and less immediately tangible, was the so-called 'clash of civilizations' thesis (Huntington 1993), linked to a cultural or constructivist turn in International Relations theory. This characterization made the point that 'civilizations', often loose regions and their accompanying cultures, could not be homogenized and had creative and fragmentary power. Regions drew on and supported normative frames that could be complementary or competitive to global order. In this sense regionalism, construed as a response to the global 'other', extended the project that had commenced with the early Third World regionalisms and the second post-Cold War wave. Regionalism thus provided a vehicle for alternative conceptions of order and security, hence the 'Asian Way' or 'African solutions to African problems'.

Third, from a more practical perspective, it became clear that existing multilateral structures, given the new demands placed upon them, would need buttressing. Nowhere was this more apparent than in the area of conflict resolution. In calling for the revival of Chapter VIII provision, UN Secretaries-General were not advocating regionalism per se, but burden-sharing (Boutros Ghali 1992). The UN both lacked the necessary resources and the commitment of major states to act as a global security provider, creating vacuums that regional powers and institutions could fill (Weiss, Forsythe and Coate 2004, Price and Zacher 2004). Hence 'new' security regionalism must also be understood in terms of UN capacity, the disinterest of great powers in costly external interventions and maintaining their former alliance systems. It represented the further development of a self-help system for weaker states to cope with the new security environment. It also permitted stronger regional powers greater scope to set local agendas within a legitimate institutional framework.

The third wave of security regionalism was characterized by two main developments: the establishment or upgrading of security provision in existing institutions and the creation of new ones. Like the third, and not unrelated wave of democratization, there were few regions which did not participate. New institutions, like the ARF or CIS were formed in the Asia-Pacific region and in the former Soviet space. China entered into regional security arrangements for the first time, as a member of the ARF and the Shanghai Cooperation Organization (SCO) (see below). Major constitutional changes were introduced in a number of existing institutions, notably in Europe, the Americas and Africa, where additional protocols, treaties and conventions were signed relating to conflict prevention and management, human rights and democracy. Much has been written about the nature and purpose of this 'new' regionalist moment, and its varied and arguably novel dimensions (Soderbaum and Shaw 2003, Farrell, Hettne and Lagenhove 2005). However one regards it – and there is a case to be made for continuity as well as change – the quantitative evidence is noteworthy.

A brief glance at some of these institutions helps to illustrate this point. First, in Europe the EU's moves, since 1992, to develop a Common Foreign and Security Policy (CFSP) and then a European Security and Defence Policy (ESDP) have been well documented. If plans for an EU rapid reaction force have been delayed (Dinan 2005), forces from EU member states have been involved in a growing number of peace operations inside and outside Europe. The wider Europe has seen the development of the CSCE into the OSCE, following the Paris Summit of 1990, marking its move from a more informal conference to a formal organization, acquiring permanent institutions and operational capabilities. Comprising 56 member states it was, in 2011, the largest regional security organization in the world, (followed by the African Union) conducting over a dozen different peace operations and political missions (www.osce.org).

NATO has proved to be an extraordinarily resilient security institution (see Chapter 23, this volume). Overcoming early doubts about its post-Cold War rationale, it attracted new members and has engaged in 'out of area' operations from Kosovo to Afghanistan and Libya. Within the former Soviet bloc, there has been institution-building in the security area (CIS, CSTO, CACO) to fill gaps left by the demise of Cold War structures. East European and Baltic states have also looked west for association and membership of existing structures like the EU and NATO. Russia, like China, was party to the establishment of the SCO in 2001 (successor to the Shanghai Five), which has provided a forum where Central Asian states can engage with China and discuss issues of mutual concern (Allison 2004). In 2011 both Iran and Pakistan were aspiring to full membership. The lesser-known Economic Cooperation Organization (ECO), of which Iran and Turkey are key players, was expanded in 1992 to include Afghanistan and the six predominantly Muslim republics of the former USSR.

In the Asia Pacific, the creation, in 1994, of the ARF, a cross-regional association of 25 states including China, Russia, Japan, the EU and the USA, gave substance to ideas of a broader multilateral security forum in Asia. ASEAN, with the admission of Cambodia in 1999, includes all Southeast Asian countries, no small feat considering the severity of earlier regional rivalries. Wider regional fora like APEC and the ASEAN+3 framework have been slow to develop any significant security capacity though the wider East Asia region is proving, like others, to be increasingly active in the multilateral arena (Prantl forthcoming).

Important changes, often underrated, have taken place in African institutions. In its 1991 summit the OAU made regional integration a priority and established mechanisms for conflict management. During the 1990s, ECOWAS, SADC, IGAD and CEMAC underwent major restructuring, assuming greater politico-security roles including peacekeeping. Finally, in the Constitutive Act of the African Union (AU) the framework was laid for an African Parliament, Court of Justice, Peer Review Mechanism and African Standby Force, providing the pillars for a potentially far more robust pan-regional institution.

Latin America has also seen important new institutional developments. Mercosur was set up in 1991; initially as a trade agreement, but one which expanded by 1998 to include commitments to regional democracy and wider security cooperation. The OAS Santiago Declaration (June 1991) also made the link between democracy and security; followed up by the Interamerican Democratic Charter in 2001. CARICOM in 2001 established a Regional Task Force on Crime and Security to address the security issues arising from illicit drugs, arms and money laundering. NAFTA currently lacks any tripartite security mechanism, though from a community perspective it has been instrumental in consolidating Mexican democracy. Security, though, given border and illicit trafficking concerns, is an inescapable feature of US–Mexico relations. UNASUR, founded in 2008, is the most recent institutional addition to the Americas with an explicit emphasis on South American unity and security.

## Contemporary challenges

Regional institutions have grown in number, expanded their roles and membership, and gained increased international recognition. The next section discusses two core areas of activity: peace operations and the coordination of anti-terrorism and WMD policies. These by no means exhaust the different types of security activities undertaken by institutions since the Cold War, but provide some useful indicators of their roles and effectiveness.

### Peace operations

Regional actors, not always formal regional institutions, have been active in a variety of solo and combined peace operations since the 1990s, many in conjunction with the UN (Weiss 1998). This is in contrast to the Cold War where regional organizations played relatively minor roles. In 2010 of a total of some 40 peacekeeping operations nearly half were conducted by regional organizations. Of some 50 political (civilian) missions, again just under half were carried out by regional organizations. The range of these operations is wide: from enforcement missions, like those of NATO in Afghanistan, or more recently Libya, to election monitoring or institution-building, like those of the EU or OSCE in Bosnia-Herzegovina.

The demand for peace operations and the fact that the UN is not always the 'mediator of choice' (Hampson 2004) have encouraged regional organizations to take on more roles in this area. In the expanding field of multilateralism, regional actors are becoming much more significant players.

From the involvement of an offshoot group of ECOWAS in Liberia's civil war in 1990 which led to a joint UN peacekeeping operation in 1993 (UNOMIL), there has been steady and growing involvement of regional organizations in different aspects of peacekeeping in Africa. Peace operations have been undertaken in Burundi, the Comoros, Côte d'Ivoire, Central African Republic, DR Congo, Guinea-Bissau, Lesotho, Sierra Leone, Somalia, and Sudan, under the auspices of ECOWAS, SADC CEMAC and the AU.

The same is true of the wider Europe. Since the early 1990s the UN and European groups like the EU, OSCE, CIS and NATO have been involved in numerous peace operations in the Yugoslav and Soviet successor states. Such groups were brought together in Bosnia in the 1995 Dayton Accord, and in 1999 in Kosovo, where NATO was the major security provider, with the OSCE and EU working in the areas of democratization, institution-building and economic reconstruction. In Georgia a UN mission works with the OSCE and CIS; the latter has also been involved in operations in Moldova and Tajikistan.

Outside Europe, EU forces have been engaged in monitoring missions in Indonesia and peace support operations in the DR Congo and Chad. Under a UN mandate, NATO took over the coordination of the International Security Assistance Force in Afghanistan in 2003, its first mission outside the Euro-Atlantic area. In the Americas, an OAS mission has supported democratic governments in Haiti, and since 2004, in Colombia, the organization has been involved in monitoring the demobilization of paramilitary groups in the country's civil conflict. The Pacific Islands Forum in 2003 authorized the sending of a Regional Assistance Mission to the Solomon Islands to restore order following inter-communal violence in the late 1990s.

In South Asia and the Middle East there has been relatively little action by local security institutions. In the former, SAARC is a highly unequal organization and lacks a shared ideology or perception of threat. The latter, in contrast, has seen LAS efforts to mediate during the Lebanese crisis in 2006 and broad support for a Saudi-sponsored peace initiative in the Israel–Palestine conflict. The ICO has yet to take on a major peacekeeping role in this or other regions though it has provided observers and monitoring missions to Islamic countries in conflict. The EU, however, launched a police mission in Palestine in 2006 and has been the major supplier of aid to the Palestinian Authority. And following events in the Arab Spring of early 2011, it was a European initiative that led to multilateral intervention in Libya. Though neither the League of Arab States, nor the Gulf Cooperation Council was directly involved in the subsequent intervention, their support was critical for the UN Security Council resolution that authorized it. Future developments in the region are likely to depend increasingly on regional stakeholders and institutions.

Overall, despite a short-term decline in the numbers of regional peacekeepers and operations in 2006–2007 (CIC 2007) there has been a new phase of growth driven by the start-up of missions in Africa and parts of Central Asia and the expansion and reinforcement of NATO and EU operations in Afghanistan and the DR Congo respectively. With the AU's operation in Darfur, Sudan (2004–2007), and a new AU mission in Somalia (2007–present) the role of regional institutions in ever more complex peace operations looked set to continue. This situation is partly the result of incremental growth, development and learning of institutions in the post-Cold War period. It also reflects the severity of regional security concerns and the absence of other security providers, generating a high demand for regional action. Core regional states, aware of the opportunities of shaping regional security policy, have been increasingly willing to provide leadership.

As in the past, doubts have been expressed about the growth of security regionalism, both inside the UN and in the wider policy-making community (Job 2004). Issues of legitimacy and impartiality, as well as that of primacy in the relationship between the UN and regional actors have been highlighted. In the latter case the problem has been that regional organizations have conducted operations without prior authorization of the UN Security Council – the ECOMOG operation in Liberia and NATO in Kosovo are two examples. Questions have also been asked about the tendency of strong regional powers to impose their own security agendas without sufficient regard to fellow members: Russia in the CIS, Nigeria in ECOWAS, Australia in the PIF, or the US in NATO are some examples. Nevertheless, given the present international environment and the limited capacity of older multilateral frameworks like the UN, the search for 'regional solutions to regional problems' and tendency for regional institutions to play more active multilateral roles looks set to continue.

## Terrorism and WMD

Terrorism and WMD proliferation are not new but they have been classed as core security threats by dominant states and thus captured the centre of the security debate, demanding appropriate institutional responses. This has posed new challenges to security institutions, already in the process of readjustment after the Cold War.

A number of established regional institutions – NATO, the OAS, Mercosur, the OAU and the EU for example – already had anti-terrorist provision in place. Regions are arguably well positioned to react to, monitor and deter terrorist activity, and most regional organizations have responded to events since 9/11, by incorporating new institutional mechanisms. The OAS and Mercosur have strengthened their existing arrangements: the Inter-American Committee Against Terrorism and Terrorism Working Group respectively, both in place since the 1990s (Oelsner 2009). The AU has adopted an additional protocol on the prevention and combating of terrorism. The founding document of the SCO, singled out terrorism, separatism and extremism as 'three evils' to confront, reflecting concerns of members like Russia and China. Through the establishment of a Regional Anti-Terrorist Structure (RATS), based in Tashkent, it has continued to develop its capacity in this area. NATO has endorsed a new Concept for Defence against Terrorism; finally the EU in 2004 appointed a Counter-Terrorism Coordinator and in 2005 adopted a broader Counter-Terrorism Strategy.

The potential for regional organizations to act in this area is highlighted by the difficulties faced by the UN in articulating a common position. Once again, however, the results vary. There is less of a tension between the UN and regional organizations in respect of anti-terror operations, yet it remains to be seen how far states will entrust such core security concerns to international institutions. NATO and the EU are both illustrative of how individual state capabilities are not matched at the appropriate institutional level (Keohane 2008). For developing country organizations, regardless of their capacity, the securitization of terrorism could also be seen as distracting attention from other more pressing regional security and development goals. It is a reminder of how key system players (the US and the EU for example) can still dominate and constrain security options worldwide.

The issues regarding WMD are similar in some ways, though this has long been the domain of multilateral action and treaties, less of regional agencies. Many regional institutions today publicize commitments to non-proliferation and uphold the enforcement of existing multilateral treaty regimes. The EU, since 2003, has had in place an anti-proliferation policy to strengthen and universalize the existing multilateral system, and sustain a non-proliferation regime, though two EU states are themselves nuclear powers (European Security Strategy 2003). It has sponsored the EU-3 process which has sought to engage Iran on the issue of nuclear proliferation.

ASEAN, South Pacific and Latin American states support nuclear-free zones through long-standing treaties. Twenty-four Latin American countries in 1967 signed the Latin American Nuclear Free Zone Treaty at Tlatelolco. ASEAN's summit in 1995 saw the signature of the Treaty on Southeast Asian Nuclear Weapon-Free Zone (SEANWFZ). The Pelindaba Treaty establishing a nuclear-free zone among African states came into effect in 2009. While there are rational arguments supporting such cooperation for the regions in question, one must ask what role in enforcing these regimes has been played by external actors (like the US or China for example), and whether or not regional regimes could ever be fully effective in restraining the ambitions of an aspiring nuclear state.

Though the issue of WMD, like terrorism, could represent a new growth area with great possibilities for security cooperation, evidence shows that in this high politics arena, security matters are still more likely to be handled outside regional frameworks – by the P-5, strong regional powers and existing multilateral frameworks.

## Assessing the growth of regional security institutions

Regional security is an area in which explanations for cooperation diverge widely, with realists predicting only low levels of cooperation, and liberals more optimistic given the possibilities of shared transaction costs, common culture and understanding that can all facilitate functional cooperation.

The empirical record examined here suggests that security cooperation has been achieved across a wide range of issues, and regional institutions have generated more orderly relationships between states. Three features of this process stand out. First, a major driver of regionalism in security affairs has been changes in the international system, with states responding to shifts in the global and regional balances of power. This is illustrated by considering the timing and content of three main waves of security regionalism. All were responses to the new balance of power in the international system with institutions designed to enhance and consolidate the position of both strong and weak states. Cooperation was a means of increasing security, but also influence and bargaining power. Although middle or rising powers have become more autonomous since the Cold War, the latest developments in the third wave, post-9/11, also show how regional organizations, in adapting to recent threats like terrorism, are still responding to the security imperatives of the dominant global powers. On the other hand the new assertiveness of regional actors across a wider range of issues also suggests how the security environment itself is changing and more players can have a stake in multilateral security management.

Second, states and other actors evidently attach value to regional institutions. If explanations of power-balancing are useful in explaining the start-up and changing functions of institutions, they are only part of the story. Institutions are not mere epiphenomena. They have survived and developed new functions, adjusting to changing conditions, including regime change and state type. In providing more predictable bases for cooperation and negotiation in an interdependent world, they have become useful tools of diplomacy and statecraft. These changes are, in part, the result of an incremental growth in functions and ideas about cooperation, a process of learning and dialogue, but also new institutions or charters for new purposes in a changing world order. Neither ECOWAS nor SADCC had succeeded as economic or development institutions before they developed a security profile. They responded to new challenges. The same is partly true of Europe. If security spill-over has occurred, this development has much to do with local threats, and the desire of the EU to reposition itself as a great power and counterbalance the US.

Third, regional institutions draw upon and foster common identity that influences their capacity to cooperate (Barnett 1998). As constructivists argue, they have also become recognized as repositories and factories of norms (Duffield 2006). The notion of a European, Asian or African style of crisis management is of increasing significance in a more multipolar world in which concepts of security and society are contested. Both the language and form that regionalism takes reflect the identity and culture of states: regional institutions and regional security are therefore what states make of them. Yet it is also important to remember that states seek achievable security against external threats. While identity is important, regions also need to project their power and influence, and attend to their own security concerns in a way that preserves regional autonomy and order. The pro-sovereignty norm in ASEAN; the non-intervention tradition in the Americas; and the expansion of AU instruments are all about self-help and awareness of the benefits and limits of collective action. Regional institutions are therefore best seen as vehicles for coping with a security predicament, for alleviating state weakness in a competitive international environment (Ayoob 1995). Here, it is worth recalling the influential 'Responsibility to Protect' idea, which highlights the salience of security regionalism: 'Those states which can call upon *strong regional alliances*, internal peace and a strong and independent civil society seem best placed to benefit from globalization' (ICISS 2001: 7, italics added).

## Conclusion

This chapter has argued that useful distinctions can be made between regionalism under bipolarity, unipolarity and multipolarity. In all cases regionalism in security affairs must be understood as a response to the dominant security order – whether through balancing or bandwagoning behaviour. The way in which the functions of regional organizations, and their memberships, have shifted in line with dominant security trends supports this. Regional institutions also provide useful normative frameworks, conditioning members' behaviour and signalling to outsiders. Yet the propensity of institutions to switch roles in response to systemic changes suggests also the close correlation between material interests and collective behaviour. On the other hand, their survival and maintenance indicate that states value institutions and are willing to bear their costs even during periods of uncertainty and failure. The low institutional death rate and revival or expansion of previously dormant institutions demonstrates this.

Under multipolarity the trend towards further regional conflict management and increasingly sophisticated regional provision is set to continue. The UN, as highlighted in the *2005 World Summit Outcome* document, is likely to encourage rather than supplant the roles of regional organizations in the near future. The consequences of the over-extension of US power seen in Iraq, Afghanistan and elsewhere, demonstrate the demand for alternative sources of action. Declining unipolarity and the rise of new powers have promoted a more multipolar order, one in which multilateralism is a new, more competitive space in which regional capabilities and identities will be important. Security is undergoing a process of regionalization, producing changes in the old multilateral system. Strong states will find increasingly useful roles for regional institutions, and weak states will be pulled into their orbit.

## Further reading

Paul F. Diehl and Joseph Lepgold (eds.), *Regional Conflict Management* (Rowman and Littlefield, 2003). A useful survey of different regional approaches to conflict management from around the world.

David Lake and Patrick Morgan (eds.), *Regional Orders. Building Security in a New World* (Pennsylvania State University Press, 1997). One of the earlier attempts to theorize about regional security institutions illustrated with some case studies from around the globe.

Richard Price and Mark Zacher (eds.), *The United Nations and Global Security* (Palgrave, 2004). An excellent survey of how the UN has attempted to tackle a variety of security challenges.

Chester A. Crocker, Fen Osler Hampson and Pamela Aall (eds.) *Rewiring Regional Security in a Fragmented World* (US Institute of Peace Press, 2011). A comprehensive overview of how regional arrangements around the world engage in conflict management issues.

Centre for International Cooperation, *Annual Review of Global Peace Operations* (Lynne Reinner, annual since 2006). An annual statistical review of peace operations (both UN and non-UN) with short analytical essays discussing particular themes and missions.

# The United Nations

Thomas G. Weiss and Danielle Zach

## Abstract

In this chapter, students will learn about the principal organs of the United Nations (UN) and their role in maintaining international peace and security – the world body's primary mandate. It provides an overview of the UN system as well as a short history of its contributions to security studies. It also addresses key threats confronting the globe in the early twenty-first century – such as terrorism, mass atrocities, and weapons of mass destruction – and assesses the UN's capacity to meet these security challenges.

## Introduction

The United Nations was conceived during the Second World War and born in June 1945. This second experiment in universal international organization followed the failed League of Nations that had emerged after the First World War – the so-called war to end all wars. The mass death and destruction, unconscionable atrocities and human suffering caused by a further round of great-power armed conflict prompted a further effort to institutionalize collective security. The UN embodies the latest attempt at international cooperation 'to save succeeding generations from the scourge of war'.

The world organization's hierarchy of functions and tasks is reflected in the principles and values of the UN Charter – the world organization's 'constitution' (Simma 2002). The Preamble expresses the main purpose, the maintenance of international peace and security, and to that end it outlawed the use of force except in self-defence or with express authorization from the Security Council. Indeed, such other main tasks as ensuring respect for human rights and promoting economic development were seen more as instrumental to the primary security function rather than as crucial in themselves. The Charter's foundation is state sovereignty – the sanctity of a state's monopoly on the use of force and authority over a population within defined territorial borders. As Article 2(7) clearly states, 'Nothing contained in the present Charter shall authorize the United Nations to intervene in matters which are essentially within the domestic jurisdiction of any state'.

While the UN's founders had high hopes that the world body would play a central role in managing the majority of the globe's security affairs, the onset of the US–Soviet rivalry quickly dashed such aspirations. Other than buffer forces and observers, or 'peacekeepers', the UN's security machinery was essentially marginalized for most of the Cold War. It was not until the Iron Curtain fell and later the Soviet Union imploded that the UN assumed a substantial role in international peace and security.

At the beginning of the twenty-first century, the UN comprises nearly every country on the planet. To be precise, 193 states are members, a nearly fourfold increase from the original 51 in 1945. The organization's global legitimacy constitutes one of its fundamental strengths.

When discussing the past, present and future of the United Nations, it is crucial to distinguish between the three facets of the UN: the inter-governmental institution (the 'first UN'), the administrative entity (the 'second UN'), and the collection of nonstate actors that routinely engage the world body (the 'third UN') (Kennedy 2006, Weiss and Daws 2007, Weiss *et al.* 2010). The first UN is an arena for state decision-making and negotiation. Member states constitute the world organization and fund its activities. Although actors other than states are increasingly involved in security issues (as part of the problem and the solution), states remain the dominant actors in the realm of international peace and security.

The second UN comprises career and long-serving staff members serving in myriad departments, agencies, programmes and commissions. The Secretariat, headed by the Secretary-General, is the core of the administrative apparatus. The lack of commitment, resources and political will among member states often inhibits the international civil service's ability to effect change. The second UN nonetheless wields considerable moral force and has some autonomy and marked achievements.

By contrast, the third UN comprises NGOs, academics, experts, consultants and independent panels that are not formally part of the world body but are regularly involved in its various activities and influence the first and second UNs. Their contribution to international peace and security is much less pronounced than in other areas of the UN's work such as development. They have, however, made contributions on lobbying for innovations on such issues as international criminal justice and the ban on landmines.

This chapter begins by discussing the Security Council before examining the General Assembly and the Secretariat and its Secretary-General. In relationship to security studies, these are the three most relevant of the UN's six principal organs. The Economic and Social Council (ECOSOC), the International Court of Justice (ICJ) and the Trusteeship Council are treated only briefly as are other relevant parts of the UN system, or the 'extended family'. An analysis follows of contemporary security threats – including failed states, terrorism, nuclear proliferation and genocide – and the UN's capacity to grapple effectively with these grave challenges to international peace and security. To facilitate understanding of the UN's complex web of relationships and acronyms, an organizational diagram is given in Figure 25.1.

At the outset, it is important to circumscribe the term 'security' given considerable debate, in this book and elsewhere (MacFarlane and Khong 2006), about the distinction between the more traditional notion of military security from threats external to the state and the more comprehensive notion of human security that uses individuals as the metric. The latter usage connotes a broad range of issues affecting human well-being – including development and sustainability – but is not the focus here, which is the UN's effort to address immediate and violent threats to human life.

## The Security Council

The preeminent UN organ with responsibility for maintaining international order, as stated in Charter Article 24(1), is the Security Council. Unlike its defunct predecessor the League of Nations, the UN was designed to have military 'teeth' to ensure compliance with its decisions about security (Bailey and Daws 1998, Malone 2004, Luck 2011). This section details the council's composition and powers; the post-Cold War expansion of tasks; the impact of US hegemony; and the increased access of nonstate actors.

### Composition

Unlike the General Assembly, which includes all member states, the Security Council is an exclusive forum. The victors of the Second World War have always comprised the five permanent members (P-5): China, France, Russia (formerly the Soviet Union), the United Kingdom and the United States. In addition to not needing to be elected (i.e. occupying permanent seats), they can also veto any resolution. This special status was a tactical compromise to circumvent the pitfalls of the League of Nations – to ensure great-power

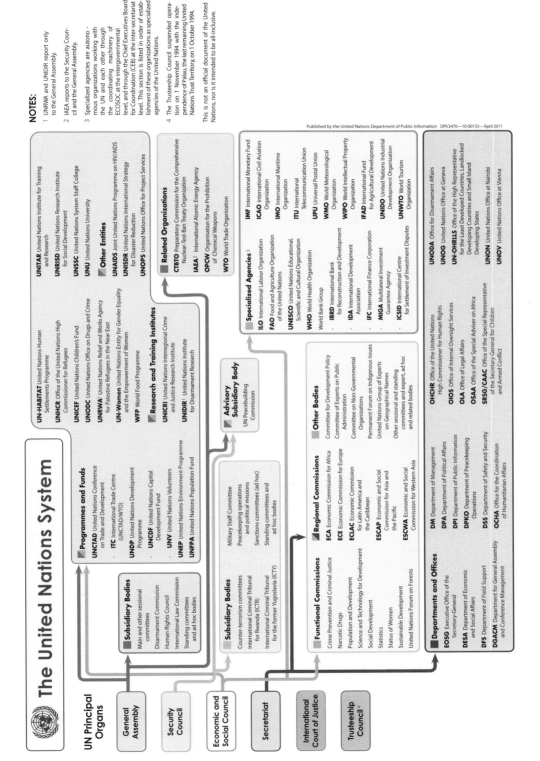

*Figure 25.1* The United Nations System

Published by the United Nations Department of Public Information   DPI/2470—10-00133—April 2011

**NOTES:**

1  UNRWA and UNIDIR report only to the General Assembly.

2  IAEA reports to the Security Council and the General Assembly.

3  Specialized agencies are autonomous organizations working with the UN and each other through the coordinating machinery of ECOSOC at the intergovernmental level, and through the Chief Executives Board for Coordination (CEB) at the inter-secretariat level. This section is listed in order of establishment of these organizations as specialized agencies of the United Nations.

4  The Trusteeship Council suspended operation on 1 November 1994 with the independence of Palau, the last remaining United Nations Trust Territory, on 1 October 1994.

This is not an official document of the United Nations, nor is it intended to be all-inclusive.

cooperation and to avoid making matters worse by launching war against a major power. The Security Council now also includes ten rotating members (there were six from 1945 to 1965) that are elected for two-year, non-renewable terms and cannot veto decisions.

Given the fundamental changes in world politics over the past six-and-a-half decades, it is no surprise that the council's permanent membership does not mirror the contemporary distribution of power, globally or regionally. While defeated and occupied in 1945, Germany and Japan are now world heavyweights – the second and third largest financial contributors to the UN's regular budget after the United States – but do not have a commensurate voice in the Security Council. Neither do such regional powers as Brazil, India, Nigeria, Egypt and South Africa. Over the years, the council's anachronistic composition and veto privileges have been heatedly debated and targeted for reform. Given the political impossibility of garnering consensus on proposed reforms, however, such efforts have been futile – as the outcome of the 2005 World Summit vividly illustrates (Weiss 2005).

### Powers

The Security Council's specific powers are codified in Chapters VI–VIII of the Charter. Chapter VI, 'Pacific Settlement of Disputes', invests the council with the authority to call disputing parties to resolve their conflict through peaceful means such as fact-finding, good offices, negotiation, arbitration and judicial settlement. It further grants the council the right to investigate disputes that might endanger international peace and security and to recommend terms of settlement.

By contrast, decisions under Chapter VII – 'Action with Respect to Threats to the Peace, Breaches of the Peace, and Acts of Aggression' – are compulsory rather than voluntary. Unlike the League of Nations, which had no such powers, Chapter VII endows the Security Council with coercive authority – that is, it can compel compliance through decisions binding on member states and not merely proffer pious recommendations. In response to what the council deems a threat to international peace and security, it may impose diplomatic and economic sanctions on belligerents or even authorize military force. Article 43 envisaged that members would enter into special agreements with the UN to make available armed forces, assistance and facilities on call; and Article 46 called for the creation of a powerful overseer, the Military Staff Committee. Neither has materialized. Military forces are assembled on a case-by-case basis.

Chapter VIII, 'Regional Arrangements', encourages such organizations to engage in peaceful dispute settlement before involving the Security Council and requires that they seek the council's authorization before undertaking coercive action. It also grants the council the power to delegate enforcement to regional bodies, which the UN has increasingly done over the past two decades to compensate for its own lack of military wherewithal.

## The Security Council's task expansion

Excessive veto use, mostly by the Soviet Union for the first half of the Cold War and the United States for the second, stymied the Security Council. However, the UN was able to carve out a role in security matters through the invention of so-called peacekeeping operations (see Chapter 26, this volume). These were dubbed 'Chapter VI and a half' operations because such measures were not explicitly mentioned in the Charter, but they fall somewhere between Chapters VI and VII. Consisting of civilians and borrowed soldiers and police from member states under the command of the United Nations, the goal of such operations is to help keep a lid on conflicts by monitoring ceasefires, interpositioning troops between belligerent forces and maintaining disengagement zones. UN peacekeepers are also known as 'blue berets' or 'blue helmets' because of their distinctive headgear (such soldiers otherwise wear national uniforms). They are deployed with the consent of warring parties and do not use force except in self-defence.

Between 1948 and 1988, the Security Council approved 13 operations. Over that four-decade period, the UN deployed some 500,000 peacekeeping personnel to places as far-flung as West New Guinea, Cyprus, India and Pakistan, Israel, Egypt, Syria, Lebanon and the Dominican Republic. While not all operations were successful, blue berets were crucial to sustaining peace in many places, and in 1988 they received the Nobel Peace Prize.

By contrast, the Security Council invoked Chapter VII a mere five times in that same period. Twice it authorized the use of force: in 1950 on the Korean peninsula in defence of the south against the communist north – only possible because the Soviet Union had boycotted the council; and in 1960 in newly independent Congo – an outpost where major powers had few strategic interests. Once it invoked Chapter VII to impose a ceasefire between Israel and its Arab neighbours and twice to impose sanctions – against Rhodesia and South Africa – motivated largely by human rights violations by white-minority regimes. The latter two cases may be seen as a precursor to the council's intimate linkage of human rights with international peace and security in the post-Cold War era.

The end of the East–West rivalry made cooperation among the P-5 more feasible, thus revitalizing the Security Council as the guardian of world peace. Several new operations began in 'flashpoints' of the East–West struggle (Afghanistan, Cambodia, Angola, Namibia, El Salvador and Nicaragua), but the real breakthrough came from the invocation of Chapter VII authorizing military force to roll back Iraqi aggression against Kuwait in 1990. The dramatic decline in vetoes is also illustrative of changes in council dynamics in the new era: between 1946 and 1986 the veto was wielded 212 times, as compared to 44 times between 1987 and 2008. The number of resolutions also doubled in half the time, 593 in 40 years versus 1,010 in the next 20.

What became known as 'second-generation' peacekeeping included electoral assistance, human rights monitoring, and even weapons collection, activities once seen as within the domestic jurisdiction of states. However, these operations were still based on the principle of consent, and peacekeepers remained bound by restrictions on the use of force.

The 1990s witnessed a radical shift in the nature of UN operations, from peacekeeping to peace enforcement, as well as an ever-widening scope for what the council judged to be a 'threat to international peace and security' (the basis for decisions; see also Chapter 26, this volume). Breaking new ground, the council called interference with humanitarian action and violence against civilians 'threats to international peace and security'; it authorized military operations to such war-torn places as Bosnia, Somalia, Rwanda, Kosovo and the Democratic Republic of the Congo (DRC). In Haiti, the council even determined that the overthrow of a democratically elected president and accompanying instability were a threat to the peace. In contrast to earlier peacekeeping, these new operations were authorized under Chapter VII and thus were coercive rather than consensual.

After Kosovo in 1999 – other than a small British deployment in Sierra Leone in 2000 and a smaller essentially French one in eastern Congo in 2003 – there was no substantial multinational military effort. The post-11 September nadir in coercive protection lasted until Security Council resolution 1973 of March 2011, which authorized 'all necessary measures' against Libya to protect civilians. That same month, the UN Security Council authorized the 'use of all necessary means' to carry out its mandate to protect civilians in Côte d'Ivoire. However, UN soldiers on the ground did little until action led by the 1,700-strong French Licorne force.

While the top three financial contributors to UN peace operations were the United States, Japan and the United Kingdom, according to 2010 published statistics the top troop-contributing countries to UN missions were Pakistan, Bangladesh, India, Nigeria and Egypt. The majority of UN military personnel come from two regions: Central and South Asia (36.7 per cent) and Africa (33.8 per cent) (CIC 2010). Lacking its own capacity to deploy military operations, however, the world body often authorizes coalitions of the willing or regional bodies – such as the African Union, Economic Community of West African States and the North Atlantic Treaty Organization (NATO) – to assume command of such missions. At the end of 2009, NATO alone had 84,000 peacekeepers in the field, accounting for 88 per cent of military personnel in non-UN-led missions (CIC 2010). Extending beyond any traditional interpretation of Chapter VII, the world body has even assumed what some see as 'neocolonial' administrative and coercive responsibilities of a state, as in post-conflict East Timor and Kosovo. European organizations have been especially helpful partners in the UN Interim Administration Mission in Kosovo.

In addition to the use of military force, the Security Council has increasingly relied on two other coercive measures – economic sanctions and international criminal prosecution. Indeed, in the post-Cold War period, the council imposed dozens of sanctions, including against such nonstate actors as the Union for the Total Independence of Angola and al-Qa'ida. First levied in this period against Saddam Hussein's Iraq in 1990, blanket trade sanctions were at the centre of controversy due to their devastating humanitarian impact. In response, the council began applying only targeted sanctions via arms embargoes, financial asset freezes, travel bans and commodity boycotts (Cortright and Lopez 2000).

International criminal tribunals were another invention. In the wake of genocide and other crimes against humanity in the former Yugoslavia and Rwanda, the council established judicial bodies to try those responsible for heinous acts in the conduct of war. These tribunals have had mixed results. After fifteen years, neither has completed their cases, while many of the key perpetrators remain free. In addition to criticisms about effectiveness and costs, some have questioned whether they actually inhibit peacebuilding and national reconciliation. Nonetheless, the war crimes tribunals have contributed to the development of international criminal law – for example, that rape can be a form of genocide – as well as the 1998 creation of the International Criminal Court and other judicial efforts in East Timor, Cambodia and Sierra Leone. The pace and the cost of such prosecutions – as of mid-2011, the ICC had as yet to pronounce a decision on any of the persons indicted – make this coercive measure appear pale in comparison with military force.

In sum, an increasingly active council in the post-Cold War era was willing to consider massive human rights abuses, forced displacement, purposeful starvation, and even the overthrow of an elected government as threats to international peace and security. In January 2000, the HIV/AIDS pandemic was identified as a threat to international peace and security (see Chapter 22, this volume), and in April 2007 the council debated whether climate change constituted such a menace (see Chapter 21, this volume).

The definition of what is 'essentially within the domestic jurisdiction' of states is changing, and the principle of state sovereignty along with it. This was evident at the 2005 World Summit, when some 150 heads of state and government endorsed the 'responsibility to protect' (R2P), which re-frames sovereignty as contingent rather than absolute (see Chapter 32, this volume). If a state is manifestly unwilling or unable to protect its people from ethnic cleansing or mass killing, it forfeits its sovereignty; and the responsibility for protecting citizens falls on the international community of states. In 2006, the Security Council endorsed R2P in resolution 1674 regarding the protection of civilians in armed conflict. It applied the doctrine in early 2011 by calling upon Libya to protect its civilian population and then authorizing a no-fly zone by a coalition of the willing when it failed to do so.

## US hegemony

The end of the Cold War facilitated Security Council action, but the switch from a bipolar to a unipolar world left the United States unchallenged as the remaining superpower. With military expenditures equal to the rest of the world combined, Washington's approval, or at least acquiescence, is essential to political as well as operational functioning of the world body in the security arena.

The reality of asymmetric US power is that even a diminished hegemon may choose to 'go it alone', which generates legitimacy crises for the United Nations. The US-led invasion of Iraq in 2003 without council approval, and in the face of worldwide opposition, is a vivid illustration. Finessing the council in the Iraq case, however, should be seen in historical context. The United States has vacillated between multilateral and unilateral urges not merely since 1945 but since the Senate refused to join the League of Nations, the brainchild of US president Woodrow Wilson (Luck 1999). Addressing a number of priority security threats (including terrorism and nuclear proliferation) would seem, by definition, to require multilateral cooperation even for a superpower. This was clearly the position of the Barack Obama administration in early 2011, as articulated by UN ambassador Susan Rice, who asserted that it would be not only 'immoral' but 'dangerous' to be indifferent to cross-border problems and thus 'short-sighted' to hold back funds for the UN given its huge responsibilities in peacekeeping and other areas.

## Increased access by actors other than states

While states remain the gatekeepers of international peace and security, NGOs and other actors have become more visible and numerous in the post-Cold War era, and the Security Council has responded by providing them with more access. In contrast to ECOSOC, which through Charter Article 71 can grant NGOs consultative status – thereby allowing these groups to attend meetings and even make statements and propose agenda items – no equivalent arrangement exists between such groups and the Security Council. Thus, while civil society organizations were for decades engaged in UN activities, their official participation until recently was limited to matters pertaining to development, human rights, humanitarianism and environment.

The council's expanded definition of threats to international order to include human rights violations and humanitarian disasters opened up avenues for NGOs to have a voice in security matters. The council in the early 1990s initiated greater dialogue between states and nonstate actors. The so-called Arria formula (named after the Venezuelan ambassador who launched the experiment during his presidency) has become a standard procedure, and humanitarian and human rights organizations have been able to offer country and issue-specific knowledge, practical expertise and information about on-the-ground developments.

In the early post-Cold War period, council presidents also began briefing the media, thereby drawing public attention to the body's negotiations and decisions. Celebrities have contributed to enhancing the council's visibility, as they have used their status to cast a spotlight on issues such as humanitarian crises and the plight of women and children in armed conflict. They have even made statements before the Security Council, urging members to halt atrocities in war-torn countries.

# The General Assembly

The General Assembly is a more inclusive arena for deliberations by states than the Security Council. Indeed, each UN member state has equal status in the body and one vote – concrete evidence of the 'sovereign equality of all its Members' called for in Article 2(1). Unlike the Security Council which can make binding decisions, however, the General Assembly's resolutions are always 'recommendations'. They are adopted by a simple majority, except for those identified as concerning 'important questions', which require two-thirds of the members present and voting. According to Article 18, these include 'recommendations with respect to the maintenance of international peace and security [and] the election of the non-permanent members of the Security Council'.

Charter Articles 11–12 grant the General Assembly the ability to discuss such issues and make recommendations to states and to the council, but not while a dispute or situation is being considered by the Security Council. In practice, the assembly has considered conflicts regardless.

When the council is unable to act due to actual or threatened vetoes, the General Assembly has served as an alternative avenue for addressing security issues. Resolution 377(V), titled 'Uniting for Peace' (UfP), was a watershed. It created a parallel authority in the assembly by establishing:

> procedures by which a simple majority of the Security Council on a procedural vote (not subject to veto) or a majority of UN member states can convene the Assembly in 'emergency special session' on twenty-four hours' notice to consider and develop collective responses to a crisis when the Security Council has been unable to act.
>
> (Peterson 2007: 104)

While the assembly cannot make binding decisions, through UfP it can endorse coercive actions. Adopted in 1950, it was a means to allow what many saw as 'blue-washed' US military action in Korea – originally authorized under Chapter VII – to continue despite the Soviet Union's return to the council after an earlier boycott due to Taiwan's occupancy of the 'Chinese seat'. Over the years, this procedure has been used sporadically (ten instances to be exact), the last time being against Israel in 1997 for its policies in the occupied territories.

Since decolonization, the so-called global South (what formerly was called the 'Third World') constitutes a strong majority in the General Assembly. Thus, smaller and weaker member states – and even middle powers when not elected to the council – prefer the democratic assembly in which they have a role in security matters. In particular, the Non-Aligned Movement (NAM)

– the 115 developing countries that form a bloc – has staunchly defended self-determination, sovereignty and nonintervention, which are linked to many Security Council deliberations. Moreover, Third World resistance to white-minority rule in Rhodesia and South Africa was important in mobilizing international action against those rogue regimes, which eventually led to action by the council. Similarly, the global South has consistently advocated in the assembly for the Palestinian cause in spite of council action (or inaction); over the past six decades, the assembly has passed a never-ending stream of resolutions concerning Israel and the occupied territories.

The General Assembly's endorsement of the responsibility to protect in 2005 contributed to the emergence of consensus around the norm as did its debate during its 'interactive dialogues' in 2009–2011, which resulted in a growing show of support for its implementation (see Chapter 32, this volume).

## The Secretariat

International civil servants comprise the UN's administrative apparatus, or Secretariat. At the helm is the Secretary-General, who is appointed by the assembly on the recommendation of the council. In reality, the P-5's veto power makes the selection process for the secretary-general into an exercise in geographic horse-trading (the position rotates from region to region, usually after two terms) in which the qualifications of the individual candidates are a secondary concern (Newman 1998, Gordenker 2010). Indeed, as Brian Urquhart has argued, efforts are made to select a candidate who 'will not exert any troubling degree of leadership, commitment, originality, or independence' (Urquhart 1987: 227–228). Charter Article 100, however, requires that the organization's top civil servant and other UN personnel perform their duties independent of governments, and it obliges member states 'not to seek to influence them in the discharge of their responsibilities'. In order to fulfil his (not yet her) mandate for security matters, it is essential that the Secretary-General does not incur the wrath of any of the P-5. The ill-fated first incumbent Trygve Lie – who resigned after Moscow's opposition to his conduct in Korea – once described the post as 'the most impossible job in the world' (Rivlin and Gordenker 1993) (see Box 25.1).

While the largest financial contributors to the world body often complain that the second UN is a sprawling bureaucracy, such criticisms are exaggerated. The UN Secretariat itself employs some 30,500 personnel to administer the affairs of the globe. If one considers the nine bodies of the UN proper that have special status in matters of appointment – the largest being the UN Children's Fund (UNICEF), UN Development Programme (UNDP), UN High Commissioner for Refugees (UNHCR) and World Food Programme (WFP) – the international civil service comprises about 56,000 staff worldwide. Similarly, the UN's regular budget is limited in light of the tasks that fall under the organization's purview. Although it has risen from $21.5 million in 1945 to $5.17 billion in 2010, when adjusted for inflation, the change is not nearly

---

## BOX 25.1 SECRETARIES-GENERAL OF THE UNITED NATIONS, 1946–2011

Trygve Lie (Norway) February 1946–April 1953

Dag Hammarskjöld (Sweden) April 1953–September 1961

U Thant (Burma, now Myanmar)* November 1961–December 1971

Kurt Waldheim (Austria) January 1972–December 1981

Javier Pérez de Cuéllar (Peru) January 1982–December 1991

Boutros Boutros-Ghali (Egypt) January 1992–December 1996

Kofi Annan (Ghana) January 1997–December 2006

Ban Ki-moon (Republic of Korea) January 2007–

*Note*: *Acting Secretary-General, November 1961–November 1962

---

as substantial (Myint-U and Scott 2007: 126–8). The regular budget certainly appears paltry when compared to annual US confectionary and alcohol expenditures – $27 billion and $70 billion, respectively.

For security studies, it is important to note that these figures do not include the world body's peacekeeping personnel and budget. In early 2011, the UN had nearly 100,000 troops, military observers and police engaged in 15 operations. Meanwhile the July 2010 to June 2011 peacekeeping budget reached an all-time high of $7.83 billion – about one month's expenditures by the United States during its rebuilding of Iraq in some years or less than half the annual operating budget of the New York City Board of Education. Despite the magnitude of operations, Department of Peacekeeping Operations (DPKO) staff represent about 5 per cent of total Secretariat personnel; and the Department of Political Affairs (DPA) has only about 250 employees. Together they have fewer employees than the Department of Public Information (Myint-U and Scott 2007: 127).

The Secretariat and the Secretary-General play crucial roles in security matters because they are charged with carrying out Security Council decisions. The organization's executive head routinely engages in preventive diplomacy, dispute mediation, negotiations and fact-finding, and is the person to whom UN-sponsored forces report. His authority derives from Charter Article 99, which grants him the power to call the Security Council's attention to 'any matter which in his opinion may threaten the maintenance of international peace and security'. Article 99 has been invoked on only three occasions – by Dag Hammarskjöld in 1960, in the wake of decolonization in the Congo; by Kurt Waldheim in 1979, in response to the Iranian hostage crisis; and by Javier Pérez de Cuéllar in 1989, during the escalation of armed conflict in Lebanon. Given the fruitlessness and potential embarrassment of invoking the article without P-5 support, secretaries-general have usually pursued 'quiet diplomacy', pressing their position with states behind the scenes.

Some have played more visible roles in enhancing the Secretariat in matters of international peace and security, partly because of their personalities but also the international political context during their tenures (Ramcharan 2008). Despite Cold War constraints, Lie managed to bolster his investigatory and conflict prevention responsibilities. Hammarskjöld was the intellectual force (along with Canadian minister Lester Pearson) behind the creation of Chapter VI peacekeeping operations. Under his direction, the first ever armed peace mission, the UN Emergency Force, was launched in 1956 in response to the Suez Canal crisis. Meanwhile, U Thant carved out a role for the Secretary-General as an independent mediator, while Pérez de Cuéllar – whose tenure extended into the post-Cold War period – enhanced the 38th floor's (the top floor of the UN's headquarters in Manhattan) capacity for fact-finding and observation, oversaw the initial expansion of peacekeeping, and helped quell turmoil in such Cold War flashpoints as Central America, Afghanistan, Cambodia and southern Africa. He was in office when UN peacekeepers were awarded the 1988 Nobel Peace Prize.

Boutros Boutros-Ghali, the sixth head of the world body, was one of the most influential in the security arena. His intellectual contribution was the forward-looking *An Agenda for Peace* – following the first ever meeting in his first month in office of the Security Council at the level of head of state and government – that 'still defines the conceptual framework through which (for better or worse) the UN thinks about its work in the political field, formalizing concepts such as peacebuilding, early warning, preventive deployment and peace enforcement' (Myint-U and Scott 2007: 94). He oversaw the development of more muscular peace missions and was responsible for pushing the council to action in Somalia – where the first enforcement mission under UN command and control was launched – and pushing for the first ever preventive deployment mission in Macedonia. He also reorganized the Secretariat, including the establishment of two crucial departments: the Department of Political Affairs – responsible for conflict prevention and political analysis – and the Department of Peacekeeping Operations – responsible for the operational dimensions of UN missions.

Secretary-General Kofi Annan, who received the Nobel Peace Prize in 2001, also left a considerable legacy. As under-secretary-general for peacekeeping operations in the 1990s, he had more direct experience with the practical dimensions of peace operations than his predecessors and devoted the bulk of his time to peacekeeping management rather than mediation and diplomacy. He also was the first Secretary-General to take a visible and public position on controversial human rights positions, including the responsibility to protect. He was intimately involved in the dramatic expansion in peace operations, taking a leading advocacy role in calling for humanitarian intervention and in overseeing the UN's quasi-state role in post-conflict Kosovo and East Timor (Annan 1999c). The widespread opposition to the US-led war in Iraq without Security Council approval, instances of peacekeepers' sexual exploitation of women and children, and the Oil-for-Food Programme scandal involving his son, however, clouded the end of Annan's second term.

In January 2007, Ban Ki-moon became the eighth Secretary-General and was re-elected to the post in June 2011. Unsurprisingly he stays out of the media spotlight in the exercise of his duties. He has, however, sought to advance the R2P agenda and created positions and a new office for the prevention of genocide and the responsibility to protect. Ban's form of 'invisible' diplomacy means that his use of the bully pulpit usually follows rather than precedes pronouncements by major powers and regional organizations.

## Other UN organs and actors

The three other principal organs – ECOSOC, the ICJ and the Trusteeship Council – are less central to understanding the UN's relevance for security studies. ECOSOC's purview spans economic, social, cultural, education and health as well as human rights. Charter Article 65 grants ECOSOC the power to 'furnish information' to the Security Council and requires it to assist the council upon request. Historically the link between these two bodies has been weak, even non-existent.

In the late 1990s, however, the Security Council sought to engage ECOSOC with a possible role in the UN's post-conflict peacebuilding. Resolution 1212 of November 1998 formally called upon ECOSOC to assist Haiti with a long-term sustainable development programme, and in response ECOSOC created an Ad Hoc Advisery Group to make recommendations and implement them. In collaboration with the Security Council, ECOSOC also created a working group on Guinea-Bissau. However, ECOSOC's ineffectiveness prompted the High-level Panel on Threats, Challenges and Change (2004) to recommend the creation of a new body. In late 2005 the Security Council and General Assembly approved similar resolutions calling for the creation of the Peacebuilding Commission to address coordination problems that often hamper efforts at building lasting peace. The initial five years of work by this commission indicates that it has helped add value in a number of countries where multiple inputs were required in the aftermath of conflict (Jenkins 2012).

The International Court of Justice may be considered as part of the world body's peaceful settlement of disputes machinery. However, disputing states must voluntarily consent to the court's jurisdiction, and decisions normally take years. Given that states generally consider peace and security matters too important to be settled by 15 jurists and too urgent to wait, the ICJ has not handed down decisions or opinions that have actually resolved armed conflicts. Even when such cases are brought before the court, moreover, compliance with the ICJ's ruling is not obligatory – as illustrated by the US's refusal to implement the judgment of *Nicaragua vs. the United States*.

The Trusteeship Council, the successor of the League of Nations Mandates system, was established to oversee the transition from foreign to self-rule in colonies, a topic linked to international peace and security. For decades it worked closely with the General Assembly and, in areas designated as 'strategic', the Security Council. The last remaining 'trust territory', Palau, became independent in 1994, and so this principal organ is now dormant. The 2005 World Summit agreed to eliminate the Trusteeship Council, but this would require a Charter amendment, hardly likely.

The UN's own funds and programmes – especially the largest humanitarian players the UNDP, UNICEF, the UNHCR and the WFP – are often present on the landscape in security crises and work side-by-side with UN soldiers. The specialized agencies depicted in Figure 25.1 are part of the UN system; but they are more peripheral to security studies for two reasons: they are not directly responsible to the UN Secretary-General, and their main activities are in economic and social development.

## Twenty-first century challenges

In the new millennium, the UN finds itself amidst a sea change in security affairs. While interstate disputes (its original justification) will always pose threats to international order, intrastate conflicts – often linked into elaborate arms, trade and drug trafficking networks – are widespread and constitute substantial threats to regional and even global stability. Alongside changes in warfare and the security problems posed by so-called failed states, the world organization confronts the intertwined threats of terrorism and weapons of mass destruction (WMDs).

### Changes in the nature of war and UN responses

The UN's mechanisms to prevent and confront armed conflict were conceived in the aftermath of two large-scale wars involving world powers. Since 1945, however, intrastate conflicts have become commonplace and lethal. One explanation is superpower rivalry, which fueled many conflicts during the Cold War. Its end, however, also meant that the abundant financial and military aid flowing from the United States and Soviet Union to their respective Third World clients dried up, given the diminished geostrategic significance of these allies on a fundamentally reconfigured international stage. Hence, the resources used to sustain fragile regimes through coercion and patronage led to turmoil in some parts of the global South and even state collapse, as in Somalia. The implosion of Yugoslavia and the Soviet Union, moreover, produced some 20 new countries, and the redrawing of territorial boundaries generated tensions within and between successor states. A second explanation for intrastate wars is globalization, particularly technological change and rapid economic interactions, which have made borders porous. Neoliberal structural adjustment policies similarly have curtailed resources for patronage, by requiring cuts in public sector employment, collective goods and subsidies.

Contemporary conflicts are thus waged and funded differently from most previous interstate wars. In contrast to hierarchically organized standing armies, a variety of actors participate directly in warfare – including such entities as criminal gangs and militias – via decentralized networks. Belligerents fight for control over territory and access to resources in the midst of civilian populations who are often the targets of violence rather than so-called collateral damage. While the numbers are disputed by some, in many recent wars civilians have constituted as much as 90 per cent of victims, a reversal from the beginning of the twentieth century when the ratio of military to civilian deaths typically was 9:1 and a change from the Second World War when similar numbers of civilians and soldiers died. Ethnic cleansing, forced displacement, mass rape, scorched earth campaigns, purposeful starvation and attacks on humanitarian aid workers are a standard bill-of-fare. These tactics are not 'new', but their coming together and intensity are more apparent than in the past (Kaldor 2007b), and this quantitative change is often sufficient enough to constitute a qualitative change.

The accompanying humanitarian emergencies adversely affect the security of neighbouring countries. Massive refugee populations are financially burdensome and menacing; and camps may serve as grounds for launching cross-border attacks – as illustrated by the concept of the 'refugee warrior'. In countries that already have precarious ethnic balances, the influx of particular groups may be destabilizing – a key concern, for instance, surrounding the influx of Kosovar Albanians into Macedonia in 1999.

Another source of instability arises from the economics of financing such violence. The war economies sustaining many civil wars reflect plunder, smuggling, drug trafficking and the sale of other illicit commodities. Those who benefit have an interest in continued violence not peace, especially because criminal trade networks operate globally. Failed states, moreover, can serve as havens for terrorists whose calculations are not based on cost–benefit analysis.

Peace enforcement operations were a key UN response to the actual and potential international instability emanating from war-torn societies (see also Chapter 26, this volume). As mentioned earlier, the UN has proved incapable of conducting large-scale military operations as illustrated by the failures to halt massive killings and displacement in Bosnia and Somalia. The United Nations has relied on coalitions of the willing and regional organizations – options that are not without their problems. With the exception of NATO and the European Union, regional bodies generally are ill-equipped militarily. In addition to operational issues, making use of subcontracted forces also raises questions of accountability. The involvement of regional heavyweights in neighbouring country conflicts can shift local balances of power and serve interests other than human protection. NAM rhetoric often emphasizes, for example, that humanitarian intervention may be veiled neocolonial tactics.

In places where valuable natural resources, such as diamonds, constitute the basis for sustaining war economies, the Security Council has imposed commodity embargoes on states as well as nonstate actors, and investigative panels have been created to monitor compliance. Here as elsewhere, however, noncompliance with council sanctions is a considerable obstacle to their effectiveness.

In addition to addressing conflicts once they erupt, the UN has attempted to focus on the phases before and after wars. Over the past decade, the world body has increasingly engaged in conflict prevention, particularly since the council's failure to respond to the Rwandan genocide. UN secretaries-general have been at the forefront of such efforts. Boutros-Ghali's seminal *An Agenda for Peace* emphasized the importance of preventive diplomacy, while Secretary-General Annan's *Prevention of Armed Conflict* pledged to 'move the United Nations from a culture of reaction to a culture of prevention' (Annan 2001: 1). Ban's *Implementing the Responsibility to Protect* also emphasized prevention among R2P's three pillars (Ban 2009).

A crucial component of conflict prevention entails tackling the so-called root causes of conflict, which have economic, social, environmental and institutional origins. Hence, structural prevention involves efforts to foster socioeconomic development and good governance. In a 2006 report, Annan expanded the concept to include 'systemic prevention', which aims to address international-level factors that enhance the risk of conflict such as the global illicit trade in small arms. Given the extensive scope, structural prevention is a nebulous concept that is hard to implement; it involves virtually every acronym in the UN system.

At the other end of the spectrum, post-conflict peacebuilding missions aim to assist countries to make the transition from violence to peace and prevent the recurrence of warfare. Core tasks include: weapons collection; elections monitoring; assistance with rebuilding governmental institutions; judicial reform; training of police forces; and human rights monitoring. In the most drastic cases, the UN along with other international organizations has sometimes assumed core state functions.

The record of such efforts is seen by many to be positive – if one measures success as the absence of recurrent large-scale violence. However, in some places, such as Central America, crime is endemic and levels of socioeconomic inequality have increased, while in others, such as Cambodia, democratic rule is precarious. Overall, the extent to which peacebuilding missions have created conditions for lasting peace is mixed, and a general conclusion is that longer-term commitments are required (Paris 2004, Jenkins 2012).

### Terrorism

Al-Qa'ida's attacks on US territory brought into stark relief the destructive capacity of nonstate actors in a globalizing world. Terrorism, however, has been on the UN's agenda for decades. Indeed, the General Assembly – serving as the lead UN actor due to the Cold War stalemate in the Security Council – has addressed it since 1972. Although unsuccessful in reaching an agreed-upon definition of terrorism, the assembly, particularly its Sixth Committee, has facilitated 13 international legal conventions spanning such issues as hijacking, bombings and use of nuclear material.

The spate of terrorist bombings in the late 1980s and 1990s spurred the Security Council to act. It imposed sanctions on rogue states such as Libya

– which was shielding suspects in the bombing of Pan-Am flight 103 – and Afghanistan – which was providing sanctuary to Osama bin Laden and al-Qa'ida. In the wake of 11 September, the council for the first time deemed self-defence a legitimate response to a terrorist attack in resolution 1368, thereby endorsing the US war in Afghanistan to overthrow the Taliban regime. Subsequently, resolution 1373 required all states to implement specified measures to combat terrorism, including changes to national legislation, and established the Counter-Terrorism Committee (CTC) to monitor their implementation. In 2004, the council was concerned about terrorists acquiring nuclear capabilities. It passed binding Chapter VII resolution 1540 that requires states to ensure appropriate measures to control and account for nuclear, biological and chemical weapons. Kofi Annan established a Policy Working Group to explore how the UN should respond to terrorism. He also convened the High-level Panel on Threats, Challenges and Change (2004) to recommend a comprehensive UN approach to security, including anti-terrorism. He also called attention to human rights violations perpetrated in the name of fighting terrorism – Guantánamo Bay and Abu Ghraib being hallmarks.

After three decades of grappling with this issue, the 2005 World Summit still was unable to agree on a definition of terrorism. The lack of consensus among member states is especially problematic in light of the Security Council's authorization of self-defence as a response to terrorism (Boulden and Weiss 2004).

### Disarmament and nonproliferation

Disarmament and nonproliferation were central at the UN's establishment. The Charter refers to the regulation of armaments, specifying roles for the General Assembly, Security Council and Military Staff Committee, while Articles 11 and 47 allude to disarmament.

Key components of the UN's machinery are the General Assembly, the Disarmament Commission, and the permanent Conference on Disarmament, which is an autonomous forum that reports to the assembly and is linked to the Secretariat. The UN, however, has not been a major player, although it has been crucial in the development of norms. Its main contribution has been facilitating the negotiation of international treaties, the most important being the Nuclear Non-Proliferation Treaty (NPT), the Chemical Weapons Convention (CWC), and the Biological Toxins and Weapons Convention (BWC). In 1996, the General Assembly adopted the Comprehensive Test Ban Treaty (CTBT), but it has not yet entered into force. The world body also cooperates with the International Atomic Energy Agency (IAEA), a specialized agency, which conducts inspections to verify that nuclear materials and activities are not used for military purposes, the Organization for the Prohibition of Chemical Weapons (OPCW), and the Prep Com for the Nuclear-Test-Ban-Treaty Organization (CTBTO) (see Chapter 27, this volume).

The United Nations directly engaged in a coercive disarmament operation in Iraq following the Gulf War, when the Security Council established intrusive weapons inspections bodies, first the UN Special Commission (UNSCOM) and subsequently the UN Monitoring, Verification and Inspections Commission (UNMOVIC). Given the failure of the United States to locate WMDs in Iraq following its invasion in 2003, the world body was seemingly successful in overseeing the destruction of Saddam Hussein's arsenal.

The majority of contemporary war-related deaths stem from small arms (see Chapter 29, this volume). Since the late 1990s, the UN has stepped up its nonproliferation efforts in this arena. The world body, however, has been unsuccessful in negotiating a legally binding treaty. By contrast, parallel advancements took place outside the UN to ban anti-personnel landmines, which culminated in the Ottawa Convention. This initiative was spearheaded by nongovernmental organizations and negotiated outside of the Conference on Disarmament.

## Conclusion

Dag Hammarskjöld is widely reported to have remarked, 'The purpose of the UN is not to get us to heaven but to save us from hell'. The United Nations has played an essential role in diffusing interstate and intrastate disputes, responding to humanitarian emergencies, and elaborating norms for human rights. Over almost seven decades, the world organization has demonstrated considerable creativity in navigating the constraints of power politics. However, so long as states fail to provide requisite resources and delegate authority, the UN's capacity to fulfil its mandate will remain highly circumscribed.

## Further reading

Thomas G. Weiss, David P. Forsythe, Roger A. Coate and Kelly-Kate Pease, *The United Nations and Changing World Politics* (Westview Press, 6th edition, 2010). An up-to-date text about the world organization.

Thomas G. Weiss and Sam Daws (eds.), *The Oxford Handbook on the United Nations* (Oxford University Press, 2007). A compendium of 40 original essays as Secretary-General Ban Ki-moon took the helm.

For concise and current treatments of the three principal organs discussed here with relevance for security studies, see the volumes from the Global Institutions Series: Edward C. Luck, *UN Security Council: Promise and Practice* (Routledge, 2nd edition, 2012); M.J. Peterson, *The UN General Assembly* (Routledge, 2005); Leon Gordenker, *The UN Secretary-General and Secretariat* (Routledge, 2nd edition, 2010); Rob Jenkins, *Peacebuilding: From Concept to Commission* (Routledge, 2012).

Center for International Cooperation, *Global Peace Operations 2010* and *Review of Political Missions 2010* (Lynne Rienner, annual). A statistical and analytical overview of the UN's military and political operations.

# Peace Operations

Michael Pugh

## Abstract

In this chapter, students will learn about the evolution of, and political debates surrounding, contemporary peace operations. Peace operations range from small observation and monitoring missions to large peace-building initiatives in war-torn societies. At one extreme, some observers contend that it includes combat falling short of outright belligerency: peace enforcement. This chapter traces the shift in peace operations discourse and packaging since the mid-1990s. Reforms that make peace operations a handmaiden to 'human security', enlightened governance and liberalization have as much to do with ideological conviction and the quest to maintain hierarchy as with technical and operational requirements. Peace operations reflect power distribution in the international system and, as a form of crisis management, serve to sustain rather than transform the global system.

## Introduction

This chapter focuses on the agency of peace operations. It contends that while peacekeeping by blue berets was largely a vision-less response to international crisis management, peace operations have been increasingly co-opted into grand intentions to bring about liberal peace. This is a highly problematic enterprise, in terms of both meaning and practice. In part this expansiveness occurs in a permissive environment because peace missions are ill-defined, have various purposes (from preventing conflict to transforming war-torn societies), and are undertaken by a bewildering range of actors, from the Commonwealth of Independent States (CIS) to the African Union (AU). For Western states and the UN, the expansion of peace missions forms a key part of a broad project to confer liberal privileges on societies at war by implementing 'responsibility to protect civilians', 'good governance', 'human security' and 'capacity-building'.

The circumstances and nature of peace operations have changed considerably since the Cold War. First, informed consent by hosts was such a critical variable in the deployment of traditional peacekeepers that it could be convincingly argued that state sovereignty was left intact, indeed protected by restrictive status of forces agreements and memoranda of understanding. However, state sovereignty is now considered contingent on unthreatening behaviour, human rights adherence and 'good governance'. So-called weak and failed states are to be relieved of sovereignty and accorded 'shared sovereignty' (Krasner 2005). Second, the small post-war missions – 45 observers along the 500-mile ceasefire line in Jammu and Kashmir after 1949; the modest six-month executive role in West New Guinea when a UN 'tsar' ran the territory without a budget backed by only 1,500 troops – have been eclipsed by ambitious deployments. Only the 20,000-strong Congo mission in the 1960s seems to be regarded as a precursor of current deployments, and is cited as a Cold War oddity. The contrast has been starkest in the Lebanon where 4,500 UNIFIL troops were operating under a broad 1978 mandate until after Israel's aggression in 2006, when the guarantors of a ceasefire decided that a 15,000-strong force was needed. Third, there are many more actors competing for roles and claiming special dispensations arising from regional interest or expertise, from a moral high-ground or from a particular use of power. Fourth, in contemporary operations, peacekeepers are seemingly engaged in everything from civilian protection to conflict resolution, support for police raids on fraudsters to backing up 'peace' agreements with a coercive presence.

## Language and meaning

The chapter begins with a discussion of language and typologies to show that peacekeeping has been subsumed into a broader notion of peace operations. A discourse framework has been constructed that facilitates the imposition of liberal norms and values to sustain Western hegemony in the international system, irrespective of the nationalities contributing peacekeeping troops and other personnel. The subsequent section provides a snapshot of peace operations from the mid-1990s and discusses the reforms instigated to cope with the predicaments presented by civil wars and the resurgence of demand for peace operations from 2003. The reforms led to peace operations having a more visionary rationale than old-style peacekeeping. Three issues that exercise policy-makers and practitioners in contemporary operations are discussed – standards of professionalism, hybrid missions and the so-called 'public security gap'. Finally, the chapter considers the future prospects of this activity.

First, however, it is important to unpack the confusion of terminology. In this field, language and meaning has particular importance for three main reasons. First, use of the term 'peace' as an adjective suggests these 'operations' are always beneficial and something quite distinct from war. Indeed, US military doctrine fashioned 'peacekeeping' as a category of 'Operations Other Than War', but managed also to make it a subcategory of 'stability operations' – which in Iraq and Afghanistan was indistinguishable from combat. François Debrix (1997) points out that this labelling is designed to camouflage the inadequacies of such operations in bringing about either an absence of war (negative peace) or contributing to structural change that will embed non-violence in the system (positive peace). In his view, peace operations represent a simulacra, or image, of peace. Some so-called peace operations may of course bring respite from violent conflict but this is by no means assured and such interventions may make matters worse, as clearly happened in Iraq. In similar vein, Oliver Richmond concludes that peace has not been imagined in a way that avoids hegemonic imposition: peace operations bring about a 'virtual peace' (Richmond 2005). David Chandler formulates a more radical critique, basing his thesis around Zaki Laïdi's notion of post-ideological meaningless (Laïdi 1998: 8–9, 110). Laïdi's argument that commitments are contingent, and that states interact to evade rather than engage, is applied by Chandler to demonstrate that engagement in the name of good governance and other vague agendas facilitates the evasion of both responsibility and the discharge of power (Chandler 2006: 18). Otherwise, why would potential contributors have to be bullied and cajoled into sending troops to the Lebanon, Afghanistan and the Sudan?

On the contrary, however, peace operations may be considered as agencies of liberal peace, contributing to the prevailing structures of power, not least when reifying technical and administrative involvement in so-called weak or failed states. As with Cold War peacekeeping, peace operations engage in ordering and tidying up violent conflict in the international system. By the turn of this century, however, more expansive peace operations were co-opted into ambitious designs based on liberal norms and values (Jacoby 2007).

Second, such operations have been deployed where there is no peace to secure, where ceasefires break down or, as in Afghanistan, where war continues in some areas if not in all. And so the adjective can be a misleading one, as these missions have to use violence 'to bring peace'. The oxymoron then commonly employed is 'peace enforcement'.

Third, for practical operational reasons, especially in multinational contexts, it is essential to clarify the meaning of such operations so that military and civilian personnel have common frames of reference. But the linguistic grounds have been shifting. The UK's Ministry of Defence and Foreign and Commonwealth Office, for example, use the term Peace Support Operations, implying that such operations are not ends in themselves but supportive – whereas the US uses the term Peace Operations. Even more confusing, the annual review of UN peacekeeping, sponsored by the UN Department of Peacekeeping Operations (DPKO) was entitled *Annual Review of Global Peace Operations* (Center on International Cooperation 2006). Finally, the UN Secretary-General Ban Ki-moon persuaded the DPKO to create a Department of Field Support (DFS).

The umbrella term 'peace operations', therefore, includes a wide range of activities. UK government departments categorize them according to general objectives: conflict prevention; peacekeeping; peacemaking; peace enforcement; and peacebuilding. As some of these issues are discussed elsewhere in this volume, the analysis here will be confined largely to the use of uniformed (military and police) forces for peacekeeping and enforcement missions permitted under Chapter VI and Chapter VII respectively of the UN Charter (items 3 and 4 in Box 26.1).

---

### BOX 26.1  THE UN'S CATEGORIES OF PEACE OPERATIONS

1  **Conflict prevention**: the application of structural or diplomatic measures to keep intra-state or inter-state tensions and disputes from escalating into violent conflict.

2  **Peacemaking**: measures to address conflicts in progress and usually involves diplomatic action to bring hostile parties to a negotiated agreement.

3  **Peacekeeping**: a technique designed to preserve the peace, however fragile, where fighting has been halted, and to assist in implementing agreements achieved by the peacemakers. . . . peacekeeping has evolved from a primarily military model of observing cease-fires and the separation of forces after inter-state wars, to incorporate a complex model of many elements – military, police and civilian – working together to help lay the foundations for sustainable peace.

4  **Peace enforcement**: the application, with the authorization of the Security Council, of a range of coercive measures, including the use of military force. . . . to restore international peace and security.

5  **Peacebuilding**: measures targeted to reduce the risk of lapsing or relapsing into conflict by strengthening national capacities at all levels for conflict management, and to lay the foundation for sustainable peace and development . . . by addressing the deep-rooted, structural causes of violent conflict in a comprehensive manner.

*Source*: United Nations DPKO (2008: 17–18).

## Surge, retraction, resurgence

The pattern of UN deployments changed dramatically in the decade after the mid-1990s. In July 1993, the UN was deploying 78,444 uniformed personnel, one-third of them in the Balkans. The number fell away after the débâcles in Somalia and Bosnia and Herzegovina. By the late 1990s the number of personnel on UN operations had fallen to below 15,000. Clearly, the UN had found it extremely difficult to adjust to the demand for peace enforcement in internal conflicts. Beginning in October 2003, however, five major ventures were underway in Liberia, Côte d'Ivoire, Haiti, Burundi and the Sudan. The Democratic Republic of Congo operation (MONUC) expanded to a force of 21,000 (until downsized in mid-2010 and replaced by MONUSCO) and a considerable expansion of UNIFIL in the Lebanon occurred in the wake of Israel's aggression in mid-2006 (see Figure 26.1).

By 2010, the UN was deploying 83,414 troops, 2,224 military experts (formerly called observers) and 13,958 police, a total of 98,596 personnel in 15 missions (with additional personnel in one political/peacebuilding missions, UNAMA: see Figure 26.2). Only the US has a greater global military deployment than the UN. Of the 116 contributing countries, the main suppliers continued to be Bangladesh and Pakistan (with over 10,000 uniformed personnel each), India (with about 8,700), followed by Nigeria, Egypt and Nepal (with over 5,000 each). Some previously supportive participants in UN

*Figure 26.1* Missions administered by the Department of Peacekeeping Operations

*Note*: *political or peace-building mission

peacekeeping had virtually dropped out, or confined their contributions to military experts and police. In 2010, New Zealand had only one soldier on UN service, Australia nine and Canada a mere 16 (excluding military observers/experts). The US supplied only 12 troops (but 55 police). These token troop contributions were completely overshadowed by those of relative newcomers such as China (1,892) and Rwanda (3,494). Latin American states also became more prominent in the wake of crises in Haiti. The UK with 275 troops provided a similar number as Mongolia, the Ukraine and Guatemala. The US, the UK and its former 'dominions', along with some European states, were of course otherwise engaged in (largely fruitless) warlike operations in Afghanistan.

Lack of resources has been an abiding concern of the UN, as demands rose and states were reluctant to participate in risky ventures. The budget for operations had grown from $1.5 billion in 2000 to $7.25 billion for 2010–2011, about one-hundredth the size of the US defence budget. The only states allocated more than 5 per cent of the UN's peacekeeping budget were: the US (which unilaterally and progressively reduced its contribution from 31.7 per cent in 1993 to 25 per cent in 2007), Japan (19 per cent), Germany (9 per cent), the UK and France (7 per cent each) and Italy (5 per cent). But in 2010 peacekeeping was about $3.2 billion short in contributions and the UN judged that it was owed $431 million for peacekeeping by the US, a figure contested by the Barack Obama administration (AFP 2010). Indeed, UN operations were conducted on the cheap, the US Accountability

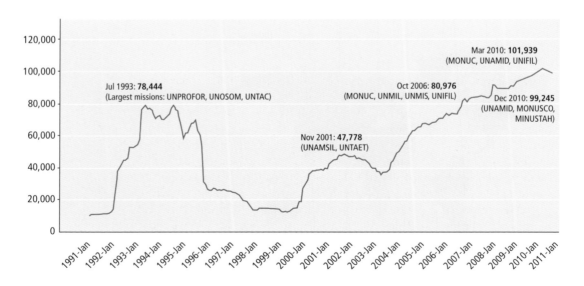

*Figure 26.2* Uniformed personnel in UN peacekeeping, 1991–2011

*Source*: UN Department of Peacekeeping Operations

Office estimating that to run the Haiti mission (MINUSTAH) would cost double if conducted unilaterally (US GAO 2007: 2).

Under such resource pressures, accompanied during the Bush Administration by the scarcely concealed contempt and hostility of the US towards the global organization, and towards former Secretary-General Kofi Annan in person, the UN could be more easily kept on a leash. Nevertheless, the UN strived to catch up with the evolving conflict environment and attempted to institute reforms congenial to its most powerful member states.

## Reforms

As a consequence of the surge in the early 1990s and the bruising experiences in Somalia, Rwanda and Bosnia and Herzegovina, Kofi Annan, himself a former Under Secretary-General for Peacekeeping, gave full support to a reconceptualization of peacekeeping. He pronounced in July 1997 that without sufficient resources or political will to endow the UN with capabilities to act under Chapter VII of the Charter, ad hoc coalitions of 'the willing' would be the most effective mechanism for enforcement missions. Reiterating the view of his predecessor Boutros Boutros-Ghali, Annan argued that: 'Cooperation with regional organizations will be intensified and regional organizations will increasingly become partners of the United Nations in all activities related to the maintenance of international peace and security' (Annan 1997). In part, the future of intervention would lie in hybrid operations, or contracted-out enforcement as in the Balkans. This was reinforced by an interrogation of peacekeeping in 2000 by the Secretary-General's experienced Special Representative and Special Adviser, Lakhdar Brahimi.

### Brahimi's report

First, Brahimi contended that UN forces must be able to defend themselves effectively, and that this should include impartial defence of the mandate. In the light of Lt. Gen. Roméo Dallaire's distressing experience in Rwanda (Dallaire 2004), Brahimi suggested that peacekeeping needed to be more flexible and robust. If peacekeeping forces could move up a gear to enforcement and back again without losing their impartiality and without having to rely on the wholesale consent of all parties in a host country, this, it was imagined, would answer the Rwandan problem of low-level, but effective, resistance to feeble UN missions by determined armed groups. The assumption that resisters could be invariably intimidated by robustness into peaceable behaviour always seemed dubious. Second, if flexible toughness was the new mantra, then far more consultation with troop contributors had to be instituted to avoid a form of peacekeeping 'taxation without representation'. This could side-step disputes about the use or misuse of national units in fraught situations, such as that which arose in Srebrenica, when Dutch troops compounded the Bosniak government's abandonment of this designated 'safe area' by failing to protect the civilian population. Third, mandates would need to reflect the resources available. Funds should be released for the planning and start-up of missions, even before a mandate had been agreed. If commitments by states were not forthcoming then mandates should be limited.

The Brahimi concept, welcomed by those Western militaries engrossed in doctrine development such as the French and British, was seriously flawed in its assumptions. First, it assumed that a strategy could be devised for both peacekeeping and enforcement by the same forces, as if they were part of a spectrum of force (whereas peacekeeping belongs on a spectrum of non-force). Moreover, the analysis rested on a misrepresentation of the potential effectiveness of enforcement, when the critical failure was not operational but political will (see Berdal 2001: 67, Johnstone 2006: 5, Tardy 2011). Second, based on a dubious projection of the Rwanda model of conflict it assumed that peace could be secured by military means and without widening resistance. Subsequently, robust forces spent as much effort on force protection as on protecting civilians. The UN Mission in Sudan, for example, originally aimed to have 10,000 peacekeepers, of whom 4,000 were for force protection (UNMIS 2006).

Third, the concept fell foul of nationalism, especially the unwillingness of states to see their forces put in harm's way under a UN command – an issue that almost paralysed NATO strategy when the US–UK aerial bombing in Kosovo would have put any ground troops at risk of Serbian retaliation. The Clinton Administration had already signalled disengagement after its disaster in Mogadishu by issuing Presidential Decision Directive 25 of 22 February 1996, which reinforced US opposition to placing troops under UN control.

Fourth, as Bellamy, Williams and Griffin point out (2004: 170), if international forces were to plan for their exits, an imposed peace would have to be part of a broad strategy involving multiple agencies that would address root causes and establish a non-violent future in war-torn societies. A liberal ideology had to be activated with a package of transformation policies – an assemblage construed by academics as the 'liberal peace' (see Richmond 2005, Duffield 2007). Concerned with democratization, rule of law and economic reconstruction, the roots of liberal peace are traceable to a global modernization project of the early Cold War years in US foreign policy (Jahn 2007), or even further back to Woodrow Wilson after the First World War. Where the UN or non-UN coalitions had administrative control, as in Bosnia and Herzegovina, Kosovo, Timor Leste and Afghanistan, the ideology could be applied directly, the presence of military forces providing the means to enforce it (Chesterman 2004).

Enforcing preferred norms of governance and socio-economic development was a grave contravention of norms declared since the Second World War that asserted the right of every state to 'choose its political, economic, social and cultural system, without interference in any form by another State' (Declaration 1965). A normative shift towards a less pluralist conception and more universalistic and individualistic conception of rights appears to have occurred in the late 1990s. It culminated in a consensus that states had a moral duty, though not a legal right, to protect civilians from gross abuse in other countries if their own state failed to do so (see Chapter 32, this volume).

Coalitions were taking matters into their own hands anyway and bypassing UN peacekeeping. Sierra Leone was a case in point. In February 2000, the UN Assistance Mission for Sierra Leone (UNAMSIL) was provided with a Chapter VII mandate to protect civilians, though without sufficient resources to do so. The Revolutionary United Front (RUF) took some 500 peacekeepers hostage in May 2000. But rather than strengthen UNAMSIL, the UK sent an independent combat force of paratroopers and marines to secure Freetown and drive the RUF back. This division of labour, with the UN subcontracting, underwriting or turning a blind eye to enforcement by freelance entrepreneurs seemed a practical solution. Indeed, the Annan/Brahimi reforms acknowledged a growing division between 'enforcers' and 'peacekeepers' as the spectrum strategy proved untenable in Sierra Leone. It also enabled states such as Canada and Australia to be more selective about contributing forces to the UN and perhaps to have a louder political voice in regional frameworks than was the case in New York.

## Guéhenno goals

Towards the end of 2005 the Under Secretary-General for Peacekeeping, Jean-Marie Guéhenno, noted that the Brahimi reforms were intended to give the UN the capacity to launch one new large operation a year. There were three in 2004 (Côte d'Ivoire, Haiti and Burundi), and between 2000 and 2005 there had been a fivefold increase in personnel in the field (Guéhenno 2005). In addition, the safety of mission personnel was being strained in attempting to meet the challenge of armed groups, including armed children, looters and criminal gangs. In the 44-year period 1948 to the end of 1992, there had been 918 peacekeeper fatalities. In the 17 years 10 months from January 1993 to October 2010 there were 1,832 (UNDPKO 2010).

Guéhenno's five-year plan, *Peace Operations 2010*, had five goals relating to personnel, principles, cooperation with other bodies, resources and integrated structures (see Box 26.2). Personnel policies would focus on selection, training and a review of conditions of service. Basic principles focused on the elaboration of guidelines, codes and best practices through enhanced production of policy directives, standard operating procedures and manuals. Improved partnerships with other UN and non-UN agencies and organizations would be achieved by integrated planning with these other bodies from the start of a mission, and establishing clear lines of authority. In particular it would be vital to establish *modus operandi* with the newly established Peacebuilding Office and Commission and with partners in hybrid operations. The DPKO was committed to supporting the African Union's capacity-building, to procedures for dealing with the EU's proposed 'battle groups' in support of peace missions, and to cooperation with NATO and the World Bank. Resources were needed to strengthen operational capacity in three areas: policing (with a 25-person Standing Police Capacity), rapidly

---

## BOX 26.2  PEACE OPERATIONS 2010

**Goal 1**: Recruit, prepare and retain high quality personnel.

**Goal 2**: Set out doctrine and establish standards.

**Goal 3**: Establish effective partnerships, integrated missions and predictable frameworks of cooperation.

**Goal 4:** Secure essential resources to improve operations, notably in rapid response and policing.

**Goal 5:** Establish integrated organizational structures at headquarters and in the field.

---

deployable military forces and enhanced information production in the field and in communicating with publics in host and troop contributing countries. Integrated organizational capacity would be achieved by establishing 'backstop teams' in DPKO for each mission, comprising specialists in political, military, police, civilian, logistic, financial, personnel and public information, and by establishing joint operation centres in the field.

### Ban's plans

These steps to deal with overstretch, underperformance and lack of resources were certainly necessary but would take five years to implement in full. In 2007, the new Secretary-General, Ban Ki-moon, proposed a more radical restructuring to cope with the expansion and complexities of peace operations. The DPKO lost its Mission Support Unit to a new Department of Field Support, which also gained resources from other parts of the UN. The new Department of Field Support was charged with administering and managing field personnel, procurement, finances and information/communications technology. Given that this reversed a merger of the political and logistic components of peacekeeping in 1993 to 1994, designed to achieve better planning and integration, this plan has to be considered a potentially risky revival of fragmentation. Ban's decision to head both departments with Under Secretaries-General but to have the head of Field Support reporting to and taking direction from the head of Peace Operations seemed a recipe for confusion and disintegration. Further, the General Assembly financed the Field Support Department for only a year initially and with 284 temporary posts, as against Ban's request for 400. Nor did developing countries allow the new department to acquire the procurement function: it being one of the powers they had left in the Department of Management.

### Standards and principles

Reports of corruption and human rights (including sexual) abuse committed by peacekeepers have damaged the reputation of peace operations since the

1990s. For example, women subject to sexual violence in conflict (inflicted on men too) were also vulnerable through poverty and diminished status to the aggressive masculinities of male-dominated peace missions (Willett 2010). In October 2000, for the first time, the UN Security Council passed a resolution (number 1325) insisting on mainstreaming gender sensitivity in peace operations. Following further reports of sexual abuse by international civilians as well as troops in the Balkans, the DRC and elsewhere, an investigation was led by Prince Ra'ad Zeid, who recommended legal steps to stamp it out (Zeid 2005). National forces, regional bodies and international training centres had invested in raising professional standards and producing manuals and codes of conduct. In November 2006, DPKO also sent Conduct and Discipline Units to the largest UN operations to instil high standards of behaviour. Thanks to resolution 1325 and Guéhenno's reforms the missions should become more professional, better trained and more effectively deployed. An effort to codify broad principles for guidance to peacekeepers in 2008 to underpin the peacekeeper's legitimacy, made it clear that human rights and the laws of armed conflict applied to peacekeeping personnel (UN DPKO 2008, 14–15).

But as scholars have pointed out, the issue is not resolved by legal measures, manuals and training alone. To begin with, less than two per cent of UN personnel in uniform were women, and they sometimes had to be kept apart from their male colleagues (Valenius 2007). An Indian paramilitary police unit of 105 women joined the Liberian mission in 2007 for crowd control and robust policing in an environment where rape has been endemic – but they did not mix with the local population either (Grewal 2007). To some extent the increased robustness expected of peace operations may have inhibited women's inclusion. However, there are two deeper causes. First, the cultural power of aggressive masculinities and essentialist views of the roles of women as victims, or as the pacifying component in peace operations, hinders inclusiveness. Second, the privileging of liberal internationalism as an apolitical and benign enterprise, while powerful UN member states engage in power politics and technical fixes, helps to maintain silences around gendered power relations (Whitworth 2004, Willett 2010).

In sum, although training, codes and standards of conduct, have probably had an impact, national militaries and civilian police have to confront challenges to their own social norms. Furthermore, it is clear that, in general, peace operations are presented as so rational and sagacious that they tend to lack an ethic that incorporates an understanding of the images of peace operations held by those subjected to them (see Pouligny 2006, Pugh 2010).

## Hybrid operations

The UN has no monopoly in peace operations, and never has had. Freelance missions have been an element in international relations, at least since coalitions were formed to manage the prolonged dismantling of the Ottoman Empire, including the international military administration of Shkodër, Albania in 1913 to 1914. Under the UN system, the US-sponsored Multinational Force and Observers in the Sinai after the Egypt–Israel Peace Treaty of 1979 is a prominent example of a non-UN mission. Although, as Trevor Findlay (2002) demonstrates, UN missions have used force, sometimes beyond self-defence, the trend has been for the UN to opt out of operations likely to involve combat, and has allowed groups of states to act as proxies. The Dayton Peace Agreement Implementation Force (IFOR) in Bosnia originally comprised 60,000 from NATO-led states; its successors, the Stabilization Force (SFOR), and EUFOR, conducted by the EU (with only 2,500 troops) also had Chapter VII mandates. NATO also supplies the troops for the UN Mission in Kosovo (UNMIK). The Economic Community of West African States has launched several missions in its region, as has the Russian-dominated CIS in the Caucasus; the African Union had 6,500 troops and police in Sudan before the UN took over in 2008; and Australian-led forces operate in the southwest Pacific.

Hybrid operations, in which regional or freelance organizations operate alongside one another, may reduce the problems arising from groups of self-appointed states policing their own interests that, wittingly or not, add to the dynamics of conflict. For example, NATO, the EU, OSCE and the UN have worked jointly, if dysfunctionally at times, as part of UNMIK. The AU and UN run a hybrid mission in Sudan, UNAMID. Many developing states, but also others such as Japan, continue to regard the UN as the most appropriate body to safeguard international peace and security because all states are represented and it embeds even the most powerful members in a system of checks and balances. Two heads of peacekeeping at the UN, Sir Marrack Goulding and Guéhenno, expressed concern that beyond Europe regional organizations are either not politically willing to conduct multilateral missions in their region (Asia and Southeast Asia) or did not have the resources and infrastructure to match the UN (Goulding 2002: 17, Guéhenno 2003: 35–36). However, the support to emerging multinational infrastructures may reduce the huge disparities between capacities in Europe and elsewhere (see Bellamy and Williams 2007: 343). Nevertheless, hybrid operations place a high premium on effective coordination, even integration, which has not often been apparent.

Although the UN has promoted hybridity, its universal legitimacy and a trend towards increased professionalism should continue to make peace missions a core function of the organization. Freelance peace missions will be only one of a range of international responses to wars and complex emergencies. Coalition forces engaged in coercion to provide security may be accompanied by UN missions. As in Chad and the Central African Republic where MINURCAT relieved EUFOR, they may be replaced by the UN in the voids created by coalitions bent on exit or unable to cope. UN deployments will still be needed where regional bodies are overstretched, lacking in infrastructure or requiring legitimacy.

## Public security gaps

Given the predilection of interventions to emphasize the establishment of rule of law, a third thorny issue became apparent in peace operations: how to deal with civil unrest and public disorder (see e.g. Oakley *et al.* 1997). Soldiers are usually the first element to arrive in a war-torn society but are inadequate for democratic policing and send a signal to local populations that brute force is the ultimate arbiter of social conflict. One answer has been to send in paramilitaries, such as the Italian *carabinieri*, operating in Bosnia and Herzegovina under military control and rules of engagement.

Another solution, with a long-standing pedigree since the peacekeeping mission in Cyprus, has been to send in civilian police. Rarely have they engaged in executive roles, Kosovo being an exception. Rather, they have concentrated on modernizing, training and supervising local police services. However, unlike many military forces, the national police forces of contributing states have not traditionally required threats abroad to justify their existence. Consequently, obtaining commitments and contributions of well-qualified officers has been highly problematic. The EU has developed expertise and a degree of competence in this field but Guéhenno's proposal for a standby UN police capacity was realised in October with a force of 25 stationed in Brindisi, Italy. Indeed, as CIVPOL transformed into UNPOL the civilian police component of peace operations rose from a strength of 5,840 in 1995 to 17,500 in 2010. However, the intrusion into rule of law issues in war-torn societies also reinforces the liberal framework of what constitutes peace and the normative values to be imposed.

A rather different 'gap' is posed by the expectations of protecting civilians in physical danger and the ability of peacekeepers to fulfil that role within their zones of operation. Although mandates have been extended to the protection of civilians – 'where appropriate' and on a case-by-case basis – in accord with Security Council resolution 1674 (2006), the resources necessary to provide civilian protection, to facilitate humanitarian assistance and to create conditions conducive to the return of displaced persons and refugees has been limited, as was demonstrated by the EUFOR operation in Chad in 2008 (Charbonneau 2009, 546–561).

## Conclusion: Future prospects

Peace operations are assumed to have a role in bringing about or maintaining conditions that reduce or eliminate violent conflict. There is some evidence for this claim. The authors of the 2005 *Human Security Report* argued that purposeful international activism, including peace operations, had been responsible for the decline in deadly civil conflicts (Human Security Centre 2005: 155). However, the evidence is largely circumstantial and one is still entitled to ask: what do peace operations represent in the early twenty-first century? Are they evidence of a grand design to simulate peace? Or will there be a post-Iraq/Afghanistan retreat into scaled-back pragmatism as a crisis of meaning afflicts the technically powerful? To help answer these questions it is relevant to boil down the impulses that construct an imagined peace, to which peace operations contribute.

For a self-styled pragmatic view George Pratt Schultz can serve as an exemplar. The neoliberal economist and Cold War diplomat who tolerated or supported dictatorships in Chile, the Philippines, Nicaragua and Haiti was a former economic adviser to Eisenhower and Nixon, Ronald Reagan's Secretary of State (1982–1989) and a Republican Party strategist. Schultz characterized his approach to Cold War politics as problem-solving. International politics, in his view, required constant attention to the obstacles, frictions and crises that arose in the quest for peace, similar to weeding a garden. The weeds are almost entirely produced by unruly others, who in the Schultz worldview included US allies who fell out of line. Cold War peacekeeping, then, was also problem-solving, but with perhaps less partiality as to the origins and outcomes of disputes.

Peace operations, modern-style, are more ambitious. And for a visionary perspective we can also turn to Schultz, honorary co-chair and subscriber to an influential Princeton University project, *Forging a World of Liberty under Law* (Ikenberry and Slaughter 2006). Signalling a retreat from the polarizing unilateralism of the Bush Administration, nevertheless the Princeton strategy had the same Wilsonian vision of a global order based on the spread of liberal democracy. In this respect the thinking behind the *Liberty under Law* strategy was a manifestation of the liberal peace, in which the weeds of the international system had to be killed off and unruly others administered and controlled to protect peace. Certainly, the strategy sought to fuse hard and 'soft power', relied less on military solutions and proposed a rediscovery of international law by the US. But it also proposed a permanent 'Concert of Democracies' led by the US to help create a 'better and safer world', retaining the impulse for changing the world in the liberal image.

In practice as well as in rhetoric, engagement in peace is accompanied by dogmatism and zeal. In addition to the co-option of peace missions into the wider project of promoting a liberal global order, authority figures have made strong efforts to embed ideals in their work. Lord Ashdown, High Representative in Bosnia and Herzegovina in the period 2002 to 2006, exemplifies the point. His reflections on his tenure in office are instructive because he lays considerable emphasis on the need for divided communities to seek a common vision beyond their immediate concerns. In the case of Bosnia and Herzegovina, the goal is membership of the EU (Ashdown 2007). The vision provides a rigorous form of conditionality introduced from the outside with no organic foundations, and serves as a rescue package that requires deferred gratification, since EU membership lies well into the future. An even more egregious instance, a component of so-called 'peace stabilization' that followed the illegal freelance invasion of Iraq, was the lengths to which Paul Bremer, the second US head of the Coalition Administration in early 2003, pursued a vision of economic development that swept aside indigenous forms of production, exchange and regulation. Bremer's fetish for deregulation, foreign direct investment, privatization (including privatization of the privatization process) and anti-protectionism was so severely disruptive and punitive against the most vulnerable sections of society that it had to be abandoned (Klein 2005).

Since the end of the Cold War, UN and non-UN peace missions continue to effect repairs, put conflicts on ice or try to resolve local and immediate issues, as they did in the past. However, they have also been co-opted into bold schemes for transformation. These have met resistance or lacked sustainability because they have been devoid of secure political foundations in war-torn societies. There is thus an emerging debate about whether the liberal peace can continue as a fantasy based on a flawed, perhaps meaningless, concept of change that actually inhibits political accountability, or whether an aggressive 'shared sovereignty' and cosmopolitan views of 'human security' and 'the responsibility to protect' will dominate the framing of peace operations. The meanings of peace missions continue to be framed as strategies to meet threats that are the product of others, usually in failed states. They represent a constancy of assumption in many quarters that the world is available for liberating by liberalism. However, the power to implement this is attenuated, and even expressed by evasion of responsibility and claims of immunity from accountability except to a socially-constructed 'international community' – the virtual signifier that often represents no more than the interests of the most powerful states in the UN system.

Nevertheless, core principles continue to be grounded in the concepts of consent, impartiality and the non-use of force except in self defence and defence of the mandate. However, the discernable shift politically has been to tie peace operation to liberal state-building in war-torn states deemed to be weak or failing. Indeed, the first core function of a multidimensional operation, according to the DPKO is to strengthen the state (UN DPKO 2008: 23).This points to contradictions: between peace- and state-building; between the state as the best guarantor of security and the non-state allegiances of populations; between involvement in building liberal foundations of a functioning state and support for local ownership; between the UN as an impartial actor and the UN as a partisan interventionist, as in MONUCs backing to DRC government's brutal armed forces and French/EUFOR support to the Déby regime in Chad. Thus it is not only an *absence* of consent that can lead peacekeeping into partiality. Further, managing the maintenance of consent is a deeply political activity when a host party to conflict becomes confident of its own capabilities and troop contributor fatigue sets in, especially under a consent-based robust mandate.

Peace operations will be dependent on maintaining credibility, on mandates matched by resources and a mission plan that can be implemented effectively. Attempts to improve integration and coordination include partnerships, not only with regional security bodies but with donors and the international financial institutions, a situation which can place peacekeepers in the inconvenient position of seeming to protect neoliberal economic reconstruction and development programmes. Redoubled efforts in 2010 to develop a universal vision of peace operations, to pursue improved integrated missions and establish a mutual accountability of 'partners' in these interventions will likely lead to more meaningful dialogue between troop and police contributing countries, the Security Council and the Secretariat. As Brahimi remarked to the General Assembly at a special meeting on peacekeeping in June 2010, 'it is not an acceptable division of responsibility that the rich contribute money and the poor contribute blood to the common cause of maintaining peace and security' (UN press release 2010, see also UN DPKO 2009).

## Further reading

Alex Bellamy and Paul Williams (eds.), *Peace Operations and Global Order* (Frank Cass, 2005). This collection of articles covers a range of conceptual and practical issues confronting peace operations in the international system. It contains various perspectives on the role of peace operations in global order by some of the foremost non-American scholars in the field.

Béatrice Pouligny, *Peace Operations Seen From Below* (Hurst, 2006). A remarkably original insight into the interactions between staff on UN operations and local interlocutors. Pouligny's research in six conflict areas investigates how local people interact with peace missions and how their daily lives are affected.

Susan Willett (ed.), *Women, Peace and Conflict: A Decade after Resolution 1325*, a special issue of *International Peacekeeping*, 17(2), 2010. Reflects on the limited progress made by women in peacekeeping in the decade since Security Council Resolution 1325 mainstreamed gender issues in peace and security.

Edward Newman and Oliver P. Richmond (eds.), *The United Nations and Human Security* (Palgrave, 2001) offers critical perspectives on multidimensional operations.

Lise Morjé Howard, *UN Peacekeeping in Civil Wars* (Cambridge University Press, 2008), is a comprehensive case-based study with an emphasis on issues of organisational learning.

## CONTENTS

# The Nuclear Disarmament and Non-Proliferation Regime

Waheguru Pal Singh Sidhu

## Abstract

In this chapter, students will learn about three contemporary challenges to institutions related to the disarmament and non-proliferation of nuclear weapons as well as efforts to overcome them. The first challenge is posed by states within the existing non-proliferation regime. The second set of challenges comes from states outside the present non-proliferation regime. The third and, perhaps, the most formidable challenge comes from non-state actors, including but not limited to terrorist groups. These three sets of challenges have generated at least three different approaches: first, to strengthen the traditional multilateral institutional approach anchored in treaty-based regimes; second, to establish non-treaty-based multilateral approaches initiated within the UN; and third, to build a set of ad-hoc, non-institutional, non-conventional approaches to address the immediate challenges of proliferation. These approaches, in turn, have led to several significant consequences for addressing disarmament and non-proliferation in future.

## Introduction

Soon after nuclear weapons first made their appearance in 1945, they emerged as the principal guarantors of international peace and security and underpinned world-order during the Cold-War. Indeed, it was the possession, or protection under the umbrella, of nuclear weapons that was widely regarded as one of the primary factors behind the long period of relative peace and stability in the international system after the Second World War. Even after the Cold War, the possession of and protection by nuclear weapons, remains the fundamental basis for world-order, evident from the continued dependence on nuclear weapons by states already possessing them and the acquisition of these weapons by new states. And yet, at least since 1 July 1968 when negotiations of the nuclear Non-proliferation Treaty (NPT) were completed and only five states (the United States, the Soviet Union, United Kingdom, France and the People's Republic of China) were known to possess nuclear weapons, there has been a desire to prevent new states from acquiring nuclear weapons and also to curb the unfettered build-up of nuclear weapons among possessor states with the ultimate objective of eventually eliminating all nuclear weapons. Thus, ironically, the NPT had the unenviable task of preventing proliferation and disarming the very weapons upon which the present world-order and international security continues to be based.

Predictably then, some scholars have argued that the NPT regime and related institutions have been far from effective in the objective of preventing proliferation and the disarmament of nuclear weapons. They point to the existing global nuclear arsenal of over 20,000 weapons and the increase in the number of states known to possess nuclear weapons from the original five in 1968 to nine in 2006 (with Israel, India, Pakistan and the Democratic People's Republic of Korea (DPRK) joining the nuclear club) as proof of the failure of the NPT. However, other scholars argue that the NPT regime has in fact been relatively effective in curbing proliferation. They note the dramatic decline in the number of nuclear weapons from around 80,000 in the late 1980s to around a quarter of that number today and the fact that only four new states (three of which – Israel, India, Pakistan – have still not signed the NPT) have acquired nuclear weapons instead of nearly 20 states that some analysts had predicted. Indeed, several states, including Bulgaria, Canada, Germany, Italy, Japan, the Netherlands, Norway and Spain, did not pursue a nuclear weapons programme despite having the technical wherewithal to do so. In addition, other states, including Argentina, Australia, Brazil, Egypt, Poland, Romania, Republic of Korea (South Korea), Spain, Sweden, Switzerland, Taiwan and Yugoslavia which had nuclear weapons programmes during the Cold War eventually abandoned them. Similarly, Libya, which was suspected of having started a clandestine nuclear weapons programme at the end of the Cold War, terminated it in 2003. Moreover, in the post-Cold War period other states, including South Africa, Belarus, Kazakhstan and Ukraine, which possessed nuclear weapons also gave them up. Clearly, the

NPT has been more successful in preventing new states from acquiring nuclear weapons than it has been in either slowing down or disarming states that already possess nuclear weapons. The latter objective is likely to be met only when nuclear weapons are de-coupled from the present world-order; an unlikely eventuality given the interest of nuclear weapons states in maintaining the status-quo despite the evolving multipolar world.

## Three caveats

This chapter is based on three essential caveats. First, contrary to conventional approaches which group nuclear weapons, along with biological and chemical weapons, into a convenient but specious category of so-called 'Weapons of Mass Destruction' (WMD), this chapter will deliberately focus only on nuclear weapons. This is primarily because biological, chemical and nuclear weapons do not belong to the same conceptual category. The lethality of chemical weapons is not significantly different from that of conventional explosives. Similarly, a variety of protective measures exist to alleviate the effects of a biological attack. In contrast, there are no effective preventive or protective measures that can mitigate a nuclear attack. Besides, although nuclear weapons are not forbidden by international law (as is the case with biological and chemical weapons), given their cataclysmic nature, the taboo against their use is so strong that it is difficult to imagine their use other than against enemy nuclear weapons. In this context, the creeping tendency to redefine the mission of nuclear weapons to counter *all* WMD has two consequences: it lumps together biological, chemical and nuclear weapons into one fuzzy conceptual category, and it weakens the nuclear taboo. If nuclear weapons are accepted as having a role to counter biological-chemical warfare, then by what logic can nuclear weapons capability be denied to a country like Iran which has actually suffered chemical weapons attacks? Therefore, this chapter focuses only on nuclear proliferation.

The second caveat is that proliferation should include both vertical (qualitative and quantitative improvement in the arsenals of states that already possess nuclear weapons) and horizontal (the quest of new states to acquire nuclear weapons) proliferation. In this context, proliferation of weapons among new nuclear states, such as the DPRK and, possibly, Iran is as much of a concern as the ongoing improvement of the nuclear arsenals of the five original nuclear weapons states, evident in efforts such as the United States' 'reliable replacement warhead' (RRW) programme, and the United Kingdom's decision to update its *Trident*-based nuclear arsenal. Moreover, today there appears to be a direct correlation between vertical and horizontal proliferation: both Iran and North Korea often cite the presence of nuclear-equipped US military forces in their respective regions as one of the primary motives behind Tehran's perceived quest and Pyongyang's evident possession of nuclear weapons.

The third caveat is that as represented in the NPT package, nuclear non-proliferation should be linked to nuclear disarmament. However, in the recent past, efforts have been made to de-link non-proliferation and disarmament, and focus only on horizontal proliferation. This is apparent in the demand for complete, verifiable and irreversible disarmament for new proliferators, such as the DPRK, without applying similar standards to the original five proliferators.

With these three caveats this chapter provides a brief overview of the three key nuclear proliferation challenges in the post-Cold War world. It then examines the three approaches being followed to address these proliferation challenges. Finally, the chapter offers some broad conclusions related to the likely consequences of the three approaches and what more could be done to facilitate disarmament and non-proliferation.

## Non-proliferation regime

Although the NPT is the lynchpin of the non-proliferation regime, the regime itself is much broader and is considered to comprise of at least the following elements: the Partial Test Ban Treaty (PTBT) and the Comprehensive Test Ban Treaty (CTBT), both of which sought to prevent nuclear proliferation by banning nuclear tests; the proposed Fissile Material Cutoff Treaty (FMCT), which seeks to ban the production of fissile material; bilateral negotiations and agreements to limit nuclear arsenals, particularly of the US and the Soviet Union/Russian Federation such as SALT I and II, the Anti-Ballistic Missile (ABM) Treaty, START I, II and III, the Intermediate-Range Nuclear Forces (INF) Treaty, and the Strategic Offensive Reductions Treaty (SORT); nuclear technology denial regimes such as the Nuclear Suppliers Group (NSG) and the Missile Technology Control Regime (MTCR); ensuring compliance of some aspects of the NPT regime through the institutions of the International Atomic Energy Agency (IAEA) and the Comprehensive Test Ban Treaty Organization (CTBTO) Preparatory Commission; and the various Nuclear Weapon Free Zones (NWFZs).

## Three challenges

The post-Cold War world has witnessed the emergence of three challenges related to the proliferation of nuclear weapons. While some of these, clearly, date back to the Cold War they nonetheless remain of particular import even today while others are more recent and might be related to the end of the Cold War.

First, there is the challenge posed by states within the existing non-proliferation regime. Here states that announced their intention to withdraw from the NPT, built and tested a nuclear weapon, such as the DPRK, pose as much of a challenge as nuclear weapons states which are seeking to develop a new generation of potentially usable nuclear weapons as outlined in the United States' National Nuclear Security Administration 'Complex 2030' plan

## BOX 27.1   MISSILES: BLIND SPOT OR ALLEY?

Nuclear weapons and missiles have a direct correlation: all the nine known nuclear weapons states possess missiles – either ballistic, or cruise or both – capable of delivering nuclear weapons. 'A ballistic missile is a weapon-delivery vehicle that has a ballistic trajectory over most of its flight path. A cruise missile is an unmanned, self-propelled weapon-delivery vehicle that sustains flight through the use of aerodynamic lift over most of its flight path' (UN Report 2002: para. 19). While all nuclear weapons states already have nuclear-tipped ballistic missiles, almost all of them also possess or are in the process of acquiring nuclear-capable cruise missiles. Conversely, however, not all ballistic and cruise missile possessing states have nuclear weapons. This poses a particular dilemma for non-proliferation: is the possession of missiles, particularly ballistic missiles, an indication of the aspiration of states to acquire nuclear weapons? The answer would have to be a qualified maybe.

In the early days of the nuclear era, missiles were seen as a *blind alley* – a distraction from the primary objective of arms control, non-proliferation and disarmament of nuclear weapons. Today, however, missiles and efforts to manage and control them are seen as a *blind spot* – a crucial gap in the existing panoply of arms control and non-proliferation that needs to be addressed.

However, unlike nuclear weapons, '[n]o universal norm, treaty or agreement governing the development, testing, production, acquisition, transfer, deployment or use specifically of missiles exists' (UN Report 2002: para. 32). Even more significantly, there is no universal norm, treaty or agreement to rid the world of missiles. Indeed, the rare cases of missile disarmament (the Intermediate-Range Nuclear Forces (INF) Treaty, Iraq, South Africa and Libya) were the result of very particular circumstances and not in adherence to any global norm or regime.

Against this backdrop and the growing salience of missiles, two trends have become evident among the international community. The first is a series of political and diplomatic initiatives (such as the INF Treaty, Missile Technology Control Regime, the Hague Code of Conduct, the Global Control System, and the three United Nations Panel of Governmental Experts) at the bilateral, regional and global levels. The second is a number of military and technological initiatives (such as the war to disarm Iraq, missile defence and the Proliferation Security Initiative). While both approaches have been limited in their effectiveness, the former is more in line with the desire for nuclear disarmament while the latter is likely to perpetuate the continued possession of nuclear weapons in the hands of some states.

(NNSA 2005), and the United Kingdom, which is updating its *Trident* strategic deterrence system (BBC 2007). Indeed, while much attention has been devoted to both Iran and the DPRK (Chubin 2006, Cha and Kang 2003), not as much consideration has been paid to the huge combined arsenals of the five nuclear weapons states within the NPT.

While for the first time ever both the United States and the United Kingdom officially revealed the size of their nuclear arsenals (US DoD 2010b, BBC 2010) the official data of national nuclear weapon stockpiles of the other seven nuclear armed states are shrouded in secrecy. With the exception of the

United States and the United Kingdom, there are still no accurate nationwide or worldwide figures for the total number of nuclear weapons (see Table 27.1 based on open sources reflecting this wide disparity). However, it is estimated that around 97 per cent of the world's nuclear arsenal of over 20,000 weapons are in the stockpiles of the United States and the Russian Federation alone (Norris and Kristensen 2006). Even more troubling, several thousands of these weapons remain on high alert and could be launched within minutes causing unimaginable death and destruction on a global scale.

While there is no doubt that some of the NPT nuclear weapon states have made significant cuts in their arsenals, the lack of transparency makes it very difficult to accurately assess whether these reductions are complete, verifiable and irreversible. This was particularly the case with the 2003 Strategic Offensive Reduction Treaty (SORT) between the United States and the Russian Federation which, as some non-nuclear NPT states pointed out, 'does not require the destruction of these weapons, does not include tactical nuclear weapons and does not have any verification provisions. The process is neither irreversible, nor transparent' (*International Herald Tribune* 2004). The situation has been rectified with the entry into force of the new START in 2011 between the United States and the Russian Federation, which supersedes SORT and also has clear verification provisions. The new START, which is expected to run until 2021 (unless it is superseded by a new treaty) also restricts the number of deployed strategic nuclear warheads to 1,550 each. However, in the absence of a similar formal, transparent and verifiable process involving the other three NPT nuclear weapon states it is almost impossible to discern the level of disarmament that might have occurred. This is probably why the 2010 NPT Review Conference categorically calls on the NPT nuclear weapon states to move 'towards an overall reduction in the global stockpile of all types of nuclear weapons' and also 'enhance transparency and increase mutual confidence' (Review Conference 2010).

Besides, despite these significant reductions in the actual number of nuclear weapons, the five nuclear weapons states are nowhere near meeting their disarmament commitments under Article VI of the NPT, which calls on these states to 'pursue negotiations in good faith on effective measures relating to cessation of the nuclear arms race . . . and to nuclear disarmament' (Treaty 1968). Indeed, even though the United Kingdom today has the smallest arsenal amongst the NPT nuclear weapon states, its decision to upgrade the Trident system means that it will retain nuclear weapons at least until the middle of this century. Similarly, both the United States and the Russian Federation, despite the massive cut in their arsenals, are likely to retain nuclear weapons until at least 2021 and beyond. The same is true of both France and China which remain the least transparent of all the five NPT nuclear states in terms of their nuclear disarmament commitments.

As one former senior US official argued, echoing the sentiments of the other NPT nuclear weapon states: 'Nuclear weapons continue to have relevance in today's world . . . several national nuclear weapons programmes were never initiated, or were halted, because security guarantees provided by a nuclear

Table 27.1 Estimates of nuclear weapons in the possession of known nuclear weapon states

| Nuclear Armed States | Official Government Figures | Arms Control Association | Bulletin of Atomic Scientists | SIPRI | Nuclear Threat Initiative |
|---|---|---|---|---|---|
| Russia | Not available | 11,400 (2,400 strategic, 2,000 tactical, 7,000 stockpile) | 12,000 (4,600 plus 7,300 in storage) | 11,000 (2,427 deployed; 8570 other) | ~12,000 (4,600 operational, 7,300 non-deployed) |
| USA | 5,113 in 2009 (Fact Sheet: Increasing Transparency in the US Nuclear Weapons Stockpile, 3 May, 2010) | 5,113 active and inactive; 3,500 retired and awaiting dismantlement | 10,104 (5,735 plus about 5,000 in reserve) | 8,500 (2,150 deployed; 6,350 other) | 5,113 (2,468 operational; 2,600 non-deployed) |
| France | Not available | Fewer than 300 strategic warheads | ~300 | 300 (290 deployed; 10 others) | ~300 operational warheads |
| China | Not available | About 240 warheads | ~240 | 240 (200 others) | ~240 (~176 operational) |
| UK | 225 warheads (UK Foreign Secretary William Hague reveals size of Trident stockpile, 26 May, 2010) | 160 deployed, total 225 | 225 | 225 (160 deployed; 65 other) | 225 (~160 deployed and 65 non-deployed) |
| Pakistan | Not available | ~70–90 warheads | ~90–110 warheads | ~90–110 | 70–90 warheads |
| Israel | Not available | ~75–200 warheads | ~80 | ~80 | 80 warheads |
| India | Not available | Upto 100 warheads | ~70 | ~80–100 | 70 warheads |
| DPRK | Not available | Plutonium for 12 warheads | ~10 | | ~10 |

armed United States convinced these states not to seek nuclear weapons' (Rocca 2007). This view, however, has been challenged by four former senior US officials who argued in an op-ed that 'reliance on nuclear weapons for this [deterrence] purpose is becoming increasingly hazardous and decreasingly effective' (Schultz *et al.* 2007). The growing desire to move towards a world without nuclear weapons was best articulated by US President Barack Obama in a 2009 speech in Prague. The ambitious Prague agenda called for a 'reduction in warheads and stockpiles . . . a global ban on nuclear testing . . . a new treaty that verifiably ends the production of fissile materials . . . strengthen the Nuclear Non-Proliferation Treaty as a basis for cooperation . . . [and] ensure that terrorists never acquire a nuclear weapon' (White House 2009). However, Obama also cautioned that the goal of a world without nuclear weapons is unlikely in the foreseeable future and 'perhaps not in my lifetime'.

In light of this statement, will the conditions ever prevail for complete nuclear disarmament? Or, is the presence of some nuclear weapons in the hands of some states essential to prevent proliferation? Finally, in the absence of nuclear guarantees, do states have the right to build nuclear weapons to ensure their own security? These dilemmas relate not only to the first set of challenges posed to the non-proliferation regime from within but also to the second set of challenges posed from states without.

The second set of challenges comes from states such as India, Israel and Pakistan which have not signed the NPT or the CTBT but also states like the China, DPRK, Egypt, Iran, Israel and the United States, which have still to ratify the CTBT. There are a variety of reasons why these states either never joined these treaties or having signed them did not ratify them, or having joined them decided to opt out and withdraw from the treaty. These reasons could vary from domestic political, technological or economic factors to regional security concerns to prestige and the desire to have a greater say in global governance. In the case of Israel and Pakistan (Cohen 1998, Weissman and Krosney 1981), both the quest for nuclear weapons and the desire to stay outside of the non-proliferation regime was primarily driven by security concerns. In the case of India, however, the reasons were apparently more complex (Perkovich 1999); they were partly related to security concerns, partly to display domestic technological prowess and partly to acquire a prominent seat in determining world affairs. In the case of the DPRK the primary factor for its apparent withdrawal from the NPT and staying out of the CTBT was probably driven by security concerns in the changed international scenario after the Cold War when it lost the protection of a collapsing Soviet Union and felt increasingly threatened by an unchecked United States. In the case of the United States the change in its attitude to the non-proliferation regime in general and the CTBT in particular came during the George W. Bush administration. Despite the subsequent regime change and Obama's declared support for the NPT regime, including the CTBT, there remains strong resistance and suspicion among the political and nuclear establishment to international treaties and arrangements. Irrespective of their motives, the presence of states with nuclear weapons outside the non-proliferation regime poses a peculiar and unique challenge. Can the regime make non-members comply with the norms and principles of the treaties even if they are not legally bound to the rules and regulations? On the other hand, can non-members behave like members of the regime in spirit if not in law? Would that be acceptable to the regime?

The third and, perhaps, the most formidable challenge comes from non-state actors, including but not limited to terrorist groups. According to UN Security Council Resolution 1540 of 28 April 2004, a non-state actor is defined as an 'individual or entity, not acting under the lawful authority of any State in conducting activities which come within the scope of this resolution'. This would include the quest of transnational or subnational fundamentalist or

## BOX 27.2 THE MAKING OF NUCLEAR WEAPONS

All nuclear weapons are made out of fissile materials, which are so-called because they are composed of atoms that can be split by neutrons in a self-sustaining chain-reaction to release enormous amounts of energy. The key fissile materials for nuclear weapons are plutonium-239 and uranium-235. While uranium occurs in nature, plutonium normally does not.

Natural uranium comprises about 99.3 per cent of uranium-238 and 0.7 per cent of uranium-235. For the purposes of making nuclear weapons this natural uranium is 'enriched' so that it comprises 90 per cent of the uranium-235 isotope. About 15 to 25 kilograms of highly enriched uranium is required to make one nuclear bomb.

Plutonium-239 is a man-made element and is the by-product of burning uranium-238 in a nuclear reactor. However, the plutonium recovered from a nuclear reactor has to be 'reprocessed' chemically before it can be used to build bombs. About six to eight kilograms of plutonium are required for one bomb.

'In mid-2009, the unofficial estimate of the global stockpile of highly enriched uranium (HEU) was 1600 ± 300 tons, enough for more than 60,000 nuclear weapons . . . and the global stockpile of separated plutonium was about 500 ± 25 tons . . . sufficient for more than 60,000 first-generation nuclear weapons' (International Panel 2009).

The explosive power of nuclear weapons is based on either splitting atoms through a process called 'fission' or combining atoms through a process called 'fusion'. The former is possible only with fissile material, like plutonium-239 and uranium-235, while the latter requires light atoms with very small mass, such as deuterium or tritium, both isotopes of hydrogen; hence a 'fusion' bomb is also called a hydrogen bomb or a thermonuclear bomb. While conventional explosives form the trigger for a 'fission' bomb, a nuclear explosion is required to trigger a 'fusion' bomb.

Since the first nuclear test on 16 July 1945 over 2,000 nuclear tests have been carried out worldwide until now. The latest nuclear test was conducted by DPRK on 25 May 2009. However, nuclear weapons have not been used for over 65 years since the United States first dropped a uranium bomb on Hiroshima on 6 August 1945 and then a plutonium bomb on Nagasaki on 9 August 1945.

cult groups, such as Aum Shinrikyo and al-Qa'ida, to develop nuclear weapons as well as the antics of nuclear scientists and entities, such as Dr A.Q. Khan, to hawk their materials and expertise. The Khan episode in particular indicates a triple proliferation threat: first there is a real concern about the ability of a weak state like Pakistan to manage and control its nuclear establishment and scientists and, as a corollary, its nuclear weapons. Second, it also highlights the possibility that states seeking a nuclear arsenal now have access to another unchecked network for acquiring nuclear weapons technology (see also chapter 29 in this volume). Third, there is also the serious possibility that armed transnational non-state actors seeking nuclear weapons (such as al-Qa'ida) might also receive the necessary know-how and expertise from the elaborate Khan network (Corera 2006, Albright and Hinderstein 2005).

Although non-state actors were known to have used biological and chemical weapons as early as the mid-1980s and sought to acquire nuclear weapons thereafter, this concern was accentuated following the events of 11 September 2001 when the phenomenon of mass terrorism became more apparent. Expert opinion is sharply divided over the threat posed by non-state actors, particularly armed non-state actors. According to Graham Allison, 'In sum, my best judgement is that based on current trends, a nuclear terrorist attack on the United States is more likely than not in the decade ahead . . . Former Defense Secretary William Perry has said that he thinks I underestimate the risk' (Allison 2006: 39). This alarmist view is challenged by other scholars who argue that 'nuclear terrorism is a less significant threat than is commonly believed, and that, among terrorists, Muslim extremists are not the most likely to use nuclear weapons' (Frost 2005: back cover).

These differences notwithstanding, it is important to note three characteristics of the use of biological, chemical and nuclear weapons by non-state actors. First, so far biological and chemical weapons have been used by non-state actors operating in the territory of their own state and *not* by transnational groups, such as al-Qa'ida in the territory of another state. This was the case of the Rajneesh group's attack in Oregon, the Aum Shinrikyo's assault on the Tokyo subway and the so-called Amerithrax attack in the US. Second, casualties caused by the use of chemical, biological and nuclear weapons by non-state actors has been minimal (far less than the daily death toll in Afghanistan and Pakistan caused by conventional means): in the Rajneesh case while 751 people were affected by salmonella poisoning, there were no deaths. The Aum Shinrikyo attacks affected 5,000 people and led to 12 deaths. In the Amerithrax case where letters containing anthrax were posted to several locations in the USA, 22 people were affected and five died. Third, so far there has been no known case of terrorism successfully using nuclear material. While one plot in England planned to use radioactive material in a conventional bomb, this 'dirty bomb' plan was nipped in the bud (BBC 2006).

To consider this threat realistically, five factors would have to be taken into account. These include the motives of the outfit (whether they are apocalyptic groups); their methods (whether they have a propensity for indiscriminate and mass-killings); access to nuclear material; the necessary monetary resources to buy nuclear material; and the expertise to manufacture and use such weapons (Zaman 2002). Given what we do know about transnational armed non-state actors, such as al-Qa'ida, and if we consider their outlook in terms of the five factors listed above, we can conclude that while there is certainly a high risk of nuclear terrorism, the probability of its occurrence is low. However, there is a higher risk and probability of the use of a radiological dispersal device (popularly called a 'dirty bomb' because it combines conventional explosives with other radioactive material, such as that used for medical or industrial purposes). Such a device when detonated would not cause a nuclear explosion but would cause radioactive material to scatter and fall over a large area, increasing panic and radioactive risk.

## Three approaches

These three sets of challenges from state parties, states not parties as well as non-state actors to the non-proliferation regime have generated at least three different approaches to address them.

First, there are the traditional multilateral institutional approaches anchored in negotiated treaty-based regimes, such as the 1963 PTBT, the 1968 NPT and the 1996 CTBT. All these treaties were concluded after a long-drawn out negotiating process. In the case of the CTBT, for instance, the idea was first proposed in the 1950s but was only taken up seriously in the early-1990s. This long delay may have been on account of the ongoing Cold War as well as the impetus of the NPT nuclear states to continue testing; the end of the Cold War and the cessation of tests by at least three of the five NPT nuclear states paved the way for the CTBT negotiations to begin. Given the complexity of negotiating treaties, such treaties are also not amenable to amendments and cannot be easily altered to adjust to the new realities. Finally, these treaties are invariably strong in setting norms and principles and in international law, but they tend to be relatively weak on enforcement. For instance, the NPT is as incapable of dissuading states from exercising the right to withdraw under Article X as it is of enforcing nuclear disarmament under Article VI. (Article X of the NPT gives each signatory the 'right to withdraw from the Treaty if it decides that extraordinary events . . . have jeopardised the supreme interests of its country' while Article VI calls on members to 'pursue negotiations in good faith on effective measures relating to the cessation of the nuclear arms race at an early date and to nuclear disarmament'.)

Despite these drawbacks the post-Cold War period was regarded as one of opportunity to strengthen the treaty-based regime. This promise was partly fulfilled in the mid-1990s following the indefinite extension of the NPT in 1995, the successful culmination of the CTBT in 1996 and adoption of the so-called '13 steps' in the 2000 NPT Review Conference. The '13 steps' suggest a set of practical measures for the 'systematic and progressive efforts' to implement Article VI of the NPT. They call for, among other things, a moratorium on nuclear testing, further unilateral reductions in the nuclear arsenals of nuclear weapons states, a reduced role for nuclear weapons in security policies, and an unequivocal undertaking by the NPT nuclear weapon states to the total elimination of their nuclear arsenals (NPT RevCon 2000: 14 para. 15). Simultaneously, the promise was also belied by the failure to make substantive progress on the Middle East resolution (a critical element of the 1995 deal to indefinitely extend the NPT), the inability to ensure the entry into force of the CTBT (partly on account of the shift in US policy and partly as a result of the Indian and Pakistani tests in 1998), and a retreat on the commitment to the '13 steps,' especially by the NPT nuclear states. The diminishing role of the multilateral approach was highlighted by the debacle of the 2005 NPT Review Conference, which 'foundered on procedural wrangling' and failed not only to produce a substantive consensus Final Document but also retracted from some of the significant agreements made in the 1995 and 2000 NPT Review Conferences, particularly the '13 steps' (Johnson 2005).

This trend appears to have continued with the 2010 NPT Review Conference; its 64-point action plan not only reiterates commitments made in previous NPT Review Conferences, notably the '13 steps' of 2000 but also lays out an even more ambitious agenda. However, the prospects of this grand plan being fulfilled have already stumbled on the political realities of nuclear weapons and the reluctance of key members states to cooperate. If the treaty-based regime was ineffective in holding member states to their commitments, it was even weaker in its efforts to deal with both non-member states as well as non-state actors.

Second, partly on account of these inherent weaknesses in the treaty-based regime, in the post-Cold War world a series of non-treaty based multilateral approaches were adopted, such as the various declarations and resolutions made by the UN Security Council and the UN General Assembly. This, of course, was not the first time that such an approach was followed: in the 1960s the UN General Assembly passed several resolutions supporting the NPT and, after further revision – concerning mainly the preamble and Articles IV and V, the General Assembly commended the draft text of the NPT, which is annexed to its resolution 2373 (XXII). Similarly, it was the General Assembly that resurrected the CTBT (after it had been blocked at the Conference on Disarmament in Geneva) by adopting a resolution (A/RES/50/245) on 10 September 1996. In April 2005 the General Assembly also adopted the *International Convention for the Suppression of Acts of Nuclear Terrorism* which addresses non-state actors.

In contrast, the UN Security Council, which had been in a debilitating paralysis during the Cold War, also became active on the issue of nuclear proliferation. The first indication of this was the various resolutions related to Iraq's invasion of Kuwait, which also established the UN Special Commission (UNSCOM) to disarm Iraq's nuclear, biological and chemical programmes. Another significant step was the Security Council's Presidential Statement of 31 January 1992 which stressed that 'proliferation of all weapons of mass destruction constitutes a threat to international peace and security' and with specific reference to nuclear weapons noted 'the decision of many countries to adhere to the [NPT] and emphasise the integral role in the implementation of that Treaty'. Ironically, this statement also highlighted the failure of the NPT nuclear states (who are also the permanent members of the UN Security Council) to keep their commitments to the Treaty. Subsequently, the Security Council passed several other resolutions related to state actors and nuclear proliferation including 1172 (1998), 1696 (2006), 1718 (2006) and 1737 (2006). A notable development was UN Security Council resolution 1887 (24 September 2009), which was the result of a special session chaired by President Obama. This is the first ever Council resolution that underlines the commitment of the NPT nuclear weapon states who are also the permanent members of the UN Security Council to Article VI of the NPT.

Pessimists have argued that this resolution was a last-ditch effort to salvage the NPT regime. They asserted that it was narrowly designed to ensure a modicum of success for the much-beleaguered NPT review conference in May 2010 and had a sell-by date of only a few months. They noted that the unprecedented reference to Article VI and a brief reference to disarmament was the only price that the five permanent nuclear members of the Security Council were willing to pay.

Optimists on the other hand, while acknowledging these omissions and commissions, nonetheless looked to the resolution as an important first step in bridging the gap between non-proliferation and disarmament. In addition, they also welcomed the resolution's efforts to highlight the clear and present danger posed by non-state actors seeking weapons of mass destruction. They argued that not only had disarmament been put back on the UN agenda but also the major powers and the original five nuclear weapons states were brought back to the UN to discuss this crucial issue.

In addition to 1887, the Security Council had previously passed several resolutions related to non-state actors and nuclear proliferation including 1373 (2001), 1540 (2004) and 1673 (2006). These resolutions are particularly innovative for two reasons: first they seek to deal with non-state actors and, second, they seek to provide stopgap arrangements to plug existing loopholes in the present treaty-based regime. UN Security Council resolution 1540 in particular is far reaching because it calls on all UN member states to 'adopt and enforce appropriate effective laws which prohibit any non-State actor to manufacture, acquire, possess, develop, transport, transfer or use nuclear, chemical or biological weapons and their means of delivery' as well as to 'take and enforce effective measures to establish domestic controls to prevent the proliferation of nuclear, chemical, or biological weapons and their means of delivery'. While the resolution has been generally welcomed given that present treaty-based regimes do not address this aspect of proliferation, there is concern that this approach of using the UN Security Council to legislate, if exercised often enough, would circumvent the negotiated approach to developing treaty-based regimes.

Third, there are a set of ad hoc, non-institutional, non-conventional approaches led by individual states or a group of states to address the immediate challenges of non-proliferation. These include the so-called preventive war against Iraq's nuclear, chemical and biological weapons in 2003, which was probably the first non-proliferation war; the US-led Proliferation Security Initiative (PSI); the EU3's negotiations with Iran; the six-party talks to address the DPRK's nuclear ambitions; and the Indo-US civilian nuclear initiative. All of these arrangements tend to be stronger on the enforcement dimension but are relatively weak in both international law as well as establishing norms and principles. Indeed, all of these initiatives are discriminatory and, predictably, do not enjoy universal adherence. Although the states behind these initiatives – primarily the NPT nuclear weapons states – have attempted to seek greater legitimacy for their actions by having these initiatives endorsed by the UN Security Council, there is concern that these initiatives might deal a fatal blow to the already weakened treaty-based non-proliferation regime. Nonetheless, given the inability of the existing formal regime to address many of the proliferation challenges of today, these ad hoc initiatives are likely to flourish.

Based on the above overview, it is evident that the liberal and institutional school would prefer strengthening the multilateral treaty-based institutions to address the non-proliferation challenges rather than opt for ad hoc and military options to deal with the present set of proliferation challenges. In contrast, the realist school would appreciate the ad hoc and unilateral or 'coalition of the willing' approaches, including the use of force, to ensure the security of the state vis-à-vis other states as well as non-state actors. However, it is equally clear that ad hoc approaches alone are unlikely to be effective either in the short- or the long-term unless they are intrinsically linked to the universally applicable treaty-based regime. This is possible only if the realists and liberals bridge their differences and seek a middle ground. Is such a compromise possible?

## Way forward

Scholars and practitioners from both the liberal and the realist schools believe that while in the short-term ad hoc and innovative approaches are likely to be preferred in addressing the most immediate challenges, such approaches should be dovetailed with the medium- to long-term objective of strengthening the global non-proliferation regime by eventually de-coupling nuclear weapons and international peace and security. For instance, among the proposals made by Shultz *et al.* (2007) are:

- Changing the Cold War posture of deployed weapons to increase warning time and reduce the danger of accidental or unauthorized use of nuclear weapons;
- Continuing to reduce substantially the size of nuclear forces in all states that possess them;

■ Eliminating short-range nuclear weapons designed to be forward deployed;

■ Achieving ratification of the CTBT;

■ Providing the highest possible security standards for all stocks of weapons . . . [and fissile material] . . . everywhere in the world;

■ Halting the production of fissile material for weapons globally;

■ Resolving regional confrontations and conflicts that give rise to new nuclear powers.

Most of these proposals are neither radical nor new but their authors are new converts from the original nuclear weapons state and, therefore, this message carries greater weight than that of other analysts. Many of these proposals form part of Obama's Prague agenda.

In addition, countries which are presently under the extended nuclear umbrella of nuclear weapons states, might consider whether their dependency on such weapons is posing a challenge for nuclear disarmament. What are the likely implications for such countries to reconsider their position and move out from under the nuclear umbrella? Would it really make them more vulnerable or less vulnerable? Would such vulnerability be worth it to start the process of nuclear disarmament rolling? What is the likely critical mass of countries required to ensure that the process of disarmament could begin and be sustained? Yet another approach to de-linking nuclear weapons and world order would be for one of the current permanent members of the UN Security Council and nuclear weapons states to give up their arsenals and become the Council's first non-nuclear weapons permanent member. What are the prospects of one of the nuclear weapons states considering that their security is unaffected even if they were to give up their nuclear arms? It would also, inevitably, set the stage for the creation of a new world order not based on nuclear weapons and would have a lasting impact on the reform of the UN Security Council. These ideas are compelling and the only missing element is the will to operationalize them. This is, perhaps, the mother of all challenges.

## ■ Further reading

*Disarmament Diplomacy* at www.acronym.org.uk/dd/index.htm. An independent, quarterly journal of the Acronym institute which provides some of the best in-depth and critical coverage of developments in disarmament negotiations, multilateral arms control and international security.

Jozef Goldblat, *Can Nuclear Proliferation be Stopped?* (Geneva International Peace Research Institute (GIPRI), 2007). An excellent, concise overview of the present state of nuclear proliferation which includes recommendations that build on, and go beyond, the '13 steps'.

Waheguru Pal Singh Sidhu and Ramesh Thakur (eds.), *Arms Control after Iraq* (UN University Press, 2006). Offers global and regional perspectives to examine the impact of the ongoing Iraq crisis on nuclear proliferation and stresses a central role for the UN in non-proliferation.

*The Bulletin of Atomic Scientists* at www.thebulletin.org/. The oldest (founded in 1945 by atomic scientists involved in the Manhattan Project) and most respected journal on all things nuclear, especially non-proliferation. Its data on nuclear arsenals of nuclear states (prepared by the Natural Resources Defense Council) is regarded as one of the most reliable.

*Nuclear Threat Initiative* (NTI) at www.nti.org/ is a one-stop website for nuclear, biological and chemical weapon programmes of different countries. The website also hosts an innovative on-line tutorial (WMD 411) which provides essential information on nuclear weapons and efforts to disarm them.

*In My Lifetime*, a film by the Nuclear World Project, at http://thenuclearworld.org/category/in-my-lifetime/

*Countdown to Zero*, a film by the Global Zero Movement, at http://www.globalzero.org/en/film

*Nuclear Tipping Point*, a film by the Nuclear Security Project of the Nuclear Threat Initiative, at http://www.nucleartippingpoint.org/film/film.html

# Private Security

Deborah Avant

## Abstract

In this chapter, students will learn about the growth of private security – security allocated through the market. The chapter explains why this development is important for the control of force and outlines a debate over its costs and benefits. It also describes the current market, compares it to other markets for violence in the past, and explains its origins. The chapter encourages students to think about how the market for force poses trade-offs to the state and non-state actors that seek to control it and how a market for force challenges some of the central assumptions in security studies.

## Introduction

It has long been common sense in security studies that the control, sanctioning and use of violence fall to states. Private security activity in the last two decades, though, lays waste to this conventional wisdom. More than one half of the people the US has deployed in Iraq and Afghanistan have been contractors working for private military and security companies (PMSCs): companies that, under contract, perform services that might otherwise be provided by military or police forces . As lawlessness followed the fall of the Iraqi government and coalition forces were stretched thin an 'army' of private personnel flooded into the country. Some were hired by the Coalition Provisional Authority (CPA) to train the Iraqi police force, the Iraqi army, and a private Iraqi force to guard government facilities and oil fields. Other PMSCs worked for the US Army translating and interrogating prisoners, or for a company called Parsons, providing security for employees rebuilding Iraq's oil fields. The role of PMSCs in the Iraqi occupation was thrust into the public eye when four private security personnel working for the US PMSC, Blackwater, were killed and mutilated on 31 March 2004 and when contracted interrogators working for CACI and Titan were among those implicated in the abuses at Abu Ghraib prison. A similarly wide range of services have been provided to the US government in Afghanistan and with comparable controversy. The US government is not the only consumer of military and security services, though. NGOs, oil companies, the United Nations (UN), and many other countries join the US as customers of PMSCs.

The role of private military and security services in Iraq is simply the latest chapter in the private security boom. While the state's monopoly on the use of force Max Weber (1964) wrote about was exaggerated from the start and there has been a role for the private sector in security for some time, since the end of the Cold War that role has grown and is larger and different now than it has been since the foundation of the modern state. PMSCs today provide more services and more kinds of services including some that have been considered core military capabilities in the modern era. Also, changes in the nature of armed conflicts have led tasks less central to the core of modern militaries (such as operating complex weapons systems and policing) to be subcontracted to PMSCs. Furthermore, states are not the only organizations that hire security providers. Increasingly transnational non-state actors (NGOs, multinational corporations, and others) are financing security services to accomplish their goals. In sum, a burgeoning transnational market for force now exists alongside the system of states and state forces.

This chapter analyses these issues in five sections. The first explains why this development is important for the control of force and outlines the debate over the market's costs and benefits. The second section describes the current market for force and provides some examples of how it works. The third section compares today's market for force to other markets for violence in the past. The fourth section describes the origins of the current market. Finally, the chapter concludes with some thoughts about how the market for force poses trade-offs to the control of force and changes the role of both states and non-state actors in security studies.

## Private security and the control of force

Why should we worry – or even care – about this transnational market? The answer is simple, private security may affect how and whether people can control violence. The existence of this market also raises some important questions for students of security studies: Does the privatization of security undermine state control of violence? Can the privatization of security enhance state control of violence? Does the privatization of security chart new ways by which violence might be collectively controlled? How does private security affect the ability to contain the use of force within political process and social norms?

It also raises questions about the language we use to talk about and analyse these developments. In keeping with the most common usage, 'private' refers to actors that are not governments. Commercial entities and NGOs thus fall into this category – however, so do vigilantes, paramilitaries and organized crime bosses. Though many use 'public' to denote governmental institutions of whatever sort, it is important to distinguish between governments that have the capacity and legitimacy to claim to work toward collective ends (strong states) and those that do not (weak states).

The implications of privatizing security for the control of force have been hotly debated. Pessimists claim that the turn to private security threatens to undermine state control and democratic processes (e.g. Silverston 1998, Musah and Fayemi 2000). In Africa, for example, Musah and Fayemi (2000: 23–26) argue that the consequences of privatizing security can be devastating. Though contemporary mercenaries attempt to distinguish themselves from the lawless 'guns for hire' that ran riot over Africa during the Cold War, their consortium with arms manufacturers, mineral exploiters, and Africa's authoritarian governments and warlords sustains the militarization of Africa. This poses 'a mortal danger to democracy in the region'. Unregulated private armies linked to international business interests threaten to undermine democracy and development in Africa.

Optimists, however, declare that private options offer solutions to intractable security problems that can operate within national interests and/or the values shared by the international community (e.g. Shearer 1998, Brooks 2000). David Shearer (1998) argued that in Africa and elsewhere PMSCs willing to take on messy intervention tasks that Western militaries were eager to avoid could help end civil conflicts that would otherwise be intractable. He argued that rather than outlawing PMSCs, the international community should engage them, give them a legitimate role and expect them to operate as professionals, according to the values held by the international social system. Doug Brooks (2003) proposed that a consortium of PMSCs could bring years of peacekeeping experience and NATO-level professionalism to protect vulnerable populations in places like the Democratic Republic of the Congo (DRC) or Darfur, Sudan; they could also train local gendarmes in policing and human rights so as to build a more professional local force.

Who is right? It turns out they both are. These two sets of arguments often hinge on different conceptions of 'control' and compare private security to different state alternatives. Privatization's effect on the capability of forces and the values they serve varies depending on the issue and context in question. Privatization sometimes leads to greater capabilities, other times to lesser capabilities and sometimes leads to more, sometimes less integration of violence with prevailing international values. Inevitably, however, privatization involves the redistribution of power over the control of violence. In effect, the shift to private guardians changes who guards the guardians.

When considering the effects of privatization in different settings, a fundamental intervening variable is the varying capacities of states. Strong states that are coherent, capable and legitimate to begin with are best able to manage the risks of privatization and harness the PMSCs to produce new public goods but at the risk of corrupting democratic processes. Weak states with ineffective and corrupt forces have the most to gain (or the least to lose) from the capacities offered by the private sector, but also are the least able to manage private forces for the public good. Attempts to harness the private sector for state building in such environments are often a desperate gamble.

## A transnational market for military and security services

Since the end of the Cold War, both demand for and supply of private military and security services grew. Demand can be found among states, international organizations, NGOs, global corporations, and wealthy individuals. The number of private security providers burgeoned during the 1990s with well over two hundred such companies making the news between 1995 and 2004. Private firms trained militaries in more than 42 countries during the 1990s. By the early twenty-first century several hundred companies globally operate in over 100 countries on six continents (Singer 2003b: 2).

Though it is hard to specify the size of the market, we have a variety of benchmarks. One set of projections within the industry suggested in 1997 that revenues from the global international security market (military and policing services in international and domestic markets) would rise from $55.6 billion in 1990 to $202 billion in 2010 (see Vines 1999: 47). In 2003 it was estimated that global revenue for this industry was over $100 billion (Singer 2003b: 2). PMSCs were also valuable commodities in their own right as those with publicly traded stocks growing at twice the rate of the Dow Jones Industrial Average in the 1990s. The Commission on Wartime Contracting (CWC), established by Congress in the US in 2008, estimates conservatively that at least $177 billion has been obligated in contracts and grants to support US operations in Afghanistan and Iraq since 2001 (see CWC 2011: 1).

What kinds of services do these firms provide? Despite the media hype, few contracts promise participation in combat. Instead, PMSCs offer three broad categories of military support: operational support, military advice and training, and logistical support. PMSCs also offer services more similar to policing, ranging from site security (armed and unarmed), crime prevention and intelligence. Singer (2003a) disaggregated these firms by the relationship of their primary services to 'the tip of the spear' in 'battlespace'. Services closest to the tip of the spear are those on the front lines of battle, typically the most

## BOX 28.1  THE EVOLUTION OF A PRIVATE MILITARY AND SECURITY COMPANY: THE EXAMPLE OF ARMORGROUP (FORMERLY DSL, NOW PART OF G4S)

ArmorGroup began as DSL, a British firm founded in 1981. DSL was purchased by a publicly held American conglomerate called Armor Holdings in 1997. Most of its employees that operate out of its London office are former British Special Air Services (SAS), but the company also draws on retired US military personnel and local personnel in its offices all over the world. In 2000 Armor Group had offices in the US, the UK, South Africa, DRC/Zaire, Mozambique, Kenya, West Africa, North Africa, Zimbabwe, Uganda, Hong Kong, Nepal, Asia, the Philippines, France, Bosnia-Herzegovina, Russia, Kazakhstan, Ukraine, Columbia, Ecuador, Venezuela and Brazil, and regional managers in Europe and the CIS, Russia, Latin America, Southern Africa, Central Africa, North Africa, the Far East, and the Middle East. In most of the regional offices, a small expatriate core with mostly British military background employs predominantly local personnel. ArmorGroup works according to local laws and with local personnel, but its behaviour in one area affects its reputation worldwide. The company's leadership claims to be keenly aware of the need to have professional standards for behaviour and monitor them closely.

ArmorGroup has worked for a variety of customers, including private businesses, INGOs and states. It provided security and logistics personnel to the UN mission in the former Yugoslavia from 1992–1995, protected BP oil property against attacks in Columbia, provided security for Bechtel in Iraq, trained Iraqi police under contract with the British Government in Basra, and also worked for such clients as De Beers, Shell, Mobile, Amoco, Chevron, CARE and GOAL.

DSL was privately held until 1997, but was publicly traded as part of Armor Holdings from 1997–2004. In January 2004, US based ArmorGroup informed the Securities and Exchange Commission that it intended to sell off its London-based affiliate DSL (renamed ArmorGroup International) to a group of its own staff. With that sale complete, it was again a privately held company. In April 2008 ArmorGroup International was purchased by G4S (formerly Group 4 Securicor), the world's largest security company. Like all PMSCs ArmorGroup fills contracts from its database, supplemented by advertisements. That is, it has a small contingent of full-time employees and a large database of individuals from which to fill specific contracts. These databases are not exclusive – persons may appear on the databases of several different firms. This means that someone could be working for ArmorGroup one week and Control Risk Group, Xe, Erinys, or a wide variety of others the next.

Sources: O'Brien 1998, ArmorGroup company literature, author's interviews.

deadly and dangerous. Figure 28.1 draws on Singer's battlespace analogy, extends it to police as well as military services and provides examples of contracts providing these services in particular settings.

A small number of contracts have stipulated services at the very tip of the spear that most closely resemble 'core' military competencies – armed operational support on the battlefield. Sandline and Executive Outcomes (EO) (both now defunct) became famous for missions that included the deployment of armed personnel on the battlefield, Sandline in Sierra Leone and Papua New Guinea and EO in Angola and Sierra Leone. EO closed its doors for business after the post-apartheid South African government passed legislation ostensibly designed to regulate the export of military services but believed by many to try and outlaw this kind of activity. Though EO employees now operate or work for a variety of firms – some new, some outside of South Africa – the firms are less public about their dealings.

Many more contracts do not raise troops or deploy personnel on the battlefield, but offer advice and training to military forces. The training programmes vary widely from the high end where PMSCs are reorganizing the force structure and training officers in battlefield scenarios to more mundane troop training, simulations, and peacekeeping training. Examples of such firms in the US include MPRI, Booz Allen and Hamilton, Cubic, and DynCorp. UK examples include ArmorGroup, Aims Limited, Gurka Security Guards, Watchguard International and Sandline. Similar firms can also be found in Canada, France, Israel, Australia, and Belgium.

There are also firms that offer operational support in the form of command and control, transport, and weapons systems. Both Sandline and MPRI suggested they could offer command and control support to UN peace

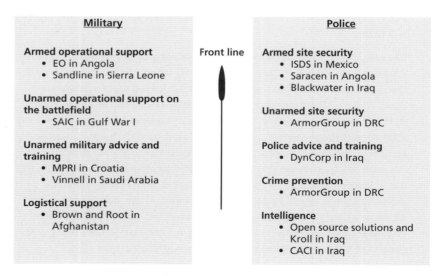

*Figure 28.1* Contracts in battlespace

*Source:* Avant 2005: 17.

missions. More common are contractors that provide support for or operate weapons and information systems on the battlefield. As the technological sophistication of weapons systems and platforms has grown, more and more contractors have been hired to work with troops to maintain and support these systems. During the 2003 war with Iraq, for instance, PMSCs also provided operational support for the B-2 stealth bomber, the F-117 stealth fighter, Global Hawk UAV, U-2 reconnaissance aircraft, the M-1 tank, the Apache helicopter, and many navy ships.

Logistics support for militaries in the field is another significant market for the private sector that has many providers. A wide variety of PMSCs offer transport, telecom, food, laundry, and other administrative services as well as setting up and taking down temporary bases and camps. Haliburton subsidiary, Kellogg, Brown and Root (a US company) has a huge presence in this market. It supported American troops in Somalia, Haiti, Bosnia, Afghanistan and the 2003 war with Iraq.

PMSCs also offer internal security services, closer to what police routinely do, such as site security, international civilian police, police training, crime prevention and intelligence. They include decades-old private security companies such as Pinkertons and Wackenhut as well as new firms in South Africa, the UK, the US, and all over Europe. For instance, virtually all US contributions to international civilian police units in the 1990s were DynCorp employees. DynCorp was also responsible for protecting Afghan president Hamid Karzai.

Harder to categorize are the contracts that offer operational capacity in counter-insurgency, anti-terrorism, and other special operations. These services, offered to states as well as multinational corporations and other non-governmental entities, work in the nebulous area that connects external and internal security. The demand for these kinds of services undoubtedly reflects the increasing concern with international criminal threats and the blurring of internal and external security (Andreas 2003).

The role of PMSCs in Iraq yielded insights into the difficulty of distinguishing between policing-type security duties and combat in a violent environment. For example, Blackwater employees providing security to US Coalition Provisional Authority administrator Paul Bremer, carried weapons, had their own helicopters and fought off insurgents in ways that were hard to distinguish from combat (Priest 2004). The CWC set forth three categories of contracted services: logistics, reconstruction (including military and police training), and security – which they highlight as a set of services requiring strict scrutiny given the controversies created by armed security guards and mobile details in Iraq and Afghanistan (CWC 2009).

A helpful way to think about the contours of markets for force more generally is set out in Table 28.1. This makes use of the distinction between the financing and delivery of security services. As the shaded boxes in Table 28.1 indicate, the term 'privatization' refers to decisions to devolve the delivery or financing of services to private entities – the two outermost rows and columns of Table 28.1. Though conventional wisdom suggests that traditional

Table 28.1 The variety of arrangements for allocating violence

| | Financing for security services | | | | |
| --- | --- | --- | --- | --- | --- |
| | National financing | Foreign national financing | Multinational financing | Private financing (for profit) | Private financing (not for profit) |
| National delivery | USA in WWII | German troops in the American Revolution | The first Gulf War | Shell financing Nigerian Forces | WWF financing park guards in DRC |
| Foreign national delivery | German troops in the American Revolution | Korean troops fighting for the USA in Vietnam | The first Gulf War | Branch group contributing to Nigerian forces in Sierra Leone | |
| Multinational delivery | NATO in Kosovo | Muslim states' contribution to Western military aid in Bosnia | UN Peacekeeping | | |
| Private delivery (for profit) | MPRI's provision of ROTC Trainers to the USA | MPRI's work for Croatia | MPRI's work for Bosnia | DSL working for Lonhro in Mozambique | DSL working for ICRC around the world |
| Private delivery (not for profit) | | | 'Green Cross' | BP financing Columbian paramilitaries | Wildaid in Asia |

Source: Avant 2005: 25

military forces are the norm, the last century has provided cases that fit in almost every box. The not-for-profit financing column is the most problematic, conceptually, as it encompasses a range of possibilities from NGOs to rebel, paramilitary, and militia forces. It is also, however, one of the more important columns. During the post-Cold War era, private (for and not-for) profit financing and delivery have been significant areas of growth.

## The current market compared

This is not the first market for force. Markets for allocating violence were common before the systems of states came to dominate world politics. Feudal lords supplemented their forces with contracted labour from the beginning of the twelfth century, and from the end of the thirteenth century, through the Peace of Westphalia in 1648, virtually all force was allocated through the market. Furthermore, the rise of the state did not immediately preclude the market allocation of violence. Early modern states both delegated control over force to commercial entities and participated in the market as both suppliers and purchasers.

Chartered companies, prominent in the seventeenth and eighteenth centuries, such as the British East India Company, were an instance of state-delegated commercial control over violence. Chartered companies were state-designated entities for engaging in long distance trade and establishing colonies. The Dutch, English, French, and Portuguese all chartered companies during this time. French companies were state enterprises forged by the king and designed to increase state power later in the game. Dutch companies were private wealth-seeking enterprises that were organized in a charter so as to enhance the Dutch profit relative to the English or (particularly) the Portuguese. The crown chartered the English companies for similar reasons. These forces were both an army and a police force for establishing order and then protecting both trade routes and new territory. Also during the early period of the state, states rented out their forces to other friendly states. These troops would arrive equipped and ready to fight under the command of the contracting government.

Even in the modern system, some states have relied on the private sector, for weapons particularly, but also for logistics support, and for a variety of services idiosyncratic to a particular conflict. The US government, for instance, has a long history of looking to the market for military services. Up until the beginning of World War II, most of these services were in the area of logistics support and weapons procurement. During the Cold War, however, the US hired firms to perform military training missions as well. The British government hired less frequently than the US from the market for military services in the modern period, but allowed its citizens to sell their services abroad. The commercial sale of security services by British citizens abroad can be traced back through the centuries (Thomson 1994: 22). More recently UK Special Air Services (SAS) personnel formed firms to sell military and security services during the Cold War. For instance, in 1967 Colonel Sir David Stirling founded WatchGuard International (O'Brien 2000). And, of course, individuals acting on their own sold a variety of services in Africa during the Cold War. Also, states still do 'rent out' their forces – to UN peacekeeping units or to other states. In the first Gulf War, for instance, US forces were subsidized by Japan. In the 2003 war with Iraq, the US paid forces from other countries to participate in the coalition.

While market allocation of security was never completely eliminated in the modern era, it was frowned upon. This led private security to be informally organized, secretive, and directed to a specific customer base. Soldiers of fortune operated in the shadows – as did the covert private military services provided to individual governments. In the current system, though, PMSCs have a corporate structure and operate openly, posting job listings on their web-sites and writing papers and articles mulling over the costs and benefits of the private sector in security (see, for example, IPOA 2007). They have sought, and received, some degree of international acceptance.

The corporate form, relative openness, acceptance, and transnational spread of today's security industry bear many similarities to the late Middle Ages and Early Modern period. There are some features of today's market, though, that are unique. First, unlike the military enterprisers of the late Middle Ages today's PMSCs do not so much provide the foot soldiers, but more often act as supporters, trainers, and force multipliers for local forces. PMSCs, then, are different from private armies – when they leave, they leave behind whatever expertise they have imparted – subject to whatever local political controls (or lack thereof) exist. Second, unlike the period of the chartered companies, states do not authorize private takeover of other territories, even though transnational corporations and INGOs finance security on their own – either by subsidizing weak states or hiring PMSCs. Thus chartered companies provided a more specific administrative and legal framework for the private use of force than is the case with private financiers today.

## Why the current market?

As suggested above, the growth of the market was tied to supply and demand. In the 1990s, the supply factors came from both local (the end of apartheid in South Africa) and international (the end of the Cold War) phenomena that caused militaries to be downsized in the late 1980s and early 1990s. Military downsizing led to a flood of experienced personnel available for contracting. Concomitant with the increase in supply was an increase in the demand for military skills on the private market – from Western states that had downsized their militaries, from countries seeking to upgrade and Westernize their militaries as a way of demonstrating credentials for entry into Western institutions, from rulers of weak or failed states no longer propped up by superpower patrons, and from non-state actors such as private firms, INGOs, and groups of citizens in the territories of weak or failed states.

The downsizing of these militaries took place in an ideological context where liberal capitalist ideas were in the ascendancy. Initially, prevailing ideas about the benefits of privatization were associated with the powerful conservative coalitions in the US and the UK in the 1980s, but the collapse of the Soviet bloc, the ensuing privatization of state-owned industries across Europe, and the endorsement of these principles by international financial institutions like the International Monetary Fund and the World Bank led privatization to be endorsed much more widely. The appeal of privatization ideas both led people to see private alternatives as obvious and affected the growth of private supply.

The end of the Cold War also had important political repercussions which influenced the market for force. Just two years into what US President George H.W. Bush called the 'New World Order,' a rash of smaller scale conflicts unleashed disorder and demands for intervention. As the clamour for a Western response grew just as Western militaries were shrinking, nascent PMSCs provided a stop-gap tool for meeting greater demands with smaller forces. For example, according to Robert Perito (2002), who served as the Deputy Director of the International Criminal Investigative Training Assistance Program at the US Department of Justice during the 1990s, this was the logic for the initial use of DynCorp to mobilize a small group of international civilian police to send to Haiti. The US had no such force and DynCorp could provide one.

The Cold War's end had a different impact in the former eastern bloc (where it led to defunct governance structures and forces, new opportunities, and a sudden opening to global flows) and in the developing world (where it abruptly ended superpower patronage – revealing the enduring difficulties of these governments and their militaries – corruption, poor standards, poor management, ethnic rivalries, etc.). In each instance, the potential for violence increased. Weak governments paved the way for ethnic mobilization, transnational criminal activity, warlords, rebels and paramilitaries, and the result ravaged civilians, enslaved children, destroyed the environment, and otherwise disrupted order and violated global norms (see Fearon and Laitin 2003). In some cases PMSCs provided tools for weak governments in the eastern bloc and the developing world (e.g. Angola, Papua New Guinea and Sierra Leone) to shore up their capabilities.

And it was not just states that took advantage of the market for force. Transnational firms in the extractive industry, particularly, are often likely to stay in dangerous areas if that is where the resources are. Unable to rely on weak states for security and often unwilling to leave, these actors have provided another pool of demand for non-state protection that PMSCs have exploited. The reason PMSCs – and not multilateral armed responses, such as those provided by the UN – have thrived is because multilateral forces have been much harder to deploy and (often because of problematic mandates) seen as less effective.

Thus, both material and ideational changes placed private military and security options on the agenda. The reluctance of states to take on the variety of missions that people have felt moved to respond to, and the poor performance of multilateral institutions have made the private alternative appear more workable, as have prevailing beliefs that private means cheaper and better.

## Conclusion

Global forces, new ideas and political choices have combined to enhance the opportunities for private delivery of and private financing for security services. As a result, a growing market for force now exists alongside, and intertwined with, state military and police forces.

This development holds significant implications for students of security studies. It also has implications for the control of force that poses states, firms and people with a number of trade-offs. Individual states can sometimes enhance the capacity of their forces, and thereby increase their control and power. At the same time, though, the market undermines the *collective* monopoly of the state over violence in world politics, and thus a central feature of the sovereign system. Without that collective monopoly, states face increasing dilemmas about whether to hire from the private sector for security and how best to regulate the export of security services.

The existence of an extensive market alternative for military services changes the options available to states for the conduct of foreign and security policies. Market alternatives, however, through government contracts or regulation, operate differently from military organizations, and advantage some portions of the government more than others. In particular, using market allocation generally advantages executives relative to legislatures, reduces transparency, and reduces the mobilization required to send public forces abroad. Furthermore, the use of market alternatives often involves the private sector in decision-making – giving those with commercial interests in policy influence over its formation and implementation. Because of these changes, the market option has made it easier to undertake adventurous foreign policies – or actions that do not have widespread support in a polity – and thus it is more likely that such actions will be taken.

The US has taken particular advantage of this market. PMSCs were particularly vital to US efforts in Iraq, where they not only supported US troops via logistics and operational support missions, but also deployed quickly to the country to train Iraqi forces and provide security as stability unravelled in the wake of Saddam Hussein's fall from power. Sometimes US decisions to use PMSCs have been more costly than using US military forces, other times less, but as one US official told me in 1999, 'it is easier to get money out of the Pentagon than people'. The US can thus use PMSCs as force multipliers for its own troops, to train and supervise other troops, and even as a tool for recruiting something like an imperial force.

Not all states have reacted to the market in the same way. For example, in contrast to the US, South Africa has eschewed the private military and security sector in its foreign policy. South Africa's efforts to sideline PMSCs led it to forego new policy tools and also decreased its ability to control the violent actions of its citizens abroad. This was particularly poignant as South African personnel and PMSCs have poured into Iraq under contract with the US to support stability operations in the wake of a war that the South African government did not support (*The Star* 2004).

Whether privatization of security in states like the US will lead to disruptive change in military effectiveness or be folded into a new process of control is the $64,000 question. In Iraq, well publicized cost overruns from outsourcing, dramatic scenes of private personnel abused and abusing, unclear coordination between public and private forces all seemed to point toward an eroding process of control. Thus far, however, the lessons the US has drawn appear to be focused on how to better regulate these forces rather than how to get rid of them. Private forces appear to have been folded into the future of American foreign policy as a necessary dimension in an era of uncertain and ever-changing threats.

As well as offering new foreign policy choices to states, privatization also shifts power over violence outside the bounds of state machinery. This is most obvious when non-state actors finance security, which accords influence over security decisions to actors both outside the territory of the state and outside of government. In individual instances, transnational financing often diffuses power over the control of force. From a broader perspective, this diffusion of power should also lead us to expect a greater variety of actors to have influence over the use of force, should predict a furthering of competing institutions with overlapping jurisdictions over force, and thus accords with many who have argued that the world is entering a neo-medieval period (see Bull 1977: 254–255, Cerny 1998).

What is often lost in contemporary commentary is the notion that the 'ideal' form of markets can only function effectively when the state is also playing its 'ideal' role. Similarly, NGOs, to play their ideal role, rely on a government. In this sense, the privatization of security does not so much transfer power from one institution (the state) to another (the market) so much as pose challenges to the way both states and markets have functioned in the modern system. Instead of focusing on ideal types of states and markets (which have little basis in historical fact), it would be more prudent to examine the variety of institutional forms that are emerging, the way they are functioning, and think about their viability in terms of the degree to which they generate mechanisms that work together, potentially generating reinforcing processes, or chafe against one another, generating continued change.

The market for force has loosened the ties between states and force and undermined states' collective monopoly on violence in the international system. This has not made states, per se, less important, but opened the way for changes in the roles states and other actors play in controlling force on the world stage. The rush to normative judgment about whether the privatization of security was 'good' or 'bad' has impeded analysis of the range of privatization's effects, the trade-offs associated with private security, and the choices available for its management. Both policy-makers and their constituents, however, would be well served by refocusing on these issues now.

## Further reading

Deborah Avant, *The Market for Force: The Consequences of Privatizing Security* (Cambridge University Press, 2005). This book provides an overview of the global market and its implications.

Simon Chesterman and Chia Lehnardt (eds.), *From Mercenaries to Markets: The Rise and Regulation of Private Military Companies* (Oxford University Press, 2007). This book brings together a range of analysts and participants in the market to examine the potential for regulation.

Elke Krahmann, *States, Citizens and the Privatization of Security* (Cambridge University Press, 2010). This books analyses the different trajectories of privatization in the US, Britain and Germany.

P.W. Singer, *Corporate Warriors: the Rise of the Privatized Military Industry* (Cornell University Press, 2003). This book suggests a typology of military firms and gives a good history of three: Executive Outcomes, MPRI and Haliburton.

PMSC websites:
DynCorp http://www.dyn-intl.com/
Triple Canopy http://www.triplecanopy.com/triplecanopy/en/home/
G4S http://www.g4s.uk.com/
MPRI http://www.mpri.com/web/

# PART 4
# CONTEMPORARY CHALLENGES

# CHAPTER 29

# The International Arms Trade

William D. Hartung

## Abstract

In this chapter, students will learn about the dynamics of the global arms trade and how they have changed substantially from the end of the Cold War to the new era marked by the 9/11 terror attacks. Sales of major combat equipment continue to pose the greatest challenge in managing relations between states. But as the proportion of wars carried on within states rather than between states has accelerated, small arms and light weapons (SALW) have become the tools of choice in most of the world's conflicts. In an era of asymmetric warfare, the 'high end' of the weapons spectrum has also become cause for increasing concern as some regional powers seek the technology to produce nuclear, chemical, and biological weapons. Using shifting United States policies as a primary example, this chapter traces the political, economic, and strategic factors driving these three strands of the arms trade: major combat systems, small arms, and technology suited to building nuclear weapons.

## Introduction

The international arms trade is intimately linked to issues of peace and security, justice and injustice, and development and underdevelopment. Arms sales can fuel regional and local conflicts, or help create balances of power that head off conflict. They provide repressive regimes with the tools they need to suppress democratic movements and commit human rights abuses. They can be used to facilitate terrorist acts, or to support oppressed populations in fighting off genocide and ethnic cleansing. They can fuel technological growth or undermine economic development. They can serve as an independent variable fueling conflict, or merely a tool used by both sides in a preexisting conflict driven by other causes. The impacts of exported weapons depend on the forces driving the trade and the circumstances under which they are used.

The dynamics of the global arms trade have changed substantially over the past five decades, from the Cold War to the war on terror. The rationales for the trade have ranged from geopolitics (cementing relations with key strategic allies) to geoeconomics (securing substantial weapons deals that serve to subsidize the defense industrial bases of arms exporting countries). These shifting justifications have mirrored changing global circumstances, as analysed below. But before addressing that crucial set of issues, a few definitions are in order.

## Three channels for arms transfers

The global arms trade is composed of three different elements: (1) the trade in major systems such as combat aircraft, tanks, and warships; (2) the trade in small arms and light weapons (SALW), from AK-47s to shoulder-fired missiles (see Hartung 2000); and (3) the trade in 'dual use' items with both civilian and military applications, including everything from shotguns and unarmed helicopters to equipment that can be used to manufacture nuclear, chemical, and biological weapons.

The trade in major conventional weapons is the best known, most lucrative, and best monitored element of the global arms business. Major arms manufacturing states such as the USA, Russia, the UK, France and China – the five permanent members of the UN Security Council – generally control between two-thirds and three-quarters of all global weapons sales in a given year. Table 29.1 shows that between 2002 and 2009, for example, these states accounted for between 69 and 82 per cent of total global arms sales agreements (Grimmett 2010: 69).

The pursuit of exports of fighter planes, tanks, military helicopters and combat ships to states in Europe, Asia, and the Middle East sparks intense competition among major suppliers. There are clear economic incentives for pursuing these deals. Sales of major combat systems not only generate revenues

*Table 29.1* Arms transfer agreements by the permanent five members of the UN Security Council, 2002–2009 (in US$m)

| | 2002 | 2003 | 2004 | 2005 | 2006 | 2007 | 2008 | 2009 |
|---|---|---|---|---|---|---|---|---|
| US | 12,914 | 14,447 | 12,670 | 12,773 | 15,955 | 24,387 | 37,186 | 22,610 |
| Russia | 5,600 | 4,300 | 8,200 | 8,200 | 14,700 | 10,600 | 5,400 | 10,400 |
| France | 600 | 2,800 | 2,900 | 5,900 | 7,700 | 2,000 | 3,100 | 7,400 |
| UK | 800 | 3,000 | 4,200 | 2,900 | 4,200 | 9,800 | 200 | 1,500 |
| China | 400 | 600 | 1,000 | 2,900 | 1,500 | 2,400 | 2,100 | 1,700 |
| World Total | 28,414 | 30,547 | 42,070 | 45,573 | 56,155 | 59,987 | 61,386 | 57,510 |
| P-5 as % World Total | (71%) | (82%) | (69%) | (72%) | (78%) | (82%) | (78%) | (76%) |

*Source*: Grimmett 2010: 69.

and profits for military firms, they contribute to the balance of trade and provide jobs in key regions and localities of the exporting state.

While economics is one driver of the trade in major conventional weapons, politics and security often have an even more important role to play. During the Cold War, the USA used arms exports to cement relationships with key regional allies such as Iran, Indonesia, Taiwan, and Brazil. These relationships involved tacit or explicit commitments to promote US security interests in their region; to develop the capacity to operate smoothly alongside US military forces in the event of a conflict; and, in a number of key cases, to provide access to military bases in the recipient country (Klare 1984: 29–30, 35). Without arms sales as a tool, it would have been difficult for the US to develop the 'global reach' that it achieved during the Cold War, and that it has maintained ever since.

During this same period, the Soviet Union made substantial arms exports, often in the form of military aid. From supporting national liberation movements in South Africa, Angola, and Central America to courting nationalist regimes in Egypt and India, Soviet exports were even more driven by political considerations than those of the West. The USSR's range of clients was much smaller than the USA's, with just 20 major clients in the Third World for most of the Cold War period. By the mid-1980s, just five clients – Angola, India, Iraq, Libya and Syria – accounted for 75 per cent of Soviet weapons exports. Of these, three – India, Iraq, and Syria – had Treaties of Friendship with the USSR (Anthony 1989: 200).

European suppliers such as France and the United Kingdom were particularly dependent on exports to sustain their capabilities to produce their own aircraft, combat vehicles and fighting ships. With more limited domestic demand, the spiraling costs of major weapons systems made exports an essential component in defence planning, with competitions with the two superpowers for sales in the Middle East and Asia taking priority. And while France continued to try to 'go it alone', other European countries such as the

UK, Germany, Italy and Spain decided to collaborate on systems like the Tornado and the European Fighter Aircraft as a way to spread costs. Taken as a group, the major European suppliers – France, the UK and Germany – rivaled Russia and the United States in their volume of arms exports during the 1980s (Anthony 1989: 198, 204–207). In some cases the urgent need to export led to desperate measures, as with the allegations of bribery in the 1986 'Al Yamamah' deal to sell scores of British planes to Saudi Arabia (Corbin, 2007).

More details of the incentives for and impacts of conventional weapons sales will be supplied below. But now we must look at the second major channel of arms transfers, the supply of dual-use items. In the 1980s, the sale to Iraq of equipment and materials useful in the development of everything from medium-range Scud missiles to nuclear, chemical and biological weapons was a classic case of the 'boomerang effect' – the tendency of arms and military technology transfers to be used against the states that supplied them. Some of the supplies came from nominal Iraqi allies such as Russia and China, but large flows of dual-use items also came from the USA, France, Italy, the UK, and Germany – the states that led the opposition to Iraq in the 1991 Gulf War.

Since dual-use transfers generally involve arms-making *technology* rather than finished weapons systems, they are generally harder to track, even when exporting states put their minds (and resources) to the job. The stage for arming Iraq was set during the Iran/Iraq war (1980–1988), when a wide range of countries supplied one or both sides, including not only the major suppliers but also smaller suppliers such as Brazil, North Korea, Egypt, Jordan, and Syria. Even so, major suppliers dominated in the value of arms transferred. France (over one quarter) and the USSR (nearly one half) supplied the bulk of Iraq's weapons imports; on the other side of the ledger, China supplied about one half of Iran's imports during the war (Anthony 1989: 196–197).

The third channel of arms flows – one that has taken on particular prominence since the end of the Cold War – is the trade in SALW. The vast majority of combat deaths in the world's annual roster of two to three dozen conflicts are inflicted with these systems, which are loosely regulated and were largely ignored as a proliferation problem until the late 1990s. SALW are easy to maintain and transport, relatively cheap to purchase, and notoriously hard to track. For all of these reasons they are the weapons of choice for terrorists, separatist movements, militias, warlords and other non-state groups that are central players in the wars of the post-Cold War period, the vast majority of which are fought within countries, not between countries (see Boutwell *et al.* 1995). Control of SALW is further complicated by the fact that armed factions can seize control of natural resources such as gold, diamonds, and timber and sell them illicitly to garner funds to buy another round of armaments (see UN Security Council 2000: 11–20, 30–38, 50–61). These weapons can in turn be used to capture more territory and control more resources. This vicious cycle has had a devastating effect on a wide range of countries, and it can operate in significant part without the active involvement of major arms-supplying nations. However, there are numerous sins of omission and commission by other governments. These include turning a blind eye to the transport operations of a dealer like Viktor Bout and the accepting of bribes in exchange for the provision of falsified documents that are used to conceal the ultimate destination of a given weapons shipment (Farah and Braun 2007).

## Arms sales take off: The 1970s and 1980s

Arms sales and military aid have been tools of warfare and diplomacy from the outset of the Cold War, from US aid to Greece and Turkey to fight pro-communist partisans after World War II to British, French, and Soviet bloc exports to both sides of the 1956 Suez crisis. But weapons exports really took off in the 1970s and 1980s, when the total value of the global trade increased threefold (US ACDA 2004: 53).

The increase in arms sales was driven by two major factors. On the geopolitical side, US President Richard Nixon was looking for a way to promote US interests around the world without resorting to another major military intervention as was the case in Vietnam. The result came to be known as the Nixon Doctrine – Washington would arm regional allies to protect its security interests rather than sending US troops to confront those threats directly (Nixon 1971: 544–549). In some cases these transfers involved not only the weapons themselves but extensive training packages and the knowledge and technology needed to produce comparable systems. The second major factor was the rise in oil prices fostered by the formation of Organization of Petroleum Exporting Countries (OPEC) in 1974. Oil revenues created purchasing power that was used by Saudi Arabia, Iran, and other oil exporting states to purchase top-of-the-line fighter planes and combat vehicles from the US, Britain, France, and other suppliers (Klare 1984: 33).

During this period, the USA, the Soviet Union, and Western Europe accounted for about one-third each of the global arms trade, with the large caveat that many of the Soviet sales were in the form of military aid, not cash sales. Economic incentives to export arms rivalled geopolitical drivers during this period. One such incentive was the felt need by the Western powers to 'recycle petrodollars' – recapture additional monies spent to purchase higher-priced oil by selling expensive weapons systems to the oil-exporting states. In the USA, increased arms sales also helped smooth out the dip in military spending that came with the end of the Vietnam War; as US procurement for the war declined from 1973 to 1975, arms sales rose substantially, creating an alternative market that partly made up for declining Pentagon spending.

The administration of Jimmy Carter tried to change the dynamics of the global trade by promoting a policy of arms sales restraint. The Carter initiative built on the actions of the post-Vietnam, post-Watergate Congress, which passed the Arms Export Control Act (AECA) in 1976 in response to runaway US arms sales (see Hartung 1995: 56–62). The mid-1970s saw the USA offering excessive arms transfers to Saudi Arabia and Iran, arming both sides of the war between Greece and Turkey over Cyprus, and arming right-wing rebel groups in Angola which were allied with the apartheid regime of South Africa. The AECA gave Congress veto power over major sales of military equipment; put forward the principle that US-transferred arms should be used for defensive purposes; and stated that it would henceforth be the policy of the United States to take a leadership role in promoting arms sales restraint.

In line with this framework and in pursuit of his own beliefs, Carter campaigned for president on a pledge to take the lead in curbing the international weapons trade (United States 1978: 266–275). His most promising initiative in this regard was the Conventional Arms Transfer (CAT) talks between the USA and the Soviet Union. The talks appeared to be making progress as each major supplier honed in on regions in which it would pledge to reduce the size and scope of its arms transfers. But late in Carter's term, his National Security Adviser Zbigniew Brzezinski pulled the rug out from under the talks, in part to clear the way for the USA to offer military technology to China as part of the ongoing normalization of US–China relations. President Carter's own commitment to arms sales restraint waned as he warmed to the idea of using arms transfers as tools to reward friends and intimidate adversaries (Blechman and Nolan 1987).

In keeping with Carter's shift in emphasis, the USA armed the Shah of Iran right up to the end of his regime in 1979, when he was overthrown and replaced with a regime headed by the Ayatollah Ruhollah Khomeini. France, the UK and Germany were also major suppliers to the Shah, but their sales taken together were less than total exports to Tehran on the part of the United States (Pierre 1982: 149–150). The US arms relationship with the Shah continued despite the repressive character of his regime, in which the US-trained SAVAK intelligence service engaged in kidnappings, torture and murder in its efforts to suppress anti-regime activists (Sick 1985: 24–25).

In addition, the Carter administration offered arms packages to a wide range of states in the Persian Gulf and the Horn of Africa – including Kenya, Egypt, and Saudi Arabia – in exchange for access to military facilities that could be used by the newly forming Rapid Deployment Force, designed to ensure that there would be 'no more Irans' and 'no more Afghanistans' in the Persian Gulf region. Even Carter's greatest foreign policy achievement – the Camp David peace accords between Israel and Egypt – was sealed with a multi-billion dollar military aid package for each party to the talks. In short, Jimmy Carter was ultimately seduced by the short-term benefits of arms transfers in securing political and military support, and allowed them to trump concerns about human rights, democracy, and the fueling of regional conflicts (Hartung 1995: 82–83).

While Carter came late to the business of promoting arms sales, Ronald Reagan was a major booster from the outset of his administration. One of his first major efforts was to lobby Congress to approve a $9 billion-plus sale of Airborne Warning and Control System (AWACS) radar planes to Saudi Arabia, a fight which he won when the Senate voted 52 to 48 to support the sale (Klare 1984: 148–154). This was followed by a sale of F-16 combat aircraft to Venezuela, in contravention of a policy introduced during the Carter years that called for a virtual ban on sales of advanced US combat aircraft in Latin America. But perhaps the most important aspect of the Reagan arms sales policy was his support for covert arms sales to movements in Afghanistan, Angola, Cambodia, and Nicaragua, all of whom he described as 'freedom fighters' regardless of their actual ideologies and practices.

In Afghanistan, the USA funneled over $2 billion in weapons and training to the *mujahadin* dedicated to ousting Soviet occupiers from their country (Katzman 1993: 15). Equipment ranged from automatic rifles, to military trucks, to shoulder-fired missiles. Much of this weaponry was siphoned off by the ISI, Pakistan's military intelligence service, and transferred into conflict zones in Kashmir, India, Tajikistan, and other hot spots around the globe (Smith 1995). Osama Bin Laden, who went on to found the al-Qa'ida movement, used contacts with CIA-trained and armed *mujahadin* that he made during the Afghan war to build the foundations of his organization.

Perhaps the most publicized arms scandal of the 1980s was the Iran/Contra affair, in which the Reagan administration bartered arms with Iran to raise funds to arm the anti-government Contra militia force in Nicaragua. The operation violated a Congressional ban on aid to the Contras, and demonstrated what a determined administration can do when it chooses to use arms sales to do an 'end run' around legal restrictions. The operation was revealed to the public after Eugene Hasenfus, a low-level operative involved in delivering weapons via air to the Contras, was captured by the Sandinista government and acknowledged his role in the pro-Contra operation. A bipartisan Congressional committee that investigated the case found that Col. Oliver North had coordinated a multinational arms supply operation out of his offices around the corner from the White House. Among the other players in the scandal were Saudi Arabia, which put up $32 million to help arm the Contras, along with a 'rogues gallery' of middlemen that ranged from ex-CIA and Pentagon officials to international arms dealers like the Saudi Adnan Khashoggi and Iranian Manucher Ghorbanifar. While the scandal was ultimately uncovered, punishments for the participants were minimal and it was not at all clear that steps had been taken to prevent such an operation in the future (see Draper 1987).

## Post-Cold War dynamics

With the end of the Cold War, economic motives moved to the forefront in the Clinton administration's arms sales policy, which explicitly cited the importance of weapons exports in supporting the US defense industrial base. Even before he was elected president, Bill Clinton showed a penchant for supporting major arms deals as a way of currying favor in key states. His opponent, the incumbent George Herbert Walker Bush, announced several large deals during the stretch run of the campaign, including a $5 billion sale of F-15 combat aircraft to Saudi Arabia and a $9 billion sale of F-16 combat aircraft to Taiwan. While the Bush administration went through the motions of presenting strategic rationales for each of these deals, the real motives were made clear when candidate Bush announced the deals at major rallies in front of cheering workers in St. Louis (home to production of the F-15) and Fort Worth, Texas (where F-16s are manufactured). In Fort Worth, Bush made his remarks amidst signs saying 'Jobs For America – Thanks Mr. President' (Wines 1992). In St. Louis, he asserted that 'in these times of economic transition, I want to do everything I can to keep Americans at work' (Bush 1992).

Candidate Bill Clinton immediately put out a press release supporting the F-15 sale to the Saudis (despite objections by Israel, one of the US's strongest allies), in no small part because the planes are built in Missouri, an important 'swing state' that could have gone Democratic or Republican in the 1992 elections. Clinton's support for the Saudi sale was no anomaly; US arms sales nearly tripled in his first year in office, to $33 billion (US DoD 2003).

One of the most embarrassing – and instructive – arms sales developments of the Bush/Clinton years was the revelation that the USA and its allies had been major suppliers of arms and arms producing technologies to Iraq in the run-up to the 1991 Gulf War. While countries like France, the UK and Italy provided finished weapons systems to Saddam Hussein's regime – not to mention the then Soviet Union, the largest supplier – the USA primarily supplied arms-making technologies, from equipment used in Iraq's missile production factories to materials applicable to the production of biological weapons (Wines 1991). Indirect US impacts on the Iraqi arsenal included the transfer of US-designed cluster bombs to Baghdad via Chilean arms dealer Carlos Cardoen (Pasztor 1991).

In the wake of the 1991 war, US President Bush and British Prime Minister John Major pledged to do something to curb the burgeoning (and destabilizing) weapons trade to the Middle East. Talks were commenced involving the five permanent members of the UN Security Council, all of which had armed Iraq in the run up to the Gulf War. The aim of the talks was to reduce the levels of sales to regions of tension and to put specific curbs on the sale of ballistic missiles. Unfortunately the talks broke down when China withdrew in 1993, in part because of US and French sales of advanced combat aircraft to Taiwan, and in part due to its own specialization in missile exports, the very systems targeted for curbs in the arms sales talks (Oberdorfer 1992). One small bright spot in the post-Gulf War period was the establishment of the UN Arms Register, a voluntary system of reporting arms exports and imports which helped focus attention on the issue of the weapons trade while providing information not always available from existing governmental and non-governmental sources.

## Post-9/11 arms exports

The 11 September 2001 terror attacks on the Pentagon and the World Trade Center created yet another shift in arms sales policy. In the name of fighting the 'global war on terrorism' (GWOT), the Bush administration lifted human rights and nonproliferation restrictions on sales to countries like Pakistan, Yemen, Kazakhstan and Indonesia, and increased military aid to Georgia, the Philippines and other states viewed as potential allies in fighting terrorist networks (Hartung and Berrigan 2005: 7). The number of states receiving US military aid doubled from 2001 through 2005, and nearly three-quarters of US arms recipients were either undemocratic regimes or major human rights abusers, by criteria established by its own State Department (Hartung and Berrigan 2005: 4, 36).

This shift towards explicitly arming repressive governments in pursuit of the war on terror did not initially lead to major increases in the dollar value of US weapons sales, but by 2006 such sales had doubled, from about $10 billion per year to over $20 billion, the highest levels since the wake of the 1991 Gulf War. Major drivers of the increase in the arms market included a major sale of F-16 combat aircraft to Pakistan, a plan for re-equipping and retraining the Saudi National Guard (SANG), and substantial sales to Turkey, Egypt, and Israel (Wayne 2006). US transfers continued to skyrocket in the final years of the George W. Bush administration on into the first term of President Barack Obama, reaching record levels of over $30 billion per year by 2009 (US Department of Defense 2009). Global sales followed suit, with totals reaching over $60 billion in the same time frame (Grimmett 2010: 69). The largest deals included an unprecedented $60 billion US sale of combat aircraft, attack helicopters and other equipment to Saudi Arabia, and a sale of missile defence systems to the United Arab Emirates.

Running in parallel to these traditional exports is the largest cooperative effort ever undertaken, the F-35 combat aircraft programme, targeted to produce up to 3,000 planes for the US, the UK, and seven other partner countries. The programme has run into cost and performance problems, but even if it is cut back it will likely be the largest cooperative aircraft project ever undertaken (Drew 2011).

The sale of unmanned aerial vehicles (UAVs) is poised to become a new market, with sales by the United States to Pakistan and Israel to a series of clients in Latin America (Military.com 2011, Neged Neshek 2011, Reuters 2011). Although the versions sold to date have been unarmed surveillance aircraft, this could change over time as the demand for these systems increases in the light of their perceived success in the war in Afghanistan and counterinsurgency efforts in Yemen.

## The trade in small arms and light weapons

As noted above, the trade in SALW is a major focus of recent analysis and activity related to the global arms trade due to its centrality in enabling current conflicts and its potential and actual role in arming terrorist groups.

Most writing on SALW uses as its point of departure the definition developed by the *Report of the Panel of Governmental Experts on Small Arms*

(UN General Assembly 1997). However, the Small Arms Survey provides the most comprehensive assessment of the global trade, global stockpiles, and global impacts of SALW. It defines small arms as revolvers and self-loading pistols, rifles, and carbines, assault rifles, sub-machine guns, and light machine guns. Light weapons are heavy machine guns, hand-held under barrel and mounted grenade launchers, portable anti-tank and anti-aircraft guns, recoilless rifles, portable launchers of anti-tank and anti-aircraft missile systems, and mortars of less than 100mm caliber (Small Arms Survey 2002: 10). The Small Arms Survey estimates that there are 639 million small arms in the world, excluding light weapons like mortars or rocket-propelled grenades. Since roughly 8 million new small arms are produced each year, the market in second-hand weapons is dominant, due to the sheer size of the stockpiles.

The bulk of the world's small arms stockpile – 378 million, or nearly 60 per cent – is owned by civilians. Many of these are handguns, some of which have been acquired by terrorists or insurgents purchasing weapons from US-based gun dealers, taking advantage of the relatively lax gun control laws that prevail in the United States.

Starting in the late 1980s the Colombian government has repeatedly called for the US government to take steps to restrict the ability of Colombian drug cartels to purchase pistols and firearms in the USA. According to the head of the US Bureau of Alcohol, Tobacco, and Firearms (BATF), 87 per cent of a sampling of 292 firearms seized from Colombian drug traffickers during 1988 and 1989 were of US-origin (Isikoff 1989b). During that same time period the *Washington Post* reported that '[l]aw enforcement officials report growing evidence that agents of the cartels operating in the United States have made major new efforts to purchase large caches of semi-automatic weapons – including AR-15 and Uzi assault guns – since the August 18 [1989] assassination of Colombian presidential candidate Luis Carlos Galan.' As Jack Killorin, then spokesperson for the BATF, put it, 'what we have is a constant flow of guns out of the country using the same trail that drugs are coming into the country . . . the cocaine traffickers are not going back empty handed' (Isikoff 1989a).

The flow of weapons from the US to Mexican drug syndicates appears to be even larger than in the Colombian case. A 1993 article in the *Cleveland Plain Dealer* (18 October 1994) reported that in 1992 and 1993 Mexican authorities identified over 8,700 guns from the US, noting that 'officials on both sides of the border say the real numbers are far higher'. Among other crimes, US-origin guns were used in the killing of a Mexican Presidential candidate, the secretary-general of Mexico's Institutional Revolutionary Party (PRI), a Roman Catholic cardinal as well as the slaughter of 19 men, women and children in Ensanada.

In addition to guns in civilian hands, an additional 241 million firearms – about 38 per cent – are controlled by traditional military forces (i.e., uniformed military forces answerable to states, not private militias or other military or paramilitary organizations) (Small Arms Survey 2002: 63, 75, 79). Some of these weapons also end up in the hands of terrorists or insurgents, either through capture, theft, or corruption (i.e., sales to the groups by members of regular military forces). For example, it is suspected that weapons accumulated by al-Qa'ida members involved in the May 1993 bombing of three residential compounds in Saudi Arabia were sold to them by members of the Saudi Arabian National Guard (Finn 2003). On a larger scale, it is believed that much of the weaponry used by Chechen rebels at the height of their war with the Soviet military in the mid-1990s were *bought* from those very same Soviet personnel in a sort of 'weapons for food' programme. As one Soviet soldier asserted, 'The Chechens bought all of their weapons from us; otherwise, we wouldn't have had money to eat' (Klare 1995: note 20).

It is believed that there are 70 to 100 million copies of just one type of automatic weapon – the Russian-designed AK-47 (and its variants) – worldwide. The AK is a popular weapon with insurgents, terrorists, and armed forces alike. For example, when the US went about building a new Iraqi military in the wake of the overthrow of Saddam Hussein, it was initially decided to arm them with AK-47s, which many Iraqis were already used to – and which were less likely to jam in the windy, dusty climate of Iraq.

How do non-state groups get their hands on SALW? Two important avenues are theft or purchase from government forces, and taking advantage of lax local gun laws. But another major source of SALW destined for terrorist and insurgent groups comes from illegal, clandestine sales, commonly referred to as the black market. This market operates on a global scale, taking advantage of state-of-the-art communications, transportation, banking and brokering services.

Under this definition, covert arms transfers of the kind that the USA made to Afghan rebel groups during their war against the Soviet occupation of their country would fall into a gray area – clandestine, but permissible under US law, and sought by rebel groups seeking to oust an illegal occupying force. But even in these cases, the weapons supplied as covert sales are often left behind to become ready stockpiles for sale on the global black market. The amounts involved can be immense. For example, according to an estimate by the Congressional Research Service, the USA funnelled $2 billion in arms and training to the various Afghan rebel factions during the 1980s alone (Katzman 1993: 15). These systems were redistributed throughout South Asia and beyond, to the point that researcher Chris Smith asserted that '[t]he single most important factor in the introduction of small arms and light weapons into South Asia was the effort by the U.S. and Pakistan to arm the Afghan mujahadin resistance' (HRW 1994: 5).

Although no comprehensive figures are available, it is widely believed that the bulk of the small arms and explosives being used by the insurgency against the US/UK-led coalition in Iraq came from internal sources. Indeed, as Saddam Hussein's regime collapsed the ready availability of unguarded weapons 'precipitated what was almost certainly one of the largest and fastest transfers of small arms ever' (Small Arms Survey 2004: 44). There is evidence to suggest that members of Iraq's armed forces spread the country's weapons stockpiles to locations throughout the country prior to the US intervention on the assumption that they would end up fighting a guerilla war after US forces toppled the regime itself. The Small Arms Survey (2004: 46) has estimated that as many as 4.2 million firearms were in the hands of Iraqi military and reserve forces prior to the March 2003 US-led invasion, and that 'many of these largely military weapons were abandoned, pilfered, looted and sold to the Iraqi public after Saddam Hussein's defeat and disappearance.'

Journalist George Packer (2005: 299) noted that, '[b]etween August 2002 and January 2003, Iraqi commanders had removed weapons and equipment from bases and hidden them in farms and houses all over the countryside'. In addition, there was considerable looting of warehouses that contained these materials. One of the most deadly weapons of the war – the improvised explosive device, or IED – is described by Packer as 'a home-made bomb composed of an artillery shell or other military munitions (available at unguarded factories and ammo dumps throughout Iraq)' (2005: 299). Last but not least, several hundred thousand members of the Iraqi army – disbanded by Paul Bremer, the head of the Coalition Provisional Authority in Iraq, in May 2003 – took their weapons with them when they left military service.

A UN panel of experts that investigated violations of the arms embargo against Liberia – which has since been lifted with the advent of a democratic government there – shed further light on methods used to transport illicit weaponry. For both aircraft and ships, Liberia had long provided a lax registration process that allowed middlemen and third countries to transport weaponry and other illicit items under Liberian 'flags of convenience'. This lax system 'enabled arms trafficking networks to camouflage their operations through fake registrations, document fraud and . . . the setting up of a mystery airline with the full knowledge of Liberian authorities in order to avoid detection' (UN Security Council 2001: 33).

One of the most important needs of arms brokers and their governmental or non-governmental clients seeking illicit weaponry are real or forged end-user certificates. These allow weapons shipments to clear customs in any country on their transport route, after which they are either delivered to the country listed on the certificate and then transferred to a third country, or sent directly to a third country not listed on the certificate. Once again, the best documented cases come from West Africa. For example, a popular mechanism for getting 'small arms, missiles, helicopters and cargo aircraft' to Liberia from Eastern Europe was by using forged end-user certificates indicating that the weapons were destined for the armed forces of Guinea. In late November 2000, the Ugandan government impounded 1,250 submachine guns allegedly destined for Guinea when authorities decided based on the plane's flight plan that the shipment was heading to Liberia (UN Security Council 2001: 36, 39).

This seemingly straightforward deal involved a long chain of front companies and illicit transport operators. Among the companies involved in the attempted shipment of the 1,250 submachine guns to Liberia were Centafrican Airlines, registered in Bangui, Central African Republic and operating out of the United Arab Emirates; Pecos, an arms dealing company based in Conakry, Guinea; Vichi, 'a private agent for the Moldovan Ministry of Defence,' and MoldTransavia, companies that were chartered to fly the aircraft used in the arms shipments. The UN panel of experts that investigated the incident also learned that the aircraft used in the transfer was owned by the arms dealer Viktor Bout, and leased from his company Transavia Travel Agency of the United Arab Emirates. San Air, another UAE-registered company, supplied insurance for the deal. The majority of the companies involved were ultimately owned either by Viktor Bout, his brother Sergei, or current or former associates of Viktor Bout (UN Security Council 2001: 39–42). Until his arrest by US authorities in 2010, Bout was one of the most active players in the illicit arms trade, with involvement in deals to UNITA in Angola, the Charles Taylor regime in Liberia, and the rebels in Sierra Leone. In addition, according to intelligence documents uncovered by the International Consortium of Investigative Journalists (ICIJ 2002: 147), Bout was involved in supplying $50 million in weaponry to the Taliban during the period that they were hosting and supplying al-Qa'ida. In November 2011, Viktor Bout was convicted of conspiring to sell anti-aircraft missiles and other weapons to the Revolutionary Armed Forces of Colombia (FARC), a non-state group designated as a terrorist organisation by the US Department of Trade.

## Dangers of dual use: The A.Q. Khan network

While the transfer of SALW to terrorist organizations and other non-state actors is a going concern, their pursuit of weapons of mass destruction – and nuclear weapons in particular – is of even greater long-term concern. Even if the probabilities of terrorists getting control of a nuclear weapon are low, the consequences of their acquiring these weapons could be catastrophic, costing tens or hundreds of thousands of lives and rendering large parts of major cities or other targeted areas uninhabitable for years to come. One model for how a nuclear black market operates is the extensive nuclear smuggling network established by Pakistani nuclear scientist A.Q. Khan.

Khan is known as the father of Pakistan's nuclear bomb. Using plans he developed while working at a nuclear facility in Europe – along with a blank cheque from the Pakistani government of Zulfikar Ali Bhutto – Khan built a vast centrifuge facility at Kahuta, near Islamabad. By the early 1980s the facility was able to enrich significant quantities of uranium. By 1984, Khan claims he completed work on a nuclear bomb. He later boasted about this feat in the context of his country's lack of development, saying 'A country which could not make sewing needles [or] good bicycles . . . was embarking on one of the latest and most difficult technologies' (Edidin 2004). But he did not do it alone. He took advantage of weak export controls and loopholes in national and international regulations that focused on plants and complete systems rather than components. Using this approach, Khan was able to purchase much of what was needed for the Pakistani bomb on the open market. By the late 1970s, the US State Department was regularly expressing its concerns to European officials about particular sales to Pakistan. In addition, the CIA was monitoring Khan's dealings and subsequently revealed that Pakistan obtained one or more of almost every component needed to build a centrifuge enrichment plant (Weissman and Krosney 1981).

Sellers from all over the world congregated in Pakistan to offer price lists for high-technology goods applicable to Pakistan's nuclear programme, according to the *New York Times*. 'They literally begged us to buy their equipment . . . My long stay in Europe and intimate knowledge of various countries and their manufacturing firms was an asset,' Khan bragged (Broad *et al.* 2004). Once Pakistan had the bomb and the capacity to enrich uranium, Khan 'reversed the network' he had developed to bring nuclear components and materials into Pakistan, using the same illicit channels to disseminate nuclear know-how and plans throughout the world.

International Atomic Energy Agency director Mohamed ElBaradei (2004) describes the elaborate model Khan perfected for disseminating nuclear materials – 'nuclear components designed for one country would be manufactured in another, shipped through a third country (which often appeared to be a legitimate user) assembled in a fourth and designated for eventual turnkey use in a fifth'. The network included suppliers from all over the world – including Switzerland, the UK, the UAE, Turkey, South Africa and Malaysia. It was responsible for the transfer of nuclear weapons-related technology, centrifuge parts and blueprints to Iran, North Korea, Libya and elsewhere (Lin 2004).

According to Clary (2004), Iran was Pakistan's first major customer and Libya was its most recent. Clary asserts that Pakistan's proliferation grew steadily more complex, noting that 'sharing with Iran was fairly limited, Pakistani–North Korean cooperation was more significant, while Libya was in the midst of acquiring the most extensive 'package' when it made the strategic decision to forego weapons in 2003'.

By the time Khan supplied materials to Libya, Khan Research Laboratories was reportedly able to offer a 'turn-key' nuclear package. Robert Joseph, a nonproliferation expert serving on the US National Security Council, asserts that 'A.Q. Khan and company' was 'the principal supplier for the entire program. Khan provided the design, the technology, the expertise, and the equipment, primarily for the centrifuges. He also provided the warhead design' (in Motta 2006).

While Khan asserts that he 'transferred nuclear technology so that other Muslim countries could enhance their security', money was also a factor: Khan spent millions buying up homes and properties, including a tourist hotel in Africa that he named after his wife Henny (Broad *et al.* 2004). Officials within the Bush administration estimate that the Khan network netted $100 million for the technology it sold to Libya alone (Broad and Sanger 2004). In early 2004, the world learned what the intelligence community had long known: A.Q. Khan oversaw what Dr. ElBaradei called the 'WalMart of private sector proliferation'.

Khan was dismissed from his post amid what Pakistan's government termed an 'investigation into alleged acts of nuclear proliferation by a few individuals'. At the beginning of February 2004, Khan and as many as six nuclear scientists were detained and questioned by the military's Inter-Services Intelligence agency. Pakistani President Pervez Musharraf vowed to punish 'with an iron hand' anyone who leaked nuclear weapons secrets to foreign governments. But by 5 February Khan had been pardoned, and dubbed a national hero in Pakistan. Even worse, Musharraf announced that he would block any international probe into Pakistan's nuclear programme. During a five-year period of house arrest that ended in 2009, Khan lived on a comfortable estate, and even the text of his 12-page confession has not been public. The IAEA was not given direct access to Khan and was only able to submit written questions for the scientist to answer.

Apparently Khan's network did not function wholly independently. A study by the US Congressional Research Service concluded that 'A.Q. Khan must have had significant logistical support from elements in the Pakistani military and the civilian nuclear establishment' (Cronin *et al.* 2005).

## Prospects for restraint

The arms transfers discussed above have prompted measures to curb the trade. While past efforts such as the Conventional Arms Transfer talks between the US and the Soviet Union have ended in failure, the new initiatives have a broader constituency and are seeking a broader range of controls. This suggests that there is a greater chance that at least some of these new initiatives could be implemented.

The most extensive efforts to curb military exports have come in the area of SALW, propelled by pressure from a broad network of NGOs ranging from arms control and human rights groups to organizations representing the handicapped to humanitarian aid and global development groups. The landmark 2001 UN Conference on Curbing Illicit Trafficking of Small Arms and Light Weapons in All of Its Aspects produced a programme of action calling on UN member states to undertake voluntary efforts to institute better internal controls on the export of SALW; consider ways to mark and trace weapons so that arms involved in conflicts and human rights abuses can be traced to their source countries; and increase intelligence and law enforcement cooperation in tracking small arms transfers.

The most ambitious undertaking in the field of arms trade regulation is the proposal for a global Arms Trade Treaty, which had initial support from 153 of the then 192 UN member states and is now being pursued with a goal of finalizing a treaty by 2012. The treaty would set standards for denying sales based on violations of human rights, enforcement of existing embargoes, and destabilizing supplies to areas of conflict (Oxfam International 2011). Arguments against the treaty include the assertion that existing regulations should be better enforced first; and the claim that decisions on arms transfers should be the sovereign prerogative of individual states. Unstated rationales for opposing the treaty, from preserving 'freedom of action' to arm key allies regardless of their human rights performance to garnering the economic benefits of weapons exports without legal impediments, may be even stronger barriers to a global agreement. But a paradigm shift may be under way which can overcome even these vigorous objections.

## Conclusion

Whether or not additional restrictions are developed, the global arms trade will continue to be a major factor in the spheres of human rights, war and peace, and the economics of international trade. For this reason, it bears greater scrutiny and transparency to enable better decision-making on when arms sales are an appropriate foreign policy tool, and when they may do more harm than good.

## Further reading

Anthony Sampson, *The Arms Bazaar: From Lebanon to Lockheed* (Viking Press, 1977). The classic treatment of the often corrupt politics of international arms sales, grounded in path breaking government investigations of the mid-1970s.

Andrew J. Pierre, *The Global Politics of Arms Sales* (Princeton University Press, 1982). A primer on the motives driving major arms suppliers and recipients to engage in the weapons trade.

Douglas Farah and Stephen Braun, *Merchant of Death: Money, Guns, Planes and the Man Who Makes War Possible* (Wiley and Sons, 2007). An inside look at the operations of the illegal trade in small arms and light weapons, based on the case of the notorious arms dealer Viktor Bout.

Lora Lumpe (ed.), *Running Guns: The Global Black Market in Small Arms*, (Zed Press, 2000). Uncovers the anatomy of the illicit trade in small arms and light weapons, including analyses of small arms manufacturing, supply networks, sources of financing, and policy issues raised by the trade.

Gordon Corera, *Shopping for Bombs: Nuclear Proliferation, Global Insecurity, and the Rise and Fall of the A.Q. Khan Network* (Oxford University Press, 2006). The most detailed accounting yet of the workings of the A.Q. Khan network, a private web of manufacturers and middlemen that provided nuclear weapons technology to Libya, Iran, and North Korea, among others.

Andrew Feinstein, *The Shadow World: Inside the global armstrade* (Farrar, Straus and Giroux, 2011). An up-to-date account of the dynamics of the international arms trade, with a special focus on corrupt practices and covert deals.

Rachel Stohl and Suzanne Grillot, *The International Arms Trade* (Polity, 2009). A history of the costs and consequences of the weapons trade in the post-cold war period, including on analysis of strategies for controlling arms transfers.

# Counterterrorism

Paul R. Pillar

## Abstract

In this chapter, students will learn about the several different elements involved in combating international terrorism, including dissuading individuals from joining terrorist groups, dissuading groups from using terrorism, reducing the capability of terrorist groups, erecting physical defences against terrorist attacks, and mitigating the effects of attacks. Reducing terrorist capabilities in turn requires the use of several instruments – each with its own strengths and limitations – including diplomacy, intelligence, financial controls, criminal justice systems, and military force. Counterterrorism unavoidably raises difficult and often controversial policy issues, including conflicts with other values such as personal liberty and privacy.

## Introduction

The prominence of counterterrorism in recent years and especially during the past decade obscures how old the underlying challenges are. Terrorism dates back to ancient times. Counterterrorism, as a concerted and cooperative effort by governments to combat this tactic, is not that old, but it long predates any 'war on terror' aimed at the Islamist variety of international terrorism that is the most recent focus of attention. What could be called the first international conference on counterterrorism took place in Rome in 1898, to deal with a wave of anarchist assassinations that had been going on worldwide for several years.

Interest in counterterrorism has waxed and waned throughout modern history. That fluctuation in interest has in part reflected the rise and demise of different types of terrorist threat, such as the anarchism of the 1890s or the leftist violence that beset Europe in the 1980s. It also has reflected the political mood and milieu in individual countries. Terrorist attacks were occurring in the United States in the mid-1970s, for example, at a pace that would cause public alarm if replicated there today. But because the American public then – having just lived through the wrenching Watergate affair – was more concerned about excesses and abuses by its own government, the attacks did not stimulate major new counterterrorist initiatives (Jenkins 2003). Understanding counterterrorism requires awareness of such swings in public mood and attention, but it also requires focusing on the essential elements and issues of counterterrorism that are present regardless of the political environment.

## Basic elements

Not everything that can be done to combat terrorism ordinarily bears the label of 'counterterrorism'. Anything that cuts the roots or attenuates the causes of terrorism is properly viewed as being at least partly a counterterrorist measure, even if it is not commonly called that and even if other policy goals are involved. Scholars and politicians often disagree about the roots of terrorism. Some focus on the conditions in which would-be terrorists live. Others point to particular conflicts that become sources of rage. Still others emphasize the allure of extremist ideologies propounded by terrorist leaders and groups. Despite these differences of emphasis, they all have to do with one of the basic elements of counterterrorism, which is to reduce the motivation for individuals to join terrorist groups.

Counterterrorist policies that reflect the different ways of looking at the causes of terrorism mentioned above are not mutually exclusive. A government may, for example, promote political and social change to weaken what it regards as roots of terrorism as well as waging a battle of ideas against extremist ideologies. These two approaches both have been facets of US counterterrorist strategy focused on the Middle East, especially in the wake of al-Qa'ida's attacks in September 2001.

For several European governments, attention to the roots of terrorism has more to do with their own Muslim populations. High-profile terrorist attacks such as those against transit systems in London and Madrid have heightened attention to the status of European Muslims. Here, too, there are disagreements and differences in approach, such as between the British concept of multiculturalism and the French emphasis on assimilation. But in either case, reducing the chance that young members of these communities will gravitate toward terrorism is a goal of government policy.

Another fundamental element of counterterrorism focuses on decisions by groups on whether to conduct more terrorism. It has to do with shaping the incentives for groups to use peaceful rather than violent means to pursue their objectives. This element is not germane to all terrorist groups. It is irrelevant to a group such as al-Qa'ida, whose ultimate goals – overthrow of most of the political order in the Muslim world – are so sweeping they could never be assuaged by any negotiations, concessions, or change of policy by a government. Even with groups whose goals are more circumscribed – as was true of the now-defeated Liberation Tigers of Tamil Eelam and its objective of an independent Tamil state carved out of Sri Lanka – the conflicts of interest may still be so acute that it is extremely difficult to divert the group from its violent path.

In some instances, however, a negotiated resolution of issues in conflict can be a major part of inducing a group to cease terrorism. The most conspicuous case is the Good Friday agreement on Northern Ireland reached in 1998. Despite many fits and starts over the subsequent decade, the peace process centred on that agreement was instrumental in inducing the leadership of the Provisional Irish Republican Army to give up terrorism.

The remaining elements of counterterrorism are more commonly labelled as such. One is usually called 'incident management,' which includes anything done, once a terrorist incident occurs, to mitigate its effects. The concept of incident management first arose in response to attacks in which hostages are seized and their lives are kept in jeopardy as the terrorists voice demands, such as for the release of previously jailed comrades. Management includes communications or negotiations with the terrorists. Expertise has been developed over the years (and has been applied by police services and private security firms to terrorist as well as non-terrorist hostage situations) on how best to deal with hostage-takers. The principal objectives usually are to weaken the will of the terrorists while avoiding any move that could stimulate rash action and harm to the hostages. Ultimately, however, the outcome of such incidents depends heavily on the policy of the authorities involved toward making concessions under duress to terrorists. Some governments (e.g. Italy) have been willing to make concessions in the interest of securing safe release of hostages. Others (e.g. the United States) are opposed to such concessions on grounds that they encourage further terrorism.

Another aspect of managing such incidents involves communications with the public and the role of the press. An objective of terrorists in staging such incidents – at least as much as the specific demands they make – is to gain attention for their cause. Partly because of this, some counterterrorist officials consider it important to restrict the release of information on such incidents and to limit public attention to them. Any such restrictions, however, raise issues of freedom of the press and of the responsibility of the press and government alike to inform citizenry about important events.

A third aspect of management of such incidents is the possible use of force to rescue the hostages. A successful rescue operation avoids the difficult choices of whether to make concessions to terrorists, as well as constituting a dramatic blow against terrorism and immediate punishment of terrorists. Past failures at hostage rescue have stimulated the development of highly skilled forces trained to conduct rescue operations. Germany developed such a force after its failure to rescue Israeli athletes taken hostage at the Olympic games in Munich in 1972, as did the United States after its aborted attempt to rescue diplomatic hostages in Iran in 1980. Even well trained forces, however, face an extremely difficult task because the terrorists have the advantage of being able to inflict immediate harm on hostages. Because of this inherent difficulty, the record of hostage rescue attempts always will be mixed (see Box 30.1).

In recent years, most major terrorist incidents have involved not the seizure of hostages and the threat of inflicting harm on them, but instead the direct and unprovoked killing of innocent people, usually with bombs. In this context, 'incident management' has come to acquire a different meaning, referring primarily to emergency responses designed to tend to the wounded and to deal with any continuing hazards at the scene of the attack. The underlying purpose is still to mitigate effects of the attack; prompt medical attention for the wounded, of course, can minimize the number of deaths. Particular emphasis is now placed on responding to terrorist attacks using unconventional weapons or materials. Despite what is still the relative rarity of such attacks, the emphasis is warranted because quick measures to contain or neutralize a biological, chemical, or radiological hazard could make a substantial difference in minimizing casualties beyond those sustained immediately in the attack itself.

The measures that are most often thought of explicitly as counterterrorism – and that are the focus of the remainder of this chapter – concern efforts to curb the *ability* of terrorists to conduct attacks. These include defensive security measures designed to protect potential targets from attack. They also include a variety of offensive measures intended to reduce terrorist capabilities.

## Defence

Defensive security measures (which sometimes bear the label 'anti-terrorism') are applied at several different levels. Most specific is the protection of individual sites, be they office buildings, military bases, embassies, or any other facility that could become a target of terrorist attack. Much site-specific security is the business of the private sector – of the owners or managers of the facilities being protected. Government facilities tend to have more security per site because the security also serves other purposes (such as preserving the secrecy of sensitive activities) and because in the eyes of terrorists, official facilities are likely to have greater symbolic value as targets for attack. Related types of security include special short-term protection provided to high-profile events such as inaugurations or major sporting events and personal security given to governmental leaders or other prominent persons.

The next level of defensive measures is security provided to entire systems. The systems-level security that has played the greatest role in counterterrorism

## BOX 30.1 SUCCESSFUL AND UNSUCCESSFUL RESCUE ATTEMPTS

Attempts to rescue hostages taken by terrorists have ranged from brilliant successes to tragic failures. Some countries have experienced both types of outcome.

An example of how a rescue attempt can go horribly wrong involved the hijacking by the Abu Nidal Organization of an Egyptian airliner in 1985. A team of Egyptian commandos attempted a rescue while the plane was on the ground in Malta, beginning their operation by using explosives to blow open doors of the aircraft. In an ensuing exchange of grenades and gunfire, the interior of the plane caught fire. Fifty-six out of 88 passengers died, as did two crew members.

A conspicuous success ended one of the last of the major hostage takings, which began in late 1996 when the Tupac Amaru Revolutionary Movement (MRTA) seized the Japanese ambassador's residence in Lima, Peru. The Peruvian government negotiated with the terrorists for four months while secretly digging tunnels underneath the residence and making other preparations for a military raid. The raid began with an explosion that collapsed part of the ground floor of the building (where the MRTA members were playing a soccer game, with their 72 hostages being kept on an upper floor). All but one of the hostages were rescued unharmed. Two members of the rescue force and all 14 terrorists were killed.

is that surrounding civil aviation. The inherent vulnerabilities and mobility of airliners always will make them tempting terrorist targets. The protection given to commercial aviation today demonstrates two principles of systems-level security. First, a chink anywhere in the armour can provide an opening for attackers – which is why reported weakness in security procedures at any one airport is legitimately a concern for people elsewhere in the system. Second – and partly in recognition of the first principle – security must be multi-layered, which in the case of aviation includes everything from x-ray inspection of baggage to hardening of cockpit doors. No other systems have received as much counterterrorist attention as aviation, but obvious vulnerabilities have increased questions in recent years about the need for additional protection to other systems such as public transit and electrical power grids. Electronic systems, such as those that support banking and financial transactions, also have received added scrutiny.

The most general level of defensive security measures is the protection of an entire country, particularly by keeping terrorists, and to some extent the wherewithal for conducting terrorist attacks (especially nuclear material) outside its borders. The United States, following the 9/11 attacks, greatly increased its emphasis on homeland security. This included not only a substantial increase in expenditures but also the creation – in the largest US governmental reorganization in over 50 years – of a Department of Homeland Security. The geographic and other circumstances of each country, however, make the homeland security task different for each. For most European countries, free cross-border movement within the European Union would make it impossible for individual states to approach homeland security in the same way the United States does. (In recent years some border controls within Europe have been reinstated, although more because of concerns about immigration rather than terrorism.) Even the United States, given its long undefended border with Canada, must consider how much emphasis to place on stopping terrorists at its own borders and how much to keeping them out of North America altogether.

Defensive countermeasures work in several ways. The most obvious is the direct foiling of an attempted terrorist attack. Even if defences do not defeat an attempted attack, however, they may deter terrorists from attacking. Terrorist preparations typically include substantial study and surveillance of the intended target, to identify vulnerabilities and possible avenues of attack but also to assess security measures. Sometimes terrorists conclude from such study that the security protecting their intended target is too strong, and they stand down from their planned attack. Of course, this does not necessarily mean that they forgo terrorism altogether; they may look for an alternative target. But at least the defences complicated their planning and forestalled whatever specific objective they had hoped to achieve by hitting their primary target.

Complicating terrorists' planning like this also slows them down, providing more time in which they might be detected. This raises another general way in which security countermeasures work, which is to complement other counterterrorist efforts. Defences that force terrorists to prepare their operation in ways they might not otherwise have used may increase the chance they will be caught. Besides lengthening the time to prepare an attack, another possibility is the need to build a bigger bomb to overcome security such as blast-resistant walls or barriers that create a standoff distance. The purchases and fabrication needed for a larger bomb may be more conspicuous and detectable than the making of a smaller device.

Mention of large bombs raises a final way in which defensive measures can save lives even if they do not prevent attacks. The truck bomb that terrorists used to attack the US military housing facility at Khobar Towers in Saudi Arabia in 1996 was so powerful that it killed 19 servicemen even though it exploded some distance away in the street. In a sense, perimeter security at the facility worked; if the truck had been permitted to enter the compound, the casualty toll would have been far higher.

Defensive security measures have several inherent limitations. They are expensive. The costs are measured not just in direct monetary expenditures for security, although some commonly used methods – such as machines that are both effective and efficient in screening large volumes of luggage of air passengers – are indeed expensive. The less measurable but still significant costs come in the form of unavoidable inefficiencies imposed on the people being protected and higher costs of doing business stemming from such things as longer travel time. Some legitimate business, including government business, may be more difficult to do at all. The type of embassies that can most readily be protected from terrorist attack, for example – fortress-like compounds located away from city centres – also make it harder for the diplomats who work there to do the parts of their job requiring free and easy interaction with the local population.

The most important limitation is that not everything can be protected, even though everything is a potential terrorist target. Terrorists always will have the advantage of choosing where to attack, with that choice reflecting in part where security is strong and where it is weak. In that sense the strengthening of security countermeasures has a self-negating aspect. Whatever the form of competition, the offence always has this advantage over the defence.

## Going on the offensive

Offensive counterterrorist operations have the attraction of not surrendering the initiative to terrorists and not trying to guess where and how they will strike next. A successful security countermeasure saves from attack whatever target or potential target is being protected. A successful offensive operation that puts a terrorist cell out of business prevents it from ever attacking *any* target. This does not mean that offensive operations are an alternative to defensive efforts. Rather, they are complementary parts of a comprehensive counterterrorist programme.

Offensive counterterrorism itself involves the use of several different tools. Again, they are complements rather than alternatives to each other. Each tool has its own advantages and limitations.

The transnational nature of modern terrorism makes *diplomacy* an important tool. Enlisting the cooperation of other governments is critical to countering terrorist operations that cross international boundaries. Diplomacy's most immediate use is to obtain cooperation on specific cases. A diplomatic démarche is the channel through which to get another government to arrest a suspected terrorist, to raid a terrorist cell, or to turn over a suspect. Diplomacy also can help to drive and guide cooperation more generally between military, security, and intelligence services. As such, it provides important support to all of the other counterterrorist tools. Finally, diplomacy is the main means for containing and confronting state sponsors of terrorism.

Counterterrorist diplomacy can be either multilateral or bilateral. Multilateral diplomacy is most useful in creating a worldwide climate that recognizes terrorism as a shared problem and that is supportive of counterterrorist efforts. (Public diplomacy – communication through mass media to publics rather than to governments – also gets used for this purpose.) Multilateral diplomacy has succeeded in making that climate more conducive to counterterrorism than it was a quarter century ago, when much terrorism got overlooked or condoned out of a disinclination to criticize 'national liberation movements'.

Multilateral diplomacy also has a more practical side, in the form of a series of international conventions on terrorism that have been negotiated over the past 40 years and that establish rules and procedures on such matters as jurisdiction over hijacking incidents and the tracing of explosives. Most practical international cooperation on terrorism, however, is bilateral. Individual terrorist cases typically involve only two or three states at a time, and the handling of secret material becomes more difficult the more states that are involved.

Another tool that diplomacy has been instrumental in supporting is *financial control* in the form of freezing or seizing of terrorist assets. Getting at terrorists' money has received increased emphasis in recent years, although legal instruments for doing so have existed much longer. The United States Treasury has long had the statutory authority to freeze the financial assets of states, groups, or individuals associated with terrorism. Except for states, however – whose financial accounts are more readily identified than those of groups or individuals – the haul of frozen assets was meagre until after 9/11, when the assistance of other governments became easier to obtain. US legislation in 1996 that created a formal list of Foreign Terrorist Organizations also made it a crime to contribute financially to any organization on the list.

Despite frequently expressed hopes of curbing terrorism by removing its 'lifeblood' of money, the contribution of financial controls to counterterrorism always will be limited for two reasons. One is that much of the money associated with terrorist activity flows through channels that are extremely hard to detect and intercept. This is particularly true of the informal money transfer networks known as *hawala* that are prevalent in the Middle East and South Asia. The other reason is that most terrorism is cheap. It simply does not cost much to assemble a truck bomb or many other means of inflicting heavy casualties.

The tool that perhaps has received more emphasis than any other in discussions of counterterrorism is *intelligence* (see Chapter 16, this volume). Inquiries in the United States following the 9/11 attacks focused primarily on intelligence. One of the principal legislative responses to the attacks was a reorganization of the intelligence community that created an additional counterterrorist centre and an additional layer of supervision over the entire community. The sentiment to which such measures are a response has more to do with defence than with offence: the hope that intelligence will uncover enough details of the next major terrorist plot to enable authorities to roll the plot up before it can be executed.

That hope, although an understandable reaction to tragic events and a widespread perception of what intelligence ought to do, is largely misplaced. Unearthing the tactical details of terrorist plots must always be one of the missions of intelligence, and the occasional successes in doing so are among the most satisfying counterterrorist triumphs. But such successes always will be rare. Some terrorist plots, including some major ones, always will go undetected no matter how skilled and assiduous the intelligence operations aimed against them may be. Terrorist plots – which typically involve small numbers of operatives who can conduct their operations in secret, avoid communications or any overt actions that could reveal their plan, are highly conscious of operational security, and are ruthless toward anyone suspected of betraying them – always will be extremely difficult targets for intelligence.

Intelligence performs three other functions that make larger contributions to counterterrorism. One is to provide a more strategic sense of terrorist threats – are they increasing or decreasing, which groups or states pose the greatest dangers, and which areas of operation are of most concern. Such strategic appraisals help to guide policymaking on all aspects of counterterrorism, including security countermeasures as well as offensive operations. A second function is to provide detailed support to all the other tools. Diplomatic démarches about terrorism, for example, nearly always are based on – and very often convey – information collected by an intelligence service. Intelligence also is important in identifying and locating terrorist financial assets. And intelligence provides critical input to law enforcement and military operations, discussed below.

The third function is clearly offensive and in many ways the most important. This is the collection and analysis of information on terrorist organizations and infrastructures, enabling them to be disrupted. The information concerned is specific but not plot-specific. It involves the names and biographic data of suspected terrorists, the location and strength of terrorist cells, the location of safehouses, and the operational connections among cells and groups. Intelligence services themselves might not accomplish the actual disruption, but the information they provide enables police or internal security services to conduct raids, arrest suspects, and confiscate material. Such actions often provide leads for collecting more information, which in turn facilitates further disruption of terrorist infrastructure. This type of offensive action does not always generate headlines, unless a particularly well-known terrorist is taken into custody or killed – as was true of the raid in Pakistan by US special forces in 2011 that killed Osama bin Laden and also involved the seizure of a large amount of exploitable material (see Box 30.2). But it probably accounts for the largest portion of counterterrorist successes, including successes against important groups such as al-Qa'ida.

## Law enforcement and military force

A common, but misleading and useless, frame of reference often invoked in discussion of counterterrorism is to ask whether the problem should be considered one of 'crime' or 'war'. Nothing inherent to terrorism warrants either posing such a choice or selecting one of these labels as an alternative to the other. Terrorists clearly commit crimes (such as murder), while their political objectives give them something in common with warfare and distinguish their actions from non-political crimes motivated by greed or passion. Counterterrorist policies and practices also do not provide a basis for any 'crime versus war' choice. Both criminal justice systems and military services appropriately play roles in counterterrorism. The establishment by the United States of military tribunals to determine the guilt or innocence of terrorist suspects – a system that is inseparably part of the realms of both 'crime' and 'war' – illustrates the falsity of the dichotomy.

Most proponents of the 'crime versus war' formulation are really just arguing in code for greater emphasis to be placed on one or the other of the associated counterterrorist tools: *criminal prosecutions* or *military force*. Most often, it is proponents of military force who invoke that formulation, because 'war' has the added favourable connotation of taking the problem seriously and giving it high priority. A more useful perspective, however, is to discard the metaphysical and semantic debates and realize that criminal justice and military force are simply two additional offensive counterterrorist tools. Like the other tools such as intelligence or diplomacy, each tool has its peculiar strengths and weaknesses. And as with the others, they are best used as complements to each other as part of an integrated counterterrorist programme.

Arrest of suspected terrorists and their prosecution in a criminal court can accomplish several things. Incarcerating (or executing) a terrorist obviously prevents him from committing further attacks. A well-publicized prosecution can help to demonstrate governmental resolve. It may also strengthen deterrence of other terrorists apprehensive about getting caught. Even if not deterred, the fear of getting caught may impede or restrict their operations. A successful prosecution can satisfy the public's appetite for punishment of wrongdoers, but does so in an orderly and peaceful framework that upholds respect for the rule of law.

Use of a criminal justice system also has significant limitations. A terrorist first has to be caught, of course, before he can be prosecuted. Senior leaders who plan and direct terrorist attacks are less likely to be caught than underlings who must be at the scene of the attack. In the case of state-directed terrorism, the leaders most responsible are unlikely ever to be arrested. Deterrence may be ineffective – particularly inasmuch as leaders tend to go free – and is irrelevant to suicide bombers. A legal case that establishes beyond reasonable doubt that someone has committed terrorist crimes is more difficult to make than an intelligence case that someone is probably a terrorist. There is thus the risk of acquittal, an outcome less favorable to counterterrorism than if a terrorist had not been arrested in the first place. Accused terrorists may use a public trial as a platform for propaganda. Incarceration of convicted terrorists may stimulate further attacks, perhaps in the form of hostage-taking aimed at bargaining for the prisoners' release.

With terrorists moving and operating across international boundaries, jurisdictional issues also complicate the application of criminal justice. This has partly involved the assertion by the United States of extraterritorial jurisdiction of terrorist crimes against US interests in other countries, an assertion that is questionable under international law and that comes into conflict with the laws of the countries on whose territories the crimes were committed. Disagreements over the death penalty – opposed by the European Union, still used in the United States – have been an added complication that has impeded the extradition of, and even sharing information about, some terrorist suspects.

Some have looked to the International Criminal Court (ICC), the founding statute of which was ratified by enough states to enter into force in 2002, as a place to prosecute international terrorists while pre-empting some of these jurisdictional issues. There remain problems, however, of distinguishing terrorist crimes to be tried in the ICC from ordinary crimes that would still be tried in national courts. The handling of sensitive security-related information, which is often involved in terrorism cases and is difficult enough to use as evidence even in national courts, is another complication for the ICC.

The most successful use of military force for counterterrorist purposes was the US-led intervention in the civil war in Afghanistan following al-Qa'ida's attacks in the United States in September 2001. Notwithstanding the subsequent continued security problems in Afghanistan (where command of the international forces was later turned over to the North Atlantic Treaty Organization), the intervention did force al-Qa'ida from its main sanctuary and ousted the Taliban regime, which, as a close partner of al-Qa'ida, had become a major state sponsor of terrorism. This success helped to raise expectations, especially in the United States, about how a more aggressive use of military force might be used effectively to combat terrorism.

Some of the principal attractions of military force for this purpose are stronger versions of the attractions of using a criminal justice system. A military strike can be an even more dramatic demonstration of resolve than a prosecution. It can immediately disrupt or destroy terrorist capabilities, such as training camps, and possibly kill key terrorists. It may have deterrent effects not just on terrorist groups but also on states. And it can do all this without the administrative, evidentiary, and other legal complications that often impede criminal prosecutions.

The principal limitation of the counterterrorist use of military force is that international terrorism simply does not present very many good military targets. Afghanistan of the Taliban was a unique case. Even state sponsors in general have become a significantly smaller part of international terrorism than they were two decades ago. And with groups rather than states, most of the important preparations for terrorist attacks occur not in open air training camps but in places not readily targeted for military strikes, such as apartments in cities, including Western cities.

Further limitations parallel some of those associated with criminal prosecutions. A military attack may serve more to provoke than to deter. The US military strike on Libya in 1986 in response to a terrorist attack in Germany may have helped to provoke the much deadlier Libyan bombing of Pan American flight 103 two years later. Being subject to a military attack may rally support for an extremist group's leader, among the group's membership and possibly among a wider constituent population. Military strikes also have their own practical problems, such as access to bases and overflight of third countries.

Other drawbacks stem from the inherently destructive nature of military force. Collateral damage, including the loss of innocent lives, is almost inevitable. Such damage can alienate civilian populations, as it has to some degree as a result of military operations in Afghanistan and missile strikes in northwest Pakistan launched from unmanned US aircraft. Some will always regard the use of military force as excessive, making it at least as prone to controversy as any other counterterrorist instrument.

## Issues and choices

The expansion of counterterrorist powers and functions, even if not involving military force, frequently gives rise to public debate. This in part reflects disagreement over the effectiveness of particular measures in curbing terrorism. It also stems from unavoidable conflicts and trade-offs between counter-terrorism and other public values and goals.

The treatment of suspected terrorists has been one focus of controversy in the United States and Europe in the years since the 9/11 attacks. The controversy comes not from any reservoir of sympathy for terrorists but instead from concerns over human rights and the principle that even the guilty should be treated humanely. Another concern is that not all suspects are in fact guilty.

Issues involving the handling of suspected terrorists have spilled over international boundaries and have included reports of secret prisons in which detainees have been held incommunicado indefinitely, as well as 'renditions' in which suspects are turned over from one country's custody to another without any open legal procedure to authorize the process. Renditions have been used for many years as an efficient way to get suspected terrorists to the countries where they are most wanted for their crimes, without the pitfalls associated with a formal extradition process. They have become more controversial largely because some of the receiving countries have been known for their rough handling, including torture, of prisoners. Torture in general, even with detainees who have not been subjects of rendition, also became a more prominent issue of debate in the years. This was especially due to the use of 'enhanced interrogation' techniques under the George W. Bush administration in the United States. The relevant questions include not only whether human rights are being violated but also whether torture is effective in eliciting accurate information.

Beyond torture is the issue of assassinating individual terrorist leaders, often referred to as 'targeted killings'. Some argue that this kind of decapitation of a terrorist group or cell can be effective in preventing terrorist attacks, and that the procedure should not be considered functionally or morally different from many conventional military operations. Others emphasize what can go, and has gone, wrong in clandestine assassinations, including the killing of innocent people through mistaken identity or collateral damage. Moreover, such assassinations may constitute a stooping to the same level as terrorists, by using a procedure that in some contexts can be considered terrorism itself. Both sides can find much to adduce in the experience of Israel, which has made extensive use of targeted killings as a counterterrorist tool (Byman 2006). The killing of Osama bin Laden in 2011 was generally accepted, especially outside Pakistan, as a legitimate counterterrorist measure, given the notoriety of the target and the care that went into planning the operation (see Box 30.2).

## BOX 30.2   THE DEATH OF OSAMA BIN LADEN

On 2 May 2011, al-Qa'ida leader Osama bin Laden was killed in a raid by US special forces on a compound in Abbottabad, Pakistan. The raid, in which the US commandos reached the compound by helicopter from Afghanistan, relied on intelligence painstakingly gathered for several years and concluded a manhunt that had lasted well over a decade.

The successful raid elicited an enormous public response, including celebrations in the streets of American cities. But the operation also highlighted limitations and downsides of this type of counterterrorist use of military force. The US president ordered the raid even though the available information was far from conclusive as to whether bin Laden would be found at the compound. Questions were quickly raised after the raid about the need to kill bin Laden; the United States said that its forces were prepared to capture him but that resistance made the killing necessary.

The biggest problems involved a rapid worsening in US relations with Pakistan, where many people considered the raid a violation of sovereignty and where the Pakistani military – which had not been informed in advance – was deeply embarrassed by the operation. The location of bin Laden's hideout in central Pakistan, close to a Pakistani military academy, stoked suspicion in the West that he had received official help in staying hidden.

Debate also ensued about how much damage the killing of bin Laden inflicted on terrorist capabilities. Material seized during the raid confirmed that bin Laden's role in his last few years had been confined mostly to exhortation, not command and control. His personal following and skill as a propagandist nonetheless meant that his death was probably a significant loss to al-Qa'ida, one that cannot be fully replaced by his less charismatic successor, Ayman al-Zawahiri.

---

Most citizens never experience directly anything having to do with the controversial procedures just mentioned. But they do experience other conflicts between counterterrorism and important public values. There is unavoidable conflict with two values in particular: liberty (absence of restrictions on daily life) and privacy (avoiding governmental scrutiny of personal matters). Liberty is curtailed every time one is denied access to a formerly public place in the interest of security, or one has to empty pockets and detour through a metal detector to enter a building. Privacy is compromised when government agencies collect and exploit financial, travel, or other data on individuals in the interest of identifying possible terrorists. Issues of privacy became especially acute in the United States with the expansion of investigative activities after the 9/11 attacks. Debate centred on, for example, the Federal Bureau of Investigation's new power to require public libraries to identify which books an individual had borrowed, or the National Security Agency's interception of telephone conversations without a court warrant. The controversies eased somewhat with new legislative restrictions on communications intercepts and shifts in policy from Bush's administration to that of Barack Obama (Lynch 2010), but the underlying conflicts among social and security objectives remain.

There is no single, optimum formula for resolving these conflicts. Counterterrorism is not the only objective in public policy, nor should it be.

It is up to each country's citizenry, preferably acting through a fair process of representative government, to decide where it wishes to strike a balance between safety from terrorism and other interests and values.

A citizenry's confidence that this balance has been struck properly and in a way consistent with its values is important for the final, critical ingredient in counterterrorism: informed and sustained public support. That type of support is difficult to get. Public interest in counterterrorism is high after a major terrorist attack, but tends to wane if time passes without more such attacks. A counterterrorist programme can be effective only if government officials and private citizens alike understand that the programme must be applied consistently, coherently, and over a long time.

## Further reading

Gabriella Blum and Philip B. Heymann, *Laws, Outlaws, and Terrorists: Lessons from the War on Terrorism* (MIT Press, 2010). Examines the legal, ethical, and practical dimensions of some of the most controversial recent issues in counterterrorism.

Daniel Byman, *The Five Front War: The Better Way to Fight Global Jihad* (John Wiley and Sons, 2008). Offers a general strategy of counterterrorism.

Audrey Kurth Cronin and James M. Ludes (eds.), *Attacking Terrorism: Elements of a Grand Strategy* (Georgetown University Press, 2004). Surveys the principal counterterrorist instruments and some of the major considerations that arise in using them.

Paul R. Pillar, *Terrorism and U.S. Foreign Policy* (Brookings Institution Press, 2003). A general treatise on counterterrorism that also places the subject in a broader policy context, with particular reference to the United States.

Richard A. Posner, *Preventing Surprise Attacks: Intelligence Reform in the Wake of 9/11* (Rowman & Littlefield, 2005). Analyses the challenges of applying intelligence to counterterrorism.

# Counterinsurgency

Joanna Spear

## Abstract

In this chapter, students will learn about the theory and practice of counterinsurgency. Counterinsurgency is an old issue with new currency in the twenty-first century. The ongoing campaign in Afghanistan and the previous one in Iraq led to a new generation of writings on counterinsurgency drawing comparisons and contrasts to the campaigns of the past. Counterinsurgency is an issue area where there are many scholar-practitioners (in contrast to other areas of security studies) which gives their writings a certain immediacy and applicability. Many of these scholar-practitioners are engaged in trying to change the way that militaries understand and fight these 'hearts and minds' campaigns.

## Introduction: The current discourse on counterinsurgency

When we wrote the first edition of this book, Americans were rediscovering counterinsurgency. The ongoing campaigns in Afghanistan and Iraq had led them to ask important questions about how to defeat determined but illusive opponents in challenging environments where superior technology did not seem to be the answer. Today American military involvement in Iraq is much reduced and the counterinsurgency (COIN) operations there are broadly defined as a success. Attention is now fully focused on Afghanistan, which has become, in the words of Bob Woodward (2010), 'Obama's war'. In Afghanistan some of the techniques that seemed to work in Iraq are being applied again by some of the same military leaders. The key question today is will the strategy of 'the surge' that was employed in Iraq work in Afghanistan? The answer is far from determined and has become embroiled in the internal politics of NATO and the International Security Assistance Force (ISAF), Afghan politics, American presidential politics and battles within the Pentagon. Clearly there is more fighting being done than just in Afghanistan.

America was slow and reluctant to rediscover counterinsurgency, despite the fact that the successful US campaign against the Huq rebels in the Philippines and the Vietnam conflict were both counterinsurgencies. The reluctance seems to stem from the extremely painful national and individual experiences in the latter unsuccessful campaign. Rarely, until a speech by President Bush in August 2007, was America's own experience of battling a highly motivated, low-tech local insurgency in Vietnam discussed. So deep was the post-Vietnam amnesia of America that when COIN was discussed, the historical parallels generally made reference to *European* – not American – experiences of counterinsurgency. Thus, interestingly, the first book-length consideration of the parallels between the two US counterinsurgency operations was produced in Europe (Dumbrell and Ryan 2007). Even today, most US writings on COIN draw on campaigns other than Vietnam.

Part of the reason for the slow American rediscovery of counterinsurgency is that initially in Afghanistan there was not a strong insurgency, the Taliban seemed essentially beaten. And at the outset of the Iraq war the Bush Administration had no expectation that they would need to fight insurgents; rather they assumed that the US would be welcomed as 'liberators' – as Vice President Dick Cheney put it on *Meet the Press* (16 March 2003). Given this assumption, there was little planning for extensive Iraqi post-conflict reconstruction, let alone for counterinsurgency! Since these expectations about Afghanistan and Iraq were dashed America has been relearning counter-insurgency in both theory and practice.

A second notable feature of the current discourse on counterinsurgency is that in many of the countries militarily engaged in Afghanistan, domestic public opinion has become increasingly sceptical about continued involvement and the chances of successfully extinguishing the insurgency. For example, every military coffin being brought back from Afghanistan to Britain is being met by large respectful crowds – silent reproaches to the British Government's Afghanistan policy (Deacon, 2009). Today the mission in Afghanistan is being questioned – the rationale is no longer accepted, the Afghan central government is seen as incompetent and corrupt, the resurgence of the Taliban is worrying – and all this after a decade of international involvement. Consequently, international forces are all planning their military exits from Afghanistan. Ironically this all comes at a time when NATO/ISAF and the individual national militaries are more effectively trained and armed to undertake COIN operations than in a generation.

A third notable feature of the discourse on counterinsurgency is the fact that it is often also linked to a discussion of military learning – or, more accurately – not learning (Nagl 2005). For America, counterinsurgency was a mission that politicians and the military (apart from Special Forces) had turned their back on after Vietnam, and the wider military had devalued or forgotten much of what it knew. America has gone through the process of re-learning counterinsurgency. In Britain, the military regard themselves as good at counterinsurgency due to their colonial history, the long-term operation in Northern Ireland and their experiences as peacekeepers (which hone a comparable skill set). However, the British counterinsurgency practice in Afghanistan's Helmand province is widely seen to have failed (Wikileaks: US Embassy Cables 2008, 2009). Somehow the British military had un-learned COIN (discussed further below).

This chapter will now examine some of the key aspects of counter-insurgency. The first section discusses the state of the field and highlights some contrasts between it and other areas of security studies. The second section examines insurgency, which is the problem that counterinsurgency is designed to check. Here I discuss the differences between 'classic' insurgencies and those taking place today. The third section looks at an enduring aspect of counterinsurgency; the battle for 'hearts and minds'. The fourth section looks at the role of force in counterinsurgency (and the debate over it) and the strategies and tactics that are often involved. The fifth section discusses military learning in general while the sixth looks at doing counterinsurgency in an age of a global media. Section seven draws comparisons between counterinsurgency and so-called 'post-conflict peacebuilding'. The final section considers whether counterinsurgency is a major mission for the future.

---

### BOX 31.1  KEY DEFINITIONS

#### Insurgency

*Insurgency* is defined in British military doctrine as 'an organized movement aimed at the overthrow of a constituted government through the use of subversion and armed conflict' (UK Ministry of Defence 2004: 4). The same definition is used by NATO and the US military.

#### Counterinsurgency

*Counterinsurgency* is defined in British and NATO military doctrine as 'those military, paramilitary, political, economic, psychological, and civic actions taken to defeat insurgency' (UK Ministry of Defence 2004: 4). The US definition is subtly different; 'Those military, paramilitary, political, economic, psychological, and civic actions taken *by a government* to defeat insurgency' [emphasis added] (DOD 2007). Thus, for the US, counterinsurgency is a solely government activity, whereas Britain and NATO have a rather more freewheeling attitude.

---

## The state of the field

Writings on counterinsurgency differ in one crucial respect from most of the writings in the field of security studies; a much higher percentage of the writers are both scholars *and* practitioners. This has certain advantages, for example, the writers often display a deep understanding of military practice, communicate a real sense of the operational environment and have spent many hours pondering the successes and failures they experienced. The disadvantages can be that they are writing primarily for a military audience (and this can make it hard to follow), that they tend to assume that what works for them in one country will automatically work elsewhere (a very big assumption), and – particularly in the case of those who fought in Algeria and Vietnam – some of them are embittered by their experiences and treat writing as a form of therapy.

## The problem that counterinsurgency responds to – insurgency

Insurgency is a form of violent opposition to rule by a stronger force. It is not new with insurgents dating back to at least the Roman Empire. Other widely debated examples are the insurgency British forces encountered in the American colonies in the eighteenth century and the French resistance to Nazi rule during the Second World War.

David Kilcullen (a scholar-practitioner, see Box 31.2) has made a number of useful observations about contemporary insurgencies as compared to those that informed a lot of the 'classical' works on how to understand and prosecute counterinsurgency. In the 'classical insurgencies' of the late colonial era (*c.*1944–1980) – when much of the initial formulation of counterinsurgency took place – the insurgent groups were intent on expelling foreign forces from their territories and establishing their own sovereign states. Thus in classical insurgencies the insurgents were the instigators and the revolutionaries wanting change. Today, by contrast, the insurgents are often protecting the status quo from the changes brought by outside invaders, for example, Afghanistan, Iraq, Pakistan, and Chechnya (Kilcullen 2006/2007: 113).

In Latin America, where Che Guevara both practised and wrote about guerrilla warfare, the emphasis was on deposing local elites and replacing them with a socially just (i.e. leftist) system of government. As he wrote of guerrilla warfare in 1963, 'this form of struggle is a means to an end. That end, essential and inevitable for any revolutionary, is the conquest of political power' (Guevara 1963: 1). Thus, insurgents had clear political agendas, involving gaining control of the state, and, following Mao Zedong's strategy, often sought to prove they were fit to rule by providing an alternative governance structure to that of the colonists/oligarchs. Kilcullen points out that contemporary insurgencies do not all seek to take over and establish their own

## BOX 31.2  COUNTERINSURGENCY SCHOLAR-PRACTITIONERS

*T. E. Lawrence:* also known as 'Lawrence of Arabia' for his role in leading an Arab revolt against the Ottoman Turks in the Middle East (to provide help to Lord Kitchener by defeating this ally of Germany). More of an insurgent than a counterinsurgent, his book *The Seven Pillars of Wisdom* is a valuable account of the problems of insurgency and has been studied by those seeking to understand the psyche of insurgents.

*Roger Trinquier:* first practised counterinsurgency with the French in Indochina before moving to Algeria in 1957 as a Lieutenant Colonel. Algeria was the inspiration for *Modern Warfare: A French View of Counterinsurgency* (Trinquier 1961) which stressed the importance of winning the support of the people. He thought victory would come through: securing an area to operate from, good intelligence, gaining support in the government and general population, maintaining the initiative, and carefully managing propaganda (Tomes 2004: 18). He advocated a 'gridding system' of dividing territory into sectors that can be swept clear of insurgents, this *quadrillage* strategy used by the French in Algeria had the effect of tying down over 300,000 troops (Alexander and Keiger 2002: 15, 21).

*David Galula:* completed *Counterinsurgency Warfare: Theory and Practice* in 1964. In it he distilled his experiences in China, Greece, Indochina and Algeria into a series of principles for counterinsurgency from which strategies and tactics could be derived. He concluded that in counterinsurgency 'most of the rules applicable to one side do not work for the other' (cited in Tomes 2004: 20). He also stresses the dynamic nature of insurgency and the ways in which it will adopt new injustices to reinforce its cause. In response the counterinsurgent must be alert to potential problems and proactively solve them. Galula conceives of counterinsurgency as demanding primarily political responses.

*Frank Kitson:* rose to the rank of Commander in Chief of the British land forces and was knighted. He fought insurgencies in Kenya, Malaya, Cyprus and Northern Ireland. His controversial work *Low Intensity Operations: Subversion, Insurgency and Peacekeeping*, published in 1971, put particular stress on psychological operations against insurgents.

*David Petraeus:* a West Point graduate, he was the top graduate of the US Army Command and General Staff College Class of 1983 and won all three of the class prizes when he attended Ranger School. His career has alternated between command and staff assignments and working as an aide to some of the Army's most prominent generals. He also attended Princeton University and obtained a MA in International Relations and completed a PhD thesis on 'The American Military and the Lessons of Vietnam'. His first combat experience was in Iraq in 2003 and he later won praise for his handling of the Mosul area during the early occupation. He was the intellectual inspiration for and a major contributor to the US Army and Marine Corps *Counterinsurgency Field Manual* (2006). In January 2007 he was appointed to oversee operations in Iraq and instigated the successful 'surge' there. Following the ignominious resignation of General Stanley McChrystal in June 2010, General Petraeus took a demotion to lead US operations in Afghanistan and to implement a 'surge' strategy there (Barnes *et al.* 2010).

*John Nagl:* was an active duty officer in the US army who completed a thesis at Oxford University and then found himself in Iraq practising what he had written about. The introduction to *Eating*

*Soup with a Knife* (2005) reflects on how well his theoretical insights stood up to the reality of counterinsurgency practice. He worked with General Petraeus on the *Counterinsurgency Field Manual* and instigated its wider publication, recognizing the importance of the public accepting counterinsurgency as a key US mission. After leaving the military he was for three years President of the Center for a New American Security think tank and a member of the US Defense Policy Board. Subsequently, he joined the Faculty of the Naval Academy, where he teaches the history of modern counterinsurgency.

*David Kilcullen:* originally Australian, he worked in Baghdad with General Petraeus. He previously served in the Middle East, Southeast Asia and the Pacific and in the counterinsurgency in East Timor. His book *The Accidental Guerrilla* (2009) was well received. He is a prolific author and a thoughtful commentator on the situations he encounters and on the bigger strategic picture.

state. Rather, 'insurgency today follows state failure, and is not directed at taking over a functioning body politic, but at dismembering or scavenging its carcass, or contesting an "ungoverned space"' (Kilcullen 2006/2007: 112). Moreover, some religiously motivated insurgencies may not have a political aim; the very act of insurgency may be seen as earning God's favour (Kilcullen 2006/07: 116). Nevertheless, even if an insurgency lacks political motive, it will have political consequences.

The tactics employed by insurgents were – and still are – necessitated by their military weakness; they could not confront the opposing power directly and therefore attacked vulnerable points and then retreated amongst the local population (moving as 'fishes to the water' in Mao's classic analogy) so that they were hard to detect and punish. These insurgent tactics were hard to counter. Attempts at mass punishment of populations in response to insurgencies had the counter-productive aim of alienating the local population from the authority trying to maintain its power and legitimacy. As a consequence, a body of knowledge began to accumulate – primarily among colonial militaries – about how best to deal with these difficult insurgent tactics. Knowledge was often the result of painful learning even in ultimately successful operations. For example, the British in Malaya suffered real problems in the early years of the campaign before they honed a successful strategy.

In the classical model the insurgents live off the population, so a key aim is to isolate the insurgents from these sources of support. This would not – in itself – be a successful tactic today as in direct contrast to times past, the insurgents in Afghanistan and Iraq are often better off than the population because they receive outside funding (Kilcullen 2006/2007: 119). By contrast, today insurgents sometimes provide resources to the local population in exchange for services such as planting roadside bombs. Nevertheless, the local population remains an important source of camouflage and intelligence gathering for the insurgents, so the aim of isolating them from the people still has value.

The classical counterinsurgencies were primarily rural affairs but this is not true today, where the insurgencies of Iraq and Afghanistan are fought in urban areas, causing new headaches for the counterinsurgency forces as there are greater dangers to civilians and incentives for the insurgents to target them to seize media headlines. Thus, as General Sir Rupert Smith has put it, 'we fight among the people' (2005: 278).

Classical insurgencies were usually confined to one state or region and involved one insurgent group and one government. This was far from the case in Iraq where the array of forces that the US and its allies faced was very complex and the relationship of local groups to one another was fluid and shifting (International Crisis Group 2006). Indeed, a particular feature in Iraq was that local groups were not just fighting against the external occupiers, but also fighting amongst themselves, making conflicts less binary struggles than multi-sided violent interactions. The positive side of this is that there were opportunities for counterinsurgents to ally with local forces. For example, the alliance struck between US forces and the tribal groups of Tal Afar against units of 'Al-Qa'ida in Iraq'. The negative side is that just as alliances can shift one way, they can also shift another. The US experience in the 1980s of backing counterinsurgents in Afghanistan (including Osama Bin Laden) shows that alliances are temporary.

Another aspect of this complexity should be noted; it is no longer a traditional military handling all aspects of the counterinsurgency mission. Who undertakes counterinsurgency is now more complex too, with civilian government agencies, private security companies, aid agencies, non-governmental organizations, the media and a host of other actors playing a role (sometimes unwittingly) in the counterinsurgency campaign. This has led to clashes of organizational culture in the field, as a group pursues its activities unaware (or unconcerned about, or unwilling to contribute to) the wider counterinsurgency mission. For example, at the height of the conflict in Iraq the second largest external force in the country (after the US) were private military contractors (see Chapter 28, this volume). Their missions were specific and limited, often as simple as 'convey person A to point Y safely'. Their only concern was to complete that mission and they would run cars off the road, stop the traffic, annoy Iraqis etc. and not worry about it, even though it counteracted the larger counterinsurgency mission of winning 'hearts and minds'. This led contractors into conflicts with military and civilian authorities.

Kilcullen warns of the dangers of applying wholesale lessons from classical counterinsurgency to contemporary situations as the nature of the insurgents, the complexity of local environments and the globalization of the international system require a careful adaptation of counterinsurgency to the contemporary era. That said, he is clear that one key aspect of insurgency and counter-insurgency has not changed; it is a battle for the support of the people.

## 'Hearts and minds'

It is now a truism that successful counterinsurgency involves winning the 'hearts and minds' of the local population. This reflects the competition for the allegiance of the people. Scholar-practitioner Frank Kitson (see Box 31.2) made the insightful comment that 'Insurgents start with nothing but a cause and grow to strength, while the counterinsurgents start with everything but a cause and gradually decline in strength and grow to weakness' (Kitson 1971: 49 cited in Nagl 2005: 23).

The phrase 'hearts and minds' was initially coined by High Commissioner Gerald Templer and reflected the transformation he brought to British strategy in Malaya. His changes involved listening and responding to some of the insurgents' demands – therefore taking away from their cause and source of popularity – and ensuring the British became genuine protectors of the local population and therefore winning local support against the insurgents. Templer has come to regret that coinage; in 2010 he described it as 'that nauseating phrase'. His concern is that 'winning hearts and minds' – or WHAM as it is now being called – has come to be thought of as achieving local popularity, rather than winning legitimacy, which should be the aim (Wilton Park 2010: 6).

Despite most discussions of counterinsurgency giving a prominent place to 'hearts and minds' this does not always get translated into practice in a timely fashion: a number of counterinsurgencies lose valuable psychological ground by initially focusing on the use of force and failing to listen and respond to the local population.

There is a second front in the battle for 'hearts and minds' that is under-appreciated; the battle on the home front in the state conducting the counterinsurgency. Interestingly many insurgent groups have ultimately triumphed not because they won but because the counterinsurgents lacked the will to carry on, having lost the 'hearts and minds' of their constituents. This was true for the Soviet Union in Afghanistan, even though it was not a democracy the Soviet government realized there was insufficient popular support for continuing to prosecute the conflict (Savranskaya 2001). Time is often on the insurgents' side; because the stakes are much higher for them and they can wear down the home population's support for the counterinsurgency. The faltering domestic support for the current conflict in Afghanistan (and before that in Iraq) points to the importance of the 'hearts and minds' at home.

## The role of military force in counterinsurgency

Another scholar-practitioner is Robert Thompson who focused more on strategy than tactics and created what he called the *Five Principles of Counterinsurgency*:

1  The government must have a clear political aim: to establish and maintain a free, independent and united country which is politically and economically stable and viable.

2  The government must function in accordance with the law.

3  The government must have an overall plan.

4 The government must give priority to defeating the political subversion, not the guerrillas.

5 In the guerrilla phase of insurgency, a government must secure its base areas first.

(Thomson 1972: 50-60 cited in Nagl 2005: 29)

Even bearing in mind the points made by David Kilcullen about how the insurgents and the counterinsurgents have changed, there is still much of value here. In particular, the principle of securing base areas first and then spreading outwards – the so-called 'ink blot' (British term) or 'oil-spot' (American term) strategy was used successfully in Malaya, was used in Iraq and is currently being employed in Afghanistan.

In terms of tactics, an important part of counterinsurgency is actually *not* using force. David Galula (1964: 89) suggested that the ideal counter-insurgency campaign would be '80% political, 20% military'. He contended that the point of military power was to create the space for political progress (Galula 1964: 88). Given the centrality of 'hearts and minds' this makes perfect sense; a counterinsurgency campaign should involve politics, economics, psychology and, as necessary, military force. As Kilcullen concluded, 'This certainly remains relevant to modern counterinsurgency in the sense that non-military elements of national power remain decisive, though less well resourced than military elements' (2006/2007: 123).

Clearly, in situations where authorities are trying to win the support of the local population, the heavy-handed use of military power is likely to be counterproductive. As McFate and Jackson (2006: 15) note 'A direct relationship exists between the appropriate use of force and successful counterinsurgency'. Thus when force is used it must be precise, discriminating and accurate. All of this points to the crucial role of good intelligence in ensuring the appropriate use of force. Yet this is often a real shortcoming of counterinsurgency efforts, at least in the early stages and sometimes throughout the campaign. Moreover, intelligence is more than situational information; it is also about understanding the culture, workings and priorities of the local population (see Chapter 16, this volume). A classic feature of unsuccessful counterinsurgencies is either an underestimation of the will of the people (for example, President Johnson declared that the US could not be defeated by the 'bicycle powered economy' of Vietnam), or its motivation (the USA failed to understand conflict in Vietnam as an ongoing anti-imperialist struggle, seeing it through the Cold War lens of virulent communism and assuming if Soviet and Chinese support was ended, the war would be won).

For the US military in Iraq one of the big debates was how much to prioritize force protection as compared to protecting the local population. Initially the American military gave clear priority to force protection, in comparison to the British military operating in the (much more benign) atmosphere of Basra. Thus whereas the British were patrolling on foot and wearing berets, the American military were patrolling in armoured vehicles with heavy weaponry (Brown 2004). Although this was partly a question of differing security situations, there was also a different set of priorities for the two; the British tradition of imperial policing led them to put security of the local population as the key mission, whereas the US military prioritized force protection (possibly a manifestation of 'Vietnam Syndrome'?). The same debate has been raging in Afghanistan and in both theatres General Petraeus switched US tactics towards protecting the population.

Another facet of the use of military force is the US military's general preference for conventional warfare fought with high-technology weapons systems. As the initial invasion of Iraq showed, the US is a formidable conventional fighting machine, but in the words of a senior British officer, it is one which 'is fascinated by electronics, PowerPoint and the rhythm of battle' (Mills 2004). One of the problems of counterinsurgency is that these weapons are generally not useful in fighting urban insurgencies.

## Learning on the ground

According to Kilcullen 'the nature of counter-insurgency is not fixed but shifting' and this is because 'it evolves in responses to changes in insurgency' (2006/2007: 112). On a micro-scale this can be seen in Iraq where, for example, the use of improvised explosive devices (IEDs) has become more extensive, evolved to include follow-up small arms fire, was latterly videoed for propaganda use, and has subsequently spread to Afghanistan and Thailand (Waterman 2006). In response the counterinsurgency has shifted to meet these new and difficult challenges, but it is struggling to get ahead of the insurgents.

One of the key aspects of counterinsurgency is to allow the forces on the ground autonomy in responding to the situations that they encounter; to become what has been called 'strategic corporals' (Krulak 1999). In the UK this is generally more easily achieved due to the anti-doctrine bias in the British armed forces, where there is a tradition of having a basic set of rules, the interpretation and implementation of which is left to commanders in the field. This is thought to give British counterinsurgency flexibility and to encourage initiative (Thornton 2000). There is also a certain tradition of regimental 'lore' which is often unique to a particular regiment and reflects their history, approaches and tactics and is informally passed down to new soldiers.

For the much larger American military this is more of a challenge; the very size of the force means that there is greater reliance upon hierarchies and written doctrine and therefore traditionally there are fewer roles for individual initiative (Aylwin-Foster 2005). Moreover, whereas Nagl defines the British as a 'learning military' he sees the US military as failing to learn and adapt (2005: 191–208). This does not mean that there is not learning at the tactical level in the US military – the Iraq counterinsurgency is replete with examples of learning on the ground – but that this does not percolate upwards into doctrinal and strategic change (Gavrilis 2005). The 2007 US *Counterinsurgency Field Manual* is clear on the importance of the individual, stressing the need to 'empower the lowest levels'.

In Iraq and Afghanistan soldiers have been using the internet to share information and tactics on dealing with insurgents. This has proved invaluable when one military unit is rotating out of a theatre and wishes to pass on information to the incoming units (sometimes information that their leaders do not want passed on). However, the American authorities became concerned about who else was reading these blogs and web-posts and watching the YouTube videos and imposed restrictions on what can be posted and when – in an attempt to protect operational security (OpSec). They argue that insurgents could glean valuable intelligence from these sources (Shane 2005). The stream of secret US information being released by Wikileaks has only increased that concern. Interestingly, the British military have not done the same and seem to regard new technologies as an excellent means of ensuring quick learning about evolving insurgent tactics.

To indicate the extent of the learning challenge that the US military has faced, according to Aylwin-Foster, in 2005 there were no courses in the DOD military education system (which is extensive) solely focused on counter-insurgency (2005: 9). This situation has since been rectified. There are also a number of institutional attempts to help US forces learn. Counterinsurgency is now a part of pre-deployment training and often includes interactions with Afghan-Americans to help soldiers understand the complexity of the local environment. An important initiative is the Center for Lessons Learned at Fort Leavenworth, with 200 researchers and staff on call, who can answer questions from soldiers on the ground that need help fast. The Center prepared *A Soldiers Handbook: the First 100 Days* for those deploying to Iraq. It covered what to be alert for, IEDs, avoiding routines and complacency, how to face the dead and the injured etc. (WBEZ 2007).

Ironically, while the US has become more of a 'learning military' the British seem to have gone in the opposite direction! The British counterinsurgency campaign in Helmand Province has failed to follow their own best practices to concentrate forces to achieve an 'ink blot'. Forces were spread too thinly in 'forward operating bases' vulnerable to attack, and denied themselves the opportunity to consolidate territorial gains (Wikileaks 2008). Moreover, the British have favoured the pro-active use of force over the more sanguine political tactics advocated in COIN. Anthony King identifies a number of telling reasons for this failure: the preference for kinetic activity of the particular regiments involved, the pressure to act from local politicians, the lure of the technological force-multiplying possibilities of the Apache helicopter, deep regimental rivalries, and a military culture that rewards action with medals and thus reinforces the rush to kinetic activity (King 2010).

## Counterinsurgency in the media age

Given the centrality of the 'hearts and minds' of the local and the home populations, the media is an essential sinew of a counterinsurgency campaign. Back in the 1930s T. E. Lawrence wrote that 'The printing press is the greatest weapon in the armory of the modern commander' (cited in Nagl 2005: 24). The media has become another arena of competition between insurgents and counterinsurgents, with each trying to convince key constituents of its positions. With the globalization of the media and the technologies that facilitate it, it has become harder to control. Much contemporary counter-insurgency practice is about 'spin control'; attempting to influence how events (in and out of theatre), campaigns and progress are reported, both locally and at home. For example, when an American Pastor provocatively burnt a Koran – enraging people in Afghanistan and leading to riots and the murder of United Nations staff – General Petraeus went on Afghanistan TV and Radio to directly denounce the Pastor's activities (Sieff 2011).

A consequence of the increasing democratization of the media (anyone with a cell phone, access to the internet or a camera can be a reporter) is that everything the counterinsurgent does may be observed. This goes from the very macabre – jihadists taking videos of the destruction they cause or allied soldiers photographing the humiliation of prisoners – to citizen/journalists providing a 'bird's eye' view of what they see of the counterinsurgency. One consequence is that every move the individual soldier, contractor and official makes has to be calibrated in terms of the overall counterinsurgency; something that was desirable anyway but has become crucial, though difficult, to achieve.

## Similarities to post-conflict peacebuilding

There are a number of comparisons to draw between counterinsurgency operations and post-conflict peacebuilding which are worth noting: First, in both situations the ideal ratio between force (kinetic) and non-violent (non-kinetic) activities is the same; 20 per cent military to 80 per cent non-military elements. In each type of operation there are the same questions over the suitability of the military for doing some of these tasks – particularly the economic and political elements. In both situations the military are often the only group there in strength and inevitably find themselves undertaking tasks they are not trained for.

Second, both operations are aimed at standing up and supporting weak governments. Often the situation they encounter is where informal authorities are the only power structure and society works through patrimonial networks (tribes and clans). Consequently, some of the same dilemmas are involved, in particular the tension between doing things efficiently (that is, by the outsiders doing it – be it armies, contractors, international organizations or NGOs) and enabling local ownership. T. E. Lawrence said of the Arabs in 1917 'better [they] do it tolerably well than you do it perfectly'. We can see this dilemma clearly in Afghanistan where there is concern over the ability of the local police forces to effectively fulfill their duties. In peacebuilding operations the temptation to take over from the locals is usually overwhelming, particularly as missions often have only a short period of time to achieve 'peace' before they leave.

Third, in both counterinsurgency and peacebuilding operations there is a lot of knowledge at the tactical/operational level, but less at the strategic level, leading to a tendency to apply 'standard models' with very mixed results. In both counterinsurgency and post-conflict peacebuilding, efforts are often undermined by the same problems of lack of cultural knowledge, which rarely get addressed in time. In both situations there are attempts to learn from past operations, for example, the UN Department of Peacekeeping Operations has a Best Practices Unit, but these efforts are not very successful. Consequently, there is the same kind of sporadic learning – especially in the US which has not regarded either operation as a core mission (even though the US military ends up doing both).

Fourth, in both post-conflict peacebuilding and counterinsurgency there are similar mixes of actors involved in the operations: NGOs, international organizations, private firms, military and civilian authorities, contractors, local civil society, etc. This leads to parallel problems of coordination and the difficulty of ensuring that all actors are pursuing the same agenda.

Finally, the disarmament, demobilization and reintegration (DDR) campaigns that are an important part of peacebuilding face the same problem as counterinsurgency: how to drain away the uncommitted supporters from the fanatics who will not be swayed by alternative employment and economic opportunities.

Clearly, there are many similarities between these two types of operations. This helps to explain why forces that are regularly involved in post-conflict peacebuilding operations find the move to counterinsurgency less traumatic than militaries which are primarily focused on missions involving major wars with high-technology opponents.

## Conclusion

An important question in modern counterinsurgency is 'what constitutes victory?' A quote from former US Secretary of Defense, Donald Rumsfeld sums up the dilemma: 'We know we are killing a lot, capturing a lot, collecting arms. We just don't know yet whether that's the same as winning' (cited in Hoffman 2004: 16).

Kilcullen points to the fact that in contemporary insurgencies the continued existence of even a few insurgents armed with modern communications technologies could mean that they continue to cause significant problems, so it might not be enough to destroy an organization. Therefore, 'In modern counterinsurgency, victory may need to be re-defined as the disarming and reintegration of insurgents into society, combined with popular support for permanent, institutionalized anti-terrorist measures that contain the risk of terrorist cells emerging from the former insurgent movement' (Kilcullen 2006/2007: 123).

Within the US Pentagon there is a lively campaign being conducted to have counterinsurgency recognized as a core mission for the future. Those evangelizing for counterinsurgency want to ensure that the US does not have to go through the same painful re-learning experience in the future, but is ready, trained and able to take on the missions. Among the key counterinsurgency advocates are people like scholar-practitioners John Nagl, James Gavrillis, Thomas Hammes and David Petraeus.

These advocates are meeting spirited opposition for several reasons. First, counterinsurgency is not a mission that the military necessarily likes; operations are messy, inconclusive, can cost a lot of lives, and are in many ways 'post-heroic'. Second, the military culture of efficiency, organization and clear missions is somewhat at odds with what it takes to do successful counterinsurgency; empowering locals (even at the cost of efficiency), not really using force and stepping outside of usual roles. Third, counterinsurgency is a mission that gives the lead to the Army and Marines, and that is never going to please the Air Force and the Navy (even though both branches are providing personnel for counterinsurgency operations today). Fourth, counterinsurgency is a mission that does not require any major advanced weapons platforms (fighter aircraft, aircraft carriers, etc.) Part of the battle here comes down to concerns about the allocation of budgets. Despite US defence spending being at a historic high in terms of constant dollars, the various services are concerned that prioritizing counterinsurgency combined with the heavy cost of the campaigns in Iraq and Afghanistan and the need for austerity in a recession will lead to the diversion of funds away from weapons projects and desired future military spending (Bennett 2007). Fifth, the US record in counterinsurgency does not encourage making it a core mission; at best the record is decidedly mixed. Sixth, there are also concerns that fighting 'wars of choice' in Iraq and Afghanistan has led to the neglect of more fundamental security problems like nuclear proliferation in North Korea and Iran.

Finally, there is the political question of whether, after the bruising experiences of Iraq and Afghanistan, the US would be willing to take on new insurgencies or will it be deterred? President Obama's response to the rebellion in Libya in 2011 is a good indication of the current political landscape. Although initially supportive of a limited intervention to establish a 'no fly zone', this military involvement was then significantly scaled back, much to the chagrin of the more pro-active British and French. For now it seems the US is leery of further counterinsurgencies. However, Kilcullen has suggested that the US will be called upon to fight insurgencies until it finds a way to defeat them, so it will not have a choice.

## Further reading

A good starting point is *The U.S. Army and Marine Corps Counterinsurgency Field Manual* with Forewords by General David H. Petraeus, Lt. General James F. Amos, and Lt. Colonel John A. Nagl, and by Sarah Sewall (University of Chicago Press, 2007). This is the first time that a field manual has been published by a mainstream press and this speaks to the current interest in the issue (and can be viewed as part of the 'hearts and minds' campaign at home). A notable feature is the emphasis on understanding local culture.

John A. Nagl, *Learning to Eat Soup With A Knife: Counterinsurgency Lessons from Malaya and Vietnam* (University of Chicago Press, 2005). The title is taken from T.E. Lawrence who said 'To make war upon rebellion is messy and slow, like eating soup with a knife'.

David Kilcullen, *The Accidental Guerrilla: Fighting Small Wars in the Midst of a Big One* (Oxford University Press, 2009). A thoughtful and well-received analysis of counterinsurgency operations.

John Dumbrell and David Ryan (eds.), *Vietnam in Iraq: Tactics, Lessons, Legacies and Ghosts* (Routledge, 2007). Contains a number of interesting essays investigating the comparisons and contrasts between US involvement in these two counterinsurgencies.

There are many relevant internet blogs but their quality is hugely variable. I recommend: The Small Wars Journal blog: http://smallwarsjournal.com/blog/. This is both a good round-up of recent events and gets good quality contributions from participants such as David Kilcullen.

Other internet sites of value are the horizontal networking sites www.companycommand.com and www.platoonleader.org

See also Gary Trudeau's (creator of the 'Doonsbury' cartoon) site 'The Sandbox'. Hosted by *Slate Magazine*, for the last five years it has provided a place for soldiers to post accounts of their service in Iraq and Afghanistan: http://gocomics.typepad.com/the_sandbox/

*The Battle of Algiers* (Directed by Gillo Pontecorvo, 1966). Set during the Algerian war (1954–1962), this film follows French efforts to roll up an insurgent cell. Its actors included many locals who had lived through the civil war and it does not flinch from showing violence perpetrated by both sides. It is said that the film was watched by military officials of the Bush Administration in the aftermath of the 2003 Iraq invasion.

*Restrepo* (Co-directed by Sebastian Junger and Tim Hetherington, 2010). This documentary provides a searing account of the experiences of a US patrol in the Korengal Valley in Afghanistan.

*The War Tapes* (Directed by Deborah Scranton, 2006). Filmed by members of Charlie Company stationed in Iraq, it shows the day-to-day progress of the war and the strain it places on soldiers there.

CONTENTS

# The Responsibility to Protect

Alex J. Bellamy

▓ **Abstract**

In this chapter, students will learn about the 'responsibility to protect' principle, which seeks to rethink the relationship between security, sovereignty and human rights. It looks at the origins of the principle, the politics behind its adoption by the UN in 2005, subsequent debates at the UN about its implementation, and its role in shaping international responses to major humanitarian crises. Key questions include whether sovereignty should entail the protection of a state's population, whether states can be persuaded to take responsibility for protecting populations overseas, and what sorts of policies states should adopt in the face of mass atrocities.

▓ **Introduction**

For both realists and liberals alike, security has traditionally been understood as the purview of states and two of the principal guarantors of state security are the principles of sovereignty and non-interference. According to this perspective, security is best achieved by establishing a basic degree of international order based on each state's recognition of every other state's right to rule a particular territory and engage in external relations. This is often labelled 'Westphalian sovereignty', referring to the 1648 Peace of Westphalia which is commonly reckoned to have instituted a world order based on the right of sovereigns to govern their own people in whatever way they saw fit. This idea sits at the heart of contemporary international society's rules governing relations between states. Article 2(7) of the UN Charter prohibits the organisation from interfering in the domestic affairs of states, while Article 2(4) prohibits the threat or use of force except in self-defence or with the approval of the UN Security Council.

The value of this Westphalian system of security rests on the assumption that sovereign states are the best guardians of human security. The challenge for security studies is to explore how best to respond when sovereign states are unable to protect their citizens from genocide, mass killing or ethnic cleansing or engage in these practices themselves. This is no idle puzzle, nor is it a peripheral problem for the Westphalian system of security. According to one study, in the twentieth century alone some 262 million people were killed by their own government. This figure is six times greater than the number of people killed in battle by foreign governments during the same period (Rummel 1994). At the beginning of the twenty-first century, the Sudanese government and its Janjawiid militia were responsible for the killing of at least 250,000 and forced displacement of over two million Darfuri civilians. This is just the latest in a string of recent cases where governments have killed or supported the killing of sections of their own population. Other recent cases include mass killing in the former Yugoslavia and in East Timor and the 1994 Rwandan genocide in which approximately 1 million people were slaughtered in 100 days. As I write this chapter, reports come through daily of Libyan, Syrian and Yemeni armed forces opening fire on unarmed protestors, killing significant numbers of them. Moral indignation at such crimes forces us to ask whether such states should lose their sovereign rights in these circumstances and be subject to legitimate humanitarian intervention? And, do other states have a duty to do whatever is necessary to protect imperilled people in distant lands?

At the 2005 World Summit, the world's largest ever gathering of Heads of State and Government committed themselves unanimously to a new principle – the Responsibility to Protect, or R2P. As agreed by UN Member States, the principle rests on three equally important and non-sequential pillars (UN General Assembly 2005: paras 138–139):

I:   The responsibility of the state to protect its population from genocide, war crimes, ethnic cleansing and crimes against humanity, and from their incitement (para. 138).

II:  The international community's responsibility to assist the state to fulfil its responsibility to protect (para. 139).

III: In situations where a state has manifestly failed to protect its population from the four crimes, the international community's responsibility to take timely and decisive action through peaceful diplomatic and humanitarian means and, if that fails, other more forceful means in a manner consistent with Chapters VI (pacific measures), VII (enforcement measures) and VIII (regional arrangements) of the UN Charter (para. 139).

For the first time, governments declared themselves responsible for the protection of their populations from four of the most serious crimes and promised that in some circumstances the security of individuals and groups should be prioritized over the security of states, replacing the logic of Westphalian sovereignty with a new, human-centred, logic of responsible sovereignty.

This was no idle pledge. The UN Security Council reaffirmed R2P in 2006 (Resolution 1674) and indicated its preparedness to act in response to the four crimes (collectively labeled 'mass atrocities' in this chapter) and did so again three years later (Resolution 1894). The UN Secretary-General has issued three reports focusing on the implementation of R2P, early warning and assessment of mass atrocity threats, and the role of regional organizations respectively, and has established a new Joint Office for the Prevention of Genocide and R2P that will provide the world body with early warning advice, among other things. The General Assembly has held informal dialogues on R2P, a plenary debate, and has issued a resolution pledging to give the principle its ongoing attention. More importantly, however, R2P has been incorporated into practice. Most notably, it was used to frame the world's response to post-election massacres in Kenya (2007–2008) and to the Libyan regime's brutal response to an uprising there (2011).

The purpose of this chapter is to understand the concepts behind the R2P, the politics surrounding its adoption at the 2005 World Summit and its implementation in the UN system, and how the principle is being used to provide security for some of the world's most imperilled people and the issues this has raised. To that end, it is divided into three parts. The first provides an overview of the transformation of thinking about sovereignty and its relationship to R2P. The second section examines the adoption of R2P by world leaders in 2005 and subsequent debates about implementation. The third section considers how R2P has been used in practice.

## Sovereignty and responsibility

The idea that sovereignty entitles governments to treat their citizens however they see fit is based on a common misunderstanding of the meaning of 'absolute sovereignty', a doctrine that prevailed in Europe until the nineteenth century. 'Absolute sovereignty' is commonly understood as providing a government with *carte blanche* within its internationally recognized borders. However, in the sixteenth century, when the doctrine of absolutism was first espoused, sovereigns and lawyers distinguished between two different meanings of 'absolute sovereignty'. Yes, sovereigns had exclusive jurisdiction in their territory but they were not entitled to rule arbitrarily because sovereignty entailed responsibilities to God.

At the beginning of the industrial age in the late eighteenth century, liberals and republicans guided by beliefs in rationalism and science refused to accept that sovereigns were only answerable to God. Beginning with the American Revolution in the early eighteenth century and culminating in the principle of self-determination set out by the Versailles treaty at the end of the First World War, they insisted that sovereignty derived from the people within a state (Bukovanksy 2002). According to this doctrine, states draw their right to rule from the consent of the governed and this consent might be withdrawn if the sovereign abused its citizens or failed to guarantee their basic rights.

Following this, the horrors of the Second World War produced a somewhat contradictory response from international society because of three key factors pulling in different directions. First, fascist aggression created a strong impetus for the outlawing of war as an instrument of state policy. Second, the belief that peoples had a right to govern themselves gave impetus to decolonization under Article 1(2) but posed the problem of how to protect newly independent states from interference by the world's great powers. In addition to the ban on force, the key protection afforded to the new states was the principle of non-interference set out in Article 2(7). Finally, the Holocaust and other horrors persuaded international society to place aspirations for basic human rights at the heart of the new order (as set out in Articles 1(3), 55 and 56). The tension this created is evident in the preamble of the UN Charter which promises to 'reaffirm faith in fundamental human rights, in the dignity and worth of the human person' but also says that states must 'practice tolerance and live together in peace with one another as good neighbours'. Thus the Charter reflected a pivotal political dilemma: how should states behave in cases where maintaining faith in human rights means refusing to be a good neighbour to a tyrannical regime? For this reason, the question of humanitarian intervention was often portrayed as a debate over the priority that should be accorded to either sovereignty or human rights.

There is no space here to rehearse the debates about humanitarian intervention (see Bellamy and Wheeler 2007). Suffice it to say that during the Cold War, no right of humanitarian intervention was permitted because states were primarily concerned about maintaining as much international order as possible through adherence to the rule of non-interference. There were also deep and well-founded concerns among post-colonial states that the great powers would abuse any such right of humanitarian intervention to justify neo-imperialist activities. After the Cold War, atrocities in northern Iraq, Somalia, Bosnia and Rwanda brought a subtle but important change whereby states agreed that the UN Security Council was entitled to use its Chapter VII enforcement powers to authorize humanitarian intervention. However, a strong commitment to non-interference remained and at no time did the Security Council authorize interventions against fully-functioning sovereign states which abused their citizens.

Two events in the 1990s prompted academics, politicians and international organizations to revisit the meaning of sovereignty. In 1994, the world stood aside as the Rwandan armed forces and Hutu militia massacred approximately 1 million Tutsi and Hutu civilians. The Rwandan genocide raised questions about how international society should make good on its promise to affirm human rights by preventing genocide and mass killing and how individual states might be persuaded to commit troops and treasure to protect imperilled foreigners in such cases. Importantly, although there was no humanitarian intervention, no governments publicly argued that Rwanda's sovereignty should be privileged over concern for its citizens. In 1999, NATO bombed the Federal Republic of Yugoslavia to coerce its leader, Slobodan Milosevic, into ceasing the ethnic cleansing of Kosovar Albanians. NATO was forced to act without a UN mandate because Russia and China believed that the situation in Kosovo was not serious enough to warrant armed intervention. This case also raised two important questions: is it legitimate for states or groups of states to intervene without UN approval and, to put it crudely, how are we to make judgments about whether there has been enough killing to warrant intervention?

It was questions like these that prompted a rethink about the nature of sovereignty. An important contribution to this line of thinking was made by Francis Deng, a former Sudanese diplomat who was appointed the UN Secretary-General's special representative on internally displaced people in 1992. In a book published in 1996, Deng and his co-authors argued that:

> sovereignty carries with it certain responsibilities for which governments must be held accountable. And they are accountable not only to their own national constituencies but ultimately to the international community. In other words, by effectively discharging its responsibilities for good governance, a state can legitimately claim protection for its national sovereignty.
>
> (Deng *et al.* 1996: 1)

According to Deng, legitimate sovereignty required a demonstration of responsibility. Troubled states faced a choice: they could work with international society to improve their citizens' living conditions or they could obstruct such efforts and forfeit their sovereignty (Deng *et al.* 1996: 28). Seeing sovereignty as responsibility removed the validity of objections to international assistance and mediation based on the principle of non-interference. But at what point could a state be judged to have forfeited its sovereignty and what body has the right to decide? Deng *et al.* were sketchy on these points but they did suggest that sovereignty as responsibility implied the existence of a 'higher authority capable of holding supposed sovereigns accountable' and that this dominant authority should place collective interests ahead of the national interests of its members (Deng *et al.* 1996: 32). Clearly, the UN Security

Council most closely resembles this description, though it falls a long way short of Deng's ideal.

The divisiveness of NATO's operation in Kosovo prompted UN Secretary-General, Kofi Annan, to enter the debate in 1999. In his annual address to the General Assembly, he insisted that 'state sovereignty, in its most basic sense, is being redefined by the forces of globalization and international cooperation'. He continued:

> the state is now widely understood to be the servant of its people, and not vice versa. At the same time, individual sovereignty — and by this I mean the human rights and fundamental freedoms of each and every individual as enshrined in our Charter — has been enhanced by a renewed consciousness of the right of every individual to control his or her own destiny.
>
> (Annan 1999b)

Together, Deng and Annan pointed towards a new way of conceiving the relationship between sovereignty and human rights that recalled the long-forgotten idea that sovereignty entailed responsibilities as well as rights.

It was at this point that the Canadian government commissioned an International Commission on Intervention and State Sovereignty (ICISS) to conduct a systematic study of the relationship between sovereignty and human rights that could point to ways of advancing the debate. The ICISS is most famous for coining the phrase 'Responsibility to Protect' as a way of bridging the divide between sovereignty and human rights. After a year of consultation and research, it delivered its report in late 2001, shortly after the 9/11 attacks in the US. Borrowing from Deng's concept of sovereignty as responsibility, though without acknowledging him explicitly, the Commission argued that states have primary responsibility for protecting their populations from genocide and mass atrocities. When states were unwilling or unable to protect their citizens from grave harm, the ICISS argued that the principle of non-interference 'yields to the responsibility to protect'.

The concept of R2P was intended as a way of escaping the logic of 'sovereignty versus human rights' by focusing not on what interveners are entitled to do ('a right of intervention') but on what was necessary to protect people in dire need and the responsibilities of various actors to provide such protection. The ICISS argued that R2P was about much more than just military intervention. In addition to a 'responsibility to react' (intervene) to massive human suffering, international society also had responsibilities to use non-violent tools to prevent such suffering ('responsibility to prevent') and rebuild polities and societies afterwards ('responsibility to rebuild'). Rather than viewing sovereignty and human rights as antagonistic, R2P sees them as mutually supportive, insists that international society has a responsibility to ensure and enable this relationship to flourish, and sets out a number of ways in which this might be achieved.

The ICISS report was widely scrutinized and highly commended. For instance, Anthony Lewis (2003: 8), former columnist for the *New York Times*, commented that the report 'captured the international state of mind'. Some critics charged that the ICISS offered a right of intervention that would be abused by powerful states, that 'sovereignty as responsibility' actually diminished sovereignty by imposing Western conceptions of human rights, and that the broad spectrum of measures increased the scope for neo-imperialism (Chandler 2004). Others complained that the commission had not gone far enough. Weiss (2004) argued that it had set the bar to legitimate intervention too high by limiting it to cases of massive human suffering and therefore ruling out intervention to restore democratic governments (as the UN had authorized in Haiti in 1994) or preventive deployments. Others pointed out that the ICISS neglected gender (Bond and Sherret 2006).

The R2P concept was therefore born out of long-standing ideas about the responsibilities incumbent on sovereigns. The phrase itself was coined by an international commission that borrowed basic concepts developed by the UN's Special Representative on internally displaced people in the early 1990s in order to break the logjam in the debate about humanitarian intervention. But whatever its merits – and faults – R2P would have remained a purely academic idea had it not been adopted by member states in 2005, albeit in a very different form from that proposed by the ICISS four years earlier.

## R2P and international politics

The ICISS report was received most favourably by liberal states including Canada, the UK and Germany which had, since the Kosovo intervention, been exploring the potential for developing criteria to guide global decision-making about humanitarian intervention. The United States rejected some of the commission's ideas, especially its proposal that judgments about intervention be guided by thresholds and criteria, which it believed was unduly constraining (Welsh 2004: 180). China was even more sceptical about the whole idea and insisted that all questions relating to the use of force should defer to the Security Council, making much of the commission's work on intervention redundant. Russia agreed with the Chinese view, arguing that the UN was already equipped to deal with humanitarian crises and suggesting that R2P risked undermining the UN Charter.

Opinion outside the Security Council was also sceptical. The Non-Aligned Movement (NAM), which represents most of the world's decolonized states rejected R2P, though the 'Group of 77' (G77) developing states was more equivocal. Offering no joint position on the concept, the G77 nevertheless suggested that R2P be revised to emphasize the principles of territorial integrity and sovereignty. To make matters worse, constructive debate about R2P was hampered by the US-led invasion of Iraq. It certainly did not help that a prominent ICISS commissioner – Michael Ignatieff (2003) – initially defended the invasion on human rights grounds before changing his mind. ICISS co-chair Gareth Evans (2004) rightly argued that the 'poorly and inconsistently' argued humanitarian justification for the war in Iraq 'almost choked at birth what many were hoping was an emerging new norm justifying intervention on the basis of the principle of "responsibility to protect"'.

In preparation for a major world summit in 2005, that was expected to focus on the achievement of the Millennium Development Goals, the UN Secretary-General, Kofi Annan, created a High-Level Panel to provide him with recommendations for reforming the UN to make it better able to meet the challenge of peace and security in the twenty-first century. The panel included Gareth Evans, the ICISS co-chair and a passionate advocate of R2P, who succeeded in persuading it to endorse the concept (High-Level Panel 2004: para. 203). Annan (2005) accepted almost all the panel's recommendations, including R2P, in his own blueprint for UN reform. In important departures from the ICISS, however, the Secretary-General closed off the idea that R2P could legitimize armed intervention not authorized by the Security Council and refrained from endorsing the proposed responsibilities to 'prevent, react, and rebuild', fundamentally changing the way in which R2P was conceptualized.

Further changes were made to R2P during the negotiations leading up to the 2005 world summit. In particular, there was no mention of responsibilities to 'prevent, react and rebuild', references to the idea of criteria guiding decisions about the use of force were removed entirely, R2P intervention was made dependent on UN Security Council authorization, the thresholds at which crises would become matters of international concern were raised to cover only governments 'manifestly' failing to protect their citizens, and caveats were added to give the Security Council the flexibility to choose not to act. On the positive side, the Summit's commitment to R2P was incredibly clear and direct, and world leaders clarified what the concept applied to (genocide, war crimes, ethnic cleansing, and crimes against humanity), improving on the conceptual fuzziness of the ICISS.

Debates about implementing R2P through the UN got off to an inauspicious start. Thanks largely to lingering concerns about its potential to legitimize interference in the domestic affairs of states, some states tried to retreat from their commitment. It took six months of intense debate for the Security Council to unanimously adopt Resolution 1674, 'reaffirming' the World Summit's provisions 'regarding the responsibility to protect'. This experience persuaded some of the Council's R2P advocates to refrain from pushing the body to make greater use of the principle for fear of creating opportunities for backsliding. It proved similarly difficult to persuade the Council to refer to R2P in a non-operative paragraph in Resolution 1706 (2006) on the situation in Darfur. A paragraph indirectly referring to R2P was subsequently deleted from a draft of Resolution 1769 (2007) on Darfur, and Resolution 1814 (2008) on Somalia pointedly referred to the protection of civilians and Resolution 1674 without mentioning R2P (Strauss 2009: 307). Resistance to implementing R2P was also evident in other UN bodies. For example, when the UN Human Rights Council's High Level Mission to Darfur reported in 2007 that the government of Sudan was failing in its responsibility to protect Darfuris, the Arab Group, Asia Group and Organization of Islamic Conference all questioned the report's legitimacy and tried to prevent deliberation on its findings.

More promising signs emerged with the election of South Korean foreign minister, Ban Ki-moon as the UN Secretary-General in October 2006. Ban was personally committed to R2P and has proven to be an effective norm entrepreneur. Campaigning under the slogan of 'promise less and deliver more', Ban argued that the UN needed to close the gap between its lofty rhetoric and its often less than lofty performance. The Secretary-General appointed Edward Luck as his special Adviser on R2P. Luck's appointment represented a turning point. The Special Adviser engaged in extensive consultation with Member States based on an appropriately sharp distinction between what states had actually agreed to in relation to R2P, and a variety of alternative formulations – including that of the ICISS (Luck 2007). Many academics continue to fail to make this extremely important distinction and it is vitally important that students are aware of it. Luck's consultations encouraged the Secretary-General to identify a 'narrow but deep' approach to implementing R2P that strictly limited it to what was agreed in 2005 but 'utilized the whole prevention and protection tool kit' available to the United Nations system, regional arrangements, states, and civil society groups. Analysing in detail what states had actually agreed in 2005, the Secretary-General also identified the three pillars of R2P described earlier (Ban 2008).

In 2009, the Secretary-General released an important report, entitled *Implementing the Responsibility to Protect* (Ban 2009). It clarified the nature of the 2005 agreement and outlined a wide range of measures that individual states, regional organizations and the UN system might consider in order to implement R2P's three pillars. Some of the recommendations are summarized in Table 32.1.

The Secretary-General argued that R2P 'is an ally of sovereignty, not an adversary', that grows from the principle of sovereignty as responsibility rather than through the doctrine of humanitarian intervention (Ban 2009: para. 10(a)). As such, R2P focuses on helping states to succeed (pillar two), not just on reacting when they fail (some aspects of pillar three). Furthermore, he found that until member states decide otherwise, the R2P applies only to genocide, war crimes, ethnic cleansing and crimes against humanity and to their prevention. Expanding the principle to include natural disasters or climate change would undermine consensus and damage the principle's operational utility.

The report was subsequently debated in the General Assembly, revealing a broad consensus in support of his approach. Ninety-four speakers, representing some 180 governments (including the Non-Aligned Movement) from every region participated in the debate. Of those, only four (Cuba, Venezuela, Sudan and Nicaragua) called for a renegotiation of the 2005 agreement. The General Assembly largely agreed with the Secretary-General's

*Table 32.1* Implementing the responsibility to protect: The Secretary-General's recommendations (excerpts)

| *Pillar I:* <br> *The state's R2P* | *Pillar II:* <br> *International assistance* <br> *to the state* | *Pillar III:* <br> *Timely and decisive* <br> *response* |
|---|---|---|
| • The UN Human Rights Council could encourage states to meet their R2P obligations. | • Those inciting or planning to commit the four crimes need to be made aware that they will be held to account. | • The Security Council might use targeted sanctions on travel, financial transfers, and luxury goods, and arms embargoes. Capacity and will should be dedicated to properly implement these regimes. |
| • States should become parties to the relevant instruments of human rights law, international humanitarian law and refugee law, as well as to the Rome Statute of the International Criminal Court (ICC). | • Incentives should be offered to encourage parties towards reconciliation. | • The permanent members of the Security Council should refrain from using their veto in situations of manifest failure and should act in good faith to reach a consensus on exercising the Council's responsibility. |
| • States should assist the ICC and other international tribunals. | • Security sector reform aimed at building and sustaining legitimate and effective security forces. | • The UN should strengthen its capacity for the rapid deployment of military personnel. |
| • R2P principles should be localized into each culture and society. | • Targeted economic development assistance would assist . . . by reducing inequalities, improving education, giving the poor a stronger voice, and increasing political participation. | • The UN should strengthen its partnerships with regional organizations to facilitate rapid cooperation. |
| • States should ensure that they have mechanisms in place to deal with bigotry, intolerance, racism and exclusion. | • International assistance should help states and societies to build the specific capacities they need prevent genocide and mass atrocities. | |
| | • The UN and regional and subregional organizations could build rapidly deployable civilian and police capacities to help countries under stress. | |
| | • Where relevant crimes are committed by non-state actors, international military assistance to the state may be the most effective way of helping it to fulfil its R2P. | |

*Source*: Ban 2009

interpretation of the principle's fundamental elements. In particular, most governments welcomed the Secretary-General's report, noted that the 2005 World Summit represented the international consensus on R2P and agreed that there was no need to renegotiate that text. The challenge, the General Assembly agreed, was to implement R2P, *not* renegotiate it. The overwhelming majority also indicated their support for the Secretary-General's identification of the three pillars of the R2P and the 'narrow but deep' approach to implementing the principle (Bellamy 2011: 42–49). The Assembly passed a unanimous resolution, acknowledging the report, noting that the Assembly had engaged in a productive debate, and deciding to continue consideration of the matter (UN doc. A/RES/63/308, 7 October 2009).

Although the debate helped identify a broader consensus than thought possible in the immediate aftermath of 2005, it also exposed a number of concerns:

1 Modalities and need for an early warning capacity. Several member states worried that information-gathering and assessment by the UN violates sovereignty.

2 Respective roles of the Security Council and General Assembly and reform of the Security Council. Several of R2P's most prominent critics maintained that Security Council reform should be a prerequisite to implementation of R2P.

3 The potential for R2P to legitimize coercive interference and the lack of clarity about the triggers for armed intervention.

4 The potential for R2P to draw resources away from other UN programmes without adding additional value to the organization's work.

(Bellamy 2011: 45–49)

These are clearly issues that require careful thought and deliberation. These concerns notwithstanding, it is fair to conclude that the Secretary-General succeeded in stemming the tide of the post-2005 revolt against R2P, in presenting an account of R2P that could command a high degree of consensus, and articulating a manifesto for implementing the principle. The Security Council reaffirmed its commitment to R2P once again in Resolution 1894 (2009).

In 2010, the Secretary-General proposed the establishment of a Joint Office for the Prevention of Genocide and R2P which would have two new functions. First, it would provide early warning and assessment of situations likely to give rise to one of the four R2P crimes. Second, in the event that the crimes were thought likely or were in progress, the Joint Office would provide a convening mechanism that would bring together key UN departments and agencies to develop integrated policy advice and strategic planning.

There is also evidence that states are beginning to think about how they might integrate R2P into national policy. In 2010, the Global Centre for R2P spearheaded an initiative to encourage governments to appoint national focal points for mass atrocity prevention and response. Among other things, national focal points could:

- Provide early analysis of emerging situations;
- Provide advice directly to the executive about matters relating to the prevention of genocide and mass atrocities;
- Coordinate national responses to mass atrocities – thereby providing an atrocity lens to national decision-making;
- Spearhead cooperation with the Joint Office for the Prevention of Genocide and R2P and other relevant agencies and offices;
- Help foster international consensus on the results of early analysis;
- Make it possible for governments to respond to mass atrocities in a timely and decisive fashion;
- Collaborate with other focal points.

(Global Center 2010)

Responding to findings by the Genocide Prevention Task Force (2008), the Obama administration took the lead in this area by appointing David Pressman as Director for War Crimes Atrocities and Civilian Protection within the Office of the National Security Adviser. (In mid-2011, following Presidential Study Directive 10, Obama's administration also established a new Atrocities Prevention Board comprising inter-agency officials.) Several other countries followed suit, leading to the first meeting of national focal points in 2011. Although a modest first step, the appointment of national focal points creates the potential that an atrocity prevention lens will inform national level decision-making. Over time, this could strengthen national, regional and global decision-making.

Clearly, significant progress has been made in deepening the consensus reached in 2005 and translating that agreement into new institutional capacity. But it is one thing to agree on a principle and abstract modalities for implementation. It is another thing entirely to agree on how to respond in actual crises. The following section considers two recent and very different crises, where R2P was in evidence.

## R2P in action

### Kenya

The effective use of diplomacy in response to the ethnic violence that erupted in the aftermath of the disputed 30 December 2007 election in Kenya was widely trumpeted as an excellent early example of R2P in practice (e.g. Evans 2009: 106). While up to 1,500 people were killed and 300,000 displaced, a coordinated diplomatic effort by a troika of eminent persons, mandated by the African Union, spearheaded by Kofi Annan and supported by the UN

Secretary-General, persuaded the country's president, Mwai Kibaki, and main opponent, Raila Odinga, to conclude a power-sharing agreement and rein in the violent mobs. This prevented what many feared could have been the beginning of a much worse campaign of mass atrocities. Annan later observed that he:

> saw the crisis in the R2P prism with a Kenyan government unable to contain the situation or protect its people. I knew that if the international community did not intervene, things would go hopelessly wrong. The problem is when we say 'intervention,' people think military, when in fact that's a last resort. Kenya is a successful example of R2P at work.
>
> (cited in Cohen 2008)

Ban Ki-moon was also quick to characterize the situation as relevant to R2P and to remind Kenya's leaders of their responsibilities. On 2 January 2008, the Office of the Secretary-General issued a statement reminding 'the Government, as well as the political and religious leaders of Kenya of their legal and moral responsibility to protect the lives of innocent people, regardless of their racial, religious or ethnic origin' and urging them to do everything in their capacity to prevent further bloodshed. The Secretary-General's Special Adviser for the Prevention of Genocide, Francis Deng, also called upon Kenya's leadership to exercise their responsibility to protect, reminding them that if they failed to do so they would be held to account by the international community. These efforts were given strong diplomatic support by the UN Security Council, which issued a Presidential Statement reminding the leaders of their 'responsibility to engage fully in finding a sustainable political solution and taking action to immediately end violence (S/PRST/2008/4, 6 February 2008).

This concerted diplomatic effort prompted the two leaders to stand down and saved Kenya from a much worse fate. Reflecting on this case, Edward Luck told reporters:

> So the only time the UN has actually applied this [the R2P], was in the case of Kenya, early in 2008 after the disputed elections. When there's seven or eight hundred people ... killed, it was not clear there was full-scale ethnic cleansing, but it could well become that or even something greater, and the UN decided to apply R2P criteria and to really make it the focus of the efforts there.
>
> (Public Radio International 2009,
> see also International Crisis Group 2008)

But while those involved contend that Kenya provides an illustration of what R2P can deliver in terms of preventive action, others, such as Pauline Baker (Fund for Peace) argue that R2P itself played a marginal role. Another note of caution was sounded by AU Commissioner Jean Ping, who questioned whether it was appropriate to apply R2P in this case, suggesting that it raised serious questions as to the threshold of violence that constituted an R2P situation and potential selectivity when the response to Kenya is compared with the lack of response to the much more serious situation in Somalia.

## Libya

Although Kenya was an important early case of R2P in action, the 2011 UN-authorized NATO-led intervention in Libya was undoubtedly the highest profile and most significant use of the principle to date. Its significance lay in two areas. First, it was the first time that the UN's new institutional capacity relating to R2P was used to obvious effect. The March 2011 crisis in Libya was unexpected and escalated rapidly. Indeed, none of the world's existing genocide/atrocity risk assessment frameworks identified Libya as a risk, despite some of those lists extending to 68 countries. To its credit, the new UN Joint Office for Genocide Prevention and R2P warned of the risk of crimes against humanity in Libya *before* most non-governmental agencies did so, but even this was very late in the day. The second reason why Libya was so significant lies in the Security Council's adoption of Resolution 1973 (17 March 2011). Resolution 1973 was the first time the Council has authorized the use of force for human protection purposes against the wishes of a functioning state. However, the case also reveals that while it is possible to build international consensus on the use of force for humanitarian intervention, it is very difficult to do so and consensus is contingent on a wide range of political factors.

The roots of Libya's crisis lay in the political upheavals associated with the 'Arab Spring' protests that spread from Tunisia to Egypt and beyond. After some initial protests in mid-January, demonstrations quickly turned violent. This was partly because of the regime's crackdown and partly because defections from the government and army facilitated the establishment of an armed opposition group under the Interim National Transitional Council. Initially, the rebels enjoyed rapid successes, establishing a firm hold over the cities of Benghazi and Tobruk and declaring they had taken control of most of the country's other major cities. In late February and early March, however, Qaddafi's forces retook much of the country and by mid-March threatened to crush the rebellion's eastern epicentre in Benghazi. With direct echoes of the 1994 Rwandan genocide, Qaddafi told the world that 'officers have been deployed in all tribes and regions so that they can purify all decisions from these cockroaches' and 'any Libyan who takes arms against Libya will be executed' (ABC (Australia) 2011).

Senior UN officials framed the problem as one of human protection, warning of the imminent threat to civilians in Libya. On 22 February, the UN Secretary-General's Special Advisers on the prevention of genocide and

R2P said the regime's behaviour could amount to crimes against humanity and that it must comply with its 2005 commitment to R2P. The Secretary-General reiterated this point the following day and thus framed the crisis as a human protection problem and reminded both the Libyan authorities (to no effect) and the Security Council (to good effect) of their responsibilities. Activism by the UN secretariat and the relatively tough stance taken by regional organizations thus set the context for the Security Council's discussions of the crisis. A few days later, the Council unanimously passed Resolution 1970. Among other things, this condemned 'the widespread and systematic attacks' against civilians that 'may amount to crimes against humanity' and underlined the Libyan government's responsibility to protect its population. Acting under Chapter VII of the UN Charter, the Council demanded an immediate end to the violence and referred the situation to the Prosecutor of the International Criminal Court.

It was the 12 March declaration by the League of Arab States that proved decisive in persuading the Security Council to authorize the use of force. This called on the UN Security Council 'to impose immediately a no-fly zone on Libyan military aviation, and to establish safe areas in places exposed to shelling'. There are a number of reasons why the League adopted this decision, including:

- The meeting was driven by the pro-US Gulf Cooperation Council.
- The meeting was held in Cairo in the immediate aftermath of the overthrow of Hosni Mubarak and was chaired by the new Egyptian government.
- Qaddafi was widely distrusted across the African and Middle East and he had personally insulted key Arab personalities.
- Al Jazeera's reporting of Libyan abuses and mobilisation of opposition groups across North Africa and the Middle East established demands for action on Libya within the Arab world itself.
- Some regional governments might have calculated that turning the international spotlight onto Libya would divert attention from their own troubles.
- Arab governments might have worried about being portrayed as obstacles to human rights in a way that might have encouraged internal opposition (see Bellamy and Williams 2011).

The LAS statement persuaded the US, which had been cautious about the prospect of military action in Libya – because of concerns about military overstretch, potential casualties, budgetary implications, the potential for mission creep, absence of a clear exit strategy, and concerns about alienating states in the Middle East and elsewhere in the Muslim world – to support stronger action. Along with other factors – such as the brutal clarity of the threat, shortage of time, and lack of viable alternatives – the Arab statement also helped persuade several states that have traditionally opposed humanitarian intervention, such as China, Russia and India, to permit the Security Council to authorise intervention. Resolution 1973 passed with ten votes in favour and five abstentions (Brazil, China, Germany, India, and Russia). The Council authorized the use of 'all necessary measures . . . to protect civilians and civilian populated areas under threat of attack . . . while excluding a foreign occupation force of any form on any part of Libyan territory'.

Almost as soon as the resolution was passed differences emerged as to how it should be interpreted. NATO and several key allies, including Qatar and Jordan, interpreted the mandate as providing the basis for a wide range of military activities including the suppression of Libya's air defences, air force and other aviation capacities, as well as the use of force against Libya's fielded forces, its capacity to sustain fielded forces, and its command and control capacities on the grounds that Libya's armed forces constituted a threat to civilians. Others disagreed. Russia complained that NATO bombing exceeded the limited mandate given to it by the Council, a view shared by China. Although R2P did not begin with Libya, much depends on how the aftermath is handled. In particular, Bellamy and Williams (2011) noted four principal challenges emanating from this case:

1 Resolving contestation about how to interpret mandates.

2 The moral questions relating to the infliction of civilian casualties by armed forces mandated to protect civilians.

3 The relationship between human protection and regime change (widely seen as illegitimate by international society) in situations where the regime constitutes the principal threat to civilians.

4 Questions about the military means used to protect civilians and especially about the limits of air power, which provides only indirect protection and may come at the cost of some unintended additional harm to civilians.

## Conclusion

R2P is an attempt to reconfigure the relationship between sovereignty and fundamental human rights in a way that strengthens the protection of vulnerable populations while protecting cherished international rules about non-intervention. Traditionally it was assumed that the demands of international order required strict adherence to the principles of sovereignty and non-interference and that in cases where the security of states and individuals collided, the former should be privileged. After the Cold War, many governments and scholars argued that in grave circumstances sovereignty should be suspended and intervention permitted. This produced a complex debate about who had a right to authorize such interventions and in what circumstances.

This debate pitted sovereignty against human rights. In doing so, however, it played down both the original meaning of sovereignty and two centuries of republican thinking. From the republican perspective, sovereignty resides with the people and governments may only claim sovereign rights if they fulfill certain basic responsibilities to their people. It is this approach to sovereignty and human rights that underpins the R2P. If sovereignty is understood as interdependent with human rights, then the role of international society becomes one of enabling and supporting sovereigns in the discharge of their responsibilities to their citizens. The R2P argues that this is not just a matter of charity but a matter of responsibility, because the very foundations of sovereignty and international society are individual human rights. As a result, international society has a responsibility to ensure that sovereigns fulfill their duties to their citizens by preventing and reacting to cases of genocide, mass killing and ethnic cleansing and helping to transform societies afterwards. This responsibility was acknowledged at the 2005 World Summit and the principle has been endorsed many times since and has begun to shape both institutional design and political practice. But with practice come new challenges and difficult dilemmas, both political and operational, and much work remains to be done.

## Further reading

Alex J. Bellamy, *Responsibility to Protect: The Global Effort to End Mass Atrocities* (Polity, 2010). Examines the origins of R2P and early attempts to implement it.

Alex J. Bellamy, *Global Politics and the Responsibility to Protect: From Words to Deeds* (Routledge, 2011). Examines issues relating to implementation of R2P, focusing on the post-2005 era.

Gareth Evans, *The Responsibility to Protect: Ending Mass Atrocity Crimes Once and for All* (Brookings Institution Press, 2009). A powerful argument for R2P by one of its principal advocates.

International Commission on Intervention and State Sovereignty, *The Responsibility to Protect* (Ottawa: ICISS, 2001). The ICISS report setting out the R2P in detail.

Anne Orford, *International Authority and the Responsibility to Protect* (Cambridge University Press, 2011). An important treatise on R2P and political theory.

Nicholas J. Wheeler, *Saving Strangers: Humanitarian Intervention in International Society* (Oxford University Press, 2000). Still the best book on the norm of humanitarian intervention prior to 2000.

Also see the journal, *Global Responsibility to Protect* which is dedicated to this topic.

## CONTENTS

# Transnational Organized Crime

Phil Williams

## Abstract

In this chapter, students will learn about how transnational organized crime has emerged during the last two decades as one of a series of threats posed to national and international security by violent non-state actors. The chapter outlines what is meant by transnational organized crime then examines the rise of the phenomenon, suggesting that its emergence is inextricably linked to globalization and the weakness of states in many parts of the world. The major transnational criminal organizations are subsequently examined, with attention given to their diversity, organizational structures, and portfolios of activities. Illicit markets are also discussed. The chapter ends with a discussion of efforts to combat transnational organized crime, with particular emphasis on the strategy developed by the United States.

## Introduction

Organized crime is almost certainly one of the world's oldest professions. As Mark Galeotti has pointed out, 'in ancient Greece, olive growers whose groves had been cultivated over generations were prey to protection racketeers. Ancient Rome supported a thriving and complex underworld, from smugglers and counterfeiters to pirates and confidence tricksters' (Galeotti no date). Indeed, roaming bandits were prevalent in medieval Europe, while maritime piracy – which is currently a major problem in the Gulf of Aden and off the coast of Somalia – had earlier incarnations in the Mediterranean, South China Sea, and the Caribbean. It was in the late nineteenth and early twentieth centuries that organized crime emerged more obviously in various parts of the world: in Sicily and then in other parts of Italy; in China where secret societies with political agendas evolved into the Triads; in the United States (where organized crime has gone through a series of ethnic successions including Irish, Italian, Jewish, African-American, Caribbean, Russian, and now Mexican criminal organizations); and in Japan where the Yakuza became politically entrenched. Even so, organized crime was seen as a domestic law and order problem and not something that challenged the fabric of society.

After the end of the Cold War, transnational organized crime emerged as a new security threat. Initially, some critics contended that at most it was a 'boutique' threat. Ironically those dismissing transnational organized crime included 'hawks' who saw security threats exclusively in military terms and 'doves', who dismissed it as an artificial threat, inflated by professional Cassandras looking for a successor to the Soviet 'Evil Empire'. The hawkish assessment was confounded by experience in Iraq and Afghanistan: criminal enterprises engaged in kidnapping and extortion contributed significantly to the prevailing insecurity, while many insurgent groups used oil smuggling or heroin production to fund the struggle (Williams 2009, Peters 2011). In both instances, organized crime undermined efforts to provide sound governance. Similarly, in peacekeeping and post-war contingencies, whether the Balkans or East Timor, organized crime has often acted as a spoiler (Cockayne and Lupel 2011).

The sceptics, in contrast, have only to look at the growth of drug trafficking-related homicides in Mexico during the Fox and Calderon Administrations to recognize how wrong they were. In 2010, Mexico had twice as many drug-related killings as the number of people (civilians and military) killed in Iraq and Afghanistan combined. Even allowing for the population differences, it is clear that the number of violent deaths per hundred thousand in Mexico is on a par with these two war zones. Although Mexico could be dismissed as an aberration, it seems more plausible to suggest that it is simply the most serious example of a security challenge that has become both more urgent and more pervasive than ever before.

The emergence of organized crime as a growing threat to security was acknowledged by the United Nations in 1994 when it hosted the World Ministerial Conference on transnational organized crime in Naples. In 1995, the Clinton Administration also acknowledged the challenge, an acknowledgement enshrined in Presidential Decision Directive 42 and in Clinton's speech to the UN warning about transnational organized crime and calling for enhanced international cooperation to meet the threat. Although the Palermo Convention on Transnational Organized Crime was signed in December 2000, the attacks on New York and Washington DC on 11 September 2001 moved the focus from organized crime to terrorism. The experiences in Iraq, Afghanistan, and Mexico, however, have suggested that organized crime needs to be at the forefront of attention as it poses threats to security at various levels – the individual, the national, the regional and the global.

## Organized crime as a security threat

Threats at the individual level or to 'citizen' or 'public' security are most obvious in Latin America where many countries have higher homicide rates than Mexico. Levels of criminal violence are also high in parts of Africa. Nor is violence the only issue: human trafficking has become a problem of global proportions with women and children trafficked for commercial sex and men trafficked for forced labour (Cameron and Newman 2008). The argument that organized crime is simply about the provision of illicit goods and services desired by many people ignores the many victims of organized crime.

Threats to the state are particularly serious in Central America. In Guatemala the state is weak, a culture of impunity is pervasive, and Mexican drug trafficking organizations, especially the Zetas Organization and the Sinaloa Federation, have expanded their presence and their conflict. In El Salvador and Honduras, the gang problem is enormous. The Latin American organized crime threat has also expanded to West Africa, which has become a hub for cocaine transshipment to Europe. Groups from Mexico, Colombia, and Venezuela have established a presence in Guinea-Bissau and elsewhere, and have suborned and subverted already fragile governance structures through a mix of corruption and intimidation. Elsewhere in Africa and in regions such as Central Asia, criminal organizations use corruption to facilitate trafficking and to ensure a high level of impunity. Corruption is designed to neutralize or weaken the power of the state (especially law enforcement agencies), to undercut the judiciary, and to gain valuable intelligence. When successful, it provides safe havens from which transnational criminal organizations can operate. In some instances, organized crime develops a symbiotic relationship with state structures, or what Roy Godson (2003) termed a political–criminal nexus.

Transnational organized crime can also be understood as a threat to regional stability and to global norms. Arms traffickers, for example, undermine efforts at conflict resolution and peacemaking, while trafficking in endangered species is seriously undermining efforts to maintain biodiversity. The oil industry in countries as diverse as Russia, Nigeria, Mexico and Iraq has been infiltrated by criminal organizations, while threats from nuclear and radiological material trafficking – although less salient than in the 1990s – have not gone away. Recent increases in food prices and growing concerns over water scarcity suggest that in the not-too-distant future, transnational criminal organizations will have even more lucrative black markets in which to operate.

Yet, because this threat differs from traditional geopolitical threats, it has caught states remarkably unprepared for the challenges they face. This is not surprising: states historically have been organized and equipped to deal with military threats from one another. Challenges that arise from 'sovereignty-free' actors cannot easily be dealt with through the normal instruments of state power and influence (Rosenau 1990). Transnational criminal organizations are a particularly malevolent type of sovereignty-free actor as they undermine national sovereignty, the integrity of financial and commercial institutions, the propriety of public institutions, and the fabric of societies. They have a damaging impact on the quality of life in many states, especially developing states and those undergoing political transition. Moreover, transnational organized crime has already displayed a capacity to erode international stability by undermining efforts to establish and maintain norms, conventions and regimes in the international system.

While transnational organized crime poses many challenges, has real victims, and causes great social and economic harm (often driving out legitimate entrepreneurship) it is not an unmitigated evil. Organized crime, like youth gangs, flourishes amongst populations that are impoverished, alienated and marginalized. Consequently, some observers have highlighted the 'social contradictions' of organized crime, noting that it can bring benefits as well as inflict harm on economies and societies (Standing 2003). Organized crime in the United States has even been described as a 'queer ladder of social mobility' (Bell 1960: 129). In many other countries it is the only ladder of social mobility and economic advancement. Although many observers are reluctant to admit it, organized crime benefits a lot of people. It can act as a safety net and a safety valve, bring employment to marginalized and alienated populations and even have multiplier benefits in the economy. For states unable to attract foreign direct investment, 'dirty money' (i.e. criminal proceeds) is attractive – and certainly better than no money. Even those who demand protection money sometimes actually do provide a degree of protection to the businesses paying them, in some cases providing the only viable means of dispute settlement (Volkov 2002). As a result, in many countries organized crime is emerging as an alternate form of governance, offering protection, paternalism, and service provision to populations that are socially, politically, and economically excluded. None of this is to suggest that the benefits of organized crime outweigh the costs; it is merely to argue that the balance sheet is not nearly as one-sided as is often claimed.

## What is transnational organized crime?

Definitional issues in social science are always problematic and organized crime is no exception. Some observers see organized crime in terms of criminal organizations or criminal enterprises; others see organized crime as a set of activities rather than entities. In a further twist, some definitions offer simply a list of characteristics of organized crime while others try to capture the essence of the phenomenon. Traditional definitions emphasized the hierarchical structure of criminal organizations, although more recently the emphasis has been on criminal networks as a set of horizontal relationships rather than pyramids of command and control. The term 'organized crime' is also incorrectly used as a synonym for 'mafia'. Many observers, however, are increasingly making a distinction between mafias, which are in the business of private protection and extortion, and the broader phenomenon of organized crime that includes the provision of illicit goods and services, and smuggling or trafficking (Finkenauer 2007). Even accepting this, 'there are at least two competing definitions [of transnational organized crime] one that focuses on particular groups of people, and one that focuses on particular types of crime. Both definitions have some validity, and neither is sufficient to completely describe the global reality' (UNODC 2010: 19). Indeed, organized crime can be understood in terms of entities (criminal organizations or criminal enterprises) as well as in terms of the illicit activities that are characteristically used by these organizations but that can also be appropriated by other kinds of actor. Transnational criminal organizations are Clausewitzian in that crime is simply a continuation of business by other means. They systematically adopt criminal activities in pursuit of profit as their ultimate objective and use violence and corruption to assist in this pursuit. It is the distinctive mix of ends and means that distinguishes criminal enterprises from licit businesses. These criminal enterprises are usually pragmatic not ideological, attempt to influence politics only to protect their illegal activities, and generally, use violence in a selective and discriminate way.

Yet organized crime can also be seen as a methodology or a set of activities used by different entities – ethnic factions, organizations engaged in terrorism, insurgent groups, and even some governments – as a way of obtaining funds. For these groups, the ultimate ends are political, but criminal activities are instrumental in funding the political agendas. Some observers argue that the primary focus should be on the criminal markets not criminal organizations. In fact, both perspectives are valuable: it is necessary to understand the dynamics of illicit markets as well as the criminal organizations that operate within them.

Transnational organized crime refers to criminal organizations or activities that cross national borders and, therefore, involve the territories and laws of at least two states. The borders can be crossed by the perpetrators of criminal activities, by the products or commodities they are smuggling, by the proceeds of criminal activity which are typically laundered across multiple jurisdictions, and increasingly by digital signals, whether related to financial fraud and identity theft, to child pornography, or to coercion and intimidation through distributed denial of service attacks using bot-nets. The commodities crossing borders are stolen, counterfeit, regulated, or prohibited.

## Globalization, governance and the rise of organized crime

Globalization has a dark underside. By the end of the twentieth century, global linkages and communication webs had become both much denser – not least because technology had reduced the transaction costs – and much more rapid.

Passenger ships had largely been superseded by commercial airlines, the telephone had become both ubiquitous and mobile, and the postal service had given way across much of the world to electronic mail. Some observers have even seen globalization as the compression of time and space. As David Held has pointed out, globalization also involves flows – of people, money, commodities, information, messages, digital signals, and services – around the world. The 'space of flows' is now a global space (Held 2000). This is as true of trade – where the inter-modal container has had a profound impact in facilitating the movement of goods and commodities – as it is of the Internet which facilitates the almost instantaneous flow of information and messages. In one sense, of course, there is nothing new about flows, but they have increased in density and speed while the associated transaction costs have shrunk drastically.

Globalization has contributed to the rise of organized crime in several ways. First, it has been as empowering for organized crime as for legitimate business. Even a cursory global review reveals the extent to which criminal organizations have exploited the new opportunities presented by globalization. Russian organized crime, for example, now has a major presence in Israel, the United States, Spain, Mexico, the Caribbean, Thailand, and Macau, while the proceeds of Russian criminal activity have flowed through offshore financial centres in Cyprus, several Caribbean jurisdictions, and South Pacific islands such as Vanuatu, Nauru, and Niue. During the 1990s, Russian and Ukrainian arms dealers sold surplus weapons to competing factions in African civil wars and they continue to exploit any new opportunities. Albanian criminal organizations now control much of the vice trade in London and have become a major presence in Italy, sometimes cooperating and sometimes competing with Italian Mafia organizations. Chinese organized crime has clashed with the Yakuza in Tokyo, while the Hells Angels have fought with rival outlaw motorcycle gangs not only in the United States and Canada, but also as far afield as Scandinavia. Criminal organizations from Pakistan and the Balkans have made their presence felt in Norway, which, historically, has had very little experience of organized crime. Spain has become host to Russian, Colombian, Chinese and Moroccan criminal groups. Nigerian criminals have changed the nature of the drug market in South Africa and have become pervasive in countries as diverse as China, Thailand, Paraguay, Holland and Germany. As noted above, drug trafficking organizations from Colombia, Mexico and Venezuela have moved into West Africa, from where cocaine is moved to Europe.

In an odd way, organized crime can help to mitigate this pain. In zones of social and economic exclusion informal and illegal markets provide critical safety nets while organized crime not only offers one of the few forms of employment, but also provides a degree of governance and even provision of public goods. In the absence of opportunities in the legal economy people simply migrate to the illegal. As James Mittelman (2000: 210) notes, 'transnational organized crime groups operate below as well as beside the state by offering incentives to the marginalized segments of the population trying to cope with the adjustment costs of globalization'.

There are at least three ways in which states contribute to the rise of transnational organized crime. First, states that are weak, autocratic, or authoritarian provide fertile breeding grounds. Weak states are characterized by low levels of state legitimacy, weak border controls, poorly articulated and/or ineffective norms and rules, the subordination of the collective interest to individual interests, lack of provision for the citizenry, absence of legal regulation and protection for business, weak social control mechanisms, and the inability to carry out typical and traditional state functions with efficiency or effectiveness. Organized crime develops in response to a combination of opportunities on the one side and pressures and incentives on the other. Weak states feed all aspects of this equation, offering multiple opportunities for – and few constraints on – organized criminal activity. Ironically, organized crime can also develop in autocratic or authoritarian states typically characterized by one-party rule, little oversight of the ruling elite, an absence of checks and balances, weak civil society, and the prevalence of patron-client relations. Such states (for example, North Korea, and Serbia under Milosevic) encourage the development of organized crime, exploiting it for their own purposes. In effect, organized crime is co-opted and controlled by the state. The difficulty for many strong states, however, is that they cannot stay strong in perpetuity. When such states become weak – for whatever reason – organized crime is no longer constrained and often experiences a significant expansion. The rise of Russian organized crime after the collapse of the Soviet Union provides a dramatic example.

Second, the state is important to organized crime not for what it fails to do but for what it does. States enact laws, outlaw or regulate certain products, impose taxation and tariffs, set quotas etc., thereby providing opportunities for organized crime. The continued authority and power of the state – to determine what commodities are legal and what are illegal (prohibited or regulated), what activities are permissible and what are outlawed, what products and activities are taxed and how much they are taxed, what can be imported or exported freely – provides incentives for organized crime to circumvent laws and regulations. Peter Andreas has captured the complex dialectic between the state and organized crime, aptly describing 'the state–smuggler relationship' as 'a paradoxical one, defined by irony and contradiction' and one in which 'the smuggler is pursued by the state but at the same time is kept in business by the state' (2000: 22).

Third, states contribute to transnational organized crime and smuggling simply because of the differences among them. These differences – characterized by Nikos Passas as 'criminogenic asymmetries' – can be legal, administrative, economic, or financial in character (Passas 1998). Differential laws and regulations offer opportunities for organized crime. States that have high levels of bank secrecy, for example, are a natural attraction for money launderers seeking to hide criminal proceeds. States with high levels of wealth and a large customer base for illicit products attract transnational criminal organizations seeking lucrative markets. Ironically, even if such states have strong border control and effective law enforcement systems, organized crime will still seek access to their markets, accepting the higher risk because of the higher profits that can be generated. This explains, for example, why many organized crime groups traffic prohibited or regulated products into countries such as the United States, Canada, Japan, as well as the member countries of the European Union. At the same time, transnational criminal organizations prefer to have a home base where the state is weak and the risks are manageable. Operating from safe havens or sanctuaries of this kind, these organizations exploit the 'criminogenic asymmetries' by engaging in jurisdictional arbitrage, seeking out states that have something they can exploit, whether large markets for illicit products, bank secrecy laws, territorial access to smuggling targets (these states become transshipment states), or simply weak laws. It is no accident, for example, that alleged Russian organized crime figures have sued journalists for libel in Britain where the libel laws favour plaintiffs rather than defendants. Nor is it coincidental that criminal organizations (along with terrorist support networks) have congregated in the Tri Border Area of South America where Brazil, Argentina, and Paraguay come together; where laws and rules are weak or absent and borders are easy to cross and re-cross.

## Transnational criminal organizations

Transnational criminal organizations in the first two decades of the twenty-first century are diverse in terms of their location and reach, organizational structures, portfolio of activities, bonding mechanisms, degree of power and influence, their use of corruption and violence, and the balance between cooperation and conflict in their relationships with one another. Some are highly secretive in nature and emanate from cultures and sub-cultures that emphasize familial and kinship ties rather than obligations to the state, patron–client relationships, and loyalty to the organization. In some cases, criminal organizations are centred on family; others are based on ethnic networks; while yet others are more cosmopolitan. Some operate through top–down hierarchical structures, while others can best be understood as horizontal networks. Some criminal organizations have clearly defined structures and membership while others are much more amorphous. In a major study of organized crime in the Netherlands in the 1990s, for example, it was discovered that criminal organizations were little more than loosely knit small groups of a few people and characterized by fluid membership; with little trust and lots of defections (Fijnaut et al. 1998). At the opposite end of the spectrum are family-based organizations that are tightly knit, resistant to outsiders, and in some cases dominated by a patriarch. This diversity makes the study of organized crime both compelling and difficult. Although specialists in organized crime have argued about criminal structures for many years, there is no single, all-embracing model that fits all circumstances.

Just as organizational structures vary, so do portfolios of criminal activities, with some groups specializing and others involved in a variety of different crimes. The portfolio is more likely to be narrow in the case of Latin American criminal organizations where the business is drug trafficking and most other criminal initiatives are secondary to the drugs industry or designed to protect it. In Mexico, however, as the government has clamped down on drug trafficking, some organizations have diversified. The Zetas Organization, for example, has infiltrated Pemex (the national oil company), engaged in large-scale extortion, and even imposed taxes on illegal immigrants and counterfeit DVD vendors. Many Russian and Chinese criminal organizations or networks have long had broad portfolios of activities, incorporating many types of trafficking activities on the one side, and crimes such as extortion, theft, counterfeiting, kidnapping, and bank robbery on the other. In some countries, criminal activity also includes cybercrime, which can range from novel ways of committing old crimes such as cyber-extortion to new crimes such as 'phishing' or online identity theft, which, potentially, have very large victim pools. Most criminal organizations that are successful also have to engage in money laundering, which is designed to make the proceeds of crime appear to be legitimate. In some cases this requires simply a front company; in others the money is moved through various offshore accounts and parked in bank secrecy havens that are resistant to law enforcement probing.

The other area where criminal organizations differ is in terms of conflict and cooperation. Transnational criminal organizations operate in a competitive environment where they cannot use the legal system for redress, where the potential for violence is ever-present, and where competition either to establish monopolies (especially of force in protection rackets) or market share is endemic. In spite of the prevalence of conflict, however, criminal organizations often work with one another. Although these are often rather fragile relationships with a potential to break down, they can also be critical to the effective functioning of the organizations – providing a means of entry to new markets or new and lucrative revenue streams. In one case of women trafficking in Europe, Russian, Ukrainian, Serb, Albanian, and Italian groups worked together as part of a network that was uncovered by a law enforcement initiative known as Operation Girasole. These patterns of cooperation and conflict are highly dynamic as evident in the Mexican case.

Mexican drug trafficking organizations have always exhibited a degree of competitiveness that quickly spills over into violence. In the last decade or so, however, the violence has expanded and intensified with 15,273 drug-related killings in 2010. Part of the reason is that Mexican drug trafficking organizations have become dominant in the trafficking of cocaine and have replaced the Colombians as the major wholesalers in the United States. This has made the stakes much higher and the competition more intense and more violent. The nature of the drug trafficking organizations has also changed. The Sinaloa Federation, which is socially and economically embedded in the Sierra Madre Mountains, continues to exclusively focus on its superior position in the drug trafficking business. It is also highly expansionist and has challenged other organizations in Tijuana, Nuevo Laredo, and most recently Juarez; cities that are strategically located on the Mexico–US border. Sinaloa's major rival is the Zetas Organization, which has evolved out of a group of former Mexican army and airborne Special Forces who were hired by the former leader of the Gulf trafficking organization in the late 1990s and subsequently became the enforcement arm of the organization. The Zetas gradually became independent of the Gulf organization and in 2010 violence broke out between the two groups. Ironically, the Gulf organization, which had long been fending off the encroachment of the Sinaloa Federation, allied with its former enemy to fight its former employees. The Zetas Organization – because of its military training, proficiency in the use of weapons, and tactical skills – has given the competition among the drug trafficking organizations in Mexico a military quality that helps to explain the astounding rise of drug-related killings.

Another important organization is the Knights Templar, a group that evolved out of La Familia Michoacán, which combined a large methamphetamine enterprise with a cult-like quality, and achieved notoriety for beheading its enemies and killing members of the Federal Police. The leader, who had issued his own bible, was killed in December 2010, after which the organization subsequently split into rival factions. The Knights Templar seems to have emerged as the dominant group and exhibits the same combination of messianic religion and criminal behaviour. In other words, the Mexican drug world is a curious combination of strategic competition among big organizations combined with factional splits within some of these organizations.

There has also been an outsourcing of violence, with the Juarez organization employing a local gang, La Linea, to defend its position in Juarez against the encroachment of the Sinaloa Federation. The United States is concerned that some of the violence will spill across the border, a concern driven in part by the presence of major Mexican drug trafficking organizations in many American cities. In some instances these affiliates can be understood as branch offices; in others they are local franchises; and in yet others the relationship is that of supplier and buyer. The other key point about Mexican drug trafficking organizations is that they have expanded to other countries in Central and South America and West Africa and have also developed relationships with Italian criminal organizations.

In Italy, the Sicilian Mafia is no longer the premier criminal organization. It has been superseded by the Camorra, which is based in and around Naples, and by the 'Ndrangheta, which retains its base in Calabria while also maintaining a significant presence in Milan – a major transportation hub and host for a major Expo planned for 2015. Indeed, there have been numerous reports that the 'Ndrangheta has already succeeded in infiltrating companies and obtaining lucrative contracts related to the Milan Expo. The 'Ndrangheta's ability to exploit opportunities of this kind is particularly impressive given that it started as a local mafia organization engaged in kidnapping and extortion in Calabria, one of the poorest parts of Italy. Ironically, the 'Ndrangheta has subsequently developed into a transnational criminal organization with a significant presence in much of Western Europe, the United States, Australia, Canada, parts of Latin America and West Africa. It has become deeply involved in the cocaine trade and reportedly controls much of the drug that arrives in Europe – often through the port of Gioia Tauro.

The port – and the criminal opportunities it offers – has helped the 'Ndrangheta attain its current status as the most powerful criminal organization in Italy, in spite of the internecine feuds between various clans, one of which spilled over into Duisburg, Germany in 2007, when six men were killed while sitting at a pizzeria. Part of a long-running feud that has become known as the 'Vendetta of San Luca', the Duisburg massacre brought the 'Ndrangheta to the forefront of attention and made it a priority law enforcement target. A major investigation resulted in 300 arrests in 2010 and provided new insights into an organization long believed to be a horizontal network. Anti-mafia investigators in Reggio Calabria and Milan now claim that the 'Ndrangheta has a clear cut organizational hierarchy reminiscent of the Sicilian mafia.

If the 'Ndrangheta has something of a global presence, so too does Russian – or as it is more accurately called – Eurasian organized crime. Criminals from Russia, Georgia, Ukraine, Chechnya, and Central Asia are all too often lumped together under the term 'Russian organized crime'. This is not surprising. Russia has a long tradition of criminality centered on the 'Thieves' World' and criminal authority figures known as the *vory-v-zakone* or 'thieves professing the code'. The post-Soviet generation of Eurasian criminals, however, not only reflects the diverse nationalities brought together in the Soviet Union, but also is much more entrepreneurial than their predecessors (Serio 2008). The 1990s, when Russian criminals looted resources from much of the former Soviet Union, were characterized by considerable turmoil as criminal organizations fought for control of territory and markets. Contract killings were frequent and the *vory* were decimated by a new generation of criminals (the so-called authorities) who were interested in money rather than status and did not accept the traditional rules. Considerable violence also occurred between ethnic criminal organizations, especially Slavic and Chechen groups. Today, however, the Russian criminal world has achieved a degree of equilibrium and the number of contract killings has declined significantly.

Russian criminals have also developed an extensive presence overseas, typically in warm sunny places, such as the Caribbean, Spain's Costa Del Sol, Israel, and Thailand. In Western Europe, Russian criminal organizations are mainly involved in activities such as extortion, car theft, and smuggling of art and antiques; as well as trafficking in drugs and women (Kego and Molcean 2011). Russian criminals have also moved into cyberspace, where they have helped to pioneer large-scale credit card fraud, identity theft, and online extortion. The Russian Business Network – which disappeared off the radar in 2007 but is probably still active – is a one-stop criminal service provider and a leader in developing extortion through distributed denial of service attacks.

Nigerian criminals and fraudsters have also been very active in cyberspace where their 4-1-9 or advance fee fraud emails have become ubiquitous. Yet they have also been active in the real world, with a presence in somewhere between 50 and 100 countries. Indeed, since the early 1980s, Nigerians have developed an important global role in both heroin and cocaine trafficking. Nigerian criminals are also heavily involved in the trafficking of women to Europe for the commercial sex trade and reportedly control much of the prostitution in southern Italy. Nigerian criminal organizations are not particularly violent and tend to operate with fairly flexible structures. Some specialize in drug trafficking or financial fraud, while others appear to move from one crime to another very easily.

While other criminal organizations, including the Japanese Yakuza and various Chinese groups also deserve discussion, even more important is the idea of criminal activities and the fact that terrorists, insurgents, militias and warlords have all appropriated organized criminal activities as funding mechanisms. This is certainly the case with FARC in Colombia, which has become heavily involved in drug trafficking and more recently in illegal gold-mining. Sendero Luminoso protects coca farmers in the Apurimac and Ene river valleys and reportedly supplies Mexican drug trafficking organizations. In Iraq, insurgents used criminal activities (especially oil smuggling; extortion, kidnapping, and car theft) to fund their political and military campaigns, while also establishing links with more traditional profit oriented criminal organizations – especially Iraqi kidnapping gangs which seized hostages and sold them to al-Qa'ida in Iraq (AQI) and affiliated organizations. In Afghanistan, the Taliban has profited enormously from its linkages with the opium and heroin industry while affiliated groups such as the Haqqani network are heavily engaged in kidnapping for profit. Al-Qa'ida in the Islamic Maghreb (AQIM) has long-standing ties to Saharan smuggling gangs and its leaders have more than a decade of direct experience in smuggling everything from weapons to cigarettes. There are also cooperative linkages between criminal and terrorist groups, although they are neither as pervasive nor as strong as often claimed.

Although a focus on criminal (and even political organizations using organized crime) is both appropriate and helpful, it should not be overly exclusive. As a UN study on transnational organized crime observed, 'For many of these activities, the organizing principle is the invisible hand of the market, not the master designs of criminal organizations. Looking at the world through this broader definition, it is often the groups that come and go, while the market remains constant' (UNODC 2010: 19). The corollary is that 'strategies aimed at the groups will not stop the illicit activities if the dynamics of the market remain unaddressed' (UNODC 2010: v). An analysis of criminal organizations, therefore, can usefully be supplemented by an analysis of illicit markets.

## Illicit markets

As suggested above, one of the challenges facing states is that global flows of illicit commodities and even illegal migrants have become so large, diverse, and rapid, that states find it hard to regulate or inhibit them. Part of the reason is that the flow of licit goods has become so huge that illicit commodities can all too easily be hidden within them. These commodities tend to be either stolen (cars, art), prohibited (drugs and strategic nuclear materials), regulated (cultural property and arms), or differentially taxed (cigarettes). In all cases, differences in national laws and regulations, as well as varying price structures and market opportunities attract a variety of actors. In some illegal markets, transnational criminal enterprises operate alongside and in parallel with individuals and with ostensibly legitimate businesses that are not overly scrupulous about observing laws and regulations. In others, however, criminal organizations dominate. In most, instances, the symbiotic relationships between underworld suppliers and upper-world consumers provide a degree of connivance and collusion that facilitates operations and ensures profitability.

The most important illicit goods are drugs, which have become a problem for an increasing number of societies as many countries that were once involved only in production or transshipment have also developed large consumer markets. According to the 2011 UN World Drug Report, 'about 210 million people use illicit drugs each year, and almost 200,000 of them die from drugs' (UNWDR 2011: 8). In fact, there is no single drug market, but at least four distinct markets. The largest is for cannabis, which was reportedly consumed by 'between 125 and 203 million people worldwide in 2009' (UNWDR 2011: 13). Somewhere between 2.8 per cent and 4.5 per cent of the world population aged 15–64 had used cannabis at least once during the year (UNWDR 2011: 13). The second market in terms of prevalence of use is amphetamine-type-stimulants, which are synthetic and do not depend on cultivation. The third market and the one that is most violent is cocaine, which is supplied by Colombia, Peru, and Bolivia and has large markets in the United States ($37 billion) and Europe ($33 billion) (UNWDR 2011: 8). According to the UN estimate, the cocaine market serves somewhere between 14.2 and 20.5 million people aged between 15 and 64. (UNDWR 2011: 16) In 2009, an estimated 378 metric tons are believed to have left the Andean region for the USA, of which approximately 200 metric tons were seized. (UNDWR 2011: 21) The other major destinations were Western and Central Europe. Although mostly this was transported through direct shipments, the success of maritime interdiction has led traffickers to move drugs through West Africa (around 13 per cent of all trafficking to Europe). In 2009 about 217 metric tons of cocaine was shipped to Europe, of which almost 100 metric tons were seized (UNWDR 2011: 21). If these figures are correct the interdiction and seizure rates have significantly improved – although this has increased the intensity of the competition among suppliers and contributed to the increased violence in Mexico. The heroin market in 2009 consisted of 12 to 14 million users worldwide who consumed 375 metric tons (UNDWR 2011:15). Europe and Asia remain the key global consumption markets, and they are largely supplied by Afghan opium, while Mexican and Colombian traffickers supply the US market.

One of the characteristics of these markets is that they are typically populated by both large and small criminal organizations, although this tends to vary at different points in the supply chain. Large organizations (which are often erroneously described as cartels) receive most attention, but the market also allows for a large number of smaller players. In an important study on Colombian drug entrepreneurs in the Netherlands, for example, Damien

Zaitch discovered that although Colombian cocaine firms were engaged in all four aspects of the drug business in the Netherlands – transportation, importing, wholesale distribution, and retail selling – they were largely: 'informal, small, mutating, and decentralized. Some are individual enterprises; others adopt the form of temporary partnerships between two or three people. These coalitions are often formed solely for a single project, with some of the people involved also engaging in legal activities or in other coalitions' (Zaitch 2002: 297). This confirms a study of organized crime in the Netherlands done in the 1990s, which concluded that organized crime there was a large, amorphous, dynamic, and constantly shifting network. The broader point is that criminal organizations vary enormously in size and structure.

This is also true in other markets. Two of these markets involve the transportation of human beings. This can be human smuggling (when the aim is illegal immigration and the crime is against the state) or human trafficking (which typically involves coercion and deception and the crime is against the person). In practice, the distinction can all too easily become blurred as those who travel voluntarily (as part of an illegal immigration scheme) can nevertheless be exploited en route or at their destination. Women and children are most often trafficked for commercial sex while men are trafficked for forced labour. Most of the flows of people go from less developed countries to developed countries. Those who do the trafficking and smuggling can range from small, informal, and illegal travel agents to large criminal organizations and networks that are supplying the commercial sex trade.

Illegal arms trafficking represents another major illicit market. The large-scale supply that fuelled wars in Africa during the 1990s was organized largely by key brokers and transporters such as Victor Bout and Leonid Minin, both of whom have since been arrested. The smuggling of guns from the United States to Mexico is fuelled by the availability of weapons at gun shows in the Southwest United States, and the use of straw purchasers or front men working – directly or indirectly – for Mexican drug trafficking organizations. In the case of endangered species, the market is once again very varied, with participants ranging from Chinese triad organizations in South Africa, to individual collectors. Trafficking in art and antiquities is equally diverse, ranging from highly professional criminal organizations that are opportunistic about which products they traffic to groups that specialize in this area, to enthusiastic amateurs. In addition there are very large counterfeit markets in everything from pharmaceuticals to spare parts for airplanes and cars, to DVDs and cigarettes. Some of these markets are very organized and controlled while others are more diverse with lots of individual or small groups participating alongside the more well-known and larger organizations.

To the extent that the organizations are successful and the illicit markets are lucrative, it is necessary to launder criminal proceeds. The essence of the laundering process is to hide the criminal source of wealth and to make the proceeds appear legitimate. This is often done through several stages, usually termed placement, layering, and integration. Sometimes money is not put through the cleansing process completely, however, and is simply moved beyond the reach of national law enforcement. This is also an area where the criminal world and the licit world intersect as lawyers, accountants, bankers, and other specialists often assist in the laundering process.

## Responses to transnational crime

Assessing the response to transnational organized crime is problematic. Gaps in knowledge, the lack of a baseline, and the difficulty of clearly discerning trends make it difficult to know how well the criminals are doing and even more difficult to determine how governments are doing in response. Nevertheless, over the last two decades transnational organized crime has clearly become more diverse, more pervasive, more professional, and more violent than ever before. Mexican criminal organizations exhibit a degree of violence and ruthlessness that eclipse anything that Al Capone did. Capone was perhaps most famous for the St Valentine's Day Massacre in which 7 members of a rival organization were killed. This kind of killing has become a daily occurrence in the Mexican drug violence – and the number of people killed is typically much higher. As suggested above, globalization has empowered organized crime. Indeed, the problem for governments is that, for all intents and purposes, organized crime operates in a borderless world whereas law enforcement agencies still operate under the constraints of sovereignty. Ironically, criminal organizations have also become adept at using borders defensively and launder money through multiple jurisdictions, ensuring that even when law enforcement is able to follow the money it is rarely able to catch it.

Some progress has obviously been made in combating transnational organized crime. The large Colombian drug trafficking organizations based in Medellin and Cali were destroyed in the 1990s; the Sicilian mafia was significantly weakened; and Putin succeeded in restoring the power of the Russian state and constraining Russian organized crime. Yet much more needs to be done. Moreover, even successes against organized crime have a downside, often creating 'vacancy chains' within organizations or markets that in turn generate violence either within or between organizations (Friman 2004).

After 11 September 2001, the United States failed to pay attention to organized crime except where it was seen as working with terrorism. In July 2011, however, the United States issued a new strategy to combat transnational organized crime. This recognized the scope of the problem and established certain priorities for dealing with it. The overarching objective of the strategy is 'to reduce transnational organized crime from a national security threat to a manageable public safety problem in the United States and in strategic regions around the world' (White House 2011: 1). The strategy emphasizes actions the United States can take within its own borders to lessen the threat and impact of transnational organized crime domestically and on foreign partners. The other priority actions seek to: enhance intelligence and information sharing; protect the financial system and strategic markets against transnational organized crime; strengthen interdiction, investigations, and prosecutions; disrupt drug trafficking and its facilitation of other transnational threats; and build international capacity, cooperation, and partnerships.

The strategy is clearly a large step beyond anything that has gone before. The emphasis on enhanced intelligence is very positive, as is the mix of defensive measures to protect the financial system and offensive measures to degrade criminal organizations. Even though little of this is novel, the very existence of a new strategy will go some way towards facilitating a more effective and coordinated approach among the various departments and agencies of the US government. Yet gaps remain. Little attention is given, at least explicitly, to the need to attack both organizations and markets. And although the rhetoric of building international capacity, cooperation, and partnerships is emphasized, this has not been done very successfully in the period since the early 1990s when transnational organized crime first emerged as a security threat. Moreover, although the strategy recognizes that some countries are part of the problem rather than part of the solution, it does little to suggest how this can be changed. Perhaps most problematic of all, it offers little in the way of new resources to deal with the challenge. United States national security policy in the next decade or so will operate in a highly constrained budgetary environment. In these circumstances, it is unlikely that transnational organized crime will be given the priority the strategy rightly suggests is critical to success.

In the end a lot will depend on the ability of the United States to mobilize support among other countries. The difficulty is that the United States – in the aftermath of an ill-advised war in Iraq and an inconclusive intervention in Afghanistan, with a political system characterized by division, and an economy characterized by slow growth, fiscal restraint and austerity – is unlikely to be in a position to provide the leadership required, whether by example or through aid and assistance. What makes this even more disturbing is the fact that organized crime is ultimately a reflection of the pathologies of globalization and the failures of governance. In the next few decades, rapid uncontrolled urbanization, severe and unpredictable changes in climate, food and water shortages, failing states, energy and resource conflicts, and redistribution of global power, will accentuate these pathologies and failures. Consequently, organized crime will have even greater and more lucrative opportunities – and will pose an even greater challenge to the Westphalian state system. If shortages in food, water, and energy become the norm – and black markets become the most effective system of supply – then organized crime will become even more important, providing not only illicit goods and services but also the very staples of daily life. In these circumstances, in some countries at least, it will go from an alternative form of governance to the preferred form of governance.

## Further reading

Vanda Felbab-Brown, *Shooting Up* (Brookings Institution Press, 2009). An incisive study of the linkages between drug trafficking and insurgency and between counter-narcotics and counter-insurgency.

R. Thomas Naylor, *Wages of Crime: Black Markets, Illegal Finance, and the Underworld Economy* (Cornell University Press, 2002). A stimulating and provocative collection of Naylor's trenchant writings on organized crime and the illicit market.

Peter Andreas and Ethan Nadelmann, *Policing the Globe: Criminalization and Crime Control in International Relations* (Oxford University Press, 2006). A well-received study examining the rise of transnational organized crime and international responses by two noted specialists in illicit political economy.

Cyrille Fijanut and Letizia Paoli (eds.), *Organized Crime in Europe: Concepts, Patterns and Control Policies in the European Union and Beyond* (Springer, 2004). A comprehensive, if daunting, collection that provides detailed coverage of transnational crime in Europe.

Robert Mandel, *Dark Logic: Transnational Criminal Tactics and Global Security* (Stanford University Press, 2011). One of the few works on organized crime by an international security specialist, this valuable study explores how transnational organized crime uses violence and corruption and how it threatens human, national, and international security.

# Population Movements

Sita Bali

### Abstract

In this chapter, students will learn about the relationships between population movements and security. It begins by examining why and how population movements have come to be seen as security issues. It then outlines the types of population movements and highlights the way states normally deal with them. Attention focuses on the direct impact population movements can have on security, narrowly and traditionally defined: in the sense of security of the state from war, violence and conflict. The next section considers the effect of population movement on security, more widely defined. This includes an assessment of the impact of migration and ethnic minority communities on state foreign policy, particularly with regard to the countries of origin of migrant communities. Finally, the chapter examines the impact of ethnic minority communities on the internal social stability and cohesion of states.

## Introduction

Population movement, or the phenomenon of migration, is as old as humanity itself, and has played a crucial role in shaping the world as we know it. In recent years such migration has gained prominence on the international agenda because of its increasing scale and the consequences such movements have for international affairs, including security concerns of states.

The increase in international population movements can be attributed to several factors. First, the ubiquitous nature of state control makes many international movements a matter of concern to at least two and sometimes more states. Second, there is the rapid increase in the world's population, which is still growing. Third, globalization has brought about a revolution in communications and transportation that has made people aware of vastly differing conditions and opportunities in other parts of the world, as well as making travel to those areas easier. Finally, the world is a turbulent and unstable place, and turmoil and uncertainty play a role in motivating people to move, to escape and/or search for a better life. This is best illustrated by the consequences of the end of the Cold War and the demise of the Soviet Union, which led to massive movements of people in Europe for the first time since the end of the Second World War. Ethnic Germans and others migrating to Germany and the West in search of a better life were joined by millions fleeing war and ethnic persecution in the former Yugoslavia, for example.

According to the International Organization for Migration (IOM), the number of international migrants in the world has increased from just 75 million in 1960, to 150 million in 2000 to 191 million in 2005, to an estimated 214 million people in 2010, making up 3.1 per cent of the global population, or if they were a country, the fifth most populous country in the world. Among these were 15.4 million refugees. According to the UN High Commission for Refugees (UNHCR), another 27.5 million people were displaced from their homes but still living within their own countries (internally displaced people) at the end of 2010.

Table 34.1 World migrant numbers in selected years

| Year | Number of voluntary migrants (millions) | Number of refugees (millions) | Total migrant number (millions) |
|------|------------------------------------------|-------------------------------|----------------------------------|
| 1960 | 64.2  | 1.8  | 66    |
| 1970 | 17.5  | 2    | 81.5  |
| 1980 | 91.4  | 8.4  | 99.8  |
| 1990 | 136.6 | 17.4 | 154   |
| 2000 | 162.8 | 12.1 | 174.9 |
| 2005 | 182.3 | 8.7  | 191   |
| 2010 | 198.8 | 15.2 | 214   |

*Source:* UNHCR and IOM websites

*Table 34.2* Remittances to developing countries (in billions of US dollars)

| Year | 2000 | 2001 | 2002 | 2003 | 2004 | 2005 | 2006 | 2009 |
|---|---|---|---|---|---|---|---|---|
| Amount | 85 | 96 | 117 | 145 | 163 | 188 | 199 | 307 |

*Source:* World Bank website

This chapter examines the phenomenon of international population movement or migration, with a view to evaluating the extent and nature of the threat it represents to state security. It concentrates on outlining and analysing the various ways in which population movements can constitute a threat to the security of states, societies and individuals within them. It is thus not called upon to make the positive case for migration. But this does not mean that there is no case to argue or that population movements must always have a negative impact on sending and receiving countries, or their security. Migration can be economically beneficial to both sending and receiving countries and for the migrant. Sending developing countries benefit hugely from remittances that migrants send home, and from the easing of pressure on employment, housing and other social facilities.

The receiving country benefits from availability of labour at reasonable cost, increasing national productivity and economic growth. It acquires adventurous, entrepreneurially inclined individuals, determined to succeed in their new environment, who are more likely than average to become wealth creators and generators of employment. It may also acquire sorely needed highly trained and skilled personnel, like doctors and software engineers, without having to invest in developing their skills. The migrants benefit from better standards of living, and fulfilment of their aspirations. Host countries become home to migrants with a variety of talents from business acumen to sporting prowess to musical, literary and theatrical abilities, and can become vibrant, open, multicultural, multi-ethnic, multi-faith societies with a flourishing cultural life. Migrants can contribute to building bridges between communities at home, and strengthening ties with their countries of origin abroad.

## Population movements as a security issue

Over the last decade or so, a range of events in a number of countries have forced scholars to consider the importance of international migration in international relations. The flight of East Germans to the west through Austria and Hungary, that ultimately resulted in the demise of the East German state, coups and political instability in Fiji and Pakistan, ethnic cleansing and refugee movements in the Balkans, the rise of right-wing political forces like neo-Nazis in Germany and Jean-Marie Le Pen in France to name but a few, have contributed to this increasing interest. Changes to the international environment with the end of the Cold War and the re-envisaging of security with threats now perceived to emanate from a number of non-traditional sources such as environment and health, created space for rethinking the relationship between international relations and international migration. Within this context, there is also increasing recognition of the links between international migration and security.

The terrible events of 11 September 2001 dramatically reaffirmed the role that international migration can play in international relations generally, and in security issues in particular. When it emerged that the perpetrators of 9/11 were all temporary or illegal immigrants, the United States began to treat their immigration service as part of their national security apparatus, with sections of the PATRIOT Act being devoted to immigration policy and process, and immigration coming under the supervision of the Department for Homeland Security. As the global aims, reach and spread of al-Qa'ida became clearer, this approach was taken up in many other Western states. The case was further strengthened by the Madrid bombings (11 March 2004) and the London tube bombings (7 July 2005). It is now widely accepted in many Western states that the public policy process should explicitly treat immigration and security as intertwined, and bring a security focus to bear on matters of control and management of population movement.

Migration can pose a threat to the people and governments of both sending and receiving states, and to relations between these two countries. It can turn civil wars into international conflicts and it can cause the spread of ethnic conflict and civil unrest from one country to another. It can lead to some form of conflict, including full-scale war between countries. Migration can also play a role in facilitating terrorism. Population movements can become the cause of economic hardship and the increase in competition for scarce resources of various kinds from jobs to social housing, and can weaken existing power structures and institutions within countries, as well as threatening cultural identities and social cohesion.

## Population movements categorized

All international migrations can be divided into two categories: involuntary or forced (also called refugee movements), and voluntary or free (also called economic migration) on the basis of the motivation behind the migration. Involuntary or forced migration refers essentially to refugee flows, where for reasons of natural disaster, war, ethnic, religious or political persecution people are forced to flee their homes. The flight of thousands of Afghans to Pakistan and Iran since 1979 or the desperate journeys of black African Sudanese from their homes in Darfur would fall into this category. The exodus of starving Somalis to Kenya in search of nutrition in mid-2011 are a reminder that drought and political instability can combine in a lethal way to create famine, which in turn causes large scale refugee movements.

Voluntary migrations can be further subdivided into three main categories. The first is legal permanent settler migration of the kind that populated the

United States or created the Asian and Afro-Caribbean minorities in Britain. This kind of migration has decreased most sharply in recent years. The second kind is legal temporary migration, and includes the bulk of the voluntary migrations. This category would include the movement of people for education, business, tourism and employment, such as the temporary workers admitted to the Gulf States to service the oil powered economic boom in construction and other sectors. The third kind of voluntary migration is the illegal migration of people from one country to another, which may be temporary or permanent. This would include, for example, the clandestine movements of Mexicans and others across the long US–Mexican border. The relevance of this categorization is based on the existence of an international regime and norms to deal with involuntary or forced migrations, and the complete absence of the same with respect to voluntary or free migration.

Sovereignty is regarded as the defining characteristic of a state in our international system. It implies, among other things, that states have control and jurisdiction over what goes on within their territorial boundaries. One aspect of the exercise of sovereignty has always been a state's inviolable right to control who enters and exits from its territory. Thus states have traditionally operated a system of border controls, with policies regarding who may enter, for how long and under what conditions. With regard to free or voluntary migration, states have the full authority to decide who they will accept as entrants or immigrants. They make their decisions based on a variety of criteria including the labour and skills needed by their economies and cultural and ethnic similarities with incoming migrants. But when it comes to involuntary or refugee movements, there are some limited constraints on a state's authority, in the form of the obligations imposed on them by the 1951 Convention on the Status of Refugees.

## BOX 34.1  1951 CONVENTION ON THE STATUS OF REFUGEES

The 1951 Convention relating to the Status of Refugees is the key legal document in defining who is a refugee, their rights and the legal obligations of states. It was created in the aftermath of the Second World War to deal with displaced people in Europe, and originally intended to last just three years. But the refugee issue was not so easy to solve, and it was given permanence through the 1967 Protocol, which removed geographical and temporal restrictions from the Convention. The Convention is based on the principle of non-refoulment, laying down that no state should return a refugee to a state where their life might be in danger. It also established the now universal definition of a refugee, both now key principles of international law. The Convention provides the most comprehensive codification of the rights of refugees and lays down basic minimum standards for the treatment of refugees. The Convention is to be applied without discrimination as to race, religion or country of origin, and contains various safeguards against the expulsion of refugees. The Office of the UN High Commissioner for Refugees monitors states' compliance with the Convention.

This Convention obliges signatory states to extend asylum and protection to those facing persecution, on grounds of religion, race, nationality or political opinion. Further, implicit in the meaning of refugee lies an assumption that the person concerned is worthy of being and ought to be assisted, and if necessary protected from the cause of flight (Goodwin-Gill 1983: 1). In practice the Convention commits states to ensure that no asylum seeker is sent back to any country where they are likely to face danger to life or liberty, without their application for refugee status being given due consideration. Also relevant is the Universal Declaration of Human Rights (1948), which states in Article 14 that everyone has the right to seek and enjoy asylum from persecution, in other countries.

However, none of these agreements or practices actually guarantees anyone the right to refugee status, only the right to seek it. This is because in practice there is total acceptance in the international society of the right of every sovereign state to decide for itself who should be allowed entry to its territory. Thus, the question of whether someone is a refugee and should be treated as such by a state becomes an issue decided by the government and the courts of the country in which refuge is sought. Nevertheless, these instruments form an important part of the international consensus on the treatment of refugees, and they lay down an important universal principle that most states have come to endorse, namely that people with a well-founded fear of persecution have a right to exit from their own country, cannot be returned to their country of origin, and have international status.

For an asylum seeker to be recognized as a refugee is a political decision, and depends to some extent on the relationship between the sending and receiving countries. For instance, during the Cold War, anyone who managed to escape from any Eastern Bloc country to the West was welcomed with open arms. In fact in the United States, under the terms of the McCarran-Walter Act (1952) until 1980, a refugee was defined as a person fleeing Communist persecution. Since the end of the Cold War, as erstwhile Communist bloc citizens became free to exit from their countries, Western governments were no longer so hospitable.

Sometimes different streams of migration mix and merge over time (sometimes called the asylum–migration nexus). For example, the movement of Sikhs from the Punjab to the UK, US and Canada since the 1960s was a classic free economic migration. But then in the 1980s, when the demand for an independent Sikh state in the Punjab arose, it was violently suppressed by the Indian Government and a number of Sikh advocates of an independent Punjab were forced to leave their homeland and seek refuge elsewhere. Quite naturally, many of them found their way to the countries that were already home to Sikh migrants, where they could live amongst their kith and kin. One result of this kind of convergence of different types of migrations is that receiving state governments and their people are increasingly likely to treat all immigrants alike, once they are in the territory of the receiving state.

The one inevitable long-term consequence of international population movements, whether the movements of refugees or the free migration of people aspiring for a better life, is the creation of ethnic minority communities in the receiving countries. In most host countries, and certainly in democracies, it has become clear that once migration takes place, for whatever reasons, and whether intended to be permanent or temporary, it invariably results in at least some immigrants becoming citizens of the host country, and creating a cultural, linguistic, religious and possibly a racially distinct minority within the state. The existence of these communities has a substantial impact on security, both in the traditional sense of security of the state from violence, war and conflict, to security in the wider sense of social stability, economic prosperity and the internal politics of states; as well as on the relationship of host states with the countries from where these communities originate.

## Population movements and violent conflict

Large-scale refugee migration from one country to another usually raises serious security concerns. Refugee flows, by their very nature are the result of conflict, social and political upheaval and turmoil. It is therefore hardly surprising that they may sometimes carry that instability with them to the host country. In such circumstances, the refugee flows are both a consequence of some sort of conflict, violence or repression as well as themselves becoming the cause of conflict between their country of origin and the receiving state. When a government becomes unwilling host to a large refugee population, it is likely to take steps to ensure that the stay of the refugees is temporary, and there is every potential for conflict between sending and receiving countries in this case. Examples include the flow of Palestinians into the neighbouring Arab states in 1948, when Israel was created; the migration of East Pakistanis into India to escape the brutal attentions of the West Pakistani army in the early 1970s; and the movement of Afghans from their country to Pakistan in the wake of the Soviet invasion in the 1980s.

The receiving state will try to bring about a change in the situation or policies of the sending country government that led to the exodus, or failing that, try to bring about a complete change of government there. This usually tends to lead to some sort of conflict between the sending and receiving states. Often, receiving states get involved in the conflict in the sending state, threatening to arm or actually arming the refugees; and sometimes deploying their own armed forces. Instances abound, with the actions of various Arab governments towards the Palestinians; Pakistani involvement (with Western help) in Soviet controlled Afghanistan; and Indian arming of the Sri Lankan Tamils being cases in point. The instance that had the most far-reaching consequences was the Indian intervention in East Pakistan in 1971, which came about as a result of ten million East Pakistanis fleeing the violent suppression of their rebellion by the West Pakistani army, resulting in the formation of Bangladesh.

This strategy is not without risk. By strengthening a refugee group, the receiving country takes the chance that it will lose its ability to deal independently with the sending country, and that refugees will attempt to determine the host country's policies toward the sending country (Weiner 1995: 139). This has happened to the Arab governments which have supported the Palestinians, the Pakistanis who supported the Afghan Mujahidin, and to the Indians who supported the Tamils in Sri Lanka. The conflicts created by such movements can sometimes be protracted, often lasting as long as it may take for return of the refugees to their homeland, or the creation of some alternative permanent arrangement for their resettlement.

Recent events in Britain illustrate that it does not take a large number of refugees to have a negative impact on the security of the receiving country. Britain had given refuge to a small number of high profile charismatic and influential Islamist clerics, when they sought to escape repressive Middle-Eastern regimes which were targeting them for their extreme Islamist views. Amongst these was Sheik Omar Bakhri Mohammed who founded the Islamist student movement Al-Mohajiroun and radicalized British Muslim youth. There was Abu Hamza the Afghan war veteran and extremist preacher who converted Finsbury Park Mosque into a haven for Islamists and a recruitment centre for al-Qa'ida. There was also Abu Quatada the cleric who has been now named as al-Qa'ida's spiritual leader in Europe, whose speeches influenced several European suicide bombers including Zacharias Moussavi, the twentieth man involved in the 9/11 attacks and Richard Reid the shoe bomber. These extremist clerics helped radicalize many young British Muslims, recruited and sent British Muslims to fight in Bosnia and Chechnya, and arranged trips for terrorist training to Afghanistan for some. They and their associates must be seen as at least partly responsible for the radicalization that ultimately resulted in four young British Muslim men blowing themselves up on London's transport network on 7 July 2005, killing 51 members of the public and injuring hundreds more.

In recent years the US-led 'war on terror' has focused attention in the West on the potential security threat from some among their Muslim residents and citizens of immigrant origin. But attacks by Islamists based in the West go back to the first attack on the World Trade Center in 1993, and the bombing campaign by Islamist Algerians on the Paris Metro in the summer of 1995. Most of those involved in the attack on the Twin Towers of the World Trade Center, were temporary migrants, resident in the United States ostensibly for education or business. A number of those involved in the Madrid bombings, in terrorist trials and currently detained in various European countries, are Islamist residents of the countries they are now accused of attacking. That most of them are either refugees, immigrants themselves, or of immigrant origin presents Western liberal democracies with a significant challenge.

## Population movements and foreign policy

Immigrant or ethnic minority communities, formed by labour or refugee migration can play a significant independent political role in world politics.

Their continued political involvement in states in which they no longer live, and whose laws they are not subject to, presents a serious challenge to the sovereignty of that state. By the same token they challenge the ability of host states to exercise independent control over the direction of their own foreign and domestic policy.

Migrant communities tend to maintain a strong connection with their home countries, and turbulence or instability in those societies can find expression within the migrant community. When this happens, these communities will become involved in a range of political activities targeted at their home country. They will use all means at their disposal, to influence events at home, which could be in support of, or (more often) against their home governments. They take advantage of their unique status, being outside their home country, and not subject to its jurisdiction, to take those actions that people living in their country of origin cannot, due to fear of arrest, persecution or violence. In particular, they can join political groups proscribed in the home country, publicize the grievances, agendas and demands of these banned groups, be critical of home government actions and policies, and become the voice of a suppressed opposition. They can try and draw the attention of the wider world to the problems in their country of origin, causing at the very least embarrassment to the home governments. They raise funds within their diaspora community and provide financial support to like-minded forces, or victims of government persecution in their home country. Migrant communities will also try to enlist the support of the host government and population to further their particular political aims in their home country. Home country governments respond to all this offshore activity by putting pressure on the host state governments to restrict them, and not allow minorities to gain voice and succour. But if the migrant communities are acting within the laws of the host state, there may be little the host government can easily and legally do to restrict their activities. The consequence is deterioration in the relationship between the host and home states.

The case of the Sikh community in the UK acting in concert with the wider Sikh diaspora in other Western countries, including the US and Canada, is a good example of the phenomenon. The Sikh population in Britain, Canada and the US were deeply influenced by the politics of the Punjab and the demand for independence from India in the 1980s and early 1990s. The diaspora communities were themselves divided along the same factional lines as politicians in the Punjab, and disputes between factions as well as between the Sikhs and the Punjabi Hindu community and the Indian government were reflected within the Sikh communities abroad, particularly in the struggle for control of wealthy and influential Sikh temples in major Western cities and in a deteriorating relationship between other Indian immigrant organizations and Sikh institutions. In Britain this did spill over onto occasional but limited violence in centres with large Sikh populations, as well as leading to some high profile members of the Sikh and Punjabi communities being assassinated.

Sikh communities abroad contributed significantly to the violence in the Punjab which targeted Indian security forces and members of the Hindu community. Their major contribution was through collection and illegal transfer of funds to Punjab for those carrying out the secessionist violence in India. They also created serious problems for the Indian government by campaigning and publicising the demand for secession and independence abroad as well as highlighting cases of human rights abuse carried out by the Indian security forces. The diaspora Sikhs declared an independent state of Khalistan, established a government in exile in London, and began issuing passports and banknotes for their new country. In constituencies with large numbers of Sikhs, members of parliament were inundated with requests to raise these issues, and questions regarding the situation in Punjab and censure of the Indian government were tabled in the House of Commons. The Indian government tried to put pressure on Britain by questioning the UK government on its provision of asylum and benefits to some Sikh refugees, and by trying to get the UK to restrict the activities of the Khalistan Council and agree to an extradition treaty with India. The British government was reluctant to go down this route. The Indian government then delayed or cancelled commercial orders for defence equipment and helicopters with British firms. In general, for a considerable period through the 1980s and early 1990s, the activities of the Sikhs in the UK had the effect of damaging the long-standing and generally amicable and close relationship between Britain and India.

The success of migrant communities' attempts to recruit their host governments and populations to their cause in their home country depends to a large extent on the nature of the political system in the host country. The more open the system and the more susceptible to lobbying it is, the more likely it is that minority communities will succeed in getting their concerns on the agenda. The US is usually seen as being susceptible to such pressures, because of the openness of its political system to political lobbying. Thus, some American foreign policy stances are partially explained by the efficacy of minority community pressure on behalf of their home country. The unwavering support that the US has given Israel since its inception is a reflection of the power of the Jewish lobby in American politics. Similarly, the Greek community in the US successfully lobbied politicians to get Congress to embargo military assistance to Turkey, after the Turkish invasion of Cyprus.

Arguably, the presence of the Muslim minority population in Britain has become a factor to be considered in foreign policy decision-making. For example, the stance of the Muslim communities in various European states affected the policies of those states during the Gulf War (Collinson 1993: 15–16). In addition, the concerns of British Muslims may have helped draw attention to the suffering of Bosnian Muslims and Kosova Albanians, both situations in which Britain and other states ultimately intervened militarily to protect the Muslims. The anti-war demonstrations in London before the 2003 invasion of Iraq saw the Muslim minority, in conjunction with other interest groups make clear their opposition to Britain's participation in this action, and no doubt generated much mail for MPs in constituencies with large Muslim populations. Britain's participation in the invasion is understood to be one of the main causes of Muslim dissatisfaction and disenchantment with the former Labour government, and the ongoing war in Afghanistan extends that dissatisfaction to the current coalition government.

Migrant communities can also be used by the government of the home country to pursue its own aims, vis-à-vis the host country government. The relationship between successive Israeli governments and American Jews illustrates this point. Host governments too will try to use their ethnic minority communities to achieve their own goals, particularly those in relation to events in the country of origin of that community, with Mafia leaders, for example, assisting the Allied invasion of Sicily during the Second World War.

## Population movement and internal security

Admitting migrants has long-lasting social effects on receiving countries. It can turn more or less homogeneous societies into multicultural ones by the introduction of ethnically different people. Migrants raise social concerns because they potentially threaten to undermine the popularity and strength of the nation-state. At the moment nation-states remain the dominant unit of social organization across the globe with each state ostensibly forming a 'territorially based self-reproducing cultural and social system' (Zolberg 1981: 6). Their members are seen to share a common history, language, religion and culture that binds them into a cohesive integrated unit with a shared sense of nationhood. As citizens of one state, moving to live and work in another, migrants clearly challenge traditional notions about membership of a state, the meaning of nationality and citizenship, and the rights and duties of citizens towards their state and vice-versa. The fact that very few states fit the idealized picture of the homogenous nation-state, and that most states are cultural and social products of earlier movements of peoples, fails to register on the popular consciousness.

Migration can become a threat to social cohesion and stability if migrants or minority communities are seen to be an economic burden on society. The perceptions of migrants as welfare dependent, or so numerous and needy as to stretch local resources in housing, education, healthcare and transportation can cause resentment and hostility. Migrants are also perceived to be criminals and carriers of infectious diseases in some quarters. In advanced industrial societies, concern with the cost of welfare provision to migrants, particularly asylum seekers and refugees has become a major political issue. It is argued that the validity of the welfare state model in many of these countries, reliant on ordinary people's taxes, is threatened if the public begins to feel, rightly or wrongly, that their taxes are being used to subsidize foreigners' living expenses and healthcare, rather than taking care of those in need within the home society. Many European countries have seen a resurgence of the extreme right in politics as a consequence of this public unease about immigration and asylum. The rise of neo-Nazis in Germany, Le Pen in France, movements led by the now deceased Jorge Haider and Pym Fortuyn in Austria and the Netherlands, the British National Party and the English Defence League in the UK are all examples of the domestic political forces pushing European governments to take an increasingly hard line on immigration. These pressures have also prompted collective action from Western European countries. European Union states have tried to move towards a process of harmonization of their refugee and immigration policies. (This does not yet apply to the 10 new members who joined the Union in 2004, or Romania and Bulgaria who joined in 2007.) This has proved a more difficult and slower process than they envisaged, but some fundamental agreements are now in place. The 1990 Dublin Convention, (which came into effect in 1997) provided that an asylum seeker who has had his/her application rejected in one European country cannot seek asylum elsewhere in the European Union. Thus rejection by one member state is to be seen as a rejection by all the established members of the Union.

Most Western European states (with the exception of Ireland and the UK) have further collaborated on developing a common visa and immigration policy, the Schengen Agreement, which harmonizes rules for visa requirements, travel within their borders and removes intra European travel barriers. It also establishes a system of increased cooperation and information sharing between police and immigration authorities of member states, enabling states to cooperate on dealing with illegal immigrants, drug and people traffickers and security threats. The Amsterdam Treaty of the EU further commits member states to striving towards developing a single European Refugee and Migration policy, as does the Lisbon treaty of 2007, but this has not yet been achieved.

Most of the world's refugees originate from and remain in the developing world, and here large refugee inflows can be an immense burden, in economic terms. In the short-term they can cause quite serious distortions in the markets of the receiving countries, particularly with regard to escalating the prices of essential commodities. This is what happened in Iran in the aftermath of the Gulf War, when Kurdish and Shia refugees flocked into that country. In the long term, a developing state generally has to rely on international assistance, usually through the office of UNHCR to alleviate the burden on the economy, but is susceptible to the internal political tensions that difficult economic situations bring.

Migrants are received with hostility if they are perceived as a threat to the culture and way of life of the people in the receiving country. This tends to happen when large numbers arrive in a short period of time or when migrants are seen as holding themselves apart and being reluctant to make any efforts to integrate into the host country's way of life.

Large, long-term refugee populations can bring about significant changes in the social cohesion and stability of the host country. Pakistan's problems with increased drug addiction among its population, as well as the threats to law and order posed by the flourishing arms bazaars in Peshawar and elsewhere (what has been described as the 'Kalashnikov culture'), are laid at the door of their Afghan guests. Large numbers of refugees can also be a driving force for change within the receiving country, particularly if they are ethnically similar to their hosts, or speak a common language. The gradual 'talibanization' of parts of Pakistan, and the growing support attracted by the Islamic poltical parties, is at least in part a result of playing host, for nearly twenty years, to millions of Pashtuns from across the Durand line, that separates Afghanistan from Pakistan. Similarly, the large Palestinian presence in Lebanon contributed towards the destabilization of that country during its long civil war, and continues to do so to the present day.

Further, migration can affect political and social conditions, and even, in rare instances, fundamentally alter the nature of society in receiving countries, many years after the actual movement of people has ceased. An illustration of this can be seen in Fiji, where indenture migration created an Indian immigrant community nearly a century ago. Indo-Fijians formed nearly half of the Fijian population by 1987, and an election brought an Indo-Fijian dominated political party to power, and gave Fiji its first Indo-Fijian Prime Minister. The largely indigenous Fijian armed forces took power in a coup and tried to enshrine a new constitution ensuring political primacy for their ethnic group. The tussle for power between the two groups continues and Fiji has since experienced intermittent upheavals and further coups, the last being in 2006.

The extent and nature of integration of a migrant community, and the impact this has on 'societal security' has recently come under the microscope, particularly in European countries such as Britain, France and Denmark (see Waever *et al.* 1993: 17–40). The substantial long-established Muslim community in these and other European countries is now, in light of the global 'war on terror', being seen as a source of threat. According to the Pew Research Center, in 2009 there were approximately 38 million Muslims in Europe, with France having the largest numbers (5–6 million) forming 8–9 per cent of its population (Pew Forum 2009). Muslims make up 2.4 per cent of the population of Western Europe. Events like the attack on London transportation systems, the murder of film-maker Theo Van Gogh in retaliation for making a 'blasphemous' film about Islam and women, and riots in the suburbs of Paris as well as controversy about the publication of cartoons depicting the Prophet Mohammed as a terrorist, the law banning the use of headscarves in state institutions in France, and the increasing use of the full-face veil by young Muslim women, to name but a few, have been bitterly divisive.

In Britain, the 7/7 attacks precipitated soul-searching and debate about the supposedly divisive nature of multiculturalism as a model of integration, the importance of migrants being fluent in the language of the majority, and the common values that are needed to underpin a cohesive multi-ethnic multi-religious society. These debates are taking place against the backdrop of a difficult security situation, involving arrests and high profile trials of some young Muslims. This has made the Muslim minority defensive and unable or unwilling to acknowledge and confront the extent of radicalization amongst their number. The economic and social marginalization of Muslims, particularly Pakistanis, who on virtually every social indicator lag behind other immigrant communities, including those from the Indian subcontinent, is evident in even a cursory examination of areas in which they are concentrated, such as Britain's northern mill towns. This lack of economic and social progress is clearly relevant to the ongoing discussion. The direction taken by this national debate is crucial to future social stability in Britain.

## Conclusion

Until the world is free of repression, conflict, political instability and economic inequality it is certain that population movements will continue. In an increasingly globalized world, with easy access to information, instant communication and cheaper travel the numbers of people on the move can only increase. While most free migration post-1945 has been from the developing world to the richer world, most refugee migration has taken place within the developing world itself. Thus there is no part of the globe that is untouched by migration and unconcerned with its impact. Migration reflects the unequal and volatile nature of our world, and brings the conflicts and instability of the poor world into the streets and ultimately the policy forums of the comfortable and comparatively secure developed world. It also adds to the deprivation, instability and violence of the developing world. It raises questions of human rights, international law and state sovereignty. And it is a hotly debated, live and difficult issue in the contemporary politics of many states, both rich and poor.

Population movements cast light on the divided nature of the contemporary world. In a larger part of the world, most of Africa, Latin America, and Asia there is considerable insecurity, violence, conflict, repression and deprivation. By contrast, in Europe and North America and a few other areas including Japan, Australia and New Zealand, people enjoy prosperity and democracy. Such stark contrasts are a striking indictment of the present age and they contribute significantly to population movements. Such movements show that the rich Western countries cannot maintain their isolation from, and remain untouched by the deprivation and instability of the developing world. They provide a powerful argument for the sensible and whole-hearted participation of the powerful West in the development, both economic and political, of the rest of the planet.

The 'global war on terror' adds another dimension to this already divided world. The preoccupation in the West with preventing another 9/11 or 7/7 horror has led to the abrogation of long-established civil rights at home, and preventive military action abroad. These actions have arguably created more tensions than they have resolved, adding to destabilizing population movements in the Middle East and along the Durand line, as well as alienating different communities of their own citizens from each other, thus increasing insecurity at home.

However, it would not be appropriate or realistic to conclude that the best policy for states would be to drastically restrict migration. First, that does not deal with the fact of past migrations and their consequences, it would for example, do nothing to resolve the issues raised in the context of the 'war on terror'. Second, it would strongly signal that states see migration and migrants as a problem, which would make it more difficult to achieve desirable levels of integration of immigrants and may add to social insecurity. Opponents of immigration, such as the extreme right, would probably interpret such a signal as a licence to step up their divisive anti-immigrant activities. Third, as argued at the start, migration can have considerable economic and other benefits. Fourth, in a globalized world, open, free market societies will need to facilitate some migration to accommodate their demand for skills and labour, and to create the unrestricted environment in which cultural exchange, creativity, entrepreneurship and business can flourish. A balanced immigration policy, based on the needs of the economy and all citizens, with fair and transparent rules is the key to the management of migration in the contemporary era. And this has to be combined with policies that allow existing migrant communities opportunities for economic self-improvement, and encouragement to integrate. Migrant communities need to have a stake in their host societies and see their own rights, best interests and prosperity dependent on and tied to the rights, interests and prosperity of the larger society around them.

## Further reading

Alexander Betts and Gil Loescher (eds), *Refugees in International Relations* (Oxford University Press, 2011). A focused look at refugees from various IR perspectives.

Stephen Castles and Mark Miller, *The Age of Migration*, 3rd edition (Palgrave-Macmillan, 2003). A very useful overview of the phenomenon of population movement and its impact on international politics.

Robin Cohen, 'Diasporas and the nation-state: from victims to challengers', *International Affairs*, 1996, 72(3): 507–20. Focuses on the changing role of diasporas from forced migrants to challengers of the authority of nation-states.

Nana Poku and David Graham (eds), *Redefining Security: Population Movements and National Security* (Westport, 1998). A wide-ranging and useful collection, focused on various aspects of the security implications of migration.

Niklaus Steiner, *International Migration and Citizenship Today* (Routledge, 2009). Useful comprehensive look at the issues, with a good section on naturalization and citizenship.

Myron Weiner, *The Global Migration Crisis* (HarperCollins, 1995). Excellent, explicitly political analysis of the migration phenomenon with a special focus on security by one of the pioneers in the field.

# Energy Security

Michael T. Klare

## Abstract

In this chapter, students will learn about the various meanings of 'energy security' and consider why it has suddenly attracted so much attention from both policy-makers and the general public. In particular, international concern over the future availability of energy supplies is ascribed to doubts about the ability of energy producers to keep pace with rising world demand, the shift in the centre of gravity of world oil production from the global North to the global South, and the targeting of oil installations by terrorists, insurgents, and ethnic separatists. Various strategies for enhancing energy security are also considered.

## Introduction

Until just a decade ago, the term 'energy security' was almost unheard of outside the specialized analytical community. It now figures prominently in the policy discourse of major government officials. 'Energy security', said US President George W. Bush in March 2001, should be 'a priority of our foreign policy' and govern key elements of domestic policy (Bush 2001). Similar views have been expressed by President Barack Obama and the leaders of other industrialized states, thus highlighting the importance now being accorded the energy issue. This naturally invites a pair of obvious questions: What, exactly, is meant by energy security, and why has this aspect of security gained such prominence *now*?

## Understanding energy security

Energy is central to all human endeavours. Even the most primitive humans must consume food in order to obtain the caloric energy to hunt, gather more food and other essential materials, build shelter, and defend against predatory animals and hostile tribes; more complex societies need energy to procure food and water and to construct cities, fortifications, factories, ships, roads, railroads, and so on. The more complex and productive a society, the greater its need for energy; without adequate supplies of basic fuels, a complex society cannot maintain a high rate of industrial output, provide a decent standard of living to its citizens, or defend itself against competing powers. 'Oil is not just another commodity', Senator Richard G. Lugar of Indiana observed in November 2005. 'It occupies a position of *singular importance* in the American economy and way of life' (2005, emphasis added). It is from this perception of energy's 'singular importance' to the functioning of modern industrial societies that the concept of energy security springs.

In most Western states, the task of procuring, producing, and delivering energy to consumers is largely performed by private companies, which do so in the pursuit of profit; some of these companies, in fact, are among the most profitable in the world. But because the acquisition and delivery of adequate supplies of energy is considered so essential to the economic health of states, governments also play a significant role in key aspects of the energy procurement process – either directly, or through the activities of state-owned companies such as the China National Petroleum Corporation (CNPC) and the Oil and National Gas Corporation (ONGC) of India. The intervention of state authorities in the management of energy acquisition and distribution is typically justified in terms of 'energy security' – that is, ensuring that appropriate incentives and policy instruments are in place to impel private firms to take the steps needed to produce and deliver adequate supplies of energy to meet the nation's requirements; when the private sector proves unequal to this crucial task, the state must be prepared to step into the breach.

There is no standard, all-embracing definition of 'energy security'. Most analysts describe it as the assured delivery of adequate supplies of affordable energy to meet a state's vital requirements, even in times of international crisis or conflict. 'Put simply', explained a task force convened by the US-based Council on Foreign Relations, 'energy security' constitutes 'the reliable and affordable supply of energy' on a continuing, uninterrupted basis (Deutch and Schlesinger 2006: 3). In practice, this is usually understood to encompass the dual functions of ensuring the procurement of *sufficient supplies* of energy to meet fundamental needs as well as ensuring their *unhindered delivery* from point of production to ultimate consumer (see also Kalicki and Goldwyn 2005).

Fulfilling these dual requirements has proven enormously difficult in recent years as the worldwide demand for energy has grown – and the task is likely to prove even more challenging in the years ahead. Obtaining sufficient supplies of energy to satisfy national requirements will become more challenging because the energy requirements of most states will continue to expand as populations grow, urbanization and industrialization advance, incomes increase, and ordinary citizens acquire additional energy-consuming devices (especially automobiles). According to the most recent projections from the US Department of Energy (USDoE), combined world energy consumption is expected to grow by an astonishing 56 per cent between 2005 and 2035, jumping from 473 to 739 quadrillion British Thermal Units (BTU) per year (USDoE 2010a: 131). Procuring all of this additional energy will prove a gargantuan task on a global scale – but it will be at the national level that the job of actually generating all of the required additional fuels will largely be performed. For those officials who are delegated with responsibility for overseeing this crucial chore, energy security will to a considerable degree entail taking such measures as are deemed necessary to ensure that the nation's supply of available energy keeps expanding in consonance with rising demand.

The job of securing sufficient energy to meet national needs will fall upon the leaders of all countries, but will prove a particular challenge to the rapidly growing states of Asia. According to the USDoE (2010a: 131), an estimated 62 per cent of the growth in world energy consumption between 2007 and 2035 will be accounted for by developing Asia. China alone is expected to double its energy consumption between 2007 and 2030, while India is projected to experience similar growth; together, their net consumption is slated to jump from 98.3 to 196.8 quadrillion BTUs over this period, an increase of nearly 100 quadrillion BTUs. Obtaining all of this additional energy is sure to constitute one of the most daunting tasks facing Chinese and Indian leaders in the years to come (IEA 2007: 243–587). That China, India, and other developing countries will need to acquire vast amounts of additional energy is also a source of anxiety to leaders of the older industrial states, who worry about intensified competition for access to inadequate global stockpiles (see Klare 2008).

So far, we have been speaking of energy in the *aggregate* – of the sum of all sources of energy, including oil, natural gas, coal, nuclear power, hydro-power, and traditional sources such as wood and charcoal. As indicated, policy-makers will feel compelled to increase the *net* supply of energy, in all its forms, to satisfy rising demand in the decades ahead. But these officials also seek to avoid over-reliance on any one or two of these sources, lest a future shortage of those materials causes a severe energy crisis and resulting economic disaster. Policy-makers are also aware that growing concern over global climate change could well lead to future restrictions on the use of fossil fuels – oil, coal, and gas – whose consumption typically results in the release of carbon dioxide and other heat-trapping greenhouse gases. In terms of ensuring adequate supplies to meet future needs, therefore, energy security has also come to mean *diversifying* a state's primary sources of fuel and investing in climate-friendly alternatives – especially renewable forms of energy such as solar, biofuels, and wind power (IEA 2009: 167–361).

The second major energy challenge, ensuring the unhindered *delivery* of crucial supplies, will also grow more demanding in the years ahead because the global energy supply system (like that for many other basic commodities) has become highly globalized, with numerous suppliers around the world contributing oil, natural gas, coal, uranium, and electricity to extended, over-stretched, and often fragile networks of pipelines, transmission lines, and maritime trade routes. Aside from the normal wear and tear of overburdened infrastructure, these networks are often vulnerable to attack by terrorists, insurgents, pirates, and criminal bands – making the safe delivery of energy increasingly problematic. As the worldwide demand for energy expands and reliance on these far-flung networks grows along with it, energy security will inevitably entail increased emphasis on the protection of global delivery systems.

The protection of overseas sources of energy extends to several forms of energy but places special emphasis on petroleum – the world's single most important source of energy. According to the USDoE (2010a: 133), oil accounted for 35 per cent of the world's primary energy supply in 2007 and is expected to provide nearly as much in 2035. Although some large consumers of petroleum, including the United States and China, are able to draw on domestic oil reservoirs for at least some of their requirements, most industrial powers must import a large share of their supply, often from providers located half-way around the globe. As the demand for energy grows, the role played by these international petroleum transactions will assume ever greater significance in the energy calculations of the major energy-consuming states. The fact that so many of the supply routes used in the global transport of petroleum originate in or pass through areas of instability and conflict can only add to the degree to which the energy security problem is equated with the safe delivery of oil.

The challenge of securing sufficient energy to satisfy national needs and to ensure the safe delivery of imported oil faces many states, but arises with particular vehemence for the United States, which yearly consumes approximately one fifth of the world's total available energy supply – an estimated 2.2 billion tonnes of oil equivalent in 2009 (BP 2010: 41). With its growing population and robust economy, the United States is also expected to account for a significant share of the *additional* energy that will be required to satisfy anticipated world requirements in the decades ahead. The problem of energy security has thus become a major policy concern in Washington, prompting debate and action at the very highest levels. In February 2001, President Bush established the National Energy Policy Development Group (NEPDG) to review the country's long-term energy requirements and to devise a strategy for ensuring that its vital needs would continue to be satisfied in the decades to come. 'The goals of this strategy are clear', he explained, 'to ensure a steady supply of affordable energy for America's homes and businesses and industries' (Bush 2001).

In its final report, *National Energy Policy*, the NEPDG concluded that the United States was not adequately developing domestic sources of energy to satisfy its future needs and was becoming excessively dependent on unreliable foreign suppliers, thus exposing the country to the threat of recurring supply interruptions. The report therefore called for increased emphasis on the exploitation of domestic sources of supply – including oil derived from protected wilderness areas, such as the Arctic National Wildlife Refuge (ANWR) – along with diminished reliance on overseas suppliers. Under the rubric 'Increased Energy Security', the NEPDG announced its intent to 'lessen the impact on Americans of energy price volatility and supply uncertainty' by 'reduc[ing] America's dependence on foreign sources of petroleum'. At the same time, however, the group acknowledged that the United States cannot eliminate its reliance on foreign suppliers altogether, and so indicated that 'energy security must be a priority of U.S. trade and foreign policy' (NEPDG 2001: xv).

For the United States, as for other industrialized states that rely on imported supplies of energy, energy security thus entails a conspicuous *foreign policy* dimension, in that a principal objective of its overseas diplomacy is to establish and sustain friendly ties with key providers of oil, gas, and other fuels, thereby facilitating the procurement of these fuels by companies linked to the home country. In many cases, the maintenance of such ties has become a major responsibility of senior government officials – from the president or prime minister on down. President George W. Bush, for example, conducted several meetings with King Abdullah of Saudi Arabia in the spring of 2008 to plead for increased levels of Saudi oil output, while President Hu Jintao of China has made several trips to Africa in pursuit of increased investment opportunities for Chinese energy firms (Klare 2008: 86–87, 168–169).

President Obama, who frequently speaks of the need to reduce US reliance on foreign oil suppliers, has also engaged in such diplomacy, saying the United States will never be entirely free of such dependence. 'We're still going to have to import some oil', he declared in March 2011, 'it will remain an important part of our energy portfolio for quite some time'. This helps explain, he noted, his decision to visit Brazil a few weeks earlier. 'Part of the reason I went down there is to talk about energy with the Brazilians. They recently discovered significant new oil reserves, and we can share American technology and know-how with them as they develop these resources' (Obama 2011).

By the same token, energy security has acquired a significant *military dimension* for the United States and a number of other energy-importing states, in that senior officials perceive a need to protect overseas energy supply routes and to help defend their country's major foreign energy providers against rival forces that might seek to impose less favourable terms over the flow of oil. For Washington, the protection of friendly oil suppliers such as Saudi Arabia, and the defence of vital maritime trade routes – such as the narrow Straits of

Hormuz between the Persian Gulf and the Arabian Sea – have become major elements of national strategy (Klare 2004, Palmer 1992).

The military dimension of energy security was first accorded high-level attention in the United States in late 1979 and early 1980, when Islamic insurgents overthrew the US-backed Shah of Iran and Soviet forces intervened in Afghanistan – in both instances threatening the safety of oil deliveries from the Persian Gulf to the United States and its allies. 'The Soviet effort to dominate Afghanistan has brought Soviet military forces to within 300 miles of the Indian Ocean and close to the Straits of Hormuz, a waterway through which most of the world's oil must flow', then President Jimmy Carter told Congress on 23 January 1980. 'The Soviet Union is now attempting to consolidate a strategic position, therefore, that poses a grave threat to the free movement of Middle East oil'. This is a threat that the United States cannot abide, Carter affirmed. 'Let our position be absolutely clear: An attempt by any outside force to gain control of the Persian Gulf region will be regarded as an assault on the vital interests of the United States of America, and such an assault will be repelled by any means necessary, including military force' (Carter 1980).

This principle – widely known as the Carter Doctrine – was invoked by President George H. W. Bush in August 1990 when announcing the decision to deploy American troops in Saudi Arabia and to commence what became known as the first Gulf War (see Klare 2004: 48–53, Woodward 1991: 224–273). Some analysts also believe that the *second* Gulf War – the 2003 US-led invasion of Iraq – was also triggered by the Carter Doctrine and its injunction to employ military force whenever deemed necessary to overcome threats to the free flow of Persian Gulf oil (see Klare 2004: 94–100, Phillips 2006: 68–96, Yergin 2002). This is energy security writ large.

But energy security can have yet another meaning, particularly for states that are highly dependent for their energy supplies on one or two suppliers but are in a weak bargaining position with respect them and so vulnerable to political pressure. This is the case, for example, of the former Soviet republics that rely on Russia for much of their oil and natural gas supplies, especially Ukraine, Belarus, Georgia, and the Baltic states. On several recent occasions, the Russians have threatened to or have actually cut off the flow of energy to these states, producing widespread economic hardship. Ostensibly, these actions were prompted by disputes over the *pricing* of energy, but most Western observers believe that Moscow undertook such action to punish an unfriendly government or to extract political concessions from the country involved (Buckley 2005, Kramer 2006). For these countries, then, energy security has come to mean reducing their dependency on a single provider that can employ its dominant position in order to inflict punishment for an unwelcome decision or extract concessions of some sort.

Energy security, then, can have a variety of meanings, depending on the outlook of the particular state involved. For virtually every state on the planet, it means securing sufficient energy to meet vital needs, both now and in the future. This means, in most cases, diversifying the types of energy on which a state relies and investing in climate-friendly energy alternatives. In addition, for those states that rely to a considerable extent on imported sources of supply, energy security also incorporates a significant foreign policy dimension, in terms of maintaining friendly ties with key foreign providers; these countries must also worry about threats to the unhindered delivery of their energy supplies, and this has led, in some instances, to a decision to employ military force in the protection of overseas supply routes. Energy security can also embrace efforts to reduce reliance on a single major supplier that uses its dominant position to extract concessions or otherwise manipulate its highly dependent clients.

## Why now?

Concern over adequate supplies of energy has been a significant concern for many states for a very long time, but the concept of energy security has only gained widespread prominence and attention in recent years. Why is this? What explains the enormous attention now being devoted to the problem by senior government officials, military strategists, scholars, and the general public?

Analysis suggests that the growing emphasis on energy security reflects widespread anxiety about both key aspects of the problem: whether there will be *sufficient* supplies of energy to meet national requirements in the years ahead, and whether the supplies that are available will be safely transported from point of production to point of need. This anxiety stems from three key recent developments in the energy field, largely concerned with the global availability of petroleum. These are: (1) fears of a slowdown in future world petroleum output; (2) a shift in the centre of gravity of world oil production from the global North to the global South; and (3) the explicit targeting of oil facilities by insurgents, terrorists, and extremists.

## Intimations of global petroleum insufficiency

The first and most important source of anxiety about the future availability of adequate petroleum supplies arises from concern about the ability of the global energy industry to continually increase crude oil output to satisfy ever-rising levels of consumption. At present, the industry appears capable of satisfying global demand, which at the beginning of 2010 stood at an estimated 84 million barrels per day (mbd) (BP 2010: 11). But serious doubts have arisen in energy and policymaking circles about the industry's capacity to meet much higher levels of demand expected for the future, when many existing oil fields are expected to fall into decline. Even if net world oil output rises to a higher level in the years ahead – say 100 mbd or more – the major consuming states will still experience a condition of petroleum *insufficiency* if global demand climbs to levels substantially above that figure and the industry proves unable to boost output to those elevated levels.

Consider the long-term projections provided by the USDoE (2010a: 136, 235): according to the 2010 edition of its *International Energy Outlook* (IEO), world oil consumption is expected to jump from 86 mbd in 2007 to 111 mbd in 2035, an increase of 25 mbd. Fortunately, says the USDoE, global oil-production capacity will rise by a like amount over this period, also reaching 111 mbd in 2025. (These figures include biofuels and 'unconventional' liquids, such as those extracted from Canadian oil sands.) It is hard to argue with the projections for increased *demand*, as these are consistent with long-term trends regarding economic expansion, population growth, urbanization, global motorization rates, and so forth. Far more problematic, however, are the assumptions regarding future *production*: these are based on estimates of future output from existing wells along with predictions of new oil-field discoveries, and so entail considerably more guesswork. It is these latter calculations that have aroused scepticism and alarm among specialists in the field (Deutch and Schlesinger 2006, Deffeyes 2001, Goodstein 2004, Roberts 2004).

This scepticism arises from several observations regarding the world's net oil production capacity. The first derives from evidence that many of the world's most prolific oil fields are nearing the end of their most productive years and are about to experience a substantial decline in output. This is said to be the case for many mature fields in the older producing areas, including those in North America, East Asia, and western Siberia – but is also thought to be true of Saudi Arabia, the world's leading producer. In a widely cited book on Saudi Arabia's long-term production prospects, investment banker Matthew R. Simmons wrote that Saudi Arabian oil production 'is at or very near its *peak sustainable volume* . . . and is likely to go *into decline* in the very foreseeable future' (2005: xv). Although Simmons' conclusions have been contested by Saudi oil officials, it appears that his work, and that of other specialists who have raised doubts about the productivity of Saudi fields, has begun to influence the thinking of USDoE analysts, who have downgraded their projections of future Saudi output. In the 2004 edition of the IEO, for example, Saudi Arabian output was projected to reach 22.5 mbd in 2025; in the 2006 edition, its projected output for 2025 was reduced to 15.1 mbd; and by 2010, it had slipped again to 12.1 mbd.

Concern over the future availability of crude petroleum from existing fields led the International Energy Agency (IEA) in Paris, an affiliate of the Organization for Economic Cooperation and Development (OECD), to conduct a field-by-field analysis of the world's principal oil reservoirs. Its analysis, published in 2008 revealed that the rate of decline at mature fields was greater than many had assumed and was increasing with time (IEA 2008: 221–256). Even with massive investment in technologies aimed at prolonging the life-span of ageing fields – so-called 'enhanced oil recovery' (EOR) techniques – the depletion rate for all but the newest fields was calculated at 6.7 per cent per year (or the equivalent of 4.7 mbd when applied to 2007 production of 82.3 mbd). Taking into account a steady increase in the rate of decline, the IEA further calculated that output from existing fields would fall by an estimated 43 mbd between 2007 and 2030, producing a mammoth void in the global oil supply that will have to be filled with new production from what the IEA termed 'fields yet to be developed' and 'fields yet to be found'.

This leads to a second major reason for anxiety about the future sufficiency of global production capacity: a steady decline in the rate of *new oil-field discovery*. If the global supply of petroleum is to satisfy anticipated world demand in the years ahead, we will need to see a volume of discovery that equates to both the decline in older fields and the added consumption generated by global economic growth. But that is not what is happening. According to the US Army Corps of Engineers, the peak level of oil-field discovery occurred in the 1960s, when new reserves with approximately 480 billion barrels of oil were identified. Since then, the rate of discovery has dropped in each succeeding decade while the consumption of existing reserves has continued to climb, with net extraction overtaking reserve additions for the first time in the 1980s; it now exceeds the discovery rate by a ratio of two to one (Fournier and Westervelt 2005: 13, Deffeyes 2003: 47–51). What this means is that the world is now relying on previously discovered reservoirs for an ever-increasing share of its consumption – a pattern that can only result in the exhaustion of existing supplies and an inevitable contraction in supply.

A third and final reason for anxiety over the future availability of petroleum arises from the fact that whatever discoveries *are* being made today tend to be located in areas that are difficult to tap into for geographic, environmental, or political reasons – and thus may not be developed to their full potential. This is hardly surprising: it is a common law of resource extraction that developers first pursue mineral deposits that are close at hand, easy to extract, and relatively free of political impediments; only after all the easy-to-exploit reserves are exhausted do developers go after less appealing sites in more distant, less accessible areas. In the case of oil, with most of world's mature fields facing irreversible decline and no new fields in familiar areas left to be tapped, producers see no choice but to pursue options in remote, hazardous, and geologically challenging areas, such as the Arctic, the deep waters of the Gulf of Mexico, and North American state formations. These areas still harbour significant reserves of petroleum, but gaining access to these reserves will prove increasingly costly and problematic.

The difficulty of obtaining petroleum from remote, hard-to-reach locations has become especially evident as a result of the April 2010 *Deepwater Horizon* disaster in the US Gulf of Mexico. Although the proximate cause of the *Deepwater Horizon* explosion – which killed eleven oil workers and inundated the Gulf with millions of barrels of crude petroleum – is thought to be a combination of mechanical and managerial errors, many analysts see it as the inevitable consequence of attempting to drill in ever deeper waters with still-unproven technology. As determined by the National Commission appointed by President Obama to investigate the 2010 disaster, 'Deepwater energy exploration and production, particularly at the frontiers of experience, involve risks for which neither industry nor government has been adequately prepared'

(National Commission 2011: vii). This finding has led many governments to reconsider or postpone plans to drill in ultra-deep waters and the Arctic.

A different set of impediments have been encountered by Western companies seeking to do business in the former Soviet Union. During the tenure of Russian President Boris Yeltsin, Western firms were invited to assume the leadership of major energy projects in the newly independent Russian Federation, such as those getting started off of Sakhalin Island, in Russia's Far East. Among the companies which took advantage of this offer was Royal Dutch Shell – which, together with Mitsui and Mitsubishi of Japan, acquired control of the giant Sakhalin-2 oil and natural gas project. But when Vladimir Putin assumed the presidency in 2000, Russian officials sought to transfer control of the project to Gazprom, the state-controlled natural gas monopoly. After assailing Shell and its partners with a barrage of regulatory attacks, the consortium finally capitulated in December 2006 and sold a majority stake in the project to Gazprom for significantly less than its presumed market value. A similar fate befell Western companies that made significant investments in Kazakhstan (Klare 2008: 99–100, 122).

There is no question that giant companies firms like BP, Chevron, ExxonMobil, and Shell possess the will and technical capacity to operate in remote, difficult locations. But will the financial community be willing to risk the many billions of dollars in new equipment and technical services that will be needed to develop these problematic and demanding reservoirs? The answer may not always be 'yes'.

## A shift in the centre of gravity of world oil production

The growing emphasis on energy security is also being driven by a perception that the centre of gravity of world oil production has irrevocably shifted from safe, friendly areas of the global North to more dangerous, unfriendly areas of the global South. For most of the Petroleum Era, the production of petroleum was largely concentrated in the North, especially the United States, Canada, Europe, and the European portion of the Czarist/Soviet empire. As recently as 1950, approximately two-thirds of worldwide oil production was centred in these areas. This focus on production in the global North is hardly surprising, given the aforementioned tendency of resource producers to focus their initial efforts on the exploitation of the most readily accessible deposits, while leaving for later those deposits located in harder-to-reach, more hazardous locations. But precisely because the more accessible deposits were the first to be exploited, they are also among the first to be facing systemic exhaustion. As the demand for crude has grown, therefore, the consuming states have had no choice but to increase their reliance on providers in the global South. These producers generally entered the energy business later than their counterparts in the North, and so their fields are at an earlier stage of development and thus are capable of sustaining higher levels of production in the future. As a result, the centre of gravity of world oil production has shifted decisively from North to South and will remain there for as long as we can see into the future.

Evidence of this shift is clearly evident in the projections on future global oil output supplied by the USDoE. In 1990, producers in the global North (including the United States, Canada, the North Sea states, Australia, Russia, and a handful of others) jointly accounted for 39 per cent of total world oil output; by 2035, their combined share is expected to drop to 29 per cent. Meanwhile, the USDoE (2010a: 235) projects a significant increase in the share of world petroleum supply provided by key producing areas of the global South, notably Africa, the Caspian Sea basin, and the Persian Gulf; together, the proportion of world consumption accounted for by these three areas is expected to jump from 31 per cent in 2003 to 53 per cent in 2035.

This shift in the centre of gravity of world oil-production capacity has profound implications for the energy-seeking states because it entails a heightened risk to the uninterrupted flow of energy supplies. Although not all states of the global North are peaceful and not all states of the global South are conflict-prone, there is a greater incidence of disorder in the South than in the North. This is due partly to the endemic poverty and the high rates of youth unemployment found in many developing states – a natural source of fodder for insurgency, ethnic extremism, and criminal violence – and partly due to the legacies of colonialism, which in many cases include borders drawn to meet the convenience of imperial overlords rather than the aspirations of ethnic constituencies on the ground. These problems are often compounded by the discovery of oil in poor ex-colonial countries, where the inequitable allocation of oil revenues has often been a significant factor in disputes between the central government and ethnic or regional enclaves – such Aceh in Indonesia, Cabinda in Angola, Kurdistan in Iraq, the Niger Delta region in Nigeria, and the non-Muslim South in Sudan.

Many post-colonial states also suffer from weak governance structures and a tendency toward military strongmen and pervasive corruption; what sets the oil-producing countries apart from others like them, however, is the powerful attraction that oil revenues (or rents) have for all aspirants to state rule. Once in power, the leaders of these 'petro-states' will balk at nothing to remain in power, and thereby keep the oil rents flowing into their private bank accounts. This means that their competitors, after having been denied the opportunity to prevail at the ballot box, perceive no option save armed revolt to secure their own place at the feeding trough. The result, more often than not, is a continuous cycle of coups, palace revolts, and counter-coups – often supported by an impoverished and resentful population ready to rebel at the first sign of central government vulnerability (see Karl 1997).

The dangers of increased reliance on oil supplies from the global South were on full display in the spring of 2011 as anti-government rebellions erupted throughout North Africa and the Middle East. Beginning in Tunisia, the revolts and demonstrations spread first to Egypt and then to Bahrain, Jordan, Libya, Oman, Saudi Arabia, Syria, and Yemen. Although not all of these countries are significant oil producers, and not all of the protests were fueled by anger over the inequitable allocation of oil wealth, there was a pervasive sense that the governments involved had been able to remain in power for so many years because they could rely on a constant stream of oil rents – allowing them to maintain powerful domestic security forces – and because they enjoyed the support of major foreign oil consumers like the United States, which preferred an environment of stability. The spring of 2011 also witnessed the secession of South Sudan from the northern part of the country, a move that was accompanied by widespread fighting along the disputed border between the two territories – fighting that was widely attributed to efforts by the northern government to win concessions in negotiations over the allocation of shared oil revenues (Gettleman 2011).

## Oil facilities as a target of attack

The problem of energy security is further compounded by the fact that oil facilities have *themselves* become a target of attack by insurgents and terrorists, who often view them as a concrete expression of America's (or the West's) reassertion of an imperialist agenda in the global South. This is especially true in the Islamic world, where many Muslim activists interpret the assertive US military presence as, essentially, an expression of America's insatiable thirst for Middle Eastern oil. Needless to say, those who oppose the American presence in the Islamic world usually have other motives for doing so; however, there is no escaping the fact that the pursuit of oil has long been a key motive for the West's drive to establish a significant presence in the Middle East and that this has affected the region in ways that are often resented by many of its Muslim inhabitants. In particular, there is widespread resentment of the close association between Western governments and the authoritarian, pro-Western regimes in the region, such as the Mubarak government in Egypt (until its ouster in February 2011) and the House of Saud; the conspicuous presence of US military forces to protect these regimes only adds to this resentment (Klare 2006).

Aside from constituting a central feature of Muslim extremists' indictment of the major Western powers, oil installations are also seen by many terrorist groups as an attractive target in the struggle between militant Islam and its enemies. This is so in part because of their symbolic importance – as *the* major expression of Western intervention in the Middle East – and in part because of its critical role in sustaining the West's energy-intensive economies. Attack the oil fields and pipelines, the reasoning goes, and you not only focus attention on the imperial presence of the Western powers but also deliver a blow at their most vulnerable point – their excessive dependence on cheap Middle Eastern petroleum. 'Pipelines are very soft targets', Robert Ebel observed in 2003. 'They're easy to go after. It doesn't take a rocket scientist to figure out where you can do the most damage, both physical and psychological, with the minimum amount of effort' (cited in Vieth and Rubin 2003).

An early expression of this strategy was the October 2002 terrorist attack on a French oil tanker, the *Limburg*, while sailing off the coast of Yemen. This attack – widely attributed to al-Qa'ida – was seen as the opening salvo in a new campaign to punish and weaken the West by assaulting the exposed conduits of the global oil-supply system. The strategic nature of oil terrorism is also evident in Saudi Arabia, where al-Qa'ida and allied groups have targeted foreign firms and technicians employed by Saudi Arabia's oil industry, presumably to damage its operating capacity. The first such assault occurred on 1 May 2004, when gunmen killed five Western oil-industry workers in Yanbu, the site of a major petrochemical complex. An even more ominous assault occurred on 23 February 2006, when suicide attackers attempted to break through the outer defence perimeter of the Abqaiq oil-processing facility and detonate explosive-laden vehicles in the Kingdom's most important energy installation, potentially jeopardizing 6.8 million barrels of daily output; although the attack was foiled before the bombers could get close to the facility itself, the determination with which they carried out the assault hints at the extent to which such facilities have come to be viewed as prime targets for attack (Bahree and Cummins 2006).

Oil facilities are also a major target for attack by insurgents in Iraq and Nigeria. In both countries, rebel forces seek to weaken the prevailing government by depriving it of oil income and by demonstrating its incapacity to protect vital installations and personnel. In Iraq, efforts to increase oil exports – and thus boost government income – have repeatedly been frustrated by insurgent attacks on pipelines, pumping stations, and refineries. In February 2011, for example, armed gunmen planted bombs at Iraq's largest refinery, Beiji, starting a fire that forced it to halt operations. In Nigeria, rebels in the Niger Delta region have engaged in similar activities in a campaign to force government officials to allocate a larger share of national oil revenues to the impoverished Delta region (USDoE 2010b).

For all of these reasons – an expected slowdown in the global output of oil, the shift in the locus of oil production from North to South, and the targeting of oil facilities by terrorists, insurgents, and extremists – policy-makers have become increasingly alarmed about the future sufficiency of energy supplies and the safety of global energy flows. And it is this anxiety, more than anything else, which explains the upsurge of interest in problems of energy security. 'As the years roll by, the entire world will face a prospectively growing problem of energy supply', former US Secretary of Defense (and Energy) James R. Schlesinger told the Senate Foreign Relations Committee in November 2005. 'We shall have to learn to live with degrees of insecurity – rather than the elusive security we have long sought' (Schlesinger 2005).

## Addressing energy (in)security

As concern over the various aspects of energy *insecurity* has grown, policy-makers have developed a wide array of responses: from greater reliance on military force to protect the flow of oil to increased emphasis on the development of renewable sources of energy, particularly wind and solar power. Many politicians, especially in the United States, also favour a relaxation of environmental restraints on the exploitation of domestic sources of oil and other fossil fuels in order to reduce reliance on imported sources of supply; this is one of the major reasons given for drilling in the Arctic National Wildlife Refuge and other such protected areas. Although there is considerable debate as to which of these approaches is likely to prove most effective, there is general agreement that increased effort is needed to address the threats to energy security.

If there is anything that policy-makers agree on when it comes to addressing the problem of energy security, it is that more options are better than fewer. In terms of securing overseas sources of petroleum, for example, US policy favours maximizing the number of providers from which oil supplies are derived. 'Concentration of world oil production in any one region of the world is a potential contributor to market instability', the 2001 *National Energy Policy* affirmed. 'Encouraging greater diversity of oil production . . . has obvious benefits to all market participants' (NEPDG 2001: ch. 8, p. 6). Similarly, US policy, like that of many other states, favours reliance on many *types* of fuel, so as to avoid over-dependence on any single type, lest a future scarcity of that fuel lead to a severe energy crisis. Recognizing that growing public concern over global warming is likely to lead to curbs on the use of fossil fuels, moreover, policy-makers in many countries are coming to favour increased investment in energy alternatives, such as wind power and biofuels. Besides these generalizations, however, there is considerable debate over particular aspects of energy security, and over the degree of emphasis that should be placed on particular fuel types and energy alternatives.

One of the most contentious issues in this debate concerns the degree to which the protection of foreign energy supplies should be entrusted to military forces. For some policy-makers, especially in the United States, the growing risk to global petroleum flows has led to a greater emphasis on the use of military force to protect overseas oil suppliers and the maritime trade routes used to transport oil. 'As the world market for oil relies on increasingly distant sources of supply, often in insecure places, the need to protect the production and transportation infrastructure will grow', a Council on Foreign Relations task force observed in 2006. For this reason, the presence of American military forces is said to play a vital role in stabilizing key oil-producing regions and will be even more essential in the future. In addition, 'U.S. naval protection of the sea-lanes that transport oil is of paramount importance' (Deutch and Schlesinger 2006: 23, 30). This outlook is also reflected in the new maritime strategy adopted by the US Navy in October 2007, known as *A Cooperative Strategy for 21st Century Seapower*. Noting that '90% of world trade and two-thirds of its petroleum are transported by sea', the strategy calls on the Navy to play a greater role in the protection of global sea lanes (US Navy 2007: 5).

Some Western analysts believe that Chinese authorities are also inclined to place greater reliance on the use of military force to protect vulnerable energy supply lines. For example, the 2006 edition of the US Department of Defense's annual report on the *Military Power of the People's Republic of China* reported,

> Securing adequate supplies of resources and materials has become a major driver of Chinese foreign policy. . . . PRC strategists have discussed the vulnerability of China's access to international waterways. Evidence suggests that China is investing in maritime surface and sub-surface weapons systems that could serve as the basis for a force capable of power projection to secure vital sea lines of communication and/or key geostrategic terrain.
>
> (US DoD 2006: 1)

Although still relatively modest by comparison with comparable US efforts, these initiatives suggest that Chinese officials, too, are prepared to employ military means in safeguarding the flow of vital energy supplies (Andrews-Speed *et al.* 2002). Indeed, Chinese military officials have become increasingly vocal about their plans in this regard. 'With the expansion of the country's economic interests, the navy wants to better protect the country's transportation routes and the safety of our major sea lanes', Rear Admiral Zhang Huachen, deputy commander of the East Sea Fleet, said in an April 2010 interview with Xinhua, the state news agency. 'In order to achieve this, the Chinese Navy needs to develop along the lines of bigger vessels and with more comprehensive capabilities' (see Wong 2010).

But if some policy-makers in Washington, Beijing, and elsewhere favour the expanded use of military forces to protect the global flow of oil, others see in this approach greater *risk* rather than greater safety, and so seek to enhance energy security by sharply reducing the country's dependence on imported fuels. America's reliance on imported petroleum 'is the albatross of U.S. national security', Senator Lugar declared in March 2006. The United States, he argued, is dependent on increasingly vulnerable energy supply lines at a time when 'Al Qaeda and other terrorist organizations have openly declared their intent to attack oil facilities to inflict pain on Western economies'. To protect these facilities, he continued, the United States is spending as much as $50 billion on 'oil-dedicated military expenditures in the Middle East' – with no guarantee that these massive outlays will prove effective. Rather than persist in its adherence to this risky and futile approach, Lugar affirmed, the United States should 'speed up the transition to alternative renewable energy sources' and sharply diminish its reliance on imported petroleum (Lugar 2006).

Lugar's views have gained support from leaders of both political parties in the United States, many of whom seek to reduce US military involvement in the Middle East and believe that developing renewable and other domestic sources of energy is a necessary step in achieving that objective. 'America's dependence on oil is one of the most serious threats that our nation has faced',

Barack Obama declared in January 2009, shortly after assuming office as President. 'It bankrolls dictators, pays for nuclear proliferation, and funds both sides of our struggle against terrorism'. To eliminate this menace, he asserted, 'It will be the policy of my administration to reverse our dependence on foreign oil, while building a new energy economy that will create millions of jobs' (Obama 2009).

But while this perspective enjoys broad support from the US public, there is little agreement on what alternative forms of energy to promote in the struggle to reduce reliance on imports. As indicated, many in the United States favour increased reliance on domestic supplies of fossil fuels, including oil and natural gas derived from protected wilderness areas and the outer continental shelf (OCS). Proponents of this approach also advocate increased investment in nuclear energy, so-called 'clean coal' technology, and stepped-up extraction of natural gas from shale rock formations. Many others decry these proposals, saying increased reliance on fossil fuels will accelerate global warming and impede the (necessary) development of renewables (see Bamberger 2007).

President Obama has sought to carve out a middle ground between these positions. While opposing oil drilling in ANWR and certain other protected areas, he has allowed increased drilling in the OCS and supported both 'clean coal' and shale-gas initiatives. 'To keep reducing that reliance on imports, my administration is encouraging offshore oil exploration and production – as long as it's safe and responsible', he avowed in March 2011. Obama also supports increased reliance on nuclear power. But he has placed greatest emphasis on the development of renewable sources of energy, including advanced biofuels derived from non-food crops like switchgrass and wood chips. While these initiatives are said to have many attractions in their own right – notably, diminished emissions of greenhouse gases and the creation of jobs at home – they are always placed in the context of energy security. 'The only way for America's energy supply to be truly secure is by permanently reducing our dependence on oil' he declared. 'We've got to discover and produce cleaner, renewable sources of energy that also produce less carbon pollution, which is threatening our climate. And we've got to do it quickly' (Obama 2011).

For now, the promotion of 'energy security' – whether in the United States or in other major energy-importing countries – will largely entail efforts to reduce dependence on imported supplies (or multiply the number of suppliers) and to expand domestic sources of supply. Many countries in East Central Europe, for example, are considering the large-scale development of domestic shale gas reserves as a way of diminishing reliance on Russia, a persistent source of energy insecurity (Deutsch 2011). However, as global awareness of the detrimental effects of climate change spreads, policy-makers will come under increasing pressure to limit the consumption of fossil fuels and to increase reliance on climate-friendly alternatives. As this occurs, 'energy security' will acquire yet a new meaning – the urgent need to replace existing energy systems with others that do not release climate-altering greenhouse gases. As suggested by the International Energy Agency in 2009, 'Continuing on today's energy path, without any change in government policy, would mean rapidly increasing dependence on fossil fuels, with alarming consequences for climate change and energy security' (IEA 2009: 44). Much debate will no doubt ensue over the best way to achieve such a transition, but the sense of urgency in making one is bound to grow.

Finally, energy security may come to mean using energy in a far more frugal and self-aware manner than we – at least those of us in the more advanced industrial states – have tended to do so in the past. As supplies of certain primary fuels (especially oil and natural gas) become more scarce, as the geopolitical risks of relying on these fuels become more severe, and as the environmental hazards of consuming fossil fuels more apparent, citizens around the world will naturally choose to be more deliberate in their selection and utilization of primary energy, and more inclined to avoid unnecessary or wasteful expenditures of fuel. Indeed, one can already see many signs of such voluntary restraint: the growing popularity of hybrid-electric automobiles in the United States; a preference for smaller cars and fuel-efficient diesels in Europe; the renewed popularity of bicycles in many European cities; and so on. As times goes on, such behaviour is likely to play an ever-increasing role in determining what is meant by energy security.

## Further reading

Jan H. Kalicki and David L. Goldwyn (eds.), *Energy Security* (Woodrow Wilson Center Press, 2005). A valuable collection of essays that examine the energy security region by region and from a variety of perspectives.

Michael T. Klare, *Blood and Oil: The Dangers and Consequences of America's Growing Dependency on Imported Petroleum* (Metropolitan Books, 2004). A detailed study of the close relationship between oil dependency and US foreign policy.

Kenneth S. Deffeyes, *Hubbert's Peak: The Impending World Oil Shortage* (Princeton University Press, 2001). An introduction to the problem of world oil production and its imminent decline.

US Department of Energy, Energy Information Administration, *International Energy Outlook* (US Department of Energy, annual). Annual survey of the world's energy demand and supply, with extensive statistical data.

International Energy Agency (IEA), *World Energy Outlook* (IEA, annual). Annual survey of the international energy environment, with detailed studies of particular current problems and extensive statistical data.

# PART 5
# CONCLUSIONS

# CHAPTER 36

# The Academic and Policy Worlds

James M. Goldgeier

## Contents

## Abstract

In this chapter, students will learn about the complex relationship between the academic and policy worlds related to security studies. In recent years, numerous scholars have decried the growing gap between these two worlds. While some gap between these two groups is natural – after all, academics theorize about broad patterns of world politics and practitioners have to solve particular problems of the moment – there is much that each group can offer the other. Academics can engage in in-depth study of past cases involving core security studies topics: the outbreak of war, peacebuilding and post-conflict reconstruction, deterrence, and coercive diplomacy, just to name a few. By exploring cause and effect, academics can use both their historical and theoretical knowledge to help policy-makers ask the right questions when they find themselves facing a particular challenge. Meanwhile, policy-makers can help academics understand what type of work has been most helpful to them when they seek to resolve a foreign policy problem.

## Introduction

In recent years, numerous scholars have decried the growing gap between the academic and policy worlds, some even going so far as to warn of the 'cult of the irrelevant' in security studies (Desch 2010). There will always be some gap – after all, academics theorize about broad patterns of world politics and practitioners have to solve particular problems of the moment – but there is much that each group can offer the other. Academics can engage in in-depth study of past cases involving core security studies topics: the outbreak of war, peacebuilding and post-conflict reconstruction, deterrence, and coercive diplomacy, just to name a few. By exploring cause and effect, academics can use both their historical and theoretical knowledge to help policy-makers ask the right questions when they find themselves facing a particular challenge. Meanwhile, policy-makers can help academics understand what type of work has been most helpful to them when they seek to resolve a foreign policy problem.

Particularly in the United States, academics have often contributed directly to policy by serving in government. McGeorge Bundy, Walt Rostow, Henry Kissinger, Zbigniew Brzezinski, and Condoleezza Rice all served as national security advisers after careers in academia, and another presidential adviser, Anthony Lake, started his career as a foreign service officer but joined the Clinton administration directly from an academic perch. Leading academic theorists such as Stephen Krasner, Joseph Nye, and Anne-Marie Slaughter have all occupied senior positions in government, and numerous other academics have served in mid-level positions, taking a brief leave from their university and then returning to contribute further to academic and policy debates. Each of these individuals had strongly developed and honed worldviews as well as deep substantive knowledge prior to coming into office, and they could draw on their theories and their knowledge when advising presidents and secretaries of state.

Academics have other ways of influencing the policy world. Perhaps most importantly, they train future professionals in their classes. Undergraduate and graduate students reading this textbook will be gaining theoretical and substantive knowledge that they will take with them going forward. Students may even become inspired to work in the professional world of security studies thanks to their exposure to the subject in college or graduate school. And even if they forget the details of what they learned in school, concepts are likely to remain with them, shaping how they think about cause and effect. As Joseph S. Nye, Jr. has written, 'In practice, theory is unavoidable' (2008b: 648).

Practitioners may not even be conscious of the way that their prior studies influence their day-to-day decision-making (Biersteker 2010). They will often draw on terminology drawn from the academic literature without thinking too deeply about it. For example, Professor Graham Allison's (1971) book on the 1962 Cuban Missile Crisis argued that officials favoured policies that reflected the interests of the agency or office where they worked, giving rise to the oft repeated axiom in Washington that 'Where you stand depends on where you sit'. (Allison had been the graduate student rapporteur for a faculty discussion group at Harvard University's Kennedy School that sought to bridge the gap in the 1960s after the close encounter with nuclear war during the missile crisis.) In the 1990s, policy-makers all over the world used phrases like 'the end of history' and 'the clash of civilizations' that came from Francis Fukuyama (1989) and Samuel Huntington (1993), respectively. Today, ideas related to the balance-of-power have permeated thinking about what the rise of China means for world politics.

While there has been a great deal of concern about a growing lack of policy relevance due to the increasingly abstract debate in academic International Relations theorizing in general and security studies in particular, opportunities and barriers for translating academic ideas for the policy community also depend on the political environment in which policy-makers operate. The impact of politics on policy-relevant academic work is clear if we consider the fate of International Relations theory's two main intellectual traditions – realism and liberalism see (Chapters 2 and 3 this volume) – in the American national security debate since the end of the Cold War. Academic realists, focused on the balance of power, have offered trenchant arguments against an overextension of the American military machine, and were especially clear in warning about the folly of going to war in Iraq in 2003. Leading figures in the field of international security such as John Mearsheimer and Stephen Walt (2003) explained on the pages of leading journals and newspapers why policy-makers should avoid an unnecessary war – all to no avail. Meanwhile, liberals such as Michael Doyle (1983), emphasizing the possibilities for cooperation, have promoted the idea that democracies make better international partners, leading successive administrations since the collapse of the Soviet Union to trumpet the importance of promoting freedom and democracy. While each tradition is subject to intensive debates within academia, the liberals have been much more successful over the past twenty years in shaping policy because the political environment favoured their arguments while leaving the academic realists unable to convince American policy-makers not to go to war in a number of instances.

## What is policy-relevant knowledge?

Bruce Jentleson and Ely Ratner define policy-relevant scholarship as 'research, analysis, writing and related activities that advance knowledge with an explicit priority of addressing policy questions' (2011: 8). Unfortunately for this type of endeavour, professors who seek recognition within their field inevitably focus their research efforts on publishing in top-flight peer-reviewed academic journals, which typically value theorizing for its own sake, not for the purpose of addressing policy questions. Scholarly work that addresses policy questions is more likely to be published in a policy journal, which is not valued highly by academic departments, especially when considering faculty members for tenure.

Whether academics value policy relevance or not, there is a natural connection between the two worlds. As former US deputy secretary of state James B. Steinberg has succinctly put it, 'policy making is about putting ideas into practice, and universities are about generating ideas' (2009: 3). Those ideas, Harvard scholar Stephen Walt (2005) writes, are helpful in at least four distinct ways: diagnosis, prediction, prescription, and evaluation. Policymakers have to figure out what kind of problem they confront; they have to evaluate different courses of action; they must predict what effects will result from those actions; and thus they are in need of prescriptions. Theoretical work based on historical knowledge and relying on methodological rigour can assist in these tasks.

The late Stanford professor Alexander George (1993) argued that in thinking about how academics can bridge the gap, it is important to distinguish between substantive theory and process theory. Substantive theory informs policy on specific issue areas such as deterrence, coercive diplomacy and war termination. Ideally, in George's view, the theorist can offer conditional generalizations to help policy-makers understand which strategies are likely to work in a given situation.

Consider, for example, an issue like deterrence. In the summer of 1990, Iraqi leader Saddam Hussein was massing his military forces on the border with Kuwait, a country that he did not recognize as legitimate. The result was a classic deterrence problem: how could the United States convince Saddam Hussein that the costs of invading Kuwait would far surpass any possible benefits he might receive from trying to conquer his neighbour? If the United States could convince him that the costs were prohibitive, then he would not attack. And that would mean deterrence had succeeded and war avoided.

Academic work on deterrence can assist policy-makers in those types of situations by providing theories about the strategies that have worked in the past and thus showing what is necessary to convey a clear and credible signal in order to prevent a target state from taking unwanted action, in this case the invasion of another country. In addition, academics can provide not just substantive theory but substantive knowledge about the particular target state to assist in sending a signal that will have the intended effect. Historical knowledge is also critical in thinking about when deterrence is necessary or when appeasement (giving an opponent what it wants in a single, given instance in the belief that it will not then ask for more) might actually produce an end to a crisis, rather than simply giving rise to a new one.

Academics can help policy-makers not only with substance but with process as well (Eriksson and Sundelius 2005). Most organizations have standard operating procedures to guide their activities. Research has shown that while these can increase efficiency, these procedures can decrease flexibility and lead to suboptimal outcomes in certain circumstances. Similarly, work on small group dynamics demonstrates that consensus-seeking becomes a primary value and dissenting views get stifled, often leading to fiascos like the Bay of Pigs invasion of April 1961 (Janis 1982).

Academics also have something to say about decision-making styles. Psychological experiments have demonstrated that individuals who prematurely close off their minds to alternative explanations will do a poor job analysing and forecasting and will lack the political judgment of their more open-minded colleagues (Tetlock 2005). Even understanding the necessarily probabilistic nature of any assessments of the future (I think there is a 40 per cent chance that X will occur under these conditions) is important for decision-makers who must react to evidence and adjust their approach if a policy is not working. For these reasons, Uri Bar-Joseph and Rose McDermott (2008) argue that hiring more open-minded intelligence analysts, less prone to premature cognitive closure, might be a way of preventing intelligence failures.

Decision-makers must consider whether they have the right structures and procedures in place to make a well-informed decision. Did they get all the information they needed? When a consensus emerged, was there a designated devil's advocate who could force policy-makers to take another look at a problem (George and Stern 2006)? Joseph Nye has written that when he was in the government, he utilized George's lessons to produce better decisions: 'I often remembered his cautionary words against premature closure of minds, uncertain evidence, and multiple advocacy' (2008a).

History is replete with examples of suboptimal decision-making leading to poor outcomes. Academics can help policy-makers think about how to create a process that will produce the best decision possible. This means trying to ensure that biases are reduced and a good process is in place to pursue the interests that the leaders have defined for the country. Even a good process, however, is sometimes not enough to produce a successful outcome, but a poorly organized process (for example, one in which information gets distorted and biases negatively influence assessments) is almost guaranteed to produce failure unless a decision-maker gets lucky (George 1980, Goldgeier 2010).

Despite the possibilities that exist for academics to assist policy-makers, scholars who care about policy fear that the gap is growing between the two worlds because the two cultures are so different. Academics value elegant theories and often dismiss policy-makers as partisan hacks. Policy-makers value action and dismiss academics as too removed from the real world. Because academic departments devalue practical applications, there are more and more think tanks (often hiring former academics) that are filling the void left by universities (Jentleson and Ratner 2011). Unlike the natural sciences, where there is room for both theoretical and applied work, the social sciences have generally lost interest in the applied side of the equation.

## Cold War nuclear experts

A major reason for the belief that a gap is growing between the academic and policy worlds is the nostalgia for the linkages that existed in security studies during the Cold War. Nye argues, for example, 'Through a combination of writing and consulting, [Thomas] Schelling, Bernard Brodie, Albert

Wohlstetter, William Kaufmann, and others developed and refined theories of nuclear strategy and arms control that were widely used by practitioners in the Cold War' (2008a). These individuals worked in top universities, but they also often had think tank and government connections. The advent of nuclear weapons after World War II forced officials to rethink strategy: in the nuclear age, great power war was unwinnable. Hence the United States and the Soviet Union had to engage in nuclear deterrence.

The most important concept of the nuclear era was 'Mutual Assured Destruction' or MAD. The United States and the Soviet Union kept each other from attacking through a simple premise. If one side contemplated attacking the other, it was deterred in the knowledge that an attack could produce a retaliatory response that would destroy the initial attacker. 'Go ahead and launch your missiles', each side could say. 'Whatever we have left, we will launch at you, and you will be destroyed'. Given the high costs of such a choice, no rational leader would launch an attack. Deterrence between the two nuclear superpowers worked.

While the theorists Nye cites made major contributions to our understanding of the requirements for mutual deterrence, politics undermined a central academic understanding even during the Cold War. Brodie (1946) made clear soon after the advent of atomic weapons that these were 'absolute weapons', not relative weapons. Previously in world politics, a country's confidence in its weaponry was determined by how much it possessed relative to its adversaries. Simply knowing that a nation had one thousand tanks, for example, was insufficient. What mattered was whether that nation's adversaries had five hundred tanks or five thousand tanks. Of course quality was important as well, and different weapons systems could be used to offset others, but in general weapons stockpiles could only be understood as sufficient relative to the opponent's (known) stockpiles. Whether defensive weapons had the advantage over offensive systems was also important in providing confidence in one's security (Glaser 2010).

Nuclear weapons are different. If a country possesses one thousand strategic nuclear warheads, then it does not really matter if its opponent possesses five hundred nuclear warheads or five thousand. Either way, it will be deterred from attacking, and so will its adversary. In fact, the United States has been deterred from attacking North Korea even though the latter has only a handful of nuclear weapons; after all, even one weapon launched at South Korea could destroy millions of lives.

Yet while theorists like Brodie and later Robert Jervis (1989) made a clear case for the requirements of minimum deterrence, the United States felt compelled to engage in an arms race with the Soviet Union (and vice versa) during the Cold War. This arms race had a number of causes, including the traditional security dilemma (see Chapter 10 this volume). (In the classic security dilemma, a country can build military systems for defensive purposes but since its adversary does not know for sure what its intentions are, the adversary feels compelled to respond by building its own systems in turn.) The lesson from the Cuban Missile Crisis also fostered the arms race: each side believed that American nuclear superiority and the threat of an attack forced the Soviet Union to back down. Later studies showed that President John F. Kennedy was looking for a way out of the crisis and was not prepared to launch an attack on Cuba because he feared that even one missile surviving a US attack that could then be launched at an American city was too high a price to bear (Dobbs 2008).

The main reason why arms racing occurred despite academic theories demonstrating that deterrence did not require keeping up numerically with the other side was the politics in both countries. Any leader of the United States or Soviet Union who argued that he did not need to match a build-up from the other side would have been charged with being weak and committed political suicide. Conservatives, for example, fiercely excoriated Ronald Reagan for even engaging in mutual efforts to reduce levels of nuclear weapons with Soviet leader Mikhail Gorbachev, and Reagan was the most conservative president of the modern era (Mann 2009). Reagan was appalled by what he believed was the immorality of deterrence and sought to eliminate strategic nuclear warheads. (In the end, Reagan's unwillingness to abandon his efforts to build a missile shield kept Gorbachev from agreeing to his proposals. Even though Gorbachev understood that missile defence was unlikely to work as Reagan intended, his military viewed American defensive efforts as undermining MAD.) Reagan, who believed no leader should allow his country to be held hostage by another side's nuclear weapons, was searching for a way to get out of the MAD world; conservatives (who later hailed Reagan for winning the Cold War by rebuilding the American military) thought Reagan's beliefs about eliminating strategic nuclear weapons truly were mad.

Looking back on the Cold War and arguments about minimum deterrence, Columbia University professor Robert Jervis argues that he and others failed in their efforts to convince policy-makers of the virtue of their theory, because:

> leaders in both the United States and USSR had adopted a quite different view. The point is not that we were unable to persuade leaders of the validity of our views, but that as long as we could not our theories suffered a double empirical failure. Most obviously, the arguments could not explain why the states were seeking unnecessary nuclear weapons. Furthermore, as long as statesmen held to their benighted views, then nuclear superiority, 'objectively' meaningless as it was, could have great political influence.
>
> (2008: 573)

But this self-critique is too harsh. The arguments that Jervis, Brodie and others made were important because they were conceptually correct. And occasionally leaders such as Dwight Eisenhower, Nikita Khrushchev, Reagan, Gorbachev and Barack Obama have understood that they were correct, even if they have been constrained by the political limits they have faced. No leader can afford to look weak, and no academic can fully bridge the gap if the theory is right but the politics will not allow it. Understanding this gap not between academia and policy but between academia and politics can help explain the fortunes of policy-relevant theory, such as those articulated by academic realists and liberals in the aftermath of the Cold War.

## Realism and liberalism after the Cold War

Ever since the onset of the Cold War, realism has dominated the American academic field of security studies. Hans Morgenthau, Kenneth Waltz, John Mearsheimer and others working in this tradition focus on the sources of conflict in International Relations and seek to explain the recurring pattern of balance-of-power politics and the causes of war. For realists, the fundamental problem of international politics is the lack of any central authority. States seeking to survive operate in a self-help system. Leaders cannot escape this tragic system, but they can seek to employ the tools of statecraft to maintain and even improve their state's position. National security is paramount, and the worst sin is to squander state power.

For academic realists, therefore, the emergence of the unipolar world after the collapse of the Soviet Union meant that the United States could employ a policy of greater restraint, rather than greater activism. The most powerful country in the world could easily defend its interests when necessary and could deter attacks on its homeland in the face of nuclear-armed adversaries. Command of the global commons – air, sea and space – gave the United States enormous military advantages and ensured the operation of the free trade system that so benefited the American economy (Posen 2003).

Liberals, on the other hand, were in favour of greater activism. Liberalism, which during the Cold War was prominent in the field of International Political Economy, seeks to understand how the creation of certain institutional arrangements can foster cooperation and peace. Consolidated democracies with free market economies may find themselves with competitive interests, but history suggests that those liberal states don't go to war with one another (Doyle 1983, Levy 1989). And international institutions can help states achieve cooperation that is so difficult in an anarchic world by lessening their fears that others will take advantage of them.

After the Cold War, liberals saw tremendous opportunities. In the early 1980s, political scientist Michael Doyle had resurrected the theories of eighteenth-century philosopher Immanuel Kant to demonstrate why liberal states don't go to war with one another even if they go to war against illiberal states. In 1989, Francis Fukuyama suggested that the defeat of fascism and communism in the twentieth century left liberalism as the only viable model for political and economic organization, thus ushering in the 'End of History'. Meanwhile, international institutionalists, such as G. John Ikenberry (2008), argued that the United States, by serving as a liberal hegemon, had ensured that rising powers like China would find themselves better served by integrating into the existing international order rather than seeking to undermine it as the realists would predict.

Academic realists have argued that the United States should only use force to protect its core national interests, and thus, in their view, most wars since the Soviet collapse have been unnecessary. These scholars opposed American intervention in the Balkans in the 1990s, the 2003 war in Iraq, and the 2011 Libyan war. While they agreed on the need to topple the Taliban after the attacks of 11 September, they have supported scaling back in Afghanistan more recently and opposed Barack Obama's decision to send more troops in 2009–2010. In each case, policy-makers have ignored these realist scholars, and these academics have grown increasingly frustrated that their message on American national security has gone unheeded.

While realists have opposed a number of post-Cold War American interventions, they were most vociferous in rejecting the 2003 Iraq war. Leading scholars, including Robert Art, Richard Betts, Charles Glaser, Robert Jervis, John Mearsheimer, Barry Posen, Jack Snyder, Stephen Walt, and Kenneth Waltz, took out a full-page advertisement in the *New York Times* in September 2002 to make their case. They argued that while war was sometimes necessary, 'military force should be used only when it advances U.S. national interests'. War with Iraq, they declared, 'does not meet this standard'.

They rejected every argument the Bush administration was making. There was no clear link between Saddam Hussein and al-Qa'ida, and thus Iraq was not responsible for the 11 September attacks on New York and Washington DC. Even if Saddam Hussein had nuclear weapons, deterrence would prevail since both the United States and Israel had sufficient retaliatory capabilities. Even though the United States would win the war, the costs of occupation would be significantly high. And a war against Iraq would divert American attention away from the fight against al-Qa'ida.

Since Saddam Hussein did not have nuclear weapons, the realist belief in the robustness of deterrence never needed to be tested. But their other arguments all proved correct, and their most important warnings – that occupation would be costly (even more than they probably could have even imagined) and that attention was diverted from the war on terrorism – should have had major policy relevance. It was important that someone make those arguments. And yet, their belief that containment could work against Iraq as it had against the Soviet Union had no impact on Bush administration decision-making. Scholars did have something to say, but policy-makers ignored them at their peril. And in this case, the problem was not that the arguments were too abstract or involved too many mathematical formulas or were not written in an accessible manner. The problem was that in American politics after 9/11 there was pressure to act, and anyone opposing the war in Iraq was painted as soft on terror. A number of leading Senate Democrats had opposed the 1991 Persian Gulf War, and when that war proved successful, those individuals were unable to run for president because their national security credentials had been undermined. Senate Democrats were not going to make that mistake again in 2003, and thus the carefully developed scholarly arguments against the war faced an insurmountable challenge in convincing policy-makers not to go to war. (Ironically, those Democrats who did support the war in 2003 were at a disadvantage in the 2008 presidential election given the unpopularity of the conflict over time.)

The liberals also failed in Iraq because they promoted multilateralism and a United Nations process that the Bush administration ultimately ignored (after initially going to the world body to gain support). But in general after the collapse of communism, liberal arguments providing an explanation for a more orderly and hopeful international system have had a profound policy impact. The belief that democracies do not go to war with one another led the Clinton administration to develop the theme of 'Democratic Engagement and Enlargement'. First articulated by national security adviser Anthony Lake in September 1993, this approach suggested that having succeeded in containing and defeating communism, America now needed to enlarge the community of democracies, most notably in Central and Eastern Europe. Countries like Poland and Hungary that were forced to remain behind the Iron Curtain for four decades could now join the West, thereby providing the security and stability in Central Europe that was missing at the outset of World War I, World War II and the Cold War.

This theme has continued to resonate in succeeding administrations. Although the George W. Bush team entered office determined to bring a sense of realism and power politics back to American foreign policy (Rice 2000), the president abandoned that approach after 11 September and became a staunch advocate of what became known as the freedom agenda. The identification of an 'axis of evil' (Iran, Iraq and North Korea), the justification of the Iraq war as a means of removing a dictator (after the original rationale of preventing him from using weapons of mass destruction proved irrelevant since he did not possess them), and then Bush's declaration in his second inaugural address that America's goal was to rid the world of tyranny put democratization front and centre in the American foreign policy calculus.

After the debacle in Iraq, the Obama administration came into office preaching realism, arguing that the United States needed to go back to the approach of George H.W. Bush, who had overseen the end of the Cold War with deftness, managing German unification, the first Gulf War and the collapse of the Soviet Union. But despite the discrediting of both the neoconservatives and liberal interventionists who had supported the Iraq war, President Obama was pulled inexorably back to a more liberal declaration of the purposes of American foreign policy. The 2011 'Arab awakening' may have caught the United States off guard, but the administration was soon forced to support the protestors against authoritarian regimes, even when long-standing American allies such as Egypt and Saudi Arabia complained that they were being abandoned. And the threat of overwhelming civilian casualties in the Libyan city of Benghazi led President Obama to support a NATO-led military campaign to protect innocent civilians and (despite claims to the contrary) to topple Muammar Qaddafi from power.

Liberals are at a distinct advantage in American political discourse. The realists understand the tragedy of international politics, an understanding that resonates in continental Europe but not in a country that sees itself as a 'city on a hill'. As James Kurth (1998) has argued, it is no accident that the early post-World War II realists were either German (Morgenthau, Kissinger) or had decidedly continental European attitudes (George Kennan).

For Americans, international politics is about making the world a better place. The American public is proud of its role in the two World Wars and the Cold War. US leaders from both parties speak eloquently about the universal aspirations for freedom. American power is invisible to most Americans in the expansion of democracy and markets around the world, whereas others in the world recognize that it is American power that has promoted and sustained those liberal values. Liberal arguments about values resonate in American politics; realist arguments about power do not. Although Americans want to believe their leaders are using force to defend national interests, they are not comfortable talking about national interests; they typically prefer to see their leaders explain why America is making the world a better place.

Interestingly, the academic theories articulating why liberal states don't go to war with one another may have given rise to the centrality of democracy promotion in American foreign policy (and the president most associated historically with this notion was Woodrow Wilson, a former political scientist who was undoubtedly influenced by political theorist Immanuel Kant), but they have done little to prescribe to policy-makers exactly how they should go about effecting democratic change. Wars to depose autocratic regimes are only one (costly) way to produce democracies. Despite the large number of cases of democratization since World War II, there have been few studies that can provide the kind of conditional generalizations for democracy promotion that Alexander George sought to develop for issues such as deterrence and coercive diplomacy. An exception to this trend is the recent work of Michael McFaul (2010), who as a member of the Obama administration was able to bring his academic theories to bear directly on policy discussions of democratization in the Arab world (see also Carothers 1999).

## Conclusion

Although there are numerous reasons to be concerned with the gap between academia and policy, academics have long adapted their theoretical pursuits to help their audience understand major events or trends in world affairs (Hudson 2005: 13). During the Cold War, academics studied crisis prevention and crisis management, and the foreign policy field generated voluminous studies of the Korean and Vietnam wars, various Middle East crises, and, of course, the Cuban Missile Crisis (Paige 1968, Allison 1971, Snyder and Diesing 1977, Lebow 1982). In the 1990s, scholars debated the nature of the unipolar moment (Wohlforth 1999), and considered how balance-of-power politics might be changing. While Jentleson (2002) rightly decries the limited academic work that was done on terrorism before 11 September, 2001, there has been an explosion of studies on terrorism and the role of non-state actors in world affairs over the past decade.

There has also been an explosion of actors in world politics. We have well-developed theories about state behaviour. But how do we now incorporate new knowledge about new actors using new media to create new opportunities for societies to shape policy outcomes? The entire nature of world politics is changing dramatically before our eyes. Even though scholars have been arguing about the importance of non-state actors since the 1970s, our notions of world politics were largely based on our assessment of the number of dominant powers in any given era (see Chapter 11 this volume). The world was multipolar prior to 1945, bipolar during the Cold War, and unipolar in the 1990s. How should we think about world politics today? The United States is the dominant military power, but is only one of several leading economic powers. Meanwhile, state–society relations worldwide are undergoing dramatic transformations thanks to the information technology revolution. Policy-makers will be grappling for answers, and in some cases will not even know what questions to ask, and academics will only be able to help if scholarship keeps up with the frantic pace of change taking place in the world today.

Even in the midst of massive change, scholars can also help ground the discussions of current events by drawing on their knowledge of historical analogies. Policy-makers often use analogies with past events to help sort through the information they are using to make decisions. But drawing the wrong lessons from the past can be disastrous, as was the case with American policy-makers who drew from their experiences in the Korean War to make decisions about Vietnam, which was a civil war, not an interstate conflict, thus causing the analogy to fail (Khong 1992). As revolutions swept the Arab world, people quickly started reaching for historical comparisons: was this like Europe in 1989 or Europe in 1848? Scholars can use their knowledge to help shape understandings.

As we have seen, scholars may have good theories and valid prescriptions and still be ignored. Should those academics be seen as failures, as Jervis has suggested with respect to the case of minimum deterrence? Did the academic realists who opposed the 2003 Iraq war fail? Perhaps instead we should consider the cases of policy-maker failure. Leaders could easily have understood minimum deterrence arguments, just as they should have at least considered the arguments in opposition to the Iraq war. Bridging the gap is a two-way process. Academics need to be able to explain their reasoning to a policy audience uninterested in grand theory. But when they do, policy-makers need to incorporate that reasoning in their decision-making process. They may still make a decision that goes against the academic theories; but they will at least have gone through a process that takes advantage of multiple advocacy, inside government as well as outside.

But even if academics do not sway a policy debate, we should not judge them as failures. Making well-reasoned arguments that enhance our understanding of an issue is critical for a well-informed public debate. And over time, those arguments may come to permeate the discussion. But it is important to realize that when we talk about bridging the gap between academics and policy, we cannot ignore politics. Over the past twenty years, liberals in the United States have had an easier time getting their ideas put into practice because the politics favoured them. Democracy promotion was an easier sell in the United States than non-intervention. As the American public grows weary of war and is eager to engage in nation-building at home, those political winds may shift, but those winds are unlikely to shift too much. American political attitudes, and thus policy decisions, are shaped by the belief that the country has a special role to play in fostering universal values of freedom. Those beliefs are likely to shape outcomes in profound ways, and they will shape which academic ideas get adopted, and which do not.

## Further reading

Graham T. Allison, *Essence of Decision: Explaining the Cuban Missile Crisis* (HarperCollins, 1971). Allison showed that individuals working in the national security bureaucracy could rationally pursue their professional self-interest but damage the overall effort to produce a coherent and effective foreign policy decision.

Francis Fukuyama, 'The end of history?', *National Interest*, 16 (Summer 1989): 3–18. Fukuyama was one of the first scholars to try to make sense of the post-Cold War world and argued that liberalism would now prove unchallenged in world politics.

Alexander L. George, *Bridging the Gap: Theory and Practice In Foreign Policy* (US Institute of Peace Press, 1993). George spent his career developing policy-relevant academic research and distilled the fruits of his knowledge in this concise volume.

Samuel P. Huntington, 'The clash of civilisations', *Foreign Affairs*, 72(3) (1993): 22–49. One of the most famous political scientists of the twentieth century argued that the Western and Islamic worlds were destined for conflict.

Philip E. Tetlock, *Expert Political Judgment: How Good Is It? How Can We Know?* (Princeton University Press, 2005). A psychologist, Tetlock spent two decades surveying academics to learn how theory informs policy calculations.

## CONTENTS

# What Future for Security Studies?

Stuart Croft

### ▪ Abstract

In this chapter, students will learn about potential future directions for research within security studies. Security studies has most commonly been constructed as a sub-discipline of International Relations, but also exists as a transdisciplinary sub-field in which disparate research can connect over some common epistemological, methodological and empirical commitments. This chapter identifies the porous boundaries of both the sub-discipline – with its multiple mainstreams and character – and of the sub-field. In so doing, it shows how particular structures that we use to construct our work have themselves been constructed and the underlying patterns of power they reveal; and examines some of the many locations of work that could and should be of relevance to the future development of security studies.

## ▪ Introduction: Context and scope

Following so many chapters outlining the state of the art of contemporary security studies, a final chapter can take one of a variety of directions. It can look to summarize that which has gone before; it can look to synthesize those arguments into a new whole, or series of wholes; it can develop new and innovative strands of thought; it can review, endorse, and reject aspects of the preceding analysis. There are some elements of most of those approaches in that which follows. However, the key focus is in a different area; in thinking through intellectually where we find security studies in the panoply of academic enquiry; and consequently in examining its place in both 'disciplinary' and 'transdisciplinary' locations. Since such locations do not just form 'naturally,' I seek to examine some of the power structures that underlie those locations; and then, seek to identify some of the key intellectual opportunities that currently exist to develop work in security studies now and in the immediate future. In particular, not only are there issues within the various theories of security studies in motion and under development, but there are opportunities to engage across the disciplines in looking at new geographical concepts of space and time in relation to security, and in examining the role of memory in the construction of security, insecurity and post-security structures and discourses. I am not seeking here to be comprehensive in this commission; rather to engage the interest in particular directions.

## Locating security studies

This volume has demonstrated the breadth and variety of issues and approaches to contemporary security studies. It is and has been a sub-discipline of IR that is and has been constantly contested, and one that repeatedly reinvents itself. Security studies is a sub-discipline that is both embedded within the main discipline of IR, and increasingly also a sub-field that is multidisciplinary, in the sense of being driven by the intellectual agendas of disciplines other than IR. It is also a sub-discipline that ranges in focus from detailed policy prescription for governments, to philosophical statements on the nature of 'reality'.

Security studies has been, overwhelmingly, an American sub-discipline, dominated by a series of major debates (in the sense that they have been frequently cited) between key figures. True, not all of those figures have been American by birth or even by citizenship; there has been a significant European strand. But the size of the American intellectual market has been such that the sub-discipline has been largely one in which North American concerns have been in the ascendancy. One of the stories that those in security studies (that is, those who are connected to the discipline of IR) tell about themselves is that it has been a sub-discipline that has 'evolved' in a fairly linear way (for a critique, see Smith 1999). Three steps can be identified in that contemporary narration of the sub-discipline.

The first step is in seeing security studies as having evolved from strategic studies, in which security was defined in a 'narrow' fashion: it was in essence about states, and about the military nature of insecurity. Thus, the myth has developed that security during the Cold War was 'simpler,' as something

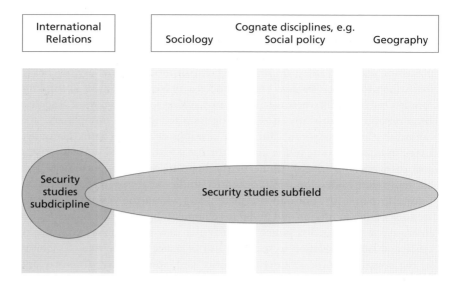

| International Relations | Cognate disciplines, e.g. | | |
| --- | --- | --- | --- |
| | Sociology | Social policy | Geography |

*Figure 37.1* Security studies as a subfield and subdiscipline

approaching nostalgia for those times has come to be the conventional wisdom in media and other circles, being regularly deployed as a straightforward rhetorical device. Charles Norchi, for instance, wrote in the *New York Times* that 'When the cold war was hot, life seemed simpler,' and Ian Thomsen wrote in the *International Herald Tribune* that 'Everything was simpler in the cold war for Americans' (Norchi 1998, Thomsen 1996). Contemporary complexity is defined and legitimized by an evolutionary metaphor: the present must be more complex than the past. Yet the flood of recent re-examinations of the Cold War period by historians would not support such a recasting of it as a period of simplicity (Gaddis 2006, LaFeber 2006, Ambrose 2006, Levering 2005).

The second step in the conventional telling of the security studies story is a period at the end of the Cold War when simplicity gave way to complexity. That complexity abroad – wars in the former Yugoslavia, genocide in Rwanda, stand-off in the Gulf, nuclear weapons development in South Asia – was matched by a debate over the broadening and widening of security studies as a sub-discipline. After a period of contestation, in which realists sought to maintain the 'narrow' definition, now there were to be a variety of referents for security – society, humanity, the individual – as well as the state, and a variety of sectors of security – economic, political, societal, environmental – to go alongside the military (above all see Buzan, Wæver and de Wilde 1998). In addition, scholars fought their own 'Cold War' as first neorealists and neoliberals fought over the meaning of security (largely in the pages of the journal *International Security* – see, for example, Jervis 1999, Waltz 2000), and then constructivists successfully struggled to become part of the (American) scholarly security studies mainstream (see the debate between Mearsheimer 1994 and Wendt 1995, also see Copeland 2006).

In the third and current phase of developments in security studies, scholars have sought to come to terms with the terrorist attacks on New York and Washington D.C. in September 2001. This has been constructed as marking the new phase of international relations and international security. Reflecting this new turn, Chris Seiple (2002: 261) argued that 'As in the early Cold War, the next five years are likely to establish patterns of global engagement and international relations that will define the next *fifty* years.' This phase emphasizes the 'newness' of issues in security studies – the novelty of mass/global terrorism, or of religion as a factor in international security. Whereas in the 1990s, the focus was on increasing the numbers of issues that could be considered under the rubric of 'security' those issues had been largely agreed upon from 2001, and in this more recent period there has been an additional and new focus towards terrorism/counter terrorism.

This 'evolution' of the sub-field appears relatively natural; but it is of course based on a construction of meanings rather than some form of independent process, in which the power to label issues and approaches as significant has been key to those developments. There has not been an 'evolution' in the sense that theories have become more sophisticated and robust. These self-images of the sub-discipline receive their authority from their repetition and reproduction in texts and in class. Yet, as familiar as this might be as a way of understanding the 'evolution' of the sub-field to those who see IR as their main discipline, it does not speak to many others who now consider themselves to be working in that sub-field of security studies. It is the case that security studies can now be found in a variety of disciplines. In sociology, where scholars examine the nature of othering and the responsibilities of cosmopolitan commitments; and in the sociology of science, the beliefs and patterns in various elite communities, such as weapons scientists. In social policy and development studies, research is conducted into relations of violence between groups, focusing on giving voice to the silenced. Such anthropological methodology – living with communities, as well as focus groups and other means of gaining insight from those beyond the governing state elite – can also be found in geography and area studies, where scholars investigate local patterns of relations throughout the world. In economics, research into arms trade patterns and probabilities of societies repeating patterns of civil violence can be found; in architecture and urban studies, work has been undertaken into how the physical environment communicates messages and affects patterns of (violent) behaviour amongst urban communities in specific places, such as Jerusalem. And of course in political science and philosophy, problems of security studies are subjected to normative theorizing, to understand the ethical commitments of various participants.

Security studies is thus now located across a variety of disciplines, although certainly the work emanating from IR still tends to predominate. It represents a vital and fluid series of areas of research, informed by a variety of theoretical and epistemological positions, but one also deeply rooted in contemporary debates about physical and structural (or symbolic) violence. In this context, two particular themes stand out. First, in terms of 'security studies – the sub-field,' one of the most dynamic areas of multidisciplinary research concerns the relationships of security, culture, images and identity. Second, in terms of 'security studies – the sub-discipline,' one of the most significant features of contemporary debate is the split between two forms of theorizing: that contained in the realism/liberalism/constructivism triangle, and the other based in various forms of critical engagement. They are reproduced in two different 'mainstreams,' that seem to have few points of contact in the contemporary research debate.

## Future directions in the sub-field

Security studies has opened up to insights from cognate disciplines in the social sciences, humanities and arts in significant ways. Beginning in the late 1990s, cultural factors became worthy of discussion in the sub-discipline (Katzenstein 1996, Duffield *et al.* 1999). This 'cultural turn' was initially a relatively 'thin' one, focusing on issues such as strategic culture and organizational culture, and in particular trying from within the discipline of IR to explain key disciplinary problems (if all units are alike, why do behaviours differ markedly?). From there, however, it was a relatively small step to introduce insights from cultural studies, anthropology, literary studies, film studies as well as gender into a 'thicker' cultural conception of security. Or, rather, security issues examined in those and other disciplines were suddenly read as relevant by some scholars who identified with the study of IR. A good deal of such development took place outside the United States, facilitated in particular by the moves to common understandings across many disciplines facilitated by shared readings of authors that spoke across traditional disciplinary boundaries: Habermas, Adorno, Horkheimer, Foucault, Derrida, Lyotard, Bourdieu. However, with the centrality of norm, identity and history construction at the centre of constructivist research projects, the broadening of interest in cultural and other factors became of widespread interest in the sub-discipline.

This focus on discourses is of course contested within the discipline of IR. But it allows analysts to understand how particular policy directions can become the norm at certain times and in certain places; the ways in which cultural practices play central roles in contemporary security studies (see Williams, M. 2007). Issues in international security are not only dealt with by governments. Common understandings are created in, with, and through wider society. Popular understandings of policy positions are constructed not only by the statements of leaders and media coverage. Debates about security can be found more widely in the media and popular culture. For example, Eric Lurio wrote a review of *The Last Samurai* arguing that the film 'is evil. Why? Ideology. The villains are the heroes and the heroes villains. Screenwriters . . . have created a profoundly reactionary and anti-American tale where ancient oppressors are seen as saintly, and those who favor democracy and liberation awful fiends . . . The sad part is that the film is sooooooo well done that it'll hurt America's international situation by giving aid and comfort to those who long to go back to the days of 1970s Bulgaria' (Lurio 2006). Such statements are important in the reproduction of shared understandings of the world across society, legitimizing the commitments of political elites. Not only do cultural representations form a context for political communication within countries, they also do so between states. For example, when the film *300* was released in the United States, it sparked popular fury in Iran. *300* narrates a (largely fictional) version of the Battle of Thermopylae between the Spartans and Persians in 480 BC. Its contemporary relevance was the reading that Persia is Iran; that the historically inaccurate construction of the two enemy societies (the film shows Spartans as free rather than slave-owning, the Persians as slave-owning rather than free . . .) is a means of dehumanizing the new (Iranian) American enemy; that *300* is part of a social campaign, preparing Americans and the West for a real war (Moaveni 2007, Mendelsohn 2007).

Examining cultural representations of security studies is particularly prominent in contemporary research on the 'war on terror' (see Martin and Petro 2006, Croft 2006). This is part of a new focus on the 'lived' or 'everyday' experience where reflection upon an experience that individuals have undergone constitutes a core element of their understanding of the world. Some lived experience may reveal a great sense of security; arguably, it was the sense that everyday security had been breached that co-constituted the powerful social shock of 9/11 in the United States and in other developed countries. As John Lewis Gaddis (2004: 80) put it, 'It was not just the Twin Towers that collapsed on that morning of September, 11 2001: so too did some of our most fundamental assumptions about international, national, and personal security.' The shock to the lived experience of Americans – and not only those in New York and Washington D.C. – dramatically inscribed socially a new security reality. Or as M. Shahid Alam put it, 9/11 was like 'an eruption, a volcanic eruption that has thrust lava and ashes from our netherworld, the dark netherworld of the Periphery, into the rich and tranquil landscape of America' (Alam 2004). This is not to argue that the developed world is a Kantian one, and the developing world a Hobbesian one (or that there are variations based on 'Mars' and 'Venus': see Elden and Bialasiewicz 2006). The developed world has its own range of insecurities, based on gender, ethnicity and class; processes of actual and of symbolic violence. Rather it is to suggest that shocks to lived experience can in security terms be powerful in reconstituting expectations.

Research that focuses on the lived experience includes that on war crimes tribunals, which rely on the eyewitness testimony of those whose lived experience has involved them in crimes against humanity as victims or as perpetrators (Gow 2003). In a similar vein, important work has been conducted on understanding, for example, how those on the receiving end of peacekeeping missions interact with their 'protectors'. That involves an anthropological commitment to working and living with those communities, both those who live in the country and with the peacekeepers themselves in the country, and to a methodology of conducting fieldwork that allows individuals to speak in their own voice (Higate 2004, Pouligny 2006). The same commitment can be seen by those working with women in political post-conflict communities, allowing groups to speak to security in their own words (Hamber *et al.* 2006). In terms of seeking to mobilize support for a particular cause, organizations seek to include their donors, to inscribe in them an experience (*Live Earth*, for example) that will shape their commitments for the future. It is possible to extend this sense of the lived experience. *Eyes on Darfur*, for example, is an Amnesty International project that uses satellite imagery to show the impact of violence in Sudan on the lives of the people in particular villages under threat (see www.eyesondarfur.org/villages.html). The method is to extend the lived experience from villager to internet user, to bring in more involvement from those not immediately involved in the conflict, but whose involvement can be developed virtually.

These considerations raise in significance the geographical dimension of security studies. Once, geography and international security were intimately connected, with the study of geopolitics made most famous by Halford Mackinder, who argued in 1904 that the Eurasian 'heartland' could only be offset by a combination of the maritime powers, a theory that connected with the work on seapower by Alfred Mahan. Such traditional geopolitics still has its advocates in contemporary strategic studies. But in parallel, a new focus in geography has developed in critical geopolitics (Ó Tuathail 1996). In this light, acts of representation and modes of narration, based on and mutually constituted by geopolitical cultures, become central. Here, geographical knowledge is deployed and reformulated in the interests of furthering particular political projects (Bialasiewicz *et al.* 2007). Gearóid Ó Tuathail (2000) has written of the 'Postmodern Geopolitical Condition', and here the work on critical geopolitics intersects with a wider sub-field in geography, that which is known as postmodern geography. In that wider sub-field, subjectivity, identity, representation and practice are key. Nigel Thrift gives full expression to this in a discussion of 'Space' which is seen to have four characteristics: that everything is spatially distributed, everything has 'its own geography'; that there are no boundaries, that all spaces are porous; all spaces are in constant motion; and that 'there is no one kind of space' (Thrift 2006: 140–141). If spatiality is not fixed (and as a consequence, Thrift argues against the view 'space [is] somehow separated from time'), the implications for thinking about the nature of security studies are profound.

Security studies at its core is concerned with a level of reality about which there is no epistemological argument. The collapse of security leads to real violence against real people, to acts of brutality that lie without any discussions of relativism. Powerful stories of loss are global in their reach. Of the numerous potent tales, the Kigali Memorial Centre, which commemorates those lost in the Rwandan genocide, holds many (www.kigalimemorialcentre.org/). These histories, perhaps particularly those of whom we learn in the children's room, are unbearable. We see photographs of the murdered, and in so doing learn of Uwase, a two-year-old whose favourite toy was her doll, who loved rice and chips, and whose best friend was her daddy. She was killed by being smashed against a wall. And then there was David Mugiraneza, a ten-year-old boy who loved football and wanted to be a doctor. He was killed by being tortured to death. When we debate security studies, we should remember Uwase; we should remember David.

Questions of political violence have never been the monopoly of IR, or indeed of the discipline/combined disciplines of political science and IR. The 'construction of the Holocaust as the central event of the twentieth century' (Kansteiner 2004: 193) has had many political and ethical consequences. One is that it is hard to find any self-defined discipline in the social sciences, arts and humanities that has not at some level engaged with the Holocaust and, therefore, with that and other issues of political violence. Perhaps, as discourses of justice, ethics, responsibility, revulsion and indeed revenge have developed following events such as the Rwandan genocide, the Yugoslav wars, the 'war on terror' and the violence in Darfur (to name but a few), issues of war and violence have become increasingly and more deeply examined by other disciplines. As IR becomes more open to other disciplines, it is clear that important new avenues of research are opening up. For example, the growth in memory studies provides opportunities for developing studies looking at the means by which memory issues affect security (from within the sub-discipline, a key text of this is Edkins 2003). Indeed, it could be argued that memory is crucial in the construction of a sense of belonging, of where we come from and where we are going, that it is at the heart of all identity debates and, as such, that should be at the heart of security studies. (This is not to argue that memory is objectively created; there are processes of the social construction of memory.) There has been a 'memory boom' in so many disciplines across the social sciences and the humanities (Huyssen 1994); it will inevitably interconnect with work on security studies. The role of memory in questions of political violence can connect those in IR with colleagues in literary studies, psychology, sociology, media studies, and a range of other disciplines. But in so doing, scholars need to take care with regard to deeply engrained arguments that exist in and between different disciplines over core concepts. For example, is trauma and its consequences – victimhood and entitlement – part of the everyday experience of human communication? Or does trauma imply 'the occurrence of some serious real or imagined injury with long-term psychological, political and moral consequences' (Kansteiner 2004)? These issues may seem some distance from international security; but given that the key 'case' surrounding such debates is the Holocaust, it is clear that they are not.

There is, then, an ongoing process of developing security studies as a sub-field, in a multidisciplinary fashion. Of course, for many years that has already been the case, in particular under the rubric of area studies. In the future, many sites of such transdisciplinary cooperation seem possible; with perhaps the organizing devices of spatiality and memory providing the most immediate, and the commitment to researching the lived experience of those affected by (in)securities.

## Future directions in the sub-discipline

There will be many in the IR sub-discipline of security studies who will simply see much of the discussion above as being irrelevant to them; that issues of space (including time) and memory are simply not matters of international security. For such colleagues, disciplinary power is the key, and that disciplinary power resides in the academic mainstream. Much of that mainstream is defined in, through and by the American intellectual market; what can be published in the mainstream US journals and academic publishing houses, and therefore what is likely to sell to the mass audience courses in American universities. Thus, a scholar outside North America is likely to be asked by a possible book publisher to consider how his/her volume might be seen to be attractive in that US market place. It is an economic (but also socially constructed) 'reality'. And so a mainstream is constructed towards which scholarship must be oriented to count as being at the heart of a discipline. A discipline, sub-discipline or sub-field is, of course, itself socially constructed, as are the main components of each, and as are those texts that are seen to be central to the definition of that intellectual terrain. In this way, that which is seen to be 'core' or 'mainstream' security studies is driven by social factors.

In terms of the sub-disciplinary mainstream, then, it is clear that one future avenue lies with the development of particular projects. That mainstream is not and never has been static; it is always in motion. Thus, contemporary research considers the international relations of neoconservatism (Nuruzzaman, 2006); or develops particular nuances on existing theoretical frames, for example, the development of 'offensive realism' (Mearsheimer 200). As well as developing nuances and incremental alterations in particular theoretical veins, the mainstream has been, and is likely to continue to be, shaped by 'great debates.' There is a long history of how many 'great debates' there have been in IR scholarship – it is one of the self-images of the discipline. In terms of the security studies mainstream, we have seen a great debate in the 1990s between realism and liberalism; and then a great debate in which realism and liberalism (the 'neo-neo' synthesis) debated whether constructivism could be part of that mainstream (or, rather, what form of constructivism could be seen to be recognized as such). Famously, the Fiftieth Anniversary edition of *International Organization* contained an editorial in which constructivism was legitimized as a part of IR (even in its 'critical' guise), but postmodernism was not. As Katzenstein, Keohane and Krasner (1998: 678) asserted, in 'contrast to conventional and critical constructivism, postmodernism falls clearly outside of the social science enterprise, and in international relations research it risks becoming self-referential and disengaged from the world, protests to the contrary notwithstanding.' One of the functions of the widely cited 'Seizing the middle ground: constructivism in world politics' (Adler 1997) was to distinguish constructivism from the (unacceptable) postmodernist turn in IR, thus making constructivism's entry into the (American) mainstream easier. One of the functions of Wendt's *Social Theory of International Politics* was to consolidate a methodological legitimacy (in the eyes of the US mainstream) for constructivism (Wendt 1999). Realist acceptance came with Stephen Walt's 'International Relations: One World, Many Theories' article, which included a graphic showing the three pillars of the international relations/international security house to be realism, liberalism and constructivism (Walt 1998: 38). That, then, creates a new 'neo/neo/neo' synthesis in some ways, in terms of a mainstream that is self-referential and acts to exclude other modes of thought. Perhaps the nuances of those positions will be battled out in the future over which theory can most adequately explain the importance of religion/religious forces in world politics and security studies.

The mainstream is always in motion both in terms of the developments of individual theoretical streams and in terms of the patterns of contestation between different theories. But in constituting a mainstream, it creates boundaries between it and the 'non-mainstream'. Following Thrift, we should not over-emphasize the solidity of these boundaries; there is a porosity which allows for interaction. But this distinction between the mainstream and that outside is constituted in a variety of ways; an article may be written for *International Security* or for *Security Dialogue*; it is unlikely that there is a piece that could without amendment straddle both. The nature of security studies panels is very different at the *American Political Science Association* conference in relation to the *Standing Group on International Relations of the European Consortium on Political Research* conference. And so on. Security studies continues to operate in different ways inside and outside American circles (see most famously on this Wæver 1998).

One way in which there is some porosity between the mainstream and that outside is where particular ideas/schools/writers are taken up outside their defined territory. Thus it would be quite normal for American scholars, or American journals, to refer to securitization theory/the Copenhagen School/Ole Wæver. Awareness, however, does not constitute acceptance in the mainstream. But if we are to consider another 'mainstream' – that outside the United States – it is very clear that securitization theory/the Copenhagen School/Ole Wæver is about as mainstream as it is possible to get. Thus, the sub-discipline of security studies is overlaid with many mainstreams: differently global, differently regional and sometimes differently national, with porosity between all.

The non-American English language sub-discipline of security studies comprises a mainstream of four distinctive theoretical constructs. (I am here resisting the temptation to describe this as the 'European mainstream', but will shortly give ground to that.) Each seeks to be 'critical' in some form. Thus, we have a 'critical quadrangle' of the Copenhagen School; the Welsh School; the Paris School; and the human security school. Intriguingly from a critical geopolitics perspective, most seek to attach a geographical label, except for 'human security'. On the one hand, this labelling refers simply to where sets of ideas were generated: in debates in Copenhagen, Aberystwyth, and Paris respectively. It also covers each with some of the reflected legitimacy of the labelling of the 'English School' of IR (recalling that many in that school were not English). It also marks each as being critical in the sense of being non-American in origin and nature (see Van Munster 2007).

The 'critical quadrangle' comprises four theoretical perspectives each with one key 'brand' in terms of the intellectual debate. For the Copenhagen School, the brand is securitization (see Chapter 5 this volume). This focuses on a specific rhetorical structure, in which an issue is identified as threatening survival, requiring a response to be urgent, outside of the norm, and that the 'audience' has to be convinced. In such an approach, existential threats, and thus securitizing moves, can be found in sectors other than the military. Hence the Copenhagen School focuses on the politics of the exception. The Paris School in contrast focuses on the politics of unease, on the ordinary rather than the exceptional in policy practice (see Chapter 9 this volume). Here the brand is insecuritization (*insécurisation*), a process by which elites and government authority lower the threshold of acceptability of others; a means by which external threat and internal life are connected through policies over terror and migration, enacted by the police, border officials, and judiciary; where a variety of discourses are connected into a patchwork of insecurities allowing the transfer of practices from one policy frame to another (Bigo 1995, 2005). For the Welsh School, as Ken Booth first stated powerfully 15 years ago, the leitmotif is emancipation; indeed, security is emancipation (Booth 1991a, Chapter 7 this volume). Emancipation is therefore the goal of security practice (Booth ed. 2005). Rather than stressing the role of speech acts or the role of state agencies, securitization or insecuritization, the Welsh School would place individuals at the centre of security studies. Finally, there is a fragmented body of literature committed to achieving 'human security' (Newman 2001, Chapter 19 this volume). Perhaps the very fragmentation of that work has been a result of the lack of geographical signifier, allowing a greater access to the use of the term than is the case with 'Copenhagen', 'Welsh' or 'Paris'. Rather like the Welsh School, though, the commitment is to the individual level of security, and so perhaps the term that best sums up the 'brand' of the human security school is 'humanization'.

So here are the four brand concepts of the 'critical quadrangle': securitization; insecuritization; emancipation; and humanization. There is often a determination to identify this 'critical quadrangle' in contradistinction to American thought, and in some ways as a contribution to the construction of a European mode of thinking (Case Collective 2006). But of course such ideas as those discussed here can be found in other parts of the non-European but English speaking world, notably in Australia and in terms of human security, Canada. Rather like the 'other' 'American' mainstream, the 'critical quadrangle' mainstream is also dominated by two different forms of theoretical development. Each of the four theories has scholars engaged in the development of the particular theoretical perspectives themselves. And in addition, a new literature is emerging in which 'bridges' between the four are identified and explored (e.g. Floyd 2007, Browning and McDonald 2007).

Perhaps one of the key distinguishing features, however, of the 'critical quadrangle' in relation to the 'American' mainstream is scale. There are enormous numbers of scholars who would see themselves as contributing to the US mainstream; many in terms of theoretical development, many more as 'technicians,' implementing a template from one of the theoretical perspectives in relation to a particular case study. In contrast, the number of scholars in the Copenhagen, Welsh, or Paris schools is far fewer. In part that reflects the size of the 'IR industry' in North America in relation to others; in part it reflects the exclusionary dimension of a geographical label (if I am not based in department x in city/town y, can I really be a part of the school? What is the mechanism of being included?). And perhaps partly it reflects the relative unwillingness of scholars in Europe to site themselves in particular intellectual spaces. In addition, one of the key distinctions between these two particular mainstreams is that the one labeled 'American' tends to emphasize methodology, while that which sometimes labels itself as 'European' demonstrates a greater interest in epistemology.

## Security studies, porous boundaries and the struggle for coherence

There are many directions to the future of security studies. Some will be within the sub-discipline, within particular theories, and as scholars seek to understand and construct intellectual linkages between theories. As well as development within the sub-discipline, there will undoubtedly continue to be linkages between the sub-discipline and other disciplines, as the sub-field of security studies continues with processes of connection. These boundaries are of course all constructs, and as such, can and will be reconstituted. We seek to encapsulate sets of ideas through labels and categories – as I have in this chapter – when there is so much porosity, so much fluidity, and so much contestation between those ideas and their advocates. The desire to impose order on this is evident in this volume. Indeed, this is a recurrent theme in security studies – the production of volumes that seek to encapsulate the intellectual range of work that can be described as 'security studies'. This book stands as one contribution. The International Studies Association's 'Compendium' project seeks to impose some form of order on all the sub-fields of IR, with a series of volumes – including one on security studies – to be produced from 2008 onwards. There have been a variety of other examples over the years (e.g. Collins 2007, Terriff *et al.* 1999). This desire for codification is in part driven by teaching needs: if we are not able to set some boundaries around security studies, how might we teach it? And yet, again following Thrift, this is a process that can at best only provide a snapshot of thinking and research at a particular point in space and time. That which comprises security studies is always in motion in space – within the 'American' and 'European' mainstreams, and between those and other 'places' of research – and time, as issues rise and fall in importance in academic, policy and public discourses, demanding or resisting attention. And the boundaries between security studies and other areas are always porous, thus allowing the construction of new forms of thinking about these issues; or at least, in allowing that sense of 'newness' to be shared by a number of likeminded researchers. Security – as with so many social concepts – is an essentially contested concept (Buzan 1991: 7). Perhaps, then, we should embrace the fluidity of debate, and worry less about the importance of encapsulating the social reality of security studies.

# References

ABC Australia (2011), 'Defiant Qaddafi issues chilling call', *ABC* (Australia), 23 February.

Abraham, Itty (1998), *The Making of the Indian Atomic Bomb* (London: Zed Books).

Abrahamsen, Rita and Michael C. Williams (2009), 'Security beyond the state', *International Political Sociology*, 3(1): 1–17.

Acharya, Amitav (2000), *The Quest for Identity. International Relations of Southeast Asia* (Oxford: Oxford University Press).

Acharya, Amitav (2001), 'Human security: East versus West', *International Journal*, LVI(3): 442–60.

Acharya, Amitav and Alastair I. Johnston (eds.) (2007), *Crafting Cooperation* (Cambridge: Cambridge University Press).

Adamsky, Dima (2010), *The Culture of Military Innovation* (Stanford: Stanford University Press).

Adelman, Howard (2001), 'From refugees to forced migration: The UNHCR and human security', *International Migration Review*, 35(1): 7–32.

Adger, Neil, Irene Lorenzoni and Karen O'Brien (eds.) (2009), *Adapting to Climate Change* (Cambridge: Cambridge University Press).

Adler, Emmanuel (1997), 'Seizing the middle ground: constructivism in world politics', *European Journal of International Relations*, 3(3): 319–63.

Adler, Emanuel and Michael Barnett (eds.) (1998), *Security Communities* (Cambridge: Cambridge University Press).

AFP (Associated Press Francais) (2010), 'UN says United States owes 1.2 billion dollars', 14 October, at www.alternet.org/rss/breaking_news/299453/un_says_united_states__owes_1.2_billion_dollars/comments/

Aid, Matthew M. (2009), *The Secret Sentry: The Untold History of the National Security Agency* (London: Bloomsbury).

Alam, M. Shahid (2004), 'Making sense of our times: Is there an Islamic problem?', *The Electronic Intifada*, 14 October, at http://electronicintifada.net/cgi-bin/artman/exec/view.cgi/10/3231

Albright, David and Corey Hinderstein (2005), 'Unravelling the A.Q. Khan and future proliferation networks', *Washington Quarterly*, 28(2): 111–28.

Albro, Robert (2010), 'Writing culture doctrine: public anthropology, military policy, and world making', *Perspectives on Politics*, 8(4): 1087–93.

Aldrich, Richard J. (2002), *Hidden Hand: Britain, America and Cold War Secret Intelligence* (New York: Overlook).

Aldrich, Richard J. (2009a), 'US–European intelligence co-operation on counter-terrorism: low politics and constraint', *British Journal of Politics and International Relations*, 11(1): 122–40.

Aldrich, Richard J. (2009b), 'Beyond the vigilant state? Globalization and intelligence', *Review of International Studies*, 35(4): 889–902.

Alexander, Martin S. and J. F. V. Keiger (2002), 'France and the Algerian War: strategy, operations and diplomacy', *Journal of Strategic Studies*, 25(2): 1–33.

Alker, Hayward (2005), 'Emancipation in the Critical Security Studies Project' in Ken Booth (ed.), *Critical Security Studies and World Politics* (Boulder, CO: Lynne Rienner), pp. 189–213.

Alkire, Sabina (2002), 'Conceptual framework for the Commission on Human Security', at www.humansecurity-chs.org/doc/frame.html

Allison, Graham (1971), *Essence of Decision: Explaining the Cuban Missile Crisis* (New York: HarperCollins).

Allison, Graham (1999), *Essence of Decision: Explaining the Cuban Missile Crisis*, 2nd edition (New York: Longman).

Allison, Graham (2000), 'The impact of globalization on national and international security' in J.S. Nye and J.D. Donahue (eds.), *Governance in a Globalizing World* (Washington, DC: Brookings Institution Press), pp. 72–85.

Allison, Graham (2006), 'Nuclear 9/11: The ongoing failure of imagination', *Bulletin of Atomic Scientists*, 62(5): 34–41.

Allison, Roy (ed.) (2004), 'Regionalism and the changing international order in Central Eurasia', Special Issue, *International Affairs*, 80(3).

Alston, Philip (ed.) (1992), *The United Nations and Human Rights* (Oxford: Oxford University Press).

Ambrose, Stephen E, *et al.* (2006), *The Cold War: A Military History* (New York: Random House).

Amoore, Louise and Marieke De Goede (2005), 'Governance, risk and dataveillance in the war on terror', *Crime, Law and Social Change* 43: 149–73.

Andreas, Peter (2000), *Border Games: Policing the U.S.–Mexico Divide* (Ithaca, NY: Cornell University Press).

Andreas, Peter (2003), 'Redrawing borders and security in the 21st Century', *International Security*, 28(2): 78–111.

Andrew, Christopher (1995), *For the President's Eyes Only: Secret Intelligence and the American Presidency from Washington to Bush* (London: HarperCollins).

Andrew, Christopher M. (2004), 'Intelligence, international relations and "under-theorisation"' in Len V. Scott and Peter Jackson (eds.), *Understanding Intelligence in the Twenty-First Century* (London: Routledge), pp. 29–41.

Andrew, Christopher M. and Julie Elkner (2003), 'Stalin and foreign intelligence', *Totalitarian Movements and Political Religions*, 4(1): 69–94.

Andrew, Christopher M, Richard J. Aldrich and Wesley Wark (eds.) (2009), *Secret Intelligence: A Reader* (London: Routledge).

Andrews-Speed, Philip, Xuanli Liao and Roland Dannreuther (2002), *The Strategic Implications of China's Energy Needs* (Oxford: Oxford University Press for the IISS, Adelphi Paper No. 346).

Annan, Kofi (1997), *Renewing the United Nations: a Programme for Reform* (New York: United Nations).

Annan, Kofi (1999a), 'The relevance of the U.N. Security Council', in *Vital Speeches of the Day*, 65(17), 15 June.

Annan, Kofi (1999b), *Annual Report of the Secretary-General to the United Nations General Assembly* (UN doc. A/54/429).

Annan, Kofi (1999c), *The Question of Intervention: Statements by the Secretary-General* (New York: UN).

Annan, Kofi (2001), *Prevention of Armed Conflict: Report of the Secretary-General* (UN doc. A/55/985-S/2001/574).

Annan, Kofi (2005), *In Larger Freedom: Towards Development, Security and Human Rights for All* (UN doc. A/59/2005, 21 March).

Anthony, Ian (1989), 'The trade in major conventional weapons', in *SIPRI Yearbook 1989* (Oxford: SIPRI/Oxford University Press), pp. 195–210.

Aradau, Claudia, Luis Lobo-Guerrero and Rens Van Munster (2008), 'Security, technologies of risk, and the political', *Security Dialogue*, 39(2–3): 147–54.

Aron, Raymond (1978), 'War and industrial society: a reappraisal', *Millennium*, 7(3): 195–210.

ASCI (AIDS, Security and Conflict Initiative) (2009), *HIV/AIDS, Security and Conflict: New Realities, New Responses*. ASCI Final Report, at http://asci.researchhub.ssrc.org/rdb/asci-hub

Ash, Timothy Garton (2002), 'The peril of too much power', *New York Times*, 9 April.

Ashdown, Lord Paddy (2006), 'Interview: The European Union and statebuilding in the Western Balkans', *Journal of Intervention and Statebuilding*, 1(1): 107–18.

Autesserre, Severine (2010), *The Trouble with the Congo* (Cambridge: Cambridge University Press).

Avant, Deborah (2005), *The Market for Force: The Consequences of Privatizing Security* (Cambridge: Cambridge University Press).

Axelrod, Robert (1984), *The Evolution of Cooperation* (New York: Basic Books).

Axworthy, Lloyd (2001), 'Human security and global governance: putting people first', *Global Governance*, 7(1): 19–23.

Aylwin-Foster, Brigadier Nigel (2005), 'Changing the army for counterinsurgency', *Military Review*, (Nov.–Dec.): 2–15.

Ayoob, Mohammed (1995), *The Third World Security Predicament* (Boulder, CO: Lynne Rienner).

Bahree, Bhushan and Chip Cummins (2006), 'Thwarted attack at Saudi facility stirs energy fears', *Wall Street Journal*, 25–26 February.

Bailey, Sydney and Sam Daws (1998), *The Procedure of the UN Security Council*, 3rd edition (Oxford: Clarendon Press).

Baldaccini, Anneliese and Elspeth Guild (2007), *Whose Freedom, Security and Justice?* (London: Hart Publishing).

Baldwin, David A. (ed.) (1993), *Neorealism and Neoliberalism* (New York: Columbia University Press).

Balibar, Etienne (2003), 'Outlines of a topography of cruelty: citizenship and civility in the era of global violence', *Constellations*, 8(1): 15–29.

Balzacq, Thierry (2010), *Securitization Theory* (London: Routledge).

Balzacq, Thierry *et al.* (2009), 'Security practices', in Robert A. Denemark (ed.), *International Studies Online Encyclopedia* (Blackwell).

Bamberger, Robert (2007), *Energy Policy: Conceptual Framework and Continuing Issues* (Washington, DC: Congressional Research Service, 7 March).

Ban Ki-moon (2008), 'Responsible sovereignty: international cooperation for a changed world', speech given in Berlin, (UN doc. SG/SM/11701, 15 July).

Ban Ki-moon (2009), *Report of the Secretary-General, Implementing the Responsibility to Protect* (UN doc. A/63/677, 12 January).

Banks, Jeffrey S. (1990), 'Equilibrium behavior in crisis bargaining games', *American Journal of Political Science*, 34(3): 599–614.

Barash, David P. (ed.) (2000), *Approaches to Peace* (Oxford: Oxford University Press).

Barash, David, P. (ed.) (2011), *Approaches to Peace: A Reader in Peace Studies*, 2nd edition (Oxford: Oxford University Press).

Barash, David P. and Charles P. Webel (2002), *Peace and Conflict Studies* (Thousand Oaks, CA: Sage).

Bar-Joseph, Uri and Rose McDermott (2008), 'Change the analyst and not the system: a different approach to intelligence reform', *Foreign Policy Analysis*, 4(2): 127–45.

Barkawi, Tarak (2004), 'On the pedagogy of "small wars"', *International Affairs*, 80(1): 19–38.

Barkawi, Tarak (2006), *Globalization and War* (Lanham, MD: Rowman and Littlefield).

Barkawi, Tarak (2011), 'From war to security: security studies, the wider agenda, and the fate of the study of war', *Millennium*, 39(3): 701–16.

Barkawi, Tarak and Mark Laffey (eds.) (2001), *Democracy, Liberalism and War* (Boulder, CO: Lynne Rienner).

Barkawi, Tarak and Mark Laffey (2006), 'The postcolonial moment in security studies', *Review of International Studies*, 32(2): 329–52.

Barnes, Julian E., Christi Parsons and Peter Nicholas (2010), 'McChrystal out, Petraeus in', *Los Angeles Times*, 23 June, at http://articles.latimes.com/2010/jun/23/world/la-fg-mcchrystal-fired-20100624

Barnett, Michael (1998), *Dialogues in Arab Politics* (New York: Columbia University Press).

Barnett, Michael (1999), 'Culture, strategy and foreign policy change', *European Journal of International Relations*, 5(1): 5–36.

Barnett, Michael (2006), 'Building a Republican peace', *International Security*, 30(4): 87–112.

Barnett, Michael and Jack Levy (1991), 'Domestic sources of alliances and alignments', *International Organization*, 45(3): 369–95.

Barnett, Michael and Martha Finnemore (1999), 'The politics, power, and pathologies of international organizations', *International Organization*, 53(4): 699–732.

Barnett, Michael and Martha Finnemore (2004), *Rules for the World: International Organizations in Global Politics* (Ithaca, NY: Cornell University Press).

Barnett, Michael and Robert Duvall (eds.) (2005), *Power in Global Governance* (Cambridge: Cambridge University Press).

Bartelson, Jens (1995), *A Genealogy of Sovereignty* (Cambridge: Cambridge University Press).

Bartelson, Jens (2010), 'The social construction of globality', *International Political Sociology*, 4(3): 219–35.

Basaran, Tugba (2010), *Security, Law and Borders* (London: Routledge).

Battersby, Paul and Joseph M. Siracusa (2009), *Globalization and Human Security* (Lanham, MD: Rowman and Littlefield).

BBC (2006), 'Muslim convert who plotted terror', 7 November, at http://news.bbc.co.uk/go/pr/fr/-/1/hi/uk/6121084.stm

BBC (2007), 'Trident plan wins Commons support', 15 March, at http://news.bbc.co.uk/2/hi/uk_news/politics/6448173.stm

BBC (2010), 'Queen's Speech: Hague reveals size of Trident stockpile', 26 May, at http://news.bbc.co.uk/democracylive/hi/house_of_commons/newsid_8707000/8707285.stm

Beebe, Shannon and Mary Kaldor (2010), *The Ultimate Weapon is No Weapon* (New York: Public Affairs).

Bell, Daniel, (1960), *The End of Ideology*, (Cambridge, MA: Harvard University Press).

Bellamy, Alex J. (2006), 'Whither the responsibility to protect? Humanitarian intervention and the 2005 World Summit', *Ethics and International Affairs*, 20(2): 143–69.

Bellamy, Alex J. (2011), *Global Politics and the Responsibility to Protect* (London: Routledge).

Bellamy, Alex J. and Paul D. Williams (eds.) (2005), *Peace Operations and Global Order* (London: Frank Cass).

Bellamy, Alex J. and Nicholas J. Wheeler (2007), 'Humanitarian intervention in world politics' in John Baylis and Steve Smith (eds.), *The Globalization of World Politics*, 4th edition (Oxford: Oxford University Press).

Bellamy, Alex J. and Paul D. Williams (2007), 'Peace operations' in Sandra Cheldelin, Daniel Druckman and Larissa Fast (eds.), *Conflict* (New York: Continuum, 2nd edition), pp. 330–54.

Bellamy, Alex J. and Paul D. Williams (2011), 'The new politics of protection: Côte d'Ivoire, Libya and the responsibility to protect', *International Affairs,* 87(4): 825–50.

Bellamy, Alex J., Paul Williams and Stuart Griffin (2004), *Understanding Peacekeeping* (Cambridge: Polity).

Bennett, D.S. (1996), 'Testing alternative models of alliance duration, 1816–1984', *American Journal of Political Science*, 41(3): 846–78.

Bennett, John T. (2007), 'A procurement "Time Bomb": Building U.S. end strength leaves less money for arms', *Defense News*, 12 February, pp. 1 and 8.

Berdal, Mats (2001), 'Lessons not learned: The use of force in "peace operations" in the 1990s', in Adekeye Adebajo and Chandra Lekha Sriram (eds.), *Managing Armed Conflicts in the 21st Century* (London: Frank Cass), pp. 55–74.

Berdal, Mats (2003), 'How "new" are "new wars"? Global economic change and the study of civil war', *Global Governance*, 9(4): 477–502.

Bergen, Peter L. (2011), *The Longest War* (New York: Free Press).

Berger, Peter and Thomas Luckmann (1966), *The Social Construction of Reality* (London: Penguin).

Betts, Richard K. (1978), 'Analysis, war, and decision: Why intelligence failures are inevitable', *World Politics*, 31(2): 61–89.

Betts, Richard K. (2007), *Enemies of Intelligence* (New York: Columbia).

Betts, Richard K. and Thomas G. Mahnken (eds.) (2003), *Paradoxes of Strategic Intelligence* (London: Frank Cass).

Bialasiewicz, Luiza, *et al.* (2007), 'Performing security: The imaginative geographies of current US strategy', *Political Geography*, 26(4): 405–22.

Bienefeld, Manfred (1995), 'Assessing current development trends', *Canadian Journal of Development Studies*, XVI(3): 371–84.

Biersteker, Thomas (2010), 'Interrelationships between theory and practice in international security studies', *Security Dialogue*, 41(6): 599–606.

Bigo, Didier (1994), 'The European internal security field' in Malcolm Anderson and Monica Den Boer (eds.) *Policing Across National Boundaries* (London: Pinter).

Bigo, Didier (1995), 'Grands débats dans un petit monde. Les débats en relations internationales et leur lien avec le monde de la sécurité', *Cultures et Conflits*, No.19–20: 7–48.

Bigo, Didier (2005), 'La mondialisation de l'(in)sécurité ? Réflexions sur le champ des professionnels de la gestion des inquiétudes et analytique de la trans-nationalisation des processus d'(in)sécurisation', *Cultures et Conflits*, 58: www.conflits.org/document 1813.html

Bigo, Didier (2008), 'Security: A field left fallow' in Michael Dillon and Andrew Neal (eds.), *Foucault on Politics, Security and War* (London: Palgrave Macmillan).

Bigo, Didier and Daniel Hermant (1988), *La relation terroriste* (Paris: Documentation Française).

Bigo, Didier and R.B.J. Walker (2007a), 'International, political, sociology', *International Political Sociology*, 1(1): 1–5.

Bigo, Didier and R.B.J. Walker (2007b), 'Political sociology and the problem of the international', *Millennium*, 35(3): 725–39.

Bigo, Didier and Anastassia Tsoukala (2008), *Terror, Insecurity and Liberty* (London: Routledge).

Bigo, Didier and Mikael Madsen (2011), 'Bourdieu and international relations', *International Political Sociology*, 5(3): 219–24.

Bigo, Didier, *et al.*, (2006), *Illiberal Practices of Liberal Regimes* (Paris: L'Harmattan).

Bigo, Didier, *et al.*, (2008), 'The changing landscape of European liberty and security: the mid-term report of the CHALLENGE project', *International Social Science Journal*, No.192: 283–308.

Bigo, Didier, *et al.*, (2010a), *Europe's 21st Century Challenge* (Aldershot: Ashgate).

Bigo, Didier, *et al.*, (2010b), 'Borders and security: the different logics of surveillance in Europe' in Saskia Bonjour, *et al.* (eds.) *The Others in Europe* (Brussels: Presses de l'Université de Bruxelles).

Bilgiç, Ali (2010), 'Security through trust-building in the Euro-Mediterranean cooperation', *Southeast Europe and Black Sea Studies*, 10: 457–73.

Bilgin, Pinar (2002), 'Beyond statism in security studies? Human agency and security in the Middle East', *Review of International Affairs*, 2(1): 100–18.

Bilgin, Pinar (2004), 'Whose Middle East? Geopolitical inventions and practices of security', *International Relations*, 18(1): 17–33.

Bilgin, Pinar (2005), *Regional Security in the Middle East: A Critical Perspective* (New York: Routledge).

Bilgin, Pinar (2007), 'Making Turkey's transformation possible: Challenging 'security-speak' not desecuritization!', *Southeast European and Black Sea Studies*, 7: 555–71.

Bilgin, Pinar and Adam David Morton (2002), 'Historicising representations of "failed states": Beyond the cold war annexation of the social sciences?', *Third World Quarterly*, 23(1): 55–80.

Bilgin, Pinar and Adam David Morton (2004), 'From "rogue" to "failed" states? The fallacy of short-termism', *Politics*, 24(3): 169–80.

Bilgin, Pinar, Ken Booth and Richard Wyn Jones (1998), 'Security studies: The next stage?', *Nação e Defesa*, 84(2): 129–57.

Blair, Bruce and Chen Yali (2006), 'The fallacy of nuclear primacy', *China Security,* (Washington, DC: World Security Institute).

Blair, Tony (2006) 'Trident', *Hansard* (21), 4 December, at www.publications.parliament.uk

Blechman, Barry M. and Janne E. Nolan (1987), *The U.S.–Soviet Arms Transfer Negotiations* (Washington DC: SAIS, Foreign Policy Institute Case Study no. 3).

Blyth, Mark (2002), *Great Transformations: Economic Ideas and Institutional Change in the Twentieth Century* (Cambridge: Cambridge University Press).

Bond, Jennifer and Laurel Sherret (2006), *A Sight for Sore Eyes: Bringing Gender Vision to the Responsibility to Protect Framework* (New York: UN International Research and Training Institute for the Advancement of Women).

Bonditti, Philippe (2004), 'From territorial space to networks', *Alternatives*, 29(4): 465–82.

Bonelli, Laurent (2008), *La France a peur* (Paris: La Découverte).

Booth, Ken (1979), *Strategy and Ethnocentrism* (London: Croom Helm).

Booth, Ken (1991a), 'Security and emancipation', *Review of International Studies*, 17(4): 313–26.

Booth, Ken (1991b), 'Security in anarchy: Utopian realism in theory and practice', *International Affairs* 67(3): 527–45.

Booth, Ken (1995), 'Human wrongs and International Relations', *International Affairs*, 71(1): 103–26.

Booth, Ken (1997), 'Security and self: Reflections of a fallen realist', in Keith Krause and Michael C. Williams (eds.), *Critical Security Studies: Concepts and Cases* (London: UCL Press), pp. 83–119.

Booth, Ken (1999a), 'Nuclearism, human rights and constructions of security (Part 1)', *International Journal of Human Rights*, 3(2): 1–24.

Booth, Ken (1999b), 'Nuclearism, human rights and constructions of security (Part 2)', *International Journal of Human Rights,* 3(3): 44–61.

Booth, Ken (ed.) (2000), *The Kosovo Tragedy* (London: Routledge).

Booth, Ken (ed.) (2005), *Critical Security Studies and World Politics* (Boulder, CO; Lynne Rienner).

Booth, Ken (2005a), 'Critical explorations', in Ken Booth (ed.), *Critical Security Studies and World Politics* (Boulder, CO: Lynne Rienner), pp. 1–25.

Booth, Ken (2005b), 'Offensive realists, tolerant realists and real realists', *International Relations*, 19(3): 350–54.

Booth, Ken (2007), *Theory of World Security* (Cambridge: Cambridge University Press).

Booth, Ken and Nicholas J. Wheeler (2008), *The Security Dilemma: Fear, Cooperation and Trust in World Politics* (London: Palgrave-Macmillan).

Booth, Ken and Peter Vale (1995), 'Security in Southern Africa: After apartheid, beyond realism', *International Affairs*, 71(2): 285–304.

Booth Ken and Peter Vale (1997), 'Critical security studies and regional insecurity: The case of Southern Africa', in Keith Krause and Michael C. Williams (eds.), *Critical Security Studies* (London: UCL Press), pp. 329–58.

Booth, Ken and Tim Dunne (2011), *Terror in Our Time* (New York: Routledge).

Borradori, Giovanna, Jacques Derrida and Jurgen Habermas (2003), *Philosophy in a Time of Terror* (Chicago, IL: University of Chicago Press).

Boulden, Jane, and Thomas G. Weiss (eds.) (2004), *Terrorism and the UN: Before and After September 11* (Bloomington: Indiana University Press).

Boulding, Kenneth (1970), 'Limits or boundaries of peace research', *International Peace Research Association Proceedings, 3rd General Conference Volume 1* (Assen: Van Gorcum), pp. 5–19.

Boulding, Kenneth (1979), *Stable Peace* (Austin, TX: University of Texas Press).

Bourdieu, Pierre (1988), 'Vive la crise. For heterodoxy in social science', *Theory and Society*, 17: 772–86.

Bourdieu, Pierre (1996), *The State Nobility* (Stanford, CA: Stanford University Press).

Bourdieu, Pierre and Alain Accardo (1993), *La Misère du monde* (Paris: Editions du Seuil).

Bourne, John (2005), 'Total War 1: The Great War', in Townshend (ed.) (2005), pp. 117–137.

Boutwell, Jeffrey, Michael T. Klare and Laura Reed (eds.) (1995), *Lethal Commerce: The Global Trade in Small Arms and Light Weapons* (Cambridge, MA: American Academy of Arts and Sciences).

BP (2010), *BP Statistical Review of World Energy June 2010* (London: BP).

Brahimi Report (2000), *Report of the Panel on United Nations Peace Operations* (New York: UN Document A/55/305 S/2000/809, 21 August).

Brams, Steven J. (2002), 'Game Theory in Practice: Problems and prospects in applying it to International Relations' in Frank P. Harvey and Michael Brecher (eds.), *Evaluating Methodology in International Studies* (Ann Arbor, MI: University of Michigan Press), pp. 81–96.

Brams, Steven J. and D. Marc Kilgour (1988), *Game Theory and National Security* (New York: Basil Blackwell).

Brass, Paul R. (1997), *Theft of an Idol: Text and Context in the Representation of Collective Violence* (Princeton, NJ: Princeton University Press).

Brauch, Hans Günter *et al.* (eds.) (2011), *Coping with Global Environmental Change, Disasters and Security Threats, Challenges, Vulnerabilities and Risks* (Berlin-Heidelberg: Springer-Verlag).

Briggs, Chad (2010), 'Environmental change, strategic foresight, and impacts on military power', *Parameters*, Autumn: 1–15.

Broad, William J. and David E. Sanger (2004), 'Pakistan's nuclear earnings: $100 million', *New York Times*, 16 March.

Broad, William J., David E. Sanger and Raymond Bonner (2004), 'How Pakistan's network offered the whole kit', *International Herald Tribune*, 13 February.

Brodie, Bernard (1946), *The Absolute Weapon* (New York: Harcourt, Brace and Company).

Brooks, Doug (2000), 'Write a cheque, end a war', *Conflict Trends*, No.6.

Brooks, Doug (2003), 'Help for beleaguered peacekeepers', *Washington Post*, 2 June, p.A17.

Brooks, Stephen G. and William C. Wohlforth, (2008), *World Out of Balance* (Princeton, NJ: Princeton University Press).

Brown, Ben (2004), 'Reporting from Camp Dogwood', *BBC World Service News*, 11 March.

Brown, Chris (1992), 'Really existing liberalism and international order', *Millennium*, 21(3): 313–28.

Brown, Michael E. (2007), 'New global dangers', in Chester Crocker, Fen Osler Hampson and Pamela Aall (eds.), *Leashing the Dogs of War* (Washington, DC: USIP Press), pp. 39–51.

Brown, Seyom (1996), *International Relations in a Changing Global System* (Boulder: Westview Press).

Browning, Christopher S. and Matt McDonald (2011), 'The future of critical security studies', *European Journal of International Relations*. OnlineFirst publication, 27 October at http://ejt.sagepub.com/content/early/recent

Brundtland, Gro Harlem (1999), 'Why investing in global health is good politics', Speech to the Council on Foreign Relations, 6 December, at www.who.int/director-general/speeches/1999/english/19991206_new_york.html

Buckley, Neil (2005), 'Moscow seeks to wield petro-power as political tool', *Financial Times*, 23 December.

Bueno de Mesquita, Bruce (1975), 'Measuring systemic polarity', *Journal of Conflict Resolution*, 19(1): 187–216.

Bueno de Mesquita, Bruce (2002), 'Accomplishments and limitations of a game-theoretic approach to International Relations', in Frank P. Harvey and Michael Brecher (eds.), *Evaluating Methodology in International Studies* (Ann Arbor, MI: University of Michigan Press), pp. 59–80.

Bueno de Mesquita, Bruce and David Lalman (1992), *War and Reason* (New Haven, CT: Yale University Press).

Bueno de Mesquita, Ethan (2005), 'The terrorist endgame: a model with moral hazard and learning', *Journal of Conflict Resolution*, 49(2): 237–58.

Bueno de Mesquita, Ethan (2010), 'Regime change and revolutionary entrepreneurs', *American Political Science Review*, 104(3): 446–66.

Bukovansky, Mlada (2002), *Legitimacy and Power Politics* (Princeton, NJ: Princeton University Press).

Bull, Hedley (1977), *The Anarchical Society* (London: Macmillan).

Burgess, J. Peter (2011), *The Ethical Subject of Security* (London: Routledge).

Burke, Anthony and Matt McDonald (eds.) (2007), *Critical Security in the Asia-Pacific* (Manchester: Manchester University Press).

Bush, George (1992), Address to McDonnell Douglas employees, Lambert Field, St. Louis, Missouri, 11 September.

Bush, George W. (2001), 'Energy security', 2 March, at www.whitehouse.gov

Bush George W. (2002), 'President signs public health security and bioterrorism bill', Remarks by the US President at Signing of H.R. 3448, the Public Health Security and Bioterrorism Response Act of 2002, Washington, June.

Butterfield, Herbert (1951), *History and Human Relations* (London: Collins).

Butterfield, Herbert (1953), *Christianity, Diplomacy and War* (London: Epworth Press).

Buzan, Barry (1983), *People, States and Fear: The National Security Problem in International Relations* (Brighton: Wheatsheaf).

Buzan, Barry (1987), *An Introduction to Strategic Studies* (London: Macmillan).

Buzan, Barry (1991), *People, States and Fear: An Agenda for International Security Studies in the Post-Cold War Era*, 2nd edition. (London: Harvester Wheatsheaf).

Buzan, Barry (1995), 'The level of analysis problem in International Relations reconsidered', in Ken Booth and Steve Smith (eds.), *International Relations Theory Today* (Cambridge: Polity), pp. 198–216.

Buzan, Barry (2004), *The United States and the Great Powers* (Oxford: Polity).

Buzan, Barry (2010), 'Culture and international society', *International Affairs*, 86(1): 1–25.

Buzan, Barry (2011), 'A world order without superpowers: Decentered globalism', *International Relations*, 25(1): 1–23.

Buzan, Barry and Ole Wæver (2003) *Regions and Powers: The Structure of International Security* (Cambridge: Cambridge University Press).

Buzan, Barry and Lene Hansen (2009), *The Evolution of International Security Studies* (Cambridge: Cambridge University Press).

Buzan, Barry, Charles Jones and Richard Little (1993) *The Logic of Anarchy* (New York: Columbia University Press).

Buzan, Barry, Ole Wæver and Jaap de Wilde (1998), *Security: A New Framework for Analysis* (Boulder, CO: Lynne Rienner).

Buzan, Barry *et al.* (1990), *The European Security Order Recast* (London: Pinter).

Byman, Daniel (2006), 'Do targeted killings work?', *Foreign Affairs*, 85(2): 95–111.

Cameron, Sally and Edward Newman (eds.) (2008), *Trafficking in Humans* (Tokyo: United Nations University).

Campbell, David (1992), *Writing Security* (Minneapolis: University of Minnesota Press).

Campbell, Kurt, M. (2008), *Climatic Cataclysm* (Washington, DC: Brookings Institution Press).

Campbell, Kurt, M. *et al.* (2007) *The Age of Consequences* (Washington DC: CSIS and Center for a New American Security).

Carlson, Lisa J. (1995), 'A theory of escalation and international conflict', *Journal of Conflict Resolution*, 39(3): 511–34.

Carothers, Thomas (1999), *Aiding Democracy Abroad* (Washington DC: Carnegie Endowment for International Peace).

Carpenter, R. Charli (2005), ' "Women, children and other vulnerable groups" Gender, strategic frames, and the protection of civilians as a transnational issue', *International Studies Quarterly*, 49(2): 295–334.

Carr, Edward Hallett (1939/1946), *The Twenty Years' Crisis: An Introduction to the Study of International Relations* (New York: St. Martin's Press).

Carter, Jimmy (1980), 'State of the union address', 23 January, at www.jimmycarterlibrary.org

CASE Collective (2006), 'Critical approaches to security in Europe: A networked manifesto', *Security Dialogue*, 37(4): 443–87.

Castles, S. and A. Davidson (2000), *Citizenship and Migration* (London: Macmillan).

Castles, S. and G. Kosack (1985), *Immigrant Workers and the Class Structure in Western Europe*, 2nd edition (Oxford: Oxford University Press).

Center for International Cooperation (CIC) (2006–10), *Annual Review of Global Peace Operations* (Boulder, CO: Lynne Rienner).

Center for Security Studies (2011), 'Human security: genesis, debates, trends', No.90 (Zurich, Switzerland), at www.sta.ethz.ch/content/download/2510/14589/version/2/file/CSS_Analysis_90.pdf

Centre for International Cooperation and Security (CICS) (2005), *The Impact of Armed Violence on Poverty and Development* (Bradford University: CICS).

Cerny, Philip (1998), 'Neomedievalism, civil war and the new security dilemma', *Civil Wars*, 1(1): 36–64.

Cesarani, David (1996), *Citizenship, Nationality and Migration in Europe* (London: Routledge).

Cha, Victor D. and David C. Kang (2003), *Nuclear North Korea* (New York: Columbia University Press).

Chandler, David (2004), 'The responsibility to protect: Imposing the liberal peace', *International Peacekeeping*, 11(1): 59–81.

Chandler, David (2006), *Empire in Denial: The Politics of State-building* (London: Pluto).

Charbonneau, Bruno (2009), 'What is so special about the European Union? EU–UN cooperation in crisis management in Africa', *International Peacekeeping*, 16(4): 546–61.

Checkel, Jeffrey T. (1998), 'The constructivist turn in International Relations Theory', *World Politics*, 50(2): 324–48.

Checkel, Jeffrey T. (2005), 'International institutions and socialization in Europe', *International Organization*, 59(4): 801–26.

Chen, Lincoln, J. Leaning and V. Narashimhan (eds.) (2003), *Global Health Challenges for Human Security* (Cambridge, MA: Harvard University Press).

Chesterman, Simon (2004), *You, the People: the United Nations, Transitional Administration, and State-Building* (Oxford: Oxford University Press).

Chesterman, Simon (2006), 'Does the UN have intelligence?', *Survival*, 48(3): 149–64.

Chickering, Roger, Stig Förster and Bernd Grenier (eds.) (2005), *A World at Total War* (Cambridge: Cambridge University Press).

Chomsky, Noam and Carlos P. Otero (2003), *Radical Priorities* (New York: AK Press).

Chowdhry, Geeta and Sheila Nair (eds.), (2002), *Power, Postcolonialism and International Relations: Reading Race, Gender, and Class* (London: Routledge).

Christensen, Thomas J. (1996), *Useful Adversaries: Grand Strategy, Domestic Mobilization, and Sino-American Conflict, 1947–1958* (Princeton, NJ: Princeton University Press).

Christensen, Thomas J. (2006), 'Fostering stability or creating a monster? The rise of China and U.S. policy toward East Asia', *International Security*, 31(1): 81–126.

Christensen, Thomas J. and Jack Snyder (1990), 'Chain gangs and passed bucks: Predicting alliance patterns in multipolarity', *International Organization*, 44(2): 137–68.

Chubin, Shahram (2006), *Iran's Nuclear Ambitions*, (Washington, DC: Carnegie Endowment for International Peace).

CIA (2000), *The Global Infectious Disease Threat and Its Implications for the United States*, National Intelligence Estimate NIE99-17D, at www.cia.gov/cia/publications/nie/report/nie99-17d.html

CIA (2005), *Mapping the Global Future* (Washington, DC: CIA).

Clary, Christopher (2004), 'Dr. Khan's nuclear WalMart', *Disarmament Diplomacy*, 76 (March/April).

Claude, Richard Pierre and Burns H. Weston (2006), *Human Rights in the World Community*, 3rd edition (Philadelphia: University of Pennsylvania Press).

CNA Corporation (2007), *National Security and the Threat of Climate Change* (Alexandria, VA: CNA Corporation).

Cockayne, James and Adam Lupel, (2011), *Peace Operations and Organized Crime* (London: Routledge).

Cockburn, Cynthia (2010), 'Gender relations as causal in militarization and war: A feminist standpoint', *International Feminist Journal of Politics*, 12(2): 139–57.

Cocklin, Chris and Meg Keen (2000), 'Urbanization in the Pacific', *Environmental Conservation*, 27(4): 392–403.

Cogan, Charles (2004), 'Hunters not gatherers: Intelligence in the twenty-first century', *Intelligence and National Security*, 19(2): 304–21.

Cohen, Antonin, Bernard Lacroix and Philippe Riutort (2009), *Nouveau manuel de sciences politique* (Paris: La Découverte).

Cohen, Avner (1998), *Israel and the Bomb* (New York: Columbia University Press).

Cohen, Lenard J. (1995), *Broken Bonds: Yugoslavia's Disintegration and Balkan Politics in Transition* (Boulder, CO: Westview).

Cohen, R. and Z. Layton-Henry (1997), *The Politics of Migration* (London: Edward Elgar).

Cohen, Roger (2008), 'How Kofi Annan rescued Kenya', *New York Review of Books*, 55(13), 14 August.

Cohn, Carol (1987), 'Sex, death, and the rational world of defense intellectuals', *Signs*, 12(4): 687–718.

Cohn, Carol (1993), 'Wars, wimps, and women: Talking gender and thinking war', in Miriam Cooke and Angela Woollacott (eds.), *Gendering War Talk* (Princeton, NJ: Princeton University Press), pp. 227–46.

Cohn, Carol, with Felicity Hill and Sara Ruddick (2005), *The Relevance of Gender for Eliminating Weapons of Mass Destruction*. The Weapons of Mass Destruction Commission Papers, No.38, at www.wmdcommission.org/files/No38.pdf

Collier, David, Daniel Hidalgo and Andra Olivia Maciuceanu (2006), 'Essentially contested concepts: Debates and applications', *Journal of Political Ideologies*, 11(3): 211–46.

Collier, Paul (2007), 'Economic causes of civil conflict and their implications for policy' in Chester A. Crocker, Fen Osler Hampson, and Pamela Aall (eds.), *Leashing the Dogs of War* (Washington DC: US Institute of Peace), pp. 197–218.

Collier, Paul *et al.* (2003), *Breaking the Conflict Trap* (Oxford: Oxford University Press, for the World Bank).

Collins, Alan (ed.) (2007), *Contemporary Security Studies* (Oxford: Oxford University Press).

Collinson, Sarah (1993), *Beyond Borders: Western European Migration Policy towards the 21st Century* (London: RIIA and Wyndham Place Trust).

Collinson, Sarah (1995), *Migration, Visa and Asylum Policies in Europe* (London: Wilton Park Paper 107, HMSO).

Commission on Wartime Contracting (CWC) (2009), *At What Cost? Contingency Contracting in Iraq and Afghanistan: Interim Report to Congress*, (Washington, DC: CWC).

Commission on Wartime Contracting (CWC) (2011), *At What Risk? Correcting Over-reliance on Contracting in Contingency Operations* (Washington, D.C.: CWC).

Connell, R.W. (1995), *Masculinities* (Berkeley: University of California Press).

Copeland, Dale (2000), 'The constructivist challenge to structural realism: A review essay', *International Security*, 25(2): 187– 212.

Copeland, Dale (2001), *The Origins of Major War* (Ithaca, NY: Cornell University Press).

Copeland, Dale (2003), 'A realist critique of the English School', *Review of International Studies*, 29(3): 427–41.

Corbin, Jane (2007), 'Princes, planes and payoffs,' *BBC News Panorama*, 11 June.

Corera, Gordon (2006), *Shopping for Bombs: Nuclear Proliferation, Global Insecurity and the Rise and Fall of the A.Q. Khan Network* (Oxford: Oxford University Press).

Correlates of War data set, www.correlatesofwar.org

Cortright, David, and George A. Lopez (2000), *The Sanctions Decade: Assessing UN Strategies in the 1990s* (Boulder, CO: Lynne Rienner).

Cox, Robert W. (1981), 'Social forces, states, and world orders', *Millennium*, 10(2): 126–55.

Cox, Robert W. (1983), 'Gramsci, hegemony and International Relations', *Millennium,* 12(2): 162–75.

Cramer, Jane (2007), 'Militarized patriotism: Why the US marketplace of ideas failed before the Iraq War', *Security Studies*, 16(3): 489–524.

Crawford, Neta C. (2003), *Argument and Change in World Politics* (Cambridge: Cambridge University Press).

Croft, Stuart (2006), *Culture, Crisis and America's War on Terror* (Cambridge: Cambridge University Press).

Cronin, Audrey Kurth and James M. Ludes (eds.) (2004), *Attacking Terrorism: Elements of a Grand Strategy* (Washington, DC: Georgetown University Press).

Cronin, Richard P., *et al.* (2005), *Pakistan's Nuclear Proliferation Activities and the Recommendations of the 9/11 Commission* (Washington, DC: US Congressional Research Service, 24 May).

Daalder, Ivo H. (1991), *The Nature and Practice of Flexible Response* (New York: Columbia University Press).

Dabelko, Geoff (2009), 'Planning for climate change: The security community's precautionary principle', *Climatic Change* 98: 13–21.

Dalby, Simon (2002), *Environmental Security* (Minneapolis: University of Minnesota Press).

Dalby, Simon (2009), *Security and Environmental Change* (Cambridge: Polity).

Dallaire, Roméo (2004), *Shake Hands with the Devil: The Failure of Humanity in Rwanda* (London: Arrow).

Danchev, Alex (2004), 'Story development, or, Walter Mitty the undefeated', in Alex Danchev and John Macmillan (eds.) *The Iraq War and Democratic Politics* (London: Routledge), pp. 238– 60.

Dando, Malcolm (2005), *Bioterrorism: What is the Real Threat?* (London: The Nuffield Trust).

Davies, Philip (2004), 'Intelligence culture and intelligence failure in Britain and the United States', *Cambridge Review of International Affairs*, 17(3): 496–520.

Davies, Simon J. (2004), 'Community versus deterrence: Managing security and nuclear proliferation in Latin America and South Asia', *International Relations*, 18(1): 55–72.

De Goede, Marieke (2008), 'The politics of pre-emption and the War on Terror in Europe', *European Journal of International Relations*, 14(1): 161– 85.

de Nevers, R. (2007), 'NATO's international security role in the terrorist era', *International Security*, 31(4): 34–66.

de Waal, Alex (2005), 'HIV/AIDS and the military', background paper to expert seminar and policy conference *AIDS, Security and Democracy*, Clingendael Institute, The Hague, 2–4 May.

Deacon, Michael (2009), 'Wootton Bassett: town gathers for a solemn ritual that is all too familiar', *The Telegraph*, 11 July, at www.telegraph.co.uk/news/newstopics/onthefrontline/5798353/Wootton-Bassett-town-gathers-for-a-solemn-ritual-that-is-all-too-familiar.html

Debrix, François (1997), *(Re-)envisioning Peacekeeping: The United Nations and the Mobilization of Ideology* (Minneapolis: University of Minnesota Press).

Declaration on the Inadmissibility of Intervention in the Domestic Affairs of States and their Independence and Sovereignty (1965), GA Res. 2131, 20th Session, Supp. No. 14, UN doc. A/6014 (5).

Deffeyes, Kenneth S. (2001), *Hubbert's Peak: The Impending World Oil Shortage* (Princeton, NJ: Princeton University Press).

Deffeyes, Kenneth S. (2003), *Beyond Oil* (New York: Hill and Wang).

Delumeau, Jean (1989), *Rassurer et protéger* (Paris: Fayard).

Dencik, Lars (1970), 'Peace research: Pacification or revolution?' *International Peace Research Association Proceedings, 3rd General Conference, Volume 1* (Assen: Van Gorcum), pp. 74–91.

Deng, Francis M., *et al.* (1996), *Sovereignty as Responsibility: Conflict Management in Africa* (Washington, DC: Brookings Institution Press).

Denov, Miriam (2010), *Child Soldiers: Sierra Leone's Revolutionary United Front* (Cambridge: Cambridge University Press).

Department of Defense (DOD) (2007), *US Doctrine, Department of Defense Dictionary of Military Terms*, at www.dtic.mil/doctrine/jel/doddict/

Der Derian, James (1990), 'The (s)pace of International Relations: Simulation, surveillance, and speed', *International Studies Quarterly*, 34(3): 295–310.

Desch, Michael (1998), 'Culture clash: Assessing the importance of ideas in security studies', *International Security*, 23(1): 141–70.

Desch, Michael (2010), 'If, when and how social science can contribute to national security policy', Security Studies Program Seminar, MIT at, http://web.mit.edu/ssp/seminars/wed_archives_2010Spring/desch.html

Deudney, Daniel (1990), 'The case against linking environmental degradation and national security', *Millennium*, 19(3): 461–76.

Deutch, John (2011), 'The good news about gas', *Foreign Affairs*, 90(1): 82–93.

Deutch, John and James R. Schlesinger (2006), *National Security Consequences of U.S. Oil Dependency* (New York: Council on Foreign Relations, Independent Task Force Report No. 58).

Deutsch, Karl W. (1957), *Political Community in the North Atlantic Area* (Princeton, NJ: Princeton University Press).

Deutsch, Karl W. and J. David Singer (1964), 'Multipolar systems and international stability', *World Politics*, 16(3): 390–406.

Diamond, Jared (2005), *Collapse: How Societies Choose to Succeed or Fail* (New York: Viking).

Dibb, Paul (1988), *The Soviet Union: The Incomplete Superpower* (Basingstoke: Macmillan).

DiCicco, Jonathan M. and Jack S. Levy (1999), 'Power shifts and problem shifts', *Journal of Conflict Resolution*, 43(6): 675–704.

DiCicco, Jonathan M., and Jack S. Levy (2003), 'The power transition research program: A Lakatosian analysis' in Elman and Elman (eds.) (2003), pp. 109–57.

Diehl, Paul F. (2005), *The Politics of Global Governance*, 3rd edition (Boulder, CO: Lynne Rienner).

Dinan, Desmond (2005), *Ever Closer Union*, 3rd edition (Basingstoke: Palgrave).

Dittgen, Herbert and Dirk Peters (2001), 'EU and NATO: Competing visions of security in Europe'. Paper presented at the 4th Pan European International Relations Conference of the ECPR Standing Group on International Relations, University of Kent, Canterbury, 8–10 September.

Dobbs, Michael (2008), *One Minute to Midnight: Kennedy, Khrushchev, and Castro on the Brink of Nuclear War* (New York: Knopf).

Donnelly, Jack (1995), 'Realism and International Relations', in James Farr, John S. Dryzek, Stephen T. Leonard (eds.), *Political Science in History* (New York: Cambridge University Press), pp. 175–97.

Donnelly, Jack (2000), *Realism and International Relations* (Cambridge: Cambridge University Press).

Doran, Charles F. (1983), 'War and power dynamics: Economic underpinnings', *International Studies Quarterly*, 27(4): 419–41.

Doran, Charles F. (1989), 'Systemic disequilibrium, Foreign policy role, and the power cycle', *Journal of Conflict Resolution*, 33(3): 371–401.

Doran, Charles F. (2000), 'Confronting the principles of the power cycle', in Manus I. Midlarsky (ed.), *Handbook of War Studies II* (Ann Arbor, MI: University of Michigan Press), pp. 332–68.

Doran, Charles F. and Wes Parsons (1980), 'War and the cycle of relative power', *American Political Science Review*, 74(4): 947–65.

Doty, Roxanne Lynn (1993), 'Foreign policy as social construction', *International Studies Quarterly*, 37(3): 297–320.

Downs, George and David Rocke (1990), *Tacit Bargaining, Arms Races, and Arms Control* (Ann Arbor, MI: University of Michigan Press).

Dowty, Alan (1987), *Closed Borders* (New Haven, CT: Yale University Press).

Doyle, Michael (1983), 'Kant, liberal legacies, and foreign affairs, part I', *Philosophy and Public Affairs*, 12(3): 205–35.

Doyle, Michael W. (1998), *Ways of War and Peace* (New York: Norton).

Draper, Theodore (1987), *A Very Thin Line: The Iran-Contra Affairs* (New York: Hill and Wang).

Drew, Christopher (2011), 'Panel told of plan to reduce F-35 costs', *New York Times*, 24 May.

Dueck, Colin (2006), *Reluctant Crusaders: Power, Culture, and Change in American Grand Strategy* (Princeton, NJ: Princeton University Press).

Duffield, John S. (1994/95), 'NATO's functions after the cold war', *Political Science Quarterly*, 109(5): 763–87.

Duffield, John S. (1995), *Power Rules: The Evolution of NATO's Conventional Force Posture* (Stanford, CA: Stanford University Press).

Duffield, John S. (1998), *World Power Forsaken: Political Culture, International Institutions, and German Security Policy After Unification* (Stanford, CA: Stanford University Press).

Duffield, John S. (2006), 'International Security Institutions', in R. Rhodes *et al.* (eds.), *The Oxford Handbook of Political Institutions* (Oxford: Oxford University Press), pp. 635–55.

Duffield, John, Theo Farrell, Richard Price, and Michael Desch (1999), 'Isms and schisms: culturalism versus realism in security studies', *International Security*, 24(1): 156–80.

Duffield, Mark (2001), *Global Governance and the New Wars* (London: Zed Press).

Duffield, Mark (2007), *Development, Security and Unending War* (Cambridge: Polity Press).

Dumbrell, John and David Ryan (eds.) (2007), *Vietnam in Iraq: Tactics, Lessons, Legacies and Ghosts* (London: Routledge).

Dunleavy, Steve (2001), *New York Post*, 12 September.

Dupuy, Jean-Pierre (2004), *Pour un catastrophisme éclairé* (Paris: Editions du Seuil).

Dyer, Gwynne (2008), *Climate Wars* (Toronto: Random House).

Ebeling, Richard (1991), 'A New World Order: Economic Liberalism or the New Mercantilism', *Freedom Daily*, at www.fff.org/freedom/0791b.asp

Ebeling, Richard (2000), 'Market Liberalism, International Order, and World Peace: Part 2', *Freedom Daily*, at www.fff.org/freedom/1200b.asp

Eck, Kristine, Joakim Kreutz and Ralph Sundberg (2010), 'Introducing the UCDP non-state conflict dataset', unpublished manuscript, Uppsala University.

Eckhardt, William (1981a), 'Pioneers of peace research I – Lewis Fry Richardson: apostle of math', *International Interactions*, 8(3): 247–73.

Eckhardt, William (1981b), 'Pioneers of peace research II – Quincy Wright – apostle of law', *International Interactions*, 8(4): 297–317.

Eckl, Julian (2008), 'Responsible scholarship after leaving the veranda', *International Political Sociology*, 2(3): 185–203.

Edidin, Peter (2004), 'Pakistan's Hero: Dr. Khan Got What He Wanted, and He Explains How', *New York Times*, 15 February.

Edkins, Jenny (2003), *Trauma and the Memory of Politics* (Cambridge: Cambridge University Press).

Eisenstein, Z. (2004), 'Sexual Humiliation, Gender Confusion and the Horrors at Abu Ghraib,' *PeaceWomen*, at www.peacewomen.org/news/Iraq/June04/abughraib

Ekins, Paul (1992), *A New World Order: Grassroots Movements for Global Change* (London: Routledge).

ElBaradei, Mohamed (2004), 'Nuclear Non-Proliferation: Global Security in a Rapidly Changing World', Carnegie International Non-Proliferation Conference, 21 June.

Elbe, Stefan (2002), 'HIV/AIDS and the changing landscape of war in Africa', *International Security*, 27(2): 159–77.

Elbe, Stefan (2003), *The Strategic Implications of HIV/AIDS* (Oxford: Oxford University Press Adelphi Paper 357).

Elbe, Stefan (2006), 'Should HIV/AIDS be securitized? The ethical dilemmas of linking HIV/AIDS and security', *International Studies Quarterly* 50(1): 119–44.

Elbe, Stefan (2009), *Virus Alert: Security, Governmentality and the AIDS Pandemic* (New York: Columbia University Press).

Elbe, Stefan (2010), *Security and Global Health: Toward the Medicalization of Insecurity* (Cambridge: Polity).

Elden, Stuart and Luiza Bialasiewicz (2006), 'The new geopolitics of division and the problem of a Kantian Europe', *Review of International Studies*, 32(4): 623–44.

Elias, Norbert and Jean Etoré-Lortholary (1991), *La société des individus* (Paris: Fayard).

Elman, Colin (1996a), 'Horses for courses: Why *not* neorealist theories of foreign policy?' *Security Studies*, 6(1): 7–53.

Elman, Colin (1996b), 'Cause, effect, and consistency: A response to Kenneth Waltz', *Security Studies*, 6(1): 58–61.

Elman, Colin (2001), 'History, theory and the democratic peace', *International History Review*, 23(4): 757–66.

Elman, Colin (2004), 'Extending offensive realism: The Louisiana Purchase and America's rise to regional hegemony', *American Political Science Review*, 98(4): 563–576.

Elman, Colin and Miriam Fendius Elman (1995), 'Correspondence: History vs. neo-realism: A second look', *International Security*, 20(1): 182–93.

Elman, Colin and Miriam Fendius Elman (2002), 'How not to be Lakatos intolerant: Appraising progress in IR research', *International Studies Quarterly*, 46(2): 231–62.

Elman, Colin and Miriam Fendius Elman (eds.) (2003), *Progress in International Relations Theory* (Cambridge, MA: MIT Press).

Enemark, Christian P. (2010), 'Law in the time of anthrax', *Journal of Law and Medicine*, 17(5):748–60.

Enloe, Cynthia (1983), *Does Khaki Become You? The Militarization of Women's Lives* (London: South End Press).

Enloe, Cynthia (1996), 'Margins, Silences and Bottom Rungs', in Ken Booth, Steve Smith and Marysia Zalewski (eds.), *International Theory* (Cambridge: Cambridge University Press), pp. 186–202.

Enloe, Cynthia (2000a), 'Masculinity as a foreign policy issue', *Foreign Policy in Focus*, 5(36), October.

Enloe, Cynthia (2000b), *Maneuvers: The International Politics of Militarizing Women's Lives* (Berkeley: University of Southern California Press).

Enloe, Cynthia (2007a), *Globalization and Militarism: Feminists Make the Link* (Lantham: Rowman and Littlefield).

Enloe, Cynthia (2007b), 'Feminist readings on Abu Ghraib', *International Feminist Journal of Politics*, 9(1): 35–7.

Enloe, Cynthia (2010), *Nimo's War, Emma's War: Making Feminist Sense of the Iraq War* (Berkeley: University of California Press).

Ericson, R.V. (2006), 'Ten uncertainties of risk-management approaches to security', *Revue canadienne de criminologie et de justice pénale*, 48(3): 345–59.

Eriksson, Johan and Bengt Sundelius (2005), 'Molding minds that form policy: How to make research useful', *International Studies Perspectives*, 6(1): 51–71.

European Commission (2002), *Europe and the Mediterranean: Towards a Closer Partnership. An Overview over the Barcelona Process in 2002* (Luxembourg: Office for Official Publications of the European Communities).

European Security Strategy (2003), *A Secure Europe in a Better World* (Brussels: EU).

Evangelista, Matthew (1999), *Unarmed Forces: The Transnational Movement to End the Cold War* (Ithaca, NY: Cornell University Press).

Evans, Gareth (2004), 'When is it right to fight?' *Survival*, 46(3): 59–82.

Evans, Gareth (2009), *The Responsibility to Protect* (Washington, DC: Brookings Institution Press).

Eyre, Dana and Mark Suchman (1996), 'Status, Norms, and the Proliferation of Conventional Weapons: An Institutional Analysis' in Peter Katzenstein (ed.), *The Culture of National Security* (New York: Columbia University Press), pp. 79–113.

Fairnhall, David (2011), *Cold Front: Conflict Ahead in Arctic Waters* (London: I.B. Tauris).

Falk, Richard and Samuel Kim (eds.) (1980), *The War System* (Boulder, CO: Westview).

Farah, Douglas and Stephen Braun (2007), *Merchant of Death* (New York: Wiley and Sons).

Farrell, Theo (2002), 'Constructivist security studies: portrait of a research paradigm', *International Studies Review*, 4(1): 71–92.

Farrell, Theo (ed.) (2010), *Nuclear Non-Use*. Special section of *Review of International Studies*, 36(4): 819–76.

Fawcett, Louise (2005), 'The Origins and Development of the Regional Idea in the Americas', in Louise Fawcett and Monica Serrano (eds.) *Regionalism and Governance in the Americas* (London: Palgrave), pp. 27–51.

Fearon, James D. (1994), 'Domestic political audiences and the escalation of international disputes', *American Political Science Review*, 88: 577–92.

Fearon, James (1998), 'Domestic politics, foreign policy, and theories of International Relations', *Annual Review of Political Science*, 1: 289–313.

Fearon, James D. and David D. Laitin (1996), 'Explaining interethnic cooperation,' *American Political Science Review*, 90(4): 715–35.

Fearon, James D. and David D. Laitin (2003), 'Ethnicity, insurgency, and civil war', *American Political Science Review*, 97(1): 75–90.

Feaver, Peter D. *et al.* (2000), 'Correspondence: Brother, can you spare a paradigm? (or was anybody ever a realist?)', *International Security*, 25(1): 165–69.

Ferris, John (2004), 'Netcentric Warfare, C4ISR and Information Operations', in Len V. Scott and Peter D. Jackson (eds.) *Understanding Intelligence in the Twenty-First Century* (London: Routledge), pp. 54–77.

Fierke, Karin M. (1998), *Changing Games, Changing Strategies* (Manchester: Manchester University Press).

Fierke, Karin M. (2007), *Critical Approaches to International Security* (Oxford: Polity).

Fijnaut, Cyrille *et al.* (1998), *Organized Crime in the Netherlands* (The Hague: Kluwer).

Findlay, Trevor (2002), *The Use of Force in UN Peace Operations* (Oxford: Oxford University Press).

Finkenauer, James O. (2007), *Mafia and Organized Crime* (Oxford: OneWorld).

Finn, Peter (2003), 'Al Qaeda Arms Traced to Saudi National Guard; 3 Attackers Identified in Riyadh Bombing', *Washington Post*, 19 May.

Finnemore, Martha (1996), *National Interests in International Society* (Ithaca, NY: Cornell University Press).

Finnemore, Martha and Kathryn Sikkink (1998), 'International norm dynamics and political change', *International Organization*, 52(4): 887–917.

Floyd, Rita (2007), 'Towards a consequentialist evaluation of security', *Review of International Studies*, 33(2): 327–50.

Forsythe, David P. (1992), 'Democracy, war, and covert action', *Journal of Peace Research*, 29(4): 385–95.

Foucault, Michel (1971), *The Order of Things* (New York: Pantheon Books).

Foucault, Michel (2003), *Abnormal: Lectures at the Collège de France, 1974–1975* (New York: Picador).

Foucault, Michel and Michel Senellart (2007), *Security, Territory, Population* (Basingstoke: Palgrave-Macmillan).

Fournier, Donald F. and Eileen T. Westervelt (2005), *Energy Trends and Their Implications for U.S. Army Installation* (Washington, DC: U.S. Army Corps of Engineers, Engineer Research and Development Center, Construction Engineering Research Laboratory, ERDC/CERL TR-05-21, September).

Fravel, M. Taylor (2010), 'International Relations theory and China's rise', *International Studies Review*, 12(4): 505–32.

Freedman, Lawrence (1989), *The Evolution of Nuclear Strategy*, 2nd edition (New York: St. Martin's).

Freedman, Lawrence (1998), 'International security: changing targets', *Foreign Policy*, 110: 48–63.

Freedman, Lawrence (1999), 'The New Great Power Politics', in Alexei G. Arbatov, Karl Kaiser and Robert Legvold (eds) *Russia and the West* (Armonk, NY: East West Institute), pp. 21–43.

Freedman, Lawrence (2001/02), 'The third World War?', *Survival*, 43(4): 61–88.

Freedman, Lawrence (2004), 'War in Iraq: selling the threat', *Survival*, 46(2): 7–49.

Friedberg, Aaron L. (2005), 'The future of U.S.–China Relations: Is conflict inevitable?' *International Security*, 30(2): 7–45.

Friedman, Thomas (2000), *The Lexus and the Olive Tree* (London: Harper Collins).

Friman, H. Richard (2004), 'Forging the vacancy chain: Law enforcement efforts and mobility in criminal economies', *Crime, Law and Social Change*, 41(1): 53–77.

Friman, H. Richard and Simon Reich (eds.) (2007), *Human Trafficking, Human Security, and the Balkans* (Pittsburgh: University of Pittsburgh Press).

Frost, Mervyn (1986), *Towards a Normative Theory of International Relations* (Cambridge: Cambridge University Press).

Frost, Robin M. (2005), *Nuclear Terrorism after 9/11* (London: IISS, Adelphi Paper 378).

Fukuyama, Francis (1989), 'The end of history?', *National Interest*, 16: 3–18.

Fund for Peace (2011), *The Failed State Index* at www.fundforpeace.org/global/?q=fsi-grid2011

Furtado, Xavier (2000), 'Human security and Asia's financial crisis', *International Journal*, LV(3): 335–75.

Gaddis, John L. (1987), *The Long Peace* (Oxford: Oxford University Press).

Gaddis, John L. (2004), *Surprise, Security and the American Experience* (Cambridge, MA: Harvard University Press).

Gaddis, John L. (2006), *The Cold War – A New History* (New York: Penguin).

Gagnon, V.P. (1995), 'Ethnic nationalism and international conflict: The case of Serbia', *International Security*, 19(3): 130–66.

Galeotti, Mark (undated), 'Digging out a History of Organized Crime'. At www.pbs.plymouth.ac.uk/solon/journal/vol.1%20issue1%202011/Galeotti%20profile.pdf

Gallie, W.B. (1956), 'Essentially Contested Concepts', *Proceedings of the Aristotelian Society*, 56: 167–98.

Galtung, Johan (1964), 'An editorial', *Journal of Peace Research*, 1(1): 1–4.

Galtung, Johan (1969), 'Violence, peace and peace research', *Journal of Peace Research*, 6(3): 167–91.

Galtung, Johan (1971), 'A structural theory of imperialism', *Journal of Peace Research*, 8(2): 81–117.

Galtung, Johan (1975a), 'Dedication', in Johan Galtung, *Peace, Research, Education, Action* (Essays in Peace Research Volume I) (Copenhagen: Christian Ejlers), pp. 17–18.

Galtung, Johan (1975b), 'International Programmes of Behavioural Science: Research in Human Survival', in Johan Galtung, *Peace, Research, Education, Action* [Essays in Peace Research Volume I] (Copenhagen: Christian Ejlers), pp. 167–87.

Galtung, Johan (1975c), 'Peace Research' in Johan Galtung, *Peace, Research, Education, Action* [Essays in Peace Research Volume I] (Copenhagen: Christian Ejlers), pp. 150–66.

Galtung, Johan (1980), *The True Worlds: A Transnational Perspective*, (New York: Free Press/Institute for World Order).

Galtung, Johan (1981), 'Western civilisation: Anatomy and pathology', *Alternatives*, 7: 145–69.

Galtung, Johan (1988), 'Dialogues as Development', in Johan Galtung, *Methodology and Development* (Essays in Methodology Volume 3) (Copenhagen: Christian Ejlers), pp. 68–89.

Galtung, Johan (1990), 'Cultural violence', *Journal of Peace Research*, 27(3): 291–305.

Galtung, Johan (1996), *Peace by Peaceful Means* (London: SAGE and PRIO).

Galula, David (1964), *Counterinsurgency Warfare: Theory and Practice* (London: Pall Mall).

Gardam, Judith and Michelle J. Jarvis (2001), *Women, Armed Conflict and International Law* (The Hague: Kluwer Law International).

Garnett, John C. (ed.) (1970), *Theories of Peace and Security* (London: Macmillan).

Garrett, Laurie (2001), 'The nightmare of bioterrorism', *Foreign Affairs*, 80(1): 76–89.

Garrett, Laurie (2005), *HIV and National Security: Where are the Links?* (New York: Council on Foreign Relations).

Garrett, Laurie (2007), 'The challenge of global health', *Foreign Affairs*, 86(1): 14–38.

Garst, Daniel (1989), 'Thucydides and neorealism', *International Studies Quarterly*, 33(1): 3–27.

Gartzke, Erik (2005), 'Economic Freedom and Peace', in James Gwartney and Robert Lawson, *Economic Freedom of the World, Annual Report* (Canada: The Fraser Institute), pp. 29–44.

Gaubatz, K.T. (1996), 'Democratic states and commitment in international relations', *International Organization*, 50(1): 109–50.

Gavrilis, James A. (2005), 'The mayor of Ar Rutbah', *Foreign Policy*, 151: 28–35.

Geertz, Clifford (1973), *The Interpretation of Cultures* (New York: Basic Books).

Geis, Anna, Lothar Brock and Harald Muller (2006), *Democratic Wars* (Houndmills: Palgrave-Macmillan).

Geisler, Charles and Ragendra de Sousa (2001), 'From refuge to refugee: The African case', *Public Administration and Development*, 21(2): 159–70.

Gelber, Katharine and Matt McDonald (2006), 'Ethics and exclusion: Representations of sovereignty in Australia's approach to asylum-seekers', *Review of International Studies*, 32(2): 269–89.

Genocide Prevention Task Force (2008), *Preventing Genocide: A Blueprint for US Policymakers* (Washington, DC: American Academy of Diplomacy, US Holocaust Memorial Museum, and USIP).

George, Alexander L. (1980), *Presidential Decision-making in Foreign Policy* (Boulder, CO: Westview).

George, Alexander L. (1993), *Bridging the Gap: Theory and Practice in Foreign Policy* (Washington, DC: US Institute of Peace Press).

George, Alexander L. (ed.) (1991), *Western State Terrorism* (Cambridge: Polity).

George, Alexander L. and William E. Simons (eds.) (1994), *The Limits of Coercive Diplomacy*, 2nd edition (Boulder, CO: Westview).

George, Alexander L. and Eric Stern (2006), 'Harnessing conflict in foreign policy making: from devil's to multiple advocacy', *Presidential Studies Quarterly*, 32(3): 484–505.

German Advisory Council on Global Change (2008), *Climate Change as a Security Risk* (London: Earthscan).

Gertz, Geoffrey and Lawrence Chandy (2011), *Two Trends in Global Poverty* (Washington, DC: Brookings Institution, May), at www.brookings.edu/opinions/2011/0517_global_poverty_trends_chandy.aspx

Gettleman, Jeffrey (2011), 'Brinkmanship in Sudan as a Deadline Nears', *New York Times*, 6 June.

Gheciu, A.I. (2005), *NAO in the 'New Europe'* (Stanford, CA: Stanford University Press).

Ghobarah, Hazem, Paul Huth and Bruce Russett (2001), 'Civil Wars Kill and Maim People Long After the Shooting Stops'. Paper to the Kennedy School of Government, Harvard University, 1–2 December.

Gibbons, Robert (1992), *Game Theory for Applied Economists* (Princeton, NJ: Princeton University Press).

Gibbons, Robert (1997), 'An Introduction to Applicable Game Theory', *Journal of Economic Perspectives*, 11(1): 127–49.

Giddens, Anthony (1985), *The Nation-State and Violence* (Cambridge: Polity).

Giles, Wenona and Jennifer Hyndman (eds.) (2004), *Sites of Violence: Gender and Conflict Zones* (Berkeley: University of Southern California Press).

Giles, Wenona, Malathi de Alwis, Edith Klein and Neluka Silva, (eds.) (2003), *Feminists Under Fire* (Toronto: Between the Lines).

Gill, Peter (2008), 'Theories of Intelligence: Where Are We, Where Should We Go and How Might We Proceed?', in P. Gill, S. Marrin, and M. Pythian (eds.), *Intelligence Theory* (London: Routledge), pp. 208–27.

Gilpin, Robert (1981), *War and Change in World Politics* (New York: Cambridge University Press).

Gilpin, Robert (1987), *The Political Economy of International Relations* (Princeton, NJ: Princeton University Press).

Gilpin, Robert (1988), 'The theory of hegemonic war', *Journal of Interdisciplinary History*, 18(4): 591–613.

Glaser, Charles L. (1992), 'Political consequences of military strategy', *World Politics*, 44(4): 497–538.

Glaser, Charles L. (1994/95), 'Realists as optimists: Cooperation as self-help', *International Security*, 19(3): 50–90.

Glaser, Charles L. (1997), 'The security dilemma revisited', *World Politics*, 50(1): 171–201.

Glaser, Charles L. (2003), 'The Necessary and Natural Evolution of Structural Realism', in John Vasquez and Colin Elman (eds.) *Realism and the Balancing of Power*

(Upper Saddle River, N.J.: Prentice Hall), pp. 266–79.

Glaser, Charles L. (2010), *Rational Theory of International Politics* (Princeton, NJ: Princeton University Press).

Global Center for the Responsibility to Protect (2010), 'Fulfilling the Responsibility to Protect: Strengthening Our Capacities to Prevent and Halt Mass Atrocities', meeting summary, 24 September.

Godson, Roy (2003), *Menace to Society: Political Criminal Collaboration around the World* (Piscataway, NJ: Transaction).

Goldgeier, James M. (1997), 'Psychology and security', *Security Studies*, 6(4): 137–66.

Goldgeier, James M. (2010), 'Foreign policy decision-making', in Robert E. Denemark (ed.), *The International Studies Encyclopedia* (New York: Wiley-Blackwell).

Goodman, Michael S. (2007), *Spying on the Nuclear Bear* (Stanford, CA: Stanford University Press).

Goodstein, David (2004), *Out of Gas* (New York: Norton).

Goodwin-Gill, Guy (1983), *The Refugee in International Law* (Oxford: Clarendon Press).

Gordenker, Leon (1987), *Refugees in International Politics* (New York: Columbia University Press).

Gordenker, Leon (2010), *The UN Secretary-General and Secretariat*, 2nd edition (London: Routledge).

Goulding, Marrack (2002), *Peacemonger* (London: John Murray).

Gow, James (2003), *The Serbian Project and its Adversaries* (London: Hurst).

Graham, Bob (2008), *World at Risk: The Report of the Commission on the Prevention of WMD Proliferation and Terrorism* (New York, NY: Vintage).

Gray, Colin (1986), *Nuclear Strategy and National Style* (Lanham, MD: Hamilton Press).

Gray, Colin (1999), 'Strategic culture as context: The first generation strikes back', *Review of International Studies*, 25(1): 49–69.

Grewal, Shabnam (2007), 'All female UN squad a Success', *BBC*, 21 June, at http://news.bbc.co.uk/1/hi/programmes/this_world/6223246.stm

Grieco, Joseph M. (1988), 'Anarchy and the limits of cooperation', *International Organization*, 42(3): 485–508.

Grieco, Joseph M. (1993), 'Anarchy and the Limits of Cooperation', in David Baldwin (ed.), *Neorealism and Neoliberalism* (New York: Columbia University), pp. 116–40.

Grieco, Joseph M., Robert Powell and Duncan Snidal (1993), 'The relative-gains problem for international cooperation', *American Political Science Review*, 87(3): 729–43.

Griffin, Keith (1995), 'Global prospects for development and human security', *Canadian Journal of Development Studies*, XVI(3): 359–70.

Grimmett, Richard F. (2010), *Conventional Arms Sales to Developing Nations* (Washington, DC: Congressional Research Service, 10 September).

Gros, Frederic (2006), *Etats de violence* (Paris: Gallimard).

Gross, Michael (2009), *Moral Dilemmas of Modern War* (New York: Cambridge University Press).

Gruber, Lloyd (2000), *Ruling the World: Power Politics and the Rise of Supranational Institutions* (Princeton, NJ: Princeton University Press).

Guéhenno, Jean-Marie (2003), 'Everybody's Doing It', *World Today*, 59(8/9): 35–36.

Guéhenno, Jean-Marie (2005), 'Peace Operations 2010', letter to all DPKO and mission staff, New York, 30 November.

Guevara, Che (1963), 'Guerilla Warfare: A Method', *Cuba Socialista*, Havana, (September 1963), pp. 1–17. Reproduced in Che Guevara, *Guerrilla Warfare* (London: Souvenir Press, 2003).

Guild, Elspeth (2009), *Security and Migration in the 21st Century* (London: Polity).

Guild, Elspeth and Florian Geyer (eds.) (2008), *Security versus Justice?* (Aldershot: Ashgate).

Guittet, Emmanuel-Pierre (2004), 'European political identity and democratic solidarity after 9/11: The Spanish case', *Alternatives*, 29(4): 441–64.

Gurr, Ted Robert (2000), *Peoples Versus States* (Washington, DC: United States Institute of Peace).

Guzzini, Stefano (1993), 'Structural power: the limits of neorealist analysis', *International Organization*, 47(3): 443–78.

Guzzini, Stefano (1998), *Realism in International Relations and International Political Economy* (London: Routledge).

Haas, Ernst (1958), *The Uniting of Europe* (Stanford, CA: Stanford University Press).

Haas, Ernst (1993), 'Collective Conflict Management. Evidence for a New World Order?', in Thomas G. Weiss (ed.), *Collective Security in a Changing World* (Boulder, CO: Lynne Rienner), pp. 63–117.

Haas, Michael (1970), 'International sub-systems: Stability and polarity', *American Political Science Review*, 64(1): 98–123.

Haass, Richard N. (1999), 'What to do with American primacy', *Foreign Affairs*, 78(5): 37–49.

Haggerty, K.D. and R.V. Ericson (1999), 'The militarization of policing in the information age',

*Journal of Political and Military Sociology*, 27(2): 233–55.

Hamber, Brandon, *et al.* (2006), 'Discourses in transition: Re-imagining women's security', *International Relations*, 20(4): 487–502.

Hammar, Thomas (ed.) (2009), *European Immigration Policy* (Cambridge: Cambridge University Press).

Hampson, Fen Osler (2004), 'Can the UN still mediate?', in Price and Zacher (eds.) *The United Nations and Global Security* (New York: Palgrave), pp. 75–92.

Hampson, Fen Osler, *et al.* (2002), *Madness in the Multitude* (Toronto: Oxford University Press).

Hanggi, Heiner, Ralf Roloff and Jurgen Ruland (eds.) (2006), *Interregionalism and International Relations* (London: Routledge).

Hansen, Birthe (2000), *Unipolarity and the Middle East* (Richmond: Curzon Press).

Hansen, Lene (2000), 'The little mermaid's silent security dilemma and the absence of gender in the Copenhagen School', *Millennium*, 29(2): 289–306.

Hansen, Lene (2006), *Security as Practice: Discourse Analysis and the Bosnian War* (London: Routledge).

Hardin, Russell (1995), *One for All: The Logic of Group Conflict* (Princeton, NJ: Princeton University Press).

Harsanyi, John C. (1977), 'Advances in Understanding Rational Behavior', in Robert E. Butts and Jaakko Hintikka (eds.), *Foundational Problems in the Special Sciences* (Dordrecht, Holland: D. Reidel), pp. 315–43.

Hartung, William D. (1995), *And Weapons for All* (New York: HarperCollins).

Hartung, William D. (2000), 'A Tale of Three Arms Trades', in Ann Markusen (ed.), *America's Peace Dividend* (New York: Columbia International Affairs On-line), chapter 5.

Hartung, William D. and Frida Berrigan (2005), *U.S. Weapons at War* (New York: World Policy Institute).

Haslam, Jonathan (2002), *No Virtue Like Necessity* (New Haven, CT: Yale University Press).

Haywood, O. J., Jr. (1954), 'Military decision and game theory', *Operations Research*, 2: 365– 85.

Heinecken, Lindy (2003), 'Facing a merciless enemy: HIV/AIDS and the South African armed forces', *Armed Forces and Society*, 29(2): 281–300.

Heisler, O.M. and Z. Layton-Henry (1993), 'Migration and the links between social and societal security', in Ole Wæver *et al.* (eds.), *Identity, Migration and the New Security Agenda in Europe* (London: Pinter).

Held, David (1995), *Democracy and the Global Order* (Cambridge: Polity).

Held, David (2000), *A Globalizing World: Culture, Economics, Politics* (New York: Routledge).

Held, David (ed.) (2007), *Understanding Globalization* (Oxford: Oxford University Press).

Held, David *et al.* (1999), *Global Transformations* (Cambridge: Polity).

Helleiner, Eric (1994), 'Regionalization in the international political economy: A comparative perspective', *Eastern Asia Policy Papers no. 3*, University of Toronto.

Hendrickson, R.C. (2006), *Diplomacy and War at NATO* (Columbia: University of Missouri Press).

Herman, Michael (1996), *Intelligence Power in Peace and War* (Cambridge: Cambridge University Press).

Herman, Michael (2001), *Intelligence Service in the Information Age* (London: Frank Cass).

Herz, John (1950), 'Idealist internationalism and the security dilemma', *World Politics*, 2(2): 157– 80.

Herz, John (1959), *International Politics in the Atomic Age* (New York: Columbia University Press).

Hettne, Bjorn (2004), 'The new regionalism revisited' in Frederick Soderbaum and Timothy Shaw (eds.), *Theories of New Regionalism* (London: Palgrave), pp. 22–42.

Heymann, Philip B. and Juliette N. Kayyem (2005), *Protecting Liberty in an Age of Terror* (Cambridge, MA: MIT Press).

Higate, Paul (2004), *Peacekeepers and Gender: DRC and Sierra Leone* (Pretoria: Institute for Security Studies, Monograph No 91), at www.iss.org.za/pubs/Monographs/No91/Contents.html

Higgott, Richard (2006), 'International Political Institutions', in R. Rhodes *et al.* (eds.), *The Oxford Handbook of Political Institutions* (Oxford: Oxford University Press), pp. 611–32.

High-Level Panel on Threats, Challenges and Change (2004), *A More Secure World: Our Shared Responsibility* (UN doc. A/59/565, 2 December).

Highman, S. and J. Stephens (2004), 'New Details of Prison Abuse Emerge', *Washington Post*, 21 May, p.A01.

Hills, Alice (2004), *Future War in Cities* (London: Frank Cass).

Hinton, Harold C. (1975) *Three and a Half Powers: the New Balance in Asia* (Bloomington, IN: Indiana University Press).

Hirst, Paul (2002), 'Another century of conflict? War and the international system in the 21st century', *International Relations*, 16(3): 327–42.

Hobsbawm, Eric, and Terrence Ranger (eds.) (1992), *The Invention of Tradition* (Cambridge: Cambridge University Press).

Hoffman, Bruce (2004), *Insurgency and Counter-insurgency in Iraq* (The Rand Corporation: RAND Occasional Paper, June).

Hoffmann, Stanley (1965), *The State of War* (London: Pall Mall Press).

Hoffmann, Stanley (1977), 'An American social science: International Relations', *Daedalus*, 106(3): 41–60.

Holzgrefe, J.L. and Robert O. Keohane (eds.) (2003), *Humanitarian Intervention* (Cambridge: Cambridge University Press).

Homer-Dixon, Thomas (1999), *Environment, Scarcity and Violence* (Princeton, NJ: Princeton University Press).

Hooper, Charlotte (2001), *Manly States: Masculinities, International Relations and Gender Politics* (New York: Columbia University Press).

Hopf, Ted (1991), 'Polarity, the offense–defense balance, and war', *American Political Science Review*, 85(2): 475–93.

Hopf, Ted (1998), 'The promise of constructivism in International Relations theory', *International Security*, 23(1): 171–200.

Horkheimer, Max (1982), 'Traditional and Critical Theory', in *Critical Theory: Selected Essays*. Translated by Matthew J. O'Connell and others (New York: Continuum), pp. 188–243.

Horowitz, Donald L. (1985), *Ethnic Groups in Conflict* (Berkeley: University of California Press).

Horowitz, Donald L. (2000), *The Deadly Ethnic Riot* (Berkeley: University of California Press).

Howard, John W. III and Laura C. Prividera (2004), 'Rescuing patriarchy or saving "Jessica Lynch": The rhetorical construction of the American woman soldier', *Women and Language*, 27(2): 89–97.

Howard, Michael (2000), *The Invention of Peace* (London: Profile Books Ltd).

Hudson, Valerie M. (2005), 'Foreign policy analysis: actor-specific theory and the ground of international relations', *Foreign Policy Analysis*, 1(1): 1–30.

Hughes, J. Donald (2006), *What is Environmental History?* (Cambridge: Polity).

Human Rights Watch (HRW) (1994), *India: Arms and Abuses in Indian Punjab and Kashmir* (Washington, DC: HRW Arms Project).

Human Security Centre (2005), *Human Security Report, 2005: War and Peace in the 21st Century* (Oxford: Oxford University Press).

Human Security Centre (2010), *Human Security Report* (Oxford: Oxford University Press).

Human Security Report (2009), *The Shrinking Costs of War* (Canada: Simon Fraser University).

Human Security Report Project (2011), *The Human Security Gateway*, at www.humansecuritygateway.com/topicGateways.php

Hunt, Krista (2002), 'The strategic co-optation of women's rights: Discourse in the "War on Terrorism"', *International Feminist Journal of Politics*, 4(1): 116–21.

Huntington, Samuel P. (1991), 'America's changing strategic interests', *Survival*, 33(1): 35–36.

Huntington, Samuel P. (1993), 'The clash of civilisations', *Foreign Affairs*, 72(3): 22–49.

Huntington, Samuel P. (1996), *The Clash of Civilisations and the Remaking of World Order* (New York: Simon and Schuster).

Huntington, Samuel P. (1999), 'The lonely superpower', *Foreign Affairs*, 78(2): 35–49.

Huth, Paul (1988), *Extended Deterrence and the Prevention of War* (New Haven, CT: Yale University Press).

Huysmans, Jeff (1995), 'Migrants as a security problem' in R. Miles and D. Thränhardt (eds.), *Migration and European Integration* (London: Pinter).

Huysmans, Jeff (2006), *The Politics of Insecurity: Fear, Migration and Asylum in the EU* (London: Routledge).

Huyssen, Andreas (1994), *Twilight Memories: Marking Time in a Culture of Amnesia* (London: Routledge).

Hyndman, Jennifer (2001), 'Towards a feminist geopolitics', *The Canadian Geographer*, 45(2): 210–22.

Ignatieff, Michael (2003), 'Why Are we in Iraq? (And Liberia? And Afghanistan?)', *New York Times Magazine*, 7 September, pp. 2–7.

Ikenberry, G. John (2008), 'The rise of China and the future of the West: can the liberal system survive?', *Foreign Affairs*, 87(1): 23–37.

Ikenberry, G. John (2009), 'Liberal internationalism 3.0: America and the dilemmas of liberal world order', *Perspectives on Politics*, 7(1): 71–87.

Ikenberry, G. John and Anne-Marie Slaughter (dir) (2006), *Forging A World Of Liberty Under Law: U.S. National Security in the 21st Century* (Final Report of the Princeton Project on National Security, 27 September).

Imlay, Talbot (2007), 'Total war', *Journal of Strategic Studies*, 30(3): 547–70.

Innes, Michael (ed.) (2006), *Bosnian Security after Dayton* (London: Routledge).

Internal Displacement Monitoring Center (2011), *Global Overview of Trends and Developments in 2010* (March), at www.internal-displacement.org/publications/global-overview-2010

International Alert (1999), *Women, Violent Conflict and Peacebuilding*, proceedings from an International Conference, London, 5–7 May.

International Commission on Intervention and State Sovereignty (ICISS) (2001), *The Responsibility to Protect* (Ottawa: International Development Research Centre).

International Committee of the Red Cross (2001), *Women Facing War* (Geneva: ICRC).

International Consortium of Investigative Journalists (ICIJ) (2002), *Making a Killing: The Business of War* (Washington, DC: Public Integrity Books).

International Crisis Group (ICG) (2001), *HIV/AIDS as a Security Issue* (Brussels: ICG).

International Crisis Group (ICG) (2006), *In Their Own Words: Reading the Iraqi Insurgency* (ICG Middle East Report No.50, 15 February).

International Crisis Group (ICG) (2008), *Kenya in Crisis* (ICG Africa Report, No.137, 21 February).

International Energy Agency (2007), *World Energy Outlook 2007* (Paris: IEA).

International Energy Agency (2008), *World Energy Outlook 2008* (Paris: IEA).

International Energy Agency (2009), *World Energy Outlook 2009* (Paris: IEA).

*International Herald Tribune* (2004), 'Non-proliferation and disarmament go hand in hand', 2 September.

International Institute for Strategic Studies (IISS) (2011), *The Military Balance, 2011* (London: Taylor & Francis).

International Organization for Migration (IOM) (2005), *World Migration 2005: Costs and Benefits of International Migration* (IOM).

International Panel on Fissile Materials (2009) *Global Fissile Material Report*, at www.fissilematerials.org/ipfm/site_down/gfmr09.pdf

International Peace Operations Association (IPOA) (2007), http://ipoaonline.org/php/

Isaacs, Harold R. (1975), *The Idols of the Tribe: Group Identity and Political Change* (New York: Harper and Row).

Isikoff, Michael (1989a), 'Colombia Urges U.S. to Curb Flow of Semi-Automatic Guns', *Washington Post*, 8 September.

Isikoff, Michael (1989b), 'Cartels Turn to U.S. for Weapons', *Washington Post*, 2 November.

Jackson, Richard (2007), 'Introduction: The case for a critical terrorism studies', *European Journal of Political Science*, 6(3): 225–7.

Jacobs, Susie, Ruth Jacobson and Jennifer Marchbank (eds.) (2000), *States of Conflict* (London: Zed).

Jacoby, Tim (2007), 'Hegemony, modernisation and post-war reconstruction', *Global Society*, 21(4): 521–37.

Jahn, Beate (2007), 'The tragedy of liberal diplomacy, democratisation, intervention, statebuilding', *Journal of Intervention and Statebuilding*, part 1, 1(1): 87– 106; part 2, 1(2): 211– 229.

Janis, Irving (1982), *Groupthink: Psychological Studies of Policy Decisions and Fiascoes*, 2nd edition (Boston, MA: Houghton Mifflin).

Jeffreys-Jones, Rhodri (2003), *Cloak and Dollar: A History of American Secret Intelligence*, 2nd edition (New Haven, CT: Yale University Press).

Jenkins, Brian Michael (2008), *Will Terrorists Go Nuclear?* (Amherst: Prometheus Books).

Jenkins, Philip (2003), *Images of Terror* (New York: Aldine de Gruyter).

Jenkins, Robert (2012), *Peacebuilding: From Concept to Commission* (London: Routledge).

Jentleson, Bruce W. (2002), 'The need for praxis: bringing policy relevance back in', *International Security*, 26(4): 169–83.

Jentleson, Bruce W. and Ely Ratner (2011), 'Bridging the beltway-ivory tower gap', *International Studies Review*, 13(1): 6–11.

Jeong, Ho-Won (ed.) (1999), *The New Agenda for Peace Research* (Aldershot: Ashgate).

Jervis, Robert (1976), *Perception and Misperception in International Politics* (Princeton, NJ: Princeton University Press).

Jervis, Robert (1982), 'Security regimes', *International Organization*, 36(2): 357–78.

Jervis, Robert (1986), 'Intelligence and foreign policy', *International Security*, 11(3):141– 61.

Jervis, Robert (1988), 'Realism, game theory, and cooperation', *World Politics*, 40(3): 317– 49.

Jervis, Robert (1989), *The Meaning of the Nuclear Revolution* (Ithaca, NY: Cornell University Press).

Jervis, Robert (1997), *Systems Effects: Complexity in Political and Social Life* (Princeton, NJ: Princeton University Press).

Jervis, Robert (1999), 'Realism, neoliberalism, and cooperation: Understanding the debate', *International Security*, 24(1): 42–63.

Jervis, Robert (2002), 'Theories of war in an era of leading-power peace', *American Political Science Review*, 96(1): 1–14.

Jervis, Robert (2006), 'Reports, politics, and intelligence failures: The case of Iraq', *Journal of Strategic Studies*, 29(1): 3– 52.

Jervis, Robert (2008), 'Bridges, barriers, and gaps: research and policy', *Political Psychology*, 29(4): 571–92.

Jervis, Robert (2009), *Why Intelligence Fails: Lessons from the Iranian Revolution and the Iraq War* (New York: Columbia University Press).

Jervis, Robert and Jack Snyder (eds.) (1991), *Dominoes and Bandwagons* (New York: Oxford University Press).

Job, Brian (2004), 'The UN, Regional Organizations, and Regional Conflict', in Price and Zacher (eds.) (2004), pp. 227–43.

Johnson, Chalmers (2000), *Blowback: The Costs and Consequences of American Empire* (New York: Henry Holt).

Johnson, Harry (1958), *International Trade and Economic Growth* (Cambridge, MA: Macmillan).

Johnson, Rebecca (2005), 'Politics and protection: Why the 2005 NPT review conference failed', *Disarmament Diplomacy*, No.80, at www.acronym.org.uk/dd/dd80/80npt.htm

Johnston, Alastair I. (1995a), *Cultural Realism: Strategic Choice and Grand Strategy in Chinese History* (Princeton, NJ: Princeton University Press).

Johnston, Alastair I. (1995b), 'Thinking about strategic culture', *International Security*, 19(4): 32–64.

Johnston, Alastair I. (1999), 'Strategic cultures revisited: Reply to Colin Gray', *Review of International Studies*, 25(3): 519–23.

Johnston, Alastair I. (2001), 'Treating international institutions as social environments', *International Studies Quarterly*, 45(4): 487–515.

Johnstone, Ian (2006), 'Dilemmas of robust peace operations' in *Annual Review of Global Peace Operations, 2006* (Boulder, CO: Lynne Rienner), pp. 2–14.

Jones, Adam (2008), *Crimes against Humanity: A Beginner's Guide* (Oxford: Oneworld).

Jones, Garrett (2006), 'It's a cultural thing: Thoughts on a troubled CIA', *Orbis*, 50(1): 23–40.

Jupille, Joseph and James A. Caporaso (1999), 'Institutionalism and the European Union', *Annual Review of Political Science*, 2: 429–44.

Justice Africa (2004), *HIV/AIDS and the Threat to Security in Africa*, submission to the UN Secretary-General's High-Level Panel on Threats, Challenges and Change, 2 May, at www.justiceafrica.org/aids_mainpapers.htm

Kahl, Colin (2006), *States, Scarcity and Civil Strife in the Developing World* (Princeton, NJ: Princeton University Press).

Kahler, Miles (1997), 'Inventing International Relations: International Relations Theory After 1945', in Michael W. Doyle and G. John Ikenberry (eds.) *New Thinking in International Relations Theory* (Boulder, CO: Westview), pp. 20–53.

Kaldor, Mary (1997), 'Introduction', in M. Kaldor and B. Vashee (eds.), *Restructuring the Global Military Sector: Volume I: New Wars* (London: Pinter), pp. 3–33.

Kaldor, Mary (1999), *New and Old Wars: Organized Violence in a Global Era* (Cambridge: Polity Press and the 2nd edition, 2007).

Kaldor, Mary (2007a), *Human Security* (Cambridge: Polity).

Kaldor, Mary (2007b), *New and Old Wars*, 2nd edition (Oxford: Polity).

Kaldor, Mary (2010), 'Inconclusive wars: Is Clausewitz still relevant in these global times?', *Global Policy*, 1(3): 271–81.

Kalicki, Jan H. and David L. Goldwyn (2005), 'Introduction: The Need to Integrate Energy and Foreign Policy', in Jan H. Kalicki and David L. Goldwyn (eds.), *Energy Security* (Washington DC: Woodrow Wilson Center Press), pp. 1–16.

Kalyvas, Stathis N. (2001), '"New" and "old" civil wars: A valid distinction?', *World Politics*, 54(1): 99–118.

Kansteiner, Wulf (2004), 'Genealogy of a category mistake', *Rethinking History*, 8(2): 193–221.

Kant, Immanuel (1991a), 'Perpetual Peace: A Philosophical Sketch' in *Kant: Political Writings*, 2nd edition. Ed. H. Reiss (Cambridge: Cambridge University Press).

Kant, Immanuel (1991b), 'On the Relationship of Theory to Practice in Political Right', in *Kant: PoliticalWritings*, 2nd edition, edited H. Reiss (Cambridge: Cambridge University Press).

Kaplan, Robert D. (2005), *Imperial Grunts: On the Ground With The American Military* (New York: Vintage).

Kapstein, Ethan B. (1999), 'Does Unipolarity Have a Future?,' in Kapstein and Mastanduno (eds.) *Unipolar Politics*, pp. 464–90.

Kapstein, Ethan B. and Michael Mastanduno (eds.) (1999), *Unipolar Politics* (New York: Columbia University Press).

Karl, Terry Lynn (1997), *The Paradox of Plenty* (Berkeley: University of California Press).

Katzenstein, Peter J. (ed.) (1996), *The Culture of National Security* (New York: Columbia University Press).

Katzenstein, Peter J., Robert O. Keohane, and Stephen D. Krasner (1998), '*International Organization* and the study of world politics', *International Organization*, 52(4): 645–85.

Katzman, Kenneth (1993), *Afghanistan: U.S. Policy Options* (Washington, DC: Congressional Research Service Issue Brief, 29 November).

Kaufman, Stuart J. (2001), *Modern Hatreds: The Symbolic Politics of Ethnic War* (Ithaca, NY: Cornell University Press).

Kaufman, Stuart J. (2006), 'Symbolic politics or rational choice? Testing theories of extreme ethnic violence', *International Security*, 30(4): 45–86.

Kaufmann, Chaim (1996), 'Possible and impossible solutions to ethnic civil wars', *International Security*, 20(4): 136–75.

Kaufmann, Chaim (2004), 'Threat inflation and the failure of the marketplace of ideas: The selling of the Iraq war', *International Security*, 29(1): 5– 48.

Keck, Margaret E. and Kathryn Sikkink (1998), *Activists Beyond Borders* (Ithaca, NY: Cornell University Press).

Keegan, John (1994), *A History of Warfare* (London: Vintage).

Keen, David (2008), *Complex Emergencies* (Cambridge: Polity).

Kegley, Charles W. and Gregory Raymond (1994), *A Multipolar Peace? Great Power Politics in the 21st Century* (New York: St. Martin's Press).

Kego, Walter and Alexandru Molcean (2011), *Russian Speaking Organized Crime Groups in the EU* (Stockholm: Institute for Security and Development Policy).

Kennan, George F. (1951), *American Diplomacy, 1900–1950* (Chicago: University of Chicago Press).

Kennedy, Paul (1989), *The Rise and Fall of the Great Powers* (London: Fontana).

Kennedy, Paul (2006), *The Parliament of Man: The Past, Present, and Future of the United Nations* (New York: Random House).

Kennedy-Pipe, Caroline (2004), 'Whose security? State-building and the 'emancipation' of women in Central Asia', *International Relations*, 18(1): 91–107.

Kennedy-Pipe, Caroline and Penny Stanley (2000), 'Rape in War: Lessons of the Balkans Conflicts in the 1990s', in Booth (ed.) (2000), pp. 67–84.

Kent, George (2005), *Freedom from Want* (Washington, DC: Georgetown University Press).

Keohane, Daniel (2008), 'The absent friend: EU foreign policy and counter-terrorism', *Journal of Common Market Studies*, 46(1): 125–46.

Keohane, Robert O. (1984), *After Hegemony: Cooperation and Discord in the World Political Economy* (Princeton, NJ: Princeton University Press).

Keohane, Robert O. (ed.) (1986), *Neorealism and its Critics* (New York: Columbia University Press).

Keohane, Robert O. (1988), 'International institutions: Two approaches', *International Studies Quarterly*, 32(4): 379–96.

Keohane, Robert O. (1989), *International Institutions and State Power* (Boulder, CO: Westview).

Keohane, Robert O. and Joseph S. Nye (1977), *Power and Interdependence* (Boston: Little, Brown).

Keohane, Robert O. and Lisa Martin (2003), 'Institutional Theory as a Research Program', in Elman and Elman (eds.) (2003), pp. 71–107.

Khong, Yuen Foong (1992), *Analogies at War: Korea, Munich, Dien Bien Phu, and the Vietnam Decisions of 1965* (Princeton, NJ: Princeton University Press).

Khong, Yuen Foong (2001), 'Human security: A shotgun approach to alleviating human misery?' *Global Governance*, 7(3): 231–6.

Kier, Elizabeth (1995), 'Culture and military doctrine: France between the wars', *International Security*, 19(4): 65–93.

Kiernan, Ben (2007), *Blood and Soil: A World History of Genocide and Extermination from Sparta to Darfur* (New Haven, CT: Yale University Press).

Kilcullen, David (2006–07), 'Counter-insurgency Redux', *Survival*, 48(4): 111–30.

Kilcullen, David (2009), *The Accidental Guerrilla* (Oxford: Oxford University Press).

Kim, Jaechun (2005), 'Democratic peace and covert war: A case study of the US covert war in Chile', *Journal of International and Area Studies*, 12(1): 25– 47.

Kim, Woosang (1991), 'Alliance transitions and great power war', *American Journal of Political Science*, 35(4): 833–50.

Kim, Woosang (1992), 'Power transitions and great power war from Westphalia to Waterloo', *World Politics*, 45(1): 153–72.

Kim, Woosang (1996), 'Power parity, alliances, and war from 1648 to 1975' in Kugler and Lemke (eds.) (1996), pp. 93–105.

Kim, Woosang (2002), 'Power parity, alliance, dissatisfaction, and wars in East Asia, 1860–1993', *Journal of Conflict Resolution*, 46(5): 654–71.

Kindleberger, Charles P. (1973), *The World in Depression 1929–39* (London: Allen Lane).

Kindleberger, Charles P. (1981), 'Dominance and leadership in the international economy', *International Studies Quarterly*, 25(2/3): 242–54.

King, Anthony (2010), 'Understanding the Helmand campaign: British military operations in Afghanistan', *International Affairs*, 86(2): 311–32.

King, Gary and Christopher Murray (2001/02), 'Rethinking human security', *Political Science Quarterly*, 116(4): 585–610.

Kirshner, Jonathan (forthcoming), 'The tragedy of offensive realism: Classical realism and the rise of China', *European Journal of International Relations*.

Kitson, Frank (1971), *Low Intensity Operations* (Harrisburg, PA: Stackpole Books).

Klare, Michael T. (1984), *American Arms Supermarket* (Austin: University of Texas Press).

Klare, Michael T. (1995), 'Stemming the trade in small arms and light weapons', *Issues in Science and Technology* (Fall).

Klare, Michael T. (2004), *Blood and Oil: The Dangers and Consequences of America's Growing Dependence on Imported Petroleum* (New York: Metropolitan Books).

Klare, Michael T. (2006), 'Fueling the Fires: The Oil Factor in Middle Eastern Terrorism', in James J. F. Forest (ed.), *The Making of a Terrorist*, Vol.3 (Westport, CT: Praeger), pp. 140–59.

Klare, Michael T. (2008), *Rising Powers, Shrinking Planet: The New Geopolitics of Energy* (New York: Metropolitan Books).

Klein, Bradley (1988), 'Hegemony and strategic culture: American power projection and alliance defense politics', *Review of International Studies*, 14(2): 133–48.

Klein, Naomi (2005), *No War: America's Real Business in Iraq* (London: Gibson Sq.).

Kodmani, Bassma (2012), 'The Imported, Supported, and Homegrown Security of the Arab World', in Chester A. Crocker, Fen Osler Hampson, and Pamela Aall (eds.) *Rewiring Regional Security in a Fragmented World* (Washington, DC: US Institute of Peace Press), pp. 221–52.

Koremos, Barbara, Charles Lipson and Duncan Snidal (2004), *The Rational Design of International Institutions* (Cambridge: Cambridge University Press).

Kraig, Michael R. (1999), 'Nuclear deterrence in the developing world: A Game-theoretic treatment', *Journal of Peace Research*, 36(2): 141–67.

Kramer, Andrew E. (2006), 'Gazprom Threatens to Cut Off Gas as Belarus Rejects Higher Price', *New York Times*, 27 December.

Krasner, Stephen D. (2005), 'The case for shared sovereignty', *Journal of Democracy*, 16(1): 69–83.

Kratochwil, Friedrich (1993), 'The embarrassment of changes: Neo-realism as the science of realpolitik without politics', *Review of International Studies*, 19(1): 63–80.

Krause, Keith and Michael C. Williams (eds.) (1997), *Critical Security Studies* (London: UCL Press).

Krauthammer, Charles (2001), 'The Bush Doctrine: ABM, Kyoto and the New American Unilateralism', *The Weekly Standard* (Washington, DC), 6(36), 4 June.

Krebs, Ron (2005), 'One nation under arms? Military participation policy and the politics of identity', *Security Studies*, 14(3): 529–64.

Krebs, Ronald and Jennifer Lobasz (2007), 'Fixing the meaning of 9/11: Hegemony, coercion, and the road to war in Iraq', *Security Studies*, 16(3): 409–51.

Kritz, M., C. Keely and S. Tomasci (eds.) (1981), *Global Trends in Migration* (New York: The Center for Migration Studies).

Krulak, Charles C. (1999), 'The Strategic Corporal: Leadership in the Three Block War', *Marine Corps Gazette*, 83(1): 18–22.

Kubursi, Atif (2006), 'Oil and the global economy', in Rick Fawn and Raymond Hinnebusch (eds.), *The Iraq War* (Boulder, CO: Lynne Rienner).

Kugler, Jacek and A.F.K. Organski (1989), 'The Power Transition: A Retrospective and Prospective Evaluation', in Manus I. Midlarsky (ed.), *Handbook of War Studies* (Boston: Unwin Hyman), pp. 171–94.

Kugler, Jacek and Douglas Lemke (2000), 'The Power Transition Research Program: Assessing Theoretical and Empirical Advances', in Manus I. Midlarsky (ed.), *The Handbook of War Studies II* (Ann Arbor, MI: Michigan University Press), pp. 129–63.

Kugler, Jacek and Douglas Lemke (eds.) (1996), *Parity and War* (Ann Arbor, MI: Michigan University Press).

Kumar, Krishna (ed.) (2001), *Women and Civil War* (Boulder, CO: Lynne Rienner).

Kupchan, Charles A. (1998), 'After Pax Americana', *International Security*, 23(2): 40–79.

Kupchan, Charles A. (2002), *The End of the American Era* (New York: Alfred Knopf).

Kuper, Adam (1999), *Culture: The Anthropologists' Account* (Cambridge, MA: Harvard University Press).

Kuper, Leo (1981), *Genocide: Its Political Use in the Twentieth Century* (Harmondsworth: Penguin).

Kurth, James (1998), 'Inside the cave: the banality of IR studies', *National Interest*, 53: 29–40.

Kydd, Andrew H. (1997a), 'Game theory and the spiral model', *World Politics,* 49(3): 371–400.

Kydd, Andrew H. (1997b), 'Sheep in sheep's clothing: Why security seeker's do not fight each other', *Security Studies*, 7(1): 114–54.

Kydd, Andrew H. (2000), 'Trust, reassurance and cooperation', *International Organization*, 54(2): 325–59.

Kydd, Andrew H. (2001), 'Trust building, trust breaking: The dilemma of NATO enlargement', *International Organization*, 55(4): 801–29.

Kydd, Andrew H. (2005), *Trust and Mistrust in International Relations* (Princeton, NJ: Princeton University Press).

Labs, Eric J. (1997), 'Beyond victory: Offensive realism and the expansion of war aims', *Security Studies*, 6(4): 1–49.

Lacina, Bethany and Nils Peter Gleditsch (2005), 'Monitoring trends in global combat', *European Journal of Population*, 21(2–3): 145–66.

Lacroix, Bernard (1994), 'La crise de la démocratie représentative en France', *Scalpel*, No.1: 6–29.

Laderchi, Caterina R., Ruth Saith and Frances Stewart (2003), 'Does it matter that we do not agree on the definition of poverty? A comparison of four approaches', *Oxford Development Studies*, 31(3): 243–74.

LaFeber, Walter (2006), *America, Russia and the Cold War 1945–2006* (New York: McGraw Hill).

Laïdi, Zaki (1998), *A World Without Meaning* (London: Routledge, orig. 1994).

Lakatos, Imre (1970), 'Falsification and the Methodology of Scientific Research Programmes', in Imre Lakatos and Alan Musgrave (eds.), *Criticism and the Growth of Knowledge* (New York: Cambridge University Press), pp. 91–196.

Lake, David A. (2001), 'Beyond anarchy: The importance of security institutions', *International Security*, 26(1): 129–60.

Lake, David A. (2009), *Hierarchy in International Relations* (Ithaca, NY: Cornell University Press).

Lake, David A. and Patrick M. Morgan (eds.) (1997), *Regional Orders: Building Security in a New World* (University Park: Pennsylvania State University Press).

Lander, Stephen (2004), 'International intelligence co-operation: An inside perspective', *Cambridge Review of International Studies*, 17(3): 481–93.

Lasswell, Harold D. (1936), *Politics: Who Gets What, When and How* (New York: McGraw-Hill).

Latour, Bruno and Vincent Lepinay (2008), *L'économie, science des intérêts passionnés* (Paris: La Découverte).

Lauren, Paul Gordon (1998), *The Evolution of Human International Rights* (University Park: Pennsylvania State University Press).

Lawler, Peter (1995), *A Question of Values: Johan Galtung's Peace Research* (Boulder, CO: Lynne Rienner).

Lawler, Peter (2002), 'Peace research, war, and the problem of focus', *Peace Review*, 14(1): 7–14.

Layne, Christopher (1993), 'The unipolar illusion: Why other Great Powers will rise', *International Security*, 17(4): 5–51.

Layne, Christopher (2006), *The Peace of Illusions: American Grand Strategy from 1940 to Present* (Ithaca, NY: Cornell University Press).

Leander, Anna (2005), 'The power to construct international security: on the significance of private military companies', *Millennium*, 33(3): 803–25.

LeBillon, Philippe (2005), *Fuelling War: Natural Resources and Armed Conflict* (London: Routledge/ Institute for International and Strategic Studies).

Lebow, Richard N. (1982), *Between Peace and War* (Baltimore, MD: Johns Hopkins University Press).

Lee, Kelley (2003), *Health and Globalisation: An Introduction* (Basingstoke: Palgrave).

Leeds, B.A., *et al.* (2002), 'Alliance treaty obligations and provisions, 1815–1944', *International Interactions*, 28(3): 237–60.

Legro, Jeffrey W. (2007), 'What China will want: The future intentions of a rising power', *Perspectives on Politics*, 5(3): 515–34.

Legro, Jeffrey W. and Andrew Moravcsik (1999), 'Is anybody still a realist?' *International Security*, 24(2): 5–55.

Leiber, Karl A. and Darryl G. Press (2006), 'The end of MAD? The nuclear dimension of US primacy', *International Security*, 30(4): 7–44.

Lemke, Douglas (1995), 'Toward a general understanding of parity and war', *Conflict Management and Peace Science*, 14: 143–62.

Lemke, Douglas (1996), 'Small States and War: An Expansion of Power Transition Theory' in Kugler and Lemke (eds.) (1996), pp. 77–91.

Lentz, Theodore F. (1955), *Towards a Science of Peace* (London: Halycon Press).

Leon, David A. and Gill Walt (2001), *Poverty, Inequality, and Health* (New York: Oxford University Press).

Levering, Ralph B. (2005), *The Cold War: A Post Cold War History* (Wheeling, IL: Harlan Davidson).

Levy, Jack (1989), 'The causes of war: a review of theories and evidence' in P.E. Tetlock et. al. (eds.), *Behavior, Society, and Nuclear War*, vol. I. (New York: Oxford University Press), pp. 209–333.

Lewis, Anthony (2003), 'The challenge of global justice now', *Dædalus*, 132(1): 5–9.

Liberman, Peter (1993), 'The spoils of conquest', *International Security*, 18(2): 125–53.

Lieberman, Elli (1995), 'What makes deterrence work', *Security Studies*, 4(4): 833–92.

Lijphart, Arend (1985), *Power-Sharing in South Africa*, Policy Papers in International Affairs no. 24 (Berkeley: Institute of International Studies, University of California).

Lin, Shi-chin (2004), *The A.Q. Khan Revelations and Subsequent Changes to Pakistani Export Controls* (Center for Nonproliferation Studies (CNS), Monterey Institute of International Studies).

Linklater, Andrew (2005), 'Political Community and Human Security', in Ken Booth (ed.), *Critical Security Studies and World Politics* (Boulder, CO: Lynne Rienner), pp. 113–31.

Lobell, Steven E. (2009), 'Threat Assessment, the State, and Foreign Policy' in Lobell *et al.* (eds.) (2009), pp. 42–74.

Lobell, Steven E., Norrin M. Ripsman, and Jeffrey W. Taliaferro (eds.) (2009), *Neoclassical Realism, the State, and Foreign Policy* (New York: Cambridge University Press).

Lock, Edward (2010), 'Refining strategic culture: Return of the second generation', *Review of International Studies*, 36: 685–708.

Louis, William R. (1985), 'American anti-colonialism and the dissolution of the British empire', *International Affairs*, 61(3): 395–420

Lowenthal, Mark (2008), *Intelligence: From Secrets to Policy* (Washington, DC: CQ Press).

Luck, Edward C. (1999), *Mixed Messages: American Politics and International Organization 1919–1999* (Washington, DC: Brookings Institution).

Luck, Edward C. (2007), 'The responsible sovereign and the responsibility to protect', *Annual Review of United Nations Affairs 2006/2007* (Oxford: Oxford University Press).

Luck, Edward C. (2011), *UN Security Council: Promise and Practice*, 2nd edition (London: Routledge).

Lugar, Richard G. (2005), 'Opening Statement, Hearing on the High Costs of Oil Dependency', Senate Committee on Foreign Relations, 16 November, at http://foreign.senate.gov

Lugar, Richard G. (2006), Address to the Brookings Institution, Washington, DC, 13 March, at http://lugar.senate.gov

Lukes, Steven (1986), *Power* (New York: New York University Press).

Lurio, Eric (2006), 'The Last Samurai', *Greenwich Village Gazette*, 6(26): www.nycny.com/movies/last_samurai/index.html

Lynch, Marc (2010), *Rhetoric and Reality: Countering Terrorism in the Age of Obama* (Washington: Center for a New American Security).

Lynch, Marc (2011), 'Libya in its Arab context', *Foreign Policy*, 21 March, at http://lynch.foreignpolicy.com/posts/2011/03/21/keeping_libya_in_context

Lynn-Jones, Sean M. (1995), 'Offense-defense theory and its critics', *Security Studies*, 4(4): 660–91.

Lynn-Jones, Sean M. (2001), *Does Offense–Defense Theory Have a Future?* (Working Paper, Research Group in International Security, Université de Montréal).

Lyon, David (2007), *Surveillance Studies: An Overview* (Oxford: Polity).

Mabey, Nick (2007), *Delivering Climate Security* (London: Royal United Services Institute, Whitehall Paper No.69).

Mabey, Nick, *et al.* (2011), *Degrees of Risk: Defining a Risk Management Framework for Climate Security* (London: E3G).

MacEachin, Douglas (2001), *US Intelligence and the Polish Crisis, 1980–1981*. (Washington, DC: Center for the Study of Intelligence, Central Intelligence Agency).

MacFarlane, Neil S. and Yuen Foon Khong (2006), *Human Security and the UN* (Bloomington: Indiana University Press).

Mack, Andrew (2001), 'Notes on the Creation of a Human Security Report'. Paper to the Kennedy School of Government, Harvard University, 1–2 December.

Mack, Andrew (2005), *Human Security Report 2005* (New York: Oxford University Press).

Mack, Andrew (2007), *Global Political Violence: Explaining the Post-Cold War Decline* (New York: International Peace Academy Coping with Crisis Working Paper, March).

Madsen, Mikael (2011), 'Reflexivity and the international object of study', *International Political Sociology*, 5(3): 259–75.

Malone, David M. (ed.) (2004), *The UN Security Council* (Boulder, CO: Lynne Rienner).

Mann, James (2009), *The Rebellion of Ronald Reagan* (New York: Viking).

Mann, Michael (1988), *States, War and Capitalism* (Oxford: Blackwell).

Mansaray, Binta (2000), 'Women against weapons: A leading role for women in disarmament' in Anatole Ayissi and Robin-Edward Poulton (eds.), *Bound to Cooperate* (Geneva: UN Institute for Disarmament Research).

Mansfield, Edward D. (1993), 'Concentration, polarity, and the distribution of power', *International Studies Quarterly*, 37(1): 105–28.

Mansfield, Edward D. and Brian M. Pollins (2001), 'The study of interdependence and conflict', *Journal of Conflict Resolution*, 45(6): 834–59.

Mansoor, Peter (2011), 'The softer side of war: Exploring the influence of culture on military doctrine', *Foreign Affairs*, 90(1): 164–71.

Mao Zedong (1937), *On Guerrilla War* (Champaign ILL: First Illionis Paperback, 2000 print).

March, James G. and Johan P. Olsen (1989), *Rediscovering Institutions* (New York: Free Press).

Martin, Alex (2007), 'The lessons of Eastern Europe for modern intelligence reform', *Conflict, Security and Development*, 7(4): 551–77.

Martin, Alex and Peter Wilson (2008), 'The value of non-governmental intelligence: Widening the field', *Intelligence and National Security*, 23(6): 767–76.

Martin, Andrew and Patrice Petro (2006), *Rethinking Global Security* (New York: Rutgers University Press).

Martin, Lisa (1999), 'The contributions of rational choice: A defense of pluralism', *International Security*, 24(2): 74– 83.

Mastanduno, Michael (1997), 'Preserving the unipolar moment: realist theories and US grand strategy after the Cold War', *International Security*, 21(4): 51–52.

Matthew, Richard A., Jon Barnett, Bryan McDonald and Karen L. O'Brien (eds.) (2009), *Global Environmental Change and Human Security* (Cambridge: MIT Press).

Mayer, Ann (2006), *Islam and Human Rights*, 4th edition (Boulder, CO: Westview).

McAdam, Doug, Sidney Tarrow, and Charles Tilly (2001), *Dynamics of Contention* (Cambridge: Cambridge University Press).

McAnany, Patricia and Norman Yoffee (eds.) (2010), *Questioning Collapse: Human Resilience, Ecological Vulnerability, and the Aftermath of Empire* (Cambridge: Cambridge University Press).

McCalla, Robert B. (1996), 'NATO's persistence after the cold war', *International Organization*, 50(3): 445–75.

McDonald, John and John W. Tukey (1949), 'Colonel Blotto: A problem of military strategy', *Fortune*, June.

McDonald, Matt (2008), 'Securitization and the construction of security', *European Journal of International Relations*, 14(4): 563–87.

McFate, Montgomery and Andrea V. Jackson (2006), 'The object beyond war: Counterinsurgency and the four tools of political competition', *Military Review*, 86(1): 13–26.

McFaul, Michael (2010), *Advancing Democracy Abroad* (Palo Alto, CA: Hoover Institution).

McInnes, Colin (2001), 'Fatal attraction: Airpower and the West', *Contemporary Security Policy*, 22(3): 28–51.

McInnes, Colin (2002), *Spectator-Sport War: The West and Contemporary Conflict* (Boulder, CO.: Lynne Rienner).

McInnes, Colin (2006), 'HIV/AIDS and security', *International Affairs*, 82(2): 315–26.

McInnes, Colin (2011), 'HIV, AIDS and conflict in Africa: why isn't it (even) worse?', *Review of International Studies*, 37(2): 485–509.

McInnes, Colin and Simon Rushton (2010), 'HIV, AIDS and security: Where are we now?', *International Affairs*, 86(1): 225–45.

McKenna, Thomas M. (1998), *Muslim Rulers and Rebels* (Berkeley: University of California).

McRae, Robert G. and Donald Hubert (2001), *Human Security and the New Diplomacy* (Kingston and Montreal: McGill-Queen's University Press).

McSweeney, Bill (1996), 'Identity and security: Buzan and the Copenhagen School', *Review of International Studies*, 22(1): 81–93.

McSweeney, Bill (1999), *Security, Identity and Interests: A Sociology of International Relations* (Cambridge: Cambridge University Press).

Mearsheimer, John J. (1983), *Conventional Deterrence* (Ithaca, NY: Cornell University Press).

Mearsheimer, John J. (1990), 'Back to the future: Instability in Europe after the Cold War', *International Security*, 15(1): 5–56.

Mearsheimer, John J. (1994/95), 'The false promise of International Institutions', *International Security*, 19(3): 5–49.

Mearsheimer, John J. (2001), *The Tragedy of Great Power Politics* (New York: W.W. Norton).

Mearsheimer, John J. (2006), 'China's unpeaceful rise,' *Current History*, 105(690): 160–62.

Mearsheimer, John J. and Stephen M. Walt (2003), 'An unnecessary war', *Foreign Policy*, No.131: 51–59.

Mello, Patrick (2010), 'In search of new wars', *European Journal of International Relations*, 16(2): 297–309.

Mendelsohn, Daniel (2007), 'Duty', *New York Review of Books*, 54(9), 31 May, at www.nybooks.com/ articles/article-preview?article_id=20231

Merle, Renae (2006), 'Census Counts 100,000 Contractors in Iraq', *Washington Post*, 5 December, p.D1.

Mernissi, Fatima (1989), *Doing Daily Battle: Interviews with Moroccan Women*. Trans. M.J. Lakeland (New Brunswick, NJ: Rutgers University Press).

Midlarsky, Manus and Ted Hopf (1993), 'Polarity and international stability', *American Political Science Review*, 87(1): 173–180.

Miguel, E. (2006), 'Global poverty, conflict and insecurity', *The Brookings Blum Roundtable*, 2 August.

Military.com (2011), 'Northrop Pushing the Export of Spy Drones,' 2 April.

Miller, Steven E. (2010), 'The hegemonic illusion? Traditional strategic studies in context', *Security Dialogue*, 41(6): 639–48.

Milliken, Jennifer and Keith Krause (2002), 'State failure, state collapse, and state reconstruction', *Development & Change*, 33(5): 753–74.

Mills, Greg (2004), 'Relearning the Lessons of Vietnam and Malaya', *Straits Times* (Singapore), 29 January.

Mises, Ludwig von (1949), *Human Action: A Treatise on Economics* (Inning-on-Hudson, NY: The Foundation for Economic Education).

Mitchell, Ronald B. (2006), 'Institutional design and the relative effectiveness of international environmental agreements', *Global Environmental Politics*, 6(3): 72–89.

Mittelman, James (2000), *The Globalization Syndrome* (Princeton, NJ: Princeton University Press).

Mitzen, Jennifer (2006), 'Ontological security in world politics: State identity and the security dilemma', *European Journal of International Relations*, 12(3): 341–70.

Moaveni, Azadeh (2007), '300 sparks an outcry in Iran' *Time Magazine*, 13 March, at www.time.com/time/world/article/0,8599,1598886,00.html

Modelski, George (1963), 'The study of alliances: a review', *Journal of Conflict Resolution*, 7(4): 769–76.

Modelski, George (1978), 'The long cycle of global politics and the nation-state', *Comparative Studies in Society and History*, 20(2): 214–35.

Modelski, George and Patrick M. Morgan (1985), 'Understanding global war', *Journal of Conflict Resolution*, 29(3): 391–417.

Moore, Jonathan (1996), *The UN and Complex Emergencies* (Geneva: UNRISD).

Moran, Daniel (ed.) (2011), *Climate Change and National Security* (Washington DC: Georgetown University Press).

Moravcsik, Andrew (2001), *Liberal International Relations Theory* (Cambridge, MA: Harvard University Press).

Morgenthau, Hans (1948), *Politics Among Nations: The Struggle for Power and Peace*, 1st edition (New York: A.A. Knopf).

Morgenthau, Hans (1985), *Politics Among Nations: The Struggle for Power and Peace*, 6th edition (New York: McGraw-Hill).

Morrow, James D. (1994), *Game Theory for Political Scientists* (Princeton, NJ: Princeton University Press).

Morsink, Johannes (1998), *The Universal Declaration of Human Rights* (University Park: University of Pennsylvania Press).

Moser, Caroline O.N. and Fiona C. Clark (eds.) (2001), *Victims, Perpetrators or Actors? Gender, Armed Conflict and Political Violence* (London: Zed).

Motta, Mary (2006), 'Reporters Get First-Hand Look at Libyan WMD', *VOA News*, 14 March.

Mueller, John (2000), 'The banality of ethnic war', *International Security*, 25(1): 42–70.

Mueller, John (2006a), 'Is there still a terrorist threat? The myth of the omnipresent enemy', *Foreign Affairs*, 85(5): 2–8.

Mueller, John (2006b), *Overblown* (New York: Free Press).

Mueller, John (2010), *Atomic Obsession. Nuclear Alarmism from Hiroshima to al-Qaeda* (Oxford: Oxford University Press).

Munkler, Herfried (2004), *The New Wars* (Cambridge: Polity).

Musah, A-F. and K. Fayemi (2000), 'Africa: In Search of Security', in A-F Musah and K. Fayemi (eds.), *Mercenaries: An African Security Dilemma* (London: Pluto), pp. 13–42.

Myint-U, Thant, and Amy Scott (2007), *The UN Secretariat: A Brief History (1945–2006)* (New York: International Peace Academy).

Nafziger, E. Wayne and Juha Auvinen (2002), 'Economic development, inequality, war and state violence', *World Development*, 30(2): 153–63.

Nagl, John A. (2005), *Learning to Eat Soup With A Knife* (Chicago: University of Chicago Press).

Nantais, Cynthia and Martha F. Lee (1999), 'Women in the United States military: protectors or protected?', *Journal of Gender Studies*, 8(2): 181–91.

Narlikar, Amrita (2010), *New Powers and How to Manage Them* (New York: Colombia University Press).

Nash, John (1951), 'Non-cooperative games', *Annals of Mathematics*, 54(2): 286–95.

National Advisory Committee on Criminal Justice Standards and Goals (NACCJSG) (1976), *Report of the Task Force on Disorders and Terrorism* (Washington DC: US Government Printing Office).

National Commission on the BP Deepwater Horizon Oil Spill and Offshore Drilling (National Commission) (2011), *Deep Water: The Gulf Oil Disaster and the*

*Future of Offshore Drilling* (Washington, DC: National Commission).

National Energy Policy Development Group (NEPDG) (2001), *National Energy Policy* (Washington, DC: The White House, 17 May).

National Film Board of Canada (1997), *Chronicle of a Genocide Foretold: Part 2, 'Kigali: "We Were Cowards".* (Ottawa: National Film Board of Canada).

National Nuclear Security Administration (NNSA) (2005), *Future of the Nuclear Weapons Complex*, at www.nnsa.doe.gov/docs/Future_of_the_Nuclear_Weapons_Complex.pdf

National Nuclear Security Administration (NNSA) (2007), 'NNSA Releases Report on Plans for Future of the Nuclear Weapons Complex', at www.nnsa.doe.gov/docs/newsreleases/2007/PR_2007-2-2_NA-07-03.htm

Navari, Cornelia (2006), 'Globalization and security: much ado about nothing?', in William Bain (ed.), *The Empire of Security and the Safety of the People* (Abingdon: Routledge), pp. 116–38.

Neal, Andrew W. (2009), *Exceptionalism and the Politics of Counter-terrorism* (New York: Routledge).

Nef, Jorge (2002), *Human Security and Mutual Vulnerability* (Ottawa: International Development Research Centre).

Neged Neshek (2011), 'Israel and the Rise of Drone Warfare', at www.negedneshek.org/exports/uavs/israel-and-the-rise-of-drone-warfare/

Neufeld, Mark (2004), 'Pitfalls of emancipation and discourses of security: reflections on Canada's 'Security with a Human Face", *International Relations*, 18(1): 109–23.

Newell, Peter and Matthew Paterson (2010), *Climate Capitalism* (Cambridge: Cambridge University Press).

Newman, Edward (1998), *The UN Secretary-General From The Cold War To The New Era* (Basingstoke: Macmillan).

Newman, Edward (2001), 'Human security and constructivism', *International Studies Perspectives*, 2(3): 239–51.

Newman, Edward (2004), 'The "New Wars" debate: A historical perspective is needed', *Security Dialogue*, 35(2): 173–89.

Newton, Allen (2011), 'The "Talking Cure": Intelligence, counter-terrorism doctrine and social movements', *Intelligence and National Security*, 26(1): 120–131.

Nicholas, Peter (2011), 'Samantha Power, Long a Critic of U.S. Foreign Policy, Now Helps Shape It', *Los Angeles Times*, 30 March.

Nicolson, Harold (1939), *Diplomacy* (London: Oxford University Press).

Niebuhr, Reinhold (1940), *Christianity and Power Politics* (New York: Scribner's).

Niou, Emerson, Peter Ordeshook and Gregory F. Rose (1989), *The Balance of Power* (Cambridge: Cambridge University Press).

Nixon, Richard (1971), 'Informal Remarks by Richard Nixon in Guam with Newsmen', 25 July 1969 in *Public Papers of the Presidents of the United States – Richard Nixon, 1969* (Washington, DC: US Government Printing Office).

Nizamani, Haider K. (2008), 'Our Region Their Theories: A Case for Critical Security Studies in South Asia', in Navnita C. Behera (ed.) *International Relations in South Asia* (Delhi: Oxford University Press) pp. 90–109.

Non-Aligned Movement (2005), 'Statement By Chairman of the Non-Aligned Movement Concerning the Draft Outcome Document of the High-Level Plenary Meeting of the General Assembly', 21 June.

Norchi, Charles (1998), 'Cold War Reheated' *New York Times*, 20 September, at www.nytimes.com/books/98/09/20/reviews/980920.20norchit.html

Norris, Robert J. and Hans M. Kristensen (2006), 'Nuclear Notebook: Global Nuclear Stockpiles, 1945–2006', *Bulletin of Atomic Scientists*, 62(4): 64–6.

North, Douglass, C. (1990), *Institutions, Institutional Change and Economic Performance* (Cambridge: Cambridge University Press).

Nuruzzaman, Mohammed (2006), 'Beyond the realist theories: "Neo-conservative realism" and the American invasion of Iraq', *International Studies Perspectives*, 7(3): 239–53.

Nye, Joseph (1968), *International Regionalism* (Boston: Little Brown and Co.).

Nye, Joseph (1971), *Peace in Parts* (Boston: Little Brown and Co.).

Nye, Joseph (2004), *Soft Power: The Means to Success in World Politics* (New York: Public Affairs).

Nye, Joseph (2008a), 'Bridging the gap between theory and policy', *Political Psychology*, 29(4): 593–602.

Nye, Joseph (2008b), 'International relations: the relevance of theory to practice', Christian Reus-Smit and Duncan Snidal (eds.), *The Oxford Handbook of International Relations* (Oxford: Oxford University Press), pp. 648–59.

Ó Tuathail, Gearóid (1996), *Critical Geopolitics* (London: Routledge).

Ó Tuathail, Gearóid (2000), 'The postmodern geo-political condition: states, statecraft, and security at the millennium', *Annals of the Association of American Geographers*, 90(1): 166–78.

O'Brien, Kevin (1998), 'Freelance forces: Exploiters of old or new-age peacebrokers?' *Janes Intelligence Review*, 10(8): 42–6.

O'Brien, Kevin (2000), 'PMCs, myths, and mercenaries', *Royal United Service Institute Journal*, (February), pp. 59–64.

O'Halpin, Eunan (2005), 'Evidence from the Butler and Hutton Reports: The British case for confronting Iraq', *Irish Studies in International Affairs*, 16(1): 89–102.

O'Neill, Barry (1994a), 'Sources in Game Theory for International Relations Specialists', in Michael D. Intriligator and Urs Luterbacher (eds.), *Cooperative Models in International Relations Research* (Boston: Kluwer), pp. 9–30.

O'Neill, Barry (1994b), 'Game Theory Models of Peace and War', in Robert J. Aumann and Sergiu Hart (eds.), *Handbook of Game Theory*. Vol.2 (Amsterdam: Elsevier), pp. 995–1090.

O'Neill, Barry (2007), 'Game Models of Peace and War: Some Recent Themes', in Rudolf Avenhaus and I. William Zartman (eds.), *Diplomacy Games* (Berlin: Springer), pp. 25–44.

Oakley, Robert, B., Michael J. Dziedzic and Eliot M. Goldberg (1997), *Policing the New World Disorder* (Washington, DC: National Defense University).

Obama, Barack (2009), 'From Peril to Progress', Remarks by the President on Jobs, Energy, and Climate Change, the White House, Washington, DC, 26 January, at www.whitehouse.gov

Obama, Barack (2011), 'Remarks by the President on America's Energy Security', Georgetown University, Washington, DC, 30 March, at www.whitehouse.gov

Oberdorfer, Don (1992), '1982 Arms Policy with China Victim of Bush Campaign, Texas Lobbying', *Washington Post*, 4 September.

Oelsner, Andrea (2009), 'Consensus and governance in Mercosur. The evolution of the South American security agenda', *Security Dialogue*, 40(2): 191–212.

Olsson, Christian (2009), Conquérir "les coeurs et les esprits"? Usages et enjeux de légitimation locale de la force dans les missions de pacification extérieures (Bosnie, Kosovo, Afghanistan, Irak; 1996–2006) (PhD thesis, Sciences Po Paris).

Omand, David (2006), 'Ethical guidelines in using secret intelligence for public security', *Cambridge Review of International Affairs*, 19(4): 613–28.

Omand, David (2009), *The National Security Strategy: Implications for the UK Intelligence Community* (London: Institute for Public Policy Research).

Oneal, John and Bruce Russett (1997), 'The classical liberals were right: Democracy, interdependence, and conflict 1950–85', *International Studies Quarterly*, 41(2): 267–93.

Onuf, Nicholas (1989), *World of Our Making* (Columbia: University of Southern California Press).

Organski, A.F.K. (1958), *World Politics*, 1st edition (New York: Knopf).

Organski, A.F.K. (1968a), *World Politics*, 2nd edition (New York: Knopf).

Organski, A.F.K. (1968b), 'Power Transition', in David L. Sills (ed.), *International Encyclopedia of the Social Sciences*, Vol. 12 (New York: The Macmillan Company and The Free Press), pp. 415–18.

Organski, A.F.K. and Jacek Kugler (1980), *The War Ledger* (Chicago: University of Chicago Press).

Osgood, Robert E. (1962), *NATO, the Entangling Alliance* (Chicago: University of Chicago Press).

Osgood, Robert E. (1968), *Alliances and American Foreign Policy* (Baltimore, MD: Johns Hopkins Press).

Osiander, Andreas (1998), 'Rereading early twentieth century IR theory: Idealism revisited' *International Studies Quarterly*, 42(3): 409–32.

Overy, Richard (2005), 'Total War 2: The Second World War', in Townshend (ed.) (2005), pp. 138–157.

Owen, John M. (1996), 'How Liberalism Produces Democratic Peace', in M.E. Brown, S. Lynn-Jones and S. Miller (eds.), *Debating the Democratic Peace* (Cambridge, MA: MIT Press), pp. 116–56.

Oxfam International (2011), 'Why We Need a Global Arms Trade Treaty', at www.oxfam.org/en/campaigns/conflict/controlarms/why-we-need-global-arms-trade-treaty

Oye, Kenneth A. (1986), *Cooperation Under Anarchy* (Princeton, NJ: Princeton University Press).

Özet, Aylin (2010), 'Civil Society and Security in Turkey – Communities of (in)Security and Agency', *GCST-New Voices* 3, at www.securitytransformation.org/bli.php?id=176

Packer, George (2005), *The Assassin's Gate: America in Iraq* (New York: Farrar, Straus and Giroux).

Paige, Glenn D. (1968), *The Korean Decision* (New York: Free Press).

Palme, Olaf (1982), 'Introduction', in The Report of the Independent Commission on Disarmament and Security Issues, *Common Security: A Blueprint for Survival* (London: Pan).

Palmer, Michael A. (1992), *Guardians of the Gulf* (New York: Free Press).

Pape, Robert A. (1996), *Bombing to Win: Air Power and Coercion in War* (Ithaca, NY: Cornell University Press).

Paris, Roland (1997), 'Peacebuilding and the limits of liberal internationalism', *International Security*, 22(2): 54–89.

Paris, Roland (2001), 'Human security: Paradigm shift or hot air?', *International Security*, 26(2): 87–102.

Paris, Roland (2004), *At War's End: Building Peace After Civil Conflict* (Cambridge: Cambridge University Press).

Pascal, Cleo (2010), *Global Warring: How Environmental, Economic and Political Crises will Redraw the World Map* (Toronto: Key Porter).

Pasha, Mustapha Kamal (1996), 'Security as hegemony', *Alternatives*, 21(3): 283–302.

Passas, Nikos (1998), 'Globalization and transnational crime: Effects of criminogenic asymmetries', *Transnational Organized Crime*, 4(3–4): 22–56.

Pasztor, Andy (1991), 'Investigators Say Chilean Dealer Smuggled U.S. Weapons to Iraq', *Wall Street Journal*, 20 November.

Perito, Robert (2002), *The American Experience with Police in Peacekeeping Operations* (Clementsport, NS: Canadian Peacekeeping Press).

Perkovich, George (1999), *India's Nuclear Bomb* (Berkeley, CA: University of California Press).

Peters, Gretchen (2011), 'The Afghan Insurgency and Organized Crime', in Whit Mason (ed.), *The Rule of Law, Missing in Inaction* (New York: Cambridge University Press).

Peterson, M.J. (2005), *The UN General Assembly* (London: Routledge).

Peterson, V. Spike and Anne Sisson Runyan (1999), *Global Gender Issues*, 2nd edition (Boulder, CO: Westview).

Pew Forum on Religion & Public Life (October 2009), at http://pewforum.org/Mapping-the-Global-Muslim-Population.aspx

Philipose, L. (2007), 'The politics of pain and the end of empire', *International Feminist Journal of Politics*, 9(1): 60–81.

Phillips, Kevin (2006), *American Theocracy* (New York: Viking).

Pierson, Paul (1996), 'The path to european integration. A historical institutional analysis', *Comparative Political Studies*, 29(2): 123–63.

Pillar, Paul R. (ed.) (2003), *Terrorism and U.S. Foreign Policy* (Washington DC: Brookings Institution Press).

Pincus, W. and S. Barr (2007), 'CIA Plans Cutbacks, Limits on Contractor Staffing', *Washington Post*, 11 June.

Pocock, Chris (1989), *Dragon Lady: The History of the U-2 Spyplane*. (Shrewsbury: Airlife).

Pollitt, Katha (2001), 'Where are the women?', *The Nation*, 22 October.

Poore, Stuart (2003), 'What is context? A reply to the Gray-Johnston debate on strategic culture', *Review of International Studies*, 29(2): 279–84.

Posen, Barry (1993), 'The security dilemma and ethnic conflict', *Survival*, 35(1): 27–47.

Posen, Barry (2003), 'Command of the commons: the military foundation of U.S. hegemony', *International Security*, 28(1): 5–46.

Posner, Richard A. (2005), *Preventing Surprise Attacks: Intelligence Reform in the Wake of 9/11* (Lanham, MD: Rowman & Littlefield).

Pouligny, Béatrice (2006), *Peace Operations Seen From Below* (London: Hurst).

Powell, Robert (1991), 'Absolute and relative gains in international relations theory', *American Political Science Review*, 85(4): 1303–20.

Powell Robert (2002), 'Bargaining theory and international conflict', *Annual Review of Political Science*, 5: 1–30.

Powell Robert (2003), 'Nuclear deterrence theory, nuclear proliferation, and national missile defense', *International Security*, 27(4): 86–118.

Power, Samantha (2003), *A Problem from Hell* (New York: Harper Perennial).

Powers, Francis Gary (1971), *Operation Overflight* (London: Hodder and Stoughton).

Prantl, Jochen (forthcoming), *Whither Liberal Institutions? European Union, NATO and United Nations* (Oxford: Oxford University Press).

Price, Richard (2008), 'Moral limit and possibility in world politics', *International Organization*, 62(2): 191–220.

Price, Richard and Christian Reus-Smit (1998), 'Dangerous liaisons? Critical international theory and constructivism', *European Journal of International Relations*, 4(3): 259–294.

Price, Richard and Mark Zacher (eds.) (2004), *The United Nations and Global Security* (New York: Palgrave).

Price-Smith, Andrew (2009), *Contagion and Chaos* (Cambridge, MA: MIT Press).

Priest, Dana (2004), 'Private Guards Repel Attack on US Headquarters', *Washington Post,* 6 April, p.A1.

Priest, Dana and Bill Arkin (2011), *Top Secret America* (Boston: Little and Brown).

Public Radio International (2009), 'The Responsibility to Protect', 7 March, at www.pri.org/stories/world/global-responsibility-to-protect.html

Pugh, Michael (2010), 'Accountability and Credibility: assessing host population perceptions and expectations', in Cedric de Coning, Andreas Øien Stensland and Thierry Tardy (eds.), *Beyond the 'New Horizon'*, proceedings from a seminar on 'UN Peacekeeping Future Challenges', Geneva, 23–24 June, pp. 56–65.

Pugh, Michael and W.P.S. Sidhu (eds.) (2003), *The United Nations and Regional Security* (Boulder, CO: Lynne Rienner).

Pumphrey, Carolyn (ed.) (2008), *Global Climate Change: National Security Implications* (Carlisle, PA: U.S. Army War College).

Quackenbush, Stephen L. (2006), 'National missile defense and deterrence', *Political Research Quarterly*, 59(4): 533–41.

Quackenbush, Stephen L. (2010), 'General deterrence and international conflict', *International Interactions*, 36: 60–85.

Ramcharan, Bertrand G. (2008), *The UN and Preventive Diplomacy* (Bloomington: Indiana University Press).

Ranciere, Jacques (2006), *On the Shores of Politics* (London: Verso).

Raphael Lemkin (1944), *Axis Rule in Occupied Europe* (Washington, DC: Carnegie Endowment for International Peace).

Rapoport, Anatol (1968), 'Introduction', in Carl Von Clausewitz, *On War*. Edited by Anatol Rapoport. (London: Penguin), pp. 11–80.

Rasler, Karen and William R. Thompson (1983), 'Global wars, public debts, and the long cycle', *World Politics*, 35(4): 489–516.

Rasler, Karen and William R. Thompson (1985), 'War making and state making', *American Political Science Review*, 79(2): 491–507.

Rasler, Karen and William R. Thompson (1991), 'Technological innovation, capability positional shifts, and systemic war', *Journal of Conflict Resolution*, 35(3): 412–42.

Rasler, Karen and William R. Thompson (1994), *The Great Powers and Global Struggle, 1490–1990* (Lexington, KT: University Press of Kentucky).

Rasler, Karen and William R. Thompson (2000), 'Global War and the Political Economy of Structural Change', in Manus I. Midlarsky (ed.), *The Handbook of War Studies II* (Ann Arbor, MI: Michigan University Press), pp. 301–31.

Rasler, Karen and William R. Thompson (2001), 'Malign autocracies and major power warfare', *Security Studies*, 10(3): 46–79.

Ray, James Lee (2003), 'A Lakatosian View of the Democratic Peace Research Program', in Elman and Elman (eds.) (2003), pp. 205–43.

Rees, Wyn and Richard J. Aldrich (2005), 'Contending cultures of counterterrorism: Transatlantic divergence or convergence?' *International Affairs*, 81(5): 905–25.

Reisman, Michael W. and James E. Baker (1992), *Regulating Covert Action* (New Haven, CT: Yale University Press).

Report of the Commission on Human Security (2003), *Human Security Now* (New York: UN).

Reus-Smit, Christian (2002), 'Imagining society: Constructivism and the English School', *British Journal of Politics and International Relations*, 4(3): 487–509.

Reuters (2011), 'US to Supply Pakistan with 85 Mini-drones', 21 April.

Reveron, Derek S. and Kathleen A. Mahoney-Norris (2011), *Human Security in a Borderless World* (Boulder, CO: Westview).

Review Conference of the Parties to the Treaty on the Non-Proliferation of Nuclear Weapons (NPT RevCon) (2000), *Final Document:* NPT/CONF. 2000/28 (Parts I and II).

Review Conference of the Parties to the Treaty on the Non-Proliferation of Nuclear Weapons (NPT RevCon) (2010), *Final Document:* NPT/CONF. 2010/50 (Vol.I).

Rice, Condoleezza (2000), 'Campaign 2000: Promoting the national interest', *Foreign Affairs*, 79(1): 45–62.

Richelson, Jeffrey T. (2006), *Spying on the Bomb* (New York: W.W. Norton).

Richmond, Oliver (2005), *The Transformation of Peace* (Basingstoke: Palgrave).

Richter-Montpetit, M. (2007), 'Empire, desire and violence: A queer transnational feminist reading of the prisoner "abuse" in Abu Ghraib and the question of "gender equality"', *International Feminist Journal of Politics*, 9(1): 38–59.

Rieff, David (1996), *Slaughterhouse: Bosnia and the Failure of the West* (New York: Simon and Schuster).

Riker, William H. (1962), *The Theory of Political Coalitions* (New Haven, CT: Yale University Press).

Rivlin, Benjamin, and Leon Gordenker (1993), *The Challenging Role of the UN Secretary-General* (Westport, CT: Praeger).

Roberts, Adam (2005), 'Against War', in Townshend (ed.) (2005), pp. 317–340.

Roberts, Adam (2010), 'Lives and statistics: Are 90% of war victims civilians?', *Survival*, 52(3): 115–36.

Roberts, Paul (2004), *The End of Oil* (Boston: Houghton Mifflin).

Robinson, Geoffrey (2010), *'If You Leave Us Here, We Will Die': How Genocide Was Stopped in East Timor* (Princeton, NJ: Princeton University Press).

Rocca, Ambassador Christina (2007), 'Creating the Environment Necessary For Nuclear Disarmament', Statement to the Conference on Disarmament, 6 February, at www.usmission.ch/Press2007/0206 Rocca.html

Roman, Peter J. (1995), *Eisenhower and the Missile Gap* (Ithaca, NY: Cornell University Press).

Rose, Gideon (1998), 'Review: Neoclassical realism and theories of foreign policy', *World Politics*, 51(1): 144–72.

Rosenau, James (1990), *Turbulence in World Politics*, (Princeton NJ: Princeton University Press).

Rosenthal, Joel H. (1991), *Righteous Realists: Political Realism, Responsible Power, and American Culture in the Nuclear Age* (Baton Rouge, LA: Louisiana State University Press).

Rothschild, Emma (1995), 'What is security?', *Daedalus*, 124(3): 53–98.

Rothstein, Robert (1977), *The Weak in the World of the Strong* (New York: Columbia University Press).

Rousseau, David L. (2002), 'Motivations for choice: The salience of relative gains in international politics', *Journal of Conflict Resolution*, 46(3): 394–426.

Rousseau, Jean Jacques (1917), *A Lasting Peace Through the Federation of Europe and The State of War* (trans. C.E. Vaughn) (London: Constable and Co.).

Ruane, Joseph and Jennifer Todd (1996), *The Dynamics of Conflict in Northern Ireland* (Cambridge: Cambridge University Press).

Ruggie, John (1999), *Constructing the World Polity* (London: Routledge).

Rummel, R.J. (1994), *Death by Government* (New Brunswick, NJ: Transaction).

Rumsfeld, Donald (2011), *Known and Unknown: A Memoir* (New York: Sentinel).

Russet, Bruce (1967), *International Regions and the International System* (Chicago: Rand McNally).

Russet, Bruce (1993), *Grasping the Democratic Peace* (Princeton, NJ: Princeton University Press).

Russett, Bruce (1996), 'Why Liberal Peace?', in M.E. Brown, S. Lynn-Jones and S. Miller (eds.), *Debating the Democratic Peace* (Cambridge, MA: MIT Press), pp. 82–115.

Russett, Bruce and Harvey Starr (2000), 'From Democratic Peace to Kantian Peace', in M.I. Midlarsky (ed.) *Handbook of War Studies II* (Ann Arbor: University of Michigan Press), pp. 93–128.

Sabrosky, Alan (ed.) (1985), *Polarity and War* (Boulder, CO: Westview).

Sagan, Scott (1996/7), 'Why do states build nuclear weapons? Three models in search of a bomb', *International Security*, 21(3): 54–86.

Sagan, Scott and Kenneth Waltz (2003), *The Spread of Nuclear Weapons: A Debate Renewed*, 2nd edition (New York: W.W. Norton).

Said, Edward W. (1994), *Representations of the Intellectual* (New York: Pantheon Books).

Saideman, Stephen M. (2001), *The Ties That Divide: Ethnic Politics, Foreign Policy and International Conflict* (New York: Columbia University Press).

Sambanis, Nicholas, *et al.* (2002), 'Addressing Conflict: Emerging Policy at the World Bank', in Fen Osler Hampson and David M. Malone (eds.), *From Reaction to Conflict Prevention* (Boulder, CO: Lynne Rienner), pp. 321–56.

Samuel, Kumudini (2001), 'Gender difference in conflict resolution: The case of Sri Lanka', in Inger Skjelsbæk and Dan Smith (eds.) *Gender, Peace and Conflict* (London: Sage Publications).

Sarooshi, Danesh (1998), *The United Nations and the Development of Collective Security* (Oxford: Oxford University Press).

Satha-Anand, Chaiwat (1990), 'The Non-violent Crescent: Eight Theses on Muslim Non-violent Action', in Ralph E. Crow, Philip Grant and Saad E. Ibrahim (eds.), *Arab Nonviolent Struggle in the Middle East* (London: Lynne Rienner), pp. 25–40.

Savranskaya, Svetlana (ed.) (2001), *September 11th Sourcebooks Volume II: Afghanistan: Lessons from the Last War The Soviet Experience in Afghanistan: Russian Documents* (9 October). The National Security Archive at the George Washington University, at www.gwu.edu/~nsarchiv/NSAEBB/NSAEBB57/soviet.html

Schatzki, T.R., K. Knorr-Cetina and E. Savigny (2001), *The Practice Turn in Contemporary Theory* (New York: Routledge).

Schelling, Thomas C. (1960), *The Strategy of Conflict* (Cambridge, MA: Harvard University Press).

Schelling, Thomas C. (1966), *Arms and Influence* (New Haven, CT: Yale University Press).

Schlesinger, James R. (2005), 'Statement before the Senate Foreign Relations Committee', 16 November, at http://foreign.senate.gov

Schmeidl, Susanne (2002), '(Human) security dilemmas: long-term implications of the Afghan refugee crisis', *Third World Quarterly*, 23(1): 7–29.

Schmid, Herman (1968), 'Peace research and politics', *Journal of Peace Research*, 5(3): 217–32.

Schmidt, Brian and Michael C. Williams (2008), 'The Bush Doctrine and the Iraq War: Neoconservatives versus Realists', *Security Studies*, 17(2): 191–220.

Scholte, Jan Aart (2000), *Globalization: A Critical Introduction* (Basingstoke: Macmillan).

Schreuer, Christoph (1995), 'Regionalism v. Universalism', *European Journal of International Law*, 6(3): 1–23.

Schroeder, P. (1976), 'Alliances, 1815–1945: Weapons of Power and Tools of Management', in K. Knorr (ed.), *Historical Dimensions of National Security* (Lawrence: University Press of Kansas), pp. 227–62.

Schultz, George P., William J. Perry, Henry A. Kissinger, Sam Nunn (2007), 'A world free of nuclear weapons', *Wall Street Journal*, 4 January.

Schwarzenberger, Georg (1941), *Power Politics* (New York: Praeger).

Schweller, Randall L. (1993), 'Tripolarity and the Second World War', *International Studies Quarterly*, 37(1): 73–103.

Schweller, Randall L. (1994), 'Bandwagoning for profit: Bringing the revisionist state back in', *International Security*, 19(1): 72–107.

Schweller, Randall L. (1996), 'Neorealism's status-quo bias: What security dilemma?' *Security Studies*, 5(3): 90–121.

Schweller, Randall L. (2006), *Unanswered Threats: Political Constraints on the Balance of Power* (Princeton, NJ: Princeton University Press).

Schweller, Randall L. (2009), 'Neoclassical Realism and State Mobilization: Expansionist Ideology in the Age of Mass Politics', in Lobell *et al.* (eds.) (2009), pp. 227–50.

Scott, Len (2004), 'Secret intelligence, covert action and clandestine diplomacy', *Intelligence and National Security*, 19(2): 322–34.

Secret Intelligence Service (SIS) (2011), 'UK National Security Strategy', at www.sis.gov.uk/about-us/what-we-do/uk-national-security-strategy.html

Segal, Gerald (1982), *The Great Power Triangle* (London: Macmillan).

Seiple, Chris (2002), 'Homeland security concepts and strategies', *Orbis*, 46(2): 259–73.

Selten, Reinhard (1975), 'A re-examination of the perfectness concept for equilibrium points in extensive games', *International Journal of Game Theory*, 4: 25–55.

Serio, Joseph D. (2008), *Investigating the Russian Mafia* (Durham: Carolina Academic Press).

Shane III, Leo (2005), 'Military Issues Content Warning to Combat-Zone Bloggers', *Stars and Stripes*, 1 October, at http://stripes.com

Shanker, Thom (2011), 'After a Decade of War, Top Officer Directs the Military to Take Stock of Itself', *New York Times*, 8 January, at www.nytimes.com/2011/01/09/us/09mullen.html?emc=eta1

Sharman, Jason (2009), 'The bark *is* the bite: International organizations and blacklisting', *Review of International Political Economy*, 16(4): 573–96.

Sharoni, Simona (1996), 'Gender and the Israeli-Palestinian Accord: Feminist Approaches to International Politics', in Deniz Kandiyoti (ed.) *Gendering the Middle East* (Syracuse, NY: Syracuse University Press), pp. 107–26.

Shaw, Martin (1994), '"There is no such thing as society": Beyond individualism and statism in international security studies', *Review of International Studies*, 19(2): 159–76.

Shaw, Martin (2000), 'The contemporary mode of warfare? Mary Kaldor's theory of new wars', *Review of International Political Economy*, 7(1): 171–92.

Shearer, David (1998), *Private Armies and Military Intervention* (Oxford: Oxford University Press, Adelphi Paper 316).

Sheffer, Gabriel, (ed.) (1986), *Modern Diasporas in International Politics* (London: Croom-Helm).

Shepherd, Laura J. (ed.) (2010), *Gender Matters in Global Politics* (London: Routledge).

Shimshoni, Jonathan (1988), *Israel and Conventional Deterrence* (Ithaca, NY: Cornell University Press).

Shiraz, Zakia (2011), 'CIA intervention in Chile and the fall of the Allende government in 1973', *Journal of American Studies*, 45(3): 603–613.

Shorrock, Tim (2008), *Spies for Hire* (New York: Simon and Schuster).

Shpiro, Shlomo (2003), 'The CIA as Middle East peace broker?', *Survival*, 45(2): 91–112.

Shultz, Kenneth A. (2001), *Democracy and Coercive Diplomacy* (Cambridge: Cambridge University Press).

Shuman, Frederick (1933), *International Politics* (New York: McGraw-Hill).

Sick, Gary (1985), *All Fall Down* (New York: Random House).

Sieff, Kevin (2011), 'Florida Pastor Terry Jones's Koran Burning Has Far-Reaching Effect', *Washington Post*, 2 April, at www.washingtonpost.com/local/education/florida-pastor-terry-joness-koran-burning-has-far-reaching-effect/2011/04/02/AFpiFoQC_story.html

Signorino, Curt S. and Ahmer Tarar (2006), 'A unified theory and test of extended immediate deterrence', *American Journal of Political Science*, 50(3): 586–605.

Silverston, Ken (1998), 'Privatizing war', *The Nation*, 7 July.

Simma, Bruno (ed.) (2002), *The Charter of the United Nations*, 2nd edition, 2 vols. (Oxford: Oxford University Press).

Simmons, Matthew R. (2005), *Twilight in the Desert* (New York: John Wiley).

Simon, J.D. (1997), 'Biological terrorism: preparing to meet the threat', *Journal of the American Medical Association*, 278(5): 428–30.

Singer, J. David, Stuart Bremer and John Stuckey (1972), 'Capability Distribution, Uncertainty and Major Power War, 1820–1965' in Bruce M. Russett (ed.), *Peace, War, and Numbers* (Beverly Hills: Sage), pp. 19–48.

Singer, P.W. (2001/02), 'Corporate warriors: The rise of the privatized military industry and its ramifications for international security', *International Security*, 26(3): 186–220.

Singer, P.W. (2003a), *Corporate Warriors: the Rise of the Privatized Military Industry* (Ithaca, NY: Cornell University Press).

Singer, P.W. (2003b), 'Peacekeepers, Inc.', *Policy Review*, (June).

Singer, P.W. (2005), *Children At War* (London: Pantheon).

SIPRI (2011), 'World military spending reached $1.6 trillion in 2010', 16 April, at www.sipri.org/media/pressreleases/milex

*SIPRI Yearbook 2010* (Oxford: Oxford University Press).

Sjoberg, Laura (2007), 'Agency, militarized femininity and enemy others: Observations from the war in Iraq', *International Feminist Journal of Politics*, 9(1): 82–101.

Sjoberg, Laura and Caron E. Gentry (2007), *Mothers, Monsters, Whores: Women's Violence in Global Politics* (London: Zed).

Small Arms Survey (2002), *Small Arms Survey 2002: Counting the Human Cost* (Oxford: Oxford University Press).

Small Arms Survey (2004), *Small Arms Survey 2004: Rights at Risk* (New York: Oxford University Press).

Small, Melvin and J. David Singer (1982), *Resort to Arms: International and Civil War, 1816–1980* (Beverly Hills, CA: Sage).

Smil, Vaclav (2008), *Global Catastrophes and Trends: The Next Fifty Years* (Cambridge, MA: MIT Press).

Smith, Alastair (1995), 'Alliance formation and war', *International Studies Quarterly*, 39(4): 405–25.

Smith, Anthony D. (1986), *The Ethnic Origins of Nations* (New York: Blackwell).

Smith, Chris (1995), 'Light Weapons and Ethnic Conflict in South Asia', in Boutwell, Klare, and Reed (1995), pp. 61–80.

Smith, Hugo (1994), 'Intelligence and UN peace-keeping', *Survival*, 36(3): 177–97.

Smith, Michael Joseph (1986), *Realist Thought From Weber to Kissinger* (Baton Rouge: Louisiana State University Press).

Smith, Paul J. (2007), 'Climate change, mass migration and the military response', *Orbis*, 51(4): 617–33.

Smith, Rupert (2005), *The Utility of Force: The Art of War in the Modern World* (London: Allen Lane).

Smith, Steve (1996), 'Positivism and Beyond', in Steve Smith, Ken Booth and Marysia Zalewski (eds.), *International Theory* (Cambridge: Cambridge University Press), pp. 11–44.

Smith, Steve (1999), 'The increasing insecurity of security studies', *Contemporary Security Policy*, 20(3): 72–101.

Smith, Steve (2000), 'The discipline of International Relations: Still an American social science?', *British Journal of Politics and International Relations*, 2(3): 374–402.

Smith, Steve (2005), 'The Contested Concept of Security', in Ken Booth (ed.), *Critical Security Studies and World Politics* (Boulder, CO: Lynne Rienner), pp. 27–62.

Snidal, Duncan (1991a), 'International cooperation among relative gains maximizers', *International Studies Quarterly*, 35(4): 387–402.

Snidal, Duncan (1991b), 'Relative gains and the pattern of international cooperation', *American Political Science Review*, 85(3): 701–26.

Snidal, Duncan (2002), 'Rational Choice and International Relations', in Walter Carlsnaes, Thomas Riesse and Beth A. Simmons (eds.), *Handbook of International Relations* (London: Sage), pp. 73–94.

Snyder, Glenn (1958), *Deterrence by Denial and Punishment* (Princeton, NJ: Center of International Studies).

Snyder, Glenn H. (1997), *Alliance Politics* (Ithaca, NY: Cornell University Press).

Snyder, Glenn H. and Paul Diesing (1977), *Conflict Among Nations* (Princeton, NJ: Princeton University Press).

Snyder, Jack (1977), *The Soviet Strategic Culture: Implications for Nuclear Options* (Santa Barbara, CA: Rand).

Snyder, Jack (1991), *Myths of Empire* (Ithaca, NY: Cornell University Press).

Snyder, Jack (2000), *From Voting to Violence: Democratization and Nationalist Conflict* (New York: W.W. Norton).

Solomon, Norman (2001), 'The 'Wimp' Factor: Goading to Shed Blood', *Media Beat* 28, at www.fair.org/media-beat/010928.html

Spear, Joanna and Paul D. Williams (eds.) (2012), *Security and Development in Global Politics* (Washington, DC: Georgetown University Press).

Spiro, David E. (1996), 'The Insignificance of the Liberal Peace', in M.E. Brown, S. Lynn-Jones and S. Miller (eds.), *Debating the Democratic Peace* (Cambridge, MA: MIT Press), pp. 202–38.

Spirtas, Michael (1996), 'A house divided: Tragedy and evil in realist theory', *Security Studies*, 5(3): 385–423.

Squire, Vicki (2010), *Borderzones of Mobility, Security and Citizenship* (London: Routledge).

Stamnes, Eli (2004), 'Critical security studies and the United Nations preventive deployment in Macedonia', *International Peacekeeping*, 11(1): 161–81.

Stamnes, Eli and Richard Wyn Jones (2000), 'Burundi: A critical security perspective', *Peace and Conflict Studies*, 7(2): 37–55.

Standing, Andre (2003), *The Social Contradictions of Organized Crime on the Cape Flats* (Johannesburg: Institute for Security Studies Paper 74).

Steans, Jill (1998), *Feminism and International Relations* (New Jersey: Rutgers University Press).

Steffen, Will, Paul Crutzen and John R. O'Neill (2007), 'The Anthropocene: Are humans now overwhelming the great forces of nature?' *Ambio* 36(8): 614–21.

Steinberg, James B. (2009), 'Universities and public policy,' transcript of a presentation at the Presidents' National Dialogue, University of Ottawa, Canada, at www.sciencessociales.uottawa.ca/cepi-cips/eng/documents/steinberg.pdf

Stempel, John D. (2007), 'Covert action and diplomacy', *International Journal of Intelligence and Counter-intelligence*, 20(1): 122–35.

Sterling-Folker, Jennifer (2009), 'Neoclassical Realism and Identity: Peril Despite Profit Across the Taiwan Strait', in Lobell *et al.* (eds.) (2009), pp. 99–138.

Stewart, Frances (2003), 'Conflict and the millennium development goals' *Journal of Human Development*, 4(3): 325–51.

Stewart, Frances (2004), 'Development and security', *Conflict, Security and Development*, 4(3): 261–87.

Stewart, Frances and Graham Brown (2007), 'Motivations for Conflict: Groups and Individuals', in Chester A. Crocker, Fen Osler Hampson, and Pamela Aall (eds.), *Leashing the Dogs of War* (Washington, DC: US Institute of Peace), pp. 197–219.

Stewart, Frances, Valpy Fitzgerald *et al.* (2001), *War and Underdevelopment*, Vols 1 and 2 (Oxford: Oxford University Press).

Stoddard, Abby, Adele Harmer and Katherine Haver (2006), *Providing Aid in Insecure Environments: Trends in Policy and Operations* (London: Humanitarian Policy Group, HPG Report 23).

Strauss, Ekkehard (2009), ' "A bird in the hand is worth two in the Bush": On the assumed legal nature of the responsibility to protect', *Global Responsibility to Protect*, 1(3): 291–323.

Strongin, Robin and C. Stephen Redhead (2001), *Bioterrorism: Summary of a CRS/National Health Policy Forum Seminar on Federal, State and Local Public Health Preparedness* (Washington, DC: Congressional Research Service (CRS)).

Svendsen, Adam (2008), 'The globalization of intelligence since 9/11', *Cambridge Review of International Affairs*, 21(1): 131–46.

Swatuk, Larry A. and Peter Vale (1999), 'Why democracy is not enough: Southern Africa and human security in the twenty-first century', *Alternatives*, 24: 361–89.

Taliaferro, Jeffrey W. (2004), *Balancing Risks: Great Power Intervention in the Periphery* (Ithaca, NY: Cornell University Press).

Taliaferro, Jeffrey W. (2006), 'State building for future wars: Neoclassical realism and the resource-extractive state', *Security Studies*, 15(3): 464–95.

Tang, Shiping (2010), *A Theory of Security Strategy For Our Time* (Basingstoke: Palgrave-Macmillan).

Tannenwald, Nina (2007), *The Nuclear Taboo* (Cambridge: Cambridge University Press).

Tardy, Thierry (2011), 'A critique of robust peacekeeping in contemporary peace operations', *International Peacekeeping*, 18(2): 152–67.

Tavares, Rodrigo (2010), *Regional Security* (London: Routledge).

Taylor, Anita and M.J. Hardman (2004), 'War, language and gender, what new can be said? Framing the issues', *Women and Language*, 27(2): 3–19.

Teitelbaum, M.S. (1980), 'Right vs. Right: Immigration and refugee policy in the United States', *Foreign Affairs*, 59(1): 21–59.

Templer, Gerald (1960), 'Report on Service Intelligence', 16 December 1960, DEFE 23/23, UK National Archives.

Terriff, Terry, Stuart Croft, Lucy James and Patrick Morgan (1999), *Security Studies Today* (Cambridge: Polity).

Tetlock, Philip E. (2005), *Expert Political Judgment: How Good is it? How Can we Know?* (Princeton, NJ: Princeton University Press).

*The Star* (2004), 'Are We Fighting Foreign Wars?', *The Star* (Johannesburg), 10 February.

Thomas, Caroline (1987), *In Search of Security: The Third World in International Relations* (Boulder, CO: Lynne Rienner).

Thomas, Caroline (2000), *Global Governance, Development and Human Security* (London: Pluto Press).

Thomas, Caroline (2001), 'Global governance, development and human security: exploring the links', *Third World Quarterly*, 22(2): 159–75.

Thomas, Caroline (2007), 'Globalization and Development in the South', in John Ravenhill (ed.), *Global Political Economy*, 2nd edition (Oxford: Oxford University Press), pp. 410–47.

Thomas, Raju C.G. (ed.) (1983), *The Great Power Triangle and Asian Security* (Lexington, MA.: Lexington Books).

Thompson, William R. (1983), 'Uneven economic growth, systemic challenges, and global wars', *International Studies Quarterly*, 27(3): 341–55.

Thompson, William R. (1986), 'Polarity, the long cycle, and global power warfare', *Journal of Conflict Resolution*, 30(4): 587–615.

Thompson, William R. (1990), 'Long waves, technological innovation, and relative decline', *International Organization*, 44(2): 201–33.

Thomsen, Ian (1996), 'After the cold war, who's the 'enemy'?', *International Herald Tribune*, 24 July, at www.iht.com/articles/1996/07/24/oswimny.t_0.php

Thomson, Janice (1994), *Mercenaries, Pirates and Sovereigns* (Princeton: Princeton University Press).

Thornton, Rob (2000), 'The role of peace support operations doctrine in the British army', *International Peacekeeping*, 7(2): 41–62.

Thrift, Nigel (2006), 'Space', *Theory, Culture and Society*, 23(2–3): 139–46.

Thucydides (1972), *History of the Peloponnesian War* (London: Penguin Books). Trans R. Warner with an Introduction and Notes by M. I. Finley.

Tomes, Robert R. (2004), 'Relearning counter-insurgency warfare', *Parameters, US Army War College Quarterly*, 34(1): 16–28.

Tooze, Roger (2005), 'The Missing Link: Security, Critical International Political Economy, and Community', in Ken Booth (ed.), *Critical Security Studies and World Politics* (Boulder, CO: Lynne Rienner), pp. 133–58.

Tow, William T., Ramesh Thakur and In-Tayek Hyun (eds.) (2000), *Asia's Emerging Regional Order* (Tokyo: UN University Press).

Townshend, Charles (ed.) (2005), *The Oxford History of Modern War*, New edition (Oxford: Oxford University Press).

Treaty on the non-proliferation of nuclear weapons (1968), 1 July, at http://disarmament.un.org/wmd/npt/npttext.html

Treverton, Gregory (1988), *Covert Action* (New York: Basic Books).

Treverton, Gregory (2009), 'Intelligence test', *Democracy: A Journal of Ideas*, 11 (Winter), at www.democracyjournal.org/11/6667.php?page=2

Treverton, Gregory (2011), *Intelligence for an Age of Terror* (Cambridge: Cambridge University Press).

Trinquier, Roger (1961), *Modern Warfare: A French View of Counterinsurgency* at www.cgsc.edu/carl/resources/csi/trinquier/trinquier.asp

Tsoukala, Anastassia (2009), *Football Hooliganism in Europe* (Basingstoke: Palgrave-Macmillan).

Turshen, Meredeth and Clotilde Twagiramariya (eds.) (1998), *What Women Do in Wartime* (London: Zed Books).

Tuschhoff, C. (1999), 'Alliance cohesion and peaceful change in NATO', in H. Haftendorn, R.O. Keohane and C.A. Wallander (eds.), *Imperfect Unions* (Oxford: Oxford University Press), pp. 140–61.

Tversky, Amos, and Daniel Kahneman (eds.) (2000), *Choices, Values, and Frames* (Cambridge: Cambridge University Press).

Tversky, Amos, Paul Slovic and Daniel Kahneman (eds.) (1982), *Judgment Under Uncertainty* (Cambridge: Cambridge University Press).

UK Ministry of Defence (2004), *The Military Contribution to Peace Support Operations* (Joint Warfare Publication 3–50. 2nd edition, June).

ul Haq, Mahbub (1995), *Reflections on Human Development* (Oxford: Oxford University Press).

Ullman, Richard (1983), 'Redefining security', *International Security*, 8(1): 129–53.

UN (1995), *The Copenhagen Declaration and Programme of Action* (World Summit for Social Development, 6–12 March: New York: Oxford University Press).

UN (1999), *Report of the Group of Governmental Experts on Small Arms in Pursuance of General Assembly Resolution 52/38 J* (UN doc. A/54/258, 19 August), at www.iansa.org/documents/un/un_pub/reports/rep54258e.pdf

UN (2011a), *Millennium Development Goals: 2011 Progress Chart* (New York: UN Department of Economic and Social Affairs), at http://mdgs.un.org/unsd/mdg/Resources/Static/Products/Progress2011/11-31330%20(E)%20MDG%20Report%202011_Progress%20Chart%20LR.pdf

UN (2011b), *The Millennium Development Goals Report 2011* (New York: UN).

UN Department of Peacekeeping Operations (DPKO) (2008), *United Nations Peacekeeping Operations: Principles and Guidelines* (New York: Best Practices Section).

UN Department of Peacekeeping Operations (DPKO) (2009), *A New Partnership Agenda: Charting a New Horizon for UN Peacekeeping* (New York: UN).

UN Department of Peacekeeping Operations (DPKO) (2010), at www.un.org/en/peacekeeping/fatalities/documents/StatsByYear%201.pdf

UN Development Programme (1994), *Human Development Report* (New York: Oxford University Press).

UN Development Programme (1997), *Human Development Report* (New York: Oxford University Press).

UN Development Programme (2003), *Making Global Trade Work for People* (London: Earthscan), at www.undp.org/mainundp/propoor/docs.trade-jan2003.pdf

UN Development Programme (2005), *Human Development Report 2005* (New York: UN).

UN Environment Programme (UNEP) (2007), *GEO4 Global Environmental Outlook: Environment for Development* (Nairobi: UNEP).

UN General Assembly (2004), UN document A/59/565 (New York: UN).

UN General Assembly (2005), 'World Summit Outcomes' (UN doc. A/60/L.1, 20 September).

UN High Commission for Refugees (UNHCR) (2005), *Statistical Yearbook 2005: Trends in Displacement, Protection and Solutions* (New York: UN).

UN Press Release (2010), 'Secretary-general says "successful peacekeeping is a shared responsibility" as General Assembly marks tenth anniversary of Brahimi reform report', UN DOC., GA/10953, 22 June.

UN Report (2002), *The Issue of Missiles in All Its Aspects: Report of the Secretary-General* (General Assembly document A/57/229, 23 July).

UN Secretariat (2003), *The Impact of AIDS* (New York: UN, Report by the Population Division, Department of Economic and Social Affairs, 2 September).

UN Secretary-General (1999), *The Fall of Srebrenica* (UN doc. A/54/549, 15 November).

UN Secretary-General (2009), *Climate Change and its Possible Security Implications* (New York: UN).

UN Secretary-General Study (2002), *Women, Peace and Security* (New York: UN).

UN Secretary-General's High-Level Panel on Threats, Challenges, and Change (2004), *A More Secure World: Our Shared Responsibility* (New York: UN).

UN Security Council (2000), *Final Report of the Monitoring Mechanism on Angola Sanctions* (UN doc. S/2000/1225, 21 December).

UN Security Council (2001), *Report of the Panel of Experts pursuant to Security Council Resolution 1343 (2001), paragraph 19, concerning Liberia* (UN doc. S/2001/1015, 21 October).

UN Women (2010), *The Status of Women in the United Nations System and in the Secretariat (from 1 January 2008 to 31 December 2009)*, at www.un.org/womenwatch/osagi/pdf/As-of-31-December-2009.pdf

UNAIDS (2003), *On the Front Line: A review of policies and programmes to address HIV/AIDS among peacekeepers and uniformed services* (Geneva: UNAIDS).

UNCTAD (2006), *Trade and Development Report* (Geneva: UNCTAD).

UNCTAD (2010), *Trade and Development Report* (Geneva: UNCTAD).

Ungar, Sanford J. and Peter Vale (1985/86), 'South Africa: Why constructive engagement failed', *Foreign Affairs*, 64(2): 234–58.

United States (1978), *The Presidential Campaign 1976 Part 1: Jimmy Carter* (Washington, DC: US Government Printing Office).

United States (1998), *A National Security Strategy for a New Century* (Washington, DC: The White House).

UNMIS (UN Mission in Sudan) (2006), 'Military Component', at www.unmis.org/english/military.htm

UNODC (2010), *The Globalization of Crime: A Transnational Organized Crime Threat Assessment*, (Vienna, UNODC).

UNWDR, (2011), *United Nations World Drug Report 2011* (Vienna: UNODC).

Urquhart, Brian (1987), *A Life in Peace and War* (New York: Harper and Row).

US Arms Control and Disarmament Agency (ACDA) (2004), *World Military Expenditures and Arms Transfers 1972–1982* (Washington, DC: ACDA)

US Army (1990), *FM 100-20/AFP 3-20: Military Operations in Low Intensity Conflicts* (Washington, DC: Departments of the Army and Air Force, 5 December).

US Army (2007), *The U.S. Army and Marine Corps Counterinsurgency Field Manual* (Chicago: University of Chicago Press).

US Department of Defense (DoD) (2004), *Foreign Military Sales, Foreign Military Construction Sales, and Military Assistance Facts as of September 30, 2003* (Washington, DC: Defense Security Cooperation Agency).

US Department of Defense (DoD) (2006), *Military Power of the People's Republic of China 2006* (Washington, DC: DoD Annual Report to Congress).

US Department of Defense (DoD) (2010a), *Foreign Military Sales, Foreign Military Construction Sales, and Military Assistance Facts as of September 30, 2009* (Washington, DC: Defense Security Cooperation Agency).

US Department of Defense (DoD) (2010b), 'Fact Sheet: Increasing Transparency in the U.S. Nuclear Weapons Stockpile', 3 May, at www.defense.gov/news/d20100503stockpile.pdf

US Department of Energy, Energy Information Administration (2010b), 'Nigeria', Country Analysis Brief, September, at www.eia.doe.gov

US Department of Energy, Energy Information Administration (USDoE) (2010a), *International Energy Outlook 2010* (Washington, DC: USDoE).

US Department of State (2001), *Annual Country Reports on Terrorism* (Washington, DC: US Government Printing Office).

US Government Accountability Office (2007), 'Observations on Costs, Strengths, and Limitations of U.S. and UN Operations', testimony by Joseph A. Christoff before the Subcommittee of International Organizations, Human Rights, and Oversight, Committee on Foreign Affairs, House of Representatives, 13 June, GAO-07-998T.

US Navy (2007), *A Cooperative Strategy for 21st Century Seapower* (Washington, DC: Department of the Navy).

Vale, Peter (2003), *Security and Politics in South Africa* (Boulder, CO.: Lynne Rienner).

Valenius, Johanna (2007), 'A few kind women: Gender essentialism and Nordic peacekeeping operations', *International Peacekeeping*, 14(4): 510–23.

Van Creveld, Martin (1991), *On Future War* (London: Brassey's).

Van Evera, Stephen (1994), 'Hypothesis on nationalism and war', *International Security*, 19(1): 5–39.

Van Evera, Stephen (1999), *Causes of War: Vol. I: The Structure of Power and the Roots of War* (Ithaca, NY: Cornell University Press).

Van Lagenhove, Luk (2011) *Building Regions* (London: Routledge).

Van Munster, Rens (2007), 'Review essay: Security on a shoestring: A hitchhiker's guide to critical schools of security in Europe', *Cooperation and Conflict*, 42(2): 235–43.

Varshney, Ashutosh (2002), *Ethnic Conflict and Civic Life: Hindus and Muslims in India* (New Haven: Yale University Press).

Vasquez, John A. (1997), 'The realist paradigm and degenerative versus progressive research programs', *American Political Science Review*, 91(4): 899–912.

Vasquez, John A. and Colin Elman (eds.) (2003), *Realism and the Balancing of Power* (Upper Saddle River, NJ: Prentice Hall).

Vaughan, Diana (1996), *The Challenger Launch Decision* (Chicago: University of Chicago Press).

Veyne, Paul (1984), *Writing History* (Middletown, CT: Wesleyan University Press).

Vieth, Warren and Alissa J. Rubin (2003), 'Iraq Pipelines Easy Targets for a Saboteur', *Los Angeles Times*, 26 June.

Vigarello, Georges (1993), *Le sain et le malsain* (Paris: Seuil).

Vines, Alex (1999), 'Mercenaries and the Privatization of Security in Africa in the 1990s', in Greg Mills and John Stremlau (eds.), *The Privatization of Security in Africa* (Johannesburg: SAIIA), pp. 47–80.

Volkan, Vamik (1997), *Bloodlines: From Ethnic Pride to Ethnic Terrorism* (New York: Farrar, Straus & Giroux).

Volkov, Vadim (2002), *Entrepreneurs of Violence: The Use of Force in the Making of Russian Capitalism* (Ithaca, NY: Cornell University Press).

Von Neumann, John and Oskar Morgenstern (1944), *Theory of Games and Economic Behavior* (Princeton, NJ: Princeton University Press).

Wæver, Ole (1995), 'Securitization and Desecuritization', in Ronnie D. Lipschutz (ed.), *On Security* (New York: Columbia University Press), pp. 46–86.

Wæver, Ole (1998), 'The sociology of a not so international discipline: American and European developments in International Relations', *International Organization*, 52(4): 687–727.

Wæver, Ole (2000), 'The EU as a security actor', in Morten Kelstrup and Michael C. Williams (eds.), *International Relations Theory and the Politics of European Integration* (London: Routledge), pp. 250–94.

Wæver, Ole (2004), 'Aberystwyth, Paris, Copenhagen: New Schools in Security Theory and their Origins between Core and Periphery', paper presented at *International Studies Association* Conference, Montreal, 17–20 March.

Waever, Ole (2010), 'Beyond the evolution of international security studies?', *Security Dialogue*, 41(1): 659–67.

Wæver, Ole, *et al.* (1993), *Identity, Migration and the New Security Agenda in Europe* (London: Pinter).

Wagner, R. Harrison (1993), 'What was bipolarity?', *International Organization,* 47(1): 77–106.

Walker, R.B.J. (2007), 'Security, critique, Europe', *Security Dialogue*, 38(1): 95–103.

Walker, R.B.J. (2010), *After the Globe, Before the World* (London: Routledge).

Wallander, Celeste A. (2000), 'Institutional assets and adaptability: NATO after the Cold War', *International Organization*, 54(4): 705–35.

Wallander, Celeste A. and Robert O. Keohane (1999), 'Risk, threat, and security institutions', in H. Haftendorn, R.O. Keohane and C.A. Wallander (eds.), *Imperfect Unions: Security Institutions over Time and Space* (Oxford: Oxford University Press), pp. 21–47.

Walt, Stephen M. (1985), 'Alliance formation and the balance of world power', *International Security*, 9(4): 1–43.

Walt, Stephen M. (1987), *The Origins of Alliances* (Ithaca, NY: Cornell University Press).

Walt, Stephen M. (1991), 'The renaissance of security studies', *International Studies Quarterly*, 35(2): 211–39.

Walt, Stephen M. (1996), *Revolution and War* (Ithaca, NY: Cornell University Press).

Walt, Stephen M. (1997), 'Why alliances endure or collapse', *Survival*, 39(1): 156–179.

Walt, Stephen M. (1998), 'International Relations: One world, many theories', *Foreign Policy*, 110: 29–46.

Walt, Stephen M. (1999), 'Rigor or rigor mortis? Rational choice and security studies', *International Security*, 23(4): 5–48.

Walt, Stephen M. (2000), 'Containing rogues and renegades: Coalition strategies and counterproliferation' in Victor A. Utgoff (ed.), *The Coming Crisis* (Cambridge, MA: MIT Press), pp. 191–226.

Walt, Stephen M. (2002), 'The Enduring Relevance of the Realist Tradition', in Ira Katznelson and Helen V. Milner (eds.), *Political Science: State of the Discipline* (New York: W.W. Norton), pp. 197–230.

Walt, Stephen M. (2005), 'The relationship between theory and policy in international relations', *Annual Review of Political Science*, 8: 23–48.

Waltz, Kenneth N. (1954), *Man, the State and War* (New York: Columbia University Press).

Waltz, Kenneth N. (1979), *Theory of International Politics* (Reading, MA: Addison-Wesley).

Waltz, Kenneth N. (1981), *The Spread of Nuclear Weapons: More May Be Better* (London: IISS, Adelphi Paper No. 171).

Waltz, Kenneth N. (1993a), 'The emerging structure of international politics', *International Security*, 18(2): 44–79.

Waltz, Kenneth N. (1993b), 'The new world order', *Millennium,* 22(2): 187–195.

Waltz, Kenneth N. (1996), 'International politics is not foreign policy', *Security Studies*, 6(1): 54–7.

Waltz, Kenneth N. (2000) 'Structural realism after the Cold War', *International Security*, 25(1): 5–41.

Wang, Yuan-kang (2004), 'Offensive realism and the rise of China', *Issues and Studies*, 40(1): 173–201.

Wardlaw, Grant (1982), *Political Terrorism: Theory, Tactics and Counter-Measures* (Cambridge: Cambridge University Press).

Warner, Michael (2002), 'Wanted: A definition of "Intelligence"', *Studies in Intelligence*, 46(3): 15–23.

Warner, Michael (2008), 'Intelligence as Risk-Shifting', in P. Gill, S. Marrin and M. Pythian (eds.) *Intelligence Theory: Key Questions and Debates* (London: Routledge), pp. 16–33.

Waterman, Shaun (2006), 'Thai militants learn from Iraq insurgency', *United Press International*, 15 February.

Wayman, Frank W. (1984), 'Bipolarity and war: The role of capability concentration and alliance patterns among major powers 1816–1965', *Journal of Peace Research,* 21(1): 61–78.

Wayne, Leslie (2006), 'Foreign sales by U.S. arms makers doubled in a year', *New York Times*, 11 November.

WBEZ Chicago (2007), '"This American Life" show on the Center for Lessons Learned', 25 May. Podcast, at www.thislife.org/Radio_Archive.aspx#5

Weber, Max (1949), *The Methodology of the Social Sciences* (New York: Free Press).

Weber, Max (1964), *The Theory of Social and Economic Organization* (New York: Free Press).

Webersik, Christian (2010), *Climate Change and Security* (Santa Barbara, CA: Praeger).

Weiss, Thomas G. (2004), 'The sunset of humanitarian intervention? The responsibility to protect in a unipolar era', *Security Dialogue*, 35(2): 135–53.

Weiss, Thomas G. (2005), *Overcoming the Security Council Impasse* (Berlin: Friedrich Ebert Stiftung Foundation Occasional Paper 25).

Weiss, Thomas G. (ed.) (1998), *Beyond UN Subcontracting* (London: Macmillan).

Weiss, Thomas G., and Sam Daws (eds.) (2007), *The Oxford Handbook on the United Nations* (Oxford: Oxford University Press).

Weiss, Thomas G., David P. Forsythe and Roger A. Coate (2004), *The United Nations and Changing World Politics* (Boulder, CO: Westview).

Weiss, Thomas G., David Forsythe, Roger Cote, and Kelly-Kate Pease (2010), *The UN and Changing World Politics*, 6th edition (Boulder, CO: Westview).

Weissman, Steve and Herbert Krosney (1981), *The Islamic Bomb* (New York: New York Times Book Co.).

Weitsman, P.A. (2004), *Dangerous Alliances* (Stanford, CA: Stanford University Press).

Weldes, Jutta (1996), 'Constructing national interests', *European Journal of International Relations*, 2(3): 275–318.

Weldes, Jutta, Mark Laffey, Hugh Gusterson and Raymond Duvall (1999), 'Introduction', in Jutta Weldes *et al.* (eds.), *Cultures of Insecurity* (Minneapolis: University of Minnesota Press), pp. 1–33.

Welsh, Jennifer (2004), 'Conclusion' in Jennifer Welsh (ed.), *Humanitarian Intervention and International Relations* (Oxford: Oxford University Press), pp. 176–83.

Wendt, Alexander (1992), 'Anarchy is what states make of it', *International Organization*, 46(2): 391–425.

Wendt, Alexander (1995), 'Constructing international politics', *International Security*, 20(1): 71–81.

Wendt, Alexander (1999), *A Social Theory of International Relations* (Cambridge: Cambridge University Press).

Wendt, Alexander (2000), 'On the via media: A response to the critics', *Review of International Studies*, 26(1): 165–80.

Whaley, Barton (1973), *Codeword Barbarossa* (Cambridge, MA: MIT Press).

Whaley, Barton (2007), *Stratagem: Deception and Surprise in War* (Boston: Artech).

Wheeler, Nicholas J. (2000), *Saving Strangers: Humanitarian Intervention in International Society* (Oxford: Oxford University Press).

Wheeler, Nicholas J. (2008), 'To put oneself into the other fellow's place': John Herz, the security dilemma and the nuclear age', *International Relations*, 22(4): 493–509.

White House (2009), Remarks by President Barack Obama, Hradcany Square, Prague, Czech Republic, 5 April, at www.whitehouse.gov/the_press_office/Remarks-By-President-Barack-Obama-In-Prague-As-Delivered/

White House (2011), *Strategy to Combat Transnational Organized Crime* (Washington, DC: White House).

Whitworth, Sandra (1997), *Feminism and International Relations* (Basingstoke: Palgrave).

Whitworth, Sandra (2002), '11 September and the aftermath', *Studies in Political Economy*, 67(Spring): 33–8.

Whitworth, Sandra (2004), *Men, Militarism and UN Peacekeeping* (Boulder, CO: Lynne Rienner).

Whitworth, Sandra (2008), 'Feminism', in Christian Reus-Smit and Duncan Snidal (eds.), *Oxford Handbook of International Relations* (Oxford: Oxford University Press).

WHO (2007), *The World Health Report 2007* (Geneva: WHO).

WHO (2008), *Research Policy and Management of Risks in Life Sciences Research for Global Health Security: Report of the Meeting Bangkok, Thailand, 10–12 December 2007* (Geneva: WHO).

Wiebes, Cees (2003), *Intelligence and the War in Bosnia* (Munster: Lit Verlag).

Wight, Martin (1946), *Power Politics* (London: Royal Institute of International Affairs Looking Forward Pamphlet No.8).

Wight, Martin (1979), *Power Politics* (Harmondsworth: Penguin).

Wikileaks (2008), 'US Embassy Cable, Subject: Scene Setter for December 10–11, 2008 Visit to Afghanistan by Secretary of Defense, Robert M. Gates', Kabul, 9 December 2008. *The Guardian*, 'US Embassy Cable UK "Not Up To The Task" Of Securing Helmand, says US', 2 December 2010, at www.guardian.co.uk/world/us-embassy-cables-documents/181930

Wikileaks (2009), 'US Embassy Cable, Subject: 'Vice President-Elect Biden and Senator Graham', Kabul, 20 January 2009. *The Guardian*, 'US Embassy Cable Helmand Governor Criticises UK Military Strategy', 2 December 2010, at www.guardian.co.uk/world/us-embassy-cables-documents/187855

Wilkin, Peter (2002), 'Global poverty and orthodox security', *Third World Quarterly*, 23(4): 633–45.

Willett, Susan (ed.) (2010), *Women, Peace and Conflict: A Decade after Resolution 1325*, a special issue of *International Peacekeeping*, 17(2).

Williams, Michael C. (2007), *Culture and Security: Symbolic Power and the Politics of International Security* (London: Routledge).

Williams, Paul (2000), 'South African foreign policy: Getting critical?', *Politikon: South African Journal of Political Studies*, 27(1): 73–91.

Williams, Paul (2001), 'Fighting for Freetown: British military intervention in Sierra Leone', *Contemporary Security Policy*, 22(3): 140–68.

Williams Paul D. (2007), 'Thinking about security in Africa', *International Affairs*, 83(6): 1021–38.

Williams, Paul D. (2011), *War and Conflict in Africa* (Cambridge: Polity).

Williams, Paul D. (2012), 'Poverty: A Security Perspective', in Spear and Williams (eds.) (2012).

Williams, Paul D. and Alex J. Bellamy (2007), 'Contemporary Peace Operations: Four Challenges for the Brahimi Paradigm', in H. Langholtz, B. Kondoch, A. Wells (eds.), *International Peacekeeping: The Yearbook of International Peace Operations* Vol.11 (Martinus Nijhoff Publishers), pp. 1–28.

Williams, Phil (2009), *Criminals, Militias, Insurgents: Organized Crime in Iraq* (Carlisle, PA: Strategic Studies Institute).

Wilton Park (2010), *Winning "Hearts and Minds" in Afghanistan*. Report on Wilton Park Conference 1022, 11–14 March, at www.eisf.eu/resources/library/1004WPCReport.pdf

Wimmer, Andreas, Lars-Erik Cederman and Brian Min (2009), 'Ethnic politics and armed conflict: A configurational analysis of a new global data set,' *American Sociological Review*, 74(2): 316–37.

Wines, Michael (1991), 'U.S. Tells of Prewar Technology Sales to Iraq Worth $500 Million', *New York Times*, 12 March.

Wines, Michael (1992), '$8 Billion Directed to Wheat Farmers and Arms Workers', *New York Times*, 3 September.

Wiseman, Geoff (2002), *Concepts of Non-Provocative Defence* (London: Palgrave-Macmillan).

Wivel, Anders (2005), 'Explaining why state X made a certain move last Tuesday: The promise and limitations of realist foreign policy analysis', *Journal of International Relations and Development*, 8(4): 355–80.

Wohlforth, William C. (1993), *The Elusive Balance: Power and Perceptions during the Cold War* (Ithaca, NY: Cornell University Press).

Wohlforth, William C. (1999), 'The stability of a unipolar world', *International Security*, 24(1): 5–41.

Wolfers, Arnold (1952), '"National security" as an ambiguous symbol', *Political Science Quarterly*, 67(4): 481–502.

Wolfers, Arnold (1962), *Discord and Collaboration: Essays on International Politics* (Baltimore, MD: Johns Hopkins Press).

Women Against Fundamentalisms (2007), at www.gn.apc.org/waf/

Wong, Edward (2010), 'Chinese Military Seeks to Extend its Naval Power', *New York Times*, 23 April.

Woodrow, Thomas (2001), 'Time to Use the Nuclear Option', *Washington Times*, 14 September.

Woods, Ngaire (ed.) (2000), *The Political Economy of Globalization* (Basingstoke: Macmillan).

Woodward, Bob (1991), *The Commanders* (New York: Simon and Schuster).

Woodward, Bob (2010), *Obama's Wars* (New York: Simon and Schuster).

World Bank (2006), *Development and the Next Generation: World Development Report 2007* (Washington, DC: The World Bank).

World Bank (2007), *Global Monitoring Report 2007: The Millennium Development Goals* (Washington, DC: World Bank).

World Bank (2011), *Conflict, Security and Development: World Development Report 2011* (Washington, DC: World Bank).

World Commission on Environment and Development (1987), *Our Common Future* (Oxford: Oxford University Press).

World Economic Forum (2007), *Global Risks 2007: A Global Risk Network Report*, at www.weforum.org/pdf/CSI/Global_Risks_2007.pdf

Wright, Quincy (1983), *A Study of War* (Chicago: University of Chicago Press, 2nd edition).

Wyn Jones, Richard (1999), *Security, Strategy and Critical Theory* (Boulder, CO: Lynne Rienner).

Wyn Jones, Richard (2005), 'On Emancipation: Necessity, Capacity and Concrete Utopias' in Ken Booth (ed.), *Critical Security Studies and World Politics* (Boulder, CO: Lynne Rienner), pp. 215–35.

Yergin, Daniel (2002), 'A Crude View of the Crisis in Iraq', *Washington Post*, 6 December.

Zagare, Frank C. (1984), *Game Theory: Concepts and Applications* (Beverly Hills, CA: Sage University Paper Series on Quantitative Applications in the Social Sciences).

Zagare, Frank C. (1990), 'Rationality and deterrence', *World Politics*, 42(2): 238–60.

Zagare, Frank C. (1996), 'Classical deterrence theory: A critical assessment', *International Interactions*, 21(4): 365– 87.

Zagare, Frank C. (2004), 'Reconciling rationality with deterrence: A re-examination of the logical foundations of deterrence theory', *Journal of Theoretical Politics*, 16(2): 107–41.

Zagare, Frank C. (2011), *The Games of July: Explaining the Great War* (Ann Arbor: University of Michigan Press).

Zagare, Frank C. and D. Marc Kilgour (2000), *Perfect Deterrence* (Cambridge: Cambridge University Press).

Zagare, Frank C. and D. Marc Kilgour (2003), 'Alignment patterns, crisis bargaining, and extended deterrence: A Game-theoretic analysis', *International Studies Quarterly*, 47(4): 587–615.

Zagare, Frank C. and Branislav L. Slantchev (2010), 'Game Theory and Other Modeling Approaches', in Robert A. Denemark *et al.* (eds.), *The International Studies Encyclopedia* (Oxford: Wiley-Blackwell), Vol.IV, pp. 2591–610.

Zaitch, Damien (2002), *Trafficking Cocaine: Colombian Drug Entrepreneurs in the Netherlands* (The Hague: Kluwer).

Zakaria, Fareed (1998), *From Wealth to Power: The Unusual Origins of America's World Role* (Princeton, NJ: Princeton University Press).

Zakaria, Fareed (2001), 'Don't Oversell Missile Defense', *Newsweek*, 14 May.

Zalewski, Marysia (2000), *Feminism After Postmodernism* (London: Routledge).

Zaman, Rashed Uz (2002), 'WMD terrorism in South Asia: Trends and implications', *Journal of International Affairs*, 7(3), at www.sam.gov.tr/perceptions/Volume7/September-November2002/Perception_RashedUzZaman.pdf

Zartman, William I. (1985), *Ripe for Resolution: Conflict and Intervention in Africa* (New York: Oxford University Press).

Zedner, Lucia (2009), *Security* (New York: Routledge).

Zegart, Amy (2007), *Spying Blind: The CIA, the FBI, and the Origins of 9/11* (Princeton, NJ: Princeton University Press).

Zeid, Prince Ra'ad (2005), 'A comprehensive strategy to eliminate future sexual exploitation and abuse in UN peacekeeping operations' (UN doc., A/59/710, 24 March).

Zimmern, Ralph (1945), *The League of Nations and the Rule of Law* (London: Macmillan).

Zizek, Slavoj (2010), *Living in the End Times* (London: Verso).

Zolberg, A. (1981), 'International Migrations in Political Perspective', in M. Kritz *et al.* (eds.), *Global Trends in Migration* (New York: Center for Migration Studies), pp. 3–27.

Zolberg, A., A. Suhrke and S. Aguayo (1989), *Escape from Violence* (Oxford: Oxford University Press).

# Index

9/11 or 11 September 2001 attacks 10, 93, 94, 98–99,
104, 117–8, 149, 150, 161, 190, 221–3, 228–33,
235, 236, 239, 245, 332, 350, 369, 371, 391, 418,
441, 448–9, 461, 464, 468, 469, 491, 505, 517,
523, 527, 533, 563–4, 566, 573, see also terrorism
Aberystwyth, School of security studies 93, 96, 101–6,
577
Aborigines 268, see also Australia
Abu Ghraib prison, Iraq 114, 391, 426, see also torture
Abu Hamza 527
Abu Nidal Organization 461
Abu Quatada 527
Acharya, Amitav 288
Action Direct 225
Adelman, Howard 291
Afghanistan 99, 117–8, 119, 161, 177, 192, 202, 203,
216, 221, 228–33, 236, 243, 249, 269, 287, 288,
292, 302, 304, 324, 343, 350, 351, 366, 367, 368,
372, 379, 386, 391, 395, 398, 400, 405, 425, 426,
428, 431, 446–7, 449, 451, 467, 469, 471–82,
484, 485, 504–5, 514, 515, 518, 523,
526–7, 530, 531–2, 540, 563, see also ISAF,
Taliban
Africa 9, 72, 103, 105, 184, 196, 197, 245, 257, 261,
267, 268, 275, 278, 288, 292, 298, 301, 302, 306,
326, 331, 356–7, 361, 365, 367, 368, 370, 371,
380, 427, 434, 454, 505, 508, 516, 533, 539, 545,
Great Lakes 222, Horn 446, north 306, 318, 429,
500, 545, slave trade 258, southern 93, 105, 254,
318, 386, 429, sub-Saharan 100, 197, 286, 301,
302, 303, 304, 306, 308–9, 543, west 305, 429,
452, 505, 512, 515
African Union (AU) 179, 197, 257, 261, 262, 292,
356, 366, 367, 368, 369, 371, 380, 394, 401, 404,
497, 499, see also OAU
African Union Mission in Sudan (AMIS) 368, 404
airpower 204, 238
Alam, Shahid M. 573
Al-Arabiya 231
Albania 273, 403, 508, 511, ethnic Albanians 256,
273–4, 389, 490, 529
al-Bashir, Gen. Omar 257, 260, 273
Algeria 306, 474–5, 485, 527
Al-Jazeera 231, 500
Alker, Hayward 105
Alkire, Sabina 282
Alliance Treaty Obligations and Provisions project
340–3, 347
Allison, Graham 39, 172, 418, 556–7, 567

Althusser, Louis 68
al-Mahdi, Sadiq 272
Al-Mohajiroun 527
al-Nimeiri, Jafaar 272
al-Qa'ida 94, 104–5, 149–50, 173, 189, 217, 222,
223, 225, 228–30, 232, 234, 332, 380, 390–1,
418–9, 447, 451, 453, 458, 459, 465, 467, 469,
477, 514, 523, 527, 547, 563, see also 9/11 attacks,
Taliban
al-Qa'ida in Iraq (AQI) 514
al-Qa'ida in the Islamic Maghreb (AQIM) 514
al-Zawahiri, Ayman 228, 469
American Revolution 489
Americas 72, 292, 356, 359, 360, 361, 362, 365, 367,
368, 371
Amnesty International 253, 259, 305, 574
Amoco 429
Andreas, Peter 509, 519
Angola 306, 379, 380, 430, 435, 443, 446, 447, 453,
545
Annan, Kofi 42, 279, 307–8, 357, 385–6, 390, 391,
399, 401, 491, 493, 497–8
Anti-Ballistic Missile (ABM) Treaty 412
Anthropocene 313–4, 315, 317, 323
apartheid 11, 97, 100, 253, 259–60, 263, 267, 277,
287, 362, 363, 430, 434, 446, see also South
Africa
Arab Cooperation Council (ACC) 356, 363–4
Arab Maghreb Union (AMU) 356
Arab spring/awakening/revolutions (2011) 2, 232, 246,
280, 306, 357, 368, 499, 545–6, 564, 566
Arabs 95, 102, 172, 174, 177, 230, 266, 272, 286–7,
362, 368, 379, 475, 482, 494, 500, 526–7, 565–6
Arctic 316, 320, 539, 543–4
Arctic National Wildlife Refuge (ANWR) 539, 548,
550
Argentina 410, 510, see also Falklands/Malvinas
Islands
Arkin, Bill 240
Armenia 254, 276
ArmorGroup (formerly DSL) 429–30
Arms Export Control Act, US (AECA) 445–6
arms race 48–53, 55, 58, 82, 141, 148, 419, 560
Arms Trade Treaty 308, 455
Aron, Raymond 35
Arria, Diego 382
Art, Robert 563
ASEAN Regional Forum (ARF) 355, 356, 359
Ashdown, Lord Paddy 406